The Screen Media Reader

Culture, Theory, Practice

EDITED BY
STEPHEN MONTEIRO

Bloomsbury Academic
An imprint of Bloomsbury Publishing Inc

BLOOMSBURY
NEW YORK · LONDON · OXFORD · NEW DELHI · SYDNEY

Bloomsbury Academic

An imprint of Bloomsbury Publishing Inc

1385 Broadway	50 Bedford Square
New York	London
NY 10018	WC1B 3DP
USA	UK

www.bloomsbury.com

BLOOMSBURY and the Diana logo are trademarks of Bloomsbury Publishing Plc

First published 2017

Library of Congress Cataloging-in-Publication Data
Names: Monteiro, Stephen, editor of compilation.
Title: The screen media reader : culture, theory, practice / edited by
Stephen Monteiro.
Description: New York : Bloomsbury Academic, 2017. | Includes bibliographical
references and index.
Identifiers: LCCN 2016027347| ISBN 9781501311703 (paperback) |
ISBN 9781501311697 (hardback)
Subjects: LCSH: Mass media and history. | Mass media–Technological
innovations–Social aspects. | BISAC: SOCIAL SCIENCE / Media Studies.
Classification: LCC P96.H55 S37 2017 | DDC 302.23–dc23 LC record
available at https://lccn.loc.gov/2016027347

ISBN:	HB:	978-1-5013-1169-7
	PB:	978-1-5013-1170-3
	ePub:	978-1-5013-1167-3
	ePDF:	978-1-5013-1166-6

Cover design: Avni Patel

Typeset by Integra Software Services Pvt. Ltd.
Printed and bound in the United States of America

For Manisha and Dhruv

CONTENTS

List of Figures   xii
Preface   xvi
Acknowledgments   xviii
Permissions   xix
Editor's Note   xxii

Introduction   1

SECTION ONE   Screens and Their Histories   13

Introduction to Section One   15

Screen Identities   21

1   The Crack in the Electric Window   23
    Charles R. Acland

2   What Is a Screen Nowadays?   29
    Francesco Casetti

3   Current Screens   39
    Sean Cubitt

4   The Multiple   55
    Anne Friedberg

5   The Magic Mirror   67
    William Henry Fox Talbot

Evolution and Revolution   71

6   From *The Republic*   73
    Plato

7   Screenology; or, Media Archaeology of the Screen   77
    Erkki Huhtamo

8   A Screen's Genealogy   125
    Lev Manovich

9   The Ordered Mosaic, or the Screen Overtaken by
    Computation   133
    Edmond Couchot

10 Digital Media as Ornament in Contemporary Architecture
    Facades: Its Historical Dimension   143
    Uta Caspary

SECTION TWO   Images and Frames   153

Introduction to Section Two   155

The Production of Images   161

11 Description of the Process of Painting and Lighting
    in … Pictures of the Diorama   163
    Louis-Jacques-Mandé Daguerre

12 When Seeing Is Belonging: The Photography of
    Tahrir   167
    Lara Baladi

13 Building New Worlds   177
    Ron Burnett

14 On-Screen Screens 185
Brad Chisholm

15 Mobile Cinema 197
Sarah Atkinson

16 From *Swann's Way* 219
Marcel Proust

Terms of Display 223

17 From *Natural Magick: in XX Bookes* 225
Giambattista della Porta

18 Building a Cinema Theatre 229
Frederick J. Kiesler

19 Ideological Effects of the Basic Cinematographic
Apparatus 233
Jean-Louis Baudry

20 The Shape of New Media: Screen Space, Aspect Ratios,
and Digitextuality 245
Harper Cossar

21 Fit to Frame: Image and Edge in Contemporary
Interfaces 267
Stephen Monteiro

22 After the Screen: Array Aesthetics and
Transmateriality 287
Mitchell Whitelaw

SECTION THREE   Environments and Interactions   295

Introduction to Section Three   297

Moments of Interface   303

23   The Cinematograph   305
     O. Winter

24   The Face of Television   307
     Paul Frosh

25   From *Augmenting Human Intellect: A Conceptual
     Framework*   313
     Douglas Engelbart

26   It's All about the Fit: The Hand, the Mobile Screenic
     Device and Tactile Vision   319
     Heidi Rae Cooley

27   The iPhone as an Object of Knowledge   325
     Alexandra Schneider

28   The Smartphone Screen in All Its States   333
     Virginie Sonet

29   In the Flesh: Space and Embodiment in the Pornographic
     Peep Show Arcade   343
     Amy Herzog

Systems and Networks   365

30   The Other Small Screen: Moving Images at New York's
     World Fair, 1939   367
     Haidee Wasson

31   From Screen to Site: Television's Material Culture, and Its
     Place   389
     Anna McCarthy

32 Nollywood: Spectatorship, Audience and the Sites
    of Consumption   395
    Onookome Okome

33 "Culture: Intercom" and Expanded Cinema:
    A Proposal and Manifesto   417
    Stan VanDerBeek

34 The Aesthetics of the Arena: Live and Recorded   421
    Robert Edgar

35 Performative Cartography   435
    Nanna Verhoeff

Further Reading   450
Contributors   454
Index   457

LIST OF FIGURES

1 W.R. Seton, A periscope being used above a surgical operation which is projected onto a lantern screen for a lecture in the adjoining room, gouache, c. 1920. Courtesy Wellcome Library, London. Creative Commons Attribution 4.0 International license. 2

2 The individualized screens of an in-flight entertainment system on a wide-body aircraft. Photo: Marc Smith, flickr.com, Creative Commons Attribution 2.0 Generic license. 5

3 Crowd recording the Pope's visit to Naples, 2015. Photo: Raffaele Esposito, flickr.com, Creative Commons Attribution-NoDerivs 2.0 Generic license. 8

4 Cathode ray tube screens abandoned in the brush, Adelaide, Australia, 2015. Photo: Michael Coghlan, flickr.com, Creative Commons Attribution-ShareAlike 2.0 Generic license. 10

I.1 Early steps in learning to live through the screen: a toddler interacts with an iPad, 2012. Photo: Tia Henriksen, flickr.com, Creative Commons Attribution 2.0 Generic license. 16

2.1 Dashboard screens displaying camera and GPS views in a Tesla Model S, 2012. Photo: Steve

Jurvetson, flickr.com, Creative Commons Attribution 2.0 Generic license.   31

3.1   A technician services an outdoor liquid-crystal display (LCD) advertising screen, Berlin, 2008. Photo: nerdwithoutglasses, flickr.com, Creative Commons Attribution 2.0 Generic license.   45

4.1   A smartphone screen confronts a desktop screen, producing a *mise en abyme* through its camera and screencast. Photo: Alan Levine, flickr.com, Creative Commons Attribution 2.0 Generic license.   58

6.1   Capturing the setting sun through a smartphone screen, 2011. Photo: Juozas Kaziukenas, flickr.com, Creative Commons Attribution-ShareAlike 2.0 Generic license.   75

8.1   An American military radar operator interacts with the AN-FPS-115 Pave Paws phased array warning system, 1986. Photo: Don Sutherland, U.S. Air Force, public domain.   128

I.2   A baby monitor displaying the image of a crib. Photo: Pete, flickr.com, Public Domain Mark 1.0.   156

11.1   Malby & Sons, Traverse section of Arrowsmith's Diorama, patent drawing, London, 1857 [1823]. The screen and mechanisms for controlling light intensity and direction are at right.   164

12.1   The "Friday of Victory" after Hosni Mubarak's fall, Tahrir Square, Cairo, Egypt. Photo by Lara Baladi, February 18, 2011. Used by permission.   169

12.2   Protesters during a speech in Tahrir Square,
        April 8, 2011. Photo by Mosa'ab Elshamy.
        © Mosa'ab Elshamy.   171

12.3   Photoshopped NASA shot (copyright unknown),
        July 3, 2013; image circulating on Facebook in
        July 2013.   172

13.1   Inside a gaming arcade, Tokyo, 2008. Photo:
        Stéfan, flickr.com, Creative Commons Attribution-
        ShareAlike 2.0 Generic license.   182

16.1   Auguste Edouart, *The Magic Lantern*, cut paper
        and wash, 1826–61. The Metropolitan Museum of
        Art, New York, bequest of Mary Martin, 1938.   220

17.1   Lantern projection of illustrated slides, from
        Physiologia Kircheriana Experimentalis by
        Athanasius Kircher, 1680. As is often noted,
        this early image of a magic lantern mistakenly
        places the lens between lamp and slide, rather than
        between the slide and projection surface.   226

19.1   Toyogeki Movie Theater, Toyooka, Japan, 2010.
        Photo: Hashi Photo, Creative Commons
        Attribution 3.0 Unported license.   235

20.1   *Star Wars: Knights of the Old Republic II:
        The Sith Lords*, LucasArts, 2004.   254

20.2   *Star Wars: Knights of the Old Republic II:
        The Sith Lords*, LucasArts, 2004.   255

20.3   *A Bug's Life*, Pixar Animation Studios, 1998.   258

20.4   *A Bug's Life*, Pixar Animation Studios, 1998.   259

20.5   *A Bug's Life*, Pixar Animation Studios, 1998.   260

20.6 *A Bug's Life*, Pixar Animation Studios, 1998. 260

I.3 Viewing images on a smartphone with Google Cardboard, 2015. Photo: Becky Stern, flickr.com, Creative Commons Attribution-ShareAlike 2.0 Generic license. 298

23.1 Marcellin Auzolle, *Cinématographe Lumière*, lithograph, 1896. 306

24.1 Reflections in a dark television screen, 2007. Photo: Kent, flickr.com, Creative Commons Attribution-NoDerivs 2.0 Generic license. 309

27.1 Commuters using their smartphones while waiting on a metro platform, Washington, D.C., 2011. Photo: Jeffrey, flickr.com, Creative Commons Attribution-NoDerivs 2.0 Generic license. 327

31.1 A bank of TV broadcast monitors at Democratic Headquarters on election night, Washington, D.C., 1964. Photo: Marion S. Trikosko, U.S. News & World Report Magazine Photograph Collection, Library of Congress. 390

PREFACE

This book is designed as a foundational resource in the study of the screen and its cultural role. It contains some of the most important and stimulating work done in this area, while suggesting potential paths for further research and study. Through key historical and interpretative texts on the development and place of the screen in communications and the social sphere, it offers explorations of the screen as an idea, an object, and an experience through a variety of descriptive and analytical approaches. Readings have been chosen to illustrate the astonishing range and depth of the screen's applications and invocations in multiple media configurations and contexts. As such, the reader brings together texts from diverse sources that nevertheless share an interest in the screen as an element of popular culture and an agent in our understanding of the world around us. Work principally concerned with audience characteristics or the narratives that screens deliver have been left out, as these are abundantly available in other readers on visual media and communications.

A few of the essays appearing here may be familiar even to those coming from outside media studies, while other entries have had much less exposure. The decision to select existing texts rests on the desire to serve two important functions with this book. First is the need to provide historical breadth that contextualizes thinking about the screen across different stages of its development as a primary tool of visual communication. Second is the affirmation—through these examples—of the long-standing and fundamental role screens have played in scholarship as well as society, extending well beyond our often short-sighted sense of twenty-first-century screen saturation.

The contents are organized into three sections: Screens and Their Histories, Images and Frames, and Environments and Interactions. To avoid any hint of historical or technological determinism, texts within each section are not presented in strict chronological order but arranged to generate new relationships across the selections and the ideas they contain. While the three sections are organized to suggest defining characteristics of the screen and its cultural application, there is nothing definitive about this structure. Other categories and ways of organizing these essays are possible, and dialogues and correspondences can be traced across the sections. Indeed, sampling texts within and across sections without adhering to the established sequence may produce additional, valuable insights into the screen and the terms of its study. It is also expected that researchers and students may not read all the texts collected here, but rather draw from the contents as suits their specific interests and goals. It is hoped that any research or study project that commences here will continue to other books, sites, and archives. To that end, each section begins with an introduction framing the primary issues and key questions considered within that part of the reader and the book closes with a bibliography for further reading.

The opening section, Screens and Their Histories, introduces several major voices in the study of the screen. The essays gathered there may be considered founding texts for the field. They reflect multiple approaches and methodologies to studying the screen, while also introducing critical concepts that return at other points throughout the texts that follow. The middle section, Images and Frames, concentrates on those writings that examine the screen as a framing device for images and other visual information. The texts chosen here cover multiple media forms and historical periods to demonstrate recurring ideas in the form and perception of image-screen relationships. The closing section, Environments and Interactions, brings together texts examining the material and spatial properties of screens, whether strictly as objects or as components within larger technological and architectural structures. It introduces ideas concerning the functioning of screens in different contexts and the role of the viewer or user. It demonstrates the screen's dependence not only on associated technologies and telecommunication structures, but also shifting socio-economic conditions and cultural practices.

The only certainty in studying the screen is that this object of such importance to contemporary living is bound to take new forms and be employed in new ways, towards unanticipated ends, as technological, economic, and cultural pressures and expectations change. Any subsequent edition of this reader will reflect such developments. Nevertheless, even with these changes, the ideas, opinions, and methods presented in this volume should remain relevant to future considerations of the screen as both a symptom and agent of modern and contemporary visual culture.

ACKNOWLEDGMENTS

The idea—in fact, the need—for this collection arose when I developed a seminar on contemporary screen culture. I am grateful to the intrepid students in that course, whose response to the subject and its scattered literature informed my choices for the structure and contents of this book. The project has benefitted from the advice and support of several people, some of whose work appears in these pages. I am particularly indebted to Nicholas Mirzoeff and Murray Forman, both of whom have edited field-defining readers, for their valuable guidance in the earliest stages. I have also benefitted from the remarkable support of my editor at Bloomsbury, Katie Gallof, whose enthusiasm and support has never flagged, and editorial assistants Susan Krogulski, Michelle Chen, and Mary Al-Sayed. The readers for the press offered wise counsel, which I have done my best to heed in the final manuscript. I am grateful to all the authors, publishers, and organizations granting permission to publish the works presented here. I am particularly appreciative of those who were willing to do so at little or no expense. My family always has been a positive influence on my work. Manisha Iyer and Dhruv Iyer Monteiro have taught me much that I might otherwise never have learned about these "magic windows" and their diverse applications. The deepest roots of this book reach into my childhood and the many hours I spent around screens, long before I had any thought of studying them. The solid-state TV console, the drive-in, the handheld electronic games, the video arcade, the home slideshows, and the multiplex all cast their shadows here. Mindful of that, I am indebted to those guiding figures from my youth—some of them now gone—who did not equate screen time with wasted time.

PERMISSIONS

The following texts are reproduced with kind permission. Every effort has been made to trace copyright holders and obtain permission, but this has not been possible in all cases. Any omissions should be brought to the attention of the publisher.

Acland, Charles R. "The Crack in the Electric Window." *Cinema Journal* 51, no. 2 (2012): 169–173. Copyright © 2012 by the University of Texas Press. All rights reserved. Used by permission.

Atkinson, Sarah. *Beyond the Screen: Emerging Cinema and Engaging Audiences*. New York: Bloomsbury, 2014, 61–100. © Sarah Atkinson, 2014, from 'Beyond the Screen: Emerging Cinema and Engaging Audiences', Bloomsbury Academic (US), an imprint of Bloomsbury Publishing Plc.

Baladi, Lara. "When Seeing Is Belonging: The Photography of Tahrir." *Broadsheet* 43, no. 1 (2014): 65–68.

Baudry, Jean-Louis. "Ideological Effects of the Basic Cinematographic Apparatus." Translated by Alan Williams. *Film Quarterly* 28, no. 2 (1974–1975): 39–47.

Burnett, Ron. *How Images Think*. Cambridge, Mass.: The MIT Press, 2005, 2,940 word excerpt from pages 190–197. © 2004 Massachusetts Institute of Technology, by permission of The MIT Press.

Casetti, Francesco. "What Is a Screen Nowadays?" In *Public Space, Media Space*, edited by Chris Berry, Janet Harbord, and Rachel O. Moore. New York: Palgrave Macmillan, 2013, 16–40. Reproduced with permission of Palgrave Macmillan.

Caspary, Uta. "Digital Media as Ornament in Contemporary Architecture Facades: Its Historical Dimension." In *Urban Screens Reader*, edited by Scott McQuire, Meredith Martin, and Sabine Niederer. Amsterdam: Institute of Network Cultures, 2009, 65–74.

Chisholm, Brad. "On-Screen Screens." *Journal of Film and Video* 41, no. 2, Close Studies of Television: Encoding Research (1989): 15–24. Published by University of Illinois Press on behalf of the University Film & Video Association.

Cooley, Heidi Rae. "It's all about the Fit: The Hand, the Mobile Screenic Device and Tactile Vision." *Journal of Visual Culture* 3, no. 2 (2004): 133–155.

Cossar, Harper. "The Shape of New Media: Screen Space, Aspect Ratios, and Digitextuality." *Journal of Film and Video* 61, no. 4 (2009): 3–16.

Couchot, Edmond. "La mosaïque ordonnée ou l'écran saisi par le calcul." In Vidéo, edited by Raymond Bellour and Anne-Marie Duguet, *Communications* 48 (1988): 79–87, translated by Stephen Monteiro.

Cubitt, Sean. "Current Screens." In *Imagery in the 21st Century*, edited by Oliver Grau with Thomas Veigl. Cambridge, Mass.: The MIT Press, 2011, 6,760-word excerpt from pages 21–35. © 2011 Massachusetts Institute of Technology, by permission of The MIT Press.

Daguerre, Louis-Jacques-Mandé. *Historique et description des procédés du Daguerréotype et du Diorama.* Paris: Susse frères, 1839, 75–79, translated by Stephen Monteiro.

Edgar, Robert. "The Aesthetics of the Arena: Live and Recorded." In *The Arena Concert*, edited by Robert Edgar, Kirsty Fairclough-Isaacs, Benjamin Halligan, and Nicola Spelman. New York: Bloomsbury Academic, 2015, 195–206. © Robert Edgar, 2015, The Arena Concert, and Bloomsbury Publishing Inc.

Engelbart, Douglas C. *Augmenting Human Intellect: A Conceptual Framework*. Menlo Park, Calif.: Stanford Research Institute, 1962, 1, 3–6, 36–37, 68–69, 73–76. Reprinted by permission of SRI International.

Friedberg, Anne. *The Virtual Window: From Alberti to Microsoft*. Cambridge, Mass.: The MIT Press, 2006, 2,926-word excerpt from pages 228–235. © 2006 Massachusetts Institute of Technology, by permission of The MIT Press.

Frosh, Paul. "The Face of Television." *Annals, AAPSS* 625 (2009): 87–102.

Herzog, Amy. "In the Flesh: Space and Embodiment in the Pornographic Peep Show Arcade." *The Velvet Light Trap* 62 (2008): 29–43. Copyright © 2008 by the University of Texas Press. All rights reserved. Used by permission.

Huhtamo, Erkki. "Screenology; or, Media Archaeology of the Screen" (2016). © Erkki Huhtamo 2016.

Kiesler, Frederick. "Building a Cinema Theatre." *New York Evening Post*, February 2 (1929).

McCarthy, Anna. "From Screen to Site: Television's Material Culture, and Its Place." *October* 98 (2001): 93–111.

Manovich, Lev. *The Language of New Media*. Cambridge, Mass.: The MIT Press, 2001, 2,820 word excerpt from pages 95–103. © 2001 Massachusetts Institute of Technology, by permission of The MIT Press.

Monteiro, Stephen. "Fit to Frame: Image and Edge in Contemporary Interfaces." *Screen* 55, no. 3 (2014): 360–378. Used by permission.

Okome, Onookome. "Nollywood: Spectatorship, Audience and the Sites of Consumption." *Postcolonial Text* 3, no. 2 (2007): non-paginated.

Plato, *The Republic of Plato*. Translated by Benjamin Jowett. Rev. ed. London: The Colonial Press, 1901, 209–212.

Porta [Giambattista della]. *Natural Magick: in XX Bookes*. 2nd ed. London: R. Gaywood, 1658, 363–365.

Proust, Marcel. *Swann's Way*. Translated by C.K. Scott Moncrieff. New York: Henry Holt, 1922, 9–11.

Schneider, Alexandra. "The iPhone as an Object of Knowledge." In *Moving Data: The iPhone and the Future of Media*, edited by Pelle Snickars and Patrick Vonderau. New York: Columbia University Press, 2012, 49–60. Copyright © 2012 Columbia University Press. Reprinted with permission of the publisher.

Sonet, Virginie. "L'écran du smartphone dans tous ses états." *MEI* (Médiation et Information) 34 (2012): 189–199, translated by Stephen Monteiro.

Talbot, William Henry Fox. "The Magic Mirror." In *Legendary Tales: in Verse and Prose*. London: James Ridgway, 1830, 8–20.

VanDerBeek, Stan. "'Culture: Intercom' and Expanded Cinema: A Proposal and Manifesto." *TDR/The Tulane Drama Review* 11, no. 1 (1966): 38–48. © 1966 by New York University.

Verhoeff, Nanna. *Mobile Screens: The Visual Regime of Navigation*. Amsterdam: Amsterdam University Press, 2012, 149–163.

Wasson, Haidee. "The Other Small Screen: Moving Images at New York's World Fair, 1939." *Canadian Journal of Film Studies* 21, no. 1 (2012): 81–103.

Whitelaw, Mitchell. "After the Screen: Array Aesthetics and Transmateriality." *Column* 7 (2011): 50–57.

Winter, O. "The Cinematograph." *New Review* 14 (1896): 507–513.

EDITOR'S NOTE

The essays collected here closely follow their original published form. Ellipses or other minor changes, necessary for clarity or consistency, have been placed in brackets. In some cases accompanying images have been removed. Wherever feasible, original systems of reference have been maintained, though notes may be renumbered. In two cases—chapters seven and twelve—the authors have graciously taken the time to revise and update their originally published essays.

Introduction

Reflecting on the screen

Our world view is a screen view. There is little we experience today without the screen intervening in some way, from driving or cooking, to shopping or studying. The screen has entered into nearly every fold of the social fabric. Beyond the obvious examples of phones, tablets, and living-room screens, we commonly encounter screens on appliances, dashboards, gas pumps, ATMs, toys, billboards, and building facades. We literally live and die by the screen, as surgical procedures and bombing missions engage specialists guided by them, sometimes thousands of miles from the place of action. We first take visible form as a pre-natal sonogram on a screen, our sense of ourselves and others is constantly refracted through screens large and small as we make our way through the world and, once our lives are over, our interactions with screens survive us as data in global networks. Screens are in our hands or close by for all manner of everyday activity, shaping and reshaping what we do and how we do it. Over the course of a day we may have more face-to-face encounters with screens than with people. The screen is, paradoxically, our place of work and our source of leisure. It is where we go to connect to the world or to escape from it, where we go to get things done but may wind up feeling we have accomplished nothing. Whether we think of contemporary culture as rooted in images, information, data, or networks, the screen lies in our path to all of them. Contemporary culture is screen culture, and it has become nearly impossible to separate our relationship with the screen from our sense of what it is to be alive.

As a common, adaptable object embedded in our most familiar habits, however, the screen's properties—and how these affect our perception and behavior—often hardly register in our consciousness. Being there without our thinking about it has been the screen's historical charge and the root of its success. It is regularly meant to be construed as an unobtrusive, passive, and transparent conduit of sensory information such as text, images, colors, and patterns. It is intended to seem im-mediate, rather than inter-mediate. Indeed, we rarely think much about the screen except when it goes dark, gets scuffed or cracked, or falls short in the tasks we've assigned to it.

Our utter dependence on screens in daily routines and social relationships nevertheless makes them worthy of close, critical scrutiny. If we find it hard to pull ourselves away from their shiny surfaces for very long, then we had best try to understand them better. We might start by asking why they have become our primary means of exchanging and visualizing information? We should consider how they structure the data they display, as well as our actions and interactions on- and off-screen. What are their origins and their future? What does our screen reliance tell us about our systems of belief and knowledge?

This book is a step toward asking these questions, studying the available information, and formulating responses. It disrupts both the screen's presumed clarity and the mystification (that "screen magic") that often surrounds it. As the first extensive collection of writings directed at the screen as a historical, technological, social, and aesthetic entity, it marks the emergence of a new field of cultural inquiry, while also demonstrating that the parameters and research production of that field have been coalescing for quite some time. When we push ourselves to look *at* and *around* the screen rather than *through* it (which to some extent qualifies as nothing more than an illusion) we find that the objects and operations that comprise

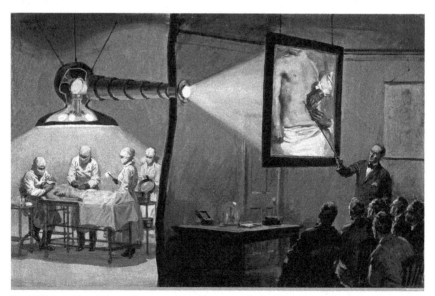

FIGURE 1 *Depiction of a periscope being used above a surgical operation, which is projected onto a lantern screen for a lecture in the adjoining room, c. 1920. Courtesy Wellcome Library, London.*

the screen and its practice are components of longer histories and wider systems of devices, apparatuses, paradigms, processes, and techniques that define visual experience and social space. The screens we face today are only the latest examples in an extensive genealogy of representation relying on modulations of light within fixed-frame surfaces. While some screen forms and applications may strike us as recent innovations, the screen has been a rich area for the exploration and explanation of diverse visual, psychological, and aesthetic experiences for centuries. Not only has the screen been the place to materialize visual representations that may haunt our thoughts, but it also haunts our experience in turn, as a concept and object that we find hard to resist for describing or engaging our world.

Screen study or screen studies

Staying true to the screen's reputation as an empty field to be filled with any sort of visual material, even when media and cultural scholars directly invoke the screen they tend to have other things in mind. On the university campus as elsewhere, the term "screen" has become a convenient catch-all used to describe the research and study of what we access through screens, perpetuating the idea of the screen as passive conduit. "Screen studies," which exists as departments, programs, and degree specializations at universities around the world, has until recently had little or no regard for the object of its title. Typically screen studies has referred to a group of associated and often overlapping areas in media research and production that includes television, film, animation, video, and even software and computing. As film and television developed into major areas of communication and media studies in the 1970s and 80s to be differentiated from primarily print and sound media, the screen arose as a hypernym acknowledging the common ground of moving-image media amid numerous qualitative and quantitative differences. By the 1990s screen studies became a sanctioned area of study at multiple institutions of higher learning, though no standard curriculum has ever emerged (Miller 2001; Hartley 2005). Screen studies programs range from a focus entirely on production to an emphasis on the history or theory of screen-based image-making. Across these differences, however, programs are consistent in their general exclusion of the screen and its properties from significant critical analysis.

This tendency to reference the screen as a media metaphor rather than a media object runs deep. Its origins may be found in the early twentieth-century use of the word "screen" in the film industry to connote cinema as a whole. At some point in the first few decades of that medium, a movie script became a screenplay and a movie star became a screen star. *Modern Screen*, founded in 1930 and one of the most successful American cinema magazines, would describe itself on its cover as having "the largest circulation of any screen magazine." While *Modern Screen* and its competitors (including *Screen Guide, Screenland*, and *Silver Screen*) offered news on everything and everyone associated with the cinema screen—actors, directors, studios, and films—there was little made of the screen itself. Like similar on-line sources today, the screen was understood merely as a convenient means of categorization, rather than an active agent in the processes of making meaning. Screens as physical objects were considered only in technical circles, such as the industry magazine *BoxOffice* or do-it-yourself publications such as *Popular Mechanics*.

In the 1970s the British film journal *Screen* became an influential source for Marxist, psychoanalytical, and feminist theories of cinema that would become known simply as "screen theory." While such theories worked through the screen's metaphorical potential, they primarily analyzed the relationship between audience, camera, and narrative content, leaving the screen's physical properties unexplored. The rise of television in popular culture and media studies required further distinction between the "small screen" and "big screen," terms which acknowledge physical differences in the screen across media, but this accomplished little in furthering interest in the screen object. In these and similar cases, using the word "screen" reinforced a metonym of cinema and moving-image culture while also reiterating the screen's connotations as a passive, immediate, practically invisible entity through which events and sensations may flow unimpeded. Paradoxically, the screen's absence is most strongly felt in such instances where its name is directly invoked.

It is only in this century that "screen studies" has begun to reflect what, on the surface, it would appear to mean: the study of the screen's material properties, its technical functioning, its historical contexts, and its cultural applications. As mobile media, graphic interfaces, convergence, digital networks, and globalization have become major topics in media studies, the screen that underlies and unites them emerges as a critical area of research. Ignoring the screen is no longer an option when our existence relies on it so heavily. Courses have been created to focus on the history and theory of the screen as a cultural object and even general courses in media and communication studies are finding the time to acknowledge the part played by the screen.

This change in outlook may derive from three factors. First, there is the exponential increase in screen forms and uses in the twenty-first century. The screen has taken too many forms, and entered into too many settings, to sustain inherited facile assumptions and generalizing definitions. Screen sizes, forms, technical specifications, and uses—once the domain of industry experts—have become topics of popular discussion and media coverage. One need only visit MacRumors or TechCrunch to discover the intricacies and stakes of these conversations. Second, the development of multiple image spaces within the screen—the possibility of numerous "windows" and layers on a screen as a common feature of contemporary screen culture—produces

FIGURE 2 *The individualized screens of an in-flight entertainment system on a wide-body aircraft. Photo: Marc Smith.*

a new relationship between image, frame(s), and screen. We distinguish the on-screen frame of a media player or other app from the screen's material frame, for example, and can open additional frames within that space while bearing in mind the relationships across them. Patrick Cederberg and Walter Woodman deftly explored this condition in their 2013 film, *Noah*, which takes place entirely within the multi-window frame of a desktop screen. Third, amid this proliferation of screen forms and frames the advent of mobile and tactile screens has fundamentally changed how we interact with screens as physical objects. Touchscreen devices literally put the screen in our hands and under our fingertips, creating an unprecedented bodily intimacy between user and object. It would be difficult to maintain perceptions of the screen as a stable window offering a view onto some space beyond when in fact we clutch it in our palm and determine what happens in that frame by tapping and caressing its surface.

In response to these changes, recent research has clouded the screen's ostensibly transparent surface. This began at the close of the twentieth century, when previously disparate visual practices and viewing contexts began to converge in the frame of the computer screen. The digitization of all forms of images brought the greatest shift in visual culture since the invention of photography and its corollary—film—over a century before. What had appeared on movie screens and TV sets could now be found on the desktop or laptop screen alongside other media—from books to newspapers and photographs—that theretofore had been uncommon or unknown in screen form. Media and screen became inseparable. Lev Manovich called for an archaeology of the screen (1998), Erkki Huhtamo expressed the need for "screenology" (2004), and Anne Friedberg wrote *The Virtual Window*, a book-length study of the conditions and aesthetics of the screen from Renaissance perspective systems to twenty-first-century desktop operating systems (2006). More recently, additional calls have been heard for the study of both the contemporary screen, as in Nanna Verhoeff's work on tactile screens in mobile and locative media (2012), and overlooked historical uses and forms, as with Haidee Wasson's work on "small screen" and "suitcase" cinema (2012a,b). Researching the screen as a common element across communicative practices has emerged as an expedient method to circumvent and perhaps dismantle misleading or unproductive distinctions among media forms.

Window or wall

On those occasions when we do talk about the screen's role in our lives, the conversation tends to follow one of two paths. Either we condemn the screen as an obstacle that takes time and attention away from more worthy pursuits, or we celebrate it as a limitless tool that allows us to do things that would otherwise be impossible. Sometimes we may take both paths in the same conversation! Of course, we need to remind ourselves that the reality of our relationship with the screen rarely nears either of these extremes.

The screen does not imprison us. It is not the bedazzling wall of a cell of our own making. If movable-type printing allowed the diffusion of knowledge on a mass scale, screen media has only intensified that process. With well over a half-trillion photos uploaded to the internet every year, two hundred million hours of video uploaded to YouTube over the same period, and billions of indexed pages of text across the internet's billion websites, it's impossible to argue that the screen is not the privileged point of access to a large portion of the sum of human knowledge.

All this potential comes at a heavy price, however. The screen interface is also the privileged point of access to *us*, serving as the frame for tracking, quantifying, and commodifying our existence. It efficiently reduces our decisions and actions to fodder for algorithms that nudge us in directions we may not otherwise go as they constantly seek to monetize our time and attention without paying us a penny in return. And that is the sanguine view. Even when we are not consciously on-line, a device's operating system often will transmit our patterns of behavior back to their manufacturers. Trying any of the numerous on-line privacy tests shows us the significant amount of information we pass through the screen before we even get started. In converting our actions into storable data, interacting with the screen—even just carrying it around as it continues to interact with the network—makes our most personal details accessible to others. The screen has become the ideal surveillance tool, not as an eye peering into our living space as George Orwell had imagined it in *1984* (though it can be that), but rather as a raster grid converting our clicks and taps into indelible strings of digits that can come back to haunt us. Lest we forget that, a major browser reminds us on its homepage that "Law enforcement stake-outs have moved beyond binoculars, bugs and bad guys. [They've] gone digital" (Mozilla). Any viable route to privacy today requires abandoning the networked screen as a first step, a seemingly simple but extreme gesture that can produce untenable social and professional isolation.

Yet significant areas of the world, particularly sub-Saharan Africa and South Asia, are off that grid, suffering that isolation due to the lack of a network or the tools to access it. A billion people in India alone do not have immediate internet access. Many of them are more concerned with obtaining clean water and sufficient cooking fuel than having a connected screen in their homes. The rise of relatively inexpensive cellular networks and the second-hand market for cellphones, however, has meant that many Indians living at the edge of poverty, such as street vendors and those providing support services, have obtained their first screen device as means to maintaining and increasing their business prospects. A laundress or knife-sharpener may not have a shop, or even a legal address, but they will have a number that you can call or text when you need them. The power of the screen indeed comes in many forms.

Screen performance is no longer just what is happening on screen and how the screen affects it. It is also the screen's movement as a portable, mobile object that penetrates into and through the spaces within which we circulate. This shift has brought into relief three binaries that have guided the screen's design, use, and meaning across history. These are production and reception, fixedness and mobility, and collectiveness and individuality. All three pairings can be considered aspects of the screen's performance—that is, both screen display and the screen-object's action in time and space—as well as aspects of screen interface.

It is worth noting here how the three pairings have developed. The contemporary screen is often a site of both production and reception, where the user selects, examines, and alters visual information. Taking photos, viewing the results, applying filters, and uploading the images to a photosharing site would be a common example. Production and reception may happen simultaneously, however, as the screen functions as a variable tool. Through the interface, whether remote command or tactile, the screen display reacts to our movements, recognizing our presence. In the case of tactile screens, this recognition is direct. The pressure or electrical discharge of our finger changes the conditions of the resistive or capacitive screen's activated layers. This distinguishes today's screens from earlier examples.

FIGURE 3 *Crowd recording the Pope's visit to Naples, 2015. Photo: Raffaele Esposito.*

The eighteenth-century screen of the phantasmagoria or the twentieth-century screen of the movie theater or television were sites of reception meant to produce a spectacle for people relatively removed from the image surface. Screen users were "viewers" and "audiences." Although someone might control the images viewed—the movie theater projectionist, the parent organizing a family slide show, the TV network scheduling executive—there were usually many others involved in the viewing process with little or no possibility of affecting the performance. One might interact with images and other audience members under these circumstances, but there was no physical interaction with the screen. Touching the surface—whether fabric, glass, or another material—was strongly discouraged or prohibited, not only because it would destroy the illusion of the presented image but also because it might damage the surface and permanently jeopardize the effect of any subsequent performance. The screen was figuratively, and often literally, out of reach. As Stanley Cavell claims in the case of the movie theater screen, the screen intercedes like a barrier that "screens me from the world it holds ... [and] screens that world from me" (1979, 24). Today's screen is not only meant to be handled, but often to be used in tandem with one's engagement with the world around them. While we can continue to consider ways screens intercede to block out our surroundings (think of all the people we see staring silently at their screens in public places), we can just as easily consider how they allow us a better understanding of those surroundings by offering an adaptable frame we can hold up to those spaces.

As a consequence of these changes, the screen's relationship to the mobilized gaze has also undergone significant transformation. For centuries the mobility embodied by screens was mainly understood as the movement of light on their surfaces, rather than the screen's movement through space. In nineteenth-century magic lantern slide shows the sensation of mobility was produced by hand-cranked animation as well as dissolves into changing scenes. Cinema added the sensation of photographic live-action as well as camera movement and editing. The screen, however, remained a stationary frame during these journeys. Viewers had to travel to the screen—whether the downtown movie theater, the suburban multiplex or the TV set placed in the living room, bedroom, or neighborhood bar or community center. In general, the sensation of mobility was produced through a stable and often prescribed viewer-screen relationship (e.g. fixed seating or furniture arrangement). The late twentieth century saw the rise of the mobile screen, first with handheld video game consoles and pocket calculators, then personal digital assistants (PDAs) and cellphones. As the processing and memory of these devices improved and wireless communication became the norm, new relationships were produced among object, image, and user mobility. Contemporary screen mobility is a complex equation often involving the screen's movement through space in addition to the user's movements in space and in relation to the screen, including direct intervention into the screen display and physical contact with its surface. Through this multivariate performance, the mobilized screen gaze may have different properties and meanings from moment to moment. Mobilized interface is a more apt description of the process, as it acknowledges the increasing movement of, and physical contact between, screen and user.

A (very) material object

Screens today are lightweight, cheap, and disposable. Yet the screen is not the inexhaustible or renewable resource that it was when it entailed a white wall or cotton cloth bearing projected images. Most contemporary screen-based devices are composed of scarce natural resources (rare earth minerals and metals) that require environmentally damaging mining often in war zones or under repressive regimes in Africa and Asia—the very places where screens themselves are in short supply. The color red of most screens requires Europium, for example, which is considered one of the scarcest elements in the universe. Other materials contributing to the screen-object are extremely hazardous and potentially deadly. As the screen has gotten brighter and more portable, it has gotten more dangerous. While traditional movie screens may be made of fabric and glass beads, cathode ray tube screens (CRTs) hold deadly toxins that are difficult to recycle, including lead, mercury, cadmium, and barium. More recent liquid crystal display (LCD), light-emitting diode (LED), and plasma screens contain lead, mercury, and cadmium, along with

FIGURE 4 *Cathode ray tube screens abandoned in the brush, Adelaide, Australia, 2015. Photo: Michael Coghlan.*

arsenic, beryllium, tetramethylammonium hydroxide, and potassium iodide. One chemical used in the manufacture of LCD screens, nitrogen trifluoride, has been found to be 17,200 times more harmful than carbon dioxide in trapping atmospheric heat.

These details are all the more unsettling when we think about the abandoned screens we find dumped along our paths, not to mention the old cellphones we may have stashed in our dresser drawer or—far worse—thrown out with the household trash. The growing ecological risk of these habits is reflected in the annual production of over forty million tons of electronic waste worldwide (equivalent to six kilograms per human). Not surprisingly, the richest countries contribute most to this problem, with the U.S. producing a quarter of all such waste (Step). As screens and screen-based devices become cheaper and therefore more disposable (despite being more durable and long-lasting from a technological perspective) they are contributing significantly to our environmental woes. American electronics chains sell tablets for $50 today, a tenth of the cost of a low-end laptop only a few years ago. Just as the world is coming to terms with greenhouse gas emissions produced by fossil-fuel-based manufacturing and transportation, it will have to find ways of slowing the consumption of screen-based devices—beginning with an ideological shift away from the screen as fashion statement—in addition to implementing effective strategies for recycling their components and materials. The screen may be one of our most adaptable communicative tools and cultural objects, but we must resist the historically entrenched tendency to look past it. Unless we curb our bad habits in manufacturing and consuming screens, we may one day find ourselves left in the dark, empty-handed.

References

Cavell, Stanley. *The World Viewed*. Second edition. Cambridge, MA: Harvard University Press, 1979.

Friedberg, Anne. *The Virtual Window: From Alberti to Microsoft*. Cambridge, MA: The MIT Press, 2006.

Hartley, John. "Is Screen Studies a Load of Old Cobblers? And If So, Is That Good?" *Cinema Journal* 45, no. 1 (2005): 101–6.

Huhtamo, Erkki. "Elements of Screenology: Toward an Archaeology of the Screen." *Iconics: International Studies of the Modern Image* 7 (2004): 31–82

Manovich, Lev. "Towards an Archaeology of the Computer Screen." In *Cinema Futures: Cain, Abel or Cable?* edited by Thomas Elsaesser and Kay Hoffmann, 27–43. Amsterdam: University of Amsterdam Press, 1998.

Miller, Toby. "Revising Screen Studies." *Television & New Media* 2, no. 2 (2001): 91–3.

Mozilla, "Get Smart on the Web: Government Surveillance." Available online: https://www.mozilla.org/en-US/teach/smarton/surveillance/ (accessed February 1, 2016).

Step, E-waste world map. Available online: http://www.step-initiative.org/step-e-waste-world-map.html (accessed February 1, 2016).

Verhoeff, Nanna. *Mobile Screens: The Visual Regime of Navigation*. Amsterdam: Amsterdam University Press, 2012.

Wasson, Haidee. "The Other Small Screen: Moving Images at New York's World Fair, 1939." *Canadian Journal of Film Studies* 21, no. 1 (2012a): 81–103.

Wasson, Haidee. "Suitcase Cinema." *Cinema Journal* 51, no. 2 (2012b): 148–52.

Screens and Their Histories

Introduction to Section One

Is there anyone who does not know what a screen is or how it works? This is a reasonable question when toddlers recognize and effectively manipulate screens before they can walk and talk. A screen could be anything from a smartphone to the side of a building, however. It has developed in different directions over the centuries, contributing to some of the oldest visual media, such as drawing (through projection tracings), as well as to most of the newest.

With its frequent appearance in the everyday, one would think the screen is relatively easy to define, even if it is often overlooked or taken for granted. We all know a screen when we see one, after all. But this is becoming less and less the case as screens increasingly mimic other forms of image systems and become embedded more deeply in other objects. Describing the screen presents a remarkably difficult task. Smartphones equipped with "transparent screen" effects and laser-projection keyboards, for example, at once diminish and amplify the screen for their users. In many circumstances it may be easier to survey one's surroundings and point to specific examples of the screen than formulate a satisfactory general description. In truth one might point just about anywhere, since nearly any material surface or object can serve as a screen. Light may be projected onto an opaque plane or pass through any semi-translucent material to produce visible forms or images. Screens, or at least screen-like occurrences, can be observed in nature, as when we watch the shadows cast on the ground by objects intercepting sunlight. Nevertheless, we tend to think of screens as products of cultural practice, designed specifically for the display of changing—usually light-based—visual information.

This section of the reader presents several approaches to explaining what screens are and how they got to be this way. Essays in the first part, entitled "Screen Identities," take on the task of identifying the screen's fundamental properties and functions, a critical exercise if one is to study the screen in greater depth. Charles Acland points out the potential obstacles in this pursuit. The screen "is not in and of itself a medium, format, or platform," he states. "Rather, it is often an in-between manifestation of all three, one that materializes how we come to see and describe the differences and connections among television, film, computers, electronic signage, and digital spaces." In

FIGURE I.1 *Early steps in learning to live through the screen: a toddler interacts with an iPad, 2012. Photo: Tia Henriksen.*

his essay, Acland supplies several examples that complicate our sense of screens and suggests that their abundance along our path often makes us less aware of them. Not only have they become part of our environment but, like plastic in the mid-twentieth century, they come to define that environment. Any attempt to impose a hierarchy of screens, then, ultimately hinders our ability to study screen culture.

Francesco Casetti explains that we have reached a critical point in the history of the screen, where the term "screen" may no longer suffice to describe our relationship with these image surfaces. The metaphors of window, frame, and mirror that imply a viewer gazing at scenes that bear a resemblance to physical reality are no longer valid. Casetti offers in their stead the metaphors of the monitor, bulletin board, and scrapbook to better convey our contemporary screen views and habits. As a frame for the continual flow of data, whether we pay attention to it or not, the screen transforms into a simple display surface for Casetti, one that presents many forms of information, from the time to texts.

No matter what information they display, or how we interact with them, screens follow certain rules determined by technical constraints and cultural patterns of organizing visual information. Sean Cubitt has charted the relation between these, exploring the ideological, ecological, and cultural consequences of the screen's development and deployment. From the mining of rare earths for color screen components to the endurance of the raster grid as the surface's organizing pattern, Cubitt demonstrates that a basic understanding of the screen's technological aspects and their political economic implications remains beyond most users. Yet, he argues, "these technological features both express a particular quality of contemporary social life and retransmit it: They are normative technologies. Here lies their importance, for such structures express the nature of public life in particular, and they rearticulate it." If we do not make an effort to question the screen and what this material object tells us about global socio-ideological dynamics, he warns, then we are only shortchanging ourselves and the possibilities for positive change.

Anne Friedberg, who wrote what may be a field-defining book for studying the screen, identifies the multiplication of on-screen frames as a defining characteristic of digital interface. Ironically, the window metaphor returns in her account of computing's contribution to the screen, but the screen-as-window is replaced by Microsoft's Windows and its derivatives. "For Alberti, the metaphor of the window implied direct, veridical, and unmediated vision, transparency of surface or aperture, and transmitted light. The computer 'window' implies its opposite," Friedberg explains. Screens guided by software manifest an increase in screen representations within the frame, breaking down the cohesion of the surface and complicating our understanding of what screen and screen space entail. It is only our direct interaction with these surfaces and frames that give them their sense and meaning.

William Henry Fox Talbot lived in the relatively screen-free environment of Victorian England. However, as one of the inventors of photography, he would make a major contribution to the technologies behind modern screen culture. In this regard his fantastical poem "The Magic Mirror" is an intriguing text. This Romantic ballad of a wizard, his daughter, and their castle centers on a veiled mirror that perfectly matches Acland's definition of the screen as "a surface for animation." The mirror not only presents moving images of an imaginary space, but also literally reshapes the world that surrounds it, as human interaction with the surface has direct— catastrophic—consequences. Is it a prophetic, cautionary tale for the screens that surround us today? That Talbot wrote his poem in 1830, several years before he embarked on the experiments leading to photography, makes it all the more remarkable, speaking to a "screen" sensibility in play behind the embryonic stages of modern visual technologies.

Understanding what the screen is rests in part on knowing what it has been as both an idea and an object. The second part of this section, "Evolution and Revolution," brings together essays that trace the varied roots of, and historical influences on, today's screens and our feelings about them. Plato's allegory of the cave opens this section because it is one of the oldest and most widely disseminated descriptions of a screen world. It would be hard to ascribe to Plato's work any direct influence on the rise of the screen or screen culture. However, this ancient conceptualization of being and knowledge where "the truth would be literally nothing but the shadows of the images" may help explain the enduring uneasiness that often accompanies our reliance on screens. The common and paradoxical belief that all screens offer both more and less in their influence on our perception finds its seed in the paradigm of Plato's imaginary cave.

Erkki Huhtamo, a pioneer in the branch of media studies known as media archaeology, considers the historical development of objects, narratives, and practices that manifest—and contribute to—the idea of the screen as visual mediation. As he states, "Identifying the inherited lurking behind the 'extraordinary' may lead to a better appreciation of 'the new'." Huhtamo introduced this endeavor in his 2004 essay "Elements of Screenology," where he effectively differentiated researching the screen from what had misleadingly been called "screen studies." In his contribution here, Huhtamo has revisited, updated, and expanded this earlier work. He offers new historical examples across several centuries while refining key aspects of his theories in demonstrating the complex histories and competing desires that have informed our understandings of—and engagement with—the screen as a cultural tool.

Unlike Huhtamo's rhizomatic approach, Lev Manovich traces a more defined, teleological evolution of the screen and screen practices. In invoking a genealogy that begins with Leon Battista Alberti's window of Renaissance painting, he describes a progression of three screen types—the classical screen of painting, the dynamic screen of cinema, and the computer screen where viewers can intervene in screen events. While this typology is a simplification that negates the historical diversity noted by Huhtamo and others, it nevertheless sets the screen and screen-like properties at the center of the development of modern visuality. In addressing the contemporary screen's debt to radar and similar technologies, he places this within ideologies of power and war, an important consideration when studying the screen's role in globalized networks susceptible to constant surveillance.

Like Manovich, Edmond Couchot sees the computer screen—or, more precisely, the digitally "computed" screen—as a significant change in our relationship to images. Where Manovich sees a shift, however, Couchot finds a rupture. The digitally ordered grid of the screen converts images into mutable things that need not have any other link to physical space. He emphasizes the significance of this by contrasting digital screens to painting and analogue photography. Where the act of recording is preeminent in both painting and photography, with digital screens it is the act of presentation that matters. Though this stance—developed in the late 1980s—might seem reactionary today, Couchot presents a condition that may help explain the fetishization of the screen today as the essence of the image.

Uta Caspary considers an entirely different history of the screen in emphasizing its architectural affinities. If screens have gotten smaller, fitting into our palms, than they have also gotten larger, with enormous outdoor examples popping up in urban settings. Caspary finds the antecedents of today's large, public screens in medieval stained glass windows and modernism's lighted glass facades. These may foreshadow and explain the current appeal of massive, "permanent" screen installations in large-scale building projects. Here screen environments and built environments amount to the same thing and screen interaction becomes a nearly permanent state.

Reference

Huhtamo, Erkki. "Elements of Screenology: Toward an Archaeology of the Screen." *ICONICS: International Studies of the Modern Image* 7 (2004): 31–82.

Screen Identities

CHAPTER ONE

The Crack in the Electric Window

Charles R. Acland

You can always rely on Marshall McLuhan to supply memorably pithy aphorisms about media culture, even if his logic soon crumbles apart in your fingers. Reading his distinction between *light on* media, like film, and *light through* media, like television, he appears to have captured a fundamental aspect organizing screen technologies, namely projection versus emission.[1] But then he extends his observation to what are ultimately untenable claims about differing levels of cognitive and emotional involvement in each. As is the case with most dichotomies, it takes only a few counterexamples to reveal the wobbliness of the split. Film can be back-projected, video can be front-projected, and both were being done for years prior to McLuhan's own technologically static projections.

McLuhan's binary prompts him to declare that projected images situate spectators in the position of the camera, whereas the emission of light from television turns viewers into screens.[2] The notion of "viewers as screens" is provocative for screen culture scholars struggling to provide workable definitions for any and all "screens." At the most basic level, regardless of the light source, our faces are the surfaces on which both projections and emissions settle. Our eyes register the light, reflected or not, and our ears receive the sound waves. One such iteration of viewers as screens—the wide-eyed child, bathed in the light of a television, computer, or film—is a conventionalized representation of absorption and hypnotic media control; it is a figuration of the innocent actually becoming a media screen. But we need not reinforce this version of what C. Wright Mills might have called the cheerfully robotic spectator. Maintaining the sensory condition of our human screen-ness—sentient bodies oriented toward audiovisual media—as a conceptual anchor helps film and media scholars avoid rigid typologies of mechanisms that stimulate sensations, which is a philosophical dead end toward which so many after McLuhan continue to dash. For all its variations, we should begin by acknowledging that the concept of the "screen" stitches together an identifiable and meaningful array of artifacts. We just seem to know what it is reflexively: a thing that glows and attracts attention with changing images, sounds, and information.

Technical specifications—screen size, aspect ratio, resolution, frame and refresh rate, brightness, color scale—might help us define what we are talking about in a specific instance, or better yet complicate what we presume we know about media. But the mechanical level only gets us so far in our job of actually understanding the related senses, sensibilities, and practices that form as a consequence of media use. All those unruly features of human existence simply can't be neatly confined and appended to medium specificity. As Raymond Williams wrote, and emphatically italicized, "*[N]o mode of production and therefore no dominant social order and therefore no dominant culture ever in reality includes or exhausts all human practice, human energy, and human intention.*"[3] The human element that exceeds structuring concepts equally speaks to the boundaries that we claim exist between media, screen-based and otherwise.

So what is a screen? The question can be situationally answered with details about scale, technology, shape, tactility, portability, and location. Erkki Huhtamo's work has effectively taken the presentist air out of our inflated thinking, pushing us to understand the centuries-long trajectory of screen culture to include billboards and spotlights.[4] Other valuable research has made inroads by focusing on urban concentrations of screens, and some have elaborated on descriptive nuances to the term "screen" that include filter, protection, barrier, and surface.[5] As this and other research shows, the category of "screen" is baffling precisely because it is not in and of itself a medium, format, or platform. Rather, it is often an in-between manifestation of all three, one that materializes how we come to see and describe the differences and connections among television, film, computers, electronic signage, and digital spaces. In contrast to McLuhan's typological claims, our critical gaze is as much directed toward the integrated qualities of all the sites and locations that we casually understand as screens as it is toward the definitive distinctions between and among them.

Studies of screen culture provide limit tests to descriptions of our technological environment as well as to the way media have settled into disciplines. As an interdisciplinary research domain, screen culture has been effective in forcing the hand of Film Studies, challenging some of its more restrictive boundaries. Television Studies and Media Studies, not to mention Sound and Video Game Studies, have been relatively versatile and attentive to changing modes of production and circulation. But Screen Studies is essentially where the dust settled after the so-called death of cinema a few years back. Film Studies, sometimes in the voice of the art-loving bully and sometimes pleading for special status, you know, for old time's sake, banked foundational claims on immutable technological qualities. And it did so even as the dominance of a single technological film condition was disappearing, or, more dramatically, as historical work of the past few decades showed us that a secure and stable cinematic apparatus likely never existed. For film theory, even the term "apparatus" lent a false impression of technological fixity to what were otherwise powerful ideological critiques. One doesn't call something fluid an "apparatus." The trope of the quiet viewer, alone in the dark, in public, with only the flickering light occupying his or her field of vision, was, in the end, a wish, a beautiful expression of what was tasteful, or perhaps magical, in the constitution of relations among spectators, situations, and moving-image technologies. In this respect, the quest and demand for an ideal screening circumstance for motion pictures was partly a battle waged against the messy humanity of moviegoers with the weapon of technological determinism linked to aesthetic purity. The secret life of the cinephile is that of a technophile. Meanwhile, the electronics industry tumbles on, selling new consumer gadgets that arrive nestled in cardboard boxes and Styrofoam packaging. This industry operates oblivious to the scholarly peregrinations of a resolute faith in spectatorial ideals, except as they can be assimilated in their most basic renditions ("more cinematic") into advantageous promotional appeals.

It is easy to see how far the film screen has come from the dream of perfect cinematic conditions. Consider some recent innovations in "production screens," a long-standing category that has not received the full historical and critical attention it deserves. […] James Cameron did the motion-capture portions of *Avatar* (2009) with a "virtual camera," which was basically a handheld monitor on which he could watch the performers.[6] This screen was fed by a grid of a hundred high-definition (HD) cameras and, by moving it, he could record the camera work he desired, including pans, tilts, and tracking. No lens to look through, no actual tracks laid for camera movement, and no individual lighting setups. Shadows came later. On the one hand, this is a good example of what D. N. Rodowick observed as the reinstatement of an existing cinematic language even as the instruments are modified.[7] On the other, it moves the screen from the endpoint of spectatorship to the position previously occupied by the industry-standard motion picture camera.

For the live-action portions of *Avatar*, Cameron experimented with the "Simulcam." This allowed people on set to see, when looking through the camera eyepiece, takes with mock-ups of green-screen and motion-capture elements. A limitation of shoots involving computer-generated images is the separation between filming personnel and digital craft workers, whose enhancements to the film appear much later. The Simulcam gives directors and directors of photography the ability to see a rough approximation of effects that will be integrated eventually, and thus they have an immediate basis for on-set decision making. Again, like the virtual camera for motion capture, one result is to reinforce an existing hierarchy of authority, such that directors and directors of photography effectively wrest back some control from the digital-effects departments and are emboldened in the digital filmmaking process. Notably, the Simulcam confounds distinctions we may have internalized as the approximate integrated image appears in the eyepiece and also on a synchronized monitor. Conventional definitions of monitor, computer, and camera are disrupted. The camera is a screen and the screen is a computer, and all are windows onto a live, virtual performance.

Given these features, which challenge some basic assumptions about our object of analysis, there is some advantage in sticking with the simplest notion of a screen—that a screen is a surface for animation. The variety of ordinary screen products and possibilities means we have to forget about measuring the "unusualness" of a screen by its distance from the flat rectangle of the theatrical environment. Barbara Klinger's and Haidee Wasson's observations about the term "nontheatrical," which sneaks in a stabilized notion of "normal" exhibition circuits, are instructive here.[8] Let us embrace the full implication of challenging presumptions about real, traditional, and proper screens, and crack through awkward boundaries between TV and not-TV, film and not-film, and computer and not-computer. The expanded, augmented, and future screens of database and installation art have already unsettled these categories, but then again so have tiny screens on the back of children's toy cameras, multiuse touchscreen electronic tablets, and automobile DVD players. Going further, we must take on the "minor" screen world of the interface on a credit card machine, the automated ticket machine at a movie theater, the portable gaming device, and the blinking roadside LED warning of construction ahead as well as those "major" sites of theatrical screens, HD television, and mobile computers. This is not to efface vastly different uses and engagements, but to draw attention to all the materials that organize our relations to signs, commerce, and each other, helping us to understand more fully what is at stake in making qualitative claims about one screen and not another. Further, we should work to ensure that Screen Studies does not become another way to prioritize visual culture, when ambient or amplified sound nearly always accompanies the glowing or reflected surface, whether through human dialogue or electronic beeps. In short, we must steer clear of an impulse to defend and police hierarchies of tasteful and artful screens—screens that reveal versus screens that conceal. Therefore, it is vital to see the continuity of processes and priorities of cultural life, and to recognize the fundamental instabilities that advanced capitalism injects into most aspects of the social and technological realm.

In the 1950s, Roland Barthes wrote of the alchemy of plastic. Present everywhere and used for so many purposes, Barthes suggested that plastic effectively subsumed all other materials: "[T]he hierarchy of substances is abolished: a single one replaces them all: the whole world *can* be plasticized."[9] The ability to be shaped and reshaped into so many things, in so many places, became the core meaning of that particular synthetic chemical compound: "More than a substance, plastic is the very idea of its infinite transformation ... [I]t is ubiquity made visible."[10] Even with fuller knowledge of its environmental impact, plastic surely still holds this position as an elemental property of our constructed contemporary existence. But "ubiquity made visible" is now a resonant description of our current screen world, too. The potential adaptability of screens into any number of media, technological, and commercial operations seems limitless. Screens are the window displays for convergence, where we see the melding of film, broadcasting, and computers into hybrid media and commerce. Mobile and monumental, miniature and massive, screens are not exactly everywhere, but they offer up—they make *visible*—notions of ubiquity, adaptability, and utility. They are a stabilized part of how we expect to meet the future. Screens are our plastic.

Notes

1   Marshall McLuhan, *Understanding Media: The Extensions of Man* (New York: McGraw-Hill, 1964), 313.
2   Ibid.
3   Raymond Williams, *Marxism and Literature* (New York: Oxford University Press, 1977), 125.
4   Erkki Huhtamo, "Elements of Screenology: Toward an Archaeology of the Screen," *Iconics: International Studies of the Modern Image* 7 (2004): 31–82; and Huhtamo, "Behind the Messages on the Wall: An Archaeology of Public Media Displays," in *Urban Screens Reader*, ed. Scott McQuire, Meredith Martin, and Sabine Niederer (Amsterdam: Institute of Network Cultures, 2009), 14–28.
5   McQuire, Martin, and Niederer, *Urban Screens Reader*; Kirsty Best, "Interfacing the Environment: Networked Screens and the Ethics of Visual Consumption," *Ethics and the Environment* 9, no. 2 (2004): 66–85; Gunther Kress, "'Screen': Metaphors of Display, Partition, Concealment and Defence," *Visual Communication* 5, no. 2 (2006): 199–204.
6   On the camera systems used in Avatar, see Jody Duncan and Lisa Fitzpatrick, *The Making of "Avatar"* (New York: Abrams, 2010); and Jody Duncan, "The Seduction of Reality," *Cinefex* 120 (2010): 68–146.
7   D. N. Rodowick, *The Virtual Life of Film* (Cambridge, MA: Harvard University Press, 2007).
8   Barbara Klinger, "Cinema's Shadow: Reconsidering Non-theatrical Exhibition," in *Going to the Movies: Hollywood and the Social Experience of Cinema*, ed. Richard Maltby, Melvyn Stokes, and Robert C. Allen (Exeter, UK: University of Exeter Press, 2007), 273–290; Haidee Wasson, *Museum Movies: The Museum of Modern Art and the Birth of Art Cinema* (Berkeley: University of California Press, 2005), 35–36.
9   Roland Barthes, "Plastic" (1957), in *Mythologies*, trans. Annette Lavers (New York: Hill and Wang, 1972), 97–99.
10 Ibid., 97.

CHAPTER TWO

What Is a Screen Nowadays?

Francesco Casetti

[...]

With the introduction of the multi-screen installation, the traditional screen seemed to signal openly that it felt constrained within its traditional confines. The time had come for it to grow, to multiply, to spread out, and this moment arrived in the 1980s and 1990s. It was precisely during these two decades that a series of extensions became common (the connection of the television set to the VCR and to the videogame console, for instance).[1] Moreover, it was primarily during this 20-year span that the screen began to constitute an essential part of new media, following a trajectory which will surely continue into the next decades. Examples of this process are the increasing presence of the computer in daily life[2] and the great success of the French Minitel—an amalgamation of the telephone and the video-screen.[3] The introduction of the portable DVD player allowed for the personal consumption of videos outside the walls of the domestic space.[4] Cellphones began to become a fixture of everyday experience with the first of the four (and counting) generations of mobile telephone technology.[5] Electronic organizers started replacing paper diaries.[6] Tablets began developing along a path that would lead to incredibly successful products, such as the Kindle and the iPad.[7] And, finally, media-facades started taking their place as a characteristic feature of many urban spaces, before acquiring the capability, as they now have, of interacting with passers-by. Indeed, media have become media-screens.

This screen explosion, which is still affecting us today, has led us to a true turning point. We find ourselves surrounded by unprecedented technological innovations: surfaces made of liquid crystals, of plasma, of LEDs, and as flexible as a piece of paper. And since they are increasingly interconnected, they are able to communicate with one another. This watershed represents a conceptual transformation as much as it does a technological fact: it is the very idea of a screen that is changing, as Lev Manovich has already suggested (Manovich, 2000, pp. 94–115). There are three aspects that I consider crucial. First, the great diffusion of screens allows media content to multiply the occasions on which it may present itself (in order to watch a film, we are no longer confined to the movie theater). Second, the fact that these screens are often connected allows for the retrieval of content independent of the situation or location in which the users find themselves (in order to watch a film, we can download it where and when we like). Finally, and more radically, the ubiquity of these screens makes possible the living or reliving of media experience in new environments and on new devices (we can feel like spectators, even by watching a film in a train on a portable DVD player). In short, this screen explosion has resulted in a diffusion of content on many platforms (spreadability), an interconnection of reception points (networking) and a reactivation of experiences in many situations (relocation). This new situation, which seems to have now arrived at a maturation point, has literally led the screen to assume a new nature. It no longer represents the site of an epiphany of the real; rather, it is a surface across which travel the images that circulate through social space. The information that surrounds us condenses on the screen, lingers for a moment, interacts with the surrounding environment and then takes off for other points in a kind of continuous movement.

New metaphors for the screen

To better understand this new situation, let us attempt once again an exercise in terminological recognition by asking: What are the key words that communicate what a screen is nowadays? There is no doubt that the old metaphors no longer work, so we must discover which other terms have supplanted them.

The first term is undoubtedly "monitor": the screen increasingly serves to inspect the world around us, to analyze and verify it—in essence, to keep it under control. The window which once restored our contact with the world has become a peep-hole through which to scrutinize reality, in the likely event that it may be hiding something dangerous.

The screen as monitor is first of all what we find in the large surveillance centers and in the security offices of apartment buildings and commercial complexes. A series of viewers form a kind of wall, which allows for the constant surveillance of every room and corridor, and, above all, every entrance/exit and every point of the external perimeter. Who is it that performs the surveillance? In many cases, members of the security staff view the monitors. However, in many 24-hour, closed-circuit systems, the images gathered by the cameras are simply recorded; there is no one watching, unless the footage is reviewed later, but only "after" something has happened. The security monitor does not necessarily imply a gaze.[8]

Such a situation takes us inevitably back to Bentham's Panopticon, which Foucault chose as the emblem of the disciplinary society (Foucault, 1979). While the Panopticon was designed so that only one individual was required to keep an eye on the entire building, in the case of security cameras, everything is observed but there are no longer any observers. Put another way, no one is looking since the end goal is not to observe (or to make known that one is being observed) but simply to gather data to be mined in case the need arises.

This same contradiction is found in an even more paradoxical form in the other example of the screen as monitor: the global positioning system (GPS). This is also an instrument used to keep territory under observation, in order to avoid possible inconveniences and to take advantage of possible opportunities.

We use it to stay on track and to arrive quickly at our destination; to avoid running out of gas and to locate the nearest service station; to avoid dying of hunger and to find a decent restaurant in the vicinity. The GPS may seem to represent the return of the observer—after all, its small screen is always in front of the driver's eyes—but the gaze it elicits differs significantly from that

FIGURE 2.1 *Dashboard screens displaying camera and GPS views in a Tesla Model S, 2012. Photo: Steve Jurvetson.*

traditionally linked to a screen. It is an intermittent gaze, activated only—and most often—in moments of need; and it is a gaze with multiple focal points, aimed both at the maps supplied by the kit and at the surrounding reality, which continues to be visible through the windshield and windows of the vehicle. These windows do still exist. In short, it is a gaze that is largely independent of the device. In this light, the GPS confirms the fact that although monitors are in constant need of new information, they do not always require an eye to scrutinize and observe them.

The second term that defines contemporary screens—replacing the metaphor of the frame, which nowadays exhibits clear limitations—is "bulletin board", or even "blackboard." In fact, in the screens that surround us, we encounter less and less frequently representations capable of restoring the texture of the world, and more and more frequently figures that function as memoranda, as signposts and, above all, as instructions for behavior.

Let us consider screens found in waiting rooms, in stations and in modes of public transport. Various messages pass across these surfaces: film and video clips, advertisements, tourism documentaries and so on. Their objective is not to offer an external reality or to alleviate the sense of oppression brought on by the closed environment in which we find ourselves confined. Rather, they are intended to help us pass the time and prepare for future actions: they inform us of the approach of a train (to the station), of whose turn it is (in the waiting room), of the weather at a destination (in an airport), of the beauty of tourist destinations (in a ticket office) and of exercises to do in order to avoid discomfort (on an airplane). More than fragments of the world, they are instructions for behavior.

The same may be said for the videos in shops and malls, which display the goods for sale on the counters and shelves. Again, what is important is not what these videos depict: the merchandise is right next to them, in plain sight. What really counts is the information that accompanies the depiction of the merchandise: we see how it is used, how much it costs, where it comes from, why it is convenient and which lifestyle it matches. It is according to this information—often evocative and emotional—that we adjust our behavior—that is, to either purchase or not to purchase the merchandise. The presence of these videos acts as a sort of veil on reality: we have ceased to look at things via their representation; we look instead at a set of directives aimed at us.

In seeming contrast to this, many homepages of institutional websites function in a similar manner. I am thinking, for example, of those of schools or universities. These relate academic life to a profusion of attractive images: they reveal a whole world to the eyes of the reader. However, these illustrations act as bridges to boxes or links that offer detailed information aimed at the various users of the site: students, professors, families and administrators. A possible life experience is transformed into a series of announcements.

Videogames offer perhaps the clearest example of the screen as bulletin board or blackboard. The image that they present consists essentially of a group of figures of variable value upon which the player must act. Their value is defined by a score that appears in an accompanying box or that flashes near a character in the game. The players choose their moves based on these values, deciding whether to confront the character, to move to another portion of the landscape, to acquire new abilities and so on. The player's moves will determine changes in value: either the value of a specific character or of the total gains or losses. This score will in turn determine new moves. Therefore the essence of the game does not lie in recognizing characters that appear on the screen: attention is concentrated above all on a set of values and on a menu of possible lines of action. The players do not find pleasure in contemplating a representation; rather they move within a forest of instructions. I would add that in many of these games—those called "shoot 'em all"—the essence of the action consists in destroying that which appears before the player. This means that the world that is represented here is not only completely abstract, reduced as it is to numeric values, but also essentially destined for decomposition. What a perfect example of the tendency of the bulletin board to disassociate itself from reality, in order to create space for a flow of information. (This does not mean that what they present is not reality: it is simply not mere physical reality. Rather, it is an entity that causes facts, possible actions, comments, values and so on to overlap. In this respect, "augmented reality" is exemplary: when I point my cellphone in front of me, I see on the screen a piece of urban landscape made up of actual buildings, supplemented by indications that help me to move within the city, as well as information about edifices belonging to the past that have since disappeared, and projects for future construction.)

The third way to better describe a contemporary screen—as an alternative to the traditional metaphor of the mirror, now obsolete—is to think of it as a "mailbox" or "scrapbook." Spectators now struggle to identify with a character or story; they prefer instead to construct images of themselves in the first person, by assembling photos, texts and comments often lifted from elsewhere and trusting these heterogeneous materials to a blog or putting them in circulation on a social network. Therefore more than identifying with someone or something else, they cut, paste, compose and send.

I mentioned blogs: the personal homepage is the first example of the screen as scrapbook. Blogs are literally mosaics of texts and figures, which accumulate day after day, narrating the life of the blogger. This is a particular kind of self-presentation: the materials that form it are only partly self-produced; often they are recuperated from elsewhere, and once they are posted on the internet they are further recyclable in order to narrate other lives. The resulting portrait is true to life, but in its dismantling and reassembling, it could also apply to anyone. This means, paradoxically, that the flow of data, news and quotations is almost more important than the representation of subjectivity: the "I" is born of the personal use of what the user finds.

In the social networks typical of web 2.0, such as Tumblr, this condition returns in an even more radical way. Thanks to the presence of a feed reader, the page is loaded with content lifted from elsewhere until it forms a kind of newspaper that contains what the user reads or in which the user is interested. The posts of other bloggers appear on the user's dashboard, and they may sometimes—though not always—add comments or corrections. This results in an enormous accumulation of citations, references and sources with a relative paucity of the user's own interventions. The user's personality continues to manifest itself within this accumulation, but this manifestation comes about as the result of a type of link to which they connect themselves, much more so than as the result of what they say directly. Precisely because of this, their voice is ultimately nothing more than a montage of others' voices—almost as if to radicalize the fundamentally dialogic and heteroglossic nature of our discourse, highlighted by Mikhail Bakhtin 80 years ago (Bakhtin, 1981).

Even when this voice is made direct, the situation is not much altered. *Twitter* and *Facebook* (the initial page—or wall—of which is also reminiscent of the bulletin board) represent interesting examples. There is more space here for an exchange of opinions; however, any personal intervention is restricted to a few possibilities (in *Facebook*: "like", "comment" and "share"). Furthermore, this intervention is limited in space and therefore often devoid of much meaning (it is difficult to imagine that a click on the "Like button" can really reveal a personality). The user's intervention depends on the material that is currently available (they speak through what they find). Finally, it reflects thoughts and opinions that are strictly dependent on the subject touched upon in a discussion: once the subject changes, nothing hinders the emergence of other orientations, except a kind of loyalty to the objects that are "collected" and that lead each "friend" to offer obsessively what is expected of them.

In conclusion, these social networks are typified by a kind of self-presentation that is based on an arrangement of material, often borrowed from others, and linked closely to contingency—or simply guided by obsession. The same arrangement may also be reassembled in order to represent other personalities (perhaps of the same individual: there is no shortage of people who live a plurality of virtual lives under different nicknames). If it evolves, it may follow a course of personal transformation ("today I am not who I was yesterday"); but often, at least it seems to me, it simply follows the progression of circumstances ("I am who I am depending on the day"). These characteristics highlight the limits of these self-presentations: their value lies in how they are displayed, not in what they say; and while they have value for an individual, this is neither exclusive nor permanent. In light of this, we could say that in the very moment in which the social network participant presents a self-portrait, they open the door to their own dissolution. More decisively, what is lost is the traditional process of identification: the social network participant no longer finds completed stories in which to project themselves; they live in the midst of a continuous flow of data, available to them for every eventuality; they adapt their life to the material that they can gather; and they make of their life a bricolage.

From the screen to the display

Monitor, bulletin board (or blackboard) and scrapbook (or mailbox): these new keywords indicate just how distant the new screens are from the old. If it is true that we continue to deal with a rectangular surface on which figures in movement appear, it is also true that this surface no longer implies a reality, an envision, a recognition. This new screen is linked to a continuous flow of data but it is not necessarily coupled to an attentive gaze, to a world that asks to be witnessed or to a subject that is reflected in what it sees. There is a connection and a disconnection: a set of figures becomes perpetually available here where we are, but it does not necessarily lead us to a stable reference, an assured addressee and a full identification.

The concept of a "display" may help to better render an idea of this new entity.[9] The display shows, but only in the sense that it places at our disposition or makes accessible. It exhibits, but does not uncover. It offers, but does not commit. In other words, a display does not involve its images in the dialectic between visible and invisible (like a window used to do), between surfaces and structure (like a frame) or between appropriation and dispossession (like a mirror). The display simply "makes present" images. It places them in front of us, in case we may want to make use of them. It hands them to us, if you will.

The display is fully realized in the form of the touch screen. Here the eye is connected to the fingers, and it is they that signal if the observer is paying attention and what kind of attention they are paying. Touch solicits the arrival of images but, even more so, it guides their flow: it associates them, it downloads them and it often deletes them; it enlarges them, moves them around and stacks them. While it is the eye that supervises the operations, it is also the hand that guides them. It is the hand that calls to the images and seizes them (Flusser, 2010, pp. 23–32). We are beyond the old situation in which spectators were immersed in a world that surprised them and held their attention from the screen. Now, spectators surprise and grab hold of the images that scurry before them, images that are not necessarily capable of restituting an empirical reality; rather, they are oriented toward supplying data and information. They are not even addressed directly to anyone in particular: it is their flow more than their capture that defines them. Finally, they are tied more closely to the hand than to the eye: it is only when they are "touched" that they find their place and define their value. The display screen makes these images present. It is here that they exit the flow and come to a halt. It is here that they become simultaneously available and practicable. We literally extract them from the screen, according to a logic that mixes push and pull.[10]

In short, we cannot look out of a display screen, nor can we fill our eyes with it, nor can we lean out of it. Instead we ask of it, as at an information window. We work on it, as at a table. We wait by it, as at a bus stop. And we find ourselves in front of something that stays with us for just as long as is necessary.

Naturally, not all the screens that surround us enter fully under the rubric of the display screen. There are still moments in which the reality around us is represented to an interested and engaged observer. This may happen on the very same devices that normally seem to negate the possibility of an epiphany. Google Earth, though it offers me maps and not territories, can lead me to rediscover the pleasure of taking a walk; Photoshop, though it offers me an image of how I would like to be, may obligate me to face myself again; a videogame, though it gives me the opportunity to abandon the world, may also give me the scripts and the characters to construct another one. Computers, cellphones and tablets are still widely used for diffusing documentations and investigations, for fostering public discussions and for constructing effective communities (as documents, for example, Paola Voci's *China on Video: Smaller-Screen Realities*, 2010). Indeed, there is still room for direct testimony that reconnects us to an exploration and to a dialog.

Although the contemporary media landscape is multi-faceted, current tendencies are moving toward the display: a surface on which we find—when we find it—a reality that goes beyond empirical data, from the moment in which samples, information and elements of possibility are mixed together; and a surface on which a gaze is trained—when there is one—that goes beyond the traditional poles of contemplation and analysis, from the moment in which it is accompanied by the manipulation of what is being observed. The epoch of the window, the frame and the mirror is largely coming to an end.

[...]

Notes

1   Anne Friedberg reminds us that in 1985 some 20% of American households had a VCR; by 1997 this had reached 88% (Friedberg, 2000). The Sony Betamax was introduced in 1975 (Cabral, 2000, p. 318) and the VHS was marketed by JVC in 1976 (Ibid., p. 317). Atari's Pong console, the first to enjoy significant success, was designed in 1966 and introduced in 1972 (Computer History Museum, 2006), while the consecration of the videogame console occurred in 1977 with the Atari 2600 (Ibid.).

2   The desktop computer began to grow in popularity at the end of the 1970s and beginning of the 1980s: the Apple II debuted in 1977 (Computer History Museum, 2006), the IBM PC in 1981 (Ibid.), the Commodore 64 in 1982 (Ibid.) and the Macintosh Portable in 1989 (Edwards, 2009), while the ThinkPad 700 came out in 1992 (Mueller, 2004, p. 33).

3   The Minitel was introduced in France in 1982 (Mancini, 2002, p. 101).

4   The DVD dates back to 1995 (Toshiba, 1995).

5   The first commercially automated cellular network (1G: first generation) was launched in Japan by NTT in 1979 (Klemens, 2010, pp. 65–66), the GSM, which represents the second generation (2G) of cellphones, came online in 1991 (Pagtzis, 2011), and 3G began operation in 2001 (BBC News, 2001).

6   Noteworthy among the early palm devices are the Tandy Zoomer (1992) and the Apple Newton Message Pad (1993) (Evans, 2011).

7   Among the early tablets was the GRiDPad, released by GRiDPad System Corporation in 1989 (Evans, 2011). The Amazon Kindle was first introduced to the market by Amazon.com's subsidiary Lab126 in November 2007 (Ibid.) Apple released the first iPad in April 2010 (Ibid.)

8   Sometimes they imply a mechanical gaze. Drones in war zones gather images that a machine examines to highlight any discrepancies with prior surveillance of a given area—and it is only after this first "gaze" that an analyst is summoned to intervene, in order to give (or not give) the order for an attack on a possible enemy.

9   Dudley Andrew reaches the same conclusion regarding the computer screen: "Monitor and display seem more apt terms than screen to designate the visual experience that computers deliver" (Andrew, 2009, p. 915).

10   On the opposition of the dimensions of push and pull, both in new media and in the wider culture, see Lull (2006).

Bibliography

Andrew, Dudley (2009) "The Core and the Flow of Film Studies," *Critical Inquiry*, 35 (Summer), 879–915.

Bakhtin, Mikhail (1981) "Discourse in the Novel," in Holquist, Michael (ed.) *The Dialogic Imagination: Four Essays* (Austin: University of Texas Press).

BBC News (2001) "First 3G Launched in Japan" (1 October) http://news.bbc.co.uk/1/hi/business/1572372.stm, date accessed April 13, 2012.

Cabral, Luís M. B. (2000) *Introduction to Industrial Organization* (Cambridge: MIT Press).

Computer History Museum (2006) Timeline of Computer History: Graphics & Games, http://www.computerhistory.org/timeline/?category=gg, date accessed April 25, 2012.

Edwards, Benj (2009) The (Misunderstood) Mac Portable Turns 20, http://www.pcworld.com/article/172420/the_misunderstood_mac_portable_turns_20.html, date accessed April 25, 2012.

Evans, Dean (2011) 10 Memorable Milestones in Tablet History, *TechRadar* (31 January), http://www.techradar.com/news/mobile-computing/10-memorablemilestones-in-tablet-history-924916, date accessed April 13, 2012.

Flusser, Vilém (2010) *Into the Universe of Technical Images*, Nancy Ann Roth (trans.) (Minneapolis: University of Minnesota Press).

Foucault, Michel (1979) *Discipline and Punish: The Birth of the Prison* (New York: Vintage).

Friedberg, Anne (2000) "The End of Cinema: Multimedia and Technological Change," in Gledhill, Christine and Williams, Linda (eds.) *Reinventing Film Studies* (London: Arnold).

Klemens, Guy (2010) *The Cellphone: The History and Technology of the Gadget that Changed the World* (Jefferson: McFarland).

Lull, James (2006) "The Push and Pull of Global Culture," in Curran, James and Morley, David (eds.) *Media and Cultural Theory* (London: Routledge).

Mancini, Anna (2002) *Ancient Egyptian Wisdom for the Internet: Ancient Egyptian Justice and Ancient Roman Law Applied to the Internet* (Lanham: University Press of America).

Manovich, Lev (2000) *The Language of New Media* (Cambridge: MIT Press).

Mueller, Scott (2004) *Upgrading and Repairing Laptops* (Indianapolis: Que).

Pagtzis, Theodoros (2011) GSM: A Bit of History, http://www.cs.ucl.ac.uk/staff/t.pagtzis/, date accessed April 13, 2012.

Toshiba (1995) DVD Format Unification, http://www.toshiba.co.jp/about/press/1995_12/pr0802.htm, date accessed April 13, 2012.

Voci, Paola (2010) *China on Video: Smaller-Screen Realities* (London: Routledge).

CHAPTER THREE

Current Screens

Sean Cubitt

It is ironic that, as our aesthetics have become more and more materialist, our awareness of screens, which are today the ubiquitous medium of reception, has shrunk to nothing. This is not to say that there are no sociologies of screens: Writers and thinkers from Virilio[1] to McQuire[2] engage in intense discussions of the impact of screens on public and domestic space. Yet there is little attention paid in media and communications to the nature of the screens as material technologies. This chapter addresses screen technologies of the early twenty-first century, from handhelds to billboards. It looks at the material construction of various screen technologies, at the fundamentals of their organization of imaging, and at the bases of the software they use. These issues may be of limited interest in themselves, but, it will be argued, these technological features both express a particular quality of contemporary social life and retransmit it: They are normative technologies. Here lies their importance, for such structures express the nature of public life in particular, and they rearticulate it. Although there is a great deal of innovation in screen design, there remains a curiously static quality to the underlying features. This chapter argues that contemporary and near-future screens have abandoned important potential screen technologies in favor of a particular genus of screens, and that this articulates with a consensus on what we expect from our communications. It concludes that the road not taken can tell us as much about the kind of world we inhabit as the road that we have pursued, and recommends the development of alternative technologies as a key to reconceptualizing the nature and role of public life. The argument is framed by discussions of the environmental limits to growth that must constrain future screen technologies, thus providing a second, ethical layer to the discussion of the mediated life of populations.

Materials

For much of the twentieth century, cathode ray tubes (CRTs) were the fundamental unit of both television and computer displays. The CRT is a glass tube with at one end an emitter of negatively charged electrons (the cathode) and at the other a positively charged anode, which attracts the beam of electrons (the cathode ray) to a flattened area covered with phosphorescent materials that light up when struck by the particles. A magnetic coil or electrostatic system focuses the electron beam, and a second magnetic deflector yoke directs the beams' flight toward the desired destination on the screen. In color CRTs, three electron guns fire beams toward phosphors that glow red, green, or blue, separated from one another by a mask. The technology, which derived from both vacuum tubes (perfected in the 1850s) and cathode rays (demonstrated in the 1870s), was first used with the goal of visual display in the Braun tube, the CRT oscilloscope demonstrated by Karl Ferdinand Braun in 1897. CRT oscilloscopes, like CRT radar screens, use phosphors, which tend to keep their glow for some time after being struck by an electron.

The phosphors in television, computer, ATM, and video-game CRTs have a shorter illumination, fading swiftly to allow the next image to differ from the one before. They use innovations pioneered by Vladimir Dzworykin in the Westinghouse and RCA laboratories in the 1920s, where he had fled the Russian Revolution. The central innovation, probably introduced by Dzworykin's mentor Boris Rosing, was the scanning of images prior to transmission. Here the difference from the oscilloscope is critical: Unlike oscilloscope and radar screens, TV and computer CRT displays are formed as grids of phosphors organized in a Cartesian X-Y surface (like graph paper) called a *raster display*. The electron gun responds to incoming signals by modulating its beams as they scan of the whole screen area regularly from left to right and from top to bottom. The level of charge as the beam strikes a given square on the grid determines the "luma" or brightness signal, with a correspondingly brighter reaction from the phosphor targeted at that specific address on the screen. Oscilloscope and radar screens, in which the intensity of the charge is kept constant, steer the electron beam directly on the X and Y axes using magnetic plates seated inside the electron gun. This allows arbitrary movement in response to incoming signals from various electronic instruments like microphones and radar telescopes. This was the type of screen used in Ivan Sutherland's Sketchpad, an invention to which we will return. This first application of the CRT has been abandoned in television and subsequently (and perhaps consequently) in computer technologies, where signals such as component or composite video and RGB are organized to match the raster grid.

The materials involved in CRTs are expensive and many of them toxic and potentially dangerous to dispose of. Color CRTs require up to 32,000 volts in the screen anode (though monochrome sets use much lower voltages): The energy requirements of such devices are intense. Since the voltage/brightness connection means that unilluminated phosphors require no charge, bright images such as the typical white of a computer word-processing package require higher degrees of energy than darker images (the avowed reason for Google's *Blackle* experiment, which reproduces Google's search pages reversed out to reduce power usage: see <http://www.blackle.com>). The glass tube is under extreme pressure—implosion as a result of the vacuum can send fragments ricocheting at lethal speeds—requiring very strong glass in substantial quantities, and often metal reinforcing bands, also under extreme tension. Recycling these components can be a risky process. The glass itself is leaded to minimize the radiation risks associated with both the high energies of the cathode ray, which generates X-rays on impact with the screen, and ions generated as a by-product of running the electron beam. This lead in the glass, the often toxic phosphors which line the screen, and the frequent use of barium in the electron gun assembly all add to the toxicity of the recycling process. Legislation in the United States and the EU prevents throwing CRTs into landfill, but cannot legislate for the recycling villages of Southern China[3] and West Africa, where most Northern hemisphere electronic equipment ends up. The Basel Action Network[4] estimated that in 2005 approximately 400,000 junk computers were arriving in Lagos alone.

Liquid crystal displays (LCDs) pose similar problems, although their power usage is much lower than CRTs, which they have largely displaced in the computer market. Overtaking CRT sales in 2004, LCDs were projected to sell 50 million units worldwide in 2008, and to double in total by 2011. Found in digital watches, mobile phones, laptops, and increasingly in flat-screen TV and monitor screens, waste LCDs constitute one of the fastest growing recycling problems of recent years, with increases in end-of-life statistics projected at 16 to 25 percent every five years. The LCD backlights are the most serious pollution hazard, as they contain significant quantities of mercury. The perfluorocompounds used in the crystals themselves have a far higher greenhouse effect than carbon dioxide: up to 22,000 times higher on the global warming potential (GWP) index.[5] While the mercury can be recovered in demanufacturing processes (so long as manufacturers, mainly based in China, Korea, and Japan, abide by regulations established in key markets like the EU), the crystals are typically incinerated. The manufacturers association has established high-heat incinerators, backed up with alkaline scrubbers to react with remaining perfluorocompounds, but these too use very significant amounts of energy (though Sharp established a "green-powered" recycling plant in 2008). Many appliances are dumped when the screens have relatively minor failures: Recyclers can frequently repair and reuse them. But many will find their way into the recycling industry, where the mercury and cadmium from the integral batteries, the indium-tin oxides used in electrodes, and the unpredictable breakdown products of the organic compounds used through the assembly, from polarization and orientation layers to screen coatings, all contribute to the hazards. The problem is exacerbated by the economics of waste recovery, which suggest that the most cost-effective method is manual disassembly.[6] Despite disputes over the toxicity of the components on LCDs, there is general agreement that they are poorly biodegradable, and are potentially significant water contaminants.

The ubiquity of LCDs in mobiles places them alongside other dangerous rare earths like selenium and germanium, pointing to a further material problem: the limit to the availability of these materials, essential to the production of chips and batteries. The levels of penetration of personal devices in the West is not sustainable across the rapidly developing markets of India and China, let alone the remaining portion of global population living in the underdeveloped world. The screens in MP3 players and digital cameras, and the other components associated with them, pose not only recycling and recovery problems but suggest that without radical change in their design, there will not be enough raw material to reproduce the West's expectation of multiple, individually owned and used devices for each member of the population. The strategic importance of rare earths has sparked fears that China, which produces 95 percent of the world's lanthanides, may be introducing export controls, placing its electronics industries in a powerful position to dominate twenty-first-century manufacturing, either through domestic firms, or by forcing transnationals to move their manufacturing to China in order to access the necessary raw materials. Though global reserves include 42 percent outside China's borders, refining capacity is limited, extraction costs are often higher, and in some instances, as with Arafura, an Australian rare earths mining company, China has moved to purchase significant shares.[7] The possibility of trade wars on a level with those currently being fought over access to oil may loom for the high-tech industries, and indeed for green technologies: Hybrid cars require up to two kilograms of rare earths for their batteries alone.

Architecture

It is clear that our "immaterial" culture is highly material, especially when we consider its ecological footprint in raw materials, in use and at end-of-life. Without delving into the manufacturing process, which would require another chapter, suffice it to point out that Dell Computers, a large but otherwise typical U.S. computer brand, uses up to 98 OEM/ODM (original equipment manufacturer/original design manufacturer) sources to produce their equipment, the vast majority in developing countries or in export-friendly free-trade zones like the notorious *maquiladoras* of the Tijuana U.S.–Mexico border country, where pay and conditions are far below developed nation standards. Screens are a typical OEM/ODM item, installed without the manufacturers' name attached, and only sometimes branded by an on-seller. For example, the disc drive in my MacBook Pro is credited to Matsushita, who almost certainly has outsourced its manufacturing offshore, while the memory manufacturer is listed as "0x127F000000000000," and the LCD has no vendor or manufacturer named in any form. As is typical of information capitalism, key brands like Apple, Matsushita, and Sony (who provide my batteries) do not manufacture components themselves, and frequently do not even own the assembly plants where the final products come together. Instead they concentrate on the core business of intellectual property: trademarking the brand, patenting hardware, and copyrighting interlinked software and content. Although corporate research and development is now also often outsourced, for example to India in the software industry, or to increasingly corporatized universities in the materials science field, core trade secrets and the development of core innovations will typically be the one area of corporate concern to be kept as close as possible to the center of operations.

This situation suggests the following important question: Is it the case that, because of the proximity of hardware innovation to corporate headquarters, there is a structural homology between the design of major components of digital devices such as screens and the corporate culture in which they are formulated? The question is not entirely naive. Isabelle Stenghers[8] points out that the history of science and technology studies has presented two competing paradigms, that of the autonomy of science and technology and that of symptomatic technology and science. In recent decades, however, the work of investigators including Stenghers and Bruno Latour[9] has increasingly suggested that the assemblage of agencies involved in scientific and technological innovation are neither rational—a presumption of the autonomist thesis—nor necessarily efficient—a correlative of the symptomatic thesis. The emerging new digital architectures, for example those of the LCD, LED (light-emitting diode), and DLP (digital light processing) screen technologies, are of necessity built on existing standards. They must, for example, be able to at least speak to component and composite video, recognize different color spaces like RGB and YPbPr, and connect to existing infrastructures such as the electricity grid, broadcast transmission wavebands, and the Internet. These accumulated elements of the environment into which new technologies emerge is also a regulated environment, and as several commentators have suggested, at both national and global levels, media regulation rarely gives evidence of a unifying policy goal. Rather, governance accumulates in layers, with regulations for each technology framed inside the policy objectives of the epoch in which it emerged: freedom of speech for the U.S. press, for example, but universality of access for telephony.[10] The regulatory environment "reflects the fact that law-makers simply wrote a new law for each new network as it arrived."[11] It is therefore perhaps understandable that, given the principle that the more deregulated a market is (and this is surely the case for the global market in electronics), the more regulations are required to govern it,[12] electronic screen design is formulated not only on the technological affordances of the day, but on the accumulated technical practices of the past, and the regulatory framework of the present, which itself is typically a historical aggregation.

We can observe this in the economics of recycling: Manual labor (and therefore, the labor of developing nations) is the most efficient way to get rid of WEEE *because*, prior to regulation, there was no incentive for manufacturers to make automated demanufacturing a possibility. Even today, regional (NAFTA, EU) and international (the Basel Framework) agreements notwithstanding, the global trade in e-waste is to all intents and purposes an export trade in toxins. This trade is the more insidious to the extent that the electronics industry depends on innovation for success. Even the biggest market, such as that for personal mobile phones, flattens out once it reaches saturation. At such junctures, the industry must innovate or die. Thus we enter a cycle of built-in obsolescence equivalent to that of the Detroit motor industry in the 1950s and 1960s. The necessary by-product of such speedy electronic obsolescence is e-waste.

This is not to say that innovation is never virtuous. The LCD is a far less power-hungry technology than equivalent CRTs, for example. It is to say, however, that innovation is never undertaken without a cost, nor is it undertaken in an environment of absolute creative freedom. As an example, let us return to the raster grid, incorporated as a core technique in the innovation of the CRT. The raster grid has its own genealogy, specifically in the development of wire photography, initially demonstrated by Edward A. Hummel and Arthur Korn in 1900 and 1907 respectively, and industrialized by Bell Labs and Associated Press in 1935. This technology, which used a rotary scanning technology related to the earliest experiments in television, produced a halftone grid of dots that assembled into a still image, transmitted over telegraph wires. The halftone process itself had been pioneered by one of the key figures in the invention of photography, William Fox Talbot, in the 1850s and in industrial use by the 1870s. Half-tone printing uses a similar grid of dots and remains the core technology of photolithography, the printing technology common to both book production and chip manufacture. The halftone's unique characteristic is that it lays its grid at a 45-degree angle to the horizontal, on the basis that the human eye sees parallel lines less acutely when they are not aligned with the horizon. With that exception, it may trace its own ancestry as far back as the Renaissance, to the engraving of lozenges for shading in intaglio printing. The significant properties of the raster grid are, then, threefold: It is aligned on the horizontal axis; it is automated; and it is attached to a clock function in which the whole screen is scanned in numerical order and refreshed at regular intervals (typically 120Hz in NTSC and 200Hz in PAL and SECAM). It is in this sense a Cartesian coordinate space, each pixel enumerated along the X and Y axes, and distinguished over set increments of duration. It is a thoroughly mathematical space, and one that has been strongly identified with both modernity and the broad cultural project of modernism.[13]

FIGURE 3.1 *A technician services an outdoor liquid-crystal display (LCD) advertising screen, Berlin, 2008. Photo: nerdwithoutglasses.*

Thus, we should not be surprised that the technical innovations of the LCD rest on a far older substrate of the grid, not least since computers are now almost universally calibrated to produce video signals designed to play out on raster screens. CRTs, however, are rather less rigid than LCDs. The scattering of phosphors on the luminescent surface is itself more random, and the illumination of one phosphor tends to blur into the light from its neighbors, so that even if the electron gun tracks over the screen in linear order, the phosphors themselves are less rigidly contained. Sony's Trinitron aperture grille system for color reproduction in CRTs was designed to limit this fuzziness, by laying a grid of vertically aligned thin black wires over the screen in order to minimize the interference between phosphors, and so increase apparent resolution. This step preceded and pointed the way toward the increasingly rigid mathematicization of the raster array, much as Fox Talbot's textile screen preceded the lined glass sheets of the industrial halftone process.

LCDs do not rely on electroluminescent phosphors for their illumination but on mercury-vapor fluorescent backlights. Requiring much less power than the high voltages associated with CRTs, they both produce far less unwanted radiation than the older technology, and are eminently suited to battery-powered personal devices like laptops and handhelds. LCDs sandwich their crystals between two layers of polarized glass, arranged so that if no voltage is applied, light cannot travel through one layer and through the next. The liquid crystals (so called because although they are liquid they retain some structural characteristics of crystals) carry light between the polarized plates and change their orientation according to whether they receive a voltage from transparent indium-tin oxide electrodes placed over the glass sheets. When charged, they untwist their "relaxed" helical shape, and the light is blocked, creating black pixels; uncharged, they let the light pass through. Small displays have a discrete pair of electrodes for each pixel. Larger displays reinforce the grid structure by supplying electrodes in rows on one side of the screen and columns in the other, so that each pixel has a unique row-column address, without requiring an independent power source. The surface on the visible side of the screen is covered in a layer of red, green, and blue color filters, one of each to each pixel, allowing millions of color combinations. There is a general feeling, however, that LCD color is less subtly graded, has a narrower gamut, and in inexpensive models is less bright than CRT screens.

The same raster grid structure is apparent in other screen technologies, such as the plasma displays competing for dominance in the domestic high-definition television market. Here noble gases (neon, argon, and xenon) contained in phosphor-coated cells are ionized and heated to a plasma by voltage difference, controlled as in large LCDs by long electrodes, in this instance in rows along the back plate and columns inside the front. The ultraviolet photons given off by the plasma then trigger the phosphors to illuminate as subpixels of red, green, and blue, as in LCD technology. Indeed, this release of photons from agitated phosphors is the basis for shadow-mask CRTs, in which a triad of red, green, and blue-emitting phosphors was first established as the basis for electronic color screens. Plasma screens use power comparably to CRTs, but the size of screen, the relative brightness, and the viewing angle are all greater than that of LCDs.

Similarly, the digital micromirror device (DMD), the chip at the heart of digital light processing projectors and rear-projection TVs, sets up an array of tiny mirrors, each corresponding to a pixel, brightly illuminated and controlled to shift very swiftly on their axes. One orientation is "on," another is "off," and rapid oscillation between the two provides grayscale by reflecting some of the light away from the screen. In single-chip DLP projectors, color wheels spinning up to ten times per frame deliver the color component of the image; three-chip projectors for high-end use a prism to split the illuminating white light, passing one of the red, green, or blue wavebands to one of the three chips, which then reflect that color component onto the screen. This too has its roots in an older color technology, the three-color Technicolor camera of 1932. Though they began with mercury-vapor arc lamps (with the same color signature as LCDs), since 2006 patented LED (light-emitting diode) technology has increasingly been applied to DLP projection, with longer life, lower power consumption and comparable illumination, at least for domestic uses. At the opposite end of the market, Texas Instruments, who devised DLP and DMD, announced in 2009 its intention to develop the technology for use in handheld devices. But again, like other emerging competitor technologies in the high-definition and projection markets such as LCoS, DLP once more reproduces the raster grid, even if it has managed to exceed competitor technologies' color gamuts, an issue to which we return in the next section. The Cartesian grid is hardwired into the architecture of the DMD chips used DLP, as it is into the screen displays of plasma and LCD. The question then becomes, does this architecture also shape the use of these devices? Is the mathematicizing instrument of the Cartesian grid, which dominates the architecture of dedicated visualization chips and screens, also the overwhelming structure of twenty-first-century visuality? If the answer is yes, then the following question must be: Does it matter? Does it matter whether our images come to us in the random spatter of silver halide molecules or the ordered arrays of the raster display? Does it tell us anything about who we are, how we live, and perhaps most of all how and what we communicate?

Protocol

In the influential book *Code and Other Laws of Cyberspace*, Lawrence Lessig[14] gave the phenomenon a catchphrase: Code is Law. He was writing specifically about the use of digital rights management (DRM) code, which at the time was threatened as a new way of preventing copyright infringements. As we have seen, copyright and other intellectual property laws are of vital significance to contemporary corporations. Lessig does not suggest that it should be otherwise, although he offers nuanced arguments concerning the degree and duration of protection that can be considered just. But he does have a lawyer's disagreement with the principle that copyright owners have the right to make it impossible to infringe on their property rights. DRM effectively does this: It undertakes to make it impossible to commit the offense of infringing copyright.

Alex Galloway[15] coined the term "protocol" to express a more widespread phenomenon. Software comes in various forms: as operating system (Windows, Linux), as applications (Adobe, Autodesk), and as protocols. Protocols are common on the Internet: SMTP is standard mail transfer protocol; HTTP indicates pages using the hypertext transfer protocol; and below such familiar protocols lie more pervasive ones, specifically the TCP/IP suite (transmission control protocol/Internet protocol), which provides layers of nested protocols (applications, transport, Internet, and link), which together allow the entire system of computers communicating with each other to perform. Drawing on Deleuze and Foucault, Galloway sees protocol as the next period in a historical process, first described by Foucault, which has seen power migrate from sovereignty (the king's right to decide the life or death of a subject) to discipline (the inculcation of rules of behavior in the individual subjects of a state), and from thence to governmentality and biopolitics (the management of populations according to statistical norms). Deleuze added a fourth period: the "societies of control," where the codes operating in society effectively determine what can and cannot be done in it—much as the highway code determines how one may or may not drive a car. Technically we are free to drive—or to behave in electronic environments—just as we please, and to take the consequences if we do something illegal. But in the emergent societies of control, and more particularly in the era of protocol as the governing feature of the Internet and so of a vast swathe of contemporary life from correspondence to global finance, we are not free to disobey. The very same protocols that allow us to disport ourselves in cyberspace also constrain us to act according to the rule-set that underpins it.

It is in this vein that we turn our attention to the parallel infrastructure of software that underlies the electronic image. We have already noted in passing one or two such infrastructural themes. One of these is the question of color gamuts, the range of colors that a given screen is able to reproduce. The visible spectrum spans the waveband between, roughly, 400 and 800 nanometers. On average, a human eye has 120 million rods and 7 million color-sensitive cones, the latter concentrated in the fovea, at the center of the field of vision where they reach densities of 60,000 per square millimeter; the equivalent numbers for digital cameras are about 20,000, and for color photographs about 30,000.[16] At their best, digital screens can reproduce only about 50 percent of the visible spectrum. To make the most of a bad business, the outlying colors are moved inward toward the reproducible sector—the gamut of the screen. But that process does not account for the acute perceptual facility we have, especially within that foveal arc of one or two degrees where we focus our attention, for distinguishing between colors. It is then not the absolute hue or saturation that is at stake but the differences between them. Screens are calibrated (as are the signals they coordinate) so that the color gamut squeezes the full spectrum into the available gamut *while preserving the relationships of difference between colors*. This would be more acceptable, perhaps, if all screens used the same algorithms to redeploy colors, and if all computers shared a single color space. Unfortunately, they do not. The manufacturers of LED versions of DLP boast a much wider gamut than is available on LCD, which in turn is widely regarded as having a poorer gamut than modern CRTs. Likewise, different chips used to gather images have different gamuts: CMOS chips, previously considered only good enough for low-resolution applications like mobile phone cameras, have found a significant place in scientific imaging, partly because of their greater gamut than their competitor CCD chips.

The fact remains that digital outputs (including both screens and printers) have a much reduced color gamut compared either to normal human vision or to older color technologies like oil paint. Worse still, in network conditions, where it is impossible to know in advance which kinds of display will be used to view some piece of content, there is no way to prepare the file for optimum viewing by the far-end user. This may be critical when the files in question are being prepared for analog media such as cinema film or color printing, and is also significant for such uses as the color branding of companies or the standardization of flags and other important insignia. Here the standard recourse is to entirely nondigital media, such as the color "chips" purchasable from the Munsell Corporation, or the printer's standard recourse, the Pantone color system, both of which use printed materials for comparisons, and a numerical reference that can be passed in a more reliable, nonvisual form, to network collaborators. The mathematicization of color, which began with Newton in the seventeenth century, resulted in its commodification at the end of the twentieth.

Can anything similar be said of the other elements composing the protocological layer of screen technology? Perhaps the most important of these are the codecs, compression-decompression algorithms used to compress signals for transport, and to "unpack" them on arrival. The codecs sit a layer below such standards as PAL and NTSC, and have historically developed in relation to emergent uses such as Internet, satellite, and high definition. They have also historically been involved, because of their importance to emerging hardware and architectures, in heavily regulated environments where design can be as much influenced by national interests (for example, in protecting domestic equipment manufacture) as by elegance or efficiency. Many codecs are in use, generally standardized through the International Organization for Standardization (ISO), and some of them are wholly proprietary. The major ones, however, are MPEG-2 and MPEG-4, both used as standard codecs for broadcast television, though MPEG-4 has much broader additional capacities, for example for high-definition applications like Blu-Ray, and for encoding and decoding bitstreams representing 3D objects and surface textures. The MPEG-4 codec was devised, like the other MPEG formats, by the Motion Picture Experts Group, now a subcommittee of the Internet Engineering Task Force, but elements of the codec are owned by 640 institutions (including the military, a feature that goes back to the 1916–1918 period when the U.S. Navy took control of all radio patents[17]) and corporations. The complexity of its organization is compounded by its composition in "Parts," sometimes referred to as "layers," many of which are optional for people implementing them in specific circumstances. Thus, few nonprofessional users will require VRML support for 3D rendering, while others will find a use for Part 13, which provides for encoding DRM in MPEG-4 signals. But what is important is not such features, nor the ownership of patents, nor even the protracted negotiations required before licenses could be agreed between the patent owners, but the fact that, as Adrian Mackenzie has it, "Codecs affect at a deep level contemporary sensations of movement, color, light and time."[18]

The MPEG codecs, which lie at the deep level of such familiar tools as Windows Media, VLC, and commercial DVDs, use "lossy" compression, a term that refers to the way the decompressed signals lose resolution and color information compared to the original uncompressed signal. Although some rare codecs do promise lossless transmission, the continuing problem of bandwidth economics continues to foster lossy standards. For terrestrial and satellite broadcast transmission, digital signals are far more efficient than analog, but competition for wavebands with cell phone and other uses makes bandwidth a valuable commodity. Even in wired environments, speed of transmission is regarded as more valuable than the quality of the received image, while the carrying capacity of laser-read discs like DVD and Blu-Ray also requires considerable compression to fit feature films plus associated extras on a single side. Of the various tools used, perhaps the most significant is vector prediction.

Common to the various MPEG codecs, and especially visible in the H 261 codec that underlies the YouTube proprietary .flv format,[19] vector prediction works by assembling pixels into blocks, macroblocks, units of 4 × 4 or 16 × 16 pixels that can be treated as average hue, saturation, and brightness values. On the presumption that, for example, green grass and blue sky areas will remain the same from frame to frame, the codec "guesses" that the next frame will be by and large similar to the current one. To aid this process, the codec interpolates key frames, in the manner developed by animators around 1915, each of which establishes the beginning and end of an action, allowing the codec to interpolate the most likely sequence of changes that will take the image from the first key frame to the last. This economically satisfying system leads to advice to users to minimize movement in the frame, which tends to demand more frequent key frames and therefore more bandwidth. The result is the self-fulfilled prophecy of YouTube populated by talking heads and minimally animated flash video, or, alternatively, slow downloads (with attendant loss of interest among downloaders) for those videos that ignore the advice.

Such technologies allow a signal to be decoded that is legible. They are good-enough technologies, confining expectations to the likely loss of resolution and color depth. The vector-prediction algorithms are based on the typical broadcast, and function both normatively, by accommodating genres, like sport, that have the greatest uptake among users, and descriptively, deploying the averaging techniques first developed by Alphonse Quetelet in the nineteenth century to establish the concept of the "average man."

Conclusions

As Mackenzie[20] notes, the way a codec "pulls apart and reorganizes moving images goes further than simply transporting images. ... Like so much software it institutes a relational ordering that articulates realities together that previously lay further apart." Quetelet's "social physics" was an ultimately successful attempt to apply the mathematicizing principles of physical sciences to the emerging idea of the social sciences. Statistical norms provided in the first instance data on the average height and weight of citizens, but then increasingly on their average opinions, habits, and behaviors. It was the sociological expression of the idea of the market that had developed out of eighteenth-century radicalism in the hands of Immanuel Kant, Adam Smith, and Jeremy Bentham, and which in Foucault's analysis would form the fundamental liberal and later neoliberal formation of biopolitics: the management of populations.[21] If on the one hand, as we have seen in the case of color gamuts, the kind of mathematicization espoused by Quetelet and later opinion pollsters tended toward commodification (of audiences as sold to advertisers, for example), on the other it had a direct impact on the concept of liberal government.

The invisible hand of the market first identified by Adam Smith is at heart the aggregate rationality of individual acts of exchange influenced by such irrational factors as advertising and brand loyalty. Though every individual act can be construed as undertaken in a free environment, averaged across the whole of a market, they become statistical probabilities, much as the likelihood of death from drunk driving or smoking-related illnesses can be calculated from actuarial records. The contention implicit in the foregoing analysis is that the raster grid of dominant screen displays is indistinguishable from the Cartesian space deployed by Quetelet and every subsequent statistical sociologist to analyze the existence of *l'homme moyen*, the average person, in the environment not only of historically accumulated technological practices, nor of the historical layering of architectures and protocols, but of a regime of commodification and power whose fundamental premise is the exchangeability of any one good for another, any one person for any other, and all possible behaviors as norms or departures form the norm: a regime of accountancy rather than accountability. At the microlevel, our technologies, this chapter has argued, take the shape of the biopolitical and information-economic structures that shape our society at the macrolevel. To call this regime a database economy is perhaps to succumb to the same demand for efficiency that characterizes government in our epoch, yet it is also a way of throwing into question what has become of the publics of such technologies, as they traverse cityscapes on the one hand decorated with huge urban screens, and on the other characterized by individuals bent into the increasingly screen-dominated intimacies of handheld devices. In materials, architectures, and protocols, we can observe the structuration of contemporary media not only by their histories and by the immediate and conscious influence of regulatory environments, but by the very shape of the social organizations in which they emerge. Contemporary innovation, while it seems to churn far faster, is only the more deeply hamstrung by the rapidly accumulating mulch of previous inventions and previous regulatory interventions.

In our haste to populate our lives, intimate and public, with screens, we have opted for the good enough over the best possible, and in the process abandoned technical trajectories that might have suggested other social and political capacities and affordances. The biopolitical management of populations that Foucault describes is entirely congruent with, and in some ways reflective of the liberal conception of the market: In both systems, innumerable interactions and exchanges are aggregated in the mass and there mathematically rendered. The Cartesian grid is the tool of choice for statistical graphing, not least because once a line has been drawn of number against time, it can be extended into the future. This is the central tool of planning, of the management of markets and populations that constitute the database economy. It not only shares the grid formation, but is the managerial expression of the kinds of vector prediction analyzed above in the H.261 codec. Prediction, foreknowledge based on statistical aggregation, the enumeration of the enumerable: These have become the ingrained characteristics of the contemporary screen in all its manifestations. All, that is, bar one: the oscilloscope screen technology utilized in early experiments in computer graphics by Ivan Sutherland, mentioned briefly in the opening pages of this chapter. Sutherland's vector screen, free from the obligation to scan the raster grid in clock time, remains an available technology still deployed in air-traffic control and scientific instrumentation. Its capacities have been ignored in the development of the Cartesian raster display. Yet the vector display is the natural way to display the vector graphics that increasingly constitute the central platform of object-oriented visualization. The loss of vector screens in the age of vector graphics, and their replacement with codecs whose central innovation comprises new tools for making vectors visible on raster displays, suggests both a concrete avenue for twenty-first-century technical innovation, and the kind of lacuna in innovation that may only be typical in situations where there is a diagrammatic or structural interchange, a homological assemblage, operating between key technologies like contemporary screens, and core values and processes of both economic and political life. The oscilloscope allows for the arbitrary. Unlike our common screens, which have become attuned to the normative workings of the database economy, the vector screen is an expression of a freedom we have sensed, that we have imagined as potential, and which still lies unrealized in the storeroom of residual media. If technologies are articulations of social formations, then genuine innovation, or turning back to follow the road not taken, may well introduce us to a new way of imagining and realizing alternative social formations. Perhaps this cannot be achieved with respect for the poor and for the ecosphere, but we know for a certainty that the road we did take has not benefited either of them. It is time to set the vector free.

Notes

1   Paul Virilio, *The Vision Machine*, trans. Julie Rose (London: BFI, 1994).

2   Scott McQuire, *The Media City: Media, Architecture, and Urban Space* (London: Sage, 2008).

3   The Basel Action Network and Silicon Valley Toxics Coalition, *Exporting Harm: The High-Tech Trashing of Asia*, <http://www.ban.org/E-waste/technotrashfinalcomp.pdf>, 2002.

4   The Basel Action Network, *The Digital Dump: Exporting High-Tech Re-use and Abuse to Africa* (photo documentary); see <http://www.ban.org/BANreports/10-24-05/index.htm>, 2005.

5   Avtar S. Matharu and Yanbing Wu, "Liquid Crystal Displays: From Devices to Recycling," in *Electronic Waste Management: Issues in Environmental Science and Technology*, ed. R. E. Hester and R. M. Harrison (Cambridge: RSC Publishing, 2008), 180–211.

6   B. Kopacek, "ReLCD: Recycling and Re-use of LCD Panels," in *Proceedings of the 19th Waste Management Conference of the IWMSA (WasteCon2008)*, October 6–10, 2008, Durban, South Africa; <http://ewasteguide.info/Kopacek_2008a_WasteCon>.

7   "China Builds Rare-Earth Metal Monopoly," *Australian*, March 9, 2009.

8   Isabelle Stenghers, *The Invention of Modern Science*, trans. Daniel W. Smith (Minneapolis: University of Minnesota Press, 2000).

9   Bruno Latour, *Aramis, or The Love of Technology*, trans. Catherine Porter (Cambridge, MA: Harvard University Press, 1996).

10 François Bar and Christian Sandvig, "U.S. Communication Policy after Convergence," *Media, Culture, and Society* 30(4) (2008): 531–550.

11 Tim Wu, "Why Have a Telecommunications Law? Anti-Discrimination Norms in Communications," *Journal of Telecommunications and High Technology Law* 5 (2006–2007): 19.

12 S. K. Vogel, *Freer Markets, More Rules: Regulatory Reform in Advanced Industrial Countries* (Ithaca: Cornell University Press, 1996).

13 Rosalind E. Krauss, *The Originality of the Avant-Garde and Other Modernist Myths* (Cambridge, MA: MIT Press, 1986).

14 Lawrence Lessig, *Code and Other Laws of Cyberspace* (New York: Basic Books, 1999); see also Lawrence Lessig, *Code v.2: Code and Other Laws of Cyberspace* (New York: Basic Books, 2006), downloadable from <http://codev2.cc>.

15 Alexander R. Galloway, *Protocol: How Control Exists after Decentralization* (Cambridge, MA: MIT Press, 2004).

16 Noboru Ohta and Alan Robertson, *Colorimetry: Fundamentals and Applications* (New York: Wiley, 2005).

17 Douglas Gomery, *A History of Broadcasting in the United States* (Oxford: Blackwell, 2008).

18 Adrian Mackenzie, "Codecs," in *Software Studies: A Lexicon*, ed. Matthew Fuller (Cambridge, MA: MIT Press, 2008), 48–55, 49.

19 Sean Cubitt, "Codecs and Capability," in *Video Vortex*, ed. Geert Lovink (Amsterdam: Institute of Network Cultures, 2008), 45–52.

20 Mackenzie, "Codecs," 48–55, 49.

21 Michel Foucault, *The Birth of Biopolitics: Lectures at the Collège de France 1978–1979*, ed. Michel Senellart, trans. Graham Burchell (Basingstoke: Palgrave Macmillan, 2004).

CHAPTER FOUR

The Multiple

Anne Friedberg

[...]

Proprietary Windows

In his 1995 memoir, *The Road Ahead*, Bill Gates recalls the transition from the command line to graphic interface. Gates describes his intention, as early as 1983, to develop graphical interface and to abandon MS-DOS: "Our goal was to create software that would extend MS-DOS and let people use a mouse, employ graphical images on the computer screen, and make available on the screen a number of 'windows,' each running a different computer program."[1] In Gates's account, the other two personal computer systems that had graphical interfaces in 1983, the Xerox Star and Apple Lisa, were proprietary and expensive: "Microsoft wanted to create an open standard and bring graphical capabilities to any computer that was running MS-DOS."[2] Despite the rhetoric of an "open standard," Microsoft attached a proprietary trademark to the term "window" and in November 1985 introduced graphical cornputing to IBM PCS (and their "clones") with a product called Windows 1.0. In the fall of 1987, Windows 2.0 added icons and resizable, overlapping windows. The software war had begun. In 1988, Apple sued Microsoft for copying the "look and feel" of the Macintosh's graphic display, but the term "windows" now belonged to Microsoft as Windows™.[3] By 1993, Windows 3.0, which was released in 1990, had sold 25 million copies. And as the media-saturated campaign for Windows 95 emphasized, by the end of its first decade, Microsoft's Windows became the most widely used operating system. [4] As David Gelernter writes: "Pushing beauty instead of old-fashioned DOS ugliness, Microsoft emerged as the uncontested leader of the desktop computing world."[5]

Like the Mac OS, the "interface" of Windows extends screen space by overlapping screens of various sizes; each "window" can run a different application; the user can scroll through a text within a "window," arrange "windows" on the screen in stacked or overlapping formations, decorate "windows" (with wallpapers, textured patterns), and conduct new forms of "window shopping."[6] The "windows" trope is emblematic of the collapse of the single viewpoint; it relies on the model of a window that we don't see through, windows that instead overlap and obscure, and are resizable and movable.

Consider the following shift in discourse from the Albertian metaphor. *Webopedia*, an online dictionary of new media terms, defines "window" as distinctly polyscenic:

An enclosed, rectangular area on a display screen. Most modern operating systems and applications have graphical user interfaces that let you divide your display into several windows. Within each window, you can run a different program or display different data.

Windows are particularly valuable in *multitasking environments*, which allow you to execute several programs at once. By dividing your display into windows, you can see the output from all the programs at the same time. To enter input into a program, you simply click on the desired window to make it the foreground process.[7]

Interface culture

Why are we rejecting explicit word-based interfaces, and embracing graphical or sensorial ones—a trend that accounts for the success of both Microsoft and Disney?

—Neal Stephenson, In the Beginning Was the Command Line

Before Microsoft adopted a graphical user interface for its Windows operating system, the "holy war" between the MAC and the MS-DOS "command line" interface was described by Umberto Eco as a struggle between Macintosh/Catholicism ("the essence of revelation is dealt with via simple formulae and sumptuous icons") and MS-DOS/Protestantism ("To make the system work you need to interpret the program yourself: a long way from the baroque community of revelers, the user is closed within the loneliness of his own inner torment").[8] The religious war between a command line and a graphic display interface pitted the word and the text against the image and icon.

In his polemical treatise *In the Beginning Was the Command Line* (1999), cyber-novelist Neal Stephenson rails against a growing global "interface culture," a monoculture with a computerized visual interface.[9] Stephenson compares the Macintosh and Windows interface: the Macintosh is "not only a superb piece of engineering but an embodiment of certain ideals about the use of technology to benefit mankind," while Microsoft's Windows equivalent is "a pathetically clumsy imitation and a sinister world domination plot rolled into one."[10] And yet, despite the competition between the Mac and Windows operating systems, Stephenson holds both systems accountable for millions of computer users becoming accustomed to a graphical interface.[11]

By mapping code onto a graphic display, the GUI interface conceals its workings, hides its code. In Stephenson's account, the graphical interface "introduced a new semiotic layer" between human and machine: "GUIs use metaphors to make computing easier, but they are bad metaphors."[12] Stephenson compares this to the Disney model of "putting out a product of seamless illusion." (Stephenson's diatribe carries with it an implicit critique of icon-based graphics as reductive cartoons.) In this way, both the Mac and Windows operating systems are in the same business: that of "short-circuiting laborious, explicit verbal communication with expensively designed interfaces."[13] Alternatively, Stephenson champions the Linux operating system because its workings are exposed and it can be customized by its user, like a tuner-car. An obvious analogy occurs here: both the Mac OS and Windows interface operate like classical Hollywood film style—concealing its workings, aiming for unreflexive illusionism—while the Linux OS operates more like an independent or avant-garde film, self-reflexive, its substrates and premises exposed. The Linux OS is computing with distanciation, as if it were an operating system designed by Bertolt Brecht. But Stephenson's polemic holds a prescient command of the global effects of interface culture, for GUIs have become the "meta-interface" found on almost any screenic device—VCRs, cell phones, car navigational systems, gaming consoles, and my favorite new screen-enabled appliance, the Samsung "Internet refrigerator."[14]

While the scale and domestic place of the television may have prepared us for the screens of the "personal" computer, computer "users" are not spectators or viewers. Immobile, with attention focused on a screen, the "user" interacts directly with the framed screen image using a device—keyboard, mouse, or in the case of touch-screens, finger—to manipulate what is contained within the parameter of the screen. Computer interfaces may have been designed to become dyadic partners in a metaphysical relationship, but complaints about the awkwardness of this liaison have targeted the interface. Brenda Laurel proclaims: "Using computers is like going to the movie theater and having to watch the projector instead of the film."[15]

Old metaphors, new screens

For Alberti, the metaphor of the window implied direct, veridical, and unmediated vision, transparency of surface or aperture, and transmitted light. The computer "window" implies its opposite: the visual field seen through a computer "window" is rarely direct (although webcams play on this function); it is mediated to a high degree through its proprietary or trademarked "software"; and its representational function is highly iconic. Computer "windows" coexist on the flat surface of a computer display. They open onto flatness or depth, image or text, moving or still content. Some "windows" open onto networked systems, some only refer to the hard drive of its base. Although computer "windows" can be "open" at the same time, they rarely serve, as the art historical double-slide projection did, as a means for comparative analysis.

So let's consider the computer user who navigates the "windows" of screen space. In the mixed metaphor of the computer screen, the computer user is figuratively positioned with multiple spatial relations to the screen. "Windows" stack *in front of* each other (if one is looking into the screen perpendicularly, as if through a window) or *on top of* each other (if one is looking into the screen as if its perpendicular is in a gravity-defying ninety-degree rotation of an angle overhead). As either a "page" or a "window," a mobile switch of position is implied in the mixed metaphor: the user switches between a recumbent (desktop view) and an upright (window) view. The

FIGURE 4.1 *A smartphone screen confronts a desktop screen, producing a* mise en abyme *through its camera and screencast. Photo: Alan Levine.*

desktop metaphor implies background and foreground layers, but seen from above. The gravity-defying space of the computer screen accustoms us to the antigravity of CGI in films such as *Crouching Tiger, Hidden Dragon*, and *The Matrix*. The computer user may switch back and forth between these layers, open and close "windows," switch activities at will. The user may not be able to see each "window" in the stack on the desktop, but this doesn't mean the program isn't there or is no longer active. The computer may be "thinking" about several things at once, it may have several applications open, different programs running in separate "windows."

Of course, the icons of the graphical user interface are reductively simple, far from high art, farther even from the screens of popular culture. The Microsoft version of the window interface did not even draw on the "deep beauty" that David Gelernter finds in software that is "simple and powerful."[16] And yet, on the fractured plane of the computer screen, the metaphor of the window has retained a key stake in the technological reframing of the visual field. The Windows interface is a postcinematic visual system, but the viewer-turned-user remains in front of (*vorstellen*) a perpendicular frame.

Multitasking, the computer "window," and the multiple screen

The distracted person (der Zerstreute), too, can form habits. More, the ability to master certain tasks in a state of distraction proves that their solution has become a matter of habit … Reception in a state of distraction … finds in the film its true means of exercise.

— *Walter Benjamin*, "The Work of Art in the Age of Mechanical Reproduction"

In an oft-cited passage from "The Work of Art in the Age of Mechanical Reproduction," Walter Benjamin draws a distinction between the modes of "reception" of painting, film, and architecture. "Painting invites the spectator to contemplation/concentration," Benjamin explains, while "Architecture has always represented the prototype of a work of art the reception of which is consummated by a collectivity in a state of distraction." The film meets this mode of reception "halfway"[17] Architectural theorists have often bridled at Benjamin's dismissive generalization about the experience of architecture and, equally, film theorists have debated this assessment of the film spectator. But "reception in a state of distraction" now seems to provide a prescient model for the multitasking computer user.

For cinema spectators, the conventions of film narrative and the protocols of theatrical exhibition encouraged cognitive focus and engagement.

(Spectators who eat loudly, make out, talk on their phones—or otherwise multitask—are targets of social opprobrium.) Although the instances of split-screen and multiple-screen filmmaking described at the beginning of this chapter suggest that the film spectator was increasingly equipped to engage with such fractures in attention, televisual spectatorship much more directly encouraged the habits of a split-attentive viewer. The television's domestic site encouraged housewives to iron and fold laundry in front of the set, families to eat dinner with the TV on in the background, children to play with toys while watching cartoons. Channel switching, aided by accessory devices like the remote, implied the inherent potential to engage in a "mode switch." By contrast, the computer user must engage with the computer screen directly, as it only responds to the user's interactive "input." Yet the computer user can—and easily does—split focus and attention to multiple tasks, since computers can now routinely run multiple applications, each open in a different window.

Multiple "windows" made computer "multitasking" possible.[18] As one Web dictionary defines "multitasking," it is "working with various computer programs at one time in order to increase your productivity and reach your intended goal."[19] The windows interface made it easy for the user to switch back and forth between two documents or two applications. In order to theorize the subjective consequences of computer multitasking, we need to first consider the technical base of multiple-screen "windows." For a computer to multitask, the computer does tasks not simultaneously but serially, and yet at a high speed. (Even a slow computer with a hundred-megahertz processor can execute a million instructions between each pair of keystrokes.) While a computer microprocessor can keep many programs running at the same time (parallel processing), the user still "crosscuts" between one or more programs in selective sequence. Just as the instrumental base for the moving image—the retinal retention of successive virtual images—produced a newly virtual representation of movement and a complex new experience of time, the instrumental base for multiscreen multi-tasking poses new questions about the computer user's experience of time.

Computer multitasking makes it possible to combine work with leisure— running an Excel spreadsheet while checking email or shopping on eBay— and hence serves to equate productivity with a fractured subjectivity.[20] A 1998 *New York Times* article reported the following statistic: "Microsoft says the average office user of Windows 95 has more than three programs running at a time. At home, more than 10 million American households now have a television and a personal computer in the same room."[21]

Screen-based multitasking is only one form of multitasking. Using multiple screens (computers and TVs) or engaging in multiple activities (talking on the phone while "watching" TV) has extended the meaning of "multitasking" to a more pervasive cultural mode. In a study of American leisure time habits in 2000, an MTV Networks/Viacom Study of Media, Entertainment, and Leisure Time reported that Americans spend time with media and entertainment 4.7 hours a day. For 2.9 of those hours, the average American simultaneously reads magazines and watches TV, listens to CDs and sends email. The results, the study reports, imply that a multitasker's average day has 29.8 hours of activity.[22] However, as another critic assesses the psychic liabilities of technologically enabled multitasking: "Technology didn't give us more time, it just upped the expectations of what we could do in the same time."[23] As a further indication of the effects of multitasking on styles of learning and thinking, consider the following advice on time management offered to college students: "Multi-window, multi-task activity is the norm for today's students. E-mail, games, and web searches are routinely managed simultaneously with writing papers or completing research assignments. Students have learned to value the pace and accessibility of video presentations and sound-bite synopses of popular culture. The slow, linear process of reading a book or attending a lecture may challenge a student's time management skills and attention to detail. While multi-tasking can be a valuable tool, so are focused attention and concentration. All are required for success in college."[24]

A George Washington University website offers the following recommendations:

Multi-window, multi-task activity breaks concentration and consumes time rapidly.

- Turn off or minimize your pop up windows. Avoid screen clutter and eliminate distractions.

- Break tasks into manageable time blocks and stick to them.

- Plan the hours of your day (or study periods) in advance. Schedule a time to return e-mail.

- Control interruptions or even schedule 10 minute breaks for 50 minute study periods.

- Make allowances for periods of relaxation.

- Exercise and strengthen your ability to sustain concentration and absorb information by gradually increasing your study time and effort until you reach an established goal.

- Create a variety of study aids to help focus your attention (e.g., index cards, tables, diagrams.)

- Allow time to stop and think about connections among course materials, facts, and findings.[25]

This discussion of multitasking implies the direct cognitive effects of multitasking behaviors. Is the fractured subjectivity of multitasking in service of productivity and efficiency? Is it a mode of technologically enhanced labor-saving for the "human motor"? Does the liberatory rhetoric associated with multitasking (you can work where you want; take your computer to the beach or the café) merely mask the increased expectations of 24/7 productivity? (Do you really want your laptop at the beach?) Just as "alibi servers" help to evade surveillance, enacting a technological illusion of being elsewhere, computer "windows" can be alibi servers for identity. In *Life on the Screen*, Sherry Turkle describes how computer windows work to produce an identity with "distributed presence": "Windows provide a way for a computer to place you in several contexts at the same time … your identity on the computer is the sum of your distributed presence."[26] Turkle portrays the computer user as a "decentralized self" who, cycling between different windows, has a fractured but multiple identity.[27] She ascribes this screen life its theoretical analogs:

> [M]ore than twenty years after meeting the ideas of Lacan, Foucault, Deleuze, and Guattari, I am meeting them again in my new life on the screen. But this time the Gallic abstractions are more concrete. In my computer-mediated worlds, the self is multiple, fluid, and constituted in interaction with machine connections; it is made and transformed by language; sexual congress is an exchange of signifiers; and understanding follows from navigation and tinkering rather than analysis. And in the machine-generated world of MUDs, I meet characters who put me in a new relationship with my own identity.[28]

As a screen-based visual system, the "windows" interface subtly exponentiates what Erwin Panofsky described as the "unique and specific possibilities" of the cinema: the *dynamization of space* and the *spatialization of time*. On the computer, we can be two (or more) places at once, in two (or more) time frames, in two (or more) modes of identity, in a fractured post-Cartesian cyberspace, cybertime.

[…]

Notes

1 Bill Gates, *The Road Ahead* (New York: Viking, 1995), 53.
2 Ibid. In 1981, Microsoft was developing a software interface it called the "Interface Manager." In 1982, Microsoft added pull-down menus and dialog boxes, as used on the Xerox Star. In a 1983 announcement, the Interface Manager was renamed "Microsoft Windows."
3 Microsoft's defense in this suit was that both Apple and Microsoft actually stole from Xerox PARC.
4 Windows went through a variety of updates and improvements in its first decade: When Windows/386 was released, Windows 2 was renamed Windows/286. There were frequent criticisms of the interface: windows could be overlapped, but were instead "tiled." Windows were not allowed to cover an area at the bottom of the screen that was reserved for "iconized"

programs. Windows 95 was the beginning of a new look for Microsoft. Its new graphical user interface (owing much to the Mac interface) was much more intuitive than the cascading style of Windows 3.1. Multitasking and increased network capability also made it a more powerful operating system for an office environment. Hackers called the Microsoft interface "Micro-sloth Windows" or "Windoze" because of its agonizingly slow speed.

5 David Gelernter, *Machine Beauty: Elegance and the Heart of Technology* (New York: Basic Books, 1998), 37.

6 Computer terminology has added a new meaning of "window shopping" to the vernacular. As defined in the Web-based *HyperDictionary*, "window shopping" is

> A term used among users of WIMP environments like the X Window System or the Macintosh at the US Geological Survey for *extended experimentation with new window colours, fonts, and icon shapes.* This activity can take up hours of what might otherwise have been productive working time. "I spent the afternoon window shopping until I found the coolest shade of green for my active window borders—now they perfectly match my medium slate blue background." *Serious window shoppers will spend their days with bitmap editors, creating new and different icons and background patterns for all to see.* Also: "window dressing," the act of applying new fonts, colours, etc.

<http://www.hyperdictionary.com/dictionary/window+shopping> (emphasis added).

7 *Webopedia* <http://www.webopedia.com/TERM/w/window.html>.

8 Eco's argument:

> The fact is that the world is divided between users of the Macintosh computer and users of MS-DOS compatible computers. I am firmly of the opinion that the Macintosh is Catholic and that DOS is Protestant. Indeed, the Macintosh is counter-reformist and has been influenced by the "ratio studiorum" of the Jesuits. It is cheerful, friendly, conciliatory, it tells the faithful how they must proceed step by step to reach—if not the Kingdom of Heaven—the moment in which their document is printed. It is catechistic: the essence of revelation is dealt with via simple formulae and sumptuous icons. Everyone has a right to salvation.
>
> DOS is Protestant, or even Calvinistic. It allows free interpretation of scripture, demands difficult personal decisions, imposes a subtle hermeneutics upon the user, and takes for granted the idea that not all can reach salvation. To make the system work you need to interpret the program yourself: a long way from the baroque community of revelers, the user is closed within the loneliness of his own inner torment.
>
> You may object that, with the passage to Windows, the DOS universe has come to resemble more closely the counter-reformist tolerance of the Macintosh. It's true: Windows represents an Anglican-style schism, big ceremonies in the cathedral, but there is always the possibility of a return to DOS to change things in accordance with bizarre decisions...
>
> And machine code, which lies beneath both systems (or environments, if you prefer)? Ah, that is to do with the Old Testament, and is Talmudic and cabalistic.

This excerpt is from an English translation of Umberto Eco's back-page column "La bustina di Minerva," in the Italian newsweekly *Espresso* (September 30, 1994).

9   Steven Johnson also uses that term in his *Interface Culture: How New Technology Transforms the Way We Create and Communicate* (San Francisco: Harper, 1997).

10   Stephenson, *In the Beginning Was the Command Line*, 23. Much of Stephenson's complaint about Microsoft is an aesthetic one, targeting the "aesthetic gaffes" and "white-trash stuff" of the Microsoft operating system ("Microsoft therefore bears the same relationship to Silicon Valley elite as the Beverly Hillbillies did to their fussy banker...they simply don't care and they are going to go on being tacky, and rich, and happy, forever"); but Stephenson also succinctly separates the Mac OS from Windows OS in terms of Apple's model of hardware monopoly compared to Microsoft's software business, which cleverly found a way of marketing a string of ones and zeros, a disk full of information in an empty box. The polemical thrust of Stephenson's essay is to unmask the GUI, and to advocate the more exposed workings of the Linux operating system.

11   There are many more distinctions to draw between the Mac version of a graphic user interface and the Windows one. In Stephenson's description, when a GUI computer crashes, the result looks like "static on a broken television set—a 'snow crash.'" But when a Windows machine crashes, "the old command line interface would fall down over the GUI like an asbestos fire curtain sealing off the proscenium of a burning opera. When a Macintosh got into trouble, it presented you with a cartoon of a bomb, which was funny the first time you saw it" (*In the Beginning*, 22).Also, the Macintosh's technical means of running its graphical user interface led to its being built in one well-designed box that contained both the "motherboard" of its processing unit and the CRT video system that mapped computer memory and commands onto its screen. Ultimately, Stephenson finds a twisted irony in this: a Mac user "couldn't open up the hood and mess around with it...Apple, in spite of its reputation as the machine of choice of scruffy, creative hacker types, had actually created a machine that discouraged hacking, while Microsoft, viewed as a technological laggard and copycat, had created a vast disorderly parts bazaar" (*In the Beginning*, 80).

12   Ibid., 64.

13   Ibid., 52.

14   Samsung's Digital Network Refrigerator (model RH2777AT) has a detachable flat-screen display that functions as photo album, message board, Internet browser, TV, and refrigerator temperature control.

15   Brenda Laurel, quoted in David Kline, "The Embedded Internet," *Wired* 4.10 (October 1996): 101.

16   Gelernter, *Machine Beauty*, 2–10.

17   Walter Benjamin, "The Work of Art in the Age of Mechanical Reproduction," in *Illuminations*, ed. Hannah Arendt, trans. Harry Zohn (New York: Schocken Books, 1969), 239–240. As Colin Rowe and Robert Slutzky write: "Painting can only imply the third dimension, architecture cannot suppress it." Colin Rowe and Robert Slutsky, "Transparency: Literal and Phenomenal," in

The Mathematics of the Ideal Villa and Other Essays, Rowe (Cambridge: MIT Press, 1977), 166.

18 A multitasking operating system makes it possible for users to run multiple applications at the same time or to run "background" processes while conducting other tasks on the computer. At first a term for computer operating systems capable of running more than one task at the same time, "multitasking" has now come to refer to humans as operating systems juggling tasks—driving while talking on a cell phone, cooking dinner while watching TV, checking email while sitting in a meeting.

19 <http://en.wikipedia.org/wiki/Computer_multitasking>.

20 Recent research suggests that human multitasking, which at first may seem to increase efficiency, actually is less efficient than focusing on one task at a time. Rubinstein, Meyer, and Evans describe how their research revealed that for all types of tasks, subjects lost time when they had to switch from one task to another, and time costs increased with the complexity of the tasks: see Joshua S. Rubinstein, David E. Meyer, and Jeffrey E. Evans, "Executive Control of Cognitive Processes in Task Switching," *Journal of Experimental Psychology— Human Perception and Performance* 27, no. 4 (2001). After a long-term study of American's use of time, with a team of researchers at the University of Maryland, College Park, Dr. John Robinson concluded: "You can't expand time, so what you try to do is deepen time by doing more things in the same period." See John Robinson and Geoffrey Godbey, *Time for Life: The Surprising Ways Americans Use Their Time* (University Park: Pennsylvania State University Press, 1997).

21 Amy Harmon, "Talk, Type, Read E-mail," *New York Times*, July 23, 1998, late edition-final, G1.

22 The MTV Networks/Viacom Study of Media, Entertainment, and Leisure Time surveyed 4,070 Americans between the ages of four and seventy. The study also reported that TV viewers are using their computers while "watching" TV 20 percent of the time; one third of those in the study have their TV in the same room as their computer; and 28 percent have visited a Web address given on TV. See Stephen Battaglio, "TV, Napster and the 29.8 Hour Day," *inside. com* (June 2000).

23 Joanne Ciulla, *The Working Life: The Promise and Betrayal of Modern Work* (New York: Crown Business Books, 2000) cited in "Multi-tasking to the Max," *USA Today*, June 7, 2000 (<http://www.usatoday.com/life/cyber/tech/cth787.htm>).

24 130130 This website, run by George Washington University, offers students guidelines for computer use. *Computer Multi-tasking and Internet Interference with College Academics* <http://gwired.gwu.edu/counsel/html/virtual-handouts/computer-multi-tasking.html>.

25 Ibid.

26 Sherry Turkle, *Life on the Screen: Identity in the Age of the Internet* (New York: Simon and Schuster, 1995), 13.

27 Cognitive theorists and artificial intelligence theorists alike have challenged the concept of a unitary "self." See, for example, Marvin Minsky, *The Society of Mind* (New York: Simon and Schuster, 1986).

28 Turkle, *Life on the Screen*, 14–15.

CHAPTER FIVE

The Magic Mirror

William Henry Fox Talbot

[...]

II

Twice fifteen years had roll'd in peace away—
Now old, and nigh to death, the Wizard lay.
With his last breath he summon'd to his side
Bertha, his only child, his joy, his pride.
Daughter! he said, this castle's stern command
Must soon be trusted to thy feeble hand:
I may not tell thee Who its builders were!
Not of this Earth ... then O my child beware,
And heed a father's dying counsel well!
In days of yore I framed a charmed Spell,
Which like a shield o'er this enchanted ground,
Sheds its protecting influence around.
Not that by this alone I caused to rise
The mighty Fabric that around thee lies,
(Far other secrets raised its banner'd walls,)
But in this Talisman they center all!
'Tis like the Clasp of a mysterious Chain,
Which if thou rendest ... all the links are vain.
Behold you Mirror ... veil'd! ... In secrecy
What it concealth, seek not Thou to see.
Tempt not the Spiritis of the viewless Deep,
Long would'st thou rue it and thy folly weep!
Raise not the veil ... a thousand forms of Death
And overwhelming Ruin lurk beneath!

[…]
His voice grew faint, and ere the morrow's sun
His eyes were dim—his earthly race was run.

III
[…]
One thoughtless month o'er Bertha's head had flown
Since that fair heritage she call'd her own—
Already Pleasure drooped her languid wing,
The weary hours Amusement caused to bring,
For ah! Her days in Folly's wild career
She past, nor cared she Wisdom's voice to hear.
Fill'd was her castle with the gay and proud,
And flatt'rers came, a mercenary crowd:
In song and dance, in feast and wassail high,
The hours were spent, and idle revelry.

It chanced one time that she remain'd alone,
For over was the feast … the guests were gone;
It was the bright and sunny month of May,
The hours seem'd long … she wearied of the day.
She traversed every hall, then went again,
For Pleasure seeking … seeking it in vain,,,
When through the Chamber dim she chanced to pass,
Where that dark curtain veil'd the Fatal Glass.

A sudden wish arose … she long'd to see …
But fear'd her father's words of mystery.
She stopp'd … drew nearer to behold the veil …
Touch'd it … then felt again her courage fail!
Three times she paused … but ah! the veil was thin,
A glorious Light was streaming from within!
It seems so lovely! Need I fear? she cried,
And with rash hand she flung its folds aside!

IV
What show'd the Mirror? In an azure sky
The Sun was shining, calm and brilliantly,
And on as sweet a Vale he pour'd his beam
As ever smiled in youthful poet's dream:
With murmur soft, a hundred mazy rills
In silver tracks meander'd down the hills
And fed a crystal Lake, whose gentle shore
Was grassy bank with dark woods shadow'd o'er.

Far in the midst a lovely Isle there lay,
Where thousand birds of Indian plumage gay

Flutter'd like sparkling gems from tree to tree,
And caroll'd wild, with Nature's minstrelsy.

A Temple's fair proportion graced the Isle,
The rippling waters that around it smile
Reflect its columns in their sportive play
And glitter in the sun's unclouded ray.

And prints of tiny footsteps on the sand
Betray'd the gambols of some fairy band
Who now were flown, but scatter'd all around
Lay many a rosy chaplet on the ground,
And baskets heap'd with blushing fruits, and flow'rs
Fragrant as those which bloom'd in Eden's bow'rs,
And golden harps and timbrels cast away
Spread on the sward in rich confusion lay,
As if that light and airy company
Had shrunk in terror from a Mortal's eye!

In rapture o'er the mirror Bertha hung,
And pleased her fancy stray'd those scenes among;
But, as she gazed, a dimness seem'd to steal
O'er the bright glass, and slowly to conceal
The distant hills: then rolling up the vale
Shrouded it o'er with Vapours wan and pale.
The Lake, the Mountains, fade in mist away,
And lurid Darkness overspreads the day.

Too late repenting, Bertha tried once more
The Mirror's faded brightness to restore:
Alas! Alas! It baffles all her skill,
The vapour on the glass falls thicker still.
To chase away the noxious dew she strives …
An instant, see! the shadowy scene revives …
But ah! how changed a picture doth it show
Of desolation, misery, and woe!

Dark frown'd the Sky, all leafless were the woods,
The brooks were swollen into raging Floods—
The gloomy lake, its beauty now no more,
Rolled long and angry billows to the shore—
Voices, not human, rose upon the blast …
Forms, not of Earth, across the Darkness past …
Fly! cried a whisper to her startled ear,
O haste and fly! the Storm of Death is near!
There shone a dazzling flash … with Echoes dread
The distant Thunder roar'd … and Bertha fled.

V
[…]
The Morning dawn'd… and nothing then was seen
That could have told, those Tow'rs had ever been;
And when the Sun uprose, his cheerful ray
Fell but on shatter'd crags and summits gray.

Evolution and Revolution

CHAPTER SIX

From *The Republic*

Plato

"And now," I [Socrates] said, "let me show in a figure how far our nature is enlightened or unenlightened: Behold! human beings living in a underground den, which has a mouth open toward the light and reaching all along the den; here they have been from their childhood, and have their legs and necks chained so that they cannot move, and can only see before them, being prevented by the chains from turning round their heads. Above and behind them a fire is blazing at a distance, and between the fire and the prisoners there is a raised way; and you will see, if you look, a low wall built along the way, like the screen which marionette-players have in front of them, over which they show the puppets."

"I see," [Glaucon replied].

"And do you see," I said, "men passing along the wall carrying all sorts of vessels, and statues and figures of animals made of wood and stone and various materials, which appear over the wall? Some of them are talking, others silent."

"You have shown me a strange image, and they are strange prisoners."

"Like ourselves," I replied; "and they see only their own shadows, or the shadows of one another, which the fire throws on the opposite wall of the cave?"

"True," he said; "how could they see anything but the shadows if they were never allowed to move their heads?"

"And of the objects which are being carried in like manner they would only see the shadows?"

"Yes," he said.

"And if they were able to converse with one another, would they not suppose that they were naming what was actually before them?"

"Very true."

"And suppose further that the prison had an echo which came from the other side, would they not be sure to fancy when one of the passers-by spoke that the voice which they heard came from the passing shadow?"

"No question," he replied.

"To them," I said, "the truth would be literally nothing but the shadows of the images."

"That is certain."

"And now look again, and see what will naturally follow if the prisoners are released and disabused of their error. At first, when any of them is liberated and compelled suddenly to stand up and turn his neck round and walk and look towards the light, he will suffer sharp pains; the glare will distress him, and he will be unable to see the realities of which in his former state he had seen the shadows; and then conceive someone saying to him, that what he saw before was an illusion, but that now, when he is approaching nearer to being and his eye is turned toward more real existence, he has a clearer vision—what will be his reply? And you may further imagine that his instructor is pointing to the objects as they pass and requiring him to name them—will he not be perplexed? Will he not fancy that the shadows which he formerly saw are truer than the objects which are now shown to him?"

"Far truer."

"And if he is compelled to look straight at the light, will he not have a pain in his eyes which will make him turn away to take refuge in the objects of vision which he can see, and which he will conceive to be in reality clearer than the things which are now being shown to him?"

"True" he said.

"And suppose once more, that he is reluctantly dragged up a steep and rugged ascent, and held fast until he's forced into the presence of the sun himself, is he not likely to be pained and irritated? When he approaches the light his eyes will be dazzled, and he will not be able to see anything at all of what are now called realities."

"Not all in a moment," he said.

"He will require to grow accustomed to the sight of the upper world. And first he will see the shadows best, next the reflections of men and other objects in the water, and then the objects themselves; then he will gaze upon the light of the moon and the stars and the spangled heaven; and he will see the sky and the stars by night better than the sun or the light of the sun by day?"

"Certainly."

"Last of all he will be able to see the sun, and not mere reflections of him in the water, but he will see him in his own proper place, and not in another; and he will contemplate him as he is."

"Certainly."

"He will then proceed to argue that this is he who gives the season and the years, and is the guardian of all that is in the visible world, and in a certain way the cause of all things which he and his fellows have been accustomed to behold?"

FIGURE 6.1 *Capturing the setting sun through a smartphone screen, 2011.
Photo: Juozas Kaziukenas.*

"Clearly," he said, "he would first see the sun and then reason about him."

"And when he remembered his old habitation, and the wisdom of the den and his fellow-prisoners, do you not suppose that he would felicitate himself on the change, and pity them?"

"Certainly, he would."

"And if they were in the habit of conferring honors among themselves on those who were quickest to observe the passing shadows and to remark which of them went before, and which followed after, and which were together; and who were therefore best able to draw conclusions as to the future, do you think that he would care for such honors and glories, or envy the possessors of them? Would he not say with Homer, 'Better to be the poor servant of a poor master,' and to endure anything, rather than think as they do and live after their manner?"

"Yes," he said, "I think that he would rather suffer anything than entertain these false notions and live in this miserable manner."

"Imagine once more," I said, "such a one coming suddenly out of the sun to be replaced in his old situation; would he not be certain to have his eyes full of darkness?"

"To be sure," he said.

"And if there were a contest, and he had to compete in measuring the shadows with the prisoners who had never moved out of the den, while his sight was still weak, and before his eyes had become steady (and the time which would be needed to acquire this new habit of sight might be very considerable), would he not be ridiculous? Men would say of him that up he went and down he came without his eyes; and that it was better not even to think of ascending; and if anyone tried to loose another [from the chains] and lead him up to the light, let them only catch the offender, and they would put him to death."

"No question," he said.

"This entire allegory," I said, "you may now append, dear Glaucon, to the previous argument; the prison-house is the world of sight, the light of the fire is the sun, and you will not misapprehend me if you interpret the journey upward to be the ascent of the soul into the intellectual world according to my poor belief, which, at your desire, I have expressed—whether rightly or wrongly God knows. But, whether true or false, my opinion is that in the world of knowledge the idea of good appears last of all, and is seen only with an effort; and, when seen, is also inferred to be the universal author of all things beautiful and right, parent of light and of the lord of light in this visible world, and the immediate source of reason and truth in the intellectual; and that this is the power upon which he who would act rationally, either in public or private life must have his eye fixed."

"I agree," he said, "as far as I am able to understand you."

"Moreover," I said, "you must not wonder that those who attain to this beatific vision are unwilling to descend to human affairs; for their souls are ever hastening into the upper world where they desire to dwell; which desire of theirs is very natural, if our allegory may be trusted."

CHAPTER SEVEN

Screenology; or, Media Archaeology of the Screen

Erkki Huhtamo

Introduction: Screen, topos, dispositive

"A covered framework, partition, or curtain, either movable or fixed, which serves to protect from the heat of the sun or of a fire, from rain, wind, or cold, or from other inconvenience or danger, or to shelter from observation, conceal, shut off the view, or secure privacy; as, a fire-screen; a folding-screen; a window-screen, etc.; hence, such a covered framework, curtain, etc., used for some other purpose; as, a screen upon which images may be cast by a magic lantern; in general, and shelter or means of concealment."

Definition of "Screen," The Century Dictionary and Cyclopedia, 1911
(orig. 1889)

A large part of our daily lives is spent staring at screens. Some of them, like cinema screens and giant outdoor displays, are located in public spaces, while others are part of our privacy. Since the mid twentieth century, television screens have become a permanent feature of millions of households around the globe. Today's television culture may seem uniform. Yet, during the "interfacial invasion" of the television set, the cultural roles and even the "nature" of television have been constantly shifting, affected by social practices, broadcasting policies and design philosophies, but also by peripherals like game consoles, video recorders and cable modems.[1] Since the late 1970s, personal computers have been competing with television screens for the users' attention. The division between big screens and small screens is often thought to coincide with the divide between public and private, yet its validity has been questioned. In *Ambient Television*, Anna McCarthy demonstrated that associating the television with domestic viewing only is misleading.[2] Both large and small screens have long been installed in public spaces, as well as in many kinds of intermediate spaces. The automobile has become almost unthinkable without screens serving purposes such as road navigation, safety and even entertainment.[3]

Ideas about the screen have been further challenged by the mass dissemination of portable devices like mobile phones and pocket game consoles, which do not easily fit within existing schemes. In daily life they physically cross the thresholds between private and public, going where their users go. Miniaturized screens display huge amounts of rapidly changing information—images, graphics and text. In spite of their minuscule size, they are further divided into software-based "windows" that appear and disappear in rapid succession. An intuitive, almost real-time relationship develops between the fingers and the streams of data traversing the palm. We leave our television sets and PlayStations behind, but portable and wearable screens have become omnipresent extensions of the body.

The basic assumption behind this article is that screens in contemporary culture cannot be fully grasped without relating them to their antecedents. This is a task for a field I call "screenology." I envision it as a branch of media studies which occupies itself not only with screens as designed artifacts, but also with their uses, intermedial relations with other cultural forms, and discourses that have enveloped them in different times and places. Screenology should investigate all these issues within relevant cultural, social and ideological frames of reference. Some groundwork has already been laid by the cinematic apparatus theorists and their followers, the "dispositive" theorists, Charles Musser's investigations of screen practice, Siegfried Zielinski's comparison of cinema and television, Margaret Morse's work on screens as gateways into virtual realities, David Morley's, Lynn Spigel's and Cecelia Tichi's studies of television viewing, Lev Manovich's genealogy of the computer screen, and more recently by Anne Friedberg's *The Virtual Window* and Giuliana Bruno's *Surface*, which the author defines as an "archaeology of migrant media."[4]

The approach propagated here is media archaeological—screenology could just as well be called "media archaeology of the screen." As it is understood here, media archaeology aims to demonstrate that seemingly unprecedented phenomena are often based on recurring patterns and schemata that have appeared in earlier contexts. Recalled from shared memory banks by marketing people, techno-utopians, hobbyists, bloggers and potentially anyone, such formulas, or *topoi* (singular: topos), get assigned ever new roles. As malleable commonplaces they can be used for many purposes—to persuade, convince, fantasize and even to frighten. Mapping the paths along which their "lives" have unfolded helps us penetrate beyond the opaque façades of media culture. Media archaeology does not belittle the changes brought forth by economic and industrial developments or by phenomena like the mass adoption of mobile phones, but it likes to point out that focusing on novelty only can be misleading. Identifying the inherited lurking behind the "extraordinary" may lead to a better appreciation of "the new."

In a sense, talking about "screens" can be misleading. Although there are such things with identities of their own, in media culture the screen is always connected with something else. It is a feature or extension of a device that serves a specific purpose, as well as part of a "media dispositive." The discussion on dispositives within media studies began in the field of film scholarship in the 1970s, particularly influenced by French developments. The word *dispositif* was translated as the "cinematic apparatus."[5] Whereas film semiotics, which was in vogue in the late 1960s, analyzed films as coded texts of signifiers and signifieds, the cinematic apparatus theory focused on the contexts and conditions within which they were received by spectators. Jean-Louis Baudry and others considered the *dispositif* as a kind of psycho-physical machinery that consisted of the technological and environmental elements of the viewing situation (the auditorium, the screen, the projection booth, the light beam of the projector, etc.), but also of the metapsychological operations taking place within the spectator's mind.[6] The configuration of the elements of the viewing situation at the same time enabled and constrained the experience.

The apparatus theory, which was eclipsed from critical discourse in the later 1980s for over two decades, is attracting scholarly attention again. It has been liberated from the psychoanalytic emphasis that typified early apparatus theory as well as from its exclusive focus on the movie theater as the normative cinematic apparatus. Perhaps reflecting the displacement of cinema from its former dominant position by other channels, devices and venues, the new apparatus theory prefers to translate *dispositif* as "dispositive" or "cine-dispositive," underlining a break with the past— or at least a reorientation. It has begun to identify, analyze and classify *different* media experiences in terms of their dispositives.[7] An example is the book *La télévision du téléphonoscope à YouTube* ("The television from the telephonoscope to YouTube," 2009), which propagated the notion *télédispositif* (tele-dispositive).[8] Indeed, it could be claimed that any media machine, even one that exists as an intention or patent drawing, includes in embryonic form a potential "dispositive"—a set of descriptions about its implementation, purpose and intended user(s).

Benoit Turquety has written, I think correctly, that "[e]ach optical machine produces a specific mode of perception."[9] This could be extended by saying that each *media* machine produces a specific mode of perception / operation / subjection / interaction, etc. Perhaps we could even drop the words "optical" and "media" and say simply: machine, or go further and replace "machine" with "artifact" or "object"? Doing so would broaden the problematics of the dispositive from media studies to cultural anthropology, psychology of perception and the behavioral sciences.

Such an enormous expansion of "the regime of the dispositive" is tempting, but might dull the concept's critical edge. For media archaeology it can be very useful, but needs to be specified before it can be applied to topics like the screen. One of the issues that led to the eclipse of apparatus theory was its a-historical emphasis. To be usefully resurrected, it needs to be historicized. In this article I will suggest that the dispositive can be conceived as a topos, a stereotypical model or schema that is reactivated by cultural agents over and over again for various purposes. Media archaeology as topos study, or topos archaeology, has occupied me since the early 1990s.[10] Late in his career Friedrich Kittler endorsed the fruitfulness of such an approach, although he never applied it broadly himself: "[M]y feeling is that rather than focusing on linear history, we should instead think about what I call 'recursive history', where the same issue is taken up again and again at regular intervals but with different connotations and results."[11]

It is important to make a distinction between a technical apparatus and a dispositive, emphasizing that these are not the same thing. A technical apparatus is—as the expression indicates—a system or mechanism concocted for a certain purpose by applying engineering skills and scientific knowledge. It may be constructed—a patent model is an example—with only a vague idea about the dispositives that might be formed around it.

From a screenological perspective the dispositive is a recurrent model that manifests itself materially, but also discursively in the cultural imagination. In a similar way, the media screens that play important roles in both technical media apparata and the dispositives enveloping them have evolved parallel with imaginary ones. Countless discursive "screens" can be found from visual and textual traditions even before the ideas were realized by technological means. To mention an example which will be discussed later, the "magic mirrors" that anticipating media screens appeared in both actual and imagined necromantic practices but also in fairytales. Inspired by scholars like Walter Benjamin, Wolfgang Schievelbusch and Carolyn Marvin, I consider imaginary manifestations of culture equally real and essential as material ones.[12] Screenology should investigate the often unpredictable relationships between the cultural imagination and the world of things. Whether conceived as mirrors, crystal balls, windows, doors, observation posts, gateways or other things, screens are situated at the liminal zone between the real and the virtual.

In what follows, I will first discuss the etymology of the word screen and its early uses. I will then explore the emergence of what I call "media screens," and move on to excavate their discursive manifestations, and their introduction into the domestic sphere. Finally, I will provide some thoughts about mobile screens—arguably their most commonly used form in contemporary media culture—and briefly ponder the current efforts to go "beyond screens," manifested by virtual reality and the projection mapping of images on physical objects and buildings. The article is anything but a final word about the topic. Rather, it offers speculations supported by evidence. In a relatively short study some omissions have been unavoidable. For example the habit of framing paintings and prints and displaying them in private and public environments has screenological interest, but will be discussed only in passing. I have concentrated on cases that can be more closely associated with technological developments, paying less attention to metaphoric proto-screens such as stories about paintings that "come alive" and communicate with humans.

Etymologies and semantic shifts

The screen can be tentatively defined as a "framed information surface," which is deliberately vague. "Fits for all" definitions are difficult to formulate, as demonstrated by an attempt by Lev Manovich, who singled out three types: (1) the classical screen, which "displays a static, permanent image" (such as a framed painting), (2) the dynamic screen, which "displays a moving image of the past" (as the cinema screen) and (3) the real-time screen, which "shows the present" (such as the television, radar and computer screens).[13] Things get confusing, when Manovich adds that the dynamic screen "is the screen of cinema, television, video." Television screens "show the present" while displaying "moving images of the past" and static images too.[14] How about computer screens? Defining the classical screen as "a flat, rectangular surface" raises counter-arguments as well. Many paintings are in round or oval frames. Some have been integrated into architectural and sculptural environments, deliberately blurring the boundary between the "within and without" of the frame.[15]

Manovich also claims that the "proportions [of screens] have not changed in five centuries; they are similar for a typical fifteenth-century painting, a film screen, and a computer screen."[16] Sweeping generalizations eschew contextualization—what is "typical" anyway? There is no universal typology of screens separate from the cultural traditions that have molded, applied and signified them. Their formal features and meanings have always been in flux. Including the rich traditions of folding screens used in China and Japan for centuries or even millennia would make things even more complex. The screen is a thoroughly historical construct which avoids easy classification. In fifteenth-century Europe there was no "typical" frame ratio, although some formats may have been more common than others depending on place, tradition and purpose. In a similar way, we might ask if the "typical" film screen is that of the 1910s silent cinema or that of the 1930s sound cinema, or the wide screen that has existed in many variants since the 1950s.[17] As a rule, standardization is counterbalanced by differentiation. The genealogy of the screen is more complex than Manovich suggests.

According to the *Oxford English Dictionary* (*OED*), the foremost authority on the evolution of the English language, the word "screen" came to use in the fourteenth and fifteenth centuries; its etymology is "difficult."[18] In his *Dictionary of the English Language*, first issued in 1755, Samuel Johnson indicated that "screen" gained figurative meanings early on. His first definition is "any thing that affords shelter or concealment," followed by "any thing used to exclude cold or light," and "a riddle to sift sand." As a verb, "to screen" is first said to mean "to shelter; to conceal; to hide," and then "to sift; to riddle." Johnson's examples include Shakespeare and Francis Bacon, who stated that "[s]ome ambitious men seem as *screens* to princes in matters of danger and envy." Talking about his "juniors by a year," Jonathan Swift characterized his old age as a "*screen*, [w]hen death approach'd, to stand between; The *screen* remov'd, their hearts are trembling." For Milton, a ridge of hills "*screen'd* the fruits of th' earth, and feats of men, [f]rom cold septentrion blasts," while the poet Nicholas Rowe used the expression: "To *screen* the wild escapes of lawless passion."

The *OED* indicates that "screen" was used early on about a "contrivance for warding off the heat of fire or a draught of air."[19] It was a "piece of furniture consisting usually of an upright board or of a frame hung with leather, canvas, cloth, tapestry, or paper, or of two or more of such boards or frames hinged together."[20] Screens like these became staples of British houses. Fire-screens were common because the open fireplace was, until the late nineteenth century, the principal source of heating. In the summer the screen was used to block its opening from view. A large variety of designs developed, making it impossible to cover the topic in detail. In the nineteenth century, there were "folding screens," "pole screens," "banner screens," "horse or cheval screens" and "face or hand screens," among others.[21] They came in different shapes and materials and were mounted on stands which stood on the floor or on a table. Some were held in hand in the manner of fans. A text from 1548 talked about "Two litle Skrenes of silke to hold against the fier," which may have referred to the latter.[22] Screens became such a familiar feature of middle and upper class homes that a writer named Anna Bache made one to recount the "adventures of a fire-screen" as an anthropomorphized narrator.[23]

Screens were routinely discussed in texts instructing the reader how to furnish the house. Their main functions were to protect the inhabitants from the scorching heat of the open fireplace (fire-screens) or from the cold air seeping in from doorways or windows (draught-screens). To best serve these purposes the screens were made movable and adjustable. Some had sliding door-like panels, while the pole screens were attached to vertical poles. They were slid up and down to position them between the flames and the sitter's face. Some screens had panels of glass embedded in them to transmit light from the fire while blocking its heat; opaque ones had sometimes a bracket for a candle on the side of the sitter. Screens were also used as room dividers "for breaking up the hard, angular lines of the four square walls that form the boundary-line of most dwelling rooms [...]."[24] They provided areas for intimate *tete-à-tete* encounters during social gatherings, guarding the conversants from the others' attention. At "sick-rooms" screens protected the patient from draught, also providing privacy "to get out of bed, either to sit in a chair, or to obey the calls of nature."[25]

Can the domestic screens of the past be related with the media screens of today? At first look they seem opposites: traditional screens protected against something and blocked the view, whereas media screens are *displays*: their role is to exhibit, to serve communication and to provide visualized information, the more and faster the better. Media culture aims at universal coverage, ultimate visibility and unlimited access; if it reaches its goals, there is no place to hide.[26] It is difficult to conceive media screens that would have been designed to refuse to display. If one is encountered, it is most likely switched off, broken, or programmed to operate fully only if a software filter is deactivated or a coin or credit card is inserted into the device it is connected with. However, media culture has many areas and applications where hiding information is practiced. These are its "black holes" or "meaningful absences" that have to do with economic, political and ideological ends. From such a perspective it could be claimed that media screens can be used to conceal even as they reveal. In practice their output is selective rather than fully open and exhaustive.

It is possible to detect seeds of media culture in-the-making by paying attention to the transformation of domestic screens into attractions for the eye. From early on they were decorated with ornaments and pictures. In the nineteenth century, instructions for do-it-yourself embellishments for screens were included in handbooks of creative pastimes for ladies. *The Young Lady's Book* (1829), among others, taught how to create landscapes and "any kind of figure, animal, or small composition" for transparent screens.[27] In the Victorian era covering the common floor-standing folding screens with collages of mass-produced pictures by combining scraps and even photographs with prints and cut-outs from illustrated magazines, finally coating the result with varnish, became a popular pastime. The proliferation of visual imagery was adapted to the domestic interior by the consumers themselves.[28] The mosaic-like screens came to co-exist with photo albums, stereoscopes and stereoviews, photographs and framed paintings and prints. The significance of the variety of visual information on screens was emphasized by *An Encyclopaedia of Cottage, Farm, and Villa Architecture* (1846):

Large fire-screens for parlours are frequently covered with odd prints, and especially portraits of men, animals, plants &c., and even with select passages from newspapers; or with conundrums, riddles, enigmas, and charades. For a large library fire-screen, nothing could be more appropriate than good maps; and, indeed, we have seen a globe raised on a pole, and sliding up and down it at pleasure, used as a small fire-screen. It is a great advantage for young persons to have frequently put in their way, such instruments of education, as globes, maps, chronological tables, tables of the heights of mountains, the lengths of rivers, &c.; for in this manner the contents of these instruments, insensibly, and without effort, impress themselves on the mind.[29]

Fire and draught screens do not deserve to be called media screens, even though later media machines such as the television set shared their identity as furniture. Still, the issue is more complex than one might think. In 1862, *The Furniture Gazette* quoted an authority, H. J. Cooper, who neatly summarized the problematics of domestic screens by stating that they "may be opaque, translucent, or transparent; concealing, obscuring, or revealing, and are an important element in the dramatic arrangement of a room or suite of rooms."[30]

The emergence of screens for public spectacles

In the *OED* the earliest example of a screen as a projection surface is from 1810: "To make Transparent Screens for the Exhibition of the Phantasmagoria."[31] Phantasmagoria was a novelty ghost show, introduced in England by Paul de Philipsthal, whose presentations began at the Lyceum along The Strand in London in October 1801.[32] The reporter of the *Monthly Magazine* was determined to reveal the secrets of the spectacle to the reader. For him the role of the screen was clear:

> The people of London [...] have, during the present month, been attracted in crowds to see an exhibition of optical images in the Strand. These ghosts and spectres, as they are called, are the simple production of a common magic-lantern, the objects from which are thrown upon the farther side of a transparent screen, which is hung between the lantern and the audience. When the lantern is brought nearer the screen, the object is diminished in size, and appears to retire; when taken farther off, the object is increased [*sic*] in size, and appear to approach the spectator.[33]

This comment was published on December 1, 1801, predating the *OED*'s information by a decade. However, the association was already familiar in the previous century. James Wood wrote about media screens in his textbook *The Elements of Optics* in 1749. It is unlikely he was the first one. The detailed entry on "screen" in Samuel Johnson's *Dictionary of the English Language* does not mention projection screens, but pays attention to what Francis Bacon (1561–1626) had written in his posthumously published *Sylva Sylvarum*: "When there is a screen between the candle and the eye, the light passeth to the paper whereon one writeth."[34] Such observations, although not directly associated with media, are part of the scientific background of screen-based media. Wood associated the screen with magic lantern projections, but he also identified it as an element of another well-known device, the camera obscura:

> If light be admitted, through a convex lens, into a darkened chamber, or into a box from which all extraneous light is excluded, and the refracted rays be received upon a screen, placed at a proper distance, inverted images of external objects will be formed upon it. And if the lens be fixed in a sliding tube, the images of objects at different distances may successively be thrown upon the screen, by moving the lens backwards or forwards, as in the magic lantern.[35]

The camera obscura existed in different forms—as a portable box-like instrument, dismountable tent and permanent room or building.[36] The latter was normally a little hut erected by the sea shore or some other scenic location, sometimes at the top of a tower. The box camera obscura had a ground glass screen (alternatively called object glass) installed horizontally on the top side of the apparatus. By means of a lens tube and an internal slanted mirror, the view from the outside was projected on it from below, making it possible to sketch it on translucent paper superimposed on the screen. In room camera obscuras the surrounding scene was projected on a round "table" from a lens and mirror combination on the roof. The optical assembly could be rotated by the participants, which allowed them to observe the surroundings "panoramically." An 1805 book explained why the horizontal screen had to be circular: "The screen, upon which the picture is received, should be placed at the focal distance of the lens, and bent into an arc of a circle, of which the lens is the centre, that when the lens is turned sideways, the picture may still be cast on the screen at the focal distance of the lens."[37]

Magic lantern projections are known to have been organized since the second half of the seventeenth century.[38] The early shows were often given by itinerant show people in private homes, which gave them an intimate quality. The audience gathered around the lanternist to enjoy his stories, illustrated by pictures and accompanied by a hurdy-gurdy or other musical instrument. Judging by existing iconographic evidence, the showman made no effort to hide the lantern or himself.[39] The instrument had to be placed fairly close to the screen, because the available light sources (candles and simple oil lamps) were weak. A compromise had to be found for the projected image between decent size and brightness. Also the spectators had to remain fairly close to the screen to perceive the images. The visible presence of the "box" from which the pictures emanated must have been an essential element of the overall attraction. How such common magic lantern shows were related with Phantasmagoria was explained by *Systematic Education* in 1817:

The *Phantasmagoria* produces an exhibition very similar to that of the Magic Lanthorn. In the common Magic Lanthorns, the figures are painted on glass, and the parts of the glass not occupied by the painting are transparent, of course the image on the screen is a circle of light having a figure upon it; but in the Phantasmagoria, all the glass is opaque, except the figure only, which being painted in transparent colours, the light shines through it; of course no light can come upon the screen but that which passes through the figure itself, consequently the figure only is visible on the screen, without any circle of light.[40]

The book also noted that "[i]n common lanthorn the representation is made on the wall, or on a sheet, but in the Phantasmagoria it is thrown upon a silk screen placed between the lanthorn and the spectator."[41] The effect was the effacement of the screen: "[A]s no part of the screen can be seen, the figure appears to be formed in the air [...]."[42] In this sense Phantasmagoria could be associated with recent phenomena like holography and virtual reality, which purport to present "free" visual illusions that cannot be traced to a framed screen.

As an internet search can easily demonstrate, the word "phantasmagoria" has a broad discursive presence in today's media culture. Its original denotation may be blurry, but it lives on in contexts that refer to frightening effects caused by unknown causes. The "discursive life" of phantasmagoria needs to be discussed elsewhere.[43] For screenology its most important legacy is the spatial configuration of its dispositive, which effaced the presence of the technical apparatus. Keeping the audience in the dark (both concretely and metaphorically) blurred the boundary between the reality of the auditorium and the world of fantasy and occult penetrating into it, creating a game of make-believe.[44]

Phantasmagoria was a manifestation of what Charles Musser has labeled "the history of screen practice."[45] He used the term to position silent cinema within a continuum of preceding spectacles involving projected images. Musser's main reference point was the "magic lantern tradition in which showmen displayed images on a screen accompanying them with voice, music, and sound effects."[46] His concept is useful, but he did not fully utilize its potential. Looking back from the vantage point of early cinema made him exclude traditions that could not be directly linked with the lineage of film projection.[47] As I explained in *Illusions in Motion*, the moving panorama was one such tradition.[48] It enjoyed widespread popularity in the nineteenth century, competing for audiences with magic lantern shows, but it was not a projection-based form. The moving panorama was a huge roll painting that was wound from one roller to another in front of the audience. It was framed by a proscenium arch or a canvas mask covering the front of the hall. A lecturer explained the changing scenes to the audience, accompanied by music and sound effects. Both magic lantern shows and moving panoramas were itinerant shows and presented in similar venues from local opera houses to churches and community halls.

Musser also excluded the shadow theater, the most ancient and widespread of all screen practices. Elaborate traditions evolved in Asian cultures from India and Indonesia to China and Korea, becoming deeply rooted in cultural, social and religious customs and values. This happened long before shadow theater was introduced to Europe via the Ottoman Empire, possibly in the early seventeenth century.[49] Generalizations are risky, but all forms of shadow theater are technically live performances: the audience sits in front of the screen, while the performers operate shadow puppets behind it. The animated shadows are projected to the screen by means of a light source.

The fact that the spectators observed the spectacle from the front, while the "machinery" remained hidden from their gazes, recalls the dispositive of Phantasmagoria. As David Brewster reminded us, in his *Fantasmagorie* Etienne-Gaspard Robertson mixed features of the magic lantern and shadow show by introducing "along with his pictures the direct shadows of living objects, which imitated coarsely the appearance of those objects in a dark night or in moonlight."[50] In Paris, the heyday of *Fantasmagorie* coincided with that of Seraphin's celebrated shadow theater at Palais-Royal. In one of those cultural parallels that beg for an explanation, the Japanese *Utsushi-e*, a spectacle which began to develop around 1800, recalled features of both Phantasmagoria and Asian shadow theater, combining them with Japanese forms of popular storytelling. Several lightweight handheld magic lanterns (*furo*) were used simultaneously behind the screen. *Utsushi-e* recalls the role of translucent rice paper screens (*shoji*) as an element of the Japanese house. The living shadow figures moving behind the *shoji* stirred the imagination of both artists and writers.[51]

The vicissitudes of the "big screen" can be traced fairly accurately from the nineteenth century onward. The demand for picture shows grew with the development of the mass society, reflecting new needs for visual education and morally sound entertainments to pacify the crowds. Magic lantern shows became increasingly sophisticated. By using magnificent biunial (double) and triunial (triple) lanterns provided with powerful illuminants like oxy-hydrogen limelight and the electric carbon-arc, clear and detailed pictures could be projected in large auditoria and even outdoors.[52] As the film industry solidified its position, the word screen became firmly associated with it, reflecting the victory of projected moving images over other alternatives. In 1910 the *Moving Picture World* wrote that "people like to see on the screen what they read about," referring to their filmic preferences. *The Screen,* written with capital letters, referred metonymically to film culture itself. When a certain Mrs. P. Campbell stated in 1920 that she felt "much too aged for Eliza on the Screen," she referred to acting in the movies, working for the film industry.[53]

Words like "silver" or "big" were added in front of "screen," expressing the expansive growth of the industry and its ambitions. "Silver screen" was evoked from the early 1920s onward in the context of the triumphant silent cinema of the "Golden Age."[54] In the late nineteenth century it had been found out that by coating the projection screen with thin silver leaf and varnishing it to prevent oxidation its luminosity was greatly increased; therefore "silver screen."[55] As had been the case with "limelight," what originated as a technical term gained metaphorical power as a description of aspects of the spectacle itself.

"Big Screen" became a commonplace expression in the late 1940s and the 1950s, when the commercial film culture was plunged into a crisis, partly because of the emergence of a competitor: the television.[56] The film industry attempted to respond to the rapidly spreading habit of watching television by technological innovations that included large screen formats known by names like Cinerama, Cinemascope, VistaVision, Cinemiracle and Todd-AO (Imax was added to the list in the end of the 1960s). For *Billboard*, big screen cinema and its wedding with 3-D and color were forms of merchandizing, "wrapping the same old product in a new package [...]."[57] Both the film and broadcasting industries resorted to the expression "big screen" in their competition for spectators. As the cinema screens became wider, television manufacturers did what they could to magnify the tiny TV screens.[58] Perusing *Life* and popular scientific magazines of the period, one gets the impression that "big screen television" was mentioned more frequently than big screen cinema, which may have to do with its position as an exciting challenger.

On the genealogy of the domestic media screen

As we have seen, all kinds of screens were used in the private residences of the bourgeoisie and the upper classes in the nineteenth century (and earlier). Most of these screens do not qualify as media screens, at least when it comes to their primary purpose. Even so, they may have inspired media-like uses. As we have seen, to recall just one example, the habit of decorating fire-screens with pictures evokes aspects of media culture. The introduction of "moonlight transparencies" (*Mondschein-Transparents*) in the late eighteenth century and the invention of the lithophane some decades later were steps forward, although they did not yet manifest a clear separation between software and hardware, which is a defining characteristic of media screens. Nevertheless, instead of more pragmatic uses, they focused the attention on the picture itself and attempted to make it animated.

Moonlight transparencies were one of the many manifestations of the vogue for transparent painting, which emerged in the second half of the eighteenth century and continued into the next.[59] Large transparencies were used as backdrops at theaters and displayed in public festivities; others appeared in intimate settings. Moonlight transparencies are often said to have been invented around 1780 by the Italy-based German artist Philipp

Hackert (1737–1807), although the claim was not unanimously accepted by contemporaries.[60] They were painted landscapes enhanced by the effect of moonlight or fire, which appeared when the picture was illuminated from the rear. The fashion spread around Europe among the *beau monde*, until the widely distributed *Journal des Luxus und der Moden* turned it into a more organized business. This Weimar-based "trend magazine" of the time was edited by Friedrich Johann Justin Bertuch and the painter and engraver Georg Melchior Kraus. In the January 1799 issue Bertuch described—under the general heading *Ameublement* (furniture)—a new way of exhibiting transparencies.[61] Earlier they had normally been either inserted in walls or observed by simply holding a candle or oil lamp behind the picture.

The description was accompanied by an illustration, which depicts a neoclassical viewing cabinet, said to be approximately 87 cm wide and 105 cm tall, and made of either mahogany or pearwood.[62] Standing on "lion's paws," it resembles a classical temple with an impressive tympanon, decorated either with a Wedgwood medaillon or a bas-relief of plaster. The tympanon folds down so that a picture can be inserted behind a pane of glass which covers the framed square opening on the front side. In the daytime it was suggested to display an (opaque) copper engraving, to be replaced in the evening by the moonlight transparency. This made sense, because the latter was said to look like a plain white surface until it was illuminated. Hidden behind the tympanon there is a smokestack, and at the rear two doors. Four oil lamps, held by rotating arms attached to two vertical iron rods (two lamps on each one above the other), have been installed inside the cabinet. Thanks to this elaborate arrangement, points of light can be directed to areas that require illumination. Each lamp has two wicks on further regulate the amount of light. Bertuch recommends the device to furnish elegantly a lady's bedroom or *Boudoir*, adding that it can be used as a night lamp too to induce a person to fall asleep romantically by a moonlit landscape.

Toward the end of the previous year *Journal des Luxus und der Moden* had already published an announcement—again under *Ameublement*—signed by Kraus.[63] It was reprinted exactly a year later, this time in the section "All kinds of Christmas presents for ladies." Kraus informed the "lovers of art and optical entertainments," whom he had for some years provided "Italian transparencies," that he had discovered a more comfortable way of presenting them by means of a lightweight portable cabinet. It was not identical with the one Bertuch described, for it was only 51 cm wide and 38 cm tall, and said to be suitable both for display and travel.[64]

Although there are references to the use of moonlight transparency cabinets, the production must have remained relatively limited, because few are known to survive. They deserve a place in an archaeology of the screen, and not only because of their resemblance to television sets. Although their dissemination was limited to the circles of the wealthy upper classes, they inspired related forms that became more affordable and reached middle-class consumers. A parallel phenomenon was the viewing boxes created for roll transparencies by the Frenchman Louis Carrogis, known as Carmontelle (1717–1806), from the early 1780s until the early nineteenth century.[65] He used them as entertainments in the salons of the aristocracy. The rolls consisted of translucent watercolor paintings. They were approximately 50 cm tall and could be as long as 42 m. Most depicted parklands and other picturesque sites frequented by the nobility of the *ancien régime*. Each was enclosed in its own view box, which had a "screen-like" opening at the front and another at the back for lighting (normally from a window which was otherwise covered by curtains). Again, it is impossible not to think about the television set. The roll transparencies were moved by a crank by Carmontelle himself, who stood next to the box telling little stories related with the painted scenes.

When it comes to moonlight transparencies, their domestic role was inherited by transparent prints, such as the British William Spooner's *Protean Views*, which made romantic imagery more widely and economically available. John Heaviside Clark's *Portable Diorama* (Samuel Leigh, 1826) was a desktop box, which allowed the users to imitate the effects of Bouton's and Daguerre's Diorama and also create their own transparencies. The lithophane was invented by the Parisian diplomat Baron Paul de Bourgoing in 1827, and soon became very popular.[66] It is a white (occasionally colored) sheet of porcelain with figural reliefs "imprinted" on it. When illuminated from behind, the almost invisible scene becomes visible and remarkably three-dimensional. Lithophanes have been produced in large quantities by porcelain factories and used for many decorative purposes in lamp shades and night lamps as well as side panels on tea warmers. Many nineteenth century homes had candle shields with lithophanes mounted in ornate wooden or metal frames. They were also inserted in table screens, where they took the place of moonlight transparencies, embedded in wall panels and hung in front of the window. Tiny erotic lithophanes were kept in pocket cases, and held out against light only momentarily.[67]

In spite of its wide cultural dissemination, especially during its heyday until the 1870s, the relevance of the lithophane for screenology is limited. Lithophanes were normally separate plaques, often with romantic genre scenes. They were kept permanently on view rather than viewed one after another. Still, the flickering flame made the image to a certain extent "alive." For the emergence of the domestic media screen actual viewings and presentations that combined entertainment and education were essential. Shadow theaters or *ombres chinoises* were used in wealthy homes already in the late eighteenth century. By the end of the nineteenth century, elaborate boxed sets were manufactured by companies like Leon Saussine in Paris and Adolf Sala in Berlin and sold in department stores for the wealthy bourgeoisie. As was the case with the small moving panoramas used at homes (also produced by both Saussine and Sala), *ombres chinoises* allowed the participants to switch between the roles of the presenter and the audience, which was impossible at public spectacles.

This seemingly insignificant feature anticipated later interactive screen practices.

Magic lanterns were sometimes used at homes by the inhabitants themselves already in the late eighteenth century. In Nuremberg, Georg Hieronimus Bestelmeier's first sales catalogue, issued in 1793, offered—beside a wooden stage for *ombres chinoises* and a camera obscura—a small tin magic lantern for private non-professional buyers.[68] Significantly, rather than about Paul de Philipsthal's spectacle, the *Oxford English Dictionary*'s reference to "Transparent Screens for the Exhibition of the Phantasmagoria" (1810) was about preparing screens for domestic projections.[69] In the nineteenth century magic lanterns were widely used at homes of the bourgeoisie, which must have stripped them of some of their mystery. *Laterna magica* became a toy the children themselves could use to project fairy tales and comic episodes on the wall. Distinctive external design was more important than the quality of lenses and illuminants, although inexpensive plain models were also shipped in the thousands by companies like the Nuremberg-based Ernst Plank. The projected image remained small and faint. Any suitable surface must have been used as the screen.

Domestic media practices: Screening or peeping?

Charles Musser's way of applying his idea of screen practice to public luminous projections limits its potential relevance for discussing domestic media uses. It does characterize magic lantern projections and the rituals of watching holiday slides and home movies, but little else. Even making a case for extending its area to *ombres chinoises* and miniature moving panoramas, and perhaps even to the silent moment of meditation in front of moonlight transparencies or lithophanes, would not cover all domestic media experiences. I have suggested that there were other practices, such as the peep practice.[70] Hiding visual sights inside boxes and giving observers an ocular access to them through a peephole was already discussed in books on "natural magic" in the seventeenth century. In the following century it gave rise to itinerant spectacles that became familiar sights at fairs and marketplaces, and were often illustrated in engravings.[71] Peeping devices also entered the homes of the upper social strata of European societies. Although they may at first have been used to playfully imitate the everyday lives of the lower classes, they gradually gained educational, entertaining and aesthetic significance suited to the interior lives within the salon.

The experience of peeping into a hole differs from observing events on a proper screen. The latter is freely visible for a group of people. From the perspective of the dispositive, the differences between watching a magic lantern projection, a presentation of *ombres chinoises* or an unrolling of

Carmontelle's roll transparencies are not very significant, even though the latter two were normally exhibited on a smaller scale and within a more clearly delineated frame. The intended experiences were social and conversational. The scenes that appeared one after another were observed, shared and commented on together.

The dispositives used in peep practice emphasized individual viewing and isolation—the peeper was, at least in theory, alone with the scene inside the box. Not only was the peeper's own body visually excluded; the same can be said about the bodies of others who may have been present. However, unless one used the peeping device alone in a solitary situation, there were factors that re-connected the peeper with the social setting. The peeper's body may be touched by others, impatiently waiting for their turn or unable to resist a temptation to make some prank on the temporarily "blinded" person. In visual cultural studies it is easy to forget that the soundscape also had an impact on the situation. At a fair the showman's explanations—a "voiceover" from the outside—was mixed with other voices and ambient sounds of all kinds. Visiting a refined public peepshow salon like the Cosmorama was a social experience as well.[72]

The immersive experiences provided by "peep media" were normally intermittent and partial rather than continuous, private and totally absorbing.[73] The designs of peeping devices anticipated various degrees of immersion, coming in different forms and sizes. The production of a visual enclosure—the separation of the picture from the physical environment where the device was located—was a common goal. Some boxes utilized miniaturized scenographic elements resembling the wing stage of the baroque theater in front of the picture frame to disguise its edges. More commonly the view—often a perspective print of a geographic location—was placed at the end of a dark "tunnel." This created an impression that the scene extended indefinitely to all directions beyond the frame. The effect was amplified by making the view transparent and transforming it by rear illumination. The views were changed either by lowering them with strings from above (like theater scenery) or by attaching them together into rolls that were operated by a hand crank.[74] In both cases the changing of the views must have been noticed by the peeper, which must have worked against a virtual reality-like impression of an alternate realm.[75]

Can we characterize the peepshow box as a screen-based medium? We can certainly say that it has a "user interface," which involves both the peeper (who peeps) and the operator (who exhibits the views). The peeper stares into a peephole fitted with a magnifying lens, the function of which could be said to be twofold. On the one hand, it separates the observer from the scene inside the box, therefore functioning in the manner of media screens. On the other hand, it magnifies the scene, pulling it forward toward the observer (or pushing the observer into the scene), effacing the sense of a framed surface. Such "de-framing" anticipated what the Panorama and the Diorama attempted without resorting to lenses. The Panorama's solution was to put the observer in the center of an enormous circular painting and hiding all its edges; the picture frame therefore disappeared and a sense of visiting an alternate reality was produced. The Diorama's solution was not unlike peepshow boxes, except on a huge scale. The audience observed a gigantic painting in the end of a dark "tunnel." Its sheer size, together with elaborate visual effects that made it "alive," turned the attention away from the fact that a "stage opening" was present.

When it comes to the peepshow box, neither the lens nor the opening where the picture is seen form a screen in a technical sense. Yet it could be suggested that a "screen" does not have to be a physical surface on which "visions" appear from an elsewhere. It could be more generally defined as a "delineated zone" that provides ocular—these days also aural and even tactile—access to experiences and information that are segregated from the observer's physical environment. The peculiar feature of the peepshow box was the effacement of the referent. The peepshow, the Panorama and the Diorama all manifested in their own ways such a sense of the virtual. It is the *elimination* of cues referring to exterior reality that converts the picture into an alternate or virtual "reality." In this sense all three countered the usual logic of the screen. Virtual reality head-mounted displays manifest the same goal, although so far they have hardly managed to efface the sense that there is something between the "reality" seen and the person experiencing it.

Peeping remained a common media practice at bourgeois homes throughout the nineteenth century. Devices like the Polyorama panoptique, which was an inexpensive miniature combination of the peepshow box and Bouton's and Daguerre's Diorama, became popular and can still be occasionally found. Much more elaborate was the Megalethoscope, which was invented and patented by the Italian photographer Carlo Ponti in the 1860s. Many seem to have been bought and shipped home by wealthy tourists, who visited Italy in the second half of the nineteenth century. The Megalethoscope was a large and bulky piece of "optical furniture" for the parlors of the bourgeoisie, meant for viewing large framed albumen photographs that produced a Diorama-like "day and night" effect. The device was produced in different finishes from relatively plain to extremely ornate. The function was always the same, but the owner's social status was reflected by the ornamentation. This anticipated design strategies applied to radio and television cabinets and even to devices like the Apple Watch. Megalethoscope was the ultimate peepshow, but not for the poor; it would not even have fitted into small apartments. It is possible that the owners never associated their Megalethoscopes with the "lowly" peep shows of the past.

The most popular nineteenth-century domestic peeping device was the stereoscope, which created a veritable "stereoscopic mania" soon after it had been introduced to the public at the Crystal Palace Exhibition in London in 1851. The production of stereoviews became a large industry and a huge variety of stereoscopes were designed, ranging from simple handheld models to elaborate floor standing cabinets that contained dozens of stereoviews attached to a lifting mechanism operated by turning knobs.[76] Although it was based on recent scientific discoveries about human vision, through the practices of use the stereoscope became connected with the already long trajectory of peep media.[77] The issues it raised are similar to those evoked by earlier forms of peeping. Did it encourage solitary and isolated uses or togetherness and social interaction? By merely assessing the stereoscope itself it would be tempting to vote for the first alternative. However, it would be a mistake to identify the configuration of a media dispositive with its uses in actual circumstances. There is no automatic equivalence between them. In fact, there is a large amount of iconographic evidence that supports the second alternative.[78] Many "self-reflective" stereoviews show the device in use at Victorian or Napoleon III era salons. Most depict emphatically social situations. Contrary to what one might expect, images depicting a single person immersed in the stereoscope alone are uncommon.[79]

This impression may have been caused by biased source material. Emphasizing the social appeal of the stereoscope was surely in the interests of the companies that produced and distributed stereoviews. Solitary introversion, especially by means of a technological contrivance, was not part of the ideology of the era, although it must have taken place in private. For the purpose of promoting a new habit it made sense to embed it within an idealized image of social life. The stereoscope thus became coated with the dominant domestic ideology. One can occasionally glimpse the reverse, for example in critical cartoons and comments ridiculing mass-marketed stereoviews as trash, but tracing the outlines of a more uniform counter discourse is not easy. The general impression remains one of unquestioning assimilation.

The stereoscope played a central, perhaps even a dominant, role in the domestic media practices of the second half of the nineteenth century, and still persisted in the early twentieth century. Screen practices like magic lantern projections came second, perhaps partly because the magic lantern had to be set up for the showings that were only possible in the evening time. Their presence in the home was intermittent. The stereoscope and its views were always ready and profited from daylight. The stereoscope offered an easy to use interface that did not require skills or preparations to operate; anyone could do it. A simple slot or tray where the stereoview was inserted took the place of the screen. Toward to end of the nineteenth century competitors started to court the domestic audiences with attractions like recorded sounds and moving images. The phonograph, the cinematograph and novelties such as the popular Kinora viewers for flip reels of moving images all had advantages over the stereoscope.

The view provided by the stereoscope was three-dimensional, but it was also tightly framed. The framing of the stereoview was normally rectangular, with a curved upper edge. Even *vues d'optique* had offered a wider field of vision. The stereoscope presented a "tunnel vision" emphasizing the depth axis without expanding the visual space laterally. This could be an advantage, giving the viewer ample time to reflect on details on different picture planes, but the lack of movement was increasingly considered a deficiency. The emergence of film culture and the gradual decline of stereoscopy took place simultaneously, which was hardly a coincidence. Finally, although it was used for armchair travel into virtual realms inside one's own parlor, the stereoscope remained an "off-line medium." This could hardly be considered a real lack in a culture where no permanent channels for domestic on-line communications existed. When inventors and popular illustrators began to envision devices for seeing at a distance by electricity in the late nineteenth century, the stereoscope was one of the models they turned to. In their imagination it was simply "wired" and converted into a "tele-peepshow." Screen practice also entered this imaginary field, claiming for attention.

"Seeing at a Distance," or discursive manifestations of the small screen

Much discursive activity and some concrete experimentation inspired by "seeing at a distance" took place during the final quarter of the nineteenth and the early twentieth centuries.[80] Optical extensions of vision like the telescope were already familiar and in practical use in many areas, including optical telegraphy and maritime communications. The real challenge was something else: applying electric technology to real-time connections between locations that were beyond direct optically enhanced eye-to-eye contacts—behind walls, mountains or oceans.[81] The "electric telescope" an obscure Irish inventor named Denis D. Redmond proposed in 1879 after experimenting with the light transmitting qualities of selenium had, in spite of its name, little to do with traditional telescopes.[82] A discursive field of fantasies, wishful thinking and inspired suggestions came into being. This development, which is often labeled the prehistory of television, proliferated for half a century before the first successful public demonstrations took place in the mid-1920s.[83]

For the media archaeology of the screen "prehistory" is a misnomer, because it does not consider television as the culmination of screen-based media. It is only one of its many forms—one that has kept metamorphosing throughout its history and is prone to be replaced and combined with other forms due to changes within broader cultural fabrics. In his substantial *Television: An International History of the Formative Years* (1998) R. W. Burns wisely speaks about "the era of speculation 1877 to c. 1922."[84] Burns grounds his discussion of the topic in a relatively cursory review of earlier visual media, pointing out for example the significance of the camera obscura, adding however that it "can show only the scenes and incidents in its immediate vicinity."[85]

The nineteenth-century media cultural imaginary was deeply influenced by visual spectacles like the Panorama as well as advances in telegraphy. By offering an all-embracing view of a surrounding artificial space and elevating the spectators' points-of-view as if above the horizon, the Panorama expressed a desire to break out from the confines of local existence and to embrace visual reality on a global scale. When it comes to telegraphy, the possibility of transmitting still images over electric telegraph wires was demonstrated by Bain in 1842 and Bakewell in 1847.[86] The first working system for transmitting images and texts over wire was the Pantelegraph (predecessor of the telephoto and the telefax). It was invented by the Italian Abbé Giovanni Caselli in the 1850s and used commercially in the next decade for verifying signatures and distributing images of wanted criminals.[87] The invention of the telephone in 1876 and the enormous publicity it received, as well as simultaneous advances in electric motors and lighting, gave technological stimuli to the evolving imaginary, which was also inspired by colonialism, international trade, the beginnings of organized tourism and other signs of dawning globalization.

An early expression of the unfolding "seeing by electricity" discourse was a cartoon by the illustrator and author George Du Maurier, published in *Punch's Almanac for 1879* as "Edison's Telephonoscope (Transmits Light as well as Sound)."[88] It depicts an elderly couple sitting at home in front of a "screen" over a fireplace, observing a group of young people play badminton "at the Antipodes" (in Ceylon). Holding a speaking horn, the male is having an audiovisual conversation with his daughter "through the wire." The illustration has often been considered a prophesy of wall-mounted flat panel screens, but it is worth reading the caption again. The device is "an electric camera-obscura," which the Pater- and Materfamilias "set up" every evening "over their bedroom mantel-piece" to communicate with their children. The reference to Edison is not random. Du Maurier may have picked the word "telephonoscope" from a device Edison was claimed to have invented, but which was something else, a "little instrument for the *use of deaf persons*, so that, without any perceptible instrument, *such as an ear trumpet*, the softest whisper may be heard."[89]

Du Maurier's telephonoscope was not permanent; it was set up for use, much like a portable camera obscura. Comparisons with wall-mounted flat panel television screens are therefore anachronistic. The camera obscura was widely understood as a device that transmitted live pictures from a location outside the "dark chamber," in other words: from beyond direct vision. It makes sense that a French inventor named Senlecq announced his intention to design "an apparatus intended to reproduce telegraphically at a distance the images obtained in the camera obscura."[90]

Similar interpretations of the word telephonoscope were given by others. Most importantly, it was adopted by the French illustrator and author Albert

Robida in his widely read prophesies of the future, *Le Vingtième Siècle* (The Twentieth Century, 1883) and *La Vie électrique* (The Electric Life, 1890).[91] Emphasizing its importance, the imaginary device was featured, with other inventions, even on the former's title page. What makes Robida's visions particularly acute is the prominent role he assigned to media and communications. The centerpiece is the *téléphonoscope*, a panacea for any communication need—"the suppression of absence, surveillance made easy, the theatre brought to your home."[92] Anachronistically speaking, it functions as both a receiver for broadcasts and a videophone. By peering into its "glass plate" (*plaque de cristal*) at home, the users can enjoy live or recorded performances from the opera or view the latest news.[93] They can also meet others remotely face-to-face.

Robida's *téléphonoscope* was not limited to indoor spaces. A memorable idea is *l'Epoque*, the newspaper of the future. It is available for home subscribers via the *téléphonoscope* as four daily editions plus a 'breaking news' service, but it can also be experienced outside the newspaper's headquarters in Paris on two "immense glass plates, twenty-five meters in diameter."[94] They stand on tall scaffolds, and can be seen from the street, viewing platforms around the newspaper building, and the windows and balconies of the neighboring houses. The *cercle du cristal* to the left of the building in Robida's illustration is dedicated to advertising. A "calligraphist" draws ads on paper, and an "ingenious electric apparatus" reproduces them on the glass plate in "gigantic characters."[95] The one on the right transmits world news as they transpire. In one of Robida's illustrations a scene from the current Chinese civil war (it is 1951) is just being transmitted. L'Epoque's roaming reporters have been armed with small pocket-telephonoscopes that evoke smartphones except that they are wired. When the device is pointed to a scene, an enlarged image appears on the huge glass plate in Paris; real time sound is also provided.

Robida could have gotten the idea from Du Maurier, although it was "in the air." The grand medium that keeps the Parisians informed about "the catastrophes, floods, earthquakes, or fires taking place in any part of the world" is rooted in nineteenth-century infomania. It is a synthesis of panoramas, stereoscopes, newspapers, illustrated magazines, billboards and telecommunications.[96] The word telephonoscope was used side by side with a related concept, "telectroscope." The former seems to have appeared more often in fictional contexts, whereas the latter was repeatedly applied to devices claimed to have been just invented and almost ready to be demonstrated in public. However, the division was not clear-cut. A mock-up of a Telephonoscope, which must have been non-functional, was exhibited at the Jubilee soirée of the Postal Telegraph office, leading a commentator to slur that "[s]eeing by electricity […] must be left to the twentieth century."[97] The notion of the telectroscope may have had its origin in an obscure source, a letter published in the *New York Sun* on March 29, 1877, written by an "Electrician." Addressed to the editor, it claimed that an "eminent scientist of this city" had invented an instrument, "by means of which objects or persons standing or moving in any part of the world may be instantaneously seen anywhere and by anybody." A lively description of the miraculous powers of "The Electroscope" [*sic*] followed:

> By means of the electroscope merchants will be able to exhibit their goods, or samples of them, to any customer supplied with the same instrument, whether in Liverpool, London, Paris, Berlin, Calcutta, Peking, San Francisco, or New Orleans. Fugitive criminals placed in the electroscope can be instantly identified by the police authorities in any part of the globe. Mothers, husbands, and lovers will be enabled to glance at any time at the very persons of their absent children, wives, or belowed ones. Painters may retain their paintings in their studio, and yet exhibit them simultaneously in all the galleries of Europe and America provided with the invention. Scholars are thus enabled to consult in their own rooms any rare and valuable work or manuscript in the British Museum, Louvre, or Vatican, by simply requesting the librarians to place the book, opened at the desired page, into this marvellous apparatus.[98]

The writer made a link with the just invented telephone, characterizing it as "the new instrument for carrying musical sounds," which he hoped would "succeed also in transmitting ordinary conversations." By combining the two instruments, he believed, it would be possible for anyone "not only actually to converse with each other, no matter how far they are apart, but also to look into each other's eyes [...]."[99] The writer further claimed that "if the invention proves successful, it will supersede in a very short time the ordinary methods of telegraphic and telephonic communication."[100] This ephemeral piece of writing, which may have been a hoax, was relayed by other publications and may have attracted the attention of the French popularizer of science, Louis Figuier, who added, either deliberately or by mistake, a "T" in front of the title.[101] Figuier, who claimed he got the information from the Boston press, "identified" the "eminent scientist" as Alexander Graham Bell, who had surged into fame by patenting the telephone (1876).[102] Although the "Electrician" extrapolated features from existing devices (likenesses of criminals had already been transmitted by Caselli's Pantelegraph, etc.), the vision was synthetic enough to set the stage for many similar claims and prophesies to come.

Whether identified as teleoscope, telectroscope or something else (such as 'Diaphote'), a vital topos was formed and evoked over and over again.[103] The "Electrician's" vision may seem to have been more about the internet than about broadcast television or traditional telecommunications, but this only demonstrates that a century before its inception, the internet was already an element of fantasies about future societies permeated by media technology—it had already begun its "life" as a topos.

Round or square?

Popular scientific magazines kept publishing repetitive descriptions about how the telectroscope might work, but its external features, including its interface design, were left to the whimsy of illustrators who visualized their ideas in magazine articles, tradecards and other popular forms of imagery. The flush of images demonstrated that human imagination does not operate in a vacuum. It is not surprising that existing media machines provided models for the inventors, writers and illustrators who were trying to give form to teleoscopes and telectroscopes. Received ideas were extrapolated to imaginary structures in a collective effort to match the requirements of a foreseen but vague communications revolution.

Attached to wires that supposedly linked it to an international communications network, the stereoscope was converted into an imaginary desktop viewer for peeking at distant realities and communicating with people far away.[104] Whether it retained its 3-D properties or had to exchange them for an electric real time connection was not specified. A related situation reappeared in the 1910s in a postcard published by the Keystone View Company, a leading manufacturer and distributor of stereoviews. The headline declares: "She Sees Her Son in France," and an additional text elaborates: "You can talk across the miles with your TELEPHONE—The WHOLE FAMILY Can See the WAR ZONE When our Representative calls to deliver your order about July 6 1921 [the date filled in]."[105] A composite photograph depicts a lady sitting in an armchair, immersed in a stereoscope. It is as if the device emits (or receives?) a "light beam" displaying a view from the front of the World War I. By associating the stereoscope with the telephone, the card purports to provide stereoviews the real time quality they were lacking. It could even be claimed that the combination anticipates television, which was nearing its first public demonstrations. The reference to "the whole family" supports this association.

The magic lantern provided another model.[106] As we have seen, magic lanterns were familiar both from public and home entertainments, so it comes as no surprise that devices for "seeing by electricity" were imagined as projectors. In January 1901, *Harper's Weekly* welcomed the new century with an article that reviewed "the future of long-distance communication."[107] It ended with a prophesy for "the child born to-day [sic] in New York city" that "when in middle age he shall visit China." A pair of illustrations shows a parade taking place on Broadway and "reproduced upon a screen, with all its movement and color, light and shade [...]." We see a large circular image being projected on a screen at a crowded Chinese city square. The writer comments: "While the American pageant passes in the full glare of the morning sun its transmitted rays will scintillate upon the screen amid the darkness of an Asian night. Sight and sound will have unlimited reach through terrestrial space."[108] The illustrations evoke a public magic lantern show, turned into a space and time defying spectacle.

When desktop tele-projectors for domestic use were depicted, their designs often resemble modernistic table lamps or searchlights more than traditional magic lanterns, which may have been found too imbued with "passeistic" Victorian connotations.[109] The devices frequently lack cases. The exposed mechanisms and the "user interfaces" look exotic, but complicated and uninviting for twenty-first-century eyes, much like the mechanized production machines at factories and offices of the time. It is difficult say how such a lack of user-friendliness should be interpreted. In contrast with the outdated non-technological pastimes within Victorian salons and nurseries, the machinic nature of these imaginary devices must have been an attribute of modernity, a way of highlighting the message the illustration purported to communicate, whether its tone was laudatory or satirical.

For some fantasy screens the models may have been less existing technological devices than semi-mythological objects like magic mirrors and crystal balls. This may have been the case in Robida's glass plates, which he never attempted to explain in terms of technology. In esoteric practices and traditions both had long been used as "windows" for peering into a future or getting connected with an elsewhere. Well known examples include Shakespeare's *Macbeth* (Act IV, Scene I) and the story *La Belle et La Bête* (1751), adapted in 1756 by Jeanne-Marie Le Prince de Beaumont from an earlier tale.

In an important book on mirrors, Jurgis Baltruisaitis discussed a mid-seventeenth-century print depicting the sorcerer Nostradamus (1503–1566) performing a mirror trick for Catherine de Medici (1519–1589), the French queen.[110] Versions of this legend have been told by Étienne-Gaspard Robertson in his *Mémoires* (1831), Fulgence Marion in *The Wonders of Optics* and others.[111] Nostradamus is said to have used a magic mirror to display for Catherine a prophesy about her three sons—would they make it to the French throne? Illustrators have depicted the situation in different ways. A very similar scene appears in Sir Walter Scott's story "My Aunt Margaret's Mirror" (1828). Two noble ladies are consulting the advice of a mysterious Paduan savant, who has a "very tall and broad mirror," where "as if it had self-contained scenery of its own, objects began to appear within it."[112] The scene was "as if represented in a picture, save that the figures were movable instead of being stationary."[113] In the print discussed by Baltruisaitis the enchanted mirror above the fireplace bears an almost uncanny resemblance to the shape and position of "Edison's Telephonoscope" in Du Maurier's cartoon. He coined the anachronistic term *téléviseur catoptrique* ("catoptric television") for cases where magic mirrors appeared as "media."[114]

It is not surprising that advertisers compared early television sets with crystal balls and magic mirrors. They were modern wizardry, "man's strangest dream come true in your home … "[115] In 1912, Alan A. Campbell Swinton, a scientist who contributed to the evolution of television, had already stated: "[I]f there could be added to each telephone instrument what would indeed be a magic mirror, in which we could see even only in monochrome the faces of those with whom we were communicating, the material advantages would be great. In addition, there would be much sentimental and other value."[116] The association became commonplace. In 1944, on the eve of the television era, a children's book looked back into the past as it anticipated the future: "If you have a magic mirror you can see a play at a theater without leaving home, you can be with friends who live in another city. The magic mirror makes everything near. What is the magic mirror? It is a *television* machine."[117] In 1940 the *Archery News* had already asked a question the media archaeologist will answer in the affirmative: "May not the magic mirror be nothing but an early conception of the possibilities of Television?"[118] To profit from such associations, the Admiral Corporation branded its receiver Magic Mirror Television.[119]

Directly or indirectly, Robida's glass discs reverberated in fantasies forty years later, as the covers of Hugo Gernsback's *Radio News*, which began appearing in 1919, demonstrate. The early issues were understandably preoccupied with radio. The magazine tried to profit from the raging wireless enthusiasm and anticipated the advent of radio broadcasting in 1922. In mid-decade television became a buzzword, which manifested itself in the covers. The first was a "maybe" spoof about "Radio Doctor," a system for conducting real time medical examinations through television, published in the April 1924 issue (the screen was square).[120] In May 1925 Gernsback ventured into "Radio in 1935" with the cover and a related article.[121] He suggested that "radio television" would be available by then. An explorer could "take along with him a portable radio station and he will be able to give a lecture right on the spot in the jungle in darkest Africa or up in the unexplored regions [...] of the Amazon." His "projector" would be "tuned at every angle so that the listeners 10.000 or 12.000 miles away will be able to see at the same time."[122] This explains the native staring from the screen. Corporations and broadcasting networks are missing from Gernsback's vision, although the model was then being set by radio broadcasting.

It is the fanciful form of the "tentative radio set of 1935" that interests us here. The neoclassical cabinet has a single dial. Its pointer is made to move by pressing one of two buttons on a wired remote controller. Releasing the button "puts the station on the loud speaker and a television apparatus begins to function at the same time."[123] A perfectly circular screen has been installed on top of the cabinet, and is held on the shoulders of two statuesque Hercules figures—the association between the screen and the Earth is easy to grasp. Is the design purely imaginary? Interestingly, Gernsback claims that "the screen itself upon which the televis[i]on picture shows may become the diaphra[g]m for the loud speaker." Indeed, he suggests a new loudspeaker design, a thin circular glass diaphragm, silvered on the inside and backed with wood covered with silver foil. It has been mounted on a table stand between two arms, which allow its angle to be freely adjusted. The surface is "made to vibrate on the electrostatic principle" and obviously to display at the same time the television picture (along unstated principles). Gernsback's fantastic loudspeaker-and-screen combination looks exactly like a standard desktop makeup mirror, but can also be associated with the iconography of the magic mirror—and Robida's discs.[124]

More illustrations appeared on the covers of subsequent issues. In May 1926 a man was shown kneeling in front of a remarkably similar receiver, proposing for a woman ambiguously smiling at him from the circular screen. The device has a separate loudspeaker embedded in a sideboard-like cabinet supporting a huge, almost freestanding circular screen, which easily evokes the graphoscope, a familiar parlor instrument for magnifying cabinet card photographs.[125] The August 1928 cover pictured another receiver with screen that looks like a desktop makeup mirror. This time it was an existing one, Charles Francis Jenkins's (1867–1934) experimental "radio-movie projector." Jenkins, who invented one of the earliest film projectors in the 1890s, also became a television pioneer, whose endeavors were avidly reported in the popular-scientific press in the 1920s and the early 1930s. The successful demonstration of his "radiovision" on June 13, 1925, with an apparatus using a rotating mirror prism as the scanner—one month after Gernsback's article on "Radio in 1935" had appeared—is considered a "first" in the United States.[126]

The Jenkins "Radiovisor" in the *Radio News* cover contained a cylindrical neon tube inside a spinning cylinder with 48 quartz rods to reproduce the transmitted image line by line. The image was then reflected by a slanted mirror to a round magnifying lens functioning as the screen. After this final appearance in *Radio News*, circular glass discs gave way to other solutions. The September 1928 issue depicted a "Televiser" in the form of a wooden sideboard, with a large square screen embedded in it. It was commented with a single word: "Soon!"[127] The November issue showed a plain wooden box-like viewer, which only has a tiny round peephole towards the top, and a few knobs and sockets at the bottom to connect it with a radio receiver and a wired remote controller. Based on a photograph, it shows Gernsback himself using a do-it-yourself television at his home in New York.[128] A detailed article instructed the diligent amateur how to construct such a mechanical scanning disc based receiver. The December 1928 issue introduced an imaginary "multiple television," a mechanical receiver that made it possible to watch three programs at once from as many tiny square screens.[129]

One gets the impression that from the late Victorian era until the first decades of the twentieth century round screens or circular images projected on screens that were otherwise rectangular dominated the media cultural imagination. Strict categorizations are always risky. Even Robida, who favored the round shape, included in *Le Vingtième Siècle* a scene where a family is watching *Le Journal Téléphonoscopique* from a wide square screen not unlike the one in Du Maurier's "Edison's Telephonoscope."[130] Why are certain formats chosen rather than others? Some topos may from time to time become more attractive than others, but there is no fit-for-all explanation for the recurrence of the round screen. Pictures and mirrors were fitted in circular and oval frames, but also in square ones. The framing of stereoviews, cabinet card portraits and carte-de-visite photographs was normally a square (with rounded corners), but Kodak's early snapshot photographs (c. 1890) were circular. The latter evoke lantern slides, which were often (but not always) physically circular or mounted within a round black matte. It is possible that the lantern slides influenced the "seeing by electricity" iconography, but the circular table top displays of public room camera obscuras, although seemingly different, may also have played a role. Besides, it is worth keeping in mind that the lenses of the familiar peepshow boxes were normally round.[131]

The interplay of circularity and quadrangularity was brought to a dynamic but open-ended synthesis by Frederick Kiesler in the modernist cinema he designed for the Film Arts Guild in New York (opened in February 1929).[132] Kiesler strove for a radical reversal of the principles of the standard movie theater, which he found derived from nineteenth-century theater houses and unsuited to the nature of film as "a play on surface," an "optical flying machine of the camera."[133] He configured the auditorium explicitly as a cine-dispositive, a "machine" for "displaying the cinematic art" in "pitch black darkness."[134] The goal was "to suggest concentrated attention and at the same time to destroy the sense of confinement that may occur easily when the spectator concentrates on the screen."[135]

Whether Kiesler could have achieved this was never demonstrated, because his plans were implemented only partially. What was realized was a funnel-shaped plain auditorium that ended in a "screen-o-scope," Kiesler's invention. It was a mechanical "shutter," which replaced the customary proscenium arch and curtains. No descriptions or images about how it was used during the screenings seem to survive. We only have a series of staged and collaged photographs by Kiesler himself. It seems that in the beginning of the show the audience stared at a large light-colored circle with a dark edge. It then opened in the manner of a "cat's eye." Two curved sections retreated to left and right revealing the screen, which had been framed by movable rectangular black masks to the produce the desired screen ratio. Kiesler's photographs show the system at different positions. In one, a horizontal rectangular screen is partly hidden by the semi-open curved sections. In others, the outer circle is fully open, while the screen has been masked into a slightly stretched vertical rectangle or narrow vertical beam. Basically it could be reduced to a tiny square dot. Whether any of these configurations was used in the actual screenings is unknown. Film formats were much more standardized than the utopian avant-garde context Kiesler created for them.

The screen-o-scope could be read symptomatically as a token of trends in screen culture, although its presence remained more discursive than material. It was an anomaly, and may have been actively used only for a very brief moment, because the Film Arts Guild had rented its cinema to another exhibitor by 1930.[136] There is a risk of over-emphasizing its role by retrospective theorizing. Giuliana Bruno has compared being inside Kiesler's theater to

> being inside a camera. The shape of the screen resembled that of a lens, and it manifested itself as a mechanical eye. The ceiling was slanted and the floor inclined, making the room, the locale of the movie house, similar to the interior of the camera obscura. Spectators were taken into this 'room' and projected towards the lens. As their eyes met with the mechanical eye of the screen, they were transported into the film and enveloped within the spatiality of the cinema.[137]

This is inspiring, but hardly matches the materialities of media culture. The dispositive of the room camera obscura (where people could indeed be "taken") was very different; it did not project, it was projected into. To claim it did is metaphorical metapsychological speech, like the fantasy of being inside a "camera."

The screen: Transitions in design

Instead of simply anticipating broadcast television, the "seeing by electricity" discourse suggested a variety of uses from the very beginning. Particularly common was the idea of the "picture-phone," a two-way person-to-person system of communication. This was an age-old topos picked up by those fascinated by the possibility of using new technology to unite people separated by distance. An example that recurs over and over again could be called the "caught in the act" topos. It is well represented in the imaginary of seeing at a distance. In a typical case, a husband somehow ends up on the television screen courting another woman, only to be detected by his wife; as a rule, a corporal punishment follows. The topos appeared many times in cartoons and picture postcards, as well as on the screen itself, including the silent film *Up the Ladder* (Edward Sloman, Universal, 1925).[138]

Even when technological advances were beginning to turn television into a *fait accompli*, in the cultural imagination broadcasting did not automatically overshadow its other potential uses. To mention just one example among many, in the silent science fiction film *High Treason* (Maurice Elwey, England, 1929) we see screens serving different purposes. While the government broadcasts propaganda to public spaces via small screens placed everywhere, flat panel screens in offices serve person-to-person communication.[139] The latter can be conveniently lowered inside the desk after the use. As we have seen, an abundance of further evidence can be found by perusing the popular scientific magazines of the 1920s and 1930s. Raymond Williams famously pointed out that television technology itself did not determine its uses.[140] They were molded by complex evolving webs of economic, social and ideological factors.

After television had been publicly demonstrated in the second half of the 1920s, fantasies had to start looking for a concrete form as products to sell. Television did not turn into a monolithic unity—for example projection-based systems remained part of its development—but its external form became a concern for industrial design, a new profession that was just beginning to emerge. As the artist Vito Acconci noted in a memorable essay,

> [i]n its early days, the TV set took, inside the house, the position of specialized furniture: the position of sculpture. It was like other furniture, but there were differences: it couldn't be sat in, like a chair; it couldn't be sat at, like a table; part of the console could, as a by-product, function like a cabinet, for storage, but not the TV-part itself. Compared to other furniture, the television set could not be used, it could only be looked at […].[141]

To become a material entity, the television set had to be given an identity by combining technological requirements, expected uses and stylistic trends. Arguably, it also had to be related to the imaginary designs internalized by generations of media users.

It is impossible to discuss the entire history of television design here. There is only room for considerations with particular screenological interest. Reviewing pictures of the early television sets from the 1920s and 1930s, it is impossible not ignore the fact that their tiny screens readily evoke the peepshow boxes of the past. This was to an extent determined by technological limitations. There were two competing television systems, the mechanical and the electronic. In mechanical television receivers the image was formed by means of a slotted disc spinning in synchrony with a similar disc in the camera and transmitter unit.[142] The image was simultaneously deconstructed and reconstructed by these discs. Even producing a small image with enough lines to make it clear required a fairly large spinning disc, which nevertheless only produced a small image. In early receivers, like the *Televisors* based on John Logie Baird's designs, the shape of the disc was echoed in the form of the cabinet. General Electric's unusual *Octagon* (USA, 1928) housed the disc in an octagonal case mounted on top of a wooden floor-standing cabinet.[143] In Western Television's *Visionette* (USA, 1929–1930), it was hidden inside a plain square wooden cabinet which had a round viewing hole on its sparsely decorated front side.[144]

In electronic television systems the image appeared on the round end of a cathode ray tube; its fluorescent "screen" was bombarded by electrons emitted by a cathode-ray gun.[145] Manufacturing large tubes was initially difficult and costly, which partially explains the small screens of the early electronic TV sets, yet they were normally bigger than the "peep holes" of the mechanical receivers. During the 1930s the roundness often gave way to a more rectangular format with curved corners. This was achieved by masking part of the cathode-ray tube's "screen." To enlarge the image, a round magnifying lens was fixed in front of it, which gave it a fishbowl look. However, the circular shape was not superseded immediately. As late as 1948 Zenith was advertising its "Television with Giant Circle Screen" as "so *sensationally* different it defies description."[146] Its circular screens persisted only until the early 1950s, while a horizontal near-rectangular format became the norm, partly thanks to larger "flattened" cathode-ray tubes. Television's competition with movie theaters and the increasing role of old serials and feature films in the broadcasting flow worked in favor of the square image frame.[147]

Although the earliest television screen formats may be partially explained by technological necessities, they should also be assessed against the media archaeological backdrop. Technical publications that commented on the new "radio pictures" in the 1930s compared television sets in a disparaging tone with the peepshow boxes of the past. The association became even more evident when the magnifying lens was used. Traces of peep media persisted in other structural features as well. Early television sets were often disguised in wooden cabinets that looked most of the time like any similar piece of furniture. When the device was not in use, the screen was hidden behind wooden doors, probably manifesting the manufacturers' and designers' doubts about the owner's willingness to permanently infect the traditional home interior with discrepant futuristic-technological elements. Such television sets presented themselves as a manifestation of the tradition of the curiosity cabinet. Instead of displaying relics, specimens or mementos, the new variety magically allowed the whole wide world enter the living room.

Even more interesting is the mirror lid console television, where the cathode-ray tube was mounted in an upright position, its screen facing upward. To watch the programs, a hinged lid on the top side had to be opened and installed in a slightly slanted position. The pictures were seen reflected from a mirror installed on its underside, which became the screen. Why such an arrangement? The obvious explanation is again the technical one. To increase the size of their display surface, cathode-ray picture tubes of the time had to be made very long. Positioning them horizontally would have made the television receiver very deep and bulky; the verticality took less room space.[148]

In all these cases the observer's contact with the image is mediated rather than direct. To find more predecessors, one could go even further back in time to the sixteenth and seventeenth century theories of catoptrics, which were demonstrated with complicated mirror tricks, or to recall the role of the magic mirror as an *Ersatz* screen. Is all this just a coincidence? Or does it imply the existence of continuities that bring hidden logics stored in the deep layers of culture to the surface, presented as potential solutions to current challenges? It could indeed be suggested that media dispositives function as topoi—persisting models that can be recalled when tasks at hand require support from tried and tested solutions. The 1920s and the 1930s were a period of experimentation. Both programming services and the number of television owners were very limited. There was no consensus about either the ideal form of the television set or about the optimum shape and size of its screen. It is therefore understandable that existing schemata—manifested in the media dispositives of the past—would be activated and tried out, whether consciously or unconsciously.

Still, one should never prioritize one explanation at the expense of others. Most cultural case histories are complex, involving webs of contributing factors. The upright cabinet television sets can also have been a reaction to stylistic trends that affect the look of things. The vertical format may have been influenced by the "skyscraper style," which was just then becoming a fad particularly in the United States. The skyscraper was adopted as a token of American "machine age" design.[149] Coated with Art Deco ornaments, its shape was transferred to many product categories from bookshelves, desk lamps and even perfume bottles to refrigerators and bakelite table clocks and radio sets. Whatever factors may have contributed, the peepshow analogy is not perfect. A peepshow box literally contained the views. They were not located on the surface of the lens but beyond it; one had to peep *through* the lens. Even though early photographs show people leaning toward television sets, they maintain some distance. The images are on the lens or just behind it. A group of people can witness them together. No one blocks the hole; there is no need to queue. The mirrors of the lid consoles also functioned as surfaces for collective viewing.

The evolution of the television screen was intimately connected with a complex configuration of factors: social groups and norms, lifestyles and viewing habits, home design, industrial strategies and transformations in media culture.[150] As television broadcasting solidified its position as a mass medium, issues like age, gender and family versus solitary viewing gained importance. So did the constitution of the program flow. Was television primarily a channel for viewing films, television series and spectator sports or a personal-participatory medium, where "talking heads" functioned as virtual personalities to identify with and commercials prompted consumers to action, albeit only on terms they themselves defined and controlled? It could be claimed that traces of the early utopias of interactive two-way television survived in the persistence of talking heads, which appeared in close-up in the living room night after night. There was no actual interaction, but faces that were about the same size as the faces of the viewers themselves could be conceived as belonging to friends or members of an extended family, as magazine advertisements for television sets often suggested. If talking heads had been the television's only *forte*, screens might have remained circular or oval, following Robida's suggestion.

The question about the distance between the viewer and the screen is important for screenology, but too complicated to be explored here in full. Magic lantern projections were "beyond the reach" of the spectators, whereas the live scenes projected in the camera obscura could—and often were expected to—be touched. When it comes to television, a habit to stay further from the television set developed hand in hand with the introduction of larger screens. Whether the invention of the remote controller was a cause or an effect of this "retreat" remains an unresolved issue.[151]

Particularly interesting is the American children's program *Winky Dink and You*, which was broadcast by CBS 1953–1957. Instead of staying passively on the sofa, the children were persuaded to come to the television set and draw with "Magic Crayons" on a transparent plastic "Magic Window" overlaid on it screen. After the program, the pictures were erased with a "Magic Eraser Mitt." All were part of the "Winky Dink Kit."[152] The program centered on the host, John Barry, who told stories and held his finger "against the screen," asking the child to follow it with the crayon. Invisible figures were thus "revealed." Throughout the program, Barry kept addressing the child in a colloquial manner, promoted the "Winky Dink Kit" and chatted with the cartoon character Winky Dink. An illusion of person-to-person interaction was created. The lack of a real conversation channels was compensated for by diverting the child's attention to the act of drawing. The model behind *Winky Dink and You* never became a standard within broadcast television, in spite of later experiments of interactive television.[153] Controlled drawing, which was not entirely different from the simultaneous fad of "paint-by-numbers," timidly gave way for acts that anticipated interactive screen use.[154] As if by chance, a bridge was built between the old habit of sketching on ground glass screen of the camera obscura and the future fad of swiping and tapping the screens of tablet computers and smartphones.

"Hi! [...] you can play along with me, and be a part of my television show," Winky Dink promised in the back cover of the "Winky Dink Kit." By drawing the viewers closer to do things with their fingers, *Winky Dink and You* anticipated television games, which appeared in the early 1970s, opening the flood gates of domestic video gaming. The game console was attached to the television set, cutting it off from the broadcast and turning it into an interactive arena with characters and actions manipulated by those sitting in its glow.

From the 1970s onward, the screen became an essential element of the personal computer, although the computer itself was not born as a screen-based medium. Many input and output methods, ranging from punched cards and magnetic tape to plotters and tele-typewriters, had been used.[155] Screens entered computing in the forms of oscilloscope tubes. Gradually they were adapted to display flight information at radar facilities, and text, numbers and graphics at offices and data centers. The computer screen was "born circular" and had that shape in Digital Equipment Corporation's famous PDP-1 (1959), the platform for *Spacewar*, the pioneering computer game and early graphics applications.[156]

As the screen was understood as essential to the computer, it underwent multiple metamorphoses. Sometimes it turned into a perfect square, at other times—as in the legendary Xerox Alto (1973)—into a stretched vertical rectangle. Rectangular horizontal CRT screens then gained ground, becoming the standard format for early personal computers. These changes were associated with technological innovation, the evolution of the graphical user interface, new task-oriented applications and modes of interactivity. Reflecting on the "art of the computer screen" in 1977, Ted Nelson foresaw how interactive screens would spread further: "Tomorrow's desk, tomorrow's automobile dashboard, tomorrow's control panel—all these will use the computer screen as a magic viewer and magic wand; a gateway to what we want to see or do."[157] As such developments took place, the "correct" position of the computer screen within homes, offices, airplanes and in countless other spaces became a task for interior design—like matching the television set with its surroundings had been decades earlier and accommodating fire screens, stereoscopes and other "Victorian things" in the previous century.[158] Unearthing the contextual logic underneath such cases is yet another task for the screenologist.

Conclusion: Toward an archaeology of the mobile screen

One of the premises behind this article is that screens have always been in flux. Not only have their material forms been changing; the same can be said about their uses and the dispositives surrounding them. There are actual screens and imagined ones. Complicated relationships have developed between them. The screen is an evasive object of study, slippery rather than stable, multiple rather than singular. All manifestations of screens deserve investigation, not only those that have been widely popular and seemed unchanging for periods of time. In the current media culture, unstable screens have turned into the mainstream. Less time is spent with location-based ones, whether they are part of the living room's media center or embedded in public spaces from auditoria to building façades. The reasons are twofold. First, most people carry screen-based devices and use them not only when they make a stop, but also when they remain in motion. Second, there is an urge to get rid of screens and to develop visual forms as if they hover freely in the air (like holograms) or to produce an impression of seamless worlds enveloping the user's entire field of vision, turning into alternate realities. That is what the developers of virtual reality head-mounted displays are trying to achieve.

Now that many people, especially younger ones, have virtually abandoned their desktop and laptop computers and switched to tablets and smartphones, the mobile touch screen has become commonplace and probably the standard manifestation of the screen for many users. Many fixed ideas seem to have been abandoned or at least folded to other shapes. Horizontal now turns vertical with a flick of the wrist. The screen is an omnipresent handheld magic mirror for selfies, a viewfinder for shooting both stills and video and a window for two-way video chatting, which fulfills, at least in principle, the nineteenth-century prophesies. Indeed, the screens of tablet computers, mobile phones and portable game consoles may seem at odds with traditions that considered screens and screen practices as stationary. Even though in the past screens were not always permanent, after they had been set up for viewing, the observer's body remained in stasis. This was a common trait between magic lantern projections, drawing sessions with a camera obscura and television spectatorship, no matter how different they may seem among themselves.

When a UCLA student keeps tapping on the smartphone when walking, a tourist continues snapping photos with an iPad while the tour guide is prompting the group to keep moving, or a driver tries to locate a destination using a GPS navigator, the situation is different. There is no stable dispositive— the elements of the situation are continuously under negotiation. The quest for bilocation—or *plurilocation*—is everything. Success in inhabiting two or more places at once has even become a survival skill. The increasing amount of time spent with media machines in a state of split attention has been suggested to have consequences for issues like concentration versus distraction and ultimately on identity formation, but they concern social psychologists more than media archaeologists.[159] A question that interests the media archaeologist is the changes in the relationship between the things within and without the frame. As the screen-based device is moved around, not only the things on the screen keep changing, but also the things around it. The only constants are the (soothing?) presence of one's own palm or the car's dashboard; but even they are continuously embedded within new "landscapes."

The issue of concentration emerges again: how is it possible to focus on things within the frame, and still master and—time and again, exclude— everything that surrounds it? This is not the place to discuss this complex issue, although it should be stated that it is related with interactivity, the fact that the user is not only watching the screen but influencing what happens within its confines. A deep immersion into a screen can be achieved *without* disguising what surrounds the frame, as simply observing gamers, and ordinary people lost in their smartphones practically anywhere easily demonstrates. This issue must be of interest for the developers of immersive virtual reality applications. Compared with augmented reality (AR), which superimposes the things that used to be outside *and* inside the frame, immersive virtual reality presents a homogeneous realm disguised as a "real world." A sense of bilocation is deliberately effaced. Nineteenth-century circular panoramas already tried to achieve this, but the visitor's body remained visibly present. Peepshows excluded it, but without offering an all-embracing view. Head-mounted displays purport to compensate for these deficiencies, while eliminating any sense of a screen.[160]

From a screenological perspective the novelty of portable and mobile screen-based devices is not as absolute as it may seem, as I have pointed out in earlier writings.[161] This becomes clear when we stop paying attention only to the technological features and overt functions of these devices, and instead focus on the practices of use and the conventions that inform and surround them. Analyzing seemingly ephemeral phenomena like the uses of hand fans within different cultures and the "languages" that have developed around them starts making sense. The same can be said about the habits of using pocketwatches and wristwatches. They are not media machines and their "screens" are not media screens, because there is no separation between the software and the hardware. Still, their uses have anticipated those of portable and wearable media machines. The issue is becoming even more important after the recent introduction of the smartwatch, which is many other things besides being a device for displaying time. The latter function is less important than those that have to do with communications and data manipulation. The smartwatch is first a media machine and only secondarily a watch. Its screen is a media screen.

Notes

1 Jonathan Crary, "Eclipse of the Spectacle," in: *Art After Modernism: Rethinking Representation*, ed. Brian Wallis (New York and Boston, Mass. : The New Museum of Contemporary Art and David R. Godine, 1984), 282–294.

2 Anna McCarthy, *Ambient Television. Visual Culture and Public Space* (Durham and London: Duke University Press, 2001).

3 Keith Naughton, "Living Room, to Go," *Newsweek*, Nov. 25, 2002, 62–66.

4 Siegfried Zielinski, *Audiovisions. Cinema and Television as entr'actes in history*, trans. Gloria Custance (Amsterdam: Amsterdam University Press, 1999, orig. 1989); Margaret Morse, *Virtualities. Television, Media Art, and Cyberculture* (Bloomington and Indianapolis: Indiana University Press, 1998, especially 71–98); David Morley, *Home Territories: Media, Mobility, and Identity* (London and New York: Routledge, 2000); Lynn Spigel, *Make Room for TV: Television and the Family Ideal in Post-war America* (Chicago, Ill.: University of Chicago Press, 1992); Cecelia Tichi, *Electronic Hearth: Creating an American Television Culture* (Oxford: Oxford University Press, 1991); Lev Manovich, "Towards an Archaeology of the Computer Screen," in: *Cinema Futures: Cain, Abel or Cable? The Screen Arts in the Digital Age*, ed. Thomas Elsaesser and Kay Hoffmann (Amsterdam: Amsterdam University Press, 1998), 27–43; Lev Manovich, *The Language of New Media* (Cambridge, Mass.: The MIT Press, 2000); Anne Friedberg, *The Virtual Window: From Alberti to Microsoft* (Cambridge, Mass.: The MIT Press, 2006); Giuliana Bruno, *Surface: Matters of Aesthetics, Materiality, and Media* (Chicago, Ill.: University of Chicago Press, 2014), 5. See also: *Fluid Screens, Expanded Cinema*, ed. Susan Lord and Janine Marchessault (Toronto: University of Toronto Press, 2007).

5   *The Cinematic Apparatus*, ed. Teresa de Lauretis and Stephen Heath (London and Basingstoke: Macmillan, 1980); *Apparatus. Cinematographic Apparatus: Selected Writings*, ed. Theresa Hak Kyung Cha (New York: Tanam Press, 1980). The work of Christian Metz epitomized the shift of emphasis from semiotics to psychoanalytic film theory, and so did the work of some early feminist film scholars.

6   A parallel development, which was not concerned with media *per se*, was Michel Foucault's adoption of the word *dispositif* to describe very large and heterogeneous ideological settings where human beings were being subjected to power. See Giorgio Agamben, *What Is an Apparatus? and Other Essays*, trans. David Kishik and Stefan Pedatella (Stanford, Ca.: Stanford University Press, 2009), 1–24. Frank Kessler, "Notes on dispositif" (2004–2007, available in different versions on the internet) provides more concrete leads.

7   François Albera and Maria Tortajada, "The 1900 Episteme," in: *Cinema Beyond Film. Media Epistemology in the Modern Era*, ed. Albera and Tortajada (Amsterdam: Amsterdam University Press, 2010), 25–44; François Albera, Maria Tortajada and Franck Le Gac, "Questioning the Word 'Dispositif.' Note on the Translation," and Albera and Tortajada, "Foreword," in: *Cine-Dispositives. Essays in Epistemology Across Media*, ed. Albera and Tortajada (Amsterdam: Amsterdam University Press, 2015), 11–14, 15–16.

8   *La télévision du téléphonoscope à YouTube: Pour une archéologie de l'audiovision*, ed. Mireille Berton and Anne-Katrin Weber (Lausanne: Éditions Antipodes, 2009).

9   Benoit Turquety, "Forms of Machines, Forms of Movement," in: *Cine-Dispositives*, 275.

10 Erkki Huhtamo, "Dismantling the Fairy Engine: Media Archaeology as Topos Study," in: *Media Archaeology: Approaches, Applications, and Implications*, ed. Erkki Huhtamo and Jussi Parikka (Berkeley: The University of California Press, 2011), 27–47.

11 John Armitage, "From Discourse Networks to Cultural Mathematics: An Interview with Friedrich A. Kittler," *Theory, Culture and Society*, Vol. 23, No. 1 (7–8 December 2006), 17–38, 32–33.

12 Walter Benjamin, *The Arcades Project*, trans. Howard Eiland and Kevin McLaughlin, ed. Rolf Tiedemann (Cambridge, Mass.: The Belknap Press, 1999); Wolfgang Schievelbusch, *Disenchanted Night: The Industrialization of Light in the Nineteenth Century* (Berkeley: University of California Press, 1988); *The Railway Journey: The Industrialization of Time and Space in the 19th Century*, translator not known (Berkeley: The University of California Press, 1986 [orig. 1977]); Carolyn Marvin, *When Old Technologies Were New: Thinking About Electric Communication in the Late Nineteenth Century* (Oxford: Oxford University Press, 1988)

13 Manovich, *Language of New Media*, 103.

14 Ibid., 96.

15 Jacques Aumont, *The Image*, trans. Claire Pajackowska (London: The British Film Institute, 1997), 106–118.

16 Manovich, *Language of New Media*, 96.

17 John Belton, *Widescreen Cinema* (Cambridge, Mass.: Harvard University Press, 1992).

18 *OED* from now on. All references are to the Second Edition, Vol. XIV, ed. J. A. Simpson and E. S. C. Weiner (Oxford: Clarendon Press, 1989), 722–725. The meanings of the French *écran* are, according to the OED, closely related to those of "screen."

19 *OED*, Vol. XIV, 722.

20 Ibid. In the nineteenth century the word "screen" was also used to refer to upright frames in which photographs were displayed, both in private houses and public exhibitions. In 1888 a person wrote about "some of the most delightful panel screens for photographs I ever set eyes on." *OED*, vol XIV.

21 J. C. Loudon, *An Encyclopaedia of Cottage, Farm, and Villa Architecture and Furniture* (London: Longman, Brown, Green, and Longmans, 1842), 350, 1072–1075, passim.

22 *OED*, vol XIV, "screen," 722.

23 Anna Bache, *The Fire-Screen, or Domestic Sketches* (Philadelphia, Penn.: W. J. & J. K. Simon, 1841). The expression "Adventures of a Fire-Screen" appears on top of each left-hand page.

24 "Screens and their Uses," *The Furniture Gazette*, Vol. XVII, New Series (Feb. 26, 1862), 119.

25 *The Family Physician: A Manual of Domestic Medicine* (London: Cassell & Co., 1886), 632.

26 An extreme example of associating screens with revealing—virtual stripping of the body—are airport security screenings.

27 *The Young Lady's Book: A Manual of Elegant Recreations, Exercises, and Pursuits*. Second Edition (London: Vizetelly, Branston, and Co., 1829).

28 Mediocre artworks were sometimes contemptuously compared with such screens. This habit was related with creating scrapbooks. See "An Introduction to the History of Scrapbooks," in: *The Scrapbook in American Life*, ed. Susan Tucker, Katherine Ott, and Patricia P. Buckler (Philadelphia, Penn.: Temple University Press, 2006), 1–25.

29 Loudon, *An Encyclopaedia of Cottage, Farm, and Villa Architecture and Furniture*. Jonathan Swift was enthusiastic about a screen he had received from a lady as a gift.

30 "Screens and their Uses," *The Furniture Gazette*, Feb. 26, 1862, 119.

31 *OED*, Vol. XIV, 722. The quotation is from *The New Family Receipt Book* (London: John Murray, 1810), and instructs the reader how to prepare such screens, obviously for domestic projections (257).

32 Heard gives October 5, 1801, as the opening date but does not mention his source. Mervyn Heard, *Phantasmagoria: The Secret Life of the Magic Lantern* (Hastings: The Projection Box, 2006), 131.

33 *The Monthly Magazine*, No. 80 [No. 5, of Vol. 12] (Dec. 1, 1801), 432. Sir David Brewster defined the Phantasmagoria like this: "The power of the magic lantern has been greatly extended by placing it on one side of the transparent screen of taffetas, which receives the images while the spectators are placed on the other side, and by making every part of the glass sliders opaque, excepting the part which forms the figures." Brewster, *Letters on Natural Magic* (London: John Murray, 1833), 80.

34 From Bacon's *Sylva Sylvarum; or a Natural History, in Ten Centuries* (posthum., 1627), in: *The Works of Francis Bacon. New Edition. In Ten*

Volumes. Vol. I (London: C. and J. Rivington et al., 1826), 337. Bacon used the spelling "skreen."

35 James Wood, *The Elements of Optics: Designed for the Use of Students in the University* (Cambridge: J. Burges, 1749). On the magic lantern and the screen, 149.

36 John Hammond, *The Camera Obscura. A Chronicle* (Bristol: Adam Hilger Ltd., 1981); Martine Bubb, *La Camera obscura: Philosophie d'un appareil* (Paris: L'Harmattan, 2010).

37 T. Hodson and I. Dougall, *The Cabinet of the Arts; being a New and Universal Drawing Book* (London: T. Ostell, 1805). Other varieties were also discussed, including book-shaped camera obscuras, which were set up in "pyramidical form" for use. "In this form the image is reflected from the mirror through the lens to a white screen placed at the bottom of the box, where it may be easily outlined with a black lead pencil, the operator standing with his back toward the object: by these means, a print, or picture, placed before the mirror, may be copied very exactly."

38 *Encyclopedia of the Magic Lantern*, ed. David Robinson, Stephen Herbert and Richard Crangle (London: The Magic Lantern Society, 2001); Deac Rossell, *Laterna Magica—Magic Lantern, Band 1/Vol. 1*, German trans. Marita Kuhn (Stuttgart: Füsslin Verlag, 2008).

39 See David Robinson, *The Lantern Image. Iconography of the Magic Lantern 1420–1880* (Nutley, East Sussex: The Magic Lantern Society, 1993); *The Lantern Image. Iconography of the Magic Lantern 1420–1880. Supplement No. 1* (Kirkby Malzeard Ripon, North Yorkshire: The Magic Lantern Society, 1997). A watercolor painting by Paul Sandby (c. 1760, British Museum) depicts a typical lantern show in an upper class salon. The audience consists of only a few people. The showman is an itinerant lanternist and a boy produces musical accompaniment. A large piece of cloth has been hung upon the wall covering the dark wallpaper and framed paintings. The projected image seems too large and detailed to have been possible to realize at then.

40 W. Shepherd, J. Joyce and Lant Carpenter, *Systematic Education: or, Elementary Instruction in the Various Departments of Literature and Science; with Practical Rules for studying Each Branch of Useful Knowledge* (London: Longman, Hurst, Rees, Orme, and Brown, 1817), 74.

41 Ibid.

42 Ibid.

43 Max Milner, *La fantasmagorie. Essai sur l'optique fantastique* (Paris: PUF Écriture, 1982); Terry Castle, *The Female Thermometer. Eighteenth-Century Culture and the Invention of the Uncanny* (New York and Oxford: Oxford University Press, 1995), 140–167.

44 In the beginning of Etienne-Gaspard Robertson's *Fantasmagorie* in Paris, the oil lamps illuminating the auditorium were put out, plunging the audience into total darkness. Only then was the screen revealed from behind curtain. The easiest way to make the screen invisible was to make it wet. To enhance the illusion, the backgrounds of the lantern slides around the figures were painted black. About the basic techniques of phantasmagoria, see *Lanterne magique et fantasmagorie. Inventaire des collections* (Paris: Musée national des techniques, CNAM, 1990). About the reception of Robertson Fantasmagorie, see Jann Matlock, "Voir aux limites du corps: fantasmagories et femmes invisibles dans les spectacles de Robertson," in: *Lanternes magiques. Tableaux*

transparents, ed. Ségolène Le Men (Paris: Réunion des Musées Nationaux, 1995), 82–99.

45 Charles Musser, "Toward a History of Screen Practice," *Quarterly Review of Film Studies*, Vol. 9, No. 1 (Winter 1984), 59–69; *The Emergence of Cinema: The American Screen to 1907. History of the American Cinema*, Vol. 1 (Berkeley, Los Angeles and London: University of California Press, 1990). The first part of the first chapter has been taken almost verbatim from the 1984 article.

46 Musser, *The Emergence of Cinema*, 15. Formulations like "[m]agic lantern is a species of lucernal microscope, its object being to obtain an enlargened representation of figures, on a screen in a darkened room" became common. *OED*, Vol. XIV, entry from 1846.

47 This recalls the teleological reading of the pre-history of cinema in C. W. Ceram (Kurt Mazur), *Archeology of the Cinema* (London: Thames and Hudson, 1965). See Erkki Huhtamo, "From Kaleidoscomaniac to Cybernerd. Towards an Archeology of the Media," *Leonardo*, Vol. 30, No. 3 (1997), 221–224.

48 See Erkki Huhtamo, *Illusions in Motion: Media Archaeology of the Moving Panorama and Related Spectacles* (Cambridge, Mass.: The MIT Press, 2013).

49 Olive Cook, *Movement in Two Dimensions* (London: Hutchinson, 1963). A major influence on the European shadow theater was the Turkish Karagöz. The influence of Chinese and Indonesian traditions was felt through trade relations. See *Theatres d'Ombres. Tradition et Modernité*, ed. Stathis Damianakos with Christine Hemmet (Paris: Institut International de la Marionette/L'Harmattan, 1986). The early global history of the shadow theater has many white spots.

50 Brewster, *Natural Magic*, 82. Robertson also used the Megascope, a device for projecting opaque three-dimensional objects.

51 For unknown reasons Japan did not develop its own shadow theater tradition. This may have to do with its geographical and cultural isolation (during the Edo era).

52 Outdoor projections were pictured in in the cover of *Frank Leslie's Illustrated Newspaper* (for examples, see Nov. 23, 1872 and Oct. 25, 1884). Erkki Huhtamo, "Messages on the Wall: An Archaeology of Public Media Displays," in: *Urban Screens Reader* (INC Reader #5), ed. Scott McQuire, Meredith Martin and Sabine Niederer (Amsterdam: Institute of Network Cultures, 2009, 15–28.

53 *OED*, Vol. XIV.

54 "Stars of the Silver Screen" was a typical expression. See *Popular Mechanics Magazine*, Vol. 40, No. 3 (Sept. 1923), 380

55 The invention (c. 1894–1895) has been attributed to the British Lewis Wright and Mr. Anderton. Wright described it in the appendix of his handbook *Optical Projection: a Treatise on the Use of the Lantern in Exhibition and Scientific Demonstration*, Third Edition (London: Longmans, Green, and Co, 1895), 427. Wright and Anderton patented their invention. "Silver screens" were also used in radiation therapy in the early twentieth century.

56 The film industry was also facing other challenges, such as an anti-trust suit against the American film industry, the rise of independent producers and the investigations of "anti-American" activities during the Cold War.

57 Lee Zhito, "Picture Business," *Billboard*, Vol. 65, No. 22 (May 30, 1953), 2. It called for "much needed distance between the movie industry and TV in their race for audience."

58 "It's Official—RCA Shows Big Screen Pic; DuMont Said to Have a Bigger One," *Billboard*, March 24, 1945, 11. The article discussed projection-based television receivers.

59 Birgit Verwiebe, *Lichtspiele. Vom Mondscheintransparent zum Diorama* (Stuttgart: Füsslin Verlag, 1997).

60 Ibid., 15–21. Verwiebe does not refer to the *Handbuch der Erfindungen*, Neunter Theil, M-N (Eisenach: Wittenbergische Buchhandlung, 1817), where its author Gabriel Christoph Benjamin Busch claims that before Hackert's arrival in Naples, Sir William Hamilton, a well-known Scottish art collector and naturalist based there, already had one, painted by a Swiss artist named Du Pain. It inspired the work of the Austrian artist Andreas Nesselthaler, whose work then inspired Hackert (361–363). This is very different version than Verbiebe's.

61 Johann Justin Bertuch, "Die Mondschein-Transparents," *Journal des Luxus und der Moden*, Vol. 14, Heft 1 (Jan. 1799), 48–50 + Pl. 3.

62 2 Pariser Fuss, 9 Zoll x 3 Fuss, 3 Zoll. Pariser Fuss is 0.324 m.

63 Georg Melchior Kraus, "Portative Mondschein-Transparents," *Journal des Luxus und der Moden*, Vol. 14, Heft 11 (Nov. 1799), 595–596.

64 Susanne Schroeder, "Le Mondscheintransparent portatif (tableau transparent portatif avec clair de lune)," in: *Lumière, transparence, opacité. Acte 2 du Nouveau Musée National de Monaco*, sous la direction de Jean-Michel Bouhours (Monaco & Milano: Nouveau Musée National de Monaco & Skira, 2006), 88–91.

65 Huhtamo, *Illusions in Motion*, 39–46.

66 The only history of the lithophane is Margaret Carney, *Lithophanes* (Atglen, Penn.: Schiffer Publishing, 2007). Another patent was taken in England in 1828 but no German patent has been discovered.

67 Véronique Willemin, *Eros Secret. Objets érotiques à transformation* (Lausanne: Editions Humus, 2006), 193; Carney, *Lithophanes*.

68 Georg Hieronymus Bestelmeier, *Pädagogisches Magazin für lehrreichen und angenehmen Unterhaltung für die Jugend. Erstes Stück* (Nuremberg: Georg Hieronymus Bestelmeier, 1793), 12 (ombres chinoises), 20 (magic lantern or laterna magica; camera obscura), plates 42, 78, 79.

69 *OED*, Vol. XIV, 722. The quotation is from *The New Family Receipt Book* (London: John Murray, 1810), 257.

70 Erkki Huhtamo, "Toward a History of Peep Practice," in: *A Companion to Early Cinema*, ed. André Gaudreault, Nicolas Dulac, Santiago Hidalgo (Chichester, West Sussex: Wiley-Blackwell, 2012), 32–51.

71 Richard Balzer, *Peepshows. A Visual History* (New York: Harry N. Abrams, 1998). The origins of peepshow boxes go back to Renaissance era experiments with perspective. Perspective boxes with illusionistic painted surfaces and mirrors were produced by Dutch painters like Samuel van Hoogstraaten in the seventeenth century. Martin Kemp, *The Science of Art: Optical Themes in Western art from Brunelleschi to Seurat* (New Haven and London: Yale University Press, 1990), 204–206.

72 Erkki Huhtamo, "Passages Through the Past: The Cosmorama and Its Cultural Context," in: *Acoustic Space, No. 14, Data Drift: Archiving Media and Data*

Art in the 21st Century, ed. Rasa Smite, Raitis Smits and Lev Manovich (Riga: RIXC, 2015), 177–195.

73 I coined the notion of peep media in: Erkki Huhtamo, "The Pleasures of the Peephole: An Archaeological Exploration of Peep Media," in: *Book of Imaginary Media: Excavating the Dream of the Ultimate Communication Medium*, ed. Eric Kluitenberg (Rotterdam: NAi Publishers, 2006), 74–155.

74 Huhtamo, *Illusions in Motion*, 35–39.

75 In baroque theaters the scenes were sometimes changed in full view of the audience without negatively affecting the experience.

76 Paul Wing, *Stereoscopes: The First Hundred Years* (Nashua, New Hampshire: Transition Publishing, 1996).

77 The scientific principle of stereoscopic vision was demonstrated in England by Charles Wheatstone in 1838 with an open device, which used two angled mirrors to reflect the two images drawn from slightly different angles to correspond with the parallax difference of the eyes. As a commodity the stereoscope was marketed in a different lenticular form, invented by Sir David Brewster. The stereoview was put inside a box and observed through a pair of lenses mounted on its side.

78 A large amount of such views are in the author's collection.

79 The stereoscope's potential as solitary armchair traveling was emphasized by Oliver Wendell Holmes, the inventor of a cheap popular stereoscope, in his writings. That normal photographs of buildings and places could serve this function as well is confirmed by a quotation from the British author W. J. Loftie: "It is pleasant to lean back in one's chair and be transported to distant countries at a glance." Cit. Asa Briggs, *Victorian Things* (London: Penguin Books, 1988), 247. Briggs writes about the stereoscope (132–133).

80 Zielinski, *Audiovisions, 54*; *La télévision du téléphonoscope à YouTube*; Huhtamo, "Seeing at a Distance'." David E. Fisher and Marshall Jon Fisher, *Tube: The Invention of Television* (San Diego and New York: Harcourt Brace & Company, 1996), 9–20 contains some information, but cannot be trusted as research. The most substantial treatment, with emphasis on technology, is R. W. Burns, *Television: An International History of the Formative Years*, IEE History of Technology Series 22 (London: The Institution of Electrical Engineers, 1998).

81 The optical telegraph can be conceived as a combination of a semaphore-based signaling system and the telescope. Patrice Flichy, *Une histoire de la communication moderne. Espace public et vie privée* (Paris: Éditions de la Découverte, 1991).

82 "An Electric Telescope," *English Mechanic and World of Science*, Vol. XXVIII, No. 724 (Feb. 7, 1879), 540. Comments by others who had similar ideas were published in subsequent issues.

83 The expression already appeared in Berthold Laufer's "The Prehistory of Television," *The Scientific Monthly*, Vol. 27, No. 5 (Nov. 1928), 455–459. The article covers old myths and stories that could be said to have anticipated television.

84 Burns, *Television*, Part I (3–140). It is followed by "The era of low-definition television 1926 to 1934."

85 Ibid., 11. As with many such short reviews, the one Burns offers is based on insufficient research and therefore dotted with mistakes, which is a pity in an otherwise meticulously researched work.

86   Burns, *Television*, 19–27; John V. L. Hogan, "The Early Days of Television," in: *A Technological History of Motion Pictures and Television*, ed. Raymond Fielding (Berkeley and Los Angeles: University of California Press, 1983), 230.

87   Edmond Couchot, *Images. De l'optique au numérique* (Paris: Hermes, 1988), 75–79.

88   Dec. 9, 1878. The same almanac also included a series of cartoons about "Edison's Anti-Gravitation Under-clothing." For De Maurier, author of *Trilby*, it was an anomaly; most of his cartoons depicted incidents of society life in salons and clubs. "Edison's Telephonoscope" was reprinted numerous times, for example as the lead image to "'Punch' and the Kinetograph," *The Illustrated American*, Vol. 7, No. 70 (June 20, 1891),224; Penn Steele, "Anticipations: How Some of Mr. Wells's Speculative Predecessors Have Fared," *The Era: A Monthly Magazine of Literature*, Vol. IX, No. 4 (April 1902), 460.

89   Frederick J. Garbit, *The Phonograph and Its Inventor, Thomas Alvah Edison. Being a Description of the Invention and a Memoir of its Inventor* (Boston, Mass.: Gunn, Bliss, and Co., 1878), 13. Original emphasis. The device seems to have remained unrealized. It is not identical with his "telescopophone," a more massive hearing aid. Neil Baldwin, *Edison: Inventing the Century* (New York: Hyperion, 1995), 91.

90   "The Telectroscope," *English Mechanic and World of Science*, Vol. XXVIII, No. 723 (Jan. 32, 1879), 509.

91   Albert Robida, *Le Vingtième siècle* (Paris: G. Decaux, 1883; Slatkine Reprints edition, Genève: Slatkine, 1981); *Le Vingtième Siècle: La Vie Électrique* (Paris: A La Librairie Illustrée, [1892]. In *Television*, Burns considers Robida's work the "most remarkable examples of prophesy in this field" (79) and reproduces several illustrations likely from secondary sources, without mention of the second book from which two of the illustrations have been taken (they have misleading second hand captions in English). Although acknowledged, Robida's work has been mostly used as a visual diversion, rather than truly analyzed.

92   Robida, *Le Vingtième siècle*, 73. Translations by the author.

93   Even daily program sheets are available for the subscribers, which brings to mind the subscriber-based Telefon Hirmondó system that began operating in Budapest, Hungary in 1893. It was imitated in the United States in 1911 by the short-lived Telephone Herald (Newark, New Jersey). Marvin, *When Old Technologies Were New*, 223–231.

94   Robida, *Le Vingtième siècle*, 199.

95   The idea comes from the contemporary practice of scraping messages on blackened glass plates and projecting them with a magic lantern. See Erkki Huhtamo, "Monumental Attractions: An Archaeology of Public Media Interfaces," in: *Interface Criticism: Aesthetics Beyond Buttons*, ed. Christian Ulrik Andersen and Soeren Bro Pold (Aarhus: Aarhus University Press, 2011), 21–42.

96   Robida, *Le Vingtième siècle,* 200.

97   *Journal of the Society of the Arts*, Vol. XLI, No. 2111 (May 5, 1893), 625.

98   The Electrician, "The Electroscope," *The New York Sun*, March 29, 1877.

99   Ibid.

100   Ibid.

101   Louis Figuier, "Le télectroscope, ou appareil pour transmettre à distance les images," in: *L'année scientifique et industrielle*, Vingt et unième année (1877) (Paris: Librairie Hachette et Cie, 1878), 80–81.

102   It was claimed Bell had deposited a sealed description of an invention for 'seeing by telegraph' with the Smithsonian Institution, which was said to have made several other inventors publicize their related projects. "Seeing by Telegraph," *English Mechanic and World of Science*, Vol. 31, No. 788 (April 30, 1880), 177.

103   Diaphote was suggested by Dr. H. E. Licks of Bethlehem, Pennsylvania in: "Visual Telegraphy," *Science: A Weekly Record of Scientific Progress*, Vol. 1, No. 1 (July 3, 1880), 14.

104   A French illustration, said to be from 1890, reproduced in: Albert Kloss, *Von der Electricität zur Elektrizität* (Basel: Birkhäuser Verlag, 1987), 245. The device is shown being used by a Western man in Far Asia, possibly communicating with the homeland from a colony. Wherever it may have been published, the illustration did not appear in *La Nature* between 1889 and 1891. Improvised peep holes and funnels were used in the early mechanical television receivers. See John Logie Baird's "peepshow," c. 1925 (Burns, *Television*, 13). Burns has published an unidentified late 1920s photograph showing a television receiver with a typical Holmes stereoviewer used as its eyepiece (ibid., 74). The device is J. L. Baird's stereoscopic receiver as we find out from another photo of it in: R. F. Tiltman, "How 'Stereoscopic' Television is Shown: John L. Baird Produces Moving Images Which Are Given the Appearance of Solidity," *Radio News*, Vol. 10, No. 5 (Nov. 1928), 419.

105   Author's collection. A variant with a male using the stereoscope in a similar pose also existed, and the same motif was used in Keystone's advertisements in *The Educational Screen* magazine.

106   The television pioneer Edouard Belin, among others, used a magic lantern as part of his experimental television equipment. See an illustration (1923) in: Laura Minici-Zotti, *Prima del cinema: Le lanterne magiche* (Venezia: Cataloghi Marsilio, 1988), 95.

107   Charles H. Sewall, "The Future of Long-Distance Communication," *Harper's Weekly*, Vol. XLV, No. 2298 (Jan. 5, 1901), 1262–1263. Sewall suggests that the seeing at a distance device, "when it comes, will probably be named 'optograph'" (ibid., 1262).

108   Ibid., 1263.

109   A tradecard, series *En l'an 2012*, Chocolat Lombart, Imprimerie Norgeu, 1912, in: Christophe Canto and Odile Faliu, *The History of the Future. Images of the 21st Century* (Paris: Flammarion, 1993), 46; Harry Grant Dart, cartoon from *Judge* (1929), reproduced in: Durant, *Predictions*, 151. See also Dart, "We'll All be Happy Then," cartoon, *Life*, Vol. LVIII, No. 1591 (Dec. 7, 1911), 1007.

110   Jurgis Baltrusaitis, *Le miroir. Révélations, science-fiction et fallacies* (Paris: Elmayan/Le Seuil, 1978), 187, see also: 206–208. About the cultural history of apparitions in mirrors, see Sabine Melchior-Bonnet, *The Mirror. A History*, trans. Katharine H. Jewett (New York and London: Routledge, 2002), 108–110, 195–196, 262–264. The trick, if it ever took place, would have happened in the summer 1556 in Paris. The source of the illustration

can be traced to Émile-Jules Grillot de Givry, *Le Musée des sorciers, mages et alchimistes* (Compiègne: Impr. de Compiègne; Paris: Libr. de France, 1929) but not further. Reference to "magic mirror of the living room" is from *The Nation's Business*, Vol. 27 (1939), 97 (only snippet view seen on Google Books).

111   Étienne-Gaspard Robertson, *Mémoires récréatifs scientifiques et anecdotiques*, Tome premier (Paris: Chez l'Auteur et la Librairie de Wurtz, 1831), 344; Fulgence Marion, *The Wonders of Optics*, trans. and ed. Charles W. Quin (New York: Charles Scribner & Co., 1871), 199–200. Illustration of a possible explanation, Fig. 56 (between 200 and 201).

112   Sir Walter Scott, "My Aunt Margaret's Mirror," in: *Waverley Novels, Vol. 40: Chronicles of Canongate. First Series. The Surgeon's Daughter. In Two Volumes.* II (Boston, Mass.: Samuel H. Parker, 1833), 224–225 (198–235).

113   Ibid., 226.

114   Baltrušaitis, *Le miroir*, 208.

115   *TV Kultur. Fernsehen in der Bildenden Kunst seit 1879*, ed. Wulf Herzogenrath, Thomas W. Gaehtgens, Sven Thomas und Peter Hoenisch (Amsterdam and Dresden: Verlag der Kunst, 1997), 146, 147, 157.

116   A[lan] A. Campbell Swinton, "Presidential Address. November 7th, 1911," *The Journal of the Röntgen Society*, Vol. VIII, No. 30 (January 1912), 7. Swinton's ideas about electronic scanning contributed to the development of television.

117   Michail Il'in and Elena Segal, *A Ring and a Riddle*, trans. Beatrice Kinkead (Philadelphia, Penn.: Lippincott, 1944), 72. Original emphasis.

118   *Archery News* (Hereford, England), Vol. 19 (1940), 36. Only a snippet view can be seen on Google Books.

119   *Questions and Answers about Admiral Magic Mirror Television*, booklet, II printing (Chicago, Ill.: Admiral Corporation, March 1948). Author's collection. An advertisement in *Life* explained that the "magic mirror" was an aluminum sheet inside the tube to make the picture "*twice* as bright as ordinary TV." *Life*, Vol. 37, No. 11 (Sept. 13, 1954), 25. The expression "the magic mirror of television" remained also in generic use, see *Television Magazine*, Vol. 13 (1956), 62.

120   It was related with a text by FIPS, "The Radio Doctor, Maybe," *Radio News*, Vol. 5, No. 10 (April 1924), 1406, 1514.

121   Hugo Gernsback, "Radio in 1935," *Radio News*, Vol. 6, No. 11 (May 1925), 2050–2051, 2086–2187.

122   Ibid., 2051.

123   Picture caption, ibid., 2050. The dial says "RADIOSCOPA" which seems Gernsback's imaginary brand name.

124   Another possible reference point are the swiveling round mirrors used in 18th-century boxed or book-shaped camera obscuras. There is one in the author's collection.

125   A comparable fantasy receiver is on the cover of *All About Television*, 1927, except that the screen is oval and emerges from table top radio receiver. The loudspeaker has been suspended from the top of the screen. H. Winfield Secor and Joseph H. Kraus, *All About Television, Including Experiments* (New York: Experimenter Pub. Co.: New York, 1927).

126 Burns, *Television*, 197, 203. Gernsback briefly mentioned Jenkins's experiments, as well as those of Edouard Belin in France (2051).

127 *Radio News*, Vol. 10, No 3 (Sept. 1928). A solitary gentleman smoking a pipe and holding a wired remote controller is watching a shopping program where a man is just presenting a woolen suit with a price tag.

128 *Radio News*, Vol. 10, No. 5 (Nov. 1928). The photograph is on page 422, included in "How to Make Your Own Television Receiver" (422–425, 466).

129 *Radio News*, Vol. 10, No. 6 (Dec. 1928). The device, which has a console-like interface was explained in "'Multiple Television'—A Forecast" (528–529, 589–590).

130 Robida, *Le Vingtième siècle*, 205.

131 In a typical late nineteenth century magic lantern show round and square slides often alternated. Many round slides were hand painted in bright colors; most animated effect slides, such as chromatropes, were round.

132 Laura McGuire, "A Movie House in Space and Time: Frederick Kiesler's Film Arts Guild Cinema, New York, 1929," *Studies in the Decorative Arts*, Vol. 14, No. 2 (Spring–Summer 2007), 45–78.

133 Frederick Kiesler, "Building a Cinema Theater" (1929), in: Kiesler, *Selected Writings*, ed. Siegfried Gohr and Gunda Luyken (Ostbildern bei Stuttgart: Verlag Gerd Hatje, 1996), 17.

134 Ibid., 17, 18.

135 Ibid., 17.

136 Ibid., 55.

137 Giuliana Bruno, *Atlas of Emotion: Journeys in Art, Architecture, and Film*, 46.

138 Richard Koszarski, "Coming Next Week: Images of Television in Pre-War Motion Pictures," *Film History*, Vol. 10, No. 2 (1998), 130.

139 A quite similar system of flat panel desktop picture phones is depicted in the cartoon "Something must be done about this television menace," published in *The Humorist* and *Television*, April 1933. Reproduced in: *TV Kultur*, 153. The speakers hold masks to hide their true feelings, an issue that was often raised in the early Internet era about users hiding behind aliases, changed identities, etc. The imaginary about television in early cinema has been discussed by Koszarski, "Coming Next Week," 128–140.

140 Raymond Williams, *Television: Technology and Cultural Form* (Glasgow: Fontana/Collins, 1974).

141 Vito Acconci, "Television, furniture & sculpture: the room with the American view," in: *Het Lumineuze Beeld/The Luminous Image*, ed. Dorine Mignot (Amsterdam: Stedelijk Museum, 1984), 15.

142 The origins of the mechanical scanning disc go back to an 1884 German patent by Paul Nipkow, who was not able to build the device. Burns, *Television*, 83–86.

143 This device (used as a kind of control monitor?) can be seen in photographs from the early WGY broadcasting studio in: Robert Hertzberg, "Television Makes the Radio Drama Possible," *Radio News*, Vol. 10, No. 6 (Dec., 1928), 525, 526.

144 *Classic TVs with Price Guide. Pre-War thru 1950s*, II printing, ed. Scott Wood (Gas City, In.: L-W. Book Sales, 1997), 82. A similar, even earlier 1929 Western Television model is pictured in: Phillip Collins, *The Golden Age of*

Televisions (Los Angeles, Cal.: W. Quay Hays/General Publishing Group, 1997), 16. For a Baird Televisor and General Electric Octagon, see 15.

145   The first cathode ray tubes were created around the turn of the nineteenth and twentieth centuries, which was also the pioneering era of X-rays. The fluorescent surfaces on which X-rays could be detected were also called screens.

146   Reproduced in: *Classic TVs*, 5. Original emphasis.

147   The round screen naturally cut away parts of the film being broadcast. Later proliferation of wide screen television sets could be partly explained by similar reasons: the screen ratio simulates that of widescreen films—at the same time original TV programs can be produced in the wider format, providing a competitive position against cinema.

148   The same issue could be raised by Ponti's Megalethoscope, which is horizontal; it would hardly have fitted into smaller rooms.

149   Paul T. Frankl's ideas and furniture design were an important influence here. Jeffrey L. Meikle, *Twentieth Century Limited: Industrial Design in America, 1925–1939*, Second Edition (Philadelphia, Penn.: Temple University Press, 2001), 30–32.

150   Spigel, *Make Room for TV*; *Welcome to the Dreamhouse: Popular Media and Postwar Suburbs* (Durhan and London: Duke University Press, 2001); Tichi, *Electronic Hearth*.

151   Zenith advertised its wired "Lazy Bones" remote controller from 1950 and introduced wireless "Flash-Matic Tuning" in 1955 for several of its 1956 models. It was followed by Zenith's "Space Commander." Advertisements in *Classic TVs*, 18, 27, 30. Philco presented a remote controller (designed by Marcel Breuer) built into the coffee table already in 1949. *Science Illustrated*, July 1949, reproduced in: *From Receiver to Remote Control: The TV Set*, ed. Matthew Geller and Reese Williams (New York: The New Museum of Contemporary Art, 1990), 60. The need to distance oneself from the television set was also justified by medical reasons: a belief that being too close may damage the eyes. This discussion could be compared to the radiation/cancer debate surrounding mobile phones.

152   The "Winky Dink Magic Television Kit" could be purchased in different versions from basic to more elaborate. The kits were manufactured by Standard Toykraft Products, Brooklyn, N.Y. The boxed "Official Super Winky Dink Television Game Kit" also included "The Winky Dink Magic Television Game Book," which allowed the child to play Winky Dink off line (a magic window that was folded over other pages was included, as well as a doodles and a Merton Game). Comic books, which included occasional frames consisting of numbers the child was supposed to connect with a pencil, were also produced.

153   Erkki Huhtamo, "Seeking Deeper Contact: Interactive Art as Metacommentary," *Convergence*, Vol. 1, No. 2 (1995), 81–104; "Push the Button, Kinoautomat will do the Rest! Media-archaeological Reflections on Audience Interactivity," in: *Expanding Practices in Audiovisual Narrative*, ed. Raivo Kelomees and Chris Hales (Newcastle upon Tyne: Cambridge Scholars Publishing, 2014), 173–188.

154   Karal Ann Marling, *As Seen on TV: The Visual Culture of Everyday Life in the 1950s* (Cambridge, Mass.: Harvard University Press, 1996), 59–62.

155   The Office of Charles & Ray Eames, *A Computer Perspective*, ed. Glen Fleck (Cambridge, Mass.: Harvard University Press, 1973).

156   Steward Brand, *II Cybernetic Frontiers* (New York: Random House, 1974), 39–59. The screen on which *Spacewar* is played, as seen in the photographs in Brand's invaluable book, is square.

157   Ted Nelson, *The Home Computer Revolution* (Theodor H. Nelson, 1977, distributed by The Distributors, South Bend, In.), 119.

158   Design manuals for media spaces are useful sources. See Philip Mazzurco, *The Media Design Book* (New York: Macmillan Publishing Company, 1984); James Wagenvoord, *Computerspace: Home Design Strategies that Work for Computers* (New York: Perigee Books, 1984).

159   Sherry Turkle, *Reclaiming Conversation: The Power of Talk in a Digital Age* (New York: Penguin, 2015).

160   Whether this can be technically achieved is doubtful. The issue has not only to do with the frame, but also the resolution of the display. In spite of improvements, the sense of artificiality persists; there is something between the wearer and the "world."

161   Erkki Huhtamo, "Pockets of Plenty. An Archaeology of Mobile Media," in: *The Mobile Audience: Media Art and Mobile Technologies*, ed. Martin Rieser (Amsterdam-New York: Rodopi), 23–38.

CHAPTER EIGHT

A Screen's Genealogy

Lev Manovich

Let us start with the definition of a screen. The visual culture of the modern period, from painting to cinema, is characterized by an intriguing phenomenon—the existence of *another* virtual space, another three-dimensional world enclosed by a frame and situated inside our normal space. The frame separates two absolutely different spaces that somehow coexist. This phenomenon is what defines the screen in the most general sense, or, as I will call it, the "classical screen."

What are the properties of a classical screen? It is a flat, rectangular surface. It is intended for frontal viewing—as opposed to a panorama for instance. It exists in our normal space, the space of our body, and acts as a window into another space. This other space, the space of representation, typically has a scale different from the scale of our normal space. Defined in this way, a screen describes equally well a Renaissance painting (recall Alberti's formulation [...]) and a modern computer display. Even proportions have not changed in five centuries; they are similar for a typical fifteenth-century painting, a film screen, and a computer screen. In this respect it is not accidental that the very names of the two main formats of computer displays point to two genres of painting: A horizontal format is referred to as "landscape mode," whereas the vertical format is referred to as "portrait mode."

A hundred years ago a new type of screen, which I will call the "dynamic screen," became popular. This new type retains all the properties of a classical screen while adding something new: It can display an image changing over time. This is the screen of cinema, television, video. The dynamic screen also brings with it a certain relationship between the image and the spectator—a certain *viewing regime*, so to speak. This relationship is already implicit in the classical screen, but now it fully surfaces. A screen's image strives for complete illusion and visual plenitude, while the viewer is asked to suspend disbelief and to identify with the image. Although the screen in reality is only a window of limited dimensions positioned inside the physical space of the viewer, the viewer is expected to concentrate completely on what she sees in this window, focusing her attention on the representation and disregarding the physical space outside. This viewing regime is made possible by the fact that the singular image, whether a painting, movie screen, or television screen, completely fills the screen. This is why we are so annoyed in a movie theater when the projected image does not precisely coincide with the screen's boundaries: it disrupts the illusion, making us conscious of what exists outside the representation.[1]

Rather than being a neutral medium of presenting information, the screen is aggressive. It functions to filter, to *screen out*, to take over, rendering nonexistent whatever is outside its frame. Of course, the degree of this filtering varies between cinema viewing and television viewing. In cinema viewing, the viewer is asked to merge completely with the screen's space. In television viewing (as it was practiced in the twentieth century), the screen is smaller, lights are on, conversation between viewers is allowed, and the act of viewing is often integrated with other daily activities. Still, overall this viewing regime has remained stable—until recently.

This stability has been challenged by the arrival of the computer screen. On the one hand, rather than showing a single image, a computer screen typically displays a number of coexisting windows. Indeed, the coexistence of a number of overlapping windows is a fundamental principle of the modern GUI. No single window completely dominates the viewer's attention. In this sense, the possibility of simultaneously observing a few images that coexist within one screen can be compared with the phenomenon of zapping—the quick switching of television channels that allows the viewer to follow more than program.[2] In both instances, the viewer no longer concentrates on a single image. (Some television sets enable a second channel to be watched within a smaller window positioned in a corner of the main screen. Perhaps future TV sets will adopt the window metaphor of a computer.) A window interface has more to do with modern graphic design, which treats a page as a collection of different but equally important blocks of data such as text, images, and graphic elements, than with the cinematic screen.

On the other hand, with VR, the screen disappears altogether. VR typically uses a head-mounted display whose images completely fill the viewer's visual field. No longer is the viewer looking at a rectangular, flat surface from a certain distance, a window into another space. Now she is fully situated within this other space. Or, more precisely, we can say that the two spaces—the real, physical space and the virtual, simulated space— coincide. The virtual space, previously confined to a painting or a movie screen, now completely encompasses the real space. Frontality, rectangular surface, difference in scale are all gone. The screen has vanished.

Both situations—window interface and VR—disrupt the viewing regime that characterizes the historical period of the dynamic screen. This regime, based on an identification of viewer and screen image, reached its culmination in the cinema, which goes to an extreme to enable this identification (the bigness of the screen, the darkness of the surrounding space).

Thus, the era of the dynamic screen that began with cinema is now ending. And it is this disappearance of the screen—its splitting into many windows in window interface, its complete takeover of the visual field in VR—that allows us today to recognize it as a cultural category and begin to trace its history. The origins of the cinema's screen are well known. We can trace its emergence to the popular spectacles and entertainments of the eighteenth and nineteenth centuries: magic lantern shows, phantasmagoria, eidophusikon, panorama, diorama, zoopraxiscope shows, and so on. The public was ready for cinema, and when it finally appeared, it was a huge public event. Not by accident, the "invention" of cinema was claimed by at least a dozen individuals from a half-dozen countries.[3]

The origin of the computer screen is a different story. It appears in the middle of this century, but it does not become a public presence until much later; and its history has not yet been written. Both of these facts are related to the context in which it emerged: As with all the other elements of modern human-computer interface, the computer screen was developed for military use. Its history has to do not with public entertainment but with military surveillance.

The history of modern surveillance technologies begins with photography. With the advent of photography came an interest in using it for aerial surveillance. Félix Tournachon Nadar, one of the most eminent photographers of the nineteenth century, succeeded in exposing a photographic plate at 262 feet over Bièvre, France in 1858. He was soon approached by the French Army to attempt photo reconnaissance but rejected the offer. In 1882, unmanned photo balloons were already in the air; a little later, they were joined by photo rockets both in France and in Germany. The only innovation of World War I was to combine aerial cameras with a superior flying platform—the airplane.[4]

Radar became the next major surveillance technology. Massively employed in World War II, it provided important advantages over photography. Previously, military commanders had to wait until pilots returned from surveillance missions and film was developed. The inevitable delay between time of surveillance and delivery of the finished image limited photography's usefulness because by the time a photograph was produced, enemy positions could have changed. However, with radar, imaging became instantaneous, and this delay was eliminated. The effectiveness of radar had to do with a new means of displaying an image—a new type of screen.

Consider the imaging technologies of photography and film. The photographic image is a permanent imprint corresponding to a single referent—whatever is in front of the lens when the photograph is taken. It

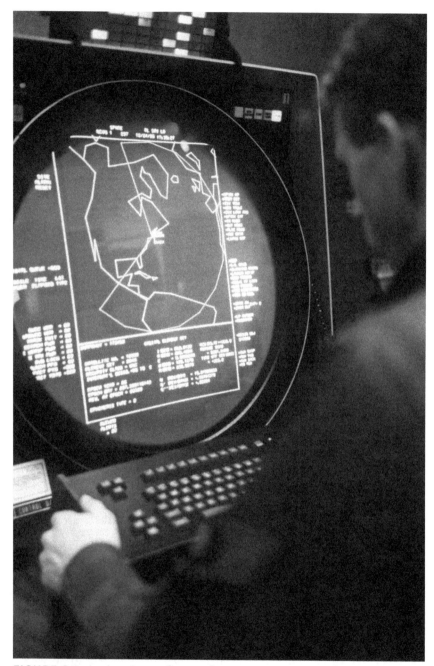

FIGURE 8.1 *An American military radar operator interacts with the AN-FPS-115 Pave Paws phased array warning system, 1986. Photo: Don Sutherland, U.S. Air Force.*

also corresponds to a limited time of observation—the time of exposure. Film is based on the same principles. A film sequence, composed of a number of still images, represents the sum of referents and the sum of exposure times of these individual images. In either case, the image is fixed once and for all. Therefore the screen can only show past events.

With radar, we see for the first time the mass employment (television is founded on the same principle but its mass employment comes later) of a fundamentally new type of screen, a screen which gradually comes to dominate modern visual culture—video monitor, computer screen, instrument display. What is new about such a screen is that its image can change in real time, reflecting changes in the referent, whether the position of an object in space (radar), any alteration in visible reality (live video) or changing data in the computer's memory (computer screen). The image can be continually updated *in real time*. This is the third type of screen after classic and dynamic—the screen of real time.

The radar screen changes, tracking the referent. But while it appears that the element of time delay, always present in the technologies of military surveillance, is eliminated, in fact, time enters the real-time screen in a new way. In older, photographic technologies, all parts of an image are exposed simultaneously, whereas now the image is produced through sequential scanning—circular in the case of radar, horizontal in the case of television. Therefore, the different parts of the image correspond to different moments in time. In this respect, a radar image is more similar to an audio record, since consecutive moments in time become circular tracks on a surface.[5]

What this means is that the image, in a traditional sense, no longer exists! And it is only by habit that we still refer to what we see on the real-time screen as "images." It is only because the scanning is fast enough and because, sometimes, the referent remains static, that we see what looks like a static image. Yet, such an image is no longer the norm, but the exception of a more general, new kind of representation for which we do not yet have a term.

The principles and technology of radar were worked out independently by scientists in the United States, England, France, and Germany during the 1930s. After the beginning of the War, however, only the U.S. had the resources necessary to continue radar development. In 1940, at MIT, a team of scientists was assembled to work in the Radiation Laboratory, or the "Rad Lab," as it came to be called. The purpose of the lab was radar research and production. By 1943, the "Rad Lab" occupied 115 acres of floor space; it had the largest telephone switchboard in Cambridge and employed four thousand people.[6]

Next to photography, radar provided a superior way to gather information about enemy locations. In fact, it provided too much information, more information than one person could deal with. Historical footage from the early days of the war shows a central command room with a large, table-size map of Britain.[7] Small pieces of cardboard in the form of planes are positioned on the map to show the locations of actual German bombers. A few senior officers scrutinize the map. Meanwhile, women in army uniforms constantly change the location of the cardboard pieces by moving them with long sticks as information is transmitted from dozens of radar stations.[8]

Was there a more effective way to process and display information gathered by radar? The computer screen, as well as most other key principles and technologies of modern human-computer interface—interactive control, algorithms for 3-D wireframe graphics, bit-mapped graphics—was developed as a way of solving this problem.

The research again took place at MIT. The Radiation Laboratory was dismantled after the end of the war, but soon the Air Force created another secret laboratory in its place—Lincoln Laboratory. The purpose of Lincoln Laboratory was to work on human factors and new display technologies for SAGE—"Semi-Automatic Ground Environment," a command center to control the U.S. air defenses established in the mid-1950s.[9] Historian of computer technology Paul Edwards writes that SAGE's job "was to link together radar installations around the USA's perimeter, analyze and interpret their signals, and direct manned interceptor jets toward the incoming bee. It was to be a total system, one whose 'human components' were fully integrated into the mechanized circuit of detection, decision and response."[10]

The creation of SAGE and the development of interactive human-computer interface were largely the result of a particular military doctrine. In the 1950s, the American military thought that a Soviet attack on the U.S. would entail sending a large number of bombers simultaneously. Therefore, it seemed necessary to create a center that could receive information from all U.S. radar stations, track the large number of enemy bombers, and coordinate a counterattack. The computer screen and other components of the modern human-computer interface owe their existence to this particular military idea. (As someone who was born in the Soviet Union and now works on the history of new media in the United States, I find this bit of history truly fascinating.)

An earlier version of the center was called "the Cape Cod network," since it received information from radars situated along the coast of New England. The center operated right out of the Barta Building on the MIT campus. Each of eighty-two Air Force officers monitored his own computer display, which showed the outline of the New England Coast and the location of key radars. Whenever an officer noticed a dot indicating a moving plane, he would tell the computer to follow the plane. To do this, the officer simply had to touch the dot with a special "light pen."[11]

Thus, the SAGE system contained all the main elements of the modern human-computer interface. The light pen, designed in 1949, can be considered a precursor of the contemporary mouse. More importantly, at

SAGE, the screen came to be used not only to display information in real time, as in radar and television, but also to give commands to the computer. Rather than acting solely as a means of displaying an image of reality, the screen became a vehicle for directly affecting reality.

Using the technology developed for SAGE, Lincoln researchers created a number of computer graphics programs that relied on the screen as a means of inputting and outputting information from a computer. These included programs for displaying brain waves (1957), simulating planet and gravitational activity (1960), and creating 2-D drawings (1958).[12] The most well-known of these programs was "Sketchpad." Designed in 1962 by Ivan Sutherland, a graduate student supervised by Claude Shannon, it widely publicized the idea of interactive computer graphics. With Sketchpad, a human operator could create graphics directly on a computer screen by touching the screen with a light pen. Sketchpad exemplified a new paradigm of interacting with computers: By changing something on the screen, the operator changed something in the computer's memory. The real-time screen became interactive.

This, in short, is the history of the birth of the computer screen. But even before the computer screen became widely used, a new paradigm emerged—the simulation of an interactive three-dimensional environment without a screen. In 1966, Ivan Sutherland and his colleagues began research on the prototype of VR. The work was cosponsored by the Advanced Research Projects Agency (ARPA) and the Office of Naval Research.[13]

"The fundamental idea behind the three-dimensional display is to present the user with a perspective image which changes as he moves," wrote Sutherland in 1968.[14] The computer tracked the position of the viewer's head and adjusted the perspective of the computer graphic image accordingly. The display itself consisted of two six-inch-long monitors mounted next to the temples. They projected an image that appeared superimposed over the viewer's field of vision.

The screen disappeared. It had completely taken over the visual field.

Notes

1   The degree to which a frame that acts as a boundary between the two spaces is emphasized seems to be proportional to the degree of identification expected from the viewer. Thus in cinema, where the identification is most intense, the frame as a separate object does not exist at all—the screen simply ends at its boundaries—whereas both in painting and television the framing is much more pronounced.
2   Here I agree with the parallel suggested by Anatoly Prokhorov between window interface and montage in cinema.
3   For these origins, see, for instance, C. W. Ceram, *Archeology of the Cinema* (New York: Harcourt, Brace and World, 1965).

4   Beaumont Newhall, *Airborne Camera* (New York: Hastings House, 1969).
5   This is more than a conceptual similarity. In the late 1920s, John H. Baird invented "phonovision," the first method for the recording and playback of a television signal. The signal was recorded on Edison's phonograph record by a process very similar to that of making an audio recording. Baird named his recording machine the "phonoscope." Albert Abramson, *Electronic Motion Pictures* (Berkeley, CA: University of California Press, 1955), 41–42.
6   *Echoes of War* (Boston, Mass.: WGBH Boston, 1989), videotape.
7   Ibid.
8   Ibid.
9   On SAGE, see the excellent social history of early computing by Paul Edwards, *The Closed World: Computers and the Politics of Discourse in Cold War America* (Cambridge, Mass.: MIT Press, 1996). For a shorter summary of his argument, see Paul Edwards, "The Closed World. Systems Discourse, Military Policy and Post-World War II U.S. Historical Consciousness," in *Cyborg Worlds: The Military Information Society*, eds. Les Levidow and Kevin Robins (London: Free Association Books, 1989). See also Howard Rheingold, *Virtual Reality* (New York: Simon and Schuster, 1991), 68–93.
10   Edwards, "The Closed World," 142.
11   "Retrospectives II: The Early Years in Computer Graphics at MIT, Lincoln Lab, and Harvard," in *SIGGRAPH '89 Panel Proceedings* (New York: The Association for Computing Machinery, 1989), 22–24.
12   Ibid., 42–54.
13   Rheingold, *Virtual Reality*, 105.
14   Quoted in ibid., 104.

CHAPTER NINE

The Ordered Mosaic, or the Screen Overtaken by Computation

Edmond Couchot

The video screen is placed horizontally before the soldering student. There is an image of a metal plate on the screen and a blowtorch in the worker's hands. The pedagogical goal of the set-up is to learn to solder quickly and well without burning fingers or wasting material. The trainee adjusts the intensity of the blowtorch through the device's thumbwheel, but no real flame emanates from the nozzle. He brings the torch to the surface of the screen, close to the spot to solder. The metal plate—its image—turns red, then goes blue, and softens. The flame is too strong, so he reduces it. The metal hardens a bit too much. The trainee increases the flame again and the metal turns the right color. He completes his soldering, then withdraws the blowtorch. Slowly the plate returns to normal.

This is what the video image becomes when the screen is controlled by a computer. The mosaic of its surface has been rigorously ordered into a matrix of numbers whose values are instantly modifiable by computation. The image can respond to the viewer, who has become more than a spectator. This response can be immediate—in "real time," as the technicians say—and can create a kind of dialogue, a conversation between the image and whoever views and manipulates it. Hence the technical term *conversational* or *interactive image* or, more generally, *dialogic image*. Unless one hangs onto faded ideas, one must admit that this image is completely different from the traditional video image, yet hard to distinguish as such in its resemblance to that image like a twin sister. It involves another system of figuration. And its use, though limited to the techno-scientific domain, is increasingly spreading within that domain and has begun to be a regular part of the researcher's daily visual universe. The general public still has only limited access to it, but access will quickly grow in the coming years. At the moment when electronic images distributed through media networks seem comfortably situated in their hegemony, a new image is emerging, belonging to a fundamentally different symbolic economy.

The embedded image

From a morphogenetic point of view the video or electronic image, in contrast to the digital image, belongs to a system of figuration that, like photography and film, consists in principal of recording—through optical means—the traces of light left by a preexisting object. The plane of representation on which the image is projected—the screen—is comparable to the plane of perspectival painting as defined in the Renaissance by Leon Battista Alberti. This system allows the automatic recording[1] of a certain image of the world—a *representation*—onto a material support. However, while the filmic (or photographic) image functions geometrically, like a *window* opening onto the world, the electronic screen displays the image in a very different way.

In effect, the window that opens in the wall allows the eye to discover—when it is invited to enter, but far enough way to escape—a continuous space, homogenous and infinite, in the direction of the view. It seamlessly prolongs the enclosed space where the eye is situated. The perspectival architectures of the Renaissance are fascinating for this reason; the tableau seems to naturally extend the room where the spectator is situated, enlarging it with a more or less significant amount of perfectly homogenous space. Similarly, the image-window of cinema urges us to leave the theatre, to forget it, by plunging through its opening. The darkness facilitates this centrifugal escape beyond the walls in constantly returning our gaze to the canvas screen. Inversely, the electronic screen does not function like a window, it is not in the wall, it does draw the gaze from the inside toward the outside. It brings the outside into the inside through a violent, centripetal movement in the very space the viewer occupies. It functions through an *effect of embeddedness*.

It is worth noting that this effect of embeddedness is not exclusive to the electronic image. Every image has a particular way of inserting itself into the space that mediates it and, according to which this is of a nature more or less foreign to the image itself, the reception space appears more or less torn, the effect of embeddedness more or less violent. A painting hanging on a wall always creates an effect of embeddedness. But this effect is more or less tempered by the frame that creates a transition between the wall and the painted space. Photographs also are embedded, in their way, in the pages of a magazine, cutting forcefully across the text. On the other hand, images that are perfectly integrated into their supports and become part of that body, such as parietal wall paintings of Magdalenian grottos or byzantine mosaics, or even a certain type of painting that seeks to emphasize the painting surface itself, do not produce an effect of embeddedness. Rather, they function through wrapping.

With television's particular way of distributing the image, the effect of embeddedness reaches its greatest intensity. The visual and audio image that the electronic screen violently introduces into the location where it is placed, without the buffer of a frame, imposes itself on the viewer by reducing surrounding space to "background." The effect is all the more noticeable as the image becomes furniture, its surface small in contrast to a painting,[2] and its light strong enough to rival daylight. The electronic screen does not give access to an exterior in the way the cinema screen does—even if its images are morphogentically the same—by leading the eye into a centrifugal movement and without a break toward an immediate outside. On the contrary, here it is the outside that erupts on the inside, forcefully spilling into the enclosed and protected living space of the viewer, within that intimacy, in an almost unstoppable flow of images or, more accurately, visual and aural events that take place elsewhere, in another space.[3]

This process of embeddedness that breaks the spatial continuity of the viewer's space and establishes a topological reversal of inside and outside produces remarkable effects on modes of image perception and the art of figuration. A generation of artists since the 1950s, beginning in the United States, have translated the effects of embeddedness of the electronic screen through diverse artistic means. Robert Rauschenberg's combine paintings are the most obvious example. Going beyond the collage, practiced since the cubists, and the readymade introduced by Duchamp, the combine-paintings are first violent inlays of heterogenic and heteroclite figurative elements on the neutral ground of a canvas whose principal function is to serve as a display unit. On this canvas that borrows ironically from the fashionable painting of the time (lyrical abstraction), Rauschenberg throws anything—all sorts of banal and quotidian objects (toothbrushes, chairs, taxidermied birds, neckties, Coke bottles…), without any hierarchy, any taste or lack thereof, or any choice, in precisely the same way the television screen projects a flood of heteroclite images from elsewhere onto the canvas ground that is the home.

It is true that Rauschenberg owes much to John Cage, from whom he applies to painting the principles of the Theory of Inclusion. For Cage, any sound could be included in a musical work. The musician should avail his perception to all sound events occurring around him, just as they present themselves in their proliferation and random incongruity, without attempting to rank them. Undoubtedly, the habit of radio (in the era of the wireless), which modified the perception of sound—lyrics, noise, and music—well before the television, strongly "inspired" this musician who knew how to translate its essence. Television prolonged and amplified this effect of inclusion or embeddedness—a word that expresses a violence more characteristic of the image—by extending it into the visual, yet it remained the same phenomenon. Art in the years following the rise of television has been essentially an art of embeddedness, of the topological turning inside-out, of the outside and the inside, of arbitrary meetings, of refusing choice and hierarchy. It is an art profoundly dependent on the event.

From scanning to computation

In relation to cinema, the electronic image—even if it morphogenetically belongs, like the film image, to a lens-based system of figuration—brings an important new element to the technology of recording: *scanning*. The principal dates back to the nineteenth century[4] and entails reducing the image produced by optical projection into a set number of thin parallel lines. The electronic screen can thus be compared to a mosaic—as Marshal McLuhan has done—a mosaic whose ordering isn't yet complete. The lines, and the points forming the lines, are not yet digitized, that is to say located exactly through discrete numerical quantities. The fact remains that it is through the *line* that we can access the image, that we can manipulate it once it is produced by a video camera lens, as the first artists interested in the electronic screen did. It is therein that scanning allows a mastery of the image that neither photography nor film can permit, since through them the image can only be captured through *shots* or fragments of shots (cut-out, coloring, collage, chemical treatment, or manipulation of exposure when printing).

Digitization—or computation—allows complete control over the ultimate physical building block of the image: the point, which is called the *pixel* in image synthesis. Thus techniques of mastering the image have passed first from the shot to the line, then from the line to the point. But the pixel is not the point, the first element of painting, as Kandinsky had analyzed it. Kandinsky's point, like painting, is part of a system of figuration that, if not entirely dependent on optics,[5] remains nevertheless that of the trace, of recording. For him the point derives from the shock of the instrument on the "originary plane" (the brush touching canvas, the pencil point touching paper, or the bite of burin on the engraving plate), contact that enriches the support and creates the form, or the different forms, of the point. Technically—and to a certain extent, aesthetically—this point is the result of the meeting of a specific surface and a preexisting object—the instrument—that leaves its trace there.

Even if the figurative forms are abstract and do not refer to any recognizable reality, such as in Kandinsky's paintings, the registration of the point testifies to a capital event: the meeting of these two realities—the instrument that inscribes and the surface that receives—orchestrated by the artist. And so this pictorial point strongly resembles the silver salt particles of photographic film that transform into metal crystals as a result of the collision of photons bouncing off the object photographed, or the electronic signal born on the photosensitive surface of an electronic tube hit by light. The image-trace bears witness to the meeting of two realities that imprint the one in the other, that collide and enrich each other. And even when this image represents nothing, it at least represents the special moment of this meeting.

Image synthesis works entirely differently. The pixel is not a point. It is not the registration of a shock between instrument and originary surface, nor the registration of a trace of light left by an object on a chemical or electronic support sensitive to light. Nor is it the shock of a beam of electrons on the luminophores of the screen, as with video images produced through "synthesizers" or electronic manipulation.[6] These operations strongly imply, in every case, the processing of a preexisting physical reality, whether materially or energy-based. The pixel comes first from language, a formal language certainly, but nevertheless a language. *It does not interpret any preexisting reality*. It visualizes abstract symbols from logical and mathematical models.

The image of the metal plate that the trainee solderer manipulates directly on the video screen is the visualization of a mathematical model *simulating* a metal plate (or the visualization of one of many models differing according to the type of metal, its thickness, etc.). It is not the faithful representation of a real, preexisting plate. One can see the radical change in system of figuration introduced by simulation. The image is no longer the image of something, the representation of a preexisting reality; it is no longer an image exactly, either. It has become a virtual "reality," that is to say parallel to physical reality, from which it takes its appearance. Above all, however, it functions like reality and substitutes for it. While the real precedes the image-trace, the model precedes the image-matrix.

The simulated image of the metal plate, in its apparent resemblance to an image that a video camera could produce by shooting a real plate but for which no one shot anything, is something other than a representation, a recording, or a trace. It contributes models and programmed algorithms to the universe of symbols that are the writing of a virtual reality ready to be realized, if one wants, through an infinity of experiences and possible manipulations. It no longer refers to that privileged moment where a pre-existing object imprints its trace on a photosensitive surface, nor to the moment when the painter's instrument enriches the originary surface. It no longer literally *re*-presents, it creates. It creates its own present from a near-infinity of possible presents.[7] The time in which the dialogical image is inscribed, or the time it generates, is no longer composed of events (televisual time *par excellence*) of present moments that take place. It is made of virtualities.

A third kind of universe

Henceforth, the mosaic of the interactive screen, ordered down to its smallest elements, no longer operates through embeddedness. The image is no longer inscribed in the space where it takes place, where the screen is situated, with the characteristic violence of televisual media that would place the outside on the inside in a constantly renewing vortex of events, whether it be from the faraway periphery in the case of televised imagery, or more or less neighboring space in the case of closed-circuit imagery. The viewer and image enter into a dialogue, they inquire and respond, they become a body, a couple, and merge into a strange being that some might call monstrous or narcissistic, uprooting themselves from both outside and inside, isolating and removing themselves from every event.

The relationship between viewer and image is no longer based on the mode of communication specific to media—communication that always tends to convey a sense of pre-existence, like the photographed object, and that one transmits to represent (by duplicating through recording) the present of events that take—or have taken—place elsewhere, outside the sphere of image and viewer. This relationship is hereafter based on a mode of switching (*commutation*), where sense is no longer conveyed via a unique source (the television antenna, the video cassette recorder) or a point of light projection (film, photography) where it is no longer received and decoded—with an inevitable uncertainty, of course—but where it develops during the exchange through direct and immediate contact, through reciprocal contamination between viewer and image.

Thus the regime of communication that governed media is followed by the regime of switching, particular to systems of dialogue where meaning emerges from conversation, in the same way the figurative regime of optical representation is succeeded by the regime of digital simulation. It is true that this succession has only just happened and there's every reason to believe that we will continue to function for a long time under a hybrid regime mixing both, each corresponding to a different and complementary symbolic economy of the image. But from this time on it is certain that the video screen is destined for other uses and that these uses cannot but strongly rattle the visual arts and culture itself. The current crisis of the image also expresses our confusion before the apparition of an image that tests the principles by which we have lived for centuries. But it expresses this rather vaguely since, among those working with images, few understand in what ways "new images" are truly new.

If digital image technologies are called upon to trigger so many consequences vis-à-vis our behavior as television has since the 1950s, we must first wait until they have made a wide impact, through simple availability, on traditional visual arts (film, television, photography, the plastic arts, etc.), an impact measured by the reactions and movements of these arts, such as already happened during the twentieth century. Outside a few very encouraging exceptions (a handful of commercials and music videos), it is clear that what we are seeing now—synthesized images in the title sequences of broadcast TV, the packaging of networks, or mostly banal feature films—is not representative of a new aesthetic, since these images lose an important part of dialogical specificity when they are put into circulation *through* traditional media. They have not yet known how to benefit from the new spatial and temporal universe opening to them, nor to go beyond a constrictive realism that appears as the only technical criterion.

Among these changes imposed by digital technologies, we can expect to see, for example, the important art of film montage profoundly revitalized, as pointed out by filmmaker Jean-Pierre Beauvais. But we can also predict the revitalization of certain visual and plastic arts, pushed to redefine themselves in reaction, just as Impressionist painting in the nineteenth century was a response to photography.[8] Above all, interactive digital technologies can produce a new and specific art of great variation, of which we currently have only a vague idea, however, though a few attempts limited by technical difficulties and material concerns (equipment costs, slow processing times, the lack of adequate simulation models, etc.) nevertheless suggest the importance. It is difficult, even absurd, to predict how the art of tomorrow will be.

But if techniques in general, and more importantly techniques of figuration, are already ways to perceive and conceive of the world, if they are aesthetics (in the etymological sense) as well as skills, perhaps it is futile to try to imagine where this art of the future will lead or, more basically, to imagine what new limitations artists will have to take into account or challenges they will have to surmount to finally attain a passing source of pleasure. For it is understood that digital technologies offer nothing in themselves that guarantee any superiority in the realm of artistic creation.

It does not seem that the greatest attraction of the digital image and processes of simulation lies in the creation of radically new, never-before-seen forms, without reference in our immediate world or link to our traditions, in a sort of hyperabstraction or hyperformalism that would only belatedly prolong an already exhausted aesthetic preoccupation. Nor, inversely, does it lie in an increased hyperrealism, toward which technologies of simulation nevertheless drive this image so strongly. Nor does it seem we can exercise over these techniques an art of *critical détournement* in the way certain artists have handled the video screen (Nam June Paik, Wolf Vostell). The computer is disconcerting in that it is indivertible. Except for the electronic palettes that are finalized rather narrowly toward a certain kind of image, and which we cannot see very well how they can be diverted, in the area of programmable three-dimensional synthesis it is difficult—and above all absurd—to want to alter the functioning of a machine that has nothing more than what has been given to it as programming. At most we can divert—or rather, use—toward artistic goals the software meant for scientific or technical use. This practice exists and does not indicate a particular critical position.

On the other hand, the means of distribution of the conventional image—how it is accessed and therefore seen—seems to hold new and great possibilities. Television has already demonstrated that the cultural upheaval brought by the electronic image derives much more from the specificity of the support (the mosaic of the screen), the means of distribution (the television network), and the possibility of being received at nearly the same moment it is generated (live transmission), than the aesthetic properties that make up the image. Yet digital techniques affect the morphogenesis of the image as much as its distribution. Interactivity between the image of a metal plate and someone learning to solder does not produce an image truly new in its forms or colors. However, the way the image is produced—the result of computation—and the way it "responds" to the person who views and manipulates it are both fundamentally new. At the moment, outside some expensive, but promising, experiences produced in the laboratory, there is little more than videogames or arcade games to offer the general public complex, interactive images.[9] We do not bemoan this. Quite the contrary, and we should remember that the cinema(tograph) began as a fairground amusement. These profound changes to the morphogenesis and distribution of the image irresistibly beckon the artist's attention.

Interactive simulation opens a paradoxical and fascinating universe to the creator. Up until now he—like everyone else—only needed to consider the outside world, the real (the surrounding things and beings) and his interior world, the imagination, moving from one to the other, nurturing one and the other. The exterior world was (and still is!) bound to entropy, to wearing down, to death, brought by the succession of events. But, through the spirit, the creator was capable of diverting the passage of time to remember the past, to project the future, and to leave behind more or less lasting traces (his works). With simulation, the artist is plunged into what might be called a third kind of universe, oscillating between the real and the imaginary, half-object, half-image, of infinite virtualities, a universe where space, and especially time, are of another essence. Nothing can diminish it, since the framework is but numbers, but everything there can constantly change, can transform. Nothing arrives, nothing is actualized once and for all. The present is not an occurrence of the future, the past, or a present that has ceased to be. The event no longer takes place, its representation no longer makes sense. Death and life, memory and oblivion are no longer what they were. What is essential to our culture becomes obsolete. For the makers of images, the exploration of this new universe will be the most passionate interior adventure to be lived in the coming years.

Notes

1 In an almost automatic way, perspective through central projection takes on—and considerably lightens—the work of the eye and the hand. The *camera*

obscura, by replacing geometry with optics, would accelerate this process of automating the image.

2   The screen produces its own light while the painting (and photo) reflects—and is totally dependent on—the light that hits it.

3   It is this effect of embeddedness that severely diminishes the meaning and aesthetic pleasure of cinema when we watch a film on a video screen. The improvishment or alteration of the cinematographic image remediated by the video screen is not only due to the loss of definition or image size. On the question of embeddedness and the new inside/outside relationship introduced by television, see Edmond Couchot, *Images—De l'optique au numérique*, Paris, Hermès, 1988, pp. 112–117.

4   Giovanni Caselli developed after 1855 an electrical system—the pantelegraph—that could transmit drawings and manuscript letters over great distances. This system employed the technical principles of scanning and synchronization that, much later, would make television possible.

5   Kandinsky's painting does not attempt to represent the world as a photograph would, but to create its own figurative objects, *abstract* objects with certain characteristics to be found in the real world (points, lines, and planes, for example, exist in nature as well as the world built by humans).

6   It is a slip in language to call these instruments "synthesizers" since in fact they do not synthesize the image through computation but influence the modulation of the video signal. They treat a physical reality (of modulated electrical energy). This holds true for all electronic manipulations that "divert" the screen from its principal technical functioning.

7   Of course we can record these images on film or videotape, but then they lose their interactivity and a large part of their originality.

8   For example the television itself, which seeks more and more this form of (non-digital) interactivity that is the participation of the viewer (real-time polling, phoning in, etc.).

9   It's worth pointing out a few very interesting efforts such as Vivarium, by Ann Marion at Apple, which allows the public to interact in real time with simulated sharks that behave much like live animals.

CHAPTER TEN

Digital Media as Ornament in Contemporary Architecture Facades: Its Historical Dimension

Uta Caspary

The question of a new aesthetics of facades in the urban environment is closely linked to the question of 'architecture as signs and systems', to take up the title of Denise Scott Brown's and Robert Venturi's latest book, published in 2004. According to Scott Brown and Venturi, 'historical precedents engaging architecture as sign embrace essentially every period or style of architecture'.[1] The surfaces of Ancient Egyptian temples were enveloped with hieroglyphics, Greek and Roman temples were richly ornamented with sculptures; both could be perceived as instances of what they call 'billboards for a proto-Information Age'.[2]

It has often been claimed that the architecture of modernity repudiated the traditional ornament or 'rhetorical element' in following both Adolf Loos' condemnation of ornament as a 'crime' against the logic of the industrial age and Mies van der Rohe's dictum 'less is more'.[3] Yet classical modernist architecture also redeveloped the ornamental in terms of material and colour compositions. Totalitarian architecture, for instance, utilised specific propagandistic and symbolically loaded icons for its purposes, while post-war-architecture experimented with a variety of facade design ranging from abstract patterns, figural mural paintings to honeycomb facades. Thus, a multi-faceted and continuous genealogy of ornament exists in the twentieth century.[4] This ongoing importance of ornamental and decorative elements, while in varying intensity, received significant impulses with postmodernism's theoretical and practical interest in architecture's narrative and communicative potential. With the 'digital turn' in the 1990s (that is, with the establishment of computer-based design and production processes), a new form of ornament was born: the electronically animated, computer-controlled ornament which as a central element of a media facade, can be transformed into huge, moving images, films or changing text-messages, thus communicating with the urban space around it.

In this article, I understand ornament as an element of a facade which cannot be separated neatly from image, writing, and – this is the focus here – digital media. I perceive a continuous interplay between image, writing, digital media and ornament to the extent that images and digital media can assume ornamental functions and that they are all united by the communicative, narrative aim of a building's facade. Ornaments provide architecture with structure and at the same time enhance its aesthetic effects. Media facades often take up ornamental principles (e.g. repetition, rhythm, and symmetry) and by doing this, they replace or expand the potential of ornament, which traditionally ranges from the purely decorative to the symbolic or functional (sun and/or view protection).

My understanding of media facades is broad: it includes facades that are based on or integrate digital media in their construction system as well as facades that correspond to media strategies or media iconography and that evolve a media-like visual effect in the viewer's eye (so-called passive media facades). In short, facades characterised by a moving, dynamic effect thanks to computerised design and production technologies.[5]

Today's discourse about media architecture widely assumes that a media facade's quality, its sensorial effect, and perceptive fascination depend on whether the facade is integrated into the building in terms of function and construction or whether it transports content or symbolic meaning.[6]

How are we to make sense of the revival of ornament in digital disguise? What do contemporary media facades communicate to us, the viewer? In trying to find answers to these and similar questions I will step back in time – not as far as Venturi, to Ancient Egypt, but to the Middle Ages – and place the comparatively young phenomenon of media facades within the tradition and theory of ornament in (mainly) European and North American architectural history.

Historical dimensions of media facades

Media architecture characterised by colour, light and moving ornaments or flickering video images has four main historical precursors. Firstly, the gothic cathedral windows of the twelfth to the fifteenth century; secondly, the *screen walls* of churches – mainly – a common practice since the twelfth century; thirdly, the origin of architecture in textile arts, as Gottfried Semper theorizes; and finally, light architecture of the early industrial age. Throughout I will pair these four historical signposts with contemporary buildings to draw out existing connections between the architectural past and present day's facades. As I focus on the conceptual, content-related dimension of media architecture, I will only touch upon technical aspects and the difference between historical facades that are mostly illuminated by daylight and today's media facades, which mainly depend on artificial light and reveal their effects only by night.[7]

Gothic cathedral windows as precursors to today's media facades

Since their appearance, media facades have been paralleled with gothic cathedral architecture.[8] Both are perceived as originating in a radical change – societal as well as technical and artistic – caused by the advent of new information technologies for the public or a mass audience. Of course, their respective contents are diametrically opposed: the iconic programme of gothic cathedral windows transmits religious information whereas media facades are nearly always of a profane aesthetic experimental character or serve commercial and advertising purposes.

The Netherlands Institute for Sound and Vision, inaugurated in 2006 in the Media Park in Hilversum near Amsterdam, seems to have been rather obviously inspired by the tall, light-transmitting, stained-glass gothic cathedral windows.[9] In this 'media cathedral', biblical scenes have been replaced by depictions of around 750 historic moments of television and film in the Netherlands, such as the Dutch Queen on a bicycle, a well-known football star, two famous comedians, etc.[10] Film clips of these images are stored in the Institute so that the facade expresses the function of the building as huge media memory. With moulds made of the digital images, thick relief glass panels were manufactured especially to achieve a tactile surface that successfully combines ornamental and iconic effects. The graphic designer and video-jockey Jaap Drupsteen worked up the images into blurred test pictures that resemble captured spirits. From a distance, the strikingly coloured facade evokes a flickering TV set in a typical Dutch living room. Although this is not a media facade in the narrow sense of the word, since there are no computer-controlled lighting effects, the impressive interplay of ornamental image and light is definitely inspired by media aesthetics. Both light refraction and reflection create a three-dimensional effect which indulges passers-by in a display of kinetic images: yet instead of being in motion itself, the facade instigates (virtual) movement in the viewer's mind – we might, therefore, want to call it a 'passive media facade'.[11]

Gothic and Renaissance screen walls as precursors to today's screen walls

The by-now widely used term *screen* (by that I mean also used in a non-Anglo-American context) can be traced back etymologically to screen walls; that is, a flat relief-like, sometimes free-standing wall (in German: *Schauwände, Schirmfassaden* or *Bildschirmwände*).[12] In Europe, such screen walls were realised in gothic and Renaissance architecture, both sacred and profane: in Italy, especially in churches, in Northern Europe, but also in townhouses.[13] These screen walls were obviously placed in front of the main construction thus implicating a rather aesthetical, narrative or symbolic function.

Famous historical screen walls in an ecclesial context include the Western facade of Santa Maria Novella in Florence, designed by L.B. Alberti (1470) or the spectacular Western facade of Lincoln Cathedral (twelfth to thirteenth centuries). This latter vast screen, made of pale yellow limestone, is built out in front of the porches 175 feet wide, thus reaching out beyond the nave's outer walls, with a high gable and corner turrets. It is covered in great bands of arcading, but the actual doorways are deeply recessed, providing an impressive effect of depth and chiaroscuro that makes it look as if the whole facade were moving. The front as a whole is a spectacular backdrop for a processional entry on feast days as well as a curtain-raiser to prodigious events within the cathedral.[14] In other examples, like Wells cathedral's screen facade (also thirteenth century), the decorative and narrative function is multiplied through sculptured figures. Similar to Hilversum, the static wall has a dynamic dimension in the eyes of the passers-by who look at the scenery of the stone screen.

For KPN Telecom's headquarters in Rotterdam, Renzo Piano designed a large screen in front of the actual wall in 1997–2000, a light wall: The facade of the building's side facing the city and the Erasmus Bridge is tilted and has a slanted pillar reaching from the ground up to the centre of the facade. The facade is clad with a green curtain wall system complemented by green lights distributed evenly over the glass facade thus showing changing patterns, moving ornaments, and simple animated sequences – smiling faces, swimming fishes, or interactive games like Tetris which are meant to encourage communication between the urban space and citizens.[15] KPN Telecom is a typical example of a contemporary media facade, which – unlike its etymological predecessors made out of stone – has no visual effect during the day.

Semper's theory of textile architecture and today's pixel facades

In his main theoretical work, *Style in Technical and Tectonic Arts, or Practical Aesthetics* from 1860/63, the architect and architectural historian Gottfried

Semper argued that all arts originated in the textile arts. The main principles of architecture can be traced back, according to Semper, to the temporary tent constructions made out of interlace, woven textiles or carpets. Semper's postulated interrelation between architecture and the textile arts seems to be an apt description of today's media facades: the digitally produced, pixelated, pixel-dissolving images shown on media facades are reminiscent of the geometrical, abstract patterns and interlaced structures of textiles and their ornamental aesthetics. The single pixel replaces the single stitch. As Tom Phillips wrote in the *Architectural Review*: 'the binary system which governs information technology is one of the most ancient staples of ornamental practice, as is the mode of visual generation by pixels in mosaic and weaving.'[16]

Chanel's new headquarters in Tokyo, designed in 2004 by Peter Marino Associates Architects (from New York), symbolizes a Semperian interdependence of texture and architecture, in combination with a market-oriented dimension typical for the present day. The building is a conceptual rendering of the iconic Chanel tweed achieved through a programmable glass facade with a massive LED display. The majority of the facade's 20-minute animations (designed by different artists and altered every three months) are also inspired by the visual world of fashion (you see models in long coats, for instance); the reduction to black and white also corresponds with Chanel's aesthetics. The tower is layered with stainless steel in glass to symbolize quilting, an icon of Chanel, and is semi-transparent during the daytime and fully transparent at night. The building, viewed from the street, appears as an immense black-and-white video wall. The curtain wall is a sophisticated 2-foot-thick layering of six components fitted onto a reinforced-concrete core: 'the high-tech illumination stitches all the elements together – and the seams don't show'.[17] All that Marino, the fashion world's architect of choice, wanted was a building that would not look like a building – 'I wanted one that would dissolve; I wanted it ever-changing. That's the face of fashion today. Nothing is static: it's not the same from 9 o'clock to 10 o'clock. It always has to be different'.[18]

Early light architecture as precursor to today's light ornaments

Artificial light is perhaps the most crucial component of media facades: especially since it allows the building come to life at night. Therefore, the forth historical precursor of today's media architecture are the luminous buildings which emerged with the widespread introduction of electricity in the late nineteenth century. Apart from its use as street lighting, artificial light was used increasingly to accentuate the symbolism and monumentality of buildings, especially of their ornamental facade details.

The earliest examples of this are the Singer Building (by Ernest Flagg, 1906–1908, demolished in 1968), the Woolworth Building (designed by Cass Gilbert as a terracotta-clad steel construction, 1910–1913) in New York and the Wrigley Building (by Graham, Anderson, Probst & White, 1920–1924) in Chicago. Powerful spotlights illuminated the skyscrapers, usually from below, creating a sensational interplay of light and shadow. Since the 1920s, illuminated signs and shop windows started to dominate the street space. Here, then, originates the close relation between media facades and commercial interests.

One of the earliest examples regarding light or media architecture in Europe is the headquarters for *De Volharding* (Perseverance), a social cooperative based in The Hague. With its big glass facade, designed in 1927/28 by Jan Willem Buijs und J.B. Lürsen, the building is reminiscent of the aesthetic of the avant-garde De Stijl-movement. Apart from a glazed stairwell and lift shaft, Buijs' design included horizontal bands of glass spandrel panels. These served as illuminated signs by night; both text and iconic messages could be changed from inside. The facade sparked a heated debate about the integration of advertising into architecture.[19] With the dawn of the industrial and later capitalist era, architecture became more and more an 'instrument for brand communication': it was used as a means of identifying a certain brand, as a signal for a company.[20] Architecture seemed to support the principles of *branding* and *corporate identity*. Whilst these terms, which originated in the USA, were introduced in Europe during the 1990s, the phenomenon itself existed before: traditional architectural ornament with its symbolic content was a predecessor of the *logo* in architecture.[21] Thanks to the opportunities opened up by digital media, architecture had re-acquired its value as a means of communicating to the public (or to use the pejorative term: a means of advertisement).

After World War II, light architecture evolved into the purely commercial architecture of Las-Vegas-Strip, which from Fifth Avenue in New York to Piccadilly-Circus in London West End uses illuminated signs, symbols, and scripture in all colours and formal variations. In their well-known 1972 study *Learning from Las Vegas*, Robert Venturi, Denise Scott-Brown, and Stephen Izenour described this kind of architecture as a spatial 'communication system'.[22]

I would now like briefly to present three examples of present-day media facades to show the variety of lighting techniques developed over the past 15 years.

The first is the light installation (or 'window raster animation') *Blinkenlights* developed by Chaos Computer Club on the Haus des Lehrers (House of the Teacher) office building at Alexanderplatz in Berlin that has been enhanced to become the world's biggest interactive computer display.[23] From 2001 to 2002, passers-by could participate in the design of the light facade playing the old arcade classic Pong on the building using their mobile phones or placing their own love letters on the screen.[24] However, interaction was limited to mostly young people in possession of the necessary technical knowledge and equipment.

The first big, permanent and non-commercial European display facade is another invention from Berlin. *BIX*, as it was called as shorthand for both *big* and *pixel*, was initiated and developed by the Berlin based media art & architecture office realities:united. It was installed on the Kunsthaus in Graz (Austria), built in 2000–2003 by Peter Cook und Colin Fournier as a multi-disciplinary venue for exhibitions, events, and other means of presenting contemporary art, new media, and photography. A matrix of 930 standard industrial fluorescent lamps is integrated into the eastern acrylic glass facade of the biomorphic building structure of the building. The lamps' brightness can be individually adjusted at an infinite variability with 20 frames per second. This allows for images, films, and animations to be displayed. Thus, the external shell of the *blob* is transformed into a communicative membrane, transmitting the internal processes of the Kunsthaus. In the absence of a recognisable boundary (the light is gradually fading away towards the edges), it looks as though the light patterns could dance freely on the outside skin of the building.

realities:united deployed the same light ring technique again from 2005 to 2007 on an office building at Potsdamer Platz. For a period of eighteen months, the eleven-storey glazed main facade hosted the light and media art installation *SPOTS*. Again, design, graphics, and animation sequences could be recreated on the facade as moving luminous images. Primarily, artistic material was displayed, creating a platform for internationally renowned artists. The client aimed to transform the unspectacular architecture into a landmark (there were still offices to rent!) and at the same time, to improve the image of the company (HVB Immobilien).

Conclusion

There are, of course, many other historical precursors, and the chosen examples might seem subjective or arbitrary to a degree. The four aspects of facades viewed historically through the concept of ornament in this article were, in summary: the facade as (1) a coloured, luminous wall, (2) a spatially relevant, narrative screen, (3) a protecting tent or perforated textile structure, and (4) a signal and brand sign.

In the present urban context, urban screens and architectural ornament have important aspects in common: the ambivalent link to function as they can be added to the building or they may be – and this is the desirable variant – fully integrated in architectural facade structures; their communicative role in urban space which is oscillating between dialogue, advertising function and artistic message; and their attempt to transform the rather static discipline of architecture into something moving and – due to the screening technique even – interactive.

The facade becomes an *interface* and ornament becomes an electronic *display*, a moving image or a transformable object. Media facades seem to accommodate the drive towards corporate design, brand familiarity and event architecture. Electronic iconography gives architecture a transitory and ephemeral dimension that enables and facilitates changeability and movement.

Against this background, I would like to encourage a form of urban architecture that strives for an ever more subtle use of media facades. The communicative or narrative role often enhanced by media facades requires careful differentiation: whereas some facades work as a perhaps slightly superficial small talk, others are able to transmit more substantial messages. Surfaces as architectural interfaces should promote interactivity and connectivity, both within themselves and with the surrounding space. As landmarks in the urban environment, they are able to mediate between public and private; they may even call for participation thus responding to the process of identification and recognition in today's societies.

Notes

1   Robert Venturi and Denise Scott Brown, *Architecture as Signs and Systems: For a Mannerist Time*, Cambridge, MA: Belknap Press, 2004, p. 24.
2   Venturi and Brown, *Architecture as Signs and Systems*, p. 24.
3   Robert Venturi, *Complexity and Contradiction in Architecture*, New York: Museum of Modern Art, 1977, p. 40.
4   Jörg Gleiter, 'Zur Genealogie des neuen Ornaments im digitalen Zeitalter. Eine Annäherung', *Arch+*, 189.10 (2008): 77–83.
5   M. Hank Haeusler, *Media Facades: History, Technology, Content*, Ludwigsburg: AVEdition 2009. Haeusler categorises the vast number of contemporary media facades according to their technical composition and distinguishes mechanical facades, projection facades, rear projection facades, illuminated facades, window raster animation, display facades and voxel facades.
6   Susanne Jaschko and Joachim Sauter, 'Mediale Oberflächen–Mediatektur als integraler Bestandteil von Architektur und Identität stiftende Maßnahme im urbanen Raum', *Arch+*, 180.09 (2006): 42–45.
7   Haeusler: *Media Facades*, p. 13. In order to distinguish media and light architecture, Haeusler stresses the dynamic aspect of the displayed graphics, text, image.
8   Martin Pawley, 'Information: Weniger ist mehr', *Arch+*, 109.08 (1991): 65.
9   The architects Neutelings Riedijk say: 'What we sought to achieve was the quality of light-transmitting cathedral windows, not just a piece of glazed and mirrored technology but a lightly tactile surface', *The Plan: Architecture & Technologies in Detail*, 19.4/5 (2007): 49.
10 Anneke Bokern, 'Flimmerkiste. Institut für Bild und Ton in Hilversum', *Baumeister*, 104.4 (2007): 86.

11   Alexander Wahl, 'Wandelbare (mediale) Gebäudefassaden', Seminar at the University of Weimar, 2001/2002, www.alexanderwahl.de/dateien/ medienfassaden/medienfassaden.html.

12   Caroline Jäger, *Europäische Architekturtraditionen: Ideen und Konzepte*, Wien: Neuer Wissenschaftlicher Verlag, 2002.

13   Günther Bindig, *Architektonische Formenlehre*, Darmstadt: Wissenschaftliche Buchgesellschaft, 1995.

14   Paul Johnson, *Cathedrals of England, Scotland and Wales*, London: Weidenfeld & Nicolson, 1990.

15   Anne Bracklow, *Markenarchitektur in der Konsumwelt. Branding zur Distinktion*, Wiesbaden: Deutscher Universitäts-Verlag, 2004, p. 142.

16   Tom Phillips, 'Ornament on Trial', *The Architectural Review*, 1274.04 (2003): 79.

17   William Weathersby, 'Peter Marino Wraps Chanel Ginza in Tokyo with a Cloak of Light', *Architectural Record*, 11 (2005): 208.

18   Jennifer Kabat, 'The Alchimist', *SPOON*, 3.4 (2005): 39.

19   After a brief period of service, the signs were never used again after the 1920s but were finally re-lit by the contemporary art movement LUST in 2000 and again at the Today's Art Festival in 2006.

20   Bracklow, *Markenarchitektur in der Konsumwelt*, pp. 7, 60.

21   Jäger, *Europäische Architekturtraditionen*, p. 134.

22   Robert Venturi, Denise Scott Brown and Steven Izenour, *Learning from Las Vegas*, Cambridge, MA: MIT Press, 1972, p. 8.

23   The existing electronic system of the building was used to produce a monochrome matrix of 18 times 8 pixels (eight storeys with 18 front windows each): A central computer linked to a bus system can control all the lamps individually, adjusting their brightness or switching them on and off, thereby showing a constantly growing number of animations during the night. See Ilka Ruby, Andreas Ruby and Philip Ursprung, *Images: A Picture Book of Architecture*, London: Prestel 2004, p. 100.

24   Blinkenlights Project Homepage, http://www.blinkenlights.net/.

Bibliography

Bindig, Günther. *Architektonische Formenlehre*, Darmstadt: Wissenschaftliche Buchgesellschaft, 1995.

Bokern, Anneke. 'Flimmerkiste. Institut für Bild und Ton in Hilversum', *Baumeister*, 104.4 (2007): 81–90.

Bracklow, Anne. *Markenarchitektur in der Konsumwelt: Branding zur Distinktion*, Wiesbaden: Deutscher Universitäts-Verlag, 2004.

Gleiter, Jörg. 'Zur Genealogie des neuen Ornaments im digitalen Zeitalter. Eine Annäherung', *Arch+*, 189.10 (2008): 77–83.

Haeusler, M. Hank. *Media Facades: History, Technology, Content*, Ludwigsburg: AVEdition, 2009.

Jäger, Caroline. *Europäische Architekturtraditionen: Ideen und Konzepte*, Wien: Neuer Wissenschaftlicher Verlag, 2002.

Jaschko, Susanne and Sauter, Joachim. 'Mediale Oberflächen – Mediatektur als integraler Bestandteil von Architektur und Identität stiftende Maßnahme im urbanen Raum', *Arch*, 180.9 (2006): 42–45.

Johnson, Paul. *Cathedrals of England, Scotland and Wales*, London: Weidenfeld & Nicolson, 1990.

Kabat, Jennifer. 'The Alchimist', *SPOON*, 3.4 (2005): 38–42.

Neutelings Riedijk Architecten. 'Hilversum', *The Plan: Architecture & Technologies in Detail*, 19.4/5 (2007): 40–57.

Pawley, Martin. 'Information: Weniger ist mehr', *Arch+*, 109.8 (1991): 65–71.

Phillips, Tom. 'Ornament on Trial', *The Architectural Review*, 1274.4 (2003): 79–86.

Project Blinkenlights Homepage, http://www.blinkenlights.net/.

Ruby, Ilka, Ruby, Andreas and Ursprung, Philip. *Images: A Picture Book of Architecture*, London: Prestel, 2004.

Semper, Gottfried. *Style in the Technical and Tectonic Arts, or Practical Aesthetics*, trans. Harry F. Mallgrave, Los Angeles, CA: Getty Research Institute, 2004.

Schittich, Christian. *Building Skins: Concepts Layers Materials*, Basel/Boston, MA/Berlin: Birkhäuser, 2001.

Venturi, Robert. *Complexity and Contradiction in Architecture*, New York: Museum of Modern Art, 1966.

Venturi, Robert, Brown, Denise Scott. *Architecture as Signs and Systems: For a Mannerist Time*, Cambridge, MA: Belknap Press, 2004.

Venturi, Robert, Brown, Denise Scott and Izenour, Steven. *Learning from Las Vegas*, Cambridge, MA: MIT Press, 1972.

Wahl, Alexander. *Wandelbare (mediale) Gebäudefassaden*, Seminar at the University of Weimar, 2001/2002, www.alexanderwahl.de/dateien/medienfassaden/medienfassaden.html.

Weathersby, William. 'Peter Marino Wraps Chanel Ginza in Tokyo with a Cloak of Light', *Architectural Record* 11 (2005): 203–208.

SECTION TWO
Images and Frames

Introduction to Section Two

We are drawn to screens by the images they bear. It has been the special qualities of screened images, such as movement, adjustment, color, and the integration of sound, that have ensured the popularity of the screen. More than any other technological object, the screen has facilitated modern culture's proliferation of images. Once images could be rendered effectively in light on a temporary support, they could be modified as frequently as desired, they could circulate to mass audiences, and they could be stored with relative ease. Thousands of images could be seen in a single confined space—the screen frame—without having to make any additional room for them.

Unlike other forms of images, the screen image is typically bright and animated. It may be produced by light coming from outside the screen, as in the case of the projected image, or it may originate in the screen's physical components, as with LCD or plasma screens. The screen has that glow of modulated light that led Cecilia Tichi to call it, in the case of the living-room television set, "the electronic hearth" (1991). Her metaphor neatly links our contemporary networked screens back to the earliest manufactured screens—metal-mesh frames placed before fireplaces to prevent flying embers. Not only did these fire screens sometimes have images woven into the mesh, but as protective surfaces they also allowed the people before them to take pleasure in the sight of the dancing flames that produced fanciful shapes and forms in light and shadow. These screened light events are now typically encased in plastic and metal, to be turned on and off as we please.

We are more likely to make and view images with the help of screens than through any other visual support. Looking at the screen has replaced looking through the viewfinder when taking photographs. Image-making and viewing become one and the same as we are already looking at the image-as-image at the moment we record it. Printing a photograph on paper, once the customary means of sharing snapshots, has become a rare act reserved for special occasions such as presenting a gift. Screen images, by their nature, are temporary images. They are visible for a fixed duration (seconds, minutes, hours), to be followed by other images. We may return to certain images again and again, such as our selfies in the cloud or a favorite on-line music video, but we don't necessarily access them on the same screen, and we may be indifferent to this eventuality.

We increasingly rely on screen images even to experience our immediate environment visually. The line between our physical surroundings and the image dissolves when we depend on rear-view screen images when backing up our car, baby-monitor images when our child is sleeping in the next room, GPS apps when navigating a city sidewalk, or video-doorbell images when someone comes to our front steps. In such circumstances screen space may augment our understanding of physical space, but it also appears that physical space is becoming an extension of screen space.

This section of the reader explores the relationship between screen and image. The first part, "The Production of Images" considers the way screen images are made and the role the screen plays in their making. It begins with Louis Daguerre's instructions for making the screens he employed in his diorama, a nineteenth-century theater show based on the slow play of light on painted fabric surfaces. The diorama was a short-lived form of entertainment that Daguerre followed with his daguerreotype photography process. However, as we can see in his description of the diorama's painting and lighting process, it set in place some of the key characteristics of contemporary screens. Most important, it involved both reflected and emitted light, the two forms of screen illumination still with us today. Indeed, its effect of real-time changes within an image—the crux of the spectacle—derived from the interface of these two forms of lighting.

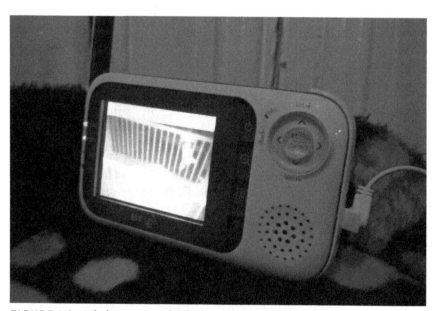

FIGURE I.2 *A baby monitor displaying the image of a crib. Photo: Pete.*

Lara Baladi's essay on the images produced and circulated during the Egyptian Revolution in 2011 considers the role played by mobile screen-based devices, placing the event and technology within larger questions of identity, politics, and globalization. Exploring our relationship to images as they relate to events in the Middle East from nineteenth-century colonial projects to today, Baladi demonstrates the evolving place of the screen. For the protests in Cairo's Tahrir Square, screens not only would contribute to producing images that circulated worldwide through social media, but they also would become the primary means of viewing them. "Here, and in the whole region during the Arab uprisings, the act of photographing became not only an act of seeing and recording, it was fully participatory," Baladi explains. If "photography meant belonging," as she asserts, the screen became a unifying object that allowed others to share in that. In essence, the screen contributed to the movement and its impact in a very intimate and powerful way.

Brad Chisholm's "On-Screen Screens" treats this topic of images of screens appearing within screen images, though toward different ends. Chisholm addresses the rise of screen images depicting screens in television and other visual media—as when news anchors in the studio interact with live images of reporters in the field—at the end of the twentieth-century. "Their presence reminds us to some degree that we are watching a film or television program," Chisholm states. This can be contrasted to the common experience today of multiple windows in graphical user interfaces (GUIs). Chisholm's observations are enlightening precisely because they focus on this multiplicity within moving-image culture during the early days of personal computing. (Microsoft Windows was still in version 2.0 when his article first appeared.) At the moment when screen culture was about to expand into laptops and cellphones, Chisholm suggests the screen and its meanings had become an object of exploration in visual narratives such as the cyberpunk series *Max Headroom* (ABC, 1987–8).

Game graphics have been particularly prone to displays of multiple screens or windows within the visual frame. The on-screen depiction of the game environment may share space with multiple areas of differing informational significance, such as dialogue boxes, maps, and statistical graphs. Ron Burnett takes up the gaming screen's visual balance between immersing gamers in an imaginary environment and distancing them from that environment through the interactive cues and mechanics of both image and hardware. Burnett's essay implies that gaming can—and should— produce new forms of screens for new types of image experience, a belief that has long driven research into consumer-grade virtual reality (VR) googles and the like.

Recent advances in consumer-grade immersive visual devices come not only from headsets such as Oculus Rift or PlayStation VR, but also decidedly low-tech do-it-yourself initiatives such as Google Cardboard. These build from the bottom up by starting with the smartphone as their primary image source. In her work on recent moving-image narratives, Sarah Atkinson has considered the growing aesthetic impact of portable screens on visual storytelling. She examines several examples of moving-image and interactive app narratives made with and for smartphones and tablets. Exploiting the specific properties of the device and its real-time interactions with networks, these narratives transform the handheld screen into an active agent in the plot's development. In further examples, Atkinson considers the production of specialized second–screen content to engage handheld screens during conventional movie screenings.

The screen's production of new image forms is at the base of Marcel Proust's evocative description of the home magic-lantern show of over a century ago. Coming early in *Swann's Way*, the first volume of Proust's monumental *In Search of Lost Time*, the event transforms the narrator's childhood bedroom into an unfamiliar world where images, objects, and architecture intermingle. The narrator's descriptions of how two-dimensional projected images take three-dimensional form on the curtain folds and doorknobs of his room remind us that the flat, rectilinear screen is no necessity, but rather a normative paradigm like any other. Proust's account shows us that inventive screen-image practices breaking that imposed frame are as likely to be found in the past as in some imagined future of the sort Burnett and others may give us.

The second part of this section, "Terms of Display" extends the consideration of the image into the particulars of screen formats and exhibition formats. Giambattista della Porta's detailed, sixteenth-century descriptions of how a magic-lantern spectacle should be arranged and what sorts of images and effects it can produce tell us that in many ways the screen has hardly changed over the past five hundred years. Porta's work is not only one of the first attempts to convey the function of the screen for making images, it also establishes the screen as a frame that should disappear from the viewer's consciousness. He suggests the screen image is more effective the less aware a viewer is of the screen's presence. In his description, a projected image "may seem to hang in a chamber" as though the screen—and its frame—never existed.

In designing movie theaters centuries later, Frederick Kiesler was still struggling with this relationship. He condemned the adaptation of the theater model to the cinema, since screen events differ fundamentally from stage events. He advocated an architecture where "the spectator must be able to lose himself in an imaginary, endless space even though the screen implies the opposite" and he built what he called the "screen-o-scope" to achieve that end. Kiesler's ideas were not widely adopted, as most exhibitors hoped to endow movie-going with the ornamental caché of the theater. Yet his ideas of the viewer isolated in complete darkness, utterly absorbed in the screen event, would appeal to film theorists as a practical explanation of cinema's psychological and ideological power. Apparatus theory, for example, would adhere to the idea of viewers lost to their surroundings in an almost Platonic engulfing darkness pierced by the bright beam of light and shadows on the surface before them.

Jean-Louis Baudry offers just such a scenario in his widely influential work on apparatus theory, an excerpt of which is reprinted here. In exploring the ideological underpinnings of the whole of commercial cinema as they manifest themselves through standard practices of exhibition, Baudry is interested in the ways the cinema has lived up to the descriptions of Porta, Kiesler, and many others. The system—from production to screen exhibition—is structured to align camera and viewing subject, thereby naturalizing the view on screen by making the viewer lose sight (sometimes in a quite literal way, as with the darkened theater) of the mechanisms at work. Cinema becomes a "sort of psychic apparatus of substitution, corresponding to the model defined by the dominant ideology," according to Baudry, where the images and narratives accessed through this system naturalize social hegemony.

Cinema today, of course, is by no means confined to dark theaters. Adaptability has become a central component of its ideological function as movies are commodities manufactured to be profitable across a range of media platforms and screen types. Nevertheless, a theater aesthetic remains through the continuation of widescreen aspect ratios and letterboxing (the horizontal bands sometimes found above and below an image to sustain widescreen ratios) into other screen circumstances. Harper Cossar explores the significance of this remediation of movie-theater visual systems in conveying the impression of cinematic images outside the movie theater. In a step beyond Kiesler's complaint, here there is an effort to lend movie-going caché to other moving-image media, such as on-line advertising and action-adventure video games, by reducing available screen space.

With the rise of widescreen televisions and portable screens, an opposite effect has also occurred. "Fit to Frame," my essay on the relationship between the image and screen edge, appears here as testimony to the consequences of trying to adapt images to all manner of screen forms. Aspect ratio and image resolution impose limits on the possibilities for screening any image, from Hollywood blockbusters to vacation videos and photos. Screen manufacturers and media software producers have found ways to mask this inconvenience by treating the image as a sort of fabric that can stretched and cropped as necessary to fill the screen's surface, a practice which inevitably deforms the image. This has ties to theories of the image and frame in other media, such as painting.

If the screen puts the image at risk on the one hand, Mitchell Whitelaw suggests that on the other hand the screen itself can be placed at risk. His exploration of "post-screen" transmateriality takes into consideration an area of art and design experimentation that has bypassed the "glowing rectangle," often via the screen's very materials and compositional strategies. Here, one could say, both image and frame can come undone, testing the limits of our understanding of what constitutes a screen. This potentially achieves a sort of deconstruction of the ideological apparatus of the networked screen in line with the sort of inquiry Baudry undertook in the cinema. Whitelaw identifies two tendencies in this process: works that focus on arrays, thereby adopting the screen's grid configuration only to test its aesthetic boundaries, and projection mapping or "extruded light" works that rely on the screen's malleability for site-specific performances.

Reference

Cecilia Tichi, *The Electronic Hearth: Creating an American Television Culture* (New York: Oxford University Press, 1991).

The Production
of Images

CHAPTER ELEVEN

Description of the Process of Painting and Lighting in ... Pictures of the Diorama

Louis-Jacques-Mandé Daguerre

These processes have been developed primarily in the pictures *Midnight Mass*, *Rockslide in the Goldau Valley*, *Temple of Salomon* and *Saint Mary's Basilica of Montreal*. All of these pictures have included day and night effects. Dissolution of forms were added to these effects, through which figures would appear in *Midnight Mass* where there had been chairs, for example, or fallen rocks would replace the view of a pleasant valley in *Goldau Valley*.

The painting process

Since the fabric must be painted on both sides, as well as lit by reflection and refraction, it is imperative to employ a very translucent material of the most uniform weave possible. Percale or calico may be used. The selected cloth must be very wide to reduce the number of seams, which are always difficult to hide, especially under the picture's strong lighting. Once the fabric is stretched each side requires at least two coats of parchment glue.

First effect

The first effect, which needs to be the lighter of the two, is executed on the front of the fabric. First the sketch is done in pencil, taking care not to blemish the fabric, whose whiteness is the only resource one has for the picture's lights, since white is not used in the execution of the first effect. The colors used are ground in oil, but applied to the fabric with turpentine, to which a bit of fatty oil should be added for the strongest shadow strokes while the rest can be applied directly. The methods used for this painting are entirely consistent with those for watercolor, with the sole difference that the colors are ground in oil instead of gum and thinned with turpentine instead of water. One cannot use white or any thickly applied opaque color whatsoever as these would produce, according to their degree of opaqueness, more or less tinted patches for the second effect. One must try to accentuate the strongest shadows on the first attempt in order to minimize any loss to the fabric's translucency.

Second effect

The second effect is painted on the back of the fabric. One must not use any other light source during the execution of this effect than that which comes from the front of the picture and penetrates the material. By this method one can perceive the forms of the first effect coming through. These forms must be either retained or eliminated. First the entire surface of the fabric is coated in a translucent white, such as Clichy white, ground in oil and

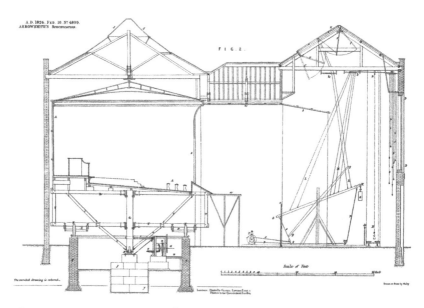

FIGURE 11.1 *Traverse section of Arrowsmith's Diorama, London, 1857 [1823].
The screen and mechanisms for controlling light intensity and direction are at right.*

thinned with turpentine. Brushstrokes are eliminated by means of a shaving brush. With this coat one can hide the seams a bit by being careful to apply it more lightly to their edges, which are always less translucent than the rest of the fabric. Once this coat has dried, one traces any changes to be made to the first effect. In the execution of the second effect, one's only concern is modulating white and black without worrying about the colors of the first picture seen through the fabric. Modulation comes from a white-based tint mixed with a small amount of peach-nut black to obtain a gray. One can determine the proper intensity by applying it to the back and looking from the front to be sure that remains imperceptible. Changes in the [color] tints are produced by the greater or lesser opacity of this [gray] tint. At some point the shadows of the first effect will interfere with the execution of the second. To remedy this inconvenience and mask these shadows, one can match up the value by means of a tint applied more or less thickly, according to the greater or lesser density of the shadows to be eliminated. One finds it necessary to push this second effect to its greatest density, since one may find the need for light tones in an area where there are strong shadows in the first [effect]. Once one has shaped the painting with these differences in the tint's opacity and obtained the desired effect, one can color it with very translucent colors ground in oil. It is another watercolor that one must make, but using less turpentine in these scumbles, which gain strength to the extent that one makes several passes and uses more fatty oil. However, for very light coloring turpentine alone is enough to spread the color.

Lighting

The painted effect on the front of the fabric is lit by reflection, that is, only by light coming from the front, and the second receives light by refraction, that is, only coming from the rear. With either effect one can employ both light sources simultaneously to modify certain parts of the picture. The light that lights the picture from the front must, as much as possible, come from above. That which lights the rear should come from vertical casements. These casements should be completely closed, of course, when viewing only the first picture. Should one need to modify any part of the first effect with the light from behind, this light must to be masked so that it hits only that area. The casements should be at least 2 m from the picture to allow unlimited modifications to the light by having it pass through color filters according to the requirements of the effect. The same method is used for the front picture. It is known that the appearance of colors of objects in general is created by the arrangement of the molecules of these objects. Consequently, all the substances used to paint have no color. They only have the property of reflecting this or that ray of light, which in itself contains all colors. The purer these substances are the more they reflect the basic colors, but never absolutely, which in fact is not necessary to reproduce the effects of nature. To understand the principles behind the making and lighting of the pictures of the aforementioned Diorama, here is an example of what happens when the light is broken down, that is to say when some of its rays are intercepted: Two colors of the greatest brilliance are coated on the fabric—one red and the other green, of about equal value. Introduce a red filter, as with a colored glass, into the light falling upon them, and the color red will reflect those rays that are red and the green will remain black. By substituting a green filter for the red filter, the opposite will occur, with the red remaining black while the green reflects the color green. But this only happens completely in cases where the filter introduced blocks the passage of all rays except one. This effect is difficult to produce completely, since in general colored materials do not reflect just one ray. Nevertheless, in the results of this experience the effects are consistent. To return to the application of this principle in the pictures of the Diorama, although these pictures essentially have only two effects painted—day on the front and night on the back—these effects, moving from one to the other only by a complicated combination of filters through which light passes, produce an infinity of other effects similar to those found in nature in its shifts from morning to evening and vice versa. One should not think it is necessary to use filters of a very intense color to produce vast shifts in color, since often a slight nuance is enough to create a great change.

CHAPTER TWELVE

When Seeing Is Belonging: The Photography of Tahrir

Lara Baladi

Photographs of Cairo's Midan Tahrir taken on the "Friday of Victory," a week after a popular uprising forced President Hosni Mubarak to relinquish power, represent a better tomorrow—the birth of a new Egypt. These images portray Liberation Square as an oasis of peace and justice, a paradise regained, an icon of freedom and renewed Egyptian identity. Have these photos of Tahrir Square replaced pictures of the pyramids as the ultimate Egyptian cliché?

In August 1990, herds of Kuwaitis sought refuge in Egypt. These tourists-in-spite-of-themselves flocked to the pyramids every day. I too was there on the Giza plateau, photographing the pyramids. My debut in photography coincided with this migration provoked by Saddam Hussein's first invasion of Kuwait.

That winter, Operation Desert Storm became the first war to be broadcast live on television. The perversity of how this invasion was represented reaffirmed Guy Debord's premise in *The Society of the Spectacle*: "All that once was directly lived has become mere representation."[1] The dark image in the convex screen was filled with occasional explosions in the night sky of an obscure city, CNN's big fat logo ever-present in the lower left corner. As this "clean," "bloodless" war was broadcast minute by minute to the world in an instantaneous mediation of unfolding events, America's overwhelming military response and its new, elaborate surveillance technologies became subject to much criticism and analysis. Jean Baudrillard, in his controversial and often-cited text on that period, went as far as to suggest that, "The Gulf War did not take place."[2] And, indeed, the images that saturated our TV screens were perceived as surreal by many and inspired a whole new market of video games where soldiers, tinged by the green glow of night vision, crawl the terrain.

A decade later, in 2001, the "casualty-free" representation of the Gulf War achieved in 1991 by CNN was turned on its head by a new generation of documentary photographers and filmmakers. 9/11 was the first major historical event to be documented by thousands of people with digital cameras, more thoroughly and effectively, as it happened, than by the mainstream media. They recorded the horror of people jumping out of windows, people covered in ashes running through the debris and carrying the wounded—trying to escape hell. But beyond recording, those who witnessed and photographed the attack on the World Trade Center in New York City contributed to the breaking of a long established monopoly on the representation of reality. Citizen journalism was born.

In a little corner shop in London, the image of a plane exploding into the twin towers flashed on TV. While gathering my groceries, I asked the shopkeeper sitting under the screen what this was. She glanced at it fleetingly over her shoulder and said, with a shrug, "It must be a film." Never in the history of cinema had a scene of this amplitude been shot. Action movies have been trying, and failing, to catch up ever since. Reality had surpassed fiction.

So the Gulf War turned warfare, for many, into a computer game. In the Wikipedia entry for "Gulf War," for example, a header reads: "'Operation Desert Storm' redirects here. For the video game, see Operation: Desert Storm (video game)." But 10 years later, the photo and film amateurs documenting the collapse of the 110-story towers in lower Manhattan re-humanized reality.

The first step toward the democratization of photography was George Eastman's invention of the Kodak camera. In 1888, with the slogan "You press the button, we do the rest," Eastman transformed a cumbersome and complicated procedure, into something easy and obtainable. Photography, until then affordable only by an elite, became even more accessible after 1975, when another Eastman Kodak engineer, Steven Sasson, came up with another major invention: the digital camera. By 2001, a majority of people in the West had one. Snapping photos was no longer the hobby of amateurs but a fully integrated aspect of most people's daily lives.

In the following decade, as cameras made their way into mobile phones (smart or not), webcams were embedded in laptop and desktop screens and people uploaded millions of images to social media sites, the global democratization of photography took on a new dimension. With the emergence of social media, mass media lost even more ground on the distribution of information. Social media, in which the user could participate in the process of selecting and distributing information and make images instantaneously available worldwide, overshadowed traditional visual media. It competed with mainstream media, thus further sharing the power by shifting the hands holding it. "The power of letters and the power of pictures distribute themselves and evaporate into the social media such that it becomes possible for everyone to act instead of simply being represented," observed the influential media artist and theorist Peter Weibel, in a recent article, "Power to the People: Images by the People."[3]

The shift was felt worldwide. When Israel attacked Lebanon in 2006, Lebanese online activists and bloggers attracted enough of the world's attention to put international pressure on Israel and help stop the war. Short-lived but devastatingly destructive, this war lasted long enough to spark the beginning of a new trend of online political activism in the whole Arab region.

On the 25th of January 2011, I was at home in Cairo with a few friends. None of us knew, beyond the unusual, eerie silence in the street, how unprecedented the protests were. To distract ourselves from the growing tension outside, we played a game of Memory, illustrated with black and white photographs from the archive of the Arab Image Foundation (AIF). As I played with these past images from the Arab world, little did I know that the history of the region, of Arab photography and of photography at large, was about to take a quantum leap.

FIGURE 12.1 *The "Friday of Victory" after Hosni Mubarak's fall, Tahrir Square, Cairo, Egypt. Photo by Lara Baladi, February 18, 2011.*

Photographing in Egypt was prohibited in many areas during the Mubarak era; I was arrested no fewer than seven times over 15 years for taking pictures in various parts of the country. Fear-mongering propaganda made people paranoid, feeding an ever-present and general suspicion of the camera, and by extension, of the "other." Complicit as societies become under dictatorship, Egyptians had for generations bowed to routine police humiliation in broad daylight, and worse brutality in the darkness of their torture chambers. Very few images of these crimes had gone public. The 2008 Mahalla protests by textile mill workers revived the notion that we had a right to see and be seen. Egyptian activist Hossam el-Hamalawy, blogged that, "the revolution will be flickrised," pointing to the need to document and disseminate the regime's repressive procedures. Seeing would mean believing and revolting for those blinded by the national media, which had concealed this repression persistently for 30 years.

This was never truer than in Tahrir Square during the 18 days of the 2011 revolution. Here, and in the whole region during the Arab uprisings, the act of photographing became not only an act of seeing and recording, it was fully participatory. At the core of the Egyptian uprising, photographing was a political act, equal in importance to demonstrating, constituting a form of civil disobedience and defiance. In the midst of the emergency, all theories on the subjectivity of photography suddenly became irrelevant. During the 18 days, people in the square took photos because they felt the social responsibility to do so. Photography became objective; photography showed the truth—yes, a Truth made of as many truths as there were protesters in the square, but nonetheless one that urgently had to be revealed at this turning point in history. The camera became a non-violent weapon aimed directly at the state, denouncing it. Photographing implied taking a stand against the regime; it was a way of reconquering territory and ultimately the country. Photographing meant belonging.

In his classic BBC series, *Ways of Seeing*, John Berger tells us, "The images come to you. You do not go to them. The days of pilgrimage are over."[4] Commenting on our experience of images in the digital age, Slavoj Žižek argued that, "what goes on today is not 'virtual reality' but the 'reality of the virtual.'"[5] A media revolution also took place in Tahrir, when the reality of the streets reached the reality on our screens. The images coming to us through our screens, finally, were "reality."

Thousands of people moved, photographed, and stood together in solidarity against totalitarianism. Protesters held above their heads signs and slogans by day, and the blue glowing lights of mobile phones, iPads, and even laptops, by night. While signifying the demand for social justice and freedom, these devices were not merely emanating a light of hope reminiscent of the dancing flames during the protests of the 1960s; they were simultaneously absorbing the ambient light, thus recording from every possible angle, in every possible quality and format, life in Tahrir.

FIGURE 12.2 *Protesters during a speech in Tahrir Square, April 8, 2011. Photo by Mosa'ab Elshamy.*

Around the world—except in China, where the government banned the word "Egypt" from its Google search engine—images of Tahrir spilled into living spaces. Transcending computers, televisions screens, and other virtual channels, the images inexorably spread the energy of the square. As Žižek said when interviewed about the Arab revolutions, "It was a genuine universal event, immediately understandable... It is every true universality, the universality of struggle."[6] People all over the world identified with the protesters in the square. Tahrir became everyone's revolution. Arab uprisings and Occupy movements followed in a chain reaction. Was image-making impacting the world and shaking its order by helping people rethink their relationship with political power?

The mainstream international media grabbed the event and sucked everything it could out of it. While it supported the crowds in Tahrir, it also diminished the revolution's momentum by referring to it in the past tense after the 18 days and moving on to other news, thus confirming McLuhan's theory that "you can actually dissipate a situation by giving it maximal coverage."[7] At this point, ordinary people had embraced the power of online images to such an extent that television news, often way behind the news on the ground, started broadcasting videos shot by amateurs or activists that had already gone viral on the web. Never, since the invention of the camera, had a historical event been so widely documented, with more videos and photos than there were protesters in the square.

The new economy brought about by digital photography has exponentially amplified photography's intrinsic factory-like quality, which is both its greatest promise and its greatest threat. On the one hand, anyone who owns a camera can produce limitless images for free. On the other hand, the abundance of rapidly distributed images is accompanied by a lack of critical distance; for example, images altered in Photoshop are mostly taken at face value.

This contributes to a general desensitization to reality. Vilém Flusser, in his 1984 book *Towards a Philosophy of Photography*, rightly warns us of the dangers of this hyper-democratization of photography in the digital age: "Anyone who takes snaps has to adhere to the instructions for use—becoming simpler and simpler—that are programmed to control the output end of the camera. This is democracy in the post-industrial society. Therefore people taking snaps are unable to decode photographs: they think photographs are an automatic reflection of the world."[8]

During the Arab uprisings, a great number of shaky and blurry mobile phone videos shot in Syria, Libya, and Bahrain, uploaded every day onto the Internet, were not "decodable." Many battle scenes, highly pixelated and graphic, resembled each other, yet nothing in them was clearly definable or recognizable in itself. Only the titles revealed the videos' content. Viewers easily disengaged from following or attempting to understand how these uprisings were evolving and, if they did, once again they relied on the mainstream media, thus handing the power back all over again.

FIGURE 12.3 *Photoshopped NASA shot, July 3, 2013; image circulating on Facebook in July 2013.*

How long will the most extensive, multi-vocal documentary ever made—that is, this extraordinary and unedited portrait of Egyptians in Midan Tahrir one finds online—survive in the ephemeral virtual archive? With most of the images of the 18 days vanishing into a bottomless pit thanks to Google's PageRank algorithm, will the vision of a possible new world people glimpsed in the Square die along with its digital traces?

Although the endless proliferation of images in Tahrir was produced for our own national consumption rather than that of a Western audience, images from the midan almost instantly turned old clichés of Egypt on their heads. The angry Arab terrorist became a dignified peace warrior. "Egypt! Help us. One world, one pain," read banners in the protests that erupted in Wisconsin in the U.S. three weeks after the Egyptian uprising. The once "dirty Arab" had transformed into a politically and socially conscious citizen. President Obama even declared in a television speech he gave after the Battle of the Camel in the midst of the 18 days: "We should raise our children to be like Egyptian youth."

In French, the word cliché means "photograph"; for the rest of the world it refers only to a stereotype that, while familiar, conceals more truths than it reveals. The most enduring Orientalist Egyptian cliché of them all, the Giza Pyramids, has been upstaged by the bird's-eye picture of a million people in Tahrir. Images of people circumambulating the tents in the center of the square resonated, at times, with images of people walking around the Kaaba in Mecca. For about a year after the revolution started, Tahrir itself was a pilgrimage site for revolution tourists.

One of the oldest debates in photography is about its relationship with death: "Photographs are a way of imprisoning reality," writes Susan Sontag in *On Photography*. "One can't possess reality ... one can't possess the present but one can possess the past."[9] The fear of loss—the fear that the vision born in Tahrir would vanish soon after President Hosni Mubarak stepped down—may have been another reason why people took images incessantly while they were there. Ultimately, photographing in Tahrir became an act of faith. As if recording the ecstatic reality of the present would remind us, in the future, of the Square's utopian promise, and help us to keep hope once the real battle began.

After January 25, 2011, the Square continued to be the center of protests, a synonym for political power and the barometer for the revolution's failure or success. Images of the square became part of our daily visual consumption routine. At times Tahrir appeared to be a parody of itself; at times the center of renewed hope.

Whether it was the revolutionaries, the Muslim Brotherhood, or the Salafis who took Tahrir, owning the Square meant owning the revolution and by extension, Egypt. As the battle for the Square worsened, Tahrir came to represent a divided nation. Rifts between Egyptians intensified during and after the first presidential campaign that followed Mubarak's toppling, in which the Brotherhood's Mohamed Morsi won under dubious circumstances and with a markedly small mandate. In the midst of economic free fall, he issued a constitutional decree granting himself virtually unchecked power. Hence, Egyptians took to the streets again, having lost all trust in his promises to support the revolution and Egypt's interests at large. Only six months into his rule, Egyptians were more bitterly divided than ever.

On June 30, Tahrir Square filled with an unprecedented number of protesters. As many other public places around the country were also being occupied with people demanding the removal of President Morsi, new bird's-eye views of Tahrir flooded the Internet and the mainstream media in ever-renewing iteration (the same but never the same). Alongside this poignant illustration of the experience of the overwhelming majority of Egyptians who, if only for a moment, united again in a common goal and spirit, a NASA photograph of Egypt from the sky—showing the Nile illuminated with a Photoshopped caption, "Egypt lights the way for the world revolution"—emerged and circulated on social media. This image, at a striking remove from the euphoria experienced on the ground, this iconic image of the Square's punctum archimedis, spread the global significance of Tahrir once again through the media.

Egypt was now defying the very core of the democratic process. Messages like the following one circulated on people's Facebook walls:

Know that almost every democracy in the world has now been dragged into this public debate about what is democratic legitimacy ... Yes, Egyptians have questioned [the] ballot box legitimacy, and YES, we asked our army to intervene when we found our political opponents bringing out their militias.

In the early days of the June 30th uprising, many Egyptians used social media to voice their anger against Western media, who were labeling the removal of President Morsi a "coup" rather than seeing it as military intervention in support of and responding to mass mobilization against his divisive and decidedly undemocratic rule.

In the days immediately following this new turn of events in Egyptian politics, 22 *Al Jazeera* journalists resigned, accusing the Qatar-based network of airing lies and misleading viewers. Reporting for *Al Arabiya*, Nada Al Tuwaijri characterized these resignations as "criticism over the channel's editorial line, the way it covered events in Egypt, and allegations that journalists were instructed to favor the Brotherhood."[10] Meanwhile, CNN's broadcasts recalled its biased coverage of the Gulf War; the network's coverage reflected its own narrative rather than the reality on the ground. CNN not only naively confused images of pro-Morsi with anti-Morsi demonstrations, but was also bluntly oblivious to the voices of the majority of the Egyptian people expressing their will. CNN's crew was thrown out of Tahrir Square, along with many other foreign journalists, because protesters refused to be misrepresented; from the start, this revolution had been about self-determination, in media as in society.

The Egyptian army regained control over the national media and gave President Morsi an ultimatum to resign. He refused. Arrested by the army, he underwent what many people would call a "show trial" and eventually received the death sentence. But as time passes, the current ruling regime imposes an increasingly aggressive form of repression against freedom of speech and a stranglehold on the media even tighter than Mubarak's.

In the wake of the uprising, the power of the image was supposedly handed back to the people, for the people. Someone even tweeted that a meteorite should fall on Tahrir. Did this message imply that Tahrir should officially be the sacred pilgrimage site for a redefined Egypt? At the time, it felt for a moment as if Tahrir could become the Mecca of a rebirthing Arab world, one in the process of seeking a new political practice and redefining democracy in ways the West has yet to imagine. Five years later, the last revolt turns out to be more like a popular movement co-opted into a full-scale counter-revolution—perhaps one more stage on Egypt's long and painful road to representative politics.

When Napoleon Bonaparte addressed his army before the Battle of the Pyramids, he said, "Soldiers! Forty centuries behold you!"

The full-force return of the military regime and the increasingly restricted spaces of resistance available to citizens have only reinforced the significance of the bird's-eye image of Tahrir. Imprinting deeper into our psyche the fact that the revolution happened; re-truing the fact that fundamental social change has been taking place in an ongoing process, against all odds; penetrating our collective memory as time passes—that image of Tahrir distilled from the mass production of images that took place in 2011 has come to represent in a way not only Egypt's uprising but all the social movements that have since followed worldwide. The bird's-eye view of Tahrir Square has become, in this way, a collective watermark of democratic longing. Even though the road to freedom seems long, this digital-age icon, by dethroning the pyramids, has brought Egypt back to the present, hopefully enduring, reiterating, and propelling it into a better future.

Notes

1   Guy Debord, *The Society of the Spectacle* (New York: Zone Books, 1995), 12.
2   Jean Baudrillard, *The Gulf War Did Not Take Place* (Bloomington: Indiana University Press, 1995).
3   Peter Weibel, "Power to the People: Images by the People," http://blog.zkm.de/en/editorial/power-people-images-people/.
4   John Berger, *Ways of Seeing* (1972; London: British Broadcasting Corporation, 2008), DVD.
5   Slavoj Žižek, *The Reality of the Virtual*, directed by Ben Wright (St. Charles, Ill.: Olive Films, 2004), DVD.
6   Slavoj Žižek, #1 *Arabian Revolution*, YouTube, June 21, 2011, https://www.youtube.com/watch?v=v9Ok0JzUL_c.

7   Marshall McLuhan, "What TV Does Best," in *Understanding Me: Lectures and Interviews*, ed. Stephanie McLuhan and David Staines (Toronto: McClelland & Stewart, 2003), 252.

8   Vilém Flusser, *Towards a Philosophy of Photography* (London: Reaktion Books, 2000), 59.

9   Susan Sontag, *On Photography* (New York: Farrar, Straus and Giroux, 1989), 163.

10   Nada Altuwaijri, " 'We Aired Lies': Al Jazeera Staff Quit Over 'Misleading' Egypt Coverage," *Al Arabiya*, July 9, 2013, http://english.alarabiya.net/en/media/2013/07/09/Al-Jazeera-employees-in-Egypt-quit-over-editorial-line-.html.

CHAPTER THIRTEEN

Building New Worlds

Ron Burnett

The links between the computer and the television screen are very suggestive of an aesthetic that is struggling to redefine flatness and three-dimensionality. Part of the struggle is located in the creation of "worlds"—the idea that worlds can be constructed by programming that introduces a whole host of variables into screen-based experiences, Yet it seems clear that games are about a creative mix of worlds and otherworldliness, Games are about gaps, and gaps are about finding a place for the player to affect the experiences he or she has. They are about role playing and imaginary projections of self into interfaces that have enough power to absorb a variety of needs and desires. In other words, they are about using the power of fantasy to allow players to see into their motivations and to hear their desires through the avatars that are generated in the screen environment (Vilhjálmsson 1997).

Games are about substitution, displacement, and the extraordinary need gamers have to reinvigorate ancient mythic stories and tales. I think there is more than a passing relationship between the medium of the computer and the desire to create complex fantasies within its screens. I would even posit that what is described as hypermedia is about the joy that comes from virtual travel, a phenomenon that has its roots in literature, art, and the relationship humans have always had with technology. (This argument might encourage critics and analysts to look at the origins of writing, storytelling, and the mapping of technology onto human bodies and into human fantasies from a different perspective.)

What does it mean to suggest that players inhabit the screen? Is the bridge among fantasy, screen, and reality such a flimsy one? Or have garners understood that the distinction itself has never been as useful as their culture and society would like them to believe? From the very beginning of the cinema, for example, screens were used as vehicles to draw audiences into other worlds. The fascination, the sheer excitement of discovering the range, depth, and infinite storytelling capacity of the cinema has not only sustained an industry, it has transformed screens into vehicles of excitement, entertainment, and learning.

The contrasting popular cultural complaint has been that viewers are victims of this process—the common argument, for example, that violent games produce violent children, I believe this point of view to be fundamentally incorrect although I am fascinated by the way it resonates as an explanation for many social ills and how it leads to all sorts of conclusions about the "value" of games, if not of the value of popular culture itself. The arguments about violence are weak in large measure because there is no way of specifying *exactly* which part of a story or a set of images has a particular effect or whether the cumulative impact of images can be measured.

Within all of this, the power to control what happens on screens, to change and transform the aesthetic of screen-based experiences has more often than not been made possible by the attentiveness of creators and producers to the needs of their audiences. Western culture has built up a vast inventory of what works and what doesn't. In this respect, garners are and have been interacting with computer games using a vast repertoire of already existing abilities and knowledge. The tone, design, and direction of computer games have been set by a host of cultural assumptions driven by the audiences that use them.

It is nevertheless important to understand that players cannot change the aesthetic of individual games unless they become the authors of the code that organizes the game's orientation, direction, and content. The movement here is along a trajectory of participation at the level of the game itself to influencing the design and appearance of the game in its next version. By now, there are many generations of games; the surprise is that there has not been even more inventiveness, more new interfaces, and more new ideas about the worlds that are generated (Schleiner 1998). Perhaps these are limitations that cannot be overcome unless screen interfaces change. The biggest challenge facing gaming companies is that they need to create more complex operating systems (game engines) for the games, which may work against transparency and simplicity. There needs to be a synergistic relationship among code, game, interface, player, and design.

Ironically, ever larger screens still remain enclosed by frames, and this may preclude the simple movement from game experience to total virtual enclosure. Perhaps this desire for the immersive experience is not as much about mastery as it is about the very character of the technology itself. In other words, the technology (and not necessarily what it does) may be the real attractor here. Immersion makes an assumption about human experience that is verified by reference to the technology itself. At the same time, flight simulators, for example, come as close to the "real" thing as is possible. American corporations now spend over $10 billion a year on three-dimensional design for a whole host of military and nonmilitary applications. Most areas of product design use digital tools to achieve their goals. *Ultima 2 Online* promotes itself as one of the most "amazing" immersive experiences in the game world, and this is largely based on assumptions about immersion. Immersion is a trope for the experiences of virtual space. Those experiences are framed by interfaces, which means that highly mediated and organized *metaphors* for seeing facilitate and encourage users to feel as if they are inside images. Ultimately, these virtual environments can only be visualized through representations, and the experiences can only be validated if participants have the will to do so. In other words, virtual spaces have no ontological foundation, and claims that suggest participants are capable of entering into virtual spaces are more than likely claims about the strength of interfaces than they are about human experience. This would even apply to the use of tele-immersive tools for medical purposes. The ability of doctors to engage with these tools will be largely dependent on the ability they have to learn how to use the interfaces that link them to patients in remote locations. The notion of presence, so crucial to games as well, is about a mental act of will to try and overcome the lack of immediacy. This requires imagination as much as it requires "presence." The confusion here is how to distinguish among the use of the tools, experience, and interpretation. Virtual spaces are, by themselves, not the medium of communications. Rather, virtual spaces are the context within which a variety of image and sound-based media operate. And participants, in ways that cannot be extrapolated from the technologies, will determine the effectiveness of those operations.

Unlike the cinema, which borrowed freely from photography, theatre, opera, music, and other traditions and media, computer games have evolved as a result of their interaction with the history of games and various forms of cultural expression. The games have been designed using categories that have links into the history of stories but not into the artistic traditions for the creation of those stories.

Many of the traditions being drawn upon are essentially linked to the capacities of the technology, which is perhaps why so many games try to generate role-playing situations and simulations. So when the creators of *Ultima 2* suggest that garners can become a "master craftsman" or a "monster" or an "expert weapon smith," they are suggesting that garners can learn to accommodate the fantasy process by reveling in their actualization of it, as well as in the immersive space that *Ultima* has created for participants.

The technology disappears so that participants can also disappear into their imaginaries. The embedded chip may well be within humans as well as outside of them, which ironically was a recurring theme of the television show *The X-Files* over a number of seasons. An important feature of *Ultima Online* is found in the many contacts people make with each other outside of the game context through conventions and other public events. This further extends the boundaries of the virtual from one context into another.

I regard the period of aesthetic experimentation in video and computer games to be in its early phase. This phase has been characterized by the incorporation of traditional styles, narrative structures, and themes into the particular look and feel of simulated gaming spaces. At the same time, an understanding of the particularities of space and time that characterize the way the games and their participants orient themselves within the screen environment is still being developed. Some of what is now going on could be described as reverse engineering. A computer animator creates an artificial world of fish in a pool. He programs them to act like real fish by first filming fish in their natural habitat. He creates his graphics by developing the drawings from the originals and then regenerating three-dimensional models with richly endowed computer-based colors. He then lets the digital fish play in their digital pool and films their behavior for a fishing game.

As Dimitri Terzopoulos (1998) puts it: "Rather than being a graphical model puppeteer, the computer animator has a job more analogous to that of an underwater nature cinematographer. Immersed in the virtual marine world, the animator strategically positions one or more virtual cameras to capture interesting film footage of the behaviors of the artificial fish" (71). The increasingly complex mediations here suggest that the creative process of producing virtual spaces has moved beyond artifice into new kinds of physical and mental environments with radically different ways of using time and dramatically new ways of envisioning the role of sight and the human body.

For example, how do participants deal with the normal sensations of space in a snowboarding game that puts them face to face with a screen large enough for them to "locate" their experiences on a mountain? The speed of descent increases with each shift of their bodies, but clearly there is neither a descent nor real speed being reached here. An argument can be made that the space being entered is an inner one, located, if that is the word, within a highly contingent imaginary sphere. This brings the body of the "player" into close contact with emotions that are linked to the "descent" even if the boundaries of the experience are ultimately of a hypothetical nature.

Here is a wonderful irony. Most games of this sort reside in a theoretical world in which a variety of hypothetical possibilities are continuously tested. The excitement and adrenaline come from the process of testing many of the inner states that are suppressed when people are on the mountain itself, as well as learning the new sensations of space and time that come with telesnowboarding.

On the mountain, the testing must be approached with great care or the player will lose his or her concentration and take a tumble. The beauty of playing at snowboarding, in an emporium devoted to virtual games or at home with a large screen and rap songs blasting over the sound system, is that players can simultaneously focus on all the elements of being within and outside the experience. This is one of the reasons why a player's sense of space is transformed. In order to really play this type of game, the participant must learn its rules and the expectations that have been built into its structure. Telepresence is about the creation of new aesthetic forms driven by photorealism and efforts to link human physical movement with responsive screen environments. In other words, telepresence is not an easy process in which to enter, nor is it foreign to other strategies that have been developed to play within any number of imaginary and real spaces.

Depending on one's perspective, these imaginary places are often miniature models of hypothetical worlds that players are asked to inhabit. The jump from presence to telepresence may be the only way to sustain the hypothetical relationship that players develop with the gaming environment. Telepresence is about playing with contingency, about the joy of testing and challenging oneself as if everything and nothing were at stake.

From an aesthetic point of view, the graphical interfaces that are designed to contain these worlds must increasingly be created according to their own rules and must allow players a smooth transition from one state of mind to another. I watched a young boy lie down on a virtual hang gliding machine at a games emporium and loudly gasp at the vista presented to him. He transited with great speed from the real to the virtual. The key word is *transit*, which means that no one could, by observation alone, fully understand how he had prepared himself for the experience or what he went through. Presumably, he had a sophisticated enough Nintendo machine to have already accepted the process of modeling, and the jump to hang gliding was merely one of many steps that he had already made in his exploration of virtual spaces and simulation.

A game is just a representational data structure with thousands of variables built into it. This structure makes it possible for certain "events," for the actual modeling, to take place. But how does that structure make it "feel" as if the screen were a useful and exciting place to create and sustain the intense relationships of a game? Can new ideas appear within this structure if the information at the core of the game is carefully organized to represent a particular design and form? These are crucial questions that require further research into the ways computer games have evolved and the synergies that have been created between images and playing.

Three-dimensional screen worlds are built on a two-dimensional foundation. The markers within those worlds must be clearly understood in order for participants to wend their way through the spatial architecture. Those markers are oriented toward simulated experiences, but what does the word *simulation* actually suggest in the context of a game? Does it imply a direct relationship between the events of the game and the world of the player? I think not.

Simulation is about a world that has a measure of autonomy built into its very grammar, but that autonomy is illusory. In simulated environments the programming can make it possible for independent choices to be made by players or users. Players use their senses in so many different ways that part of the challenge is to integrate the intensity of playing with enough self-awareness to maintain some control. This suggests that the ability to use visual signs and cues is as much about the intersections of popular culture and simulation as it is about already existing "bodies" of knowledge, As the body is transformed into digital characters capable of doing anything within the limits of the screen and within the limits of the interface, players experience a rush of power (as in the game *Grand Theft Auto 3*).

The process of getting into the games is related to the amount of time it takes to train oneself in all of the characteristics of the simulation. Perhaps this is what permits, if not encourages, the ease of movement from physical presence to telepresence. One has to be careful because simulation seems to suggest a loss of self, or a loss of control over what one defines as real to oneself. Clearly, the feelings associated with simulation are powerful. But they are limited by the interfaces and by the fact that there are always mediators among experience, fantasy, and simulation.

Could it be that the games reflect the cultural move from sensate experiences to mediated screen-based relationships? Could it be that the structure of these experiences has legitimated the ways telepresence is now accepted as an experience worth having? It may be the case that a generation that grows up with avatars, intelligent agents, and substitute worlds will lose interest in the distinctions that I am drawing here.

The flatness of the screen encourages the transposition of the games into arcades and the production of as many related toys, figurines, magazines, and texts as possible. (Books about *Myst* and *Riven* have sold hundreds of thousands of copies.)

FIGURE 13.1 *Inside a gaming arcade, Tokyo, 2008. Photo: Stéfan.*

The exigencies here are not only market-driven, but the electronic pets, Playdiums, IMAX rides, and so on are symptomatic expressions of the need to somehow bring screen experiences to another level that actualizes the physical traces of sensation even as these processes loop back again into the virtual. There could be no better evidence of the unity of these experiences than the virtual emporia I have been discussing and the increasing presence of large screen-based entertainment centers in the home.

From an analytical point of view, this once again highlights the gradual manner in which a variety of mediations support a structure that includes many levels of the real mixed in with artifice. The artifice is permanent scaffolding for buildings that will never be completed. Players don't like it when characters are killed off and can't return, because players want to keep constructing and reconstructing the scaffolding. It may be that this restructuring is actually the physical underpinning for interactive processes.

Garners discuss the interaction of the physical, visible, sensate, and screen in a holistic manner, which suggests that they are talking about a co-evolutionary process. The games evolve as players collaborate with them. Such interactions generate increasingly complex levels of play. The various components of a game, from setting the scene (exposition), facing a variety of crises, encountering obstacles and overcoming them, resolving problems and then completing the game by outwitting its structural constraints (coding), are all about the use of surrogacy to gain control over virtual environments.

All the dimensions of interaction, experience, and reconstruction that I have described and analyzed in this chapter are part of an unfolding world for which there are only temporary maps. For cultures that have been attuned to permanence and the need to preserve artifacts and experiences, this fluidity poses many challenges. Computer games are pointing toward a new process of engagement with image-worlds. At the same time, as part of the living archeological process that I mentioned earlier, all the layers of previous forms and experiences remain in place. This is as confusing as it is enticing. It could also be the site for reenvisioning the relationships humans have with the technologies they are creating and using. Crucially, computer games signal how important vantage point is, because without some perspective on subjectivity and identity, image-worlds make it appear as if players are not at the center of game experiences. The mediations among images, experiences, and players suggest a struggle with what intelligence means in digital environments.

[...]

Works cited

Schleiner, Anne-Marie. 1998. *Gendered avatars*. Available online at <http://www.
opensorcery.net/skool/games&art/avatar.html>. [Accessed January 6, 2015.
Terzopoulos, Dimitri. 1998. "Artificial life for computer animation." In *Art@
Science*, ed. Christa Sommerer and Laurent Mignonneau, 69–77. New York:
Springer-Verlag.
Vilhjálmsson, H. 1997. *Autonomous communicative behaviors in avatars*. Master's
thesis in Media Arts and Sciences, Massachusetts Institute of Technology.

CHAPTER FOURTEEN

On-Screen Screens

Brad Chisholm

There is a film from 1902 called *Uncle Josh Goes to the Motion Picture Show* in which an unsophisticated fellow sees his first movie. If you have seen this film you may recall that most of it consists of a single camera set-up. In the frame Uncle Josh can be seen seated before a motion picture screen. The central idea is that he mistakes the celluloid images for reality. While this may not have been the first film to depict a motion picture screen within a screen, it is evidence that what I call "on-screen screens" have been around for nearly 90 years. This fact alone is not especially noteworthy, but recently the inclusion of video screens within the diegesis of films and television programs has become increasingly common. I believe that along with this rise of on-screen screens comes a significant change in the way viewers make sense of the moving image arts.

A single screen image that presents diegetic space through time does so via an involved series of cues which demand a fair amount of decoding on the part of the viewer. Add additional screens and expect the viewer to perceive, cognize, reconcile, or interpret the multiple images simultaneously and you greatly complicate the viewing situation. Herbert Zettl may have been the first to systematically examine the viewing consequences of additional screens in a 1977 study which he prefaced by distinguishing multi-screens, essentially separate but adjoining monitors, from "divided" or split screens. Zettl was interested in the impact an expanded field of view would have on viewers who recognized the multi-screens as "self-contained, yet interdependent space-time entities" (6). However, mainstream narrative fiction films and television programs have rarely found a way to make use of multi-screens, and even the less drastic split screen is seldom used other than for telephone conversations or opening credit sequences. The finale of *Napoleon* (1927) and those portions of *The Boston Strangler* (1968) which use the devices have been anomalies.

Split screen variations are commonly found in non-fiction television formats. Commercials often segment the screen in order to maximize the information that can be packed into 30 seconds. Game shows such as *The Love Connection* use split screen "windows" to enable viewers to see contestant reaction shots without having to cut away from the image of the person speaking. News programs have made a similar window (one which hovers just above an anchor's shoulder) so common as to become an emblematic visual convention. Yet a split screen is not an on-screen screen. A split screen compounds demands on the viewer, but unlike an on-screen screen it can never be inside the primary space of a given shot. The anchor cannot see that hovering window. However, when an anchor looks at a monitor that is visible on the news set (whether she/he can really see the image on it or not) that monitor is an on-screen screen.[1]

Jane Feuer grappled with some of the ways such an "internal monitor" is employed in *Good Morning, America* to emphasize that program's own "liveness." She noted that when an on-screen screen is used in lieu of a shot/reverse shot between host and weatherman, the viewer is kept at arm's length from their conversation (17–18). The standard shot/reverse shot alternation is entrenched in our visual lexicon precisely because it so neatly draws the viewer into screen conversations. Devices such as the shot/reverse shot play different roles and serve different ends in non-fiction forms than in narrative fiction. It is futile, for instance, to expect eye-line matches in *The Mac Neill Lehrer News Hour* to conform to the screen direction rules used for classical narrative films. Like other devices, the on-screen screen will have different implications dependent on the form of the program in which it appears. When used on a news show the device serves, among others, the ends of immediacy and authenticity. However, immediacy is antithetical to narrative whose essence is the unfolding of story events through time, and authenticity is irrelevant to any program that presents itself as a work of fiction.

So what do on-screen screens do for narrative fiction? At times they may do little more than serve as background props in the interest of verisimilitude; in other cases they may play key roles in eliciting a self-consciousness about the medium that is lately being called "meta-television" (Olson 284). Whether blatant or not, their presence reminds us to some degree that we are watching a film or television program in which someone is, or could be, watching a film or television program. When on-screen screens and the images on them are to any degree prominent in a shot they become factors in our sense making viewing strategy because they force us to posit a diegetic world inside of and subordinate to another one.

This extra activity nuances a construct that has long been used to justify a strategy of image selection in film, that of the "best view" or "ideal observer" (Branigan 86, 136). The precedent for this filmic convention may have been set in the nineteenth century when certain novelists shifted the emphasis in their narrative rendering "from the object seen to the seer seeing" (Spiegal 82; Scholles and Kellog 241). Scholars have detected in the work of Flaubert, James, and many others an effort to establish point-of-view through the separate means of imparting knowledge via a narrator and imparting images via a "focalizer" or visualizer in the text (Genette 185–94). Such literary attention to "seeing" appears retrospectively cinematic today, but in the early years of the motion picture Hugo Munsterberg thought the new medium distinguished itself from literature and theatre by its ability to cut a selective swath through the visual field (39). In 1933 Rudolph Arnheim referred to the cinematic "necessity of deciding upon some one 'angle'" from which to render the most desirable (though not necessarily the "clearest, most obvious") view (47–48). The notion of "an observer, ideally mobile in space and time" was also called the "active observer" by V. I. Pudovkin in the 1940s and has since filtered into film studies discourse as the "ideal observer" (Pudovkin 70–71, 82; Wilson 53). The notion that the camera is placed in the ideal position to observe the most salient pro filmic material has become a fundamental of film and television practice.[2]

The concept involves not only camera placement, but timing: knowing just when to reveal something and for how long. In a nutshell, the ideal observer is what is built into films and television programs that are assembled under the "classical" strictures of the continuity editing system. It is an organizational principle that shapes both the production and the viewing of a given film or television program. It shows us who is speaking and to whom, it reveals the telling raising of the eyebrow in reaction shots, and the ticking bomb which the hero can't see.

The concept deserves further definition here, because the word "ideal" suggests too much. Ideal for whom? As practiced in Hollywood and by all purveyors of classical narrative film and video, the ideal view is that which reveals the narrative material necessary for the preferred reading of the subsequent scenes. The ideal view does not show a viewer everything essential to understanding a narrative (otherwise mysteries would be impossible). Much is withheld from this observer, but never anything that would impair the viewer's understanding of the plot according to the film's narrative design. The views of the ideal observer are classified as either: (1) objective—recorded by an omniscient yet unobtrusive camera, or (2) subjective—recorded by a camera that shows an image either precisely or approximately as a diegetic character would see it. The ideal observer can be thought of as a rationale that explains camera placement and editing decisions in the highly refined Hollywood stylistic system that uses an alternation of long, medium, and close-up shots, matches on actions and eyelines, plus a host of other devices to convey narrative as clearly as possible.

Alternatives to the ideal observer concept can be found in those films in which camera placement and editing decisions are based on priorities other than the bald rendition of narrative. Godard's *Vivre Sa Vie* (1962) is comprised of scenes shot without classical narrative consideration of the viewer. We see backs of heads, we often are not sure who is speaking, and accustomed to helpful Hollywood cut-aways and opportune close-ups, we are frequently at a loss in determining which is the critical plot material and which material is less relevant. Of course, what Godard's camera chooses to show us can be considered ideal in other ways. In the broadcast sense, wherever any filmmaker puts a camera is ideal placement for that film because the film would not be the same without it. For this reason, "implied observer" might be a more apt name for the construct. Like literature's "implied reader," it may be more or less privy to narrative information in a given work; it may be more or less classical or consistently applied (Iser, *Implied Reader* xii; Act 38).

Several aspects of the on-screen screen place special demands on the viewer in ways that precipitate a modification of the vision of the implied observer. The first and probably most common of these is a matter of "framing": borders appear between the images on the depicted screen and the rest of the primary space. These borders comprise a frame that cues the viewer to recognize that the characters in the narrative are in the presence of (and possibly viewing) a film or television show. Yet even if there are no characters in the primary space, we viewers know that the pictures on the depicted screen are supposed to represent fiction within fiction. Even though these images may be fleeting and incidental, they are a little bit like Gerard Genette's "metadiegesis," the carefully framed story within the story (228). There are many cases where these on-screen screen images depict diegetic characters who happen to get on TV as part of the plot. In *Being There* (1979), for instance, our protagonist, Chance, appears on a talk show and we see many shots of his acquaintances watching him on TV in their homes. In such cases as this, the "fiction-within-fiction" notion breaks down, but what I call "framing" does not. The television receivers that we see alert us to the status of the framed images: these are pictures of something mediated by television tubes; these are images from another space that have been composed, selected, and transmitted by characters in the fiction.

The second aspect of an on-screen screen is a tactile one that might be called the film or video "look." This does not involve image composition, rather it is the way the screen texture is manipulated so as to suggest one is watching film or video within the narrative. Heightened graininess, increased video noise or snow, and noticeable drops in resolution are common methods of achieving the film or video look. In *Where the Green Ants Dream* (1984), a character's childhood memories are depicted home-movie style through the use of heavy grain and perceptible flicker. I maintain that this tactile effect is distinct from that of framing because framing depends on us recognizing a fictional space within which is a TV or film screen. The tactile effect does not require that element. An entire shot may be filled with a single coherent image with no border to reveal it as on a screen in the narrative, but with the heightened grain or other methods of obtaining this "look" we are to understand that we are seeing an overtly mediated image that is linked to a screen within a screen, even though we cannot place it precisely on any screen within the diegetic world.

Third, on-screen screens provide a graphic, compositional aspect that is shared with the device of the split screen. This is distinct from framing in that it involves image arrangement rather than fictional levels or degrees of mediation. The graphic possibilities of an on-screen screen permit a director to make one shot function as its own shot/reverse shot. This is done in *The Manchurian Candidate* (1962) in a furious exchange between a cabinet secretary and an adversary he can see but who is off-screen to the audience. That adversary still shows up in the shot on a television monitor that the secretary cannot see, but which is in plain sight for the viewer. The more screens within a shot the more pronounced this effect becomes. In *Broadcast News* (1987) and *The China Syndrome* (1978), shots of the television control rooms that contain both preview and program monitors give viewers of those films multiple views of simultaneous events. Like the work of the cubists who sometimes explained their paintings as showing multiple views of the same thing, the on-screen screens that provide simultaneous extra angles complicate the viewing of the overall shot. Even a single monitor or film screen within a shot has the effect of doubling the graphic worlds we are asked to comprehend simultaneously.

A fourth aspect of on-screen screens might be called the "roving eye" of the diegetic camera. This is most keenly felt when we observe what are supposed to be images from a hand-held moving camera that is itself within the fiction. The movement is not essential; rather the key requirement is that the camera does exist somewhere in the diegesis. The viewer is then particularly conscious of both that camera's existence and its placement. The images from these cameras almost always rely on the framing and tactile effects explained above, but they add a sense of spying, of voyeurism, and suggest that the images are being recorded on videotape for playback at a later point in the plot. This device is often a strong means of getting one set of characters in a safe location to empathize with another set of characters who are roving through dangerous territory with their cameras. The shoulder-mounted cameras on the marines in *Aliens* (1986) are good examples.

Generally speaking, the four aspects discussed thus far are all stylistic options. One television program which generously peppered each of its episodes with examples of all four options was *Max Headroom*, broadcast intermittently by ABC in 1987 and 1988. The series blended brooding visuals with futuristic jargon in order to get a particular mix of investigative drama and satiric science fiction. Peter Wagg, the program's executive producer, admits that he and his team were "working in a different visual language" on Max. One of his associate producers describes their search for a complex style "that overloads the viewers' perceptions" (qtd. in Fisher 79). At the center of this complexity is a strategy of on-screen screen use which demands that the viewer make spatial and narrative sense out of scenes comprised of multiple diegetic spaces linked by cameras and screens within the fiction. The implied observer of a *Max Headroom* episode, then, is able to recognize the on-screen screen cues for what they are and stay on top of the narrative. Some "real" observers may not have been willing to go to that much trouble, but it is unlikely that *Max* was incomprehensible to the average American viewer. Certainly there are rapid-fire television commercials and music videos which are far more challenging. The ABC episodes appear to be toned down somewhat from the original *Max Headroom* pilot for British television, but Wagg says that once the program was on the air there was never any pressure from the network to simplify the visual rendering of the narrative. Program scheduling and problems with character appeal seem to be the more likely culprits for the low ratings.[3]

The following scene from the fourth episode of *Max Headroom* aired by ABC, "Security Systems," freely chooses from the four on-screen screen options mentioned above. Analysis makes it clear that even for this program about a reporter and his roving camera these on-screen screen options were hardly essential or endemic. The scene could as easily have been shot in a traditional fashion without a single on-screen screen.

The narrative context for the scene is as follows. Television reporter/cameraman Edison Carter is seeking entrance to the residence of a security company president whom he seeks to interview. Carter is in constant touch with his "controller," Theora Jones, who monitors his progress on her own on-screen screen. He has just angered Jones by staging an emergency helicopter landing as a ruse to gain en trance.

The sequence opens with two shots of the helicopter on the roof, where the pilot distracts security guards in order for Carter to sneak down a stairwell. Shot number three is the first on-screen screen of the 10 that appear in this 37-shot sequence. In it we see through the lens of the camera Carter carries down the stairs which descend into the building. The shot itself is brief, but is recognized for what it is by such tactile cues as the visible cam era viewfinder markings, Carter's name in the bottom right of the frame, as well as the hand-held motion, the change in resolution from the adjacent shots, and the continuity provided by the match on action from the previous shot.[4] It is like a point-of-view shot, although with the next cut we see that Carter carries his camera on his hip, is not looking through the lens, yet keeps transmitting images as he walks. Shot three could easily have been taken from Carter's direct point of view or have been replaced by an objective shot of Carter descending the stairs. So far, all that is achieved by depicting it as if through his camera is to set us up for the subsequent on-screen screen shots.

Shot four cuts efficiently with number three and is a conventional shot of Carter reaching the bottom of the stairs and proceeding down a hallway. Five is the next on-screen screen shot, this time not from Carter's camera but from a surveillance camera above him in the hall. We never see this or other such cameras at any point in the sequence. Rather we presume from the angle, the monochrome, the video noise, and the little words and numbers that say "securicam" among other things that this is indeed a surveillance camera's view. We might even presume that some character in the fiction is watching Carter's approach on those cameras, although no person is ever associated with them.

For the next 20 seconds, shots six through 21, a pattern is established alternating between objective shots of Carter proceeding down corridors, shots from his camera, shots of Jones, who is back at the network monitoring his progress, and occasional "securicam" shots similar to number five. For the first half of this portion of the scene, Jones is still angry and stands away from her station. She cannot see her monitor, yet she hears Carter and is close enough to a micro phone that they communicate. Jones talks to him and he can hear her through a speaker on his camera. There is, then, an audio link between controller and reporter independent of the on-screen images. The entire sequence could be played out with simply an audio link between controller and hero, a scenario that has been depicted in films and television shows in the past. Without the camera carried by Carter or the surveillance "eyes" the scene could have been shot using identical angles from which the on-screen screen shots are taken. This would have been entirely conventional. What wrinkle, then, is added by doctoring shots like three and five to make them appear as if on camera? For one thing, this "look" is a way of signalling to the viewer that other characters in the fiction are (or might be) gazing at the on-screen image. These are quasi point-of-view shots without the referential adjoining shot containing a face with a directed gaze. Over-the-shoulder shots are not needed to suggest that this is what somebody else is seeing. The on-screen screen has provided a shortcut for the implied observer.

Once inside the apartment of his interviewee, Valerie Towne, Carter confronts a nine-screen display upon which Towne appears. She is presumably speaking to him through this configuration from somewhere else in the apartment. In a sense the nine-screen display is akin to a window with an ornate grid pattern that stands between our protagonist and the other person. Rather than portray nine like images of her face, the configuration divides one large image of Towne among the nine screens to form a fragmented, but somehow intimidating composite. Carter turns his camera on her in Shot 28 and Jones becomes privy to the sight. In shots 29, 34, and 37 we observe the nine-screen display as Jones must be seeing it back on her monitor transmitted by Carter's camera. Carter's interview is edited conventionally with shots of him, reverse shots of the nine-screen display, and over-the shoulder shots of both him and the nine screen display cut together to carry the conversation. The on-screen screen twist is a subtle one even though the technology appears blatant. The view is from a camera on the protagonist's shoulder, not from his eyes for he does not look into a viewfinder while taping. The view of Towne is also from a camera, the one taking the image for the nine-screen display. We become ever-so-conscious of spatial displacement of the vision when we know there is a camera in the fiction.

The cameras that exist within the diegetic world, even those we never see such as the securicams or those which provide the image for Towne's nine-screen display, hold a different status than do those cam eras outside the diegesis. They are like additional characters from whom we see optical points-of-view. Granted, these would be neutral, robotic characters, but they are figures that exist as points in the diegetic space all the same. The bearing this has on the implied observer concept is twofold.

First, the notion of the classical implied observer is consistent with the "seamless" appearance of traditional Hollywood shooting and editing strategies. Thus, the camera, while able to capture the most intimate close-ups at any moment, would never appear obtrusive; it would not remind the viewer of its presence. A camera within the diegesis that transmits an image to some on-screen screen exposes itself blatantly. As far as the viewer is concerned, the camera wielded by the actor is recording the on-screen screen image. Yet the classical ideal observer concept is maintained insofar as the lens that is actually showing us the on-screen screen is not the diegetic camera at all, but a second, unobtrusive camera itself one level re moved from the fiction. The diegetic camera is not an external challenge to the tradition of the ideal view; rather it presents complications within classical confines. The presence of a camera within the fictional space makes that camera part of the narrative. Since the goal of the classical implied observer is to give narrative information absolute primacy, anyone who uses a diegetic camera presumes on the part of the viewer a basic knowledge of how cameras work. Audiences of today are understood by practitioners of the moving image arts to be able to recognize a noisy picture as that of a video screen, and to be able to associate the contraption on Carter's arm with the source of certain on-screen images. Viewers, in turn, expect a plausible source for video-generated images.

The second way in which a diegetic camera's point-of-view bears upon the classical implied observer is that the depiction of that camera's viewpoint makes viewers aware that the characters who may be observing the screen are seeing something that, while not in the same space as themselves, is not precisely the point of view of a fellow character either. That is, Jones sees through the eyes of Carter's camera, not through Carter's eyes. The implied observer or best view, then, can be selected from either: (1) an objective shot of primary space taken by a non-diegetic camera; (2) a subjective shot of primary space from the vantage point of a specific character; (3) an objective shot of on-screen screen imagery; (4) a subjective shot of on-screen screen imagery; or (5) a composite that is an objective shot (or point-of-view shot) that shows an on-screen screen somewhere within the shot. The on-screen screen has expanded the range of visual choices.

Even though on-screen screens frequently are associated with works of 1980s science fiction, the stylistic options of framing a screen within a screen, of capturing the film or video look, of graphically positioning a space within a space, and even of the roving camera eye have been around for years. *Being There* (1979) was not science fiction, yet it incorporated on-screen screens to the extent that the television itself had nearly the status of a full-blown character. *The Conversation* (1974) prefigured with audio much of the surveillance role we now see illustrated with cameras. In fact, a close precedent for Edison Carter's camera/transmitter link to Theora Jones' on-screen screen can be found in a series called *Search*, aired on NBC in the early 1970s. Filmmakers can today use these devices in more sophisticated ways than ever before. The broader palette presumes viewers have a greater familiarity with screens of all types than they have ever had. The consumer boom in video and personal computer technology of the 1980s has fueled this presumption. More and more of us sit down in front of our own computer screens every day. Young, middle-class families have made the light weight half-inch video camera a common place item. Video games occupy a significant portion of the recreation time of young people (Skirrow 113–14). As such, our vision of not only tomorrow but today is riddled with video monitors, and our films and television programs contain increasing numbers of on-screen screens.[5]

A telling shot from the *Max Headroom* sequence is number 29 for it is a screen within a screen within a screen. The shot reveals to us, through Carter's lens, Towne's image upon her nine-screen display as it must appear on Jones' monitor. Towne's face appears framed by the display in her apartment and we think she is on the premises, but she could be across the globe given the state of broadcast technology. In the apartment itself, the space between Carter's camera and the wall of monitors is not framed by a visible border, but tactile cues make it clear that we are seeing the view through the hero's camera. Here is a view of a conversation in which the depicted space contains no characters. The ideal observer usually sees a shot/reverse shot alternation in a two-person conversation, but shot 29 falls outside that pattern. If anything it approximates Jones' point-of-view as a spy privy to the interview. It is, however, a little tight to be her precise point-of-view for all we see is the framed image. Since her monitor has only a 14" screen, she would have to have her nose against the glass for shot 29 to be her optical point-of-view.

In this sequence and in many instances in which diegetic cameras are used, the implied observer is not restricted to the view through that lens. In life, were we standing next to Jones we would have to be satisfied with the images transmitted by Carter's camera, but in film and television we get to see this view as well as those we might see were we standing in the apartment with Carter. The implied observer is as omnipresent as ever in *Max Headroom*. The use of on-screen screens to render this sequence mainly adds this wrinkle: the viewer must consciously think about the source of the images in the on-screen shots. That is, while classic implied observer views attempt to make us forget to ask "where could the camera be that is showing this?" the on-screen views beg the question. We must reconcile every framed picture, every shot with that tactile or roving-eye look, and every graphic dis section of our field of vision into little screens with the idea that for every shot within a shot there must be a diegetic camera.

The resultant camera-knowledge is likely related to our society's growing familiarity with screens and cameras. Our films and television programs seem to be held to a higher level of plausibility in this regard than they were not too many years ago. The television series *Star Trek*, for example, was very cavalier about the use of diegetic cameras during the program's initial run in the 1960s. The large viewscreen on the bridge often showed images of crew members on the surface of a barren planet as if they had taken a camera down there and planted it on the ground in front of them. However, those familiar with the series know there never was a camera visible or referred to during those initial three years. The near omniscience of the bridge viewscreen was never explained. In contrast to this, the 1987–88 manifestations of *Star Trek*, set some 70 years further into the future, are careful to render on the bridge viewscreen only those images that might be recorded by a camera. There is even occasional mention of cameras in the new program, although they still are not seen. There is no longer a visual link between the bridge crew members and their mates who have beamed down into places that could not be seen by a camera. Audio communication suffices.

In his work with multi-screens, Herbert Zettl studied the ways in which different screens could foster "screen Gestalt," defined as "the perception of separate screens as an organic whole" (8). On-screen screens, it would seem, derive their visual interest from the disunity they cause. They call attention to themselves and the images upon them because they are disruptions to the space/time unity of the whole. Yet if screen Gestalt is challenged, narrative unity is recouped. The on-screen images have their role as part of the story, the space they depict is space which the viewer can position relative to the shot's primary diegetic space.

With growing frequency it is considered "ideal" to deliberately render a view as a camera would see it and as somebody would see that view on a screen. The space in such cases is not limited by the walls of the set or even the boundary of the horizon. With an on-screen screen new spaces can be revealed that permit a single shot to have the kind of limitless spatial depth otherwise only renderable with a split screen. However, unlike a split screen image, the on-screen screen also demands the viewer be conscious of the presence of a diegetic camera. This demand was subtly present even in the early Uncle Josh, but while once a novelty it is now becoming part of our most entrenched shooting, editing, and viewing strategies.

Notes

1 Split screen use in these examples as well as in television sports seems to follow logically from multi-screen use in a video production control room. Just as directors of live television can select from an array of angles and images on the

camera monitors before them, so too can viewers of split screens select from particular screen segments that appear divided in front of them.

2   An analysis of the continuity editing system used by Hollywood will reveal the great extent to which the idea of "best view" or "invisible spectator" serves as a guiding principle. For example, see Bordwell, Staiger, Thompson. Even non-Hollywood films have made famous the notion of the camera as an "invisible wit ness" that gives the viewer keen, although not omniscient, access to the diegetic world. For example, see Bazin.

3   Conversation with Peter Wagg, Oct. 21, 1988. Wagg professes to hold no bitterness about *Max Headroom*'s cancellation, and blames the poor ratings on the show's weekend time slot and also on the systems of ratings gathering in the U.S. The character appeal problem as well as an inconsistency in the way Max Headroom was himself used were suggested to me by Lilli Berko in a conversation on Oct. 19, 1988. Also see Berko.

4   While they look similar to viewfinder markings, the words and marks over the image from Carter's camera are actually supposed to be superimposed within the camera itself behind the lens.

5   In *Ulrich's International Periodicals Directory* 1987–88, vol. 2, p. 2339 (also see 1988–89, vol. 3, pp. 4894–95), the listing of U.S. consumer and trade magazines with the word "video" in the title rose from 23 to 43 in the past year [i.e. 1988–89—ed.] alone. On the matter of the increasing sophistication of the viewing audience, screen writers Carl Sautter and Sam Smiley report that the industry has acknowledged this and that writers are now instructed accordingly. At a seminar entitled "The Changing Shape of Writing in Television and Film" (Cinetex Congress, Sep. 29, 1988, Las Vegas, NV), Sautter explained that far less exposition and explanations of place and time are needed in today's films and television programs. Smiley echoed this at a subsequent workshop (UNLV, Oct. 26, 1988).

Works Cited

Arnheim, Rudolf. *Film as Art*. Berkeley, CA: U of California P, 1957.

Bazin, Andre. *Jean Renoir*. Trans. W. W. Halsey II and W. H. Simon. New York: Dell, 1973.

Berko, Lilli. "Simulation and High-Concept Imagery: The Case of *Max Headroom*." *Wide Angle* 10.4 (Fall 1988): 50–61.

Bordwell, David, Janet Staiger, and Kristin Thompson. *Classical Hollywood Cinema: Film Style and Mode of Production to 1960*. New York: Columbia UP, 1985.

Branigan, Edward. *Point of View in the Cinema: A Theory of Narration and Subjectivity in Classical Film*. New York: Mouton, 1986.

Feuer, Jane. "The Concept of Live Tele vision: Ontology as Ideology." *Regarding Television*. Ed. E. Ann Kaplan. Los Angeles, CA: AFI Monographs, 1983. 12–22.

Fisher, Bob. "Cancelled Max Headroom Leaves Legacy." *American Cinematographer* 69.2 (Feb. 1988): 77–80, 82.

Genette, Gerard. *Narrative Discourse: An Essay in Method*. Trans. Jane E. Lewin. Ithaca, NY: Cornell UP, 1980.

Iser, Wolfgang. *The Act of Reading: A Theory of Aesthetic Response.* Baltimore, MD: Johns Hopkins UP, 1978.

Iser, Wolfgang. *The Implied Reader: Patterns of Communication in Prose Fiction From Bunyan to Beckett.* Baltimore, MD: Johns Hopkins UP, 1974.

Munsterberg, Hugo. *The Film: A Psychological Study.* New York: Dover, 1970.

Olson, Scott R. "Meta-television: Popular Postmodernism." *Critical Studies in Mass Communication* 4.4 (1987): 284–300.

Pudovkin, V. I. Film *Technique and Film Acting.* Trans. Ivor Montagu. New York: Grove, 1958.

Scholes, Robert and Robert Kellogg. *The Nature of Narrative.* New York: Oxford UP, 1966.

Skirrow, Gillian. "Hellivision: An Analysis of Videogames." *High Theory/Low Culture: Analyzing Popular Television and Film.* Ed. Colin MacCabe. New York: St. Martin's, 1986.

Spiegal, Alan. *Fiction and the Camera Eye: Visual Consciousness in Film and the Modern Novel.* Charlottesville: U of Virginia P, 1976.

Wilson, George M. *Narration in Light: Studies in Cinematic Point of View.* Baltimore: Johns Hopkins UP, 1986.

Zettl, Herbert. "Toward a Multi-Screen Television Aesthetic: Some Structural Considerations." *Journal of Broadcasting* 20.4 (Winter 1977): 5–19.

CHAPTER FIFTEEN

Mobile Cinema

Sarah Atkinson

[...]

Mobile filmmaking

The emergence of the mobile phone subgenre of filmmaking has been legitimized through the proliferation of mobile phone-centric film festivals and competitions throughout the world.[1] Notable examples of the form include *Night Fishing (Paranmanjang)* (Dir: Park Chan-wook, 2011, Japan) which was shot entirely on an iPhone. The director attached a 35 mm lens to the iPhone's camera in order to achieve the filmic look. *Olive* (Dir: Hooman Khalili and Pat Gilles, 2013, USA) was shot using the Nokia N8 smartphone. In this case the filmmakers hacked the phone to disable the automatic focus and zoom functions. The phone was then mounted on various rigs including a remote-controlled helicopter. Neither *Night Fishing* nor *Olive* carries the legacy of their medium within the text; the results are cinematic in their aesthetic quality in an attempt to render imperceptible the tools of production.

Both films eschew the characteristics and mobile vernacular[2] traditionally associated with portable recording such as unstable imagery, shaky camera moves, distorted audio, and sickness-invoking motion. [... D]espite the mobile phones' portability, in these cases the use of the medium does not necessarily allow the director or camera operator to get closer to the action. The ancillary equipment attached to the phones, which are essentially deployed as data storage devices, prohibit any intimacy between the director and their subjects which would usually be facilitated by the mobile phone form.

In contrast to these examples is *SOTCHI 255* (Dir: Jean-Claude Taki, 2010) which was shot using different mobile phones in order to draw out their respective and distinctive textural aesthetics such as varying image quality and contrasting screen resolutions in order to imbue different tonalities into the fabric of the film.

Rage (2009, Dir: Sally Potter, UK) was the first ever feature film to be designed for mobile phone viewing, and one which embedded the mobile phone symbiotically into the processes of production, execution, aesthetics, distribution and consumption. The use of the mobile phone was an integral facet of the production process; although the film itself was shot using a conventional video camera held by the director, test images were taken using a mobile phone. The resultant narrative diegesis clearly implicates the mobile phone in its creation, revealing that each of the protagonists is addressing the fictional camera operator Michelangelo who is filming each of their private exchanges using his mobile phone. It transpires that Michelangelo is latterly posting these films to his website, without the informed consent of his subjects. Yet to help the audience understand and appreciate the implications of the characters' revealing on-screen disclosures, the film makes a thematic reference to the emergent notions of public and private discourses played out on line by the characters. It also invokes Anne Friedberg's observation of the 'increased centrality of the mobilized and virtual gaze as a fundamental feature of everyday life'.[3]

The film, a take on the New York fashion industry, signals another play on form and content, in which thematic concerns are expressed compositionally; the actors are shot against green-screen and the resultant aesthetics imply a photographic fashion shoot. The actors are framed in head and shoulder or facial dose-up shots invoking a first-person mobile phone aesthetic whilst also ensuring optimum visual clarity for its intended mode of viewing on a small, mobile phone screen. An intimacy between actor and director (and subsequently between character and audience) is achieved by the hyphenate writer-director also working as the camera operator. The one-to-one working environment then translates to the one-to-one viewing experience. Hand-held and uncut aesthetics also invoke both liveness and authenticity. The digitality of the film is further imbued by the vibrant palette of colours that are used for the monotone backgrounds which were sampled from an aspect of the on-screen actor, for example from an item of clothing or their eyes, rendering emotion as both a visible and tangible asset. The use of these highly saturated digitally composited backgrounds which expand the film's tonal spectrum, somehow break with the regime of verisimilitude created by the hand-held aesthetics, revealing a highly crafted and directed endeavour.

These examples where technology and technique make indelible marks on the form are what Christian Metz has referred to as 'discursive imprints' which he notes extend 'into the very text of the film'.[4]

Rage was released simultaneously as a theatrical release and also as a downloadable film via *Babelgum* (for free) to be watched on a mobile phone, in the one-to-one modality for which it was intended. The premiere of the film included a live Q and A which linked a number of the actors via synchronous video conferencing to the physical location of the British Film Institute (BFI), and thus completed the loop of the film's continuous interchange between emerging technological practices and their fusion right from conception all the way to reception and at all stages in-between.

The launch of the iPad in April 2010 opened up further possibilities and affordances for cinematic-style storytelling with its larger portable screen surface. The simplified composition necessitated by *Rage* and the small-screen size of the mobile phone was no longer an inhibiting factor for filmmakers working with portable devices.

Mobile film viewing

The widespread use of tablets initiated by the iPad's release has led to the emergence of films being created specifically for the iOS platform, making the tablet the locus of the entire experience for stand-alone pieces of cinema in their own right (and not subordinate promotional additions supporting a more substantial narrative main-event). Unique opportunities exist within this medium in which the delivery mechanism and distribution method are one in the same. This duality has been exploited by a number of filmmakers who would otherwise have been precluded from releasing their films to the public by traditionally exclusive and prohibitive distribution methods.

The Silver Goat (2012) was the first feature film to be created exclusively for the iPad, the first to be released as an app in the UK and several other countries, and the first in the world to have an iPad-only premiere melding the viewing experience with the delivery mechanism. The premiere took place on a London Route Master Bus which traversed many of the film's locations throughout the city whilst the audience members watched the film on their individual iPads.[5] *The Silver Goat* is a film told in perpetual motion, with many of the two-shot conversations taking place within uncut sequences which serve to retain a transitory continuum whilst the characters move seamlessly throughout geographic space, walking or travelling the streets of London. This thematic transience also acknowledges the mode in which it will be viewed, on a portable device where the audience member is most likely to be on the move. Furthermore, the inclusion of numerous internal monologues which reveal the interiority of the main characters also enhances the personalization of the viewing experience envisaged as a solo head-phone-wearing endeavour.

More recently *Haunting Melissa* (2013) was a film released for iOS devices by *Hooked Digital Media*. It tells the story of a recently bereaved girl, trying to uncover the truth behind her mother's death in the absence of her father. Told through first-person means, the story is presented deploying a number of techniques using mediated forms of communication that are inherent to the tablet form. We are party to webcam conversations between Melissa and her friends, video diaries (that Melissa is encouraged to make by her psychologist), instant messaging (IM) sessions, filmed action by the characters, CCTV footage and voicemail messages all of which invoke the now-familiar found footage conventions of horror films. Subjected to Melissa's one-to-one monologues via the medium of the video diary and her effusive first-person commentary as she navigates and negotiates the implied haunted spaces of her home and surrounding locale, we experience what Monika Fludernik describes as 'the mimetically motivated evocation of human consciousness',[6] an alternate way of experiencing the story which does 'not only rely on the teleology of plot'.[7] By revealing Melissa's interiority within these private exchanges, a seemingly intimate and personalized viewing experience is facilitated. The film thus exemplifies the same endemic aesthetic as *The Silver Goat* did in its use of internal monologue, invoking the singular headphone-wearing spectator.

During the IM sessions between Melissa and her friends we see the computer screen on which the exchanges are taking place, watching the messages manifest in real-time. The voice mail messages are audio-only instances whereby we listen to various messages (including those from her father), which are occasionally occluded by a sonic spectral presence, a combination of white-noise interference and a whispering female voice. This is also the audible trigger that indicates that the next piece of content is ready to view on the viewer's iPad, the app seemingly 'haunts' the viewer through these intermittent 'push' notifications,[8] which are a native feature of app-based communication devices. The disembodied haunting voice emits the name 'Melissa' from the iPad at random times throughout the experience at night or day without warning (in the same way that a new email message alert would sound). Being on the receiving end of these sonic metaphors indicative of a haunting is an unsettling experience and invokes the uncanny within the audience. Haunting pervades through all of the representational technologies deployed within the narrative. In addition to the camera, the IM message feed is similarly infiltrated by a spectral presence. In Chapter Ten, the character of Brandon chats with Melissa via the feed, but as his messages become increasingly aggressive, coupled with the fact that the message highlights are coloured black portend that all is not as it seems.

The structuring principle of *Haunting Melissa* is one of chapterized fragmentation in which episodes are released at varying temporal moments across a number of weeks. From the audience member's point of view content is released sporadically, although a predetermined schedule has been established by the filmmakers. The app's interface presents the episodic content with intermittent sub-episodic fragments in-between. Once downloaded and viewed, content can be re-watched and also bookmarked.

The app experience includes what Director Neal Edelstein has branded 'dynamic story elements' whereby subtle shifts in content occur during a secondary viewing of specific scenes. These include the appearance (and subsequent disappearance) of spectral reflections and apparitions within the videos. These mediated hauntings mark a suffusion of the story into the iPad. This is mirrored at the level of film plot; Melissa also experiences the appearances and disappearances of spectral presences that she has captured on video. In Chapter Six of the film, Melissa talks to her therapist, Dr. Carroway, to explain that the videos are different each time she watches them 'sometimes things are there, sometimes things are not there'. This is echoed in the user experience of re-watching some of the chapters, whereby the 'dynamic story elements' manipulate and change the content; again we experience a suggestive haunting of the technological apparatus. These techniques subtly implicate the unsettling presence of mobile technologies and anxieties around their use. *Haunting Melissa* can be viewed as the latest in a lineage of cultural artefacts which explore the haunting of technology. As Susan Schupli observes:

> Thomas Watson's early experiments with the telephone included using the apparatus to try and contact voices from the dead. Bell's demonstration of the first telephone, were met with skepticism and fear from an audience dislocated from their points of origin. These early metaphors of haunted technology and ghosts in the machine continue to inform contemporary notions of telepresence and disembodiment.[9]

The deployment of iOS app technology which can be updated at any time, and allows for the interpolation of additional content imbues the film viewing experience with a protean quality and signifies the conflict between the material possession (of the iPad and its constituent apps) and its arcane and evanescent nature, which can be changed at any time outside of the audience members' control. Edelstein defines this capability to make real-time edits and changes as 'the power of the application technology. It's something that could never be done in a movie or a TV show, or any other form of delivered media'.[10] Both content and form align to invoke temporality and insecurity around the veracity of media, redolent of prior debates of authenticity around the reliable indexicality of photographs and films. Impermanence is inextricably linked and embedded into these new forms. The level of control that the creators are able to assert upon the experience is countered by the audience members' unexpected engagements

Edelstein noted how one audience member had freeze-framed over a hundred instances and then uploaded them to the social media forum via *Flickr*. He stated:

> I took the body of the film and I cut it down every scene into 10 seconds, and I took all that footage and I destroyed it, and I ended up with some really fantastic weird footage that I cut into these cameras which are seemingly turning on and off, so you'd see glimpses of images, of things that are coming in the future.[11]

This particular audience member's desire to capture and share these oracular moments resonates with Mary Anne Doane's assertion (although she is applying this to close-up moments in narrative feature film) that exemplify 'a desire to stop the film, to grab hold of something that can be taken away, to transfer the relentless temporality of the narratives unfolding to a more manageable temporality of contemplation'.[12]

In the creation of these frozen instants, the audience member here engages with what Mulvey calls 'The "aesthetics of delay"' which make 'visible its materiality and its aesthetic attributes, but also engages an element of play and of repetition compulsion'.[13] Through their freeze framing, capture, annotation and discussion evidenced within surrounding social media outlets associated with the *Haunting Melissa* experience the audience's advanced engagement in their own version of textual analysis is demonstrated. The producers have since responded to these audience practices by embedding a 'screen capture' button into the interface within a subsequent version update of the app.

An exemplar of the advancement of cinematic storytelling techniques within the mobile form in its production and delivery, and an indication of audience sophistication and increasing literacy in its reception, *Haunting Melissa* is also textually underpinned by an implicit discourse of technological anxiety.

[...]

Tablet apps are also being created for other cultural forms where cinema is not the dominant media but where the product incorporates cinematic and filmic elements. *MirrorWorld*, the iPad app created by *Mirada* [...] launched in April 2013 and is based on Cornelia Funke's books *Reckless* and *Fearless*. Funke has written over twenty fantasy books aimed at young adults and the publication of her latest book was designed to coincide with the release of the *MirrorWorld* app. *Mirada* aimed to create 'a living storybook' which would far exceed the aesthetic and experiential capabilities of an illustrated eBook. *MirrorWorld* contains fifteen short stories, which all have audio narration and enhanced features such as access to recipes, storyscapes, interactive video pieces, 3D environments, animated illustrations and 3D models of the fantastical creatures.

A blend of old and new methods were employed to create this innovative constellation of additional content which includes over 110 minutes of live action with actors performing short scenes, moving illustrations, handmade sculpture and handmade custom fabric art. The content is also accompanied by its own atmospheric music score created by Icelandic film composer Atli Örvarsson which plays throughout. The meticulously fashioned app emanates audio-visual ebullience, the creation and experience of which is unencumbered by the traditional printed page. Funke expressed a profound reverence for the iPad form, over that of film adaptation. She stated:

I've been through seven movie adaptations now, none of them reflected in any way the images I had in my own head. [...] And having them shrink the work of two years to two hours, can be really painful, so it was a unique experience, it surpassed all my expectations creatively, it took it to a level that I had never expected, I'm an illustrator myself so images for me are extremely important.[14]

The premise of the *Mirror World* story is an exploration of what lays behind the mirror. The opening text states 'There a certain mirrors that offer you an opportunity' and this particular iteration will provide 'a passage to another realm'. The opening scene then activates the device's webcam in order to supplant the viewer's reflection onto the screen within the frame of a mirror. The surface of the vitreous screen/mirror can then be manipulated by the touch of the viewer's finger tips or via movement of the head which cause the surfaces of the screen to ripple like water as the underlying depths of the story are revealed, momentarily evoking the porous boundary of the interface between reader and story, phantasy and reality.

Mirror World's predisposition and predilection to the format of the book is expressed through an affinity to the formal conventions of a printed book, such as chapters, page turns and textured paper. The stories can be navigated by a contents page or through the exploration of the 3D environment of the Ogre Tavern which serves as the homepage to the experience, and can be returned to at any time. There are a number of enchanted artefacts within the tavern environment and these act as interactive diegetic portals to other forms of content and the constituent aspects of the story. When clicked, the artefacts allow the viewer to 'see the spectacle' or 'read the story', taking the viewer to another part of the experience. Unique to *Mirror World* compared to other interactive eBooks is the embedded hapticality in the use of the touch-screen form, invoking a closeness and intimacy in which the content can literally be manipulated by the viewer's finger tips and physical movements. Hapticality as defined by Laura Marks is in opposition to:

> Optical visuality [which] depends on a separation between the viewing subject and the object. Haptic looking tends to move over the surface of its object rather than to plunge into illusionistic depth, not to distinguish form so much as to discern texture. It is more inclined to move than to focus, more inclined to graze than to gaze.[15]

Mirror World represents an evolution of a textually haptic language, through various techniques. Textual hapticity is a term I used to denote a kinaesthetic perception of the on-screen representations of materials. Within *Mirror World*, this textual hapticity is imbued in the perceptible grain and colouration of the parchment upon which much of the text is read, and also through the surface of the mirror and the reflection in water. A pseudo-haptic engagement is invoked in these inherently illusory instances since the textures are obviously indiscernible through the swipes of the user on the hardened-shell of the screen. Said Funke

> they had programmed the structure of the paper, with the writing, to make it feel real [...] it's very interesting that you can work in a very 'bookish' way although you have such a modern media. And it's very unique for Mirada that they do work a lot by hand, so many of the drawings were done on paper and the sculptures were from clay.[16]

Mirror World not only induces this mode of textual hapticality as implicated by Marks, it simultaneously evokes both graze and gaze through the physically responsive modalities which it facilitates through a corporeal engagement with the screen, which serves to bring the contiguity between the story world and the reader ever closer. By holding the iPad and physically moving it around the audience's own 360-degree environment reveals aspects of *Mirror World*'s three-dimensional space giving the viewer an enhanced impression that they are physically inhabiting the space of the Ogre Tavern and the other 3D environments. The iPad transforms into a lenticular device which provides a diegetic portal into another dimension. This effect is achieved through the gyroscopic-routing feature. Combining these features, the work invokes both a figurative and literal 'look behind the mirror' positioning the iPad as the portal into the depths of the story. [...]

Second screens

'Second screen' is the relatively new term used to identify instances whereby mobile phones, smartphones, tablets or computers are used in synchronization and in subordination with a dominant 'first screen' experience. This could include text messages, tweets or posts targeted at a specific hashtag that has been published by a television programme, to view additional scenes on the web, to engage in live chats, both synchronously and asynchronously. Hitherto, this has predominantly been a practice used by television. The context within which this term will be applied in this chapter will be to cinematic second screen experiences, firstly to access factual-based content (behind-the-scenes) and secondly to experience fiction-based narrative enhancements and extensions.

Factual

The second screen apps are to be considered as the latest in the lineage of audience exposure to the omnidiegetic behind-the-scenes processes of production, a practice which started as early as the birth of cinema itself. Despite the assertion from Winifried Nöth and Nina Bishara that 'For decades, films used to conceal the traces of their production, for example the details of the film studio and the staff behind-the-scenes, as much as possible with the purpose of creating a perfect real-life illusion',[17] the antecedents of these practices as evidenced in early cinema belie this claim. The behind-the-scenes phenomena whereby '"how is it done?" outweighs "what does the film mean?"'[18] first manifested in print form and film reels, which then moved to television broadcasts, later migrating to video special features, before finding a more established home within DVD bonus features, which are recently being supplanted by Blu-ray discs. The second screen modality is the latest in this succession of technologies to present the behind-the-scenes inner-workings.

[...]

The second screen strategy increasingly also involves the launch of a free app to accompany the film's release on Blu-ray. At the time of writing a small number of these are available in the *Apple App Store*, all for free which deploy audio synchronization[19] in order to simultaneously deliver content to the second screen in a way that directly correlates with the content in the main screen. Up until recently, this technology has mainly been used in broadcasting environments and in commercial contexts. For example, the *Grey's Anatomy Sync App* launches interactive content at specific moments during the televised episodes. These include audience opinion polls, quizzes, character biographies, behind-the-scenes footage, production details and image galleries. The app has a social layer enabling live synchronous chat between fans. The accumulation of fan cultural capital is made possible by the built in 'badge-earning' capabilities which are awarded when audience members virtually check-in to in-world locations. The commercial imperative of the use of the second screen in this particular context manifests through the Lexus advertisements which intercut the show and are rendered interactive by the app.

Current free second screen examples available for iOS devices and Blu-ray - enabled film releases include *Prometheus* (2012), *Sherlock Holmes: A game of shadows* (2011), *The King's Speech* (2010), *The Amazing Spiderman* (2012), *The Smurfs* (2011) and *Total Recall* (2012). *Prometheus* has been chosen from this selection for further consideration on account of the depth of access into the layers of the process that the app facilitates through its foregrounding of the deconstruction of various spectacular sequences.

The *Prometheus* app enables two alternate ways in which to experience additional content; viewers can 'Enter the archives' to access what appears to be the entire corpus of materials relating to the film's production. Alternatively, the materials can be accessed in synchronicity and interpolated within the film itself, via the Blu-ray player and the wireless network (a manual sync can also be activated) in order to trigger the content at the relevant temporal moments within the film's diegesis – on-screen action correlates to behind-the-scenes materials. The media is delivered within a corporatized interface that reflects and enshrines the *Weyland Industries* brand identity. This viewing mode, in which the audience can constantly switch between the registers of fictionality and its construction, invokes a metafictional experiences and awareness, which as Patricia Waugh states is 'A fiction that both creates an illusion and lays bare that illusion'.[20]

The multiple types and effusive amount of additional content include the storyboards (here known as *Ridleygrams*), conceptual art, excerpts from the making-of documentary, deleted scenes and alternate takes, costume designs, vehicle designs, pre-visualizations, motion galleries and the 'Peter Weyland files' [...] amongst others. The second screen alerts the viewer when the different items became accessible at temporal moments within the film's timeline, via a countdown clock to coincide with the on-screen action. The static art works flick through in synchronization with the scene to which it originates. At the point of which we are first introduced the character of David (the A.I. robot) in the film, the 'un-boxing' advertisement [...] is triggered on the second screen. Similarly, when the characters are first introduced to the holographic representation of an aged Peter Weyland, the main feature pauses to allow the *TED Talk* to play. These were both key elements of the pre-theatrical release campaign for the film and illuminate instances whereby, as Elsaesser states, 'the production process can take on a textual form'.[21]

The app's preferences can be set to automatically freeze the main screen feature when a second screen video clip is available to view which disrupts the narrative flow and leads to a subjugated viewing experience which creates moments of what Raymond Bellour denoted as *punctum*,

> 'a kind of wound' opened up by the automaton leads to the film's mechanism, to the 'inside', which, like the inside of the beautiful doll, needs to be disguised to maintain its credibility. Film subjected to repetition and return, when viewed on new technologies, suffers from the violence caused by extracting a fragment from the whole that, as in a body, 'wounds' its integrity But in another metaphor, this process 'unlocks' the film fragment and opens it up to new kinds of relations and revelations.[22]

In addition, at certain moments the viewer is able to 'swipe' the second screen content onto the main television screen, momentarily supplanting the main film, literally subordinating it to secondary importance. The behind-the-scenes, making-of aspects of the film demonstrate the various techniques that were used, and the labour of the film set. For example, in one clip which corresponds with the crew's discovery of the alien DNA 'pods', we are shown an excerpt of the documentary which details how a ceramicist individually hand-crafted the pots, engraved them with a language and fired them to give a metallic effect.

Moreover, the omniscient nature of the *Prometheus* second screen experience leads to heightened questioning around the presence and identity of the director, in the case of *Prometheus*, the authorial presence of Ridley Scott ensures an ever-present and enduring directorial imprint as David Bordwell noted: 'Directors' statements of intent guide comprehension of the film…More broadly, the author becomes the real world parallel to the narrational presence'[23] and according to Gray such commentaries seek to 'append aura, author, and authenticity to the text'.[24] By selecting the director's commentary Catherine Grant comments that these turn 'the "original" (theatrical) experience of watching the film *as fiction* into one in which the film's existing visual track is employed as graphic illustration of a teleological story of its own production'.[25]

More recently, these authorial commentaries have permeated the exclusive cinema arena. *Looper* (2012) released an in-theatre audio commentary track online during the theatrical release phase of the film, encouraging viewers to download it onto their MP3 players to listen to in the cinema during the film screening. This was done to encourage repeat viewing (and an increase in box office revenue). At the beginning of the film, the director states: 'Please do not do this on your first viewing of the movie, that's maybe a little bit of a ploy to get your extra theater-going dollars, but regardless please, it will spoil it entirely, see it clean at least once first'.[26]

The capacity of the Blu-ray alongside the second screen facilitates the inclusion of far more content demonstrating the cumulative nature of film production which amasses so much material whilst enabling and engendering the polyvocality of a film's production through the inclusion of numerous and varied production personnel. As Paul Arthur states '[…] the form has been proliferating, and mutating, at a speed that dwarfs that of the production of "original" features'.[27]

The *Prometheus* app is also the nexus for social media discussions around the film facilitating connectivity between *Facebook*, *Twitter*, *Instant Chat* and *GetGlue*, as well as providing access to the *Internet Movie Database (IMDb)* to access cast and crew profiles. These provide opportunities for audiences to demonstrate what Klinger has referred to as their 'cinematic acumen'.[28]

There are generic apps which enable this type of activity such as *Social Commentary* which enables audiences members to add and read comments in synchronicity with the timeline of a film, independently of the authorized discourses, which other audience members can watch and contribute to whilst watching the film. These instances usurp the position of the professional expert with that of the amateur-expert hyphenate, and provide the habitus for the 'cinema fetishist' who Metz defined as 'the person who is enchanted at what the machine is capable of'.[29] Furthermore, these apps and their related practices signal a move towards 'social film', whereby the film becomes the starting point of the subsequent activity that occurs online after a film's release […].

A schismatic divides critics around the perception of these materials which on the one hand are seen as being prosaic applications, subordinate to a commercial rubric, providing audiences with a pseudo-interactive opportunity which facilitates little more than an engagement with an advertisement or product, as Jim Stewartson opined that 'Even the category "second screen" implies that these apps have an inferiority complex'[30] to on the other, those who perceive these materials to in many cases ameliorate and supersede the primary viewing experience, and to be responsive to educational imperatives.

Just as experiments took place with the inception of DVD into its interactive storytelling potential in the mid-1990s,[31] so too are experimentations into the potential of the second screen as a storytelling device starting to emerge. Some key commercial examples of interactive narrative DVDs in the 1990s included *Tender Loving Care* (1997) and *I'm Your Man* (1998),[32] latter examples in the mid-2000s include *Late Fragment* (2007) and *Switching* (2003) where more nuanced and intuitive opportunities for interaction were offered embedded into the fabric of the story. In the case of *Late Fragment*, there were looped moments where the camera angle would switch between the three characters allowing the user to choose whose pathway to follow. *Switching* tells the story of a troubled relationship between the central characters, through a constant series of loops, which the viewer navigates between using the 'enter' button on the remote control 'uniquely determining your own film experience'.[33] Despite these examples which were few and far between, the rigidity of the DVD technical architecture stymied any significant developments that evolve new narratives and dramaturgies. The advancement of iOS technologies far surpasses these limitations, thus presenting a more propitious opportunity to advance and complexify audience engagements. Untrammelled by the physicality and permanence of DVD/Blu-ray, app data can be updated and changed at any time allowing for mercurial, dynamic, story experiences that can be constantly evolved, updated and changed. The push notifications, updates and changes perpetuate an 'upgrade culture' where 'novelty itself has intrinsic value'[34] and where narrative itself can be upgraded.

Exploitation of the second screen mode as a narrative enhancement to the main event will now be discussed in the examples of the recently released *APP* and *RIDES* which represent the early and the most recent experiments of the form of dual screen simultaneous cinema.

Fiction

APP[35] (2013), a horror film created in the Netherlands and distributed in twenty countries including France, Germany and China combines a feature film with a synchronizable smartphone app. Audiences are invited to download the accompanying app prior to entering the cinema and then encouraged to access the app in the auditorium itself, an environment in which spectators are more accustomed to being asked to turn off their mobile phones. Instead the opening screen states, 'We kindly ask you to switch on your cellular phone' and 'Open the APP'. In addition to synchronized content, audience members are also able to access a number of items of behind-the-scenes content via the app.

APP's use of the second screen during the viewing of the main feature film as an enhanced delivery mechanism augments the storyline which is centred on the lead character of Anna. A smartphone app known as 'Iris' has mysteriously infiltrated her phone (the same 'Iris' app which the audience members have downloaded). The central preoccupation of the narrative is the precipitation of Anna's demise and those around her seemingly caused by the app. The second screen reveals different pieces of content in synchronization with the viewing experience of the main feature film. These momentary, brief (silent) vignettes include point of view video from Anna's camera phone, alternate cinematic angles of certain scenes, CCTV footage, text-based content (for example a news item reporting the fatality in the pre-title opening sequence) and personal text messages between the on-screen characters.

The vibration of the audience members' phone acts as the indicative trigger alerting the audience that the second screen is about to become active. This is reminiscent of an earlier novelty cinema experiment in the 1950s in which the underside of the audiences seats were fitted with a motorized device that would make the seats vibrate at specific moments in the (horror) film in order to provoke a dramatic reaction in the audience.[36]

The simulation of the app on the audience members' phone disrupts the film viewing experience, but in a way that the viewer is enabled to take on both streams of information. This is in contrast to the other second screen apps which have been discussed previously, which interrupt the flow of the film and its narrative unity and congruence, by literally pausing the main screen in order for the viewer to watch the second screen flow unimpeded. *APP*'s director explains the production process behind this:

> Confronted by a picture-in-picture, side-by-side storyline, you need to determine when you're going to produce your second screen clues or story elements without your audience being distracted or being driven away from the regular plot[ ] and so we had to re-cut some scenes so people wouldn't miss the important things [...]1 it's all dependent on timing, because your eye can only focus on one thing and not on both things exactly at the same time.[37]

The 'Iris' app literally terrorizes the film's characters (and by implication – the audience), infecting their everyday lives, through surveillance. Iris both captures and transmits Anna's private moments which are then spread like a virus to other computer systems, other people's phones and to public screens, with humiliating, violent and in some cases fatal results. In one scene a looped image of Anna undressing and entering the shower is transmitted to all screens in an electrical store, thus invoking surveillance technologies, which has a destabilizing effect on both the characters and the audience, implying not just a social anxiety towards new technologies, but presenting them as a violent, transgressive and dangerous force. A much more explicit presentation is enacted compared to the oblique and suggestive references noted in *Haunting Melissa*.

The transmission of the additional content on the second screen transforms the phone into a key expositional tool, in which synchronous diegetic portals [...] can be accessed. These moments tend to occur around instances of fraught action on the main screen and invoke a dramatic irony in which audience members gain knowledge that the on-screen characters are precluded from. Moreover, app users also have the upper hand over other members of the viewing audience who do not have access to the second screen app. A significant example of this is demonstrated in the instant message feed between the doctor and the character of Tim, Anna's disaffected ex-boyfriend, revealing a conspiratorial relationship between the two and key clues as to where Iris originated from and how Anna's brother is a key to unlocking the app's purpose. These synchronous diegetic portals function in both anileptic and proleptic modes. For example, text messages between the characters portend latter on-screen action implicating the app's prescience. In an early sequence, Anna receives a picture of a gun via the app as well as hearing telephone calls made to emergency services. The gun acts as a predictive visualization and the recorded phone calls as predictive sonifications both of which I would identify as proleptic diegetic portals. These elements reveal and premediate the future tragedy of the college professor's suicide. Furthermore, this particularly disturbing scene of the professor's demise implicates mobile phone technologies as the root cause. The event is prompted by Iris' broadcast of the professor's illicit affair with a male student which had previously been transmitted to the lecture theatre screens and the other students' mobile phones. During this scene the professor calls everyone to use their phones to record the event, thus making an explicit reference to the constant filming, logging, capturing, surveilling and sharing upon which contemporary social practices are predicated. It also makes an implicit suggestion of both the mediation and desensitization of traumatic events in the media in contemporary society.

Further levels of dramatic irony are experienced in the climactic scene, in which a charge-bar appears on the app indicating that (our) the (character's) phone is ostensibly powering up to dangerous levels. As an audience member we are aware that this signifies something is going to happen to the phone and tension inevitably builds as the digits dick down closer to zero at which point the phone explodes with fatal consequences. As a non-app user, the tension would not have been built in the same way. It is instances such as these that a new storytelling technique is being evolved, and a new dramaturgy is being developed [...]. The director confirms that the second screen enables 'a completely different dynamic on how you perceive the film. The question of the film is who is behind the app, and the audience gets a first clue of that, the first confirmation of that on the second screen'.[38] Audience members without the app would have an abstruse and recondite experience in contrast.

A social comment on the quotidian nature of the mobile phone and the protagonists' intransigence to surrender the device despite the havoc and disruption that it causes, *APP* relays the consequences of our new reliance on the ubiquitous smartphone device and its invasion of our lives and subversion of our privacy. It is suggestive of mobile technologies' transgressing the border between public and private spaces and inculcating us into acts of privacy violation. Interestingly, *APP* uses the same audio watermarking technology previously described. The original application of this technology, which still remains its predominant use, is to identify illegally filmed copies of films. The audio signal carries with it the date and the location of the cinema to identify where and when the copy had been acquired.[39] This choice of surveillance technology adds a further literal dimension to *APP* in which audience behaviours can be watched, tracked and reprimanded. Rendering the subordination of the audience in its use of the app, it is also a case of 'The text making strange its own devices'.[40] *APP* presents the deleterious effect of new technologies through its literal demonization of the technology where audience members are subjected to constant and repeated violent and transgressive invocations.

APP unifies theme, form, device and apparatus. It presents a complex interplay and interlocking between form, content and delivery engaging explicitly with anti-technology rhetoric. A cautionary tale concerning the spreadable, social media age where content proliferates in an uncontrolled way and the audience is seemingly usurped by their own technologies.

RIDES created by *Fourth Wall Studios*, currently in public beta[41] phase, has been in development for the past five years. The company has produced a number of stand-alone episodic and serialized interactive experiences designed for single-viewer mode across second and third screens via the *RIDES.tv* online channel.

The breadth of content which spans the genres of drama, horror, mystery, sci-fi and comedy has been designed to demonstrate and showcase the *RIDES* platform with a view to monetizing its use and to encourage deployment by other companies and creators, with a view to achieving massification in the longer term. *Fourth Wall Studios*, a hybrid software, production and design company, was established by the organization known as *42 Entertainment*, the creators behind many of the instances of extended cinema [...] including *The Beast, I Love Bees, Year Zero* and *The Dark Knight, Why So Serious?* campaigns. Jim Stewartson explained that the aim of *Fourth Wall Studios* is to build original content that was going to be accessible to a much broader array of audiences that would reconcile the inherent inaccessibility of ARGs. Mass-engagement has always been a problem with these abstruse experiences which tend to be, according to Stewartson, 'big open-ended 6-month things where you had to solve enigma puzzles in Swahili'.[42] In addition Stewartson commented that the problem with ARGs is that they do not traditionally work as a stand-alone entity [...] nor have they been commercially successful without the backing of a huge brand. RIDES is so called because its experiences are likened to the expectations and hermetic parameters of a amusement park ride whereby the audience member can see exactly what the entertainment proposition is before making an informed decision whether or not to engage. It's a dearly defined, circumvented experience that 'normal people could do'.

RIDES presents a platform that simultaneously utilizes all of the audience members' digital communication devices (computer, phone and tablet) within a single unified storytelling experience. This new modality responds to multi-tasking behaviours and expectations endemic in a contemporary audience that have evolved around their use in daily life whereby multiple, synchronous data inputs are managed. The RIDES experience embeds these into the fictional experiences it creates. Audience members log into the 'RIDES.tv Sync App' via which they can experience a layered content experience, led by the content on the main 'first' screen. Contemporaneous in-world text messages, phone-calls and emails imbricate throughout the experience. [...] This is achieved through the RIDES proprietary backend which facilitates a live connection between all of the audience members' devices in order to update them in real-time. Audio recognition synchronization is also enabled through a third party system. In contrast to APP, the 'rides' utilize both video and audio, enabling the viewer to access and eavesdrop on phone calls, adding a further opportunity for the invocation of dramatic irony. Bonus scene notifications which unlock additional content can be revealed and navigated to on the graphical timeline which is displayed at the foot of the main screen, both hypermediating and premediating the audience experience, providing a prescient indicator of forthcoming dual-stream (and duplicitous) storytelling moments. For example, in an episode of Redrum, a true-crime murder mystery, the plot-line is centred upon a married couple, and the husband's extramarital relations. This particular 'ride' involves a moment where an on-screen text message is sent to the wife (Lena) and is simultaneously received by the viewer of the sync app. The message reveals photographs of Lena's husband (Carl) in a compromising situation with the other woman (Courtney). The shock and dismay of her revealing these moments is implicated to the audience in their simultaneous discovery. At another moment, the app simulates a mobile phone ring simultaneously with the on-screen character's phone (Gus). The opposite side of the conversation (with Carl) can then be heard through the telephone, this then switches between characters during a scene change.

In addition, at different moments, an opinion poll is taken on (computer) screen, which allows the audience member to express who they feel is responsible for the murder. Stewartson has referred to these moments as 'multiplatform touch points' which 'create dynamic interaction'.[43] An alternate reading of these instances is that they, as in other instances thus far described, can be thought of as synchronous diegetic portals in which the phone acts as a diegetic tool in order to reveal the *real* truth of the on-screen action. In this case it reveals the illicit affair between Carl and Courtney. Moreover, it represents a further example of the narrativization of new technologies and the reflection and refraction of the anxieties surrounding their use. In this particular case it implicates the veracious quality of the new technologies and the practice of 'social surveillance'[44] in which through our voyeuristic engagement with the second screen, we as the viewer are complicit. [...]

In a moment within an episode of *Dirty Work*, the Emmy-nominated serialized comedy, the audience can listen in on the character Pete's inner thoughts via the telephone. Within several sequences of *RVC* the comedy parody of shopping channel *QVC*, the second screen enables a number of alternative vignettes to be viewed in which characters imagine themselves in alternative circumstances as visual versions of the inner monologue. These techniques of expressing character interiority have been a repeated feature of numerous mobile cinema examples, which implicitly acknowledges the single-viewer mode of viewing.

In *6–14, RIDE.tv*'s horror offering, themes of replay, repetition and looping (which are all characteristics of digital media) are played out in which the same character repeatedly re-lives the same moment in time leading to his death. The main protagonists receive a number of telephone calls that are also simultaneously played through the mobile app.

Stewartson describes *RIDES* as 'the novelization of film' on account that it can accommodate multiple and different points of view, as well as deeper insights into exposition, context and subtext and can therefore achieve a level of depth not normally attainable in single-screen media. Stewartson claims that *RIDES* provides 'a time-based way of doing that, in real-time with the story [...] it's like creating 3D for your brain'.[45] This claim [...] signifies the emergence of a digitextuality[46] in emerging cinematic practices.

Conclusion

Characteristic of any technological transformation and its resultant social practices is the inherent exploration and meaning-making behind its implications within the narrative forms themselves. This is illustrative of Marie-Laure Ryan's observations of how 'the intrinsic properties of the medium shape the form of narrative and affect the narrative experience'.[47]

Both responsive and symptomatic of emerging audience behaviours and transitory life styles, all of the examples that have been subject to consideration within this chapter are inextricably linked to the anxieties that new technologies evoke. These modern day cautionary tales about technology have all to some extent either implicitly or explicitly inferred a mistrust for technological advancement and its implications, suggestive of our coining to terms with the acceleration and velocity of information to which we are all a subject.

Within an era of dematerialization and the imminent obsolescence of tangible media forms which are being usurped by the capacity, capability and networkability of mobile media implies that the types of mobile cinema experiences considered herein and the groundswell of emerging projects in beta mean they may soon enjoy newfound prominence within the cinematic ecology. However, they also represent the challenges to be surmounted by content producers who will be expected to satisfy the voracious capacity and capabilities of these new mediums which in turn creates tensions in competing for the audience's splintering attention and ever-fleeting engagement patterns. Content creators will need to be responsive to audience expectation to move towards 'simultaneous shift' initiatives, whereby all extraneous content is made available one point in time. The mediation of process and intramedial aesthetics are at the forefront of many emerging cinematic experiences, in some cases becoming the prevalent mode of engagement by audiences decentralizing the main feature to one experience among many that audiences can engage with.

The rights to *APP* have already been bought by a Hollywood production company, with a view to producing a remake in the next two years. As soon as the trailer was released online, the telephone started to ring for the Dutch production company behind the film, indicating an industry eager to embrace, incorporate and mainstream these new technologies and techniques. Forthcoming is the five-day smartphone thriller app for Peter James' *Dead Man's Tracks* which is currently in development with *Portal Entertainment*. A *Haunting Melissa* 2.0 sequel is already planned and Cornelia Funke has recently established a new company *Breathing Books* as an enterprise through which to extend her interactive e-book oeuvre.

The emergence of touch-screen technologies in the realm of cinema has proven to be an efficacious force, signalling an acceptance of the tablet as an alternatively configured cinematic apparatus. Furthermore, these projects suggest that as audience literacy adapts to medium coalescence, this initial period of enculturation in which we are currently a part is moving into one of acculturation. The examples considered herein represent the pioneering instances which are solidifying the status of these mobile cinematic variants as both a legitimate cultural form and a legitimate object of academic study which should encourage an expansion of scholarship into this area.

[…]

Notes

1   Examples include: *Mobile Film Festival*: Germany, *Festival Pocket Film*: France, *Mobifest*: Toronto, *Ciné Pocket*: Brussels, *The Original iPhone film festival*: USA, *iPhone film festival (IFF)*: LA, USA, *indieFoneFilmFest*: USA, *International Mobil Film Festival*: San Diego, USA.

2   A term based upon Jon Dovey's 'vernacular video', in 'Time Slice: Web Drama and the Attention Economy'; in *Ephemeral Media: Transistory Screen Culture from Television to YouTube*, ed. Paul Grainge (Basingstoke: Palgrave Macmillan, 2011), 146–147. Dovey states that 'the grammar of this vernacular is characterized by affect, intimacy, desire and display' and that it is 'a new visual grammar of consumption driven by the self-constituting practices of its creators'.

3   Anne Friedberg, *Window Shopping: Cinema and the Postmodern* (Berkeley, CA: University of California Press, 1993), 4.

4   Christian Metz, *Psychoanalysis and Cinema: The Imaginary Signifier* (London: Indiana University Press, 1982), 76.

5   Stephen Johns, '*The Silver Goat* Makes World History as First Film to Have iPad Premiere'; *Metro*, 10 May 2012.

6   Monika Fludernik, *Towards a 'Natural' Narratology* (London: Routledge, 1996), 30.

7   Fludernik, *Towards a 'Natural' Narratology*, 30.

8   These are iOS automated alerts that indicate an event, such as new content or software updates for the app. These can manifest as a sound, an-onscreen message or a 'badge' (a red circle containing a numeric value that is appended to an on-screen app icon).

9   Phony CD Rom (2001, Susan Schupli).

10 In an interview with the author, 2 August 2013.

11 In an interview with the author, 2 August 2013.

12 Mary Anne Doane, 'The Close-Up: Scale and Detail in the Cinema', *A Journal of Feminist Cultural Studies* XIV no. 3, 2003:97.

13 Laura Mulvey, *Death 24x a Second: Stillness and the Moving Image* (London: Reaktion Books, 2006), 192.

14 In an interview with the author, 6 September 2013.

15 Laura Marks, *The Skin of the Film: Intercultural Cinema, Embodiment, and the Senses* (Durham, NC: Duke University Press, 2000), 162.

16 In an interview with the author, 6 September 2013.

17 Winifried Nöth, and Nina Bishara, *Self-Reference in the Media* (Berlin: Mouton de Gruyter, 2007), 20.

18 Roger Odin, 'Spectator, Film and the Mobile Phone', in *Audiences: Defining and Researching Screen Entertainment Reception*, ed. Ian Christie (Amsterdam: Amsterdam University Press, 2012), 166.

19 There are a number of commercial-based audio-watermarking systems currently available on the market which include Nielsen's Media-Sync Platform which launched in 2010, which uses audio watermarks already inserted into nearly every TV programme in the United States as part of Nielsen's industry standard TV audience ratings service. (http://www.disneyabctv.com/web/NewsRelease/DispDNR.aspx?id=020111_02). In

addition, *SyncNow* by *Civolution* is an Automatic Content Recognition (ACR) system that powers Shazam and Soundhound. For independent filmmakers, *Gracenote* has recently released an open audio finger printing Software Development Kit (SDK) for iOS and Android called 'Entourage', which enables syncing of additional content television programmes through ACR technology. See Josh Constine, 'Gracenote's New TV Sync API Could Spawn Indie Second-Screen Apps', *TechCrunch*, 19 June 2013, http://techcrunch.com/2013/06/19/second-screen-apps/. The audio creates a fingerprint of the signal and looks it up in *Gracenote*'s global video database, returning metadata and images that can be used to fuel second screen applications. Audio finger-printing works differently to the watermarking system described above, which involves the laying of an additional audio track which carries the sync track across the programme, which can be audible in some cases. Audio finger printing recognizes any part of the actual soundtrack itself; the original content doesn't need to be modified and therefore permission isn't needed for the development of accompanying apps. This could lead to fans and audience members creating their own content to distribute and sync with their favourite programmes, possibly the next technological evolution in fan-based textual production.

20 Patricia Waugh, *Metafiction: The Theory and Practice of Self-Conscious Fiction* (London: Routledge, 1984), 6.

21 Thomas Elsaesser, 'Fantasy Island: Dream Logic as Production Logic', in *Cinema Futures: Cain, Abel or Cable? The Screen Arts in the Digital Age*, ed. Thomas Elsaesser and Kay Hoffman (Amsterdam: Amsterdam University Press, 1998), 143.

22 Mulvey, *Death 24x a Second*, 179.

23 David Bordwell, *Narration in the Fiction Film* (London: Routledge, 1985), 211.

24 Jonathan Gray, *Show Sold Separately: Promos, Spoilers and Other Media Paratexts* (New York: New York University Press, 2010), 83.

25 Catherine Grant, 'Auteur Machines? Auteurism and the DVD', in *Film and Television after DVD*, ed. James Bennett and Tom Brown (London: Routledge, 2008), 111.

26 The track can be downloaded via Sound Cloud: https://sounddoud.comkcjohnso/looper-theatrical-commentary.

27 Paul Arthur, '(In)Dispensable Cinema: Confessions of a "Making-of" Addict', *Film Comment* 40 no. 4, 2004:39.

28 Klinger, 'The DVD Cinephile: Viewing Heritages and Home Movie Cultures', in *Film and Television after DVD*, ed. James Bennett and Tom Brown (London: Routledge, 2008), 26.

29 Metz, *Psychoanalysis and Cinema*, 74.

30 Jim Stewartson, 'Yes, "Transmedia" Is an Empty Buzzword … until It Isn't', *Transmedia Coalition*, 8 May 2013, http://transmediacoalition.com/jstewartson/story/yes-transmedia-is-an-empty-buzzword-until-it-isnt.

31 I explored many of these in my thesis Sarah Atkinson, *Telling Interactive Stories: A Practice-Based Investigation into New Media Interactive Storytelling* (London: School of Arts, Brunel University, 2009).

32 See Chapter Eight, Interlude: *I'm Your Man*: Anatomy of an Interactive Movie in Marie-Laure Ryan, *Narrative as Virtual Reality: Immersion and*

Interactivity in Literature and Electronic Media (Baltimore, MD: The Johns Hopkins University Press, 2001), 271–282.

33 *Switching* DVD inlay.

34 Jon Dovey, and Helen Kennedy, *Game Cultures: Computer Games as New Media* (Maidenhead: McGraw-Hill, 2006).

35 http://www.appdefilm.nl/.

36 This was called *Percepto* and was created for a specific feature 1959 film *The Tingler*, which had been written specifically to incorporate the shaking seats into the story of the film, in Mark Thomas McGee, *Beyond Ballyhoo: Motion Picture Promotion and Gimmicks* (Jefferson, NC: Mcfarland & Co, 2011), 115.

37 In an interview with the author, 12 August 2013.

38 In an interview with the author, 12 August 2013.

39 Which according to Bordwell will '…betray the theater where the video originated'. David Bordwell, *Pandora's Digital Box: Films, Files, and the Future of Movies* (Madison, WI: The Irvington Way Institute Press, 2012), 61.

40 Dana Polan, 'A Brechtian Cinema? Towards a Politics of Self-Reflexive Film', in *Movies and Methods: An Anthology*, ed. Bill Nichols (Berkeley, CA: University of California Press, 1985), 662.

41 http://rides.tv/.

42 In interview with the author, 5 August 2013.

43 http://rides.tv/about-rides/.

44 Alice E. Marwick, 'The Public Domain: Social Surveillance in Everyday Life', *Surveillance & Society* 9 no. 4, 2012:382.

45 In interview with the author, 5 August 2013.

46 Anna Everett, 'Digitextuality and Click Theory', in *New Media: Theories and Practices of Digitextuality*, ed. Anna Everett and John Thornton Caldwell (London: Routledge, 2003), 7.

47 Marie-Laure Ryan, *Narrative across Media: The Language of Storytelling* (Lincoln, NE: University of Nebraska Press, 2004).

CHAPTER SIXTEEN

From *Swann's Way*

Marcel Proust

At Combray, as every afternoon ended, long before the time when I should have to go up to bed, and to lie there, unsleeping, far from my mother and grandmother, my bedroom became the fixed point on which my melancholy and anxious thoughts were centred. Someone had had the happy idea of giving me, to distract me on evenings when I seemed abnormally wretched, a magic lantern, which used to be set on top of my lamp while we waited for dinner-time to come: in the manner of the master-builders and glass-painters of gothic days it substituted for the opaqueness of my walls an impalpable iridescence, supernatural phenomena of many colours, in which legends were depicted, as on a shifting and transitory window. But my sorrows were only increased, because this change of lighting destroyed, as nothing else could have done, the customary impression I had formed of my room, thanks to which the room itself, but for the torture of having to go to bed in it, had become quite endurable. For now I no longer recognised it, and I became uneasy, as though I were in a room in some hotel or furnished lodging, in a place where I had just arrived, by train, for the first time.

Riding at a jerky trot, Golo, his mind filled with an infamous design, issued from the little three-cornered forest which dyed dark-green the slope of a convenient hill, and advanced by leaps and bounds towards the castle of poor Geneviève de Brabant. This castle was cut off short by a curved line which was in fact the circumference of one of the transparent ovals in the slides which were pushed into position through a slot in the lantern. It was only the wing of a castle, and in front of it stretched a moor on which Geneviève stood, lost in contemplation, wearing a blue girdle. The castle and the moor were yellow, but I could tell their colour without waiting to see them, for before the slides made their appearance the old-gold sonorous name of Brabant had given me an unmistakable clue. Golo stopped for a moment and listened sadly to the little speech read aloud by my great-aunt, which he seemed perfectly to understand, for he modified his attitude with a docility not devoid of a degree of majesty, so as to conform to the indications given in the text; then he rode away at the same jerky trot. And nothing could arrest his slow progress. If the lantern were moved I could still distinguish Golo's horse advancing across the window-curtains, swelling out with their curves and diving into their folds. The body of Golo himself, being of the same supernatural substance as his steed's, overcame all material obstacles—everything that seemed to bar his way—by taking each as it might be a skeleton and embodying it in himself: the door-handle, for instance, over which, adapting itself at once, would float invincibly his red cloak or his pale face, never losing its nobility or its melancholy, never shewing any sign of trouble at such a transubstantiation.

And, indeed, I found plenty of charm in these bright projections, which seemed to have come straight out of a Merovingian past, and to shed around me the reflections of such ancient history. But I cannot express the discomfort I felt at such an intrusion of mystery and beauty into a room which I had succeeded in filling with my own personality until I thought no more of the room than of myself. The anaesthetic effect of custom being destroyed, I would begin to think and to feel very melancholy things. The door-handle of my room, which was different to me from all the other doorhandles in the world, inasmuch as it seemed to open of its own accord and without

FIGURE 16.1 *A nineteenth-century magic-lantern show in a domestic setting, 1826–61. The Metropolitan Museum of Art, New York.*

my having to turn it, so unconscious had its manipulation become; lo and behold, it was now an astral body for Golo. And as soon as the dinner-bell rang I would run down to the dining-room, where the big hanging lamp, ignorant of Golo and Bluebeard but well acquainted with my family and the dish of stewed beef, shed the same light as on every other evening; and I would fall into the arms of my mother, whom the misfortunes of Geneviève de Brabant had made all the dearer to me, just as the crimes of Golo had driven me to a more than ordinarily scrupulous examination of my own conscience.

Terms of Display

CHAPTER SEVENTEEN

From *Natural Magick: in XX Bookes*

Giambattista della Porta

Chapter VI – Other operations of a Concave-glass

Before I part from the operations of this Glass, I will tell you some use of it, that is very pleasant and admirable, whence great secrets of Nature may appear unto us. As,

To see all things in the dark, that are outwardly done in the Sun, with the colours of them

You must shut all the Chamber windows, and it will do well to shut up all holes besides, lest any light breaking in should spoil all. Only make one hole, that shall be a hand's breadth and length; above this fit a little leaden or brass Table, and glue it, so thick as a paper; open a round hole in the middle of it, as great as your little finger: over against this, let there be white walls of paper, or white clothes, so shall you see all that is done without in the Sun, and those that walk in the streets, like to Antipodes, and what is right will be the left, and all things changed; and the farther they are off from the hole, the greater they will appear. If you bring your paper, or white Table nearer, they will show less and clearer; but you must stay a while, for the Images will not be seen presently: because a strong similitude does sometimes make a great sensation with the sense, and brings in such an affection, that not only when the senses do act, are they in the organs, and do trouble them, but when they have done acting, they will stay long in them; which may easily be perceived. For when men walk in the Sun, if they come into the dark, that affection continues, that we can see nothing, or very scantly; because the affection made by the light is still in our eyes; and when that is gone by degrees, we see clearly in dark places. Now will I declare what I ever concealed till now, and thought to conceal continually. If you put a small centicular Crystal glass to the hole, you shall presently see all things clearer, the countenances of men walking, the colours, Garments, and all things as if you stood hard by; you shall see them with so much pleasure, that those that see it can never enough admire it. But if you will,

See all things greater and clearer

Over against it set the Glass, not that which dissipates by dispersing, but which congregates by uniting, by both coming to it and going from it, till you know the true quantity of the image, by a due appropinquation of the Centre; and so shall the beholder see more fitly birds flying, the cloudy skies, or clear and blue Mountains that are afar off; and in a small circle of paper (that is

FIGURE 17.1 *Lantern projection of illustrated slides, from* Physiologia Kircheriana Experimentalis *by Athanasius Kircher, 1680. As is often noted, this early image of a magic lantern mistakenly places the lens between lamp and slide, rather than between the slide and projection surface.*

put over the hole) you shall see as it were the Epitomy of the whole world, and you will much rejoice to see it: all things backwards, because they are near to the Centre of the Glass, if you set them farther from the Centre, they will show greater and upright, as they are, but not so clear. Hence you may,

If you cannot draw a Picture of a man or anything else, draw it by this means

If you can but only make the colours. This is an Art worth learning. Let the Sun beat upon the window, and there about the hole, let there be Pictures of men, that it may light upon them, but not upon the hole. Put a white paper against the hole, and you shall so long sit the men by the light, bringing them near, or setting them further, until the Sun casts a perfect representation upon the Table against it: one that is skilled in painting, must lay on colours where they are in the Table, and shall describe the manner of the countenance; so the Image being removed, the Picture will remain on the Table, and in the superficies it will be seen as an Image in the Glass. If you will,

That all shall appear right

This is a great secret; many have tried it, but none could obtain it: For some setting Plain Glasses obliquely against the hole, by reverberation against the Table, they could see some things somewhat direct, but dark and not discernible. I oft-times by putting a white paper obliquely against the hole, and looking just against the hole, could see some things direct: but a Pyramis cut obliquely did show men without proportion, and very darkly. But thus you may obtain your desire: Put against the hole a Convex-glass; from thence let the Image reflect on a Concave-glass: let the Concave-glass be distant from the Centre, for it will make those Images right, that it receives turned, by reason of the distance of the Centre. So upon the hole and the white paper, it will cast the Images of the Objects so clearly and plainly, that you will not wonder a little. But this I thought fit to let you understand, lest you fail in the work, that the Convex- and Concave-glasses be proportionable circles: how you shall do this will be here declared often. I shall show also,

How in a Chamber you may see Hunting, Battles of Enemies, and other delusions

Now for a conclusion I will add that, then which nothing can be more pleasant for great men, and Scholars, and ingenious persons to behold; That in a dark Chamber by white sheets objected, one may see as clearly and perspicuously, as if they were before his eyes, Huntings, Banquets, Armies of Enemies, Plays, and all things else that one desireth. Let there be over against that Chamber, where you desire to represent these things, some spacious Plain, where the Sun can freely shine: Upon that you shall set Trees in Order, also Woods, Mountains, Rivers, and Animals, that are really so, or made by Art, of Wood, or some other matter. You must frame little children in them, as we use to bring them in when Comedies are Acted: and you must counterfeit Stags, Boar, Rhinocerets, Elephants, Lions, and what other creatures you please: Then by degrees they must appear, as coming out of their dens, upon the Plain: The Hunter he must come with his hunting Pole, Nets, Arrows, and other necessaries, that may represent hunting: Let there be Horns, Cornets, Trumpets sounded: those that are in the Chamber shall see Trees, Animals, Hunters Faces, and all the rest so plainly, that they cannot tell whether they be true or delusions: Swords drawn will glitter in at the hole, that they will make people almost afraid. I have often shewed this kind of Spectacle to my friends, who much admired it, and took pleasure to see such a deceit; and I could hardly by natural reasons, and reasons from the Opticks remove them from their opinions, when I had discovered the secret. [...]

Chapter VII – How you may see in the dark what is light without by reason of Torches

[...]

That by night an Image may seem to hang in a Chamber

In a tempestuous night the Image of any thing may be represented hanging in the middle of the Chamber, that will terrifie the beholders. Fit the Image before the hole, that you desire to make to seem hanging in the Air in another Chamber that is dark; let there be many Torches lighted round about. In the middle of the dark Chamber, place a white sheet, or some solid thing, that may receive the Image sent in: for the spectators that see not the sheet, will see the Image hanging in the middle of the Air, very clear, not without fear and terror, especially if the Artificer be ingenious.

CHAPTER EIGHTEEN

Building a Cinema Theatre

Frederick J. Kiesler

It is interesting to note that the original theatre structure in Greece was an amphitheatre, with the action taking place in the middle and the great audience, which was composed of all kinds and classes of men, merely surrounding it. The theatre passed from this democratic state by stages into the nineteenth-century European theatre, which was essentially aristocratic, designed to accommodate relatively small audiences. Our theatre architecture derives from this latter arrangement. The Greek open theatre was forgotten and the proscenium became a frame in which the actors formed a living picture of only two dimensions.

The huge motion picture theatres on Broadway are simply adaptations of this structural outline and utterly unsuited in principle to their purpose. Practically speaking, they depict rather than concentrate, and from an esthetic viewpoint, our modern "movie palaces" defeat their own purpose. The cinema is by nature international, the most ultra-dramatic of any art, and the attempt to give an air of aristocracy in the manner of decorations and furnishings is contrary to the basic purpose of the screen.

Architecturally, there is an enormous difference between the theatre and the cinema. The cinema has all interests concentrated on a single point of two dimensions, while the theatre must have the interest dispersed in three dimensions. This means that the theatre and the cinema require two types of buildings as distinct in form and function as a butcher shop and an office building. The problem has never been approached from this angle. All that has been done has been to adapt old forms and old styles of architecture. And today, a visitor to the most modern motion picture theatre is only conscious of the increase in size and a style of decoration.

The effort in new design can take two courses. It can search for new forms and uses of colour, or it can search for new plan arrangement. The first is never more than a passing fashion and adds nothing of constructive value to the progress of art. The second is enduring in quality and fundamentally constructive in value because it creates a better machine, more perfect in operation and more effective in displaying the cinematic art.

America is a country of great inventive genius, but not, like Europe, of research in the arts. Our thoughts are too securely fastened on the grindstone of production to reflect constructively on what we are doing. In Europe the group from which I come has for years been studying these problems, and from contemporary developments it is safe to say that old forms of the cinema will slowly disappear.

The film has nothing to do with the symphonic, spatial organization of the stage elements. Its task is to break clear of all imitation of the theatre. The film has grown mature enough to create its own form of architecture which must signify 100 per cent cinema. Our age is an optical one. The rapidity of events and their brief duration require a receding apparatus that can register as speedily as possible.[1] It is the eye. The speed of light waves exceeds that of all other waves. The film is the optical flying machine of camera.

This film is a play on surface, the theatre a play in space, and this difference has not been realized concretely in any architecture, either that of the theatre or the cinema. The ideal cinema is the house of silence.

While in the theatre[,] each spectator must lose his individuality in order to be fused into complete unity with the actors. In the cinema which I have designed for the Film Arts Guild is this most important quality of the auditorium: its power to suggest concentrated attention and at the same time to destroy the sensation of confinement that may occur easily when the spectator concentrates on the screen.

The spectator must be able to lose himself in an imaginary, endless space even though the screen implies the opposite.

The film cannot exist by itself. The first radical step toward the creation of an ideal cinema is the abolition of the proscenium and all other stage platform resemblance to the theatre which we find in motion picture houses. My invention, the screen-o-scope, takes the place of these theatrical elements and supplies a new method of opening the screen which eliminates curtains. The interior lines of the theatre must focalize to the screen compelling unbroken attention on the spectator. The "visual-acoustics" must be provided for each member of the audience through the medium of a stadium floor. Pitch black darkness must rule when the screen play is on. The orchestra must be completely obscured, no draperies or decorations must be employed, since these are too strongly reminiscent of the theatre.

Notes

1   [It is likely that Kiesler referred to a "receiving," rather than "receding," apparatus, and that there was a typesetter's error in the essay's original newspaper appearance.—Ed.]

CHAPTER NINETEEN

Ideological Effects of the Basic Cinematographic Apparatus

Jean-Louis Baudry

[...]

We must first establish the place of the instrumental base in the set of operations which combine in the production of a film (we omit consideration of economic implications). Between "objective reality" and the camera, site of the inscription, and between the inscription and projection are situated certain operations, a *work*[1] which has as its result a finished product. To the extent that it is cut off from the raw material ("objective reality") this product does not allow us to see the transformation which has taken place. Equally distant from "objective reality" and the finished product, the camera occupies an intermediate position in the work process which leads from raw material to finished product. Though mutually dependent from other points of view, *découpage* [shot break-down before shooting] and *montage* [editing, or final assembly] must be distinguished because of the essential difference in the signifying raw material on which each operates: language (scenario) or image. Between the two complementary stages of production a mutation of the signifying material takes place (neither translation nor transcription, obviously, for the image is not reducible to language) precisely where the camera is. Finally, between the finished product (possessing exchange value, a commodity) and its consumption (use value) is introduced another operation effected by a set of instruments. Projector and screen restore the light lost in the shooting process, and transform a succession of separate images into an unrolling which also restores, but according to another scansion, the movement seized from "objective reality."

Cinematographic specificity (what distinguishes cinema from other systems of signification) thus refers to a *work*, that is, to a process of transformation. The question becomes, is the work made evident, does consumption of the product bring about a "knowledge effect" [Althusser], or is the work concealed? If the latter, consumption of the product will obviously be accompanied by ideological surplus value.[2] On the practical level, this poses the question of by what procedures the work can in fact be made "readable" in its inscription. These procedures must of necessity call cinematographic technique into play. But, on the other hand, going back to the first question, one may ask, do the instruments (the technical base) produce specific ideological effects, and are these effects themselves determined by the dominant ideology? In which case, concealment of the technical base will also bring about a specific ideological effect. Its inscription, its manifestation as such, on the other hand, would produce a knowledge effect, as actualization of the work process, as denunciation of ideology, and as critique of idealism.

The eye of the subject

Central in the process of production[3] of the film, the camera—an assembly of optical and mechanical instrumentation—carries out a certain mode of inscription characterized by marking, by the recording of differences of light intensity (and of wavelength for color) and of differences between the frames. Fabricated on the model of the *camera obscura*, it permits the construction of an image analogous to the perspective projections developed during the Italian Renaissance. Of course, the use of lenses of different focal lengths can alter the perspective of an image. But this much, at least, is clear in the history of cinema: it is the perspective construction of the Renaissance which originally served as model. The use of different lenses, when not dictated by technical considerations aimed at restoring the habitual perspective (such as shooting in limited or extended spaces which one wishes to expand or contract), does not destroy [traditional] perspective but rather makes it play a normative role. Departure from the norm, by means of a wide-angle or telephoto lens, is clearly marked in comparison with so-called "normal" perspective. We will see in any case that the resulting ideological effect is still defined in relation to the ideology inherent in perspective. The dimensions of the image itself, the ratio between height and width, seem clearly taken from an average drawn from Western easel painting.

[...]

Projection: The difference negated

Nevertheless, whatever the effects proper to optics generally, the movie camera differs from still photography by registering through its mechanical instrumentation a series of images. It might thus seem to counter the unifying and "substantializing" character of the single-perspective image, taking what would seem like instants of time or slices from "reality" (but always a reality already worked upon, elaborated, selected). This might permit the supposition, especially because the camera moves, of a multiplicity of points of view which would neutralize the fixed position of the eye-subject and even nullify it. But here we must turn to the relation between the succession of images inscribed by the camera and their projection, bypassing momentarily the place occupied by montage, which plays a decisive role in the strategy of the ideology produced.

The projection operation (projector and screen) restore continuity of movement and the temporal dimension to the sequence of static images. The relation between the individual frames and the projection would resemble the relation between points and a curve in geometry. But it is precisely this relation and the restoration of continuity to discontinuous elements which poses a problem. The meaning effect produced does not depend only on the content of the images but also on the material procedures by which an illusion of continuity, dependent on the persistence of vision, is restored from discontinuous elements. These separate frames have between them differences that are indispensable for the creation of an illusion of continuity, of a continuous passage (movement, time). But only on one condition can these differences create this illusion: they must be effaced as differences.[4]

FIGURE 19.1 *Toyogeki Movie Theater, Toyooka, Japan, 2010. Photo: Hashi Photo.*

Thus on the technical level the question becomes one of the adoption of a very small difference between images, such that each image, in consequence of an organic factor [presumably persistence of vision], is rendered incapable of being seen as such. In this sense we could say that film—and perhaps in this respect it is exemplary—lives on the denial of difference: the difference is necessary for it to live, but it lives on its negation. This is indeed the paradox that emerges if we look directly at a strip of processed film: adjacent images are almost exactly repeated, their divergence being verifiable only by comparison of images at a sufficient distance from each other. We should remember, moreover, the disturbing effects which result during a projection from breakdowns in the recreation of movement, when the spectator is brought abruptly back to discontinuity—that is, to the body, to the technical apparatus which he had *forgotten*.

We might not be far from seeing what is in play on this material basis, if we recall that the "language" of the unconscious, as it is found in dreams, slips of the tongue, or hysterical symptoms, manifests itself as continuity destroyed, broken, and as the unexpected surging forth of a marked difference. Couldn't we thus say that cinema reconstructs and forms the mechanical model (with the simplifications that this can entail) of a system of writing[5] constituted by a material base and a counter-system (ideology, idealism) which uses this system while also concealing it? On the one hand, the optical apparatus and the film permit the marking of difference (but the marking is already negated, we have seen, in the constitution of the perspective image with its mirror effect).[6] On the other hand, the mechanical apparatus both selects the minimal difference and represses it in projection, so that meaning can be constituted: it is at once direction, continuity, movement. The projection mechanism allows the differential elements (the discontinuity inscribed by the camera) to be suppressed, bringing only the relation into play. The individual images as such disappear so that movement and continuity can appear. But the movement and continuity are the visible expression (one might even say the projection) of their relations, derived from the tiny discontinuities between the images. Thus one may assume that what was already at work as the originating basis of the perspective image, namely the eye, the "subject," is put forth, liberated (in the sense that a chemical reaction liberates a substance) by the operation which transforms successive, discrete images (as isolated images they have, strictly speaking, no meaning, or at least no unity of meaning) into continuity, movement, meaning; with continuity restored, both meaning and consciousness are restored.[7]

The transcendental subject

Meaning and consciousness, to be sure: at this point we must return to the camera. Its mechanical nature not only permits the shooting of differential images as rapidly as desired but also destines it to change position, to move. Film history shows that as a result of the combined inertia of painting, theater, and photography, it took a certain time to notice the inherent mobility of the cinematic mechanism. The ability to reconstitute movement is after all only a partial, elementary aspect of a more general capability. To seize movement is to become movement, to follow a trajectory is to become trajectory, to choose a direction is to have the possibility of choosing one, to determine a meaning is to give oneself a meaning. In this way, the eye-subject, the invisible base of artificial perspective (which in fact only represents a larger effort to produce an ordering, regulated transcendence) becomes absorbed in, "elevated" to a vaster function, proportional to the movement which it can perform.

And if the eye which moves is no longer fettered by a body, by the laws of matter and time, if there are no more assignable limits to its displacement— conditions fulfilled by the possibilities of shooting and of film—the world will not only be constituted by this eye but for it.[8] The movability of the camera seems to fulfill the most favorable conditions for the manifestation of the "transcendental subject." There is both fantasmatization of an objective reality (images, sounds, colors) and of an objective reality which, limiting its powers of constraint, seems equally to augment the possibilities or the power of the subject.[9] As it is said of consciousness—and in point of fact we are concerned with nothing less—the image will always be image *of* something; it must result from a deliberate act of consciousness [*visée intentionelle*]. "The word intentionality signifies nothing other than this peculiarity that consciousness has of being consciousness of something, of carrying in its quality of *ego* its *cogitatum* within itself."[10] In such a definition could perhaps be found the status of the cinematographic image, or rather of its operation, the mode of working which it carries out. For it to be an image of something, it has to constitute this something as meaning. The image seems to reflect the world but solely in the naive inversion of a founding hierarchy: "The domain of natural existence thus has only an authority of the second order, and always presupposes the domain of the transcendental."[11]

The world is no longer only an "open and unbounded horizon." Limited by the framing, lined up, put at the proper distance, the world offers up an object endowed with meaning, an intentional object, implied by and implying the action of the "subject" which sights it. At the same time that the world's transfer as image seems to accomplish this phenomenological reduction, this putting into parentheses of its real existence (a suspension necessary, we will see, to the formation of the impression of reality) provides a basis for the apodicity[12] of the ego. The multiplicity of aspects of the object in view refers to a synthesizing operation, to the unity of this constituting subject: Husserl speaks of " 'aspects,' sometimes of 'proximity,' sometimes of 'distance,' in variable modes of 'here' and 'there,' opposed to an absolute 'here' (which is located—for me—in 'my own body' which appears to me at the same time), the consciousness of which, though it remains *unperceived*, always accompanies them. [We will see moreover what happens with the body in the *mise-en-scène* of projection.—J. L. B.] Each 'aspect' which the mind grasps is revealed in turn as a unity synthesized from a multiplicity of corresponding modes of presentation. The nearby object may present itself as the same, but under one or another 'aspect.' There may be variation of visual perspective, but also of 'tactile,' 'acoustic' phenomena, or of other 'modes of presentation'[13] as we can observe in directing our attention in the proper direction."[14]

For Husserl, "the original operation [of intentional analysis] is to *unmask the potentialities implied* in present states of consciousness. And it is by this that will be carried out, from the noematic point of view, the eventual *explication, definition,* and *elucidation* of what is meant by consciousness, that is, its *objective meaning*."[15] And again in the *Cartesian Meditations*: "A second type of polarization now presents itself to us, another type of synthesis which embraces the particular multiplicities of *cogitationes*, which embraces them all and in a special manner, namely as *cogitationes* of an identical self which, *active* or *passive*, lives in all the lived states of consciousness and which, through them, relates to all objects."[16]

Thus is articulated the relation between the continuity necessary to the constitution of meaning and the "subject" which constitutes this meaning: continuity is an attribute of the subject. It supposes the subject and it circumscribes his place. It appears in the cinema in the two complementary aspects of a "formal" continuity established through a system of negated differences and narrative continuity in the filmic space. The latter, in any case, could not have been conquered without exercising violence against the instrumental base, as can be discovered from most of the texts by filmmakers and critics: the discontinuity that had been effaced at the level of the image could have reappeared on the narrative level, giving rise to effects of rupture disturbing to the spectator (to a *place* which ideology must both conquer and, in the degree that it already dominates it, must also satisfy: fill). "What is important in a film is the feeling of continuity which joins shots and sequences while maintaining unity and cohesion of movements. This continuity was one of the most difficult things to obtain."[17] Pudovkin defined montage as "the art of assembling pieces of film, shot separately, in such a way as to give the spectator the impression of continuous movement." The search for such narrative continuity, so difficult to obtain from the material base, can only be explained by an essential ideological stake projected in this point: it is a question of preserving at any cost the synthetic unity of the locus where meaning originates [the subject]—the constituting transcendental function to which narrative continuity points back as its natural secretion.[18]

The screen-mirror: Specularization and double identification

But another supplementary operation (made possible by a special technical arrangement) must be added in order that the mechanism thus described can play its role effectively as an ideological machine, so that not only the reworked "objective reality" but also the specific type of identification we have described can be represented.

No doubt the darkened room and the screen bordered with black like a letter of condolences already present privileged conditions of effectiveness— no exchange, no circulation, no communication with any outside. Projection and reflection take place in a closed space and those who remain there, whether they know it or not (but they do not), find themselves chained, captured, or captivated. (What might one say of the function of the head in this captivation: it suffices to recall that for Bataille materialism makes itself headless—like a wound that bleeds and thus transfuses.) And the mirror, as a reflecting surface, is framed, limited, circumscribed. *An infinite mirror would no longer be a mirror.* The paradoxical nature of the cinematic mirror-screen is without doubt that it reflects images but not "*reality*"; the word reflect, being transitive,[19] leaves this ambiguity unresolved. In any case, this "reality" comes from behind the spectator's head and if he looked at it directly he would see nothing except the moving beams from an already veiled light source.

The arrangement of the different elements—projector, darkened hall, screen—in addition from reproducing in a striking way the *mise-en-scène* of Plato's cave (prototypical set for all transcendence and the topological model of idealism[20]) reconstructs the situation necessary to the release of the "mirror stage" discovered by Lacan. This psychological phase, which occurs between six and eighteen months of age, generates *via* the mirror image of a unified body the constitution or at least the first sketches of the "I" as an imaginary function. "It is to this unreachable image in the mirror that the specular image gives its garments."[21] But for this imaginary constitution of the self to be possible, there must be—Lacan strongly emphasizes this point—two complementary conditions: immature powers of mobility and a precocious maturation of visual organization (apparent in the first few days of life). If one considers that these two conditions are repeated during cinematographic projection—suspension of mobility and predominance of the visual function—perhaps one could suppose that this is more than a simple analogy. And possibly this very point explains the "impression of reality" so often invoked in connection with the cinema for which the various explanations proposed seem only to skirt the real problem. In order for this impression to be produced, it would be necessary that the conditions of a formative scene be reproduced. This scene would be repeated and reenacted in such a manner that the imaginary order (activated by a specularization which takes place, everything considered, in reality) fulfills its particular function of occultation or of filling the gap, the split, of the subject on the order of the signifier.[22]

On the other hand, it is to the extent that the child can sustain the look of another in the presence of a third party that he can find the assurance of an identification with the image of his own body. From the very fact that during the mirror stage is established a dual relationship, it constitutes, in conjunction with the formation of the self in the imaginary order, the nexus of secondary identification.[23] The origin of the self, as discovered by Lacan, in pertaining to the imaginary order effectively subverts the "optical machinery" of idealism which the projection room scrupulously reproduces.[24] But it is not as specifically "imaginary," nor as a reproduction of its first configuration, that the self finds a "place" in the cinema. This occurs, rather, as a sort of proof or verification of that function, a solidification through repetition.

The "reality" mimed by the cinema is thus first of all that of a "self." But, because the reflected image is not that of the body itself but that of a world already given as meaning, one can distinguish two levels of identification. The first, attached to the image itself, derives from the character portrayed as a center of secondary identifications, carrying an identity which constantly must be seized and reestablished. The second level permits the appearance of the first and places it "in action"—this is the transcendental subject whose place is taken by the camera which constitutes and rules the objects in this "world." Thus the spectator identifies less with what is represented, the spectacle itself, than with what stages the spectacle, makes it seen, obliging him to see what it sees; this is exactly the function taken over by the camera as a sort of relay.[25] Just as the mirror assembles the fragmented body in a sort of imaginary integration of the self, the transcendental self unites the discontinuous fragments of phenomena, of lived experience, into unifying meaning. Through it each fragment assumes meaning by being integrated into an "organic" unity. Between the imaginary gathering of the fragmented body into a unity and the transcendentality of the self, giver of unifying meaning, the current is indefinitely reversible.

The ideological mechanism at work in the cinema seems thus to be concentrated in the relationship between the camera and the subject. The question is whether the former will permit the latter to constitute and seize itself in a particular mode of specular reflection. Ultimately, the forms of narrative adopted, the "contents" of the image, are of little importance so long as an identification remains possible.[26] What emerges here (in outline) is the specific function fulfilled by the cinema as support and instrument of ideology. It constitutes the "subject" by the illusory delimitation of a central location—whether this be that of a god or of any other substitute. It is an apparatus destined to obtain a precise ideological effect, necessary to the dominant ideology: creating a fantasmatization of the subject, it collaborates with a marked efficacity in the maintenance of idealism.

Thus the cinema assumes the role played throughout Western history by various artistic formations. The ideology of representation (as a principal axis orienting the notion of aesthetic "creation") and specularization (which organizes the *mise-en-scène* required to constitute the transcendental function) form a singularly coherent system in the cinema. Everything happens as if, the subject himself being unable—and for a reason—to account for his own situation, it was necessary to substitute secondary organs, grafted on to replace his own defective ones, instruments or ideological formations capable of filling his function as subject. In fact, this substitution is only possible on the condition that the instrumentation itself be hidden or repressed. Thus disturbing cinematic elements—similar, precisely, to those elements indicating the return of the repressed—signify without fail the arrival of the instrument "in flesh and blood," as in Vertov's *Man With a Movie Camera*. Both specular tranquility and the assurance of one's own identity collapse simultaneously with the revealing of the mechanism, that is of the inscription of the film-work.

The cinema can thus appear as a sort of psychic apparatus of substitution, corresponding to the model defined by the dominant ideology. The system of repression (primarily economic) has as its goal the prevention of deviations and of the active exposure of this "model."[27] Analogously one could say that its "unconscious" is not recognized (we speak of the apparatus and not of the content of films, which have used the unconscious in ways we know all too well). To this unconscious would be attached the mode of production of film, the process of "work" in its multiple determinations, among which must be numbered those depending on instrumentation. This is why reflections on the basic apparatus ought to be possible to integrate into a general theory of the ideology of cinema.

Notes

1 [Travail, the process-implying not only "work" in the ordinary sense but as in Freud's usage: the dream-work.—TR.]

2 [Althusser opposes ideology to knowledge or science. Ideology operates by obfuscating the means by which it is produced. Thus an increase in ideological value is an increase in mystification.—ED.]

3 Obviously we are not speaking here of investment of capital in the process.

4 "We know that the spectator finds it impossible to notice that the images which succeed one another before his eyes were assembled end-to-end, because the projection of film on the screen offers an impression of continuity although the images which compose it are, in reality, distinct, and are differentiated moreover by variations in space and time. "In a film, there can be hundreds, even thousands of cuts and intervals. But if it is shown for specialists who know the art, the spectacle will not be divulged as such. Only an error or lack of competence will permit them to seize, and this is a disagreeable sensation, the changes of time and place of action." (Pudovkin, "Le Montage" in *Cinéma d'aujourd'hui et de demain*, [Moscow, 1956].)

5 [*Ecriture*, in the French, meaning "writing" but also "schematization" at any given level of material or expression.—TR.]

6 [Specular: a notion used by Althusser and above all by Lacan; the word refers to the "mirror" effect which by reflection (specularization) constitutes the object reflected to the viewer and for him. The body is the most important and the first of these objects.—TR.]

7   It is thus first at the level of the apparatus that the cinema functions as a language: inscription of discontinuous elements whose effacement in the relationship instituted among them produces meaning.

8   "In the cinema I am simultaneously in this action and outside of it, in this space and out of this space. Having the power of ubiquity, I am everywhere and nowhere." Jean Mitry, *Esthétique et Psychologie du Cinéma* (Paris: Presses Universitaires de France, 1965), p. 179.

9   The cinema manifests in a hallucinatory manner the belief in the omnipotence of thought, described by Freud, which plays so important a role in neurotic defense mechanisms.

10 Husserl, *Les Méditations Cartésiennes* (Paris: Vrin, 1953), p. 28.

11 Ibid., p. 18.

12 [Apodicity, in phenomenological terminology, indicates something of an ultimately irrefutable nature. See Husserl, op.cit.—TR.]

13 On this point it is true that the camera is revealed as incomplete. But this is only a technical imperfection which, since the birth of cinema, has already in large measure been remedied.

14 Ibid., p. 34, emphasis added.

15 Ibid., p. 40.

16 Ibid., p. 58.

17 Mitry, op.cit., p. 157.

18 The lens, the "objective," is of course only a particular location of the "subjective." Marked by the idealist opposition interior/exterior, topologically situated at the point of meeting of the two, it corresponds, one could say, to the empirical organ of the subjective, to the opening, the fault in the organs of meaning, by which the exterior world may penetrate the interior and assume meaning. "It is the interior which commands," says Bresson. "I know this may seem paradoxical in an art which is all exterior." Also the use of different lenses is already conditioned by camera movement as implication and trajectory of meaning, by this transcendental function which we are attempting to define: it is the possibility of choosing a field as accentuation or modification of the *visée intentionelle*. No doubt this transcendental function fits in without difficulty the field of psychology. This, moreover, is insisted upon by Husserl himself, who indicates that Brentano's discovery, intentionality, "permits one truly to distinguish the method of a descriptive science of consciousness, as much philosophical and transcendental as psychological."

19 [It is always a reflection *of* something.—TR.]

20 The arrangement of the cave, except that in the cinema it is already doubled in a sort of enclosure in which the camera, the darkened chamber, is enclosed in another darkened chamber, the projection hall.

21 Lacan, *Ecrits* (Paris: Le Seuil, 1966). See in particular "Le Stade du miroir comme formateur de la fonction du je."

22 We see that what has been defined as impression of reality refers less to the "reality" than to the apparatus which, although being of an hallucinatory order, nonetheless founds this possibility. Reality will never appear except as relative to the images which reflect it, in some way inaugurated by a reflection anterior to itself.

23 We refer here to what Lacan says of identifications in liaison with the structure determined by an optical instrument (the mirror), as they are constituted, in the prevailing figuration of the ego, as lines of resistance to the advance of the analytic work.

24 "That the ego be 'in the right' must be avowed, from experience, to be a function of misunderstanding." (Lacan, op. cit., p. 637.)

25 "That it sustains itself as 'subject' means that language permits it to consider itself as the stagehand or even the director of all the imaginary capturings of which it would otherwise only be the living marionette." (Ibid., p. 637.)

26 It is on this point and in function of the elements which we are trying to put in place that a discussion of editing could be opened. We will at a later date attempt to make some remarks on this subject.

27 *Méditerranée*, by J.-D. Pollet and Phillipe Sollers (1963), which dismantles with exemplary efficiency the "transcendental specularization" which we have attempted to delineate, gives a manifest proof of this point. The film was never able to overcome the economic blockade.

CHAPTER TWENTY

The Shape of New Media: Screen Space, Aspect Ratios, and Digitextuality

Harper Cossar

If everything is manufactured [in digital texts], then everything must be considered.

—KATHERINE SARAFIAN, PIXAR ANIMATION STUDIOS (222)

This article examines how widescreen, analog filmmaking strategies such as letterboxing have become commonplace in digital texts such as online advertising, Web-based film series, and even digital animation films from Pixar. The various delivery platforms associated with new media texts must address the spatial and aesthetic challenges presented by the various aspect ratios necessary to accommodate many monitor/screen shapes and sizes. The online and digital texts analyzed in this article use cinematic techniques (such as letterboxing) in an effort to reproduce film/video poetics and thus present their products in terms of highbrow consumption strategies. Further, many video games, regardless of whether they are of first-person shooter or sport genres, deploy cut-scenes or "cinematics."[1] These techniques ape cinematic tropes in order to blend (or mask altogether) the transition between transtextual choices such as video games based on films or televised sports (e.g., *The Godfather* or the Madden football franchise, respectively). Because online content faces many challenges—different operating systems, monitor sizes, screen resolutions, and monitor widths, not to mention download speeds—it seems that content producers want to achieve MIVI (Maximum Instantaneous Visual Impact) (Garfield 77), and the panache of letterboxing is useful to colonize monitor space. By colonization, I assert that the shift in aspect ratio and its demarcating effect within screen space requires some visual shift on the part of the viewer.[2] Colonization occurs when Academy ratio proportions are transformed without input from the viewer into a letterboxed or widescreen visual field.

Pixar Animation Studios provides an intriguing and unique example of how aspect ratios must be negotiated when shifting between analog and digital formats. Pixar recomposes each film it produces for home video outlets. Although most films shot in the CinemaScope aspect ratio (2.35:1) must undergo significant aesthetic metamorphoses and are often released into home video formats as "full screen" via pan-and-scan, Pixar's texts are digital blanks. The *mise-en-scène*[3] of a Pixar film exists only in digital form. There is no soundstage or cinematographer to consult with regard to framing aesthetics. Digital mattes are composed in both formats from the first storyboard with the home-video release in mind. Pixar's dual-format digital production strategy is the digitextual solution to a problem faced by early experimental uses of widescreen in such films as *The Big Trail* (1930) and *The Bat Whispers* (1930).[4] *The Big Trail* and *The Bat Whispers* were shot in both wide and Academy ratios *simultaneously*. This process of concurrent production with multiple formats had recently been deemed necessary with the advent of sound filmmaking where multiple versions of films were produced in various languages to facilitate distribution to overseas ancillary markets. *The Big Trail* was filmed in two cinematographic formats, but it was also shot (with different casts) in at least four other languages to compensate for the European markets on which Hollywood relied so heavily in the silent era (Crafton 428–29).

In an *American Cinematographer* article from 1930, Arthur Edeson comments on the formal differences between the wide (70 mm) version (which Edeson shot) and Lucien Androit's Academy ratio version of *The Big Trail*. Edeson states,

> In working on such a picture as *The Big Trail,* 70 millimeter is a tremendously important aid for the epic sweep of the picture demands that it be painted against a great canvas. Grandeur gives us such a canvas to work with, and enables us to make the background play its part in the picture…The background thus plays a vitally important role in the picture—a role which can only be brought out completely by being shown as 70 millimeter film can show it. Lucien Androit…did a superb piece of work, but the medium with which he was working could not begin to capture the vast sweep of the story and its background as did the Grandeur. Working in 35mm film, he was simply unable to dramatize the backgrounds as did the larger film, for in 35mm he could not attempt to adequately show both the vast backgrounds and the intimate foreground

action in a single shot as the Grandeur cameras can. (9)

Edeson believed the Grandeur (widescreen) version of the film to be superior because of its aesthetic "advantages" over the Academy version. The Grandeur version is visually superior for Edeson because it captures the "epic sweep" of the narrative, and the 70 mm version allows "vast backgrounds and the intimate foreground action in a single shot." Edeson lists the deficiencies of the Academy version and suggests stylistic differences between the 70 mm and 35 mm versions. By stating that Androit's 35 mm version is "simply unable to dramatize" visual material with the same impact that Grandeur does, Edeson asserts that Grandeur, and thus widescreen, is altogether different aesthetically from conventional Academy ratio practices. In a February 1930 *American Cinematographer* article criticizing the usefulness of the Grandeur 70 mm process, cinematographer William Stull's remarks echo those of Edeson but announce even more specifically the stylistic changes necessary when shifting between widescreen and Academy ratios. Stull writes,

Viewed from a practical viewpoint, the Grandeur proportions (2.10:1) offer many advantages to all concerned. The director can film his spectacular scenes or stage dancing numbers to their best advantage, with fewer cuts—and no need of close-ups. The cameraman has greater scope in his composition, and considerable advantages in his lighting. For instance, the present disproportionately high sets necessitated by the more nearly square picture have made such things as backlighting increasingly difficult ... Similarly, the art directors are confronted with grave problems in the design and artistic ornamentation of the higher sets ... In Grandeur, all of these problems are reduced ... The cinematographer's task is lightened inasmuch as the sets do not have to be made nearly so high, allowing the back-lightings to strike at more effective and natural angles. (43)

Although Edeson may simply be stating that his Grandeur version is superior to that of Androit's Academy version of *The Big Trail* and thus possibly becoming part of the promotional machine for Grandeur and Fox, Stull has no such impetus. Both cinematographers echo what widescreen critics will characterize as the hallmarks of wide filmmaking in the 1950s—fewer cuts within horizontally composed frames, complete with bravura camera movement.

Edeson and Stull's comments propose an interesting set of binaries. If wide filmmakers have a choice between cutting into close-up *or* shooting in long shot, the wide filmmaker will opt not to cut because early widescreen filmmakers believed that close-ups were no longer needed. Campbell MacCullough reiterates this point in *Motion Picture* by stating that with "new" widescreen aspect ratios, "the close-up will be done away with because the medium shot of the players will be large enough to show their expressions without thrusting enormous countenances registering gargantuan passion or shedding tears the size of marbles into the very faces of the spectator" (109).

Historically, in the Academy ratio, the first camera setup of a scene is usually a master long shot to establish space and screen direction. The subsequent coverage of the action is divided into closer framed shots that maintain screen direction and hypothetically will drive the action with tempo in postproduction editing. *The Big Trail* opposes this paradigm, according to both Edeson's and Stull's assessment of the new technology's aesthetic demands.

If cinema's history can be compared to, say, painting, then prior to 1953's advent of widescreen filmmaking, cinema existed as a portrait-only operation with a premium placed on vertical compositions. This is not to say that landscape shots were not possible or that laterally oriented *mise-en-scène* did not exist. Cinematic texts, with very few exceptions, were composed in only one shape: the almost square Academy ratio. Before 1953, cinema's shape is that of portraiture; after 1953, cinema's shape is landscape. Widescreen was quite simply a break from previous stylistic norms because the shape of the frame itself was drastically reconfigured. Modern, digital filmmaking strategies are reintroducing viewers and producers alike to the differences between Academy ratio texts viewed on traditionally shaped monitors such as TVs and computer screens. The question must be asked, then, what spatial aesthetic strategies are appropriated from traditional (analog) widescreen filmmaking in digitextual forms such as online ads, computer mediated texts, and digital films? Further, how do content providers navigate the production of widescreen texts that are being viewed on 4:3 television or computer/PDA monitors? A historical example such as *The Big Trail* is a useful text for historicizing how filmmakers have negotiated shifts in aspect ratios between versions of a given text. How might such an example be adapted to interrogate the flexibility of digital texts where aspect ratios and *mise-en-scène* can be manipulated with much greater ease?

In a podcast from the Australian Film, Television and Radio School, Guy Gadney discussed the services his company (Bigpond.com) delivers to large numbers of the Australian audience. Gadney draws attention to the blurring line between live video on broadband and TV but points to much higher levels of "synchronized interactivity" via broadband. For Gadney, widescreen is exemplary of the heightened experience an online content producer can provide.

We've just made a move to widescreen…Rather than just having a little box on the Internet which everyone is used to peering into and thinking "Oh, that's a bit of a lousy experience, but hey it's the Internet," we said no, we're not going to do that. We want every piece of video to be shot, encoded and put up in widescreen…To the user, what they see is something more televisual…Just by making that psychological move…away from existing paradigms on the Internet…we were very easily able to change something into an experience which was very much more cinematographic. ("Broadband Futures")

Gadney points to the interactive nature of online content production, but he seems particularly excited about the transition to widescreen and speaks of it in glowing terms. For Gadney, the encoding of video into a widescreen format (via letterbox masking) equates television and cinema. The logic here is that through the appropriation of cinematic aspect ratios and replication of cinematic screen space (i.e., widescreen), other formats are elevated to a higher-brow visual look.

In an article discussing the rise of the DVD format and its subsequent "home theater" aficionados, James Kendrick argues a similar case with regard to aspect ratio snobbery. The author examines discussions of DVD aspect ratios on the Home Theater Forum (www.hometheaterforum.com) and notes that home theater enthusiasts view modified aspect ratio (MAR) DVD releases as violations of "the artistic integrity of the films" and "an insult to cinematic art…a subversion of the use for which the format was intended" ("Aspect Ratios" 60–61). Kendrick continues that for these DVD proselytizers of original aspect ratios (OAR), "there is only one way a film can be presented, and that is in the aspect ratio in which the film was originally presented in theaters" (61). Any manipulations of the OAR are considered bastardizations and cultivate derogatory rhetoric such as the naming of the "full screen" format (1.33:1) as "fool screen." The cineastes Kendrick describes consider knowledge of OARs to be cultural capital that they can lord over the non-initiated, run-of-the-mill video store patrons. The "black bars" of letterboxing carry some transtextual meaning that denotes a cinematic and thus higher-brow experience. The larger point being made here, but not explicitly expressed, is that post-1953, widescreen implicitly *means* cinema.

In a discussion of the aesthetics of computer window size, Jay David Bolter and Richard Grusin submit that a windowed environment does not attempt to unify any point of view (33). I submit that by segregating areas of monitor space via letterboxing, content producers narrow the viewable monitor area in an effort to present a focal point, in much the same way as formalist montage editing directs spectators' gaze. Computer monitor workspace is colonized by the video game or online ad interface; the letterbox masking isolates the workspace portion of the monitor from the letterboxed portion that video game and ad producers want viewers to consume. Why would advertisers and online content producers be willing to sacrifice such valuable visual real estate? First, by redrawing the frame boundaries within a monitor's visual field, online content producers focus a user's attention to that which has been colonized and segregated. Second, there seems to be an indication that screen shape (and therefore its spatial form) has a certain essential nature; that is, certain shapes indicate cinema (widescreen), and certain other shapes indicate television or computer workspace (Academy ratio or 4:3). This phenomenon is easily observed in the examples of Gadney's transition to widescreen for Bigpond content and, to a lesser degree, Kendrick's elucidation of the aspect ratio wars fought by home theater buffs.

Additionally, video game producers provide cut-scenes (or cinematics) at the beginning of gaming narratives and periodically throughout the gaming experience to deliver narrative. Sports games utilize the letterboxed view when something extraordinary—a shot or play—is worthy of spectatorship. The 4:3 monitor view collapses to a letterbox view. When this occurs, a remarkable transformation takes place that is virtually untapped with regard to media studies; the participant playing the game is cued by an aesthetic shift in aspect ratio and simply *becomes a spectator.*

New media providers use the widescreen cache associated with letterboxing to cue participation or spectatorship. The letterboxing of ads not only employs the colonization of monitor real estate but also signifies a cultural consumption strategy associated with cinema.[5] In addition, video game and other online content providers use the letterbox aesthetic to cue players/viewers when it is appropriate to participate and when to simply watch and consume. These new media directions offer the ontological possibilities associated with digital convergence not in terms of technology but in light of aesthetics. Whereas the CinemaScope films of the 1950s could be consumed only in their intended aspect ratio in a CinemaScope theater, online films or letterboxed video games colonize and convert any monitor's format into the desired aspect ratio.

Why would media content producers and specifically advertisers use letterbox techniques for media such as television and online content when they will most likely be viewed in a 4:3 aspect ratio monitor? Media producers of such ads confess that the goal is to make "their work more 'cinematic'... with the look and feel of a feature film" (Vagoni 49). Jay David Bolter and Richard Grusin deem such poaching as remediation. The process of remediation occurs when one medium is represented via another medium, and the authors suggest this process is "the defining characteristic of the new digital media" (45). If this is true, then digital content producers such as Guy Gadney of Bigpond use the physical and stylistic rupturing characteristics of widescreen itself as product differentiation

Everything in the realm of new media is "remediated"; the aesthetic strategies from one medium are recycled into another. This is particularly salient with letterboxing as a production device in the online advertising campaigns (Cossar, "Taking a Wider"). Widescreen aesthetics via letterboxing are exploited in two online advertising campaigns, BMW Films (*Star*) and Buick (*Tiger Trap,* which even uses a multi-screen technique). Both campaigns were launched on the Internet, and both are long-form (six to eight minutes) cinematic ads. They are useful texts to examine because unlike their thirty-second and minute-long counterparts, they have the added benefit of having already captured their audience, and therefore the letterboxing device cannot be reduced to merely an attention grabber.

Widescreen criticism

In "CinemaScope: Before and After," Charles Barr argues that widescreen cinema challenges spectators to be "alert," but should strive for a "gradation of emphasis" regarding its implementation (11). Barr contends that widescreen cinema (specifically CinemaScope) offers the possibility of "greater physical involvement" for the spectator and a "more vivid sense of space" (4). Essentially, Barr's essay reifies the notions that André Bazin put forth regarding the "myth of total cinema"—widescreen cinema allows for fewer edits and thus longer takes, which Bazin and Barr claim allows for the spectator's deeper perceptual submersion within the visual narrative. Previously, I have noted that such changes in screen shape and film space resulted in a number of aesthetic changes in early widescreen films: lower set heights, lower camera levels, and less camera movement and therefore fewer edits.[6] Barr further explains that in widescreen "peripheral vision orients us and makes the experience so vivid…this power was there even in the 1:1.33 image, but for the most part remained latent" (11). It is important to note here that Barr (like Bazin) is speaking exclusively of the new spatial norms of widescreen *theatrical* exhibition. The expansion of screen area for the CinemaScope theatrical experience was a new spatial norm, and it contrasts nicely with the stylistic shifts involved in producing online texts in widescreen-esque formats such as letterbox. Essentially, what Barr saw as stylistic ruptures to adapt to new spatial norms occurs in reverse with new media widescreen texts; online content producers contract and colonize screen area (physical rupture) to create a focal point in the 4:3 monitor. In addition, Barr isolates one of the primary claims of most widescreen critics: the larger screen area of a theatrically projected CinemaScope film encouraged audiences to perform new viewing practices.

The questions posed by Gadney and Kendrick amount to new media updates of the queries put forward by Bazin and Barr to analog film production and exhibition; what (and how) does widescreen *mean* in digital and online formats? If Barr's assertion that the widening of the frame in fact results in "greater physical involvement" and encourages viewers to "interpret" and/or "read the shot," then widescreen's deployment by the online content producers makes perfect sense. However, Barr also contends that the hallmark of widescreen images is a more open frame with a "greater…impression of depth" and an image that is "more vivid, and involves us more directly " (10). Barr claims that this power either was not present in the Academy ratio or "remained latent." If the 4:3 image does not allow for "greater physical involvement," then the TV advertising industry is compelled to colonize and letterbox material to provide a focal point to market their wares. Letterboxed content begins with film-to-video transfers that are proprietary to television. However, when this process of letterboxing is appropriated (remediated) to nonproprietary formats such as online media, the process of letterboxing *itself* has meaning. What does letterboxed content in formats with "no such imperative" mean, and how is this accomplished aesthetically? Does it follow normative trends for close-ups, landscapes, camera angles, and movement, or does it remediate other mediated strategies?

A first consideration is a new media text's *mise-en-scène* and how it changes in a letterboxed frame. Letterboxed texts manipulate spatial relationships (and their subsequent reading) when widescreen space is composed *for* a native Academy ratio space. Once the "initial" attention is achieved (MIVI), viewers are left with content that has different, unwarranted aspect ratio. For example, most computer monitors or television screens present a 4:3 aspect ratio. Therefore, like letterboxed films on VHS or DVD, available monitor space is masked, often without input from the consumer. An authorial choice to constrict and ration available monitor space is deployed. A consumer has a choice (often unbeknownst to them) between a widescreen or full-screen format for a film or video, and this is especially true with the proliferation of DVD formats that often offer both formats on a single disc.[7] Consumers then may *choose* how much monitor (TV or computer) space they are willing to "sacrifice" for viewing the text.

Texts *created* as letterboxed often do offer such an aesthetic olive branch; the decision to colonize monitor space has been made by the media producers, and consumers must view the matted content.[8] In the case online texts such as BMW Films and Buick, audiences have sought out their ads in cyberspace rather than having been snared by MIVI or some other broadcast attention-grabber. In sum, content producers take a nod from the cultural capital associated with letterboxed films and "remediate" this aesthetic tradition by appropriating a consumer's screen space. Through poaching this cinematic visual style, the ads are equated with cinematic formats, and by association the advertisers create the visual link between their products and previous consumption of other media (cinema) with similar aesthetic characteristics. The "more professional" and "stylized" look of widescreen that creates a suspension of "naturalism" is also a useful tool for advertisers who appropriate the letterbox format to appeal to what Pierre Bourdieu calls enculturated "manifested preferences" (Kendrick, "Aspect Ratios" 63). For Bourdieu, the acquisition of certain tastes is inextricably bound with the classification of where one ranks in the social hierarchy, and ultimately with power and class. Bourdieu's notion of cultural capital and letterboxing's association with the "highbrow artistic merit"[9] of quality films is significant, but "manifested preferences" cannot solely explain why advertisers willingly surrender so much vital and expensive visual real estate. Consumers usually view letterboxed ads on traditional 4:3 monitors via either television or computer monitors, and it is here that online content providers stake their claim.

Content producers need to achieve MIVI and employ the panache of letterboxing to colonize monitor space and create a focal point. Lev Manovich suggests that the need for creating a focal point is paramount within new media screen space. Manovich writes that "rather than showing a single image, a computer screen typically displays a number of coexisting windows ... No single window dominates the viewer's attention" (97). The multi-windowed, new media environments of modern computer graphical user interfaces need physically ruptured visual spaces before any one focal point can be privileged over any other.

In a discussion of the aesthetics of computer window size, Jay David Bolter and Richard Grusin submit,

> [A] windowed interface does not attempt to unify the space around any one point of view. Instead, each text window defines its own verbal, each graphic window its own visual, point of view. Windows may change scale quickly and radically, expanding to fill the screen or shrinking to the size of an icon ... [The user] oscillates between manipulating the windows and examining their contents ... (33)

Both Manovich and Bolter and Grusin suggest that a windowed environment by design cannot unify any point of view. New media content producers colonize monitor space and black out certain areas and thus create a focal hub. By redrawing the frame boundaries within a monitor's visual field, content producers focus a user's attention to that which has been colonized and segregated. Because a user may "oscillate wildly" from window to window, the letterboxed window collapses and segregates what appears onscreen. Video game manufacturers have faced similar challenges and deployed colonizing widescreen aesthetics for other reasons.

Video games and letterboxing

In many sports-themed video games, extraordinary events (shots, hits, catches, etc.) are accompanied by spectacle that points to cinematic poetics; the game's aspect ratio physically shifts from traditional Academy ratio proportions (4:3) to widescreen dimensions, and more specifically to a letterboxed view. The full-screen 4:3 visual field is squeezed vertically to focus the gamer's attention to a specific area within the gaming interface. The colonized visual field redirects the gamer's gaze, and "cinematic" flourishes accompany the colonization, such as an aural heartbeat pounding and slow-motion graphics to further enhance the exceptional quality of the "event." By deploying a letterboxed view, a role change for the gamer signals a shift from participatory to spectatorial.

Cut-scenes are narrative events often signified by a shift in composition of the visual space, an alteration of the frame's *mise-en-scène*. The widescreen aesthetics of letterboxing occurs when something extraordinary is taking place, and viewers should observe. Geoff King and Tanya Kryzwinska note that the collapse to letterboxing at specific times during game play may cue players to stop participating/gaming and simply watch. King and Kryzwinska state that "the move into gameplay from cut-scenes…[is] typically presented in a letterbox format to create a 'cinematic' effect… [T]he change in aspect ratio marks a movement from introductory exposition to the development of the specific narrative events to be depicted in the film" (17). These so-called cinematics are visual cues that cue players' reactions during game play. The colonization that occurs when the gaming interfaced becomes letterboxed signals to gamers to stop playing and observe narrative as a cinematic experience. These cues are not always appreciated or even understood by gamers. The frame grabs from *Star Wars: Knights of the Old*

FIGURE 20.1 Star Wars: Knights of the Old Republic II: The Sith Lords, *LucasArts, 2004.*

FIGURE 20.2 Star Wars: Knights of the Old Republic II: The Sith Lords, *LucasArts, 2004.*

Republic II: The Sith Lords in Figures 20.1 and 20.2[10] display the colonizing changes in interface; the shift is from participatory gaming (full frame) to an observational, cut-scene that comes complete with subtitles.

Widescreen aesthetics in cinema are well established at this point in film history, whereas trials with widescreen aspect ratios in new media environments seem to be just beginning. The demarcating effects from other software and/or windows on the computer screen require viewers to redirect their gaze, and in this way mimic the choices of widescreen filmmakers who experiment with spatial and stylistic shifts. The colonization of computer workspace by video game or online ad interfaces isolates the workspace portion of the monitor from the letterboxed. The consumption portion is physically ruptured to privilege the areas video game and ad producers want viewers to consume.

André Bazin prophesied that the "fin du montage" in widescreen films would create a new kind of cinematic experience—one where the filmmakers did not guide the spectator's gaze, but rather viewers were liberated and free to roam about the wide visual field. New media content authors mimic widescreen aesthetic choices for quite opposite reasons. Filmmakers and video distributors (i.e., letterboxing films) have long understood the importance of retaining control of the visual frame regardless of display format. Video gamers actively participate during the course of game play, but cut-scenes cue gamers with physical shifts in screen space to drop their controllers and consume the "cinematics." Advertisers have a mode of production (colonizing screen space) by which they may cue viewers *when* to consume by controlling the visual fields we gaze upon. Content producers understand that letterboxed visuals mean *something* different than traditional 4:3 ratios, and analyzing these examples provides cursory steps in evaluating how those meanings are visually communicated.

Pixar, screen space, and digital filmmaking

New media content producers use cinematic tropes to endow their texts with filmic significance and activate notions of highbrow experiences. A hallmark of online and digital textual creations is the almost limitless aesthetic freedom and manipulability of *mise-en-scène*. This final section addresses the inherent differences of spatial allocation between traditional analog film production and the infinitely alterable digitexts such as those of Pixar. These animated, digitextual creations provide an excellent case study for the possibilities of digital tools and how they affect and influence cinematic aesthetics choices with regard to screen space.

In a discussion of analog versus digital filmmaking traditions, Stephen Prince outlines several key factors that delineate these separate schools. First, analog cinema is a "photomechanical" medium that creates "its images arising from chemistry, darkroom and processing lab(s)" that are then "fixed in analog form on a celluloid surface" and exhibited (25). Katherine Sarafian, a producer at Pixar Animation Studios, notes that the filmmaker's toolbox has undergone a distinctive change with the advent of digital filmmaking choices, and therefore the workflow progression must be factored into the production equation as well. Digital filmmakers, and animators in particular, do not use the same production processes as did the analog cinema producers for the majority of the twentieth century. Traditional analog filmmakers rely on a division of labor and hierarchy of processes. Obviously, there is the progression from preproduction throughout production and then finally to postproduction and distribution. Producers, directors, and screenwriters must communicate a range of visions for aesthetic and economic concerns before a production shoot can begin, not to mention the coordination of talent that must be secured. When the production process actually begins, artisans from lighting technicians to set dressers, cinematographers, and the like must be employed and managed to produce usable footage. Then the editor and producer/director must oversee the postproduction elements that may vary from special effects work to editing to digital compositing.

Pixar's artists produce digital texts without human actors (except voiceovers) and that represent a paradigmatic shift from traditional filmmaking techniques. There is no celluloid, camera, lighting, or soundstage.

The digital toolbox of Pixar artists is composed of hard drives, keyboards, mice, stylus pens, digital shot recorders, playback monitors, and earphones, in addition to various proprietary software packages such as Renderman.

In a discussion of cinema within the context of digital technologies, Lev Manovich writes, "[A]s traditional film technology is universally being replaced with digital technology, the logic of the filmmaking process is being redefined" (300). Specifically with regard to production, Manovich argues, "in traditional filmmaking, editing and special effects were strictly separate activities" (301). Digital cinema and animation in particular recontextualizes the notion of production and workflow and thus leads to spatial and stylistic shifts with regard to screen shape. As Manovich asserts, "production just becomes the first stage of post-production" for new media and digitextual products (303). The very process of analog/traditional filmmaking splinters with multiple variables introduced throughout the process that may impact the final cut. Pixar Animation Studios follows a very different production model than that of traditional analog filmmaking. How is screen space affected with regard to such revolutionary production strategies? Pixar's video release of *A Bug's Life* (1998) provides an excellent case study.

The epigraph of this article speaks to the conceptual shift in digital filmmaking that Pixar's texts represent. Sarafian observes that everything must be created in Pixar's digital worlds. The implications for screen space within such a shift are revealing. Pixar's productions begin as digital blanks, and upholding Greg Smith's (1999) notion of the "invariant" shape of the film or television screen,[11] their texts are infinitely flexible and alterable. *A Bug's Life* was Disney's (Pixar's distributor) first animated feature release on DVD, and the production staff at Pixar made a significant choice with regard to aspect ratio. Pixar's staff chose to "reframe" *A Bug's Life* for home video release in full frame (1.33:1) by "adapting" the OAR (2.35:1). The reframing process is uncommon in film history, and it shares a lineage to the aforementioned pan-and-scan debacles with regard to OARs.

In the early days of home video (not to mention early television broadcasts of widescreen texts), VHS-formatted releases of films were panned and scanned to accommodate the width of the filmic text to the narrow television frame.[12] This process involves a flying spot scanner that projects a target onto the filmic image (a "spot") and pans and scans accordingly as that spot moves. As noted by John Belton, the pan and scan process essentially is a recomposing of filmic text, because "extraneous" footage would be scanned over or often cropped out completely. Pixar's reframing project presents one alternative to such destructive—and what Kendrick's home theater enthusiasts call "subversive"—video transfer processes ("Aspect Ratios" 61).

Realizing that their widescreen compositions would suffer on "fool" frame releases, Pixar's production team decided to reframe the film using four processes: restaging, frame height adjustments, cropping, and scanning. These processes warrant a bit of explanation, but the concept is clear: with digital filmmaking tools, Pixar's artists control the recomposition of their product in the video transfer process and control any compositional changes. The process of video transfer usually flows from film to video. The digital process includes yet another step from digital to film to video. For Pixar, the subsequent loss of quality is unnecessary because the process can simply be digital to digital with the DVD format. Therefore, Pixar produced two versions of *A Bug's Life* for home video release; each version was controlled and created by Pixar's production team and therefore retains the original integrity of composition, framing, and blocking.

Bill Kinder, editorial supervisor of *A Bug's Life,* says that "the reframing project is Pixar's way of solving the filmmaker's riddle 'how do you fit a rectangular peg in a square hole?'" (*A Bug's Life* DVD, 1998).[13] Textual examples from the different versions of *A Bug's Life* illuminate the differences possible in dual formats when production is controlled by the filmmakers and not a third party. The four reframing processes in *A Bug's Life* provide answers to the anecdotal query that begins this article. If one examines films produced in dual formats, the aesthetic disparities between the two are revelatory with regard to widescreen poetics, framing strategies, and screen space. Pixar's initial reframing process is to restage. In restaging, characters and their accoutrements are moved closer together in the frame. This stage is exemplary of the infinite possibilities of digital filmmaking and animation in particular. Pixar's filmmakers have infinite control and flexibility within the frame. Although a widescreen composition may lend itself to more airy blockings and negative space, full-frame compositions necessitate more intimate compositions.

Upon initial inspection, the full-frame version of *A Bug's Life* seems to simply have been "zoomed" in. However, a careful analysis of perspectival balance yields not-so-subtle differences in restaging. Note the obvious curvature of the leaf in Figure 20.3 and how it provides masking to create a focal point within the wide frame. The masked composition above the leaf is essentially all that remains in the full-frame version.

FIGURE 20.3 A Bug's Life, *Pixar Animation Studios, 1998.*

This two-tiered compositional strategy of restaging represents Pixar's digitally updated version of the analog problem faced by experimental widescreen films such as *The Big Trail* and *The Bat Whispers*.[14] Rather than reshoot entire films in multiple formats (and with multiple actors in the case of *The Big Trail*), Pixar's filmmakers can simply frame for both formats simultaneously.

Arthur Edeson's Grandeur (1930 widescreen process) compositions in *The Big Trail* tend to be perpendicular during conversations and dialogue scenes, whereas Lucien Androit's Academy version has the camera at slightly oblique angles to foreground the depth of field or simply to provide a more stylized composition. The Pixar filmmakers are following similar aesthetic edicts here with their restaging shots originally composed for widescreen. Also, as with Edeson on *The Big Trail* and Robert Planck on *The Bat Whispers*, the widescreen (theatrical) version takes precedence over the full-frame version and therefore dictates initial *mise-en-scène* decisions. Figure 20.4 not only evidences the reframing process and restaging but also is exemplary of Pixar's second process of reframing for the Academy ratio release—frame height.

The process of frame height is the most significant example of what this article aims to examine: the spatial differences between widescreen and Academy ratio screen shapes and the resulting content produced for each. The process of frame height keeps the original 2.35:1 frame intact but adds new artwork to the top and bottom of the frame to fill vacant areas. Thus, the wide frame necessitates the elongation of the frame and therefore more lateral artwork and shorter frame heights. Pixar artists then use the wide frame as a template, and in concert with restaging, they also verticalize the frame to fill the now-taller composition area. Certainly this example echoes Edeson and Stull's comments with regard to vertical sets and lighting trends associated with Academy ratio films. William Stull's (1930) comments equally apply to both the experimental widescreen texts of 1930 and Pixar's frame height adjustments for *A Bug's Life*.

FIGURE 20.4 A Bug's Life, *Pixar Animation Studios, 1998.*

FIGURE 20.5 A Bug's Life, *Pixar Animation Studios, 1998.*

Note the additional sand striations that extend downward into the foreground and the upper tree and sky sections that were added for the full frame release (Figure 20.5).

Certainly the argument can be waged that although a cameraman may have greater *lateral* scope within the wide frame, he certainly lacks *vertical* range. This example embodies the essential question posed by this article: what do widescreen content producers lose or gain by elongating the horizontal axis of the frame at the expense of vertical area, and how does new media deal with such challenges? The widescreen composition at the left in Figure 20.5 can only be said to be more cinematic than the full-frame composition because of its shape. The Academy ratio composition on the right actually contains more visual information (though framed more closely) because of its additional frame height.

The final two processes of Pixar's reframing methods are the crop and the scan. The crop is similar to the recomposition of a still image that has been manipulated either in a darkroom or with digital editing software.

FIGURE 20.6 A Bug's Life, *Pixar Animation Studios, 1998.*

The image is cropped when the left, right, or both edges of the frame are truncated with no camera movement. A scan accomplishes the same feat but does so with a lateral movement (Figure 20.6).

The final two processes are similar to the recompositions of a traditional pan-and-scan process, but no third party does the panning and scanning. Pixar's authors retain control of the integrity of the image.

The Pixar reframing process is unique. Images that are composed laterally as opposed to vertically exhibit distinct textual, compositional, and aesthetic strategies. This article explores a number of traditional analog filmmaking decisions and strategies to incorporate cinematic (i.e., widescreen) aesthetics into traditional Academy ratio tropes, but Pixar reduces the differences to a set of "either-or" processes. Compositions that are composed for the wide screen must undergo (1) a restaging or re-blocking of graphical elements or (2) an adjustment in frame height to compensate for the geometric changes in proportions, or (3) portions of the image must simply be truncated altogether. Differences in widescreen and Academy ratio proportions can be summarized thus: elements that are strung out along the wider staging area in a widescreen format must be compressed for the full frame; sets and lighting must be manipulated to compensate for the additional vertical frame space required in the full frame; and when all else fails, portions of the widescreen image must simply be sacrificed and lopped off to accommodate the more narrow but more vertical full frame.

New media aesthetics can be likened to an artistic palette of choices. The palette metaphor is pervasive in many graphics programs because of its adaptability. Once users know and understand the concept of the metaphorical choice menu (the palette), then the palette's refunctionalization for many programs is simplified. The flexibility of the Pixar texts recognizes that with a few adjustments, new media texts can be both full-screen and widescreen simultaneously. Whereas Edeson and Planck faced decisions of staging, lighting, and so on and how compositions would ultimately be affected, digital filmmaking tools erase the dilemma of choice: all options are infinitely flexible. Digital texts do not face the choice of either widescreen or full screen, but must negotiate both simultaneously. Therefore, as the Pixar examples display, *mise-en-scène* issues are left open for maximum flexibility. Whereas directors might string a group of actors or actions across the width of an early 1950s CinemaScope frame to "justify" the new format's width, new media texts can both foreground the width of the 2.35:1 theatrical aspect ratio release and restage, recompose, and alter frame height to better suit the Academy ratio home video version.

New media and digitexts can be said to have certain hallmarks. First, new media content producers ape the cinematics of traditional filmmaking to associate their texts with higher-brow consumables (i.e., via cinematic shape). Through the process of colonization, new media content producers provide focal points within a computer-mediated interface, and these spatial alterations of screen space from full frame to widescreen may cue viewers when to consume and when to participate. The cinematic letterboxing of texts where there is no imperative speaks to the power and clout of the wide frame and its associated formal aesthetic properties. Other cinematic techniques associated with widescreen filmmaking—lateral compositions and multiple-image screens such as those of *Star* and *Tiger Trap*—further endow the new media texts with filmic attributes, thus fulfilling the new media producers' goal of referencing cinematic film texts.

Pixar's example is at once fascinating and flummoxing. Pixar's four-phase process of reframing (particularly the processes of restaging and frame height) seems to be a touchstone for this essay that signals a progression of ultimate flexibility for the "inflexible" frame. The final two processes of crop and scan, however, demonstrate that widescreen aesthetics can always be sacrificed to a full-frame physical norm of televisions and computer monitors.[15] Pixar's reframing processes for home video formats physically alter the original cinematic text. The role of authorship is significant because, in an effort to retain the integrity of the original text and utilize the infinite flexibility of new media textual palettes, Pixar's authors control the physical and stylistic rupturing processes of restage, frame height, and crop and scan.

The goal of this article is to enumerate and critique the various uses and manifestations of traditional, analog filmic poetics at play in constructions of new media screen space. Certain texts, such as online ads or video games, demarcate screen space to revivify and hail cinematic aspect ratios, suggesting that letterboxing connotes cinema itself and thus is somehow more established. However, Pixar must create texts for multiple screen shapes and then negotiate how to accommodate such various screen spaces. Pixar seems to be at the leading edge of digitextual creations that demand multiple delivery platforms, and therefore Pixar's artists must constantly negotiate screen space allocations for all their aesthetic decisions. The new frontier of screen space possibilities lies not only in digitexts such as the ones discussed within this article but in the farthest reaches of transtextuality.[16] Video games, online digital films, and other texts that hail "cinematic" form represent new potentialities for spatial/screen shape inquiries. It is growing more difficult to discern where cut-scenes originate from; does *Doom* (2005) the film ape *Doom* the video game, or is it drawing on previous game-based films for its aesthetic strategies? Does *The Matrix*'s many transtextual manifestations—video games, comic books, graphic novels, traditional and/or online films—strive for the cinematic caché associated with widescreen, or are the producers simply defining an easily adaptable and transferable stylistic look? Further research is needed in the area of screen shape and space because the convergence of mediated spaces is ever-growing, and digitextual artists and critics must continue to negotiate the new spatial challenges ahead.

Notes

1   Portions of this essay build on previous research. See Cossar ("Taking a Wider"). Cinematics and cut-scenes are often used to interrupt game play or may advance plot, present character development, or provide background information, often though not exclusively in a letterboxed format.

2   Colonization in video games, such as cut-scenes of cinematics, can be turned off by entering a game's preferences menu. To do so obviously requires a recognition that such a transformation has occurred, and thus colonization is still relevant.

3   *Mise-en-scène* here refers to the traditional notion in analog filmmaking of the content that is composed before the camera, such as set design, costume, lighting, and the blocking of props and actors.

4   For a more thorough discussion of production strategies associated with analog dual-format (Academy and widescreen ratios) films, see Cossar ("Snake and Funerals").

5   Kendrick summarizes this point very well as he adapts Pierre Bourdieu's "manifested preferences" to the argument of home video format "wars" ("Aspect Ratios" 63).

6   See Cossar ("Snakes and Funerals").

7   Initially, the laserdisc formats were among the only home video outlets to offer consumers releases in their original aspect ratios. The Criterion Collection in particular releases films only in their OAR as a matter of principle (see Kendrick, "What Is the Criterion?"). DVD formats increasingly offer consumers a choice of either a widescreen or full-screen version separately, or with both formats packaged into one "flipper" disc. For further reading on laserdisc technologies, see Winston (126–43).

8   Increasingly, as Internet browsers and their dependent plug-ins become more sophisticated, there are media viewers that strip away the black bars from a letterboxed AVI or MPEG file, allowing viewers to consume the text in a long, horizontal window. This article does not account for such applications, but rather applies only to letterboxed content as the black bars serve as the colonizing lines of demarcation in the monitor's surface space.

9   "Highbrow" in this context is the same as used by Lawrence Levine in his exhaustive study of such cultural constructs. See Levine.

10 [Figures numbers have been changed from the original.—Ed.]

11 Smith argues that *The Maxx* television program (MTV, 1995) utilizes the "comic-ness" of its animated background by deploying "the most noticeable advantage comic books have over television ... a variably sized and shaped frame" (35). Smith contends that the television show's lineage from the printed page is the concept of varying panel size within the "invariant frame" of the 1.33:1 aspect ratio television screen (41). "The limitation which kept television from exploring the broader use of frames-within-the-frame was not a technical one, but a conceptual one" (41).

12 Letterboxing for home video release was not popularized until Woody Allen secured a contractual agreement with United Artists in 1985 that gave him control over the video versions of his work, and Allen's *Manhattan* (1979) was the first home video released in the letterbox format. See Belton.

13   Certain "traditional" filmmakers such as Gus Van Sant are now experimenting with shooting films in two formats given digital filmmaking's ease of aspect ratio shifts. Van Sant's films *Gerry* (2002), *Elephant* (2003), and *Last Days* (2005) were all shot full-frame (open matte), but the DVD releases feature matted widescreen versions as well.

14   See Cossar ("Snakes and Funerals" 84–130).

15   This "norm" is slowly changing as HDTV and widescreen aspect ratio computer monitors continue to be ushered in. Apple Computer even goes so far as to suggest that its Cinema Display monitors offer verisimilar possibilities that are not feasible with traditional 4:3 monitors. Apple's online store claims that "the widescreen Apple Cinema Display line offers a natural format for arranging documents the way your brain processes them—longer wide than high. So you can easily fit palettes, timelines, extra windows and more right in your viewing area" (http://www.shopwiki.com/Apple+Cinema+Display+20).

16   See Jenkins.

References

A Bug's Life, Collector's Edition DVD Special Features. Dir. John Lasseter. Walt Disney Home Video, 1998. DVD.

Barr, Charles. "CinemaScope: Before and After." *Film Quarterly* 16.4 (Summer 1963): 4–24. Print.

Bazin, André. "Fin du Montage." *Cahiers du Cinema* 31 (Jan. 1954); reprinted in Velvet Light Trap 21 (Summer 1985): 14–15. Print.

Belton, John. *Widescreen Cinema*. Cambridge: Harvard UP, 1992. Print.

Bolter, Jay David, and Richard Grusin. *Remediation: Understanding New Media*. Cambridge: MIT P, 2002. Print.

Cossar, Harper. "Snakes and Funerals: Widescreen Aesthetics and American Films." Diss. Georgia State U, 2007. Print.

"Taking a Wider View: The Widescreen Aesthetic in Online Advertising." *Journal of New Media and Culture* 3.1 (Winter 2005): n. pag. Web. 11 Apr 2009.

Crafton, Donald. *The Talkies: American Cinema's Conversion to Sound 1926–1931*. Berkeley: U of California P, 1997. Print.

Edeson, Arthur. "Wide Film Cinematography." *American Cinematographer* (Sept. 1930): 8–9, 21. Print.

Gadney, Guy. "Broadband Futures." LAMP, Australian Film Television and Radio School. Sept. 7, 2005. Podcast.

Garfield, Bob. "Innovation Boxes Out Effective Approach in Mercedes-Benz Ads." *Advertising Age* 11 (May 1992): 77. Print.

Jenkins, Henry. *Convergence Culture: Where Old and New Media Collide*. New York: NYU P, 2007. Print.

Kendrick, James. "Aspect Ratios and Joe Six-Packs: Home Theater Enthusiasts Battle to Legitimize the DVD Experience." *Velvet Light Trap* 56 (Fall 2005): 58–70. Print.

"What Is the Criterion? The Criterion Collection as an Archive of Film as Culture." *Journal of Film and Video* 55.2–3 (Summer–Fall 2001): 124–39. Print.

King, Geoff, and Tanya Kryzwinska. *Screenplay: Cinema/Videogames/Interfaces*. New York: Wallflower, 2002. Print.

Levine, Lawrence. *Highbrow/Lowbrow: The Emergence of Cultural Hierarchy in America*. Cambridge: Harvard UP, 1990. Print.

MacCullough, Campbell. "High, Wide and Handsome." *Motion Picture* 39.5 (June 1930): 70–72, 109–12. Print.

Manovich, Lev. *The Language of New Media*. Cambridge: MIT P, 2001. Print.

Prince, Stephen. "The Emergence of Filmic Artifacts: Cinema and Cinematography in the Digital Era." *Film Quarterly* 57.3 (2004): 24–33. Print.

Sarafian, Katherine. "Flashing Digital Animations: Pixar's Digital Aesthetic." *New Media: Theories and Practices of Digitextuality*. Ed. Anna Everett and John T. Caldwell. New York: Routledge, 2003. 209–24. Print.

Smith, Greg M. "Shaping *The Maxx*: Adapting the Comic Frame to Television." *Animation Journal* 8.1 (Fall 1999): 32–53. Print.

Stull, William. "Seventy Millimetres." *American Cinematographer* (Feb. 1930): 9, 42–43. Print.

Vagoni, Anthony. "Out of the Box." *Advertising Age* (8 Nov. 1999): 48–50. Print.

Winston, Brian. *Media Technology and Society: A History: From the Telegraph to the Internet*. New York: Routledge, 1998. Print.

CHAPTER TWENTY-ONE

Fit to Frame: Image and Edge in Contemporary Interfaces

Stephen Monteiro

Images elicit different requirements and uses in everyday life, yet most are conveyed and viewed by the same means: as digital formats on screen-based devices. Under these circumstances, the contemporary image has increasingly served to reaffirm the screen that harbours its presence. A fetishization of the frame manifests itself in the conspicuous marketing emphasis on the aesthetics of the screen-object. The dual trend towards reducing device thickness and increasing screen size (as percentage of surface area) contributes to this material aesthetics. It occurs despite the appearance of reducing the object while simultaneously maintaining the images that the object bears. Phones, tablets, televisions and monitors may now strike us as pure screens: unadorned, millimetres-thick, flush-edged, devoid of buttons, lights or any other distractions from surface and shape.[1] 'What we're going to do', Apple chief executive Steve Jobs publicly pledged when unveiling the iPhone in 2007, 'is get rid of all these buttons and just make a giant screen. A giant screen.'[2]

By privileging the screen, the object is reinforced while the image must adapt. Filling the screen surface with the image has become a priority, even when this risks alterations to the image's original aspect ratio or internal, formal relationships. The image becomes eminently convertible in contemporary interfaces, there to be stretched, compressed and rotated to conform to all manner of screen frames in a proliferation of formats and dimensions developed for any number of devices and browsers. The image can be adeptly pinched and pulled by fingertips on touchscreens, whether handheld or desktop. As tablet users turn and tilt the screen in their hands, the image will spin to match the object's new orientation, punctuating its deference to the frame as defining form. Larger desktop and wall displays continue to rely on keyboard strokes and remote-control commands to similarly reshape and resize the image to cover a portion or the entirety of the screen, but out-of-the-box default settings on these displays may automatically adjust the image signal to stretch visuals across the entire screen like a mesh or membrane. The resulting image may appear strained and shallow in its new aspect ratio, but the viewer may also perceive it as taut as a drum-skin in a frame delivering on a promise of plenitude.

No image comes up short in this situation, regardless of the input data. By filling the frame, the image asserts screen shape and size as the dominant properties of the visual experience. Whenever an image dragged across a touchscreen 'rubber-bands' upon release to fill the frame, or a television cycles through display options that stretch, contract and crop the image as the user scrolls through the menu with a remote, one is constantly reminded of the frame's continuous, guiding presence. This presence asserts itself over modifiable images that decreasingly bear any relation to the physical laws and formal properties of three-dimensional space, despite the advent of high-definition and related image features designed to reinforce notions of 'realism'.

In *Mobile Screens: the Visual Regime of Navigation*, Nanna Verhoeff argues that the advent of touchscreen interfaces has 'add[ed] to the dynamic space of the screen' in the viewer–image relationship. 'The screen, here, becomes a thin, but essential and visible membrane', Verhoeff claims. 'Its materiality has become quite literally the surface we need, the surface we touch, trace and imprint.'[3] Touchscreen has had a profound effect on the triangulated relationship of user, image and screen. As Verhoeff's evocation of 'essence' and 'need' demonstrate, the visual experience of the image becomes bound into tactile recognition of the screen, reciprocated by the screen's recognition of touch. In turn, the activated image recognizes the screen and its frame by reacting to touch commands and displaying itself in ways that maximize recognition of the frame (by turning ninety degrees, perhaps, or zooming into – or out of – full-screen mode). Tactile interface leads to the adjustment of the image, often signalled by a slight delay of repositioning – deliberately coded into the aesthetics of the interface – that visually suggests an initial *separation* of the image from the frame before performing its *reattachment*. The display modes available with remote command screens may create a similar perception of the image conforming to the frame, though this is often through visual cues differing from those found in touchscreen interfaces.

That these cues span varying screen types, uses and experiences indicates a fundamental change in the apprehension and function of the image in contemporary society. With the frequent and indifferent modification of digital images to fit screens, the screen itself may become the message. The rhetoric of the images it harbours is modified in part to reinforce this message by complying with surface and frame edge. With the frame as their primary organizing reference, browser windows, apps and images 'snap' into place (to use Microsoft's term in describing this feature in recent versions of its Windows operating system). While initiatives like 3D television have failed to gain widespread acceptance, the surface has risen to prominence. The marketing of screens and screen devices increasingly foregrounds superficiality: Microsoft calls its tablet simply 'Surface'; Indian electronics manufacturer Micromax names its line of smartphones and tablets 'Canvas'; Apple equips its iPhones and iPads with 'Retina' display, invoking the light-sensitive surface of the inner eye. 'You're actually touching your photos, reading a book, playing the piano. Nothing comes between you and what you love', Apple claims, conveniently negating the retinal reference's connotations of both surface and mediation.[4]

In this discourse, it appears all that matters, whether literally or figuratively, is the threshold of frame and surface that together bear the image. It is a matter of case over content and form over function, as images seem to fall perfectly (even when pushed or pulled by device settings) into the space of the frame. These processes, where any perceived image resistance finally succumbs to the guiding edge of the frame, adhere to Alexander R. Galloway's theorization of contemporary digital interfaces. In *The Interface Effect*, Galloway suggests such interfaces reify mediatic difference and convergence, producing 'an "agitation" or generative friction between different formats'. He explains, 'Since any given format finds its identity merely in the fact that it is a container for another format, the concept of interface and medium quickly collapse [*sic*] into one and the same thing'. Raising the possibility of *intra*face as a dynamic relationship between edge and centre within interfaces, Galloway surmises that 'all media evoke … liminal transition moments in which the outside is evoked in order that the inside may take place'.[5] An intraface aims to assert medium specificity when this might otherwise appear endangered. The image–screen relationships indicated above amount to a digital interface's intraface by consistently referencing the outside through a performance of inside. Their properties suggest a digital specificity precisely by articulating convergence within the field of the screen.

Galloway likens digital (and other) interfaces to windows and doors, a comparison that binds them to the long history of conceptualizing images and screens as windows and frames. The painting's frame is fitted to its image support, for example, as a window might be constructed to frame a view. Jacques Derrida theorizes this frame as a *parergon*, which mediates between the image and the world outside its edges.[6] In the cinema, the screen is designed to receive multiple image formats. Modifications to the projector can adjust the source image's projected size, preserving the aspect ratio while avoiding any need to reframe the image through cropping. The cinema screen as a framing device is perceived as an arbitrary break in the view of a photographically reproduced world that in the viewer's mind continues unimpeded beyond the frame. '[W]hat the screen shows us seems to be part of something prolonged indefinitely into the universe', André Bazin claims in 'Painting and cinema'.[7] Any possibility of abolishing the frame altogether in the viewer's perception would appear beneficial to the experience, bringing the moving image closer to the terms of ordinary visual cognition in a three-dimensional world. The appeal of this possibility is so persistent that such disparate film cultures as 1950s commercial widescreen production and 1960s expanded cinema share this concern, despite their opposing ideological stances.

With the inanimate photographic or painted image, according to Bazin, 'The picture frame polarizes space inwards.... A [picture] frame is centripetal, the screen centrifugal.'[8] The contemporary screen image's constant adaptation to the frame through expansion and rotation corresponds no better to much of modernist image-making, however, than it does to the model of modern screen imagery just described. Indeed, a guiding concern of avant-garde painting in the twentieth century was often the relationship between image and surface, or the material interface of canvas and paint, which accentuated the planar face of the object. Yet the contemporary screen image suggests neither an infinite universe beyond the frame nor an inward concentration on the image that would draw attention away from the frame, such as can be found in cubist, abstract expressionist, or colour-field works. Instead, it affirms the organizing presence of the screen edge. Not surprisingly, this affirmation recalls certain structuralist film and video productions of the 1960s and 1970s.[9] Yet it also finds relevant historical and theoretical kinship in a more unlikely neo-avant-garde partner: minimalist painting. As it developed from the late 1950s and through the 1960s, minimalism emphasized the whole over the part by placing a premium on object and shape rather than image and illusion. Particularly in 'hard-edge' painting, minimalism's pictorial incident was centrifugal to the extent that its visual forms not only deferred to but also referenced the object's overall shape. 'The whole picture becomes the unit', as Lawrence Alloway notes.[10] This affinity and its significance will be revisited more extensively later in this essay; for now, I shall revisit the image on screen.

'How the world is framed may be as important as what is contained within that frame', Anne Friedberg posits in *The Virtual Window*.[11] Certainly features that resize or crop the image to fit its frame conspire to adulterate the screen image by disfiguring or abridging internal formal relationships in systematic ways. As these shortcuts become increasingly standardized – and their consequences increasingly common – it becomes necessary to consider the aesthetics of frame-oriented image processing. This requires examining the cultural and technological constraints that both explain and shape the contemporary frame and the image it circumscribes. From the theory and history of art and film to descriptions in advertising and manufacturers' manuals, the relationship of the image to the screen frame can be described and understood in differing ways. Nevertheless, important overlaps relating to the fetishization of screen over image in contemporary visual culture emerge across these distinct discourses.

Amid mounting dependence on the digitally recorded, stored and displayed image, an intense investigation of the theory of the screen, its frame and the relationship of both to the image can also measure the consequences of this recent turn for visual and aesthetic theory. As Vivian Sobchack points out, the various screens confronting the contemporary viewer 'solicit and shape our presence to the world, our representation in it, and our sensibilities and responsibilities about it'. Accordingly, 'Each differently and objectively alters our subjectivity while each invites our complicity in formulating space, time, and bodily investment as significant personal and social experience'.[12] Recent changes in screen form and image display undoubtedly affect our sensibilities and responsibilities. The shift in emphasis from image to screen fosters new understandings of the image as part of a larger apparatus, where its screen status is always contingent and provisory. By recalling historical conceptualizations of the properties of filmic, televisual and digital models of display alongside differing understandings of the role of the frame, as well as early ideas of the networked image, one can begin to map the changing interdependence of screen and image as a performance of contemporary networked visuality.[13]

While transmission and exhibition of the image on screen-based devices have made it subject to the specifications of the screen, it is only with the onset of digitization as the primary means of image production and conservation that the screen has become the frame for nearly all images. With printing becoming an infrequent choice (or even an option), the aesthetics of the image's mode of presentation, rather than its creation, has become more and more critical. The still image has become animated, less presented than *performed* in its durational invocation on the screen from a base string of binary code passing through a processor. The moment the interface is interrupted or closed, this image reverts to simple code until the next occasion of access. In the relative permanence of the screen as the site through which nearly all images are retrieved and experienced, the image must conform in new ways to the aesthetics of the frame of performance. No longer bound to the formal compositional relationships established at the moment of its making, the image is reimagined at the moment of its exhibition. It becomes an approximation upon every iteration.

A brief examination of manufacturers' descriptions and guidelines for screen-based devices, shown below, reveals the variety of approaches that nevertheless converge in an overemphasis on screen-filling images as aesthetically and technologically superior. Indeed, the first entry in a recent Microsoft list of tips for 'that "world's coolest power user" feeling' is to convert 'maximized' image size to 'full screen' when using Windows.[14] Microsoft is not alone in its stance. Advertisements and user manuals from a range of manufacturers of screen-based devices imply that images displayed at less than full-screen are undesirable and even harmful. Their descriptions of screen display and image options demonstrate this bias towards full-screen display regardless of the properties of the source image.

Under the heading 'Welcome to the world of BRAVIA', Sony's manual for that series of high-definition LCD televisions explains that most HD signals use a 16:9 aspect ratio that 'fills your BRAVIA screen, maintaining a crisp, clear, vivid picture'. The 'standard-definition' 4:3 signal, on the other hand, is 'boxy'. 'You will see black bars on the sides', the manual informs owners, warning that 'picture quality may not be as sharp as with HD sources'. These descriptions misleadingly imply that the image's ability to fill the screen renders it 'crisp, clear, vivid', and that falling short of that will result in decreased resolution. The opposite is just as likely to be true, however, depending on signal quality and original aspect ratio. A further note suggests that 'You can use the Wide Mode function of the TV to adjust the 4:3 image to fit the entire screen', without explaining that the adjustment will distort the image and alter formal relationships, as the manual's accompanying illustration demonstrates.[15]

An LG Electronics manual for that manufacturer's series of LCD televisions cautions viewers that anything other than the full-screen image display mode may cause irreparable damage to the device. Its list of primary features includes HD television, Dolby, Clear Voice, HDMI and ISF technologies, but it closes with an advisory note on image burn. 'When a fixed image…is displayed on a TV for an extended period, it can become permanently imprinted on the screen. This phenomenon is known as "image burn" or "burn-in" [and] is not covered under the manufacturer's warranty', LG states. 'Image burn can also occur on the letterboxed areas of your TV if you use the 4:3 aspect ratio setting for an extended period of time.'[16] In other words, watching 4:3 images in their intended format risks ruining the television.

Samsung's online customer support for its LED televisions explains that basic options of 'zoom', 'wide fit', 'screen fit', 'smart view' and image aspect ratios of 16:9 and 4:3 produce differing effects depending on the ratio of source images. The 16:9 option will 'also stretch a 4:3 aspect ratio to fit your screen', while 4:3 will generate black bars on the left and right for 4:3 source images. The 'zoom' will 'zoom in, or crop, a 4:3 image so it will fit the 16:9 screen with no stretching', but the image will 'lose information on the top and bottom of the screen. Such [sic] as sports scores, tickers, station logos, etc.' 'Wide fit' will 'stretch and zoom a 4:3 program to display it with little distortion and little cut off', while only the last options listed – 'screen fit' and 'smart view' – will either display the source image without scaling or reduce a 16:9 image by 25–50 per cent.[17] That the loss of visual information is exemplified by disappearing sports scores and news tickers reflects an understanding of the televised image as a flexible ground upon which other information can be displayed, with a priority on text over image. Zoom loses that data, but wide fit will retain it while stretching content, implying that nearly nothing is lost in that mode.

The Gateway series of widescreen, flat-panel LCD monitors in 1.76:1 aspect ratio includes similar wide, zoom and letterbox options to match source-image aspect ratios, but it supplements these with a 'panoramic' mode. While the wide and zoom options stretch or crop the image, panoramic mode 'uses selective distortion to stretch a standard broadcast or full-frame image to fill the entire screen'. 'Unlike Wide mode', the Gateway manual informs readers, 'Panoramic mode stretches only the left and right sides of the image, and leaves the center of the image distortion-free'.[18]

When Steve Jobs presented the iPhone at Macworld 2007, he demonstrated its capacity for screening films by displaying an excerpt from a Disney blockbuster in cropped, full-screen mode. Jobs double-tapped to demonstrate widescreen, with its horizontal letterbox bars, before tapping back out to full-screen. 'Now this is a widescreen movie, so I just double-tap and I can see the whole thing here, or I can fill up the screen, whichever I like', he explained. In a paradoxical exercise of alternative plenitudes, Jobs suggests a choice of two absolutes with the iPhone: the 'whole' image or the 'full' image, which may seem to bear the same semantic value but are visually distinct. 'Full', as his performance of the device implies, may be preferable to 'whole'.

The issues raised by these multiple manufacturers' descriptions reflect those that commonly affect the display of images on most digital, image-based devices today. The consumer can infer from these statements that any image less than full-screen, contrary to logic, is prone to diminished sharpness and may have the nasty consequence (at least in one case) of frying the screen. At best, the image that does not fill the screen is quaint; at worst, it is defective or corrosive, to be corrected or neutralized by stretching it to the frame edge.

The possibility and frequency of filling the frame regardless of the source image's initial aspect ratio and size implies that the frame-within-a-frame of letterbox is generally unacceptable. This may run contrary to the everyday presence in digital displays of frames within frames with multiple open windows. Yet with these multiple frames the 'empty' space surrounding them may be perceived as meaningful space rather than a void. Browser window content exists within the context of other available windows and the desktop as a whole, which may bear a base image in 'stretch' mode as its 'wallpaper', as is often the case with Microsoft Windows and Apple OS and iOS (in fact, with the release of iOS 7 in 2013, Apple's operating system began stretching or resizing these images automatically).[19]

In 2009, Microsoft's Windows 7 operating system introduced a new relationship between user, screen and application window with the addition of its 'Snap' and 'Peek' functions. Snap matches up two windows side-by-side to divide equally (and fill) screen space. Users drag separate windows to the left and right edges of the screen until the outline of an expanded window appears, allowing the windows to fit snugly into opposite sides of the screen frame.[20] Snap is meant to simplify interface by eliminating size difference and overlap when working between files and applications, thereby avoiding previous hierarchical relationships that might resemble papers strewn across a desk. Snap instead offers the perception of eliminating the desktop altogether and filling the screen area, leaving no 'extra' or 'dead' space. In designing this interface, Microsoft went so far as to set an automatic blowup of a window, filling the entire screen, when a user drags the window's top edge into the vicinity of the screen's top edge. Triggered by the user's recognition of the frame edge, the feature gives the perception of maximum screen field efficiency, where nothing is lost, occluded or wasted. Clicking on the right corner of the bottom taskbar of Windows 7, on the other hand, activates Peek, which will make *all* open files and applications magically disappear, like a mirage, to reveal the underlying desktop. 'Peek gives you the power of X-ray', Microsoft marketing hyperbolizes, 'so you can peer past all your open windows straight to the Windows 7 desktop'.[21] Microsoft's decision to retain Snap and Peek in Windows 8 (despite a major operating system overhaul to provide a common interface for touchscreen and cursor-based computing) and Windows 10 implies the utility of both features for Windows users.

The history of the image, of course, is yoked to the frame. No image exists – large or small – without a corresponding edge or limit. Images have always been prone to recropping and other formal interventions to meet the requirements of diverse media and contexts. Negative-based photographs regularly underwent retouching, pushed exposure in development, conversion from one format to another (such as 16 mm to 35 mm), or reduction to greyscale or halftone. These images were subject to variable presentation formats on cinema screens and television sets. From widescreen ratios of 2.55:1 or 1.85:1 to the 1.33:1 Academy ratio, films were modified for television broadcast. Beginning with the 1961 US airing of *How to Marry a Millionaire* (Jean Negulesco, 1953), a Twentieth Century Fox CinemaScope feature, strategies including pan-and-scan and cropping became common when presenting theatrical releases on television.[22] If the letterbox method of adding black bands to the top and bottom of the screen retained the widescreen image in its entirety, pan-and-scan abridged it by displaying a portion of the image and moving the frame as necessary over the original picture field. The image was fragmented, truncated, cropped and trimmed as necessary to retain the 'principal' visual information of the shot, while adjusting it for a differing frame. The screen image was an excerpt or 'recomposing of the filmic text',[23] like a film converted into closeups, with a new, tighter framing that seemingly brought the viewer closer to the image and action. These changes did not affect the formal relationships of the objects on screen, however. Recent trends in electronic and digital framing strategies are fundamentally different because they adjust those relationships in the source image, often in ways that may go undetected by the viewer.

Recalling the image–frame relationships produced by two divergent yet related episodes in post-World War II visual culture may help demonstrate the radical change this shift signals. CinemaScope's introduction of anamorphic widescreen techniques to commercial cinema in the 1950s and 'expanded cinema' alternatives to commercial exhibition as imagined by Stan Vanderbeek a decade later represent ideologically opposed approaches to the image that nevertheless share a desire to dissolve frame and emphasize the visual data of the picture plane. In both formats the image could be seen to undergo distortions, yet these are embedded primarily in intermediate processes (with anamorphic projection) or the accumulation and arrangement of images (with Vanderbeek's Movie-Drome), rather than in the body of the visible image itself.

Beginning with CinemaScope, it is worth noting that the stretch deformation so common to contemporary images on screen-based devices functions inversely to the principles of this earlier widescreen process. CinemaScope relies on an anamorphic lens, fixed to both camera and projector, that first compresses the widened 2.55:1 image field onto the standard 35 mm film 1.33:1 frame at the moment of exposure then, at the time of exhibition, reverses the process as the projector's anamorphic lens expands the compressed image to fill the 2.55:1 screen. When Twentieth Century Fox introduced the process in 1953, it emphasized that CinemaScope minimized image distortion: 'for the first time in film history, one seat in a theatre becomes the equal of any other', the souvenir programme for the first CinemaScope release declares. 'Whether front, middle, side or rear, distortion of the screen is now a thing of the past.'[24]

Indeed, the studio provided illustrations for the press and exhibitors that demonstrated the difference between the image on the film strip and the theatre screen. This marketing ploy allowed viewers to understand the primordial importance of values in the *exhibited* image rather than the *source* image, as the exhibited image at the moment of performance (and not its material source) more faithfully represented the object relationships of the profilmic event.

CinemaScope and other widescreen efforts aimed to diminish or, as was the case with Cinerama's three-projector display, abolish frame edges from the viewer's perception. As Erkki Huhtamo explains, Cinerama's aspect ratio of up to 2.77:1 meant that 'the expansion of the screen reached a paradoxical conclusion: by covering the spectators' total field of vision the screen in a sense disappeared'.[25] By potentially losing the frame, the viewer before these enlarged screens could become one with the depicted scene as it became the only visual information at hand. Writing about the much more common experience of CinemaScope, Charles Barr explained in 1963 that

> it is not only the horizontal line which is emphasized in CinemaScope (this is implied by critics who concentrated on the shape of the frame qua *shape* – as though it were the frame of a painting...). The more open the frame, the greater the impression of depth: the image is more vivid, and involves us more directly.[26]

While widescreen televisions, computers and handheld devices seek to offer a seeming plenitude of the image by widening the screen, the deformation of the image in fact reasserts the presence of the frame as a defining factor in the composition's properties. The development of widescreen cinema did, to some extent, bring such instability into film production at the level of the frame, since the theatre screen would have to support multiple formats. As Bazin notes in 'Will CinemaScope save the film industry?', French film industry leaders urged in 1953 that filmmakers 'concentrate the "useful" part of the image in the central portion of the frame' so that theatres featuring 'panoramic' screens could use projector masks to 'hide the "useless" part of the image' and produce a full-screen image for the viewer.[27] This operation recalls today's relationship between device settings and screen aspect ratios as, for example, when the 'panoramic' mode of Gateway monitors selectively distorts the image by leaving the centre of the image undisturbed while 'stretching' its flanks.

These earlier aesthetic strategies of cinema screen display sought to offer experiences that would engulf the viewer in images free of visible distortion. Distortion was pushed out to the frame edge itself, which was meant to be at or beyond the limits of the viewer's perception. At the point where the image lost its edge for the viewer, it would transmogrify from framed image to environment. Nevertheless, like the contemporary aesthetic tension between screen and image, these efforts at breaking frame were driven by economic strategies of commodification and consumption. The difficulty of seeing 'the whole thing' contributed to the appeal of watching widescreen films at the cinema.

At about the time that *How to Marry a Millionaire* and widescreen cinema began to conform to the limiting frame of network television, expanded cinema emerged as a competing effort at breaking the frame, born of avant-garde strategies of radical political and ideological transformation. Vanderbeek, a leading figure in this pursuit, argued in 1966 for a system of worldwide communication rooted in a 'picture-language based on motion pictures' that would allow a utopian free flow of human knowledge across cultures by 'stor[ing] and transfer[ring] image materials, motion pictures, television, computers, video-tape, etc.'[28] In this articulation of expanded cinema, the image could escape the frame, in theory, by existing within a vast visual ecology freed from the constraints of commercial use and proprietary restrictions.

For this system to work, Vanderbeek called for the invention of the 'experience machine or "culture-intercom"', an audiovisual device combining image technologies such as cinema, television and the computer. Highly suggestive of digital networks today, this system would be capable of supporting an 'image velocity' produced through a continuous dense flow of amassed visual material, Vanderbeek claimed, that would allow vast epistemologies amounting to the whole of human culture to be 'compressed into such an aspect ratio that the audience could grasp the flow of man, time, and the forms of life that has led up to this very moment, using the past and immediate present to help realize the likely future'.[29]

Vanderbeek's prototype for the experience machine was not the handheld device that increasingly mediates contemporary networked image experiences, but rather the collective viewing apparatus of the Movie-Drome, a screen-domed cinema where multiple overlapping projections spread images across the curved surface in quick succession to create a 'rapid panoply' collage. Movie-Dromes would be both interfaces and networked databases, receiving, storing and sending vast amounts of image data via satellite and other high-speed communications systems. This material would be programmed for communal viewing as a 'feedback presentation', with the possibility for simultaneous 'intra-communitronic' dialogue with other Movie-Dromes or additional live performance. Each recorded image in these interconnected, networked presentations was to lend itself to association with other, frequently changing, images. As in widescreen cinema, once spectators lay on the floor under the dome, the frame of the device would be almost entirely absent, as 'almost the complete field of view is taken up by the dome-screen'. Under these circumstances, the view of the screen is always partial: the viewer must choose where to turn the gaze. 'The audience takes what it can or wants from the presentation and makes its own conclusions', Vanderbeek asserted. 'Each member of the audience will build his own references and realizations from the imageflow.' 'Compression', as Vanderbeek described it, is not a property of the image or the frame-edge, but rather a product of the multiplication and rapid succession of images within the experience machine. The field of the screen is filled with images of different sizes, in varying placements, juxtaposed with yet more images. No edge or frame is seen as inviolable or sovereign. The image becomes both a fragment and part of a whole. It can remain legible as discrete image, even as it enters into the patchwork fabric of presentation. While the image is not stretched or deformed, the vast screen is filled with images that would seem to push the frame to bursting.

'The purpose and effect of such image flow ... is both to deal with logical understanding and to penetrate to unconscious levels', Vanderbeek proposed, suggesting nothing less than 'to reach for the emotional denominator of all men, the non-verbal basis of human life, thought, and understanding, and to inspire all men to goodwill and "inter-and intro-realization"'. The collage of images, where the 'individual is exposed to an overwhelming information experience' in the seemingly free flow of images around and through each other, 'would access the unconscious and free the mind'.[30]

The culture-intercom embodied in Vanderbeek's Movie-Drome is antithetical to today's frame dominance, in which images are adapted to the needs of their frame and reinforce its determinant role. As Vanderbeek argued, humanity needed to 'quickly find some way for the level of world understanding to rise to a new human scale. This scale is the world.'[31] While globalization would seem to hold the promise of such an eventuality, with screen-based personal communication devices facilitating world-scale understanding through the unimpeded circulation of images, the screen-centric nature of these devices and how we use them undermines precisely those goals. Today's networked screens do not offer the free-flowing collaged interface of interpenetrating images envisioned by Vanderbeek, but rather work as containers that reinforce intraface. While they may harbour multiple images, at any given moment they may display a discrete image adjusted to the parameters of the frame, to be followed by another image adjusted in turn. Each image, closely tied to the user's handling of the apparatus, reinforces the device as primary to the experience. The apparent plenitude of the image, enforced by the proclivity of devices to match them to screen dimensions, discourages the sort of open reading across images – or even of the recognition of difference in images – essential to Vanderbeek's idea of a new scale of understanding. Friedberg explains that 'Like the window, the screen is at once a surface and a frame – a reflective plane onto which an image is cast and a frame that limits its view'.[32] In exploring this definition, she cites Derrida's theorization of the parergon as a critical step. It is worth exploring the concept of the parergon in some detail here, as it remains applicable to the changing function of the screen frame and its edge. Working from Immanuel Kant's use of the term in his *Critique of Judgement*, Derrida describes the parergon as 'that which is not internal or intrinsic, as an integral part, to the total representation of the object but which belongs to it only in an extrinsic way as a surplus, an addition, an adjunct, a supplement'. The frame serves that function and remains as important to the functioning and understanding of the image-as-image as it does to the visual information the image contains. 'The parergon inscribes something which comes as an extra, *exterior* to the proper field', Derrida states, 'but whose transcendent exteriority comes to play, abut onto, brush against, rub, press against the limit itself and intervene in the inside only to the extent that the inside is lacking. It is lacking *in* something and it is lacking *from itself*'. He elaborates:

> Parerga have a thickness, a surface which separates them not only (as Kant would have it) from the integral inside, from the body proper of the ergon, but also from the outside, from the wall on which the painting is hung, from the space in which statue or column is erected, then, step by step, from the whole field of historical, economic, political inscription in which the drive to signature is produced.[33]

As Derrida points out, the parergon informs the ergon (the work) through its own formal beauty. If it is not formally beautiful – as in a decorated or gilded frame – it descends into distracting adornment.[34] In certain circumstances relating to the frame–image relationship enacted by today's screens, the relationship has been reversed. Not only is the screen device's prevailing austere modernist form far from adornment, but one could point to the image it houses as fulfilling that role. The frame is more formally beautiful when juxtaposed against the often deformed image it harbours. It is this deformation, in fact, that can work to emphasize the formal beauty of the frame. If the contemporary image is a simulacrum that need not refer to any existing or perceived 'original', as appears to be the case when it circulates and recirculates through the vast sprawl of today's telecommunications networks, then the image is available to (and should) be modified to enhance the aesthetic value of the material object before us.

Significantly, Derrida's analysis stems from Kant's exploration of the garment as a parergon on religious or mythological figures, as with sculpted drapery on statues. Derrida playfully asks, 'Where does a parergon begin and end. Would any garment be a parergon? ... What to do with transparent veils[?]'[35] From this musing he launches into an image, citing the transparent veil in Lucas Cranach's *Lucretia* of 1533. This invocation of the textile unexpectedly intersects Derrida's pursuit with Stanley Cavell's theory of the cinema screen. Cavell argues that the screen produces a frame more closely related to the frame of a loom or a house than to a picture frame. It acts as a 'mould' or 'form' for the image rather than a border. 'Because it is the field of a photograph, the screen has no frame; that is to say, no border', Cavell claims. 'Its limits are not so much the edges of a given shape as they are the limitations, or capacity, of a container. The screen *is* a frame; the frame is the whole field of the screen – as a frame of film is the whole field of a photograph.' When projected onto this surface, Cavell explains,

> successive film frames are fit flush into the fixed screen frame [which] results in a phenomenological frame that is indefinitely extendible and contractible, limited in the smallness of the object it can grasp only by the state of its technology, and in largeness only by the span of the world.[36]

The cinema screen has no frame, as Cavell argues, because it *is* frame. Frame and image bear a one-to-one correspondence – where one ends, so must the other. In the cinema, for example, it makes no sense to speak of screen space that is *not* image space. With a monitor, however, this is not only possible but also points to a relatively common occurrence. Today's screen frames are closer in form to the painting's frame than they are to the cinema screen, yet they may act as moulds or loom frames, fitting (refitting, custom-fitting) the image to their form. They therefore function outside these opposed actions.

If the picture frame directs attention to the interior, and the cinema (and traditional television) screen acts as a window on an expansive exterior world, the new frame–image relationship directs attention to the frame as delimiting edge and shaping container. In this regard it relates less to the frame of figurative, illusionistic painting that Bazin had in mind than to the framing edge of the painting as object. The painting on canvas is first of all an object in itself, bounded by the fabric surface's adherence to the foundational structure of the stretcher frame underneath. In a way, then, the deformations of the contemporary screen image – despite the presence of a figurative image – relate strongly to the tenets of 1960s minimalism, particularly hard-edge painting, and its exploration of the image field as wholly determined by, and dependent upon, the shape of the object supporting it.

As critic and artist Donald Judd claims of such painting – in terms very close to Cavell's description of the cinema screen – 'A rectangle is a shape itself … it determines and limits the arrangement of whatever is on or inside of it'.[37] Some hard-edge painters associated with minimalism, such as Sam Francis and Jo Baer, emphasized shape's determining role by painting only near or along the edges, where the plane of the canvas met its end. Others, including Kenneth Noland and Frank Stella, reflected the overall shape of the canvas within the image area through painted bands repeating the frame's geometric form. Robert Rosenblum explains that

> Stella's paintings seemed to iron out the pictorial space … the picture was no longer an illusion above or behind its surface but rather the flat surface itself. … The picture could no longer be reduced to major and minor components but had to be accepted as a whole.[38]

Michael Fried explores the terms of this relationship in his essay 'Shape as form'. Calling the 'silhouette of the [painting's] support' the 'literal shape', on the one hand, and the 'outlines of elements in a given picture' the 'depicted shape', on the other, Fried explains that the flattened 'optical illusionism' found in mid-century abstract expressionist painting was followed by an increasingly overt correspondence between literal and depicted shape in works by Stella and Noland.[39] Beginning with standard rectangular canvases, before embarking on other shapes, the stripe-based paintings of both artists demonstrated, according to Fried, that 'the burden of acknowledging the shape of the support is borne by the depicted shape or, perhaps more accurately, by the relationship between it and the literal shape – a relation that declares the primacy of the latter'. Like the lateral elongation of screen images in widescreen modes, the framing edge appears to generate the depicted shape within the image: 'It is as though depicted shape has become less and less capable of venturing on its own, of pursuing its own ends'. It is, Fried continues,

> as though unless, in a given painting, depicted shape manages to participate in, by helping to establish, the authority of the shape of the support, conviction is aborted and the painting fails. In this sense depicted shape may be said to have become dependent upon literal shape – and indeed unable to make itself *felt* as shape except by acknowledging that dependence.[40]

Of course, the deference of image to screen shape in current visual practices bears no obvious visual resemblance to the minimalist dissolution of image into a reductive repetition/reiteration of object form in a most basic and literal manner. Nevertheless, it moves the visual rhetoric of the image into a formal recognition of screen as object. To the extent that depicted forms are converted to compensate for that object's shape, they reiterate the edge of the screen within the image. Lateral emphasis in the frame may produce lateral distortion in the image, thereby accommodating *and* emphasizing the frame's horizontal stress.

In engaging frames of painting and cinema, the differing theoretical perspectives examined here – deconstruction (Derrida), analytical philosophy (Cavell) and modernist formalism (Fried) – introduce a corollary pairing of frame and fabric. The veil or drapery as a parergon, the frame as a loom, the image-object as canvas on stretchers – all represent ways of envisioning the relationship between the edge and the surface of the work. Of course, painting and cinema have long relied on stretched fabric as their support: painting from the fifteenth century onwards regularly employed canvas fixed to wooden splints. The cinema has made use of diverse natural and synthetic fabrics on metal or wooden frameworks, stretched taut to minimize image distortion. Each system has a different relationship to the images it bears, however. In painting, the completed image can be stretched after the fact, for example, although this may produce irreparable fissures and cracking. In cinema, stretching screen materials promotes an evenness of image while loose fabric will generate optical aberrations. The digital image, on the other hand, will not crack when stretched, and the screen device that bears it will ensure a uniformly smooth surface. Yet over-magnification will break down the image to discrete pixels that emphasize the flatness of the image while straining the illusion of spatial representation in ways similar to the stretch modes of the devices examined here. Pixelation reveals that, as one engages metaphors of the frame as loom or mould, it is imperative to recognize the electronic image as being in a constant state of performance when on screen. The image is animated, even if visibly still, within the flux of the system as data are continually received, sent and processed by the screen device and network to produce and sustain this visual performance. Lev Manovich goes so far as to claim that the conversion of images to screen display means that the traditional image simply no longer exists, replaced by device operations that only suggest a stable image before our eyes:

> it is only by habit that we still refer to what we see on the real-time screen as 'images' ... a static image ... is no longer the norm, but the exception of a more general, new kind of representation for which we do not yet have a term.[41]

Sobchack asserts that the electronic experience of the image 'has neither a point of view nor a visual situation, such as we experience, respectively, with the photograph and the cinema'. Presence of the image loses stable bearings, as electronic presence randomly disperses its being *across* a network, its kinetic gestures describing and lighting on the surface of the screen rather than inscribing it with bodily dimension....Images on television screens and computer terminals seem neither projected nor deep. Phenomenologically they seem, rather, somehow 'just there' as we (inter) face them.[42]

These conditions may help to explain the digital image's constant deference to the screen frame. As point of view and visual situation become relative and unstable through the ineluctable adjustability of images in digital form, the material device of the screen, whether grasped in the hand, propped on the desk or bolted to the wall, becomes the stable presence upon which the image can appear to detach and adhere before adjustments of device orientation or viewing format require it to detach and adhere anew in a revised relationship to the screen.

Understanding the edge as frame tends to flatten representational space into a simple image surface while reinforcing the edge as that surface's definitive limit. The history of modernist painting is often understood as a shift from the metaphor of the window to the material reality of the picture frame and image surface. This trajectory culminates in works like Stella's, which repeat the contours of the edge within the image area through patterns that are not only informed by but also articulate the object's unifying shape. The current possibilities for manipulating the image on contemporary screens create situations that can reinforce either frame or edge. Stretching the image to fill the screen surface reinforces the frame like the parergon of drapery, for example. Increasing image size in tactile devices to then push the image around its surface, like a weightless tissue floating just under the frame, reinforces the edge as that of a viewfinder or window.

It was at the moment that painting was considered as an object with a shape rather than strictly as an image, Cavell notes, that 'shapes became forms, not in the sense of patterns, but in the sense of containers'.

> A form could then *give* its shape to what it contained. And content could transfer its significance as painting to what contains it. The space *pervades*, like gravity, or energy, or air....This is not, as far as we yet know, a possibility of the film or screen frame – which only repeats the fact that a film is not a painting.[43]

As Judd bluntly states, 'The main thing wrong with painting is that it is a rectangular plane placed flat against the wall'. The historical avant-garde saw the edge of that plane as a boundary to which it would react rather than as a presence to accentuate. In later, postwar American painting, according to Judd, 'The parts are few and so subordinate to the unity as not to be parts in an ordinary sense. A painting is nearly an entity, one thing, and not the indefinable sum of a group of entities and references.' The plane becomes primary. 'Everything on or slightly in the plane of the painting must be arranged laterally.'[44] The screen device has followed a similar path. Its image can be stretched in ways to produce forms with greater lateral orientation, emphasizing the screen's rectangle as the determining form over any regard for original relationships between the components of the composition. Under these circumstances, the relationships between these forms become secondary to the affirmation of the expanse of the screen that contains them.

More and more, then, the frame and the need to fill its form dictate the terms of viewing. The image, as Sobchack writes, becomes incidental, 'just there', fortuitously present for the screen device that contains it. Even if the screen image has always been susceptible to the specifications and conditions of devices and networks – changes in projection brilliance, television colour settings, broadcast signal strength, and so on – it has taken on a greater plasticity as its compositional relationships become variable. In the trend towards filling the screen, an enlarged or reformatted image appears preferable to one occupying less screen space but displaying the original aspect ratio and compositional relationships. It is implied that a larger image of lower resolution is preferable to a smaller, sharper one.

In the range of screen settings and interface options, a tension develops at the border of the image, on the ideological threshold between frame and edge. The frame serves to mediate image–environment relationships, while the edge marks the abrupt break between the two. As Carla Gottlieb notes, 'an edge does not possess the same binding power as a frame or line; it is merely a termination'.[45] Certain options or functions, such as recalculating aspect ratio to cover the entire screen surface, would appear to privilege the edge. Any deformations that are incurred in that case have been determined by the edge. Those options that enlarge the image to match up to the horizontal or vertical edge suggest framing or matting through inevitable horizontal or vertical cropping.

In those instances where the user becomes aware of the image's modification or distortion to conform to the shape of the frame, the frame rises to the surface, however momentarily, as the defining feature of the visual experience. When the image changes orientation or the internal relations of the world it depicts are deformed, the user realizes the limits of the image and its edge. Would, for example, a spectator watching laterally stretched images visualize the depicted world's continuation beyond that frame as equally stretched? If so, the experience follows Bazin's description of the centrifugal screen extending that world indefinitely. If not, it corresponds more closely to the situation presented in minimalist painting, where depicted shape describes a direct relationship to the literal shape of the object.

Unlike the earlier technologies and media of painting, cinema and television, however, the haptic screen interface of contemporary devices introduces a fundamental difference. The hard-edge paintings of Stella or Baer create visual correspondences that urge the spectator to comprehend the painting primarily as an object, for example, yet they neither require nor compel physical handling any more than a remote-controlled television. Many screen-based image devices depend upon viewers touching the screen to activate and direct the image experience. What remains fundamental even in this case, however, is an image–frame relationship that appears to extend beyond the power of the viewer's intervention. While the alignment of screen and image edge may be prompted by a finger gesture, the image's 'popping' or 'snapping' or 'rubber-banding' into place appears as the automatic and inevitable deference of image to frame. The image may be there to be shaped and reshaped by the action of the hand, but it is the containing edge of the frame that ultimately guides the performance.

Notes

1   LG Electronics' 55EM960V OLED TV, for example, has a 140 cm screen display but a depth of only 4 mm.

2   Steve Jobs, 'iPhone: Apple reinvents the phone', 2007, <http://www.youtube.com/watch?v=9hUIxyE2Ns8> accessed 27 June 2014.

3   Nanna Verhoeff, *Mobile Screens: The Visual Regime of Navigation* (Amsterdam: Amsterdam University Press, 2012), p. 65.

4   Apple, 'It's brilliant. In every sense of the word', <http://www.apple.com/sa/ipad/features/#ipadblack> accessed 27 June 2014. In introducing iPhone, Jobs bubbled, 'You can touch your music. You can just touch your music. It's so cool.' Jobs, 'iPhone'.

5   Alexander R. Galloway, *The Interface Effect* (Cambridge: Polity Press, 2012), pp. 31–32.

6   Jacques Derrida, *The Truth in Painting* (Chicago, IL: University of Chicago Press, 1987), pp. 37–81.

7   André Bazin, 'Painting and cinema', in *What Is Cinema?*, Volume I, ed. and trans. Hugh Gray (Berkeley, CA: University of California Press, 1967), p. 166.

8   Ibid.

9   Examples that overtly address the screen edge would include Malcolm Le Grice's *Horror Film* (1971), a triple-projection performance piece where a live, mobile performer frames the projected light with his hands, and Richard Serra's *Frame* (1969), in which Serra places a sheet of paper before the camera and attempts to trace the frame based on spoken descriptions from his off-screen cameraman.

10   Lawrence Alloway, 'On the edge', *Architectural Design*, vol. 30, no. 4 (1960), p. 165.

11   Anne Friedberg, *The Virtual Window: From Alberti to Microsoft* (Cambridge, MA: MIT Press, 2006), p. 1.

12   Vivian Sobchack, *Carnal Thoughts: Embodiment and Moving Image Culture* (Berkeley, CA: University of California Press, 2004), pp. 136–37.

13   This exploration of visuality conforms to Nicholas Mirzoeff's theorization of that term as describing the means of making historical processes perceptible to authority, in *The Right to Look* (Durham, NC: Duke University Press, 2011).

14   Microsoft, '6 Useful Windows tricks', <http://www.microsoft.com/athome/
     setup/windowstricks.aspx#fbid=woOSjc9w0PJ> last accessed 8 January 2013.

15   Sony, *LCD Projection TV: Operating Instructions, KDF-37H1000 BRAVIA*
     (Sony Corporation, 2007), p. 6.

16   LG Electronics, *LCD TV Owner's Manual 19LD350-55LD520* (LG
     Electronics, n.d.), p. 8.

17   Samsung, 'How to change the picture settings on your LED TV', <http://www.
     samsung.com/us/support/howtoguide/N0000000/9488/0/N/3/M//> accessed 27
     June 2014.

18   Gateway, *FHD2400 24-Inch Widescreen LCD Monitor User Guide* (Irvine,
     CA: Gateway, 2007), p. 14.

19   Kif Leswing, 'Fix the ugly iPad wallpaper Apple messed up', *Wired*, 20
     November 2013, <http://www.wired.com/2013/11/fix-ioswallpapers/>
     accessed 27 June 2014; Sarmistha Acharya, 'iOS 7.1: fix wallpaper zooming
     issues with Perspective Zoom', *International Business Times*, 23 March 2014,
     <http://www.ibtimes.co.uk/ios-7-1-fix-wallpaper-zooming-issuesperspective-
     zoom-1441444> accessed 27 June 2014.

20   Microsoft, 'Arrange Windows side by side on the desktop using Snap', <http://
     windows.microsoft.com/en-US/windows7/Arrangewindows-side-by-side-on-
     thedesktop-using-Snap> accessed 27 June 2014.

21   Microsoft, 'Windows 7 features: Peek', <http://windows.microsoft.com/is-is/
     windows7/products/features/peek> accessed 27 June2014.

22   See John Belton, *Widescreen Cinema* (Cambridge, MA: Harvard University
     Press, 1992), pp. 211–28.

23   Harper Cossar, 'The shape of new media: screen space, aspect ratios, and
     digitextuality', *Journal of Film and Video*, vol. 61, no. 4 (2009), p. 11.

24   *Twentieth Century Fox Presents a CinemaScope Production The Robe* (New
     York, NY: Ogden Printing Company, 1953), p. 11. In an August 1953 industry
     advertisement created to reassure exhibitors, Fox claimed that the two screens
     approved for CinemaScope, the Miracle Mirror Screen and Magniglow
     Astrolite Screen, were 'precisely designed to reflect and distribute the light
     evenly over the large surface required for CinemaScope projection, thus
     making every seat a good seat because the picture is uniformly bright from
     any seat in the theatre'. See reproduction in Robert E. Carr and R. M. Hayes,
     Wide Screen Movies: A History and Filmography of Wide Gauge Filmmaking
     (Jefferson, NC: McFarland, 1988), p. 62.

25   Erkki Huhtamo, 'Elements of screenology: towards an archaeology of the
     screen', *ICONICS: International Studies of the Modern Image*, no. 7 (2004),
     pp. 31–82; <http://wro01.wrocenter.pl/erkki/html/erkki_en.html> accessed 27
     June 2014.

26   Charles Barr, 'CinemaScope: before and after', *Film Quarterly*, vol. 16, no. 4
     (1963), p. 9.

27   André Bazin, 'Will CinemaScope save the film industry', *Film-Philosophy*,
     vol. 6, no. 2 (2002), <http://www.film-philosophy.com/vol6-2002/n2bazin>
     accessed 27 June 2014.

28   Stan Vanderbeek, '"Culture: intercom" and expanded cinema: a proposal and
     manifesto', *The Tulane Drama Review*, vol. 11, no. 1 (1966), p. 41.

29   Ibid., p. 45.

30   Ibid., pp. 47–48.

31 Ibid., p. 39.
32 Friedberg, *The Virtual Window*, p. 1.
33 Derrida, *The Truth in Painting*, pp. 60–61.
34 34 For a similar argument specific to cinema architecture and the screen, see Siegfried Kracauer, 'Cult of distraction: on Berlin's picture palaces', in *The Mass Ornament: Weimar Essays*, ed. and trans. Thomas Y. Levin (Cambridge, MA: Harvard University Press, 1995), pp. 323–28.
35 Ibid., p. 57.
36 Stanley Cavell, *The World Viewed: Reflections on the Ontology of Film*, 2nd edn (Cambridge, MA: Harvard University Press, 1979), pp. 24–25.
37 Donald Judd, 'Specific objects', *Arts Yearbook*, vol. 8 (1965), p. 75.
38 Robert Rosenblum, 'Frank Stella: five years of variations on an "irreducible" theme', *Artforum*, vol. 3, no. 6 (1965), pp. 22–23, reprinted in *On Modern American Art* (New York, NY: Harry N. Abrams, 1999), p. 164.
39 Michael Fried, 'Shape as form: Frank Stella's irregular polygons', *Artforum*, vol. 5, no. 3 (1966), pp. 18–27, reprinted in *Art and Objecthood: Essay and Reviews* (Chicago, IL: University of Chicago Press, 1998), p. 77.
40 Ibid., p. 81.
41 Lev Manovich, *The Language of New Media* (Cambridge, MA: MIT Press, 2001), p. 100.
42 Sobchack, *Carnal Thoughts*, pp. 158–59.
43 Cavell, *The World Viewed*, p. 232, n. 13.
44 Judd, 'Specific objects', pp. 75–76.
45 Carla Gottlieb, *Beyond Modern Art* (New York, NY: EP Dutton, 1976), p. 126.

CHAPTER TWENTY-TWO

After the Screen: Array Aesthetics and Transmateriality

Mitchell Whitelaw

Glowing rectangles

For all the diversity of the contemporary media ecology—network, broadcast, games, mobile—one technical form is entirely dominant. Screens are everywhere, at every scale, in every context. As well as the archetypal "big" and "small" screens of cinema and television, we are now familiar with pocket- and book-sized screens, public screens as advertising or signage, urban screens at architectural scales. As satirical news site *The Onion* observes, we "spend the vast majority of each day staring at, interacting with, and deriving satisfaction from glowing rectangles".[1]

Formally and technically these screens vary—in size and aspect ratio, display technology, spatiotemporal limits, and so on. They are united however in two basic attributes, which are something like the contract of the screen. First, the screen operates as a mediating substrate for its content—the screen itself recedes in favor of its hosted image. The screen is self-effacing (though never of course absent or invisible). This tendency is clearly evident in screen design and technology; we prize screens that are slight and bright—those that best make themselves disappear. Apple's "Retina" display technology claims to have passed an important perceptual threshold of self-effacement, attaining a spatial density so high that individual pixels are indistinguishable to the naked eye.[2] The second key attribute of contemporary digital screens is their tendency to generality. The self-effacing substrate of the screen is increasingly a general-purpose substrate—unlinked to any specific content type; equally capable of displaying anything—text, image, website, video, or word-processor. This attribute is coupled of course to the generality of networked computing; since the era of multimedia the computer screen has led the way in modeling itself as a container for anything (just as the computer models itself a "machine for anything"). The past decade has simply seen this general-purpose container proliferate across scales and contexts, ushering us into the era of glowing rectangles.

However, over the past decade in design and the media arts, a wave of practice has appeared which, as this paper will argue, resists the dominance of the glowing rectangle. Given the near-total cultural saturation of the screen, this is unsurprising, given the ongoing cultural dance of fringe and mainstream in which this practice participates. This is not simply a story of resistance however. In proposing and describing two particular strains of "post-screen" practice, this paper aims firstly to outline the shared terms of their relationship with the screen, and in the process develop a more detailed sense of these conceptual devices of generality, outlined above, and its opposite, specificity. Secondly, and more briefly, it outlines a theorisation of this practice, invoking transmateriality, an account of the paradoxical materiality of (especially digital) media, and Gumbrecht's notion of presence.

Arrays

During the opening ceremony of the 2008 Beijing Olympics, a huge grid of drummers assembled in the stadium, each standing before a large square *fou* drum, a traditional Chinese instrument.[3] Each drum was augmented with white LEDs mounted on its surface, triggered with each drum stroke. The drummers formed a vast array of discrete audiovisual elements, precisely choreographed in the style of these spectaculars. Human pixels, but coarse and resolutely human; at one point the drummers desynchronised entirely, forming a thunderous grid of flickering light. In a ceremony created for the (broadcast) screen—to the infamous extent of splicing computer-animated fireworks into its telecast in place of real ones—the drummers were a moment of involution. Their array echoed all the other, more conventionally self-effacing screens threaded through the event; but it also inverted some of their key attributes. Firstly its substrate, instead of receding behind "content", came forward; if anything substrate and content were one and the same. Secondly, while this array nods towards the generality of the screen in its choreographed patterns—which like the patterns on a screen could be "anything at all"—it veers strongly in the opposite direction, towards the here and now, what I will call *specificity*.[4] The poetics of this array rely on the specificity of its elements—the drummers, drums, and their solid-state illumination—rather than the patterns that play across it.

The drummers are one popular example of a formal trope we can find throughout media arts and design practice over the past decade. Daniel Rozin's 1999 *Wooden Mirror* is one of the earlier examples. *Wooden*

Mirror is an array of square wooden tiles embedded in a large octagonal frame, along with a bundle of custom electronics. The tiles are fitted with servomotors, so that each one can tilt up and down on its horizontal axis. As its angle to the light changes, each tile appears brighter or darker. Rozin wires up the array to a videocamera, to complete the mirror circuit: the brightness of pixels in the incoming image drives the angle of the tiles. Given the overtly visual logic of the work, it's interesting that its sound is equally striking: the wooden tiles clatter like mechanical rainfall, sonifying the rate of change of the image; as the image becomes still, the clatter dies off to a low twitching. Again, this array emphasises the material presence of its substrate. The tonal "generality" of the wooden mirror is functional enough to be familiar, but the coarse mechanical clattering of these pixels makes them inescapably specific.

Rozin has made many similar mirrors; notable is *Trash Mirror* (2001) where the individual elements—irregularly shaped pieces of rubbish—are packed into a freeform mosaic. This array moves one more step away from the homogeneous generality of the digital screen. Here the elements are irregular in size and shape, but also carry their own specific textures and colours. In *Mirrors Mirror* (2008), the regular grid returns, but the array elements are themselves replaced by mirrors; as these tilt they reflect different parts of the environment. Here the location of the tonal "content" in the array is, like the image source, deferred to the environment. In a familiar digital screen, image elements are luminous modules whose colour value is independent and absolute. In Rozin's *Wooden Mirror* that value becomes relative—tonality is based on self-shading, which depends on the lighting of the work. In *Mirrors Mirror* this relativity is multiplied; each element will reflect a different portion of the environment, depending on both its angle and the viewpoint of the observer. In many cases these media art arrays depart from the two-dimensional grid entirely. Robert Henke and Christopher Bauder's *ATOM* (2007–8) is an eight-by-eight grid of white helium balloons, each one fitted with LED illumination and tethered to a computer controlled winch. The grid becomes a mobile, configurable light-form, tightly coupled with Henke's electronic soundtrack in live performance. This array lowers its resolution drastically, and limits its generality in one dimension (monochrome elements), but extends its reach (literally) into a third axis. ART+COM's 2008 kinetic sculpture at the BMW museum uses a similar configuration, but a higher "resolution"—in this case 714 metal spheres are suspended from motorised cables, forming a smoothly undulating matrix—a sort of programmed corporate ballet. *Cloud* (2008), a sculpture in Heathrow airport by London art and design firm Troika, illustrates another permutation: here a 2D array forms the skin of a large three-dimensional sculptural form. In this case, the elements are electromagnetic flip-dots—components often used in airport signage before it was overtaken by glowing rectangles. As in Rozin's *Mirrors*, Troika consciously exploits the materiality, gestural character and the sound of these retro-pixels. rAndom International's 2010 *Swarm Light* demonstrates a "saturated" 3D array. The work consists of three cubic arrays of white LED lights, each ten elements per side; these cubic volumes host a flowing, flickering "swarm" of sound-responsive agents which traverse the space, brightening or dimming the array as they move.

The work of British designers United Visual Artists offers a useful longitudinal study in post-screen imaging; in particular, their work addresses one of the central technical players in this field, LED lighting. UVA's first project involved a huge LED array that formed the stage set of Massive Attack's 100th Window tour. Unlike more screenful video backdrops, this low-res grid had an inescapable presence, hung directly behind the band and looming over the stage. Rather than an image machine, UVA treat the grid as a luminous dot-matrix for the twitching alphanumeric characters of real-time data. In subsequent work, UVA develop this approach in a number of directions, but digitally articulated light—enabled by the LED— is a recurring theme. In *Monolith* (2006), UVA use a pair of large, full-colour LED screens, but treat them as a dynamic light source rather than a substrate for images; subtle gradients and washes of colour spill over the audience and into the installation environment, coupled with generated sound. In *Volume* (2006), another installation piece, the array elements are long vertical LED strips, again treated as generators of pattern, colour and sound; the work forms an interactive field as each element responds to nearby activity. In the context of this steady dismemberment of the screen, UVA's latest work *The Speed of Light* is notable in that it leaves LED arrays aside entirely. Instead it uses installed lasers manipulated into dynamic, walk-in calligraphy, as if light had been finally prised away from its digital substrate, and turned loose in the environment.

Beyond their formal similarities, these arrays share some core approaches and contexts which provide a coherent portrait of a sort of post-screen practice. These works adopt one key feature of the screen—the "generality" of an articulated substrate—but trade it off to varying extents for more "specificity"—exploiting the local, particular materiality of the work and its environment. This specificity is also technological, reflecting a practice that crafts hard- and software into idiosyncratic configurations, rather than using off-the-shelf infrastructure. Light is a strong theme, in particular the solid-state, digitally addressable light of the LED (essentially a free-floating pixel). However, the optical in these arrays is always tightly coupled with other modalities, especially sound, which is either a cherished byproduct of the array mechanism (as in Rozin's *Mirrors* and Troika's *Cloud*) or generated by the array elements themselves (as in the drummers and UVA's *Volume*). A quality of liveness is linked with the turn to specificity and being-in-the-environment; from the "live data" of UVA's Massive Attack show, to the live interaction and generation of their later installations, to the live video driving Rozin's *Mirrors*. Performance and temporary installation are the dominant forms here—emphasising the intensified moment, rather than the any-time of static content.

Projection mapping and extruded light

In one sense these arrays present a disintegration of the screen—they pull its elements apart and embed them in the environment. In another strain of media arts practice, something like the converse occurs, though with what I will argue are similar interests and agendas. In this approach screen-like technologies are used intact, rather than decomposed; but their function and their relationship to the environment are transformed. These works reverse-engineer the digital image, exploiting its digital (general) malleability in order to fit it to a specific environment.

The work of Norwegian artist HC Gilje illustrates one trajectory of this second post-screen approach. Gilje's work from the late 1990s was in live digital video, with his ensemble 242.pilots. This practice was linked to the burgeoning activity in experimental electronic music at the time; here again, performance, improvisation, and the intensified moment—what Gilje calls an "extended now"—are central concerns, though the work is strongly screen-focused in its results.[5] In Gilje's work over the following decade, he demonstrates another path towards the post-screen. Gilje's *nodio* (2005–) is a custom software system for distributing video content across collections of linked "nodes". In *drifter* (2006) these nodes are manifest as a ring of twelve screens which form a linked audiovisual interspace. With *dense* (2007) these nodes take on a more sculptural presence—hanging strips of fabric illuminated from both sides with a tailored videoprojection. Here Gilje adapts the screen technology of the video projector to a sculptural environment, pushing it one step away from image and towards illumination. The work also depends on a specific material surface—the translucent weave of the fabric enables the double-sided layering of pattern.

shift (2008) develops this approach: a technique known as projection mapping, in which the projected image is reverse-engineered to fit a specific surface. In *shift* Gilje's nodes are simple rectangular boxes, constructed from plywood. Using more custom software, the artist illuminates a cluster of these boxes with precisely mapped projected images. The coupled sound emanates from speakers housed in each box, so the objects are again audiovisual (and acoustically distinct) nodes; Gilje composes material for this environment in search of what he terms "audiovisual powerchords"—moments of intense juxtaposition and interplay. In *blink* (2009), Gilje dispenses with the boxes, instead treating the bare installation space. Simple, geometric elements—angular lines and bands of tone and colour—are reflected and modulated by the space itself, diffusing from irregular polished floorboards and painted walls. The work plays the room with articulated light, carefully matched to its geometry in a way that heightens our awareness of the interplay of space, light and materials.

Projection mapping has recently flourished in "visualist" practice across art, design and performance contexts; trompe-l'oeil architectural facades are one popular genre, manipulating the built environment by rendering it with a tailored skin of articulated light (see for example Urbanscreen's *Kubik 555*). German designers Grosse 8 and Lichtfront demonstrate a logical extension of the technique, using multiple projectors to create an "augmented sculpture" in the round. Another notable example is *Scintillation* (2009) by Xavier Chassaing, a digital stop-motion film in which projection mapping is used to layer a domestic environment with luminous swirls of particles, igniting the petals of an orchid and tracing the curves of a moulded plaster cornice. As in Gilje's *blink*, *Scintillation* emphasises the ambience of the projected light—reflections and diffusions are heightened by hand-held macro cinematography, artfully producing an impression of material texture. But in the process it raises some interesting problems for our analytical premise—a shift from the screenful image to something more live and specific. For *Scintillation* is absolutely a work of filmmaking, here projection mapping—the tailored materialisation of the image—is deployed as a technique for producing generalisable, substrate-independent image content.

The final example in this survey addresses the same tension. In their recent short film *Making Future Magic*, London design agency Berg give an ingenious demonstration of both the material turn of post-screen imaging and its recuperation as image content. Berg developed an animation technique combining multiple-exposure stop-motion with a hand-held source of articulated light—specifically the glowing rectangle of the moment, Apple's iPad. 3D forms are digitally modelled and animated, then decomposed into sequences of 2D slices. These slices are then replayed into the environment, and thus recomposed into 3D forms, by moving an iPad screen over successive still frame exposures. As Berg term it, this is "extruded light"—as in UVA's latest work, it's as if light itself has been unpinned from its substrate. The results are a beguiling combination of loose, organic light painting with simple 3D geometry and DSLR imaging. As Berg frame the work, it fits entirely within the post-screen turn proposed here. Responding to a brief around "a magical version of future media", Berg are "exploring how surfaces and screens look and work in the world...finding playful uses for the increasingly ubiquitous 'glowing rectangles'...".[6] Again the material embeddedness of this articulated light is emphasized—the way it reflects from puddles and diffuses through foliage. Screen as object in the world, rather than window to somewhere else. As in *Scintillation*, however, the inescapable irony is that the outcomes of this work are entirely bound up with screenful images—with the generalising infrastructures and distribution pipelines of social image sharing, print-on-demand, and networked video.

Transmateriality and presence culture

To recap briefly: the ubiquitous digital screen is characterised by both generality—an ability to display any content at all—and self-effacing slightness—it tries to make itself disappear as a neutral substrate for content. In contrast to these tendencies, this paperdescribes two distinct but parallel strains of "post-screen" practice in the media arts and design. Arrays mimic the grid configuration of the screen, but lower its resolution and emphasise the material presence of the array elements—their local and individual specificity is balanced with their malleable generality (their ability to carry anything-at-all). Projection mapping and "extruded light" practices also emphasise specificity, materiality and a local, performative being-in-the-world, but they do so by different means—exploiting the malleability of the digital screen (and the computational representations it hosts) in order to make it intensely site-specific. To the extent that they both adapt and resist the attributes of our familiar glowing rectangles, we could describe these practices as post-screen, but this "post" is nothing like a conscious critique, let alone a revolutionary break. However hard they may pull towards specificity and local materiality, they are readily—by design or necessity—recaptured as screen fodder.

Both these post-screen tendencies and their screenful recuperation can be usefully framed through the notion of transmateriality, a concept that attempts to capture a fundamental duality in digital (and other) media: they are everywhere and always material, yet often function as if they are immaterial.[7] In a transmaterial view, media always operate as local material instances (this is their aspect of *specificity*) yet retain the ability to hold specificity at bay—resisting the contingencies of flux—to create a functional *generalization* in which this pixel is the same as that one, the email I send is the same as the one you receive, and one node on the network is much the same as any other.

In the glowing rectangle paradigm, functional generality is entirely dominant. The work considered here, on the other hand, revels more in the pleasures and practices of specificity—the clatter of servo-actuated wood or the play of light on this particular wall. In their push towards liveness (of interaction or data), performativity, their integration of sound, and their emphasis on evanescent materiality, these works evoke what Hans Ulrich Gumbrecht would call "presence culture"—that mode of apprehending the world which is characterised by fleeting but intense moments of being, and a sense of being part of the world of things, rather than outside it, looking in. Gumbrecht constructs presence in opposition to a dominant "meaning culture", in which the essence of material things can be obtained only through interpretation. Gumbrecht describes the relationship between these poles as one of dynamic oscillation. "Presence phenomena" become "effects of" presence, "because we can only encounter them within a culture that is predominantly a meaning culture.... [T]hey are necessarily surrounded by, wrapped into, and perhaps even mediated by clouds and cushions of meaning".[8]

In exactly the same way we find an inevitable oscillation here between screen and postscreen. We can align the screen with generality and meaning culture, and the post-screen with specificity and presence culture; but here too the post-screen is evanescent and elusive, instead existing largely within the dominant screen culture. However, this is not to discount the utopian aspirations of a post-screen practice, which might instead be located through the perspective of transmateriality. For in echoing the screen, or in literally bending it to the local, present and specific, these works operate as reminders of the ubiquitous and everyday materiality of our media, of the fact that depite appearances, every glowing rectangle is already local and specific. If that specificity is latent, then these works demonstrate practical strategies for making it explicit; from hardware hacking to modular LEDs and custom software, they participate in what I have termed "expanded computing",[9] using the malleability of digital media to reactivate its presence—and thus our presence, too—in the world of things.

Notes

1   "Report: 90% of Waking Hours Spent Staring at Glowing Rectangles", *The Onion*, 2009 <http://www.theonion.com/article/report-90-of-waking-hours-spent-staring-at-glowing-2747> [accessed January 25, 2016].

2   Apple Computer, "iPhone 4—Learn about the High-resolution Retina Display", 2010 <http://www.apple.com/iphone/features/retina-display.html> [accessed October 5, 2010].

3   See for example *BEIJING OLYMPIC GAMES OPENING CEREMONY 2008*, 2008 <http://www.youtube.com/watch?v=JsDY1Ha83M8&feature=youtube_gdata_player> [accessed January 25, 2016].

4   See Whitelaw, Mitchell, "Right Here, Right Now: On HC Gilje's Networks of Specificity", in *Retrospective Catalogue 2009*, ed. by Anne Szefer Karlsen (Hordaland Art Centre, 2010), pp. 82–84.

5   Gilje, HC, "Within the Space of an Instant", in *Get Real: Real-Time + Art + Theory + Practice + History*, ed. by Morten Søndegaard, Pap/DVD (George Braziller, 2005).

6   Berg, "Making Future Magic: light painting with the iPad", 2010 <http://berglondon.com/blog/2010/09/14/magic-ipad-light-painting/> [accessed January 25, 2016].

7   See Whitelaw, Mitchell, "Notes on Transmateriality" *(the teeming void)*, 2008 <http://teemingvoid.blogspot.com/2008/03/notes-on-transmateriality.html> [accessed January 25, 2016].

8   Gumbrecht, Hans, *Production of Presence: What Meaning Cannot Convey* (Stanford University Press, 2003), 105–106.

9   Whitelaw, Mitchell, "Transduction, Transmateriality, and Expanded Computing" *(the teeming void)*, 2009 <http://teemingvoid.blogspot.ca/2009/01/transduction-transmateriality-and.html> [accessed January 25, 2016].

Environments and Interactions

Introduction to Section Three

We may think of screens as discrete objects containing worlds of their own, but even without cables or cords they remain tethered objects. Since the invention of cinema at the end of the nineteenth century, screens have functioned as the endpoints of vast networks now extending into nearly all environments to shape fundamentally the actions around them. In the classic example of the movie theater, the screen that is seemingly isolated in darkness is the interface for a network that not only extends into the social circumstances of the audience and viewing space but also reaches far back into the production and distribution systems of media industries.

We find screens in places today where they would have seemed unimaginable only a few years before. Their eminent portability means nearly every space is a potential screen context. Screens are small but durable; they may run on little energy, but they remain bright. They have become style accessories and status symbols. This may have already been the case with the living-room television console or the desktop computer, as when Apple advertised its iMac as "Chic. Not geek" in 1998 by emphasizing the gently rounded profile of the cathode-ray tube monitor, suggesting the screen-object would make you cool before you even turned it on. Smartphones have only enhanced that sentiment as screen form—whether curved, beveled, or bendable—becomes a marketing feature. Indeed, with the smartphone and similar screen-based devices the screen has absorbed much of the object behind it and now accounts for the greater part of the visible surface and physical heft of wafer-thin devices.

This change in the design of screen objects reflects their greater reliance on wireless networks for their functioning. Where screen objects once needed to have physical capacity to store data, most of this responsibility has been delegated to the network and its various "clouds." Tap an icon, pull up a website, log into our account: we have little or no idea where our photos, videos, and writings may be stored physically. Indeed, they are likely scattered across servers around the world, traveling thousands of miles in a millisecond to come back to us. Under these circumstances, the screen has taken on unprecedented importance as an affective device. It is the frame within which we realize, retrieve, and experience the stuff of our lives.

FIGURE 1.3 *Viewing images on a smartphone with Google Cardboard, 2015.*
Photo: Becky Stern.

As these networks become larger, denser, and faster, the screen responds in its portability to allow us to retrieve this "stuff" wherever we are. Mobility has become a major factor in the recent development of the screen. We can argue that the network's ubiquity in many parts of the world transforms these places into screen-based environments where having a mobile screen is increasingly necessary to accomplish even the most routine tasks, from making a phone call to paying the rent. Typically our mobile, networked screen reflects our surroundings for us through locative media. The screen may display a better awareness of where we are than we ourselves possess.

It is often not adequate to speak of "the" screen in these contexts, as interactions may take place across several screens at once. Thus the term "second screen" has emerged to describe the process of working across screens, as when watching a wall-mounted TV while using a tablet. There is even talk of the third and fourth screens. This increasingly networked aspect of the screen also contributes to the screen's scarcity—even outright absence—in those parts of the world where telecommunications networks are hard to maintain or non-existent. Indeed, we could say the presence of a screen in an environment is a strong indication of the network's invisible presence. When we are struggling to access the network—as perhaps when arriving at an airport—to whom do we turn for help? Typically the nearest person interacting with a screen in their hands. And, not surprisingly, anti-media and anti-technology movements of the last half-century have regularly prescribed turning off the screen as the first and most effective step in breaking the network's grip on everyday life.

This section of the reader focuses on our interactions with screens as access points to these networks. The first part, "Moments of Interface," considers the screen's relationship to the body, whether as an object to be manipulated, as in the case of portable touchscreens, or one triggering specific bodily reactions or stances, as with the pornographic peep show. A brief but evocative description of one of the first public film screenings in Britain, in 1896, provides telling clues into cinema's early relationship to the body through shifting impressions of the screen. As lights—whether the house lights or the bright light of the projector—go on and off between the short (less than a minute) films, the screen becomes an object of fascination. What seems a decorative "empty back-cloth" at one moment "quivers into being" in the next, then returns to its inanimate state before breaking again into life with the next reel.

Paul Frosh considers the television set's ability to play a similar role when on and off. For Frosh, the TV screen introduces face-to-face encounters under both circumstances. This sensation is produced by TV's frequent depiction of people facing the audience in medium or close-up shots. Reality shows' use of "confessional" interviews is one such case. Through Frosh's analysis, the TV set becomes the materialization of the head, the screen its face. Even when the set is turned off, Frosh points out, the head of the viewer can appear reflected in its surface. The TV screen becomes an object of interaction under all circumstances, constantly confronting viewers and profoundly shaping the sense of self.

If our interactions with movie or TV screens today often are accompanied by the second screen of a digital device in our hands, we should acknowledge the role Douglas Engelbart played in transforming computing into a routine, screen-based practice. When Engelbart was a researcher at the Stanford Research Institute in the 1960s, computers were inscrutable, room-sized machines. Engelbart imagined a new relationship between these instruments and people, one facilitated by the screen. "Augmenting Human Intellect" is the description of his vision. Engelbart designed the computer mouse and other components of human-computer interaction, so perhaps it comes as little surprise how closely the scenarios he describes in his essay (written as part of a report for the US military) resemble those taking place between people and digital screens today, such that his ideas may appear to have been thoroughly absorbed into cultural practice.

A significant difference between Engelbart's proposal and interactive screens today is that Engelbart describes a tabletop screen interface, while we frequently rely on handheld devices. For Heidi Rae Cooley, the production of screens for the hand introduces a new relationship between screen and user. Exploring the idea of "fit," Cooley considers how the screen can become a material extension of its user, as though it were a part of the body. "The hand and the device undergo a 'becoming one'," she explains. This intimacy can produce an unprecedented attachment to the personal screen, reaching levels of sensory engagement that often have little or nothing to do with what is on screen. One example would be the urge to tap the screen simply to wake it up from sleep mode, rather than to use it, as though it were a crossed arm going numb.

Such gestures would be part of the "emerging new order of visual and sensory perception" that Alexandra Schneider finds with touchscreen smartphones such as the iPhone. Schneider's essay considers Apple's phenomenally successful device a "theoretical object" and concentrates on the new relationships between touch and vision that such screens put into place. These relationships, she finds, may have unexpected affinities with earlier forms of visual culture, "reintroduc[ing] and relegitimiz[ing] the once-common link of vision and touch."

Focusing less on material interaction than situational conditions of use, Virginie Sonet describes the different modes of watching moving images on the smartphone. Developing the categories of the ambiance-screen and communication-screen to differentiate viewing (and listening) strategies found in her research on French subjects, Sonet demonstrates how smartphone users employ the screen alternately to keep themselves company and interact with those around them. While Sonet's research does not encompass all forms of smartphone use, it nevertheless provides insights regarding the portable screen's adaptability in relation to multiple forms of moving-image entertainment, from the amateur clip to full-length movies.

Very different ideas of screen sharing and isolation emerge in Amy Herzog's groundbreaking work on pornographic peepshows. By interviewing film distributors, studying booth layouts, and analyzing the films themselves, Herzog demonstrates the significant relationship between image and viewer body established by the screen's context. Meant to facilitate sexual activity, the peepshow booth is built to produce a strong correspondence between viewing body and viewed body. In an instance of media archaeology, Herzog traces the roots of the peepshow in the Panoram, a failed 1940s screen device meant to function like a visual jukebox. Unsuccessful in bars, train stations, and similar public settings, the Panoram's design was ideally suited to screening short pornographic films for individual viewers.

The second part of this section, "Systems and Networks," concludes the reader with research into the screen's enduring role as the visual entryway into larger economic and cultural networks. Through the example of moving-image exhibition strategies at the 1939 World's Fair, Haidee Wasson demonstrates the screen's diversity of types and uses even before its rivalry with television took full form. A leading figure in the study of the screen, particularly in twentieth-century film culture, Wasson focuses on the important role that small, portable screens played at the fair and within interwar visual culture more generally. Her essay demonstrates that revisiting earlier practices through a "film screen archeology" sensitive to those contexts that have not made their way into media histories not only provides a better sense of what the screen has been, but also may allow a clearer understanding of what is—and is not—new about twenty-first-century screen culture.

What Wasson has done in film studies, in many ways Anna McCarthy has achieved for the study of television. Through her work on "ambient television" from the mid-twentieth century to today, McCarthy has noted an astonishingly wide range of circumstances where the TV set and video monitor have functioned. McCarthy considers the "placeness" of television through such characteristics as live broadcast or the physical arrangement of the screen in the social environment. As she explains, "[television's] material form is profoundly *site-specific*." This specificity, in which the screen acts as a privileged point or threshold to the network, can inform both the content of the screen and the activity that surrounds it.

Screen placement and audience experience are also at the heart of Onookome Okome's examination of Nollywood. In considering the intersection of narrative and exhibition patterns in the Nigerian film industry, Okome notes the essential role of street-corner viewing. In cities such as Lagos, street-side video parlors and stalls make the screen a public meeting point for a collective gaze. The Nollywood imaginary and the social circumstances of the postcolonial public sphere overlap as on-screen narratives of hardship resonate with audiences enduring the hardships of street viewing, such as standing throughout the screening amidst the bustle of city life. The screen's presence "remaps" these sites and their social significance as the images emanating from rows of stalls become a catalyst for casual conversation and interaction within this urban flux of commercial and transportation networks.

Working and writing on the collective screen experience in the 1960s, when commercial film and television were deeply entrenched and intertwined networks, Stan VanDerBeek devised a rival, networked communications system that he similarly hoped might bring audiences together in new ways. VanDerBeek called his project "an experience machine or 'culture-intercom'." In a set-up that combines multi-projection cinema practices with real-time networks of still and moving images, the culture-intercom is meant to educate and inform by creating new, and sometimes overwhelming, juxtapositions of images drawn from the whole of human visual culture. One could say VanDerBeek's project anticipates the interactive visual networks of today, where images are constantly brought together in new arrangements. It certainly serves as an example of early thinking about media convergence, as his system would "develop new image-making devices, and store and transfer image materials, motion pictures, television, computers, video-tape, etc.," from which would be gathered the images that appeared on the dome-screen of VanDerBeek's proposed "movie-drome."

The mass image network of today, of course, is the internet, not the culture-intercom. However, one context where the screen continues to serve large gatherings is the arena, where it provides an interface for sporting events and concerts. Robert Edgar explores the pivotal role the screen plays in large-scale concerts, where it often becomes the primary means for viewing and engaging performers on a far-off stage. These moments are often recorded on cellphones, creating a confrontation between screen formats in simultaneous acts of production, reception, and exhibition. Edgar contrasts this experience to that of the concert film, where the event is planned and recorded for subsequent exhibition in contexts significantly different from the original setting. In both instances, the screen has become a critical presence, shaping our expectations and understandings of the event and its legacy.

While Edgar considers the way screens intercede in and mediate large, preconceived events, Nanna Verhoeff's work on performative cartography focuses on how our mobile screens and their supporting software and network links mediate everyday spatial encounters. Relying on real-time access to networked data, "The hybrid interface of the gadget not only allows for navigation within the machine, and on the screen, but also within the physical space surrounding the device. It provides an interface for navigating bits, pixels, and spatial coordinates," Verhoeff explains. This ties the screen closely to ideas of ambient and locative media, as well as augmented reality. Writing about the "mobile screening environment," Verhoeff demonstrates ways the screen is a visual interface with the environment that synthesizes information gathered from the device's camera, compass, motion sensor, and other features. This visual performance of screenspace informs our experience—even our basic idea—of the world immediately surrounding us.

Moments of
Interface

CHAPTER TWENTY-THREE

The Cinematograph

O. Winter

[...]

When the first rude photograph was taken, it was already a miracle; but stability was the condition of its being, and the frozen smirk of an impossible tranquillity hindered its perfection. Even the "snap-shot," which revealed poses indiscoverable to the human eye, was, at best, a mere effect of curiosity, and became, in the hands of Mr. Muybridge[1] and others, the instrument of a pitiless pedantry.

But, meantime, the moving picture was perfected, and, at last, by a skilful adaptation of an ingenious toy, you may contemplate life itself thrown moving and alert upon a screen. Imagine a room or theatre brilliant with electric lights and decorated with an empty back-cloth. Suddenly the lights are extinguished, and to the whirring sound of countless revolutions the back-cloth quivers into being. A moment since it was white and inanimate; now it bustles with the movement and masquerade of tremulous life. Whirr! And a train, running (so to say) out of the cloth, floats upon your vision. It draws up at the platform; guards and porters hustle to their toil; weary passengers lean through the window to unfasten the cumbrous door; sentimentalists hasten to intercept their friends; and the whole common drama of luggage and fatigue is enacted before your eyes.

The lights leap up, and at their sudden descent you see upon the cloth a factory at noon disgorging its inmates. Men and women jostle and laugh; a swift bicycle seizes the occasion of an empty space; a huge hound crosses the yard in placid content; you can catch the very changing expression of a mob happy in its release; you note the varying speed of the footsteps; not one of the smaller signs of human activity escapes you. And then, again, a sudden light, and recurring darkness. Then, once more, the sound and

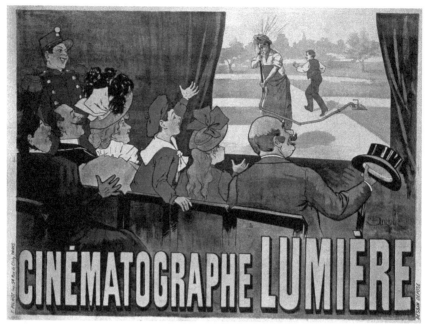

FIGURE 23.1 *Cinématographe publicity poster, 1896.*

flicker of machinery; and you see on the bare cloth a tumbling sea, with a crowd of urchins leaping and scrambling in the waves. The picture varies, but the effect is always the same – the terrifying effect of life, but of life with a difference.

[…]

Notes

1 [Eadweard J. Muybridge (1830–1904), English-American pioneer in photographic motion studies and inventor of the zoopraxiscope, an early system for projecting moving images. – Ed.]

CHAPTER TWENTY-FOUR

The Face of Television

Paul Frosh

[…]

To speak physiognomically of the face of an object is to anthropomorphize it, certainly; but it is also to claim that the object's physical appearance is a countenance to be read, an expression of the matrix of forces that materially produced it and, moreover, of those that constantly reproduce its identity and meanings as a particular kind of object. In the case of an (audio)visual medium such as television, physiognomy has an additional and very obvious resonance: for the object does not simply have surfaces, but one of those surfaces is also a screen—an interface upon which are projected moving pictures and, among them, human faces. To reflect physiognomically upon television, then, is to think about the meanings of television's physical design, the nature of its visual interface, and the psychosocial significance of its relentless display of images.

Three rudimentary observations about the face of television guide this article.[1] These concern the importance of the human face as a televisual image, the reflectivity of the television screen, and television's physical appearance as a kind of box. These observations are underpinned by a central assumption: for all the dynamics of change and flux that have characterized the medium since its inception, and despite the fact that historically speaking, "television's identity is a highly unstable affair" (Uricchio 2004), the importance of the human face, screen-reflectivity, and box like design do remain meaningfully stable across the era of mass-broadcast television. And a concomitant assumption of this generalized physiognomy of classic television is that changes in physical design, screen display, and representational practices are altering the face of the medium today.

[…]

Nonreciprocity and serial aggregation

The pervasiveness of faces on television normalizes and domesticates a paradoxical communicative structure: nonreciprocal face-to-face communication. Such a communicative structure means that one can be face-to-face with another person and not pay him any attention, since the appearance of his face, even when accompanied by direct verbal address, is an indication of his nonpresence at the location of viewing. This relationship seems to bear some affinity with the kinds of nonattentive visual encounters that characterize actual physical proximity and copresence in modern public spaces (especially in cities)—such as Simmel's (1997/1910) analysis of mental life in the metropolis and Goffman's "civil inattention" (1963).[2] Indeed, television appears to introduce such nonattentive mechanisms for apprehending unknown others into the home.[3]

Television's domestication of inattentive relations with strangers invites a powerful critique: that it is a dire extension, by a major socializing agent (television), of forms of alienation into the private sphere; that it encourages the art of "mis-meeting" (Bauman 1990), which de-ethicalizes others by turning them into mere background figures, and perhaps even establishes inattentive nonintimacy as an appropriate mode of behavior within the home. There is, however, an alternative assessment: that nonreciprocal face-to-face communication promotes a desirable cosmopolitanization of the home, allowing the faces of strangers to appear in the sphere of intimacy without creating alarm or triggering a defensively hostile response (because these faces can be safely ignored, without offending them in turn).[4]

[…]

The face behind the screen

When I watch my conventional, seven-year-old cathode-ray-tube (CRT) television, I obviously see the colors and forms, figures, and faces of programming content. But I also see something else—especially when the set is turned off: my own reflection and that of the viewing space in which I am located. In fact, it is difficult to remember a time when I did not see my own reflection in the television, and I have occasionally noticed my own children preening before the screen.

[…]

How do I look on my television? My image appears to emanate from the darkened depths of the set. The screen does not just reflect me; it also presents a mirror image of the three-dimensional space in which I am located. This is important since it constitutes the space behind the screen as a world in depth. The screen appears not only as a surface upon which

FIGURE 24.1 *Reflections in a dark television screen, 2007. Photo: Kent.*

images are projected but also as the translucent barrier to an anterior space—a space of representation (the illusion of three dimensions) that is mapped onto the physical space of the cathode ray tube. Unlike cinema, then, the space behind the television screen does not appear to be virtual: the screen is not a surface showing only the illusory representation of a three-dimensional world but a looking-glass onto the (inhabitable) inside of the television set itself.

The appearance of a world in depth behind the television screen is, therefore, not simply an effect of the optical illusion of three dimensions that characterizes the pictures shown on television. Instead, the pictorial illusion is made continuous with the reflected image of the viewer and his or her setting (walls, sofas, coffee tables), as though both take turns to occupy the same delimited space—a space that is mapped onto the physical depth of the television set. When the television is turned off, and the broadcast image disappears, the space it occupied is filled by the reflection. This gives the inhabitable "inside" of the television, the world in depth on the other side of the glass, a semblance of permanence. And this sense of a permanent world-space inside the television intersects powerfully with one of the most obvious aspects of television's physical exterior: its appearance as a kind of container.

Television as a container

The conventional, predigital television set—whether designed to look like a conventional sideboard in a family room, or as a minimalist square with its own legs, or even as a portable five-inch model from the 1970s—is designed as a box: hence the colloquialism "What's on the box tonight?"

Boxes contain things, even if it is only air. What, in representational terms, does the televisual box contain? It contains, first and foremost, space behind the screen, augmenting the sense of permanent depictive depth already aroused by the screen's reflective surface. This space can be understood as a backstage to the images the screen displays, a behind-the-scenes location from which the pictures come, along with the people who appear in them. Television in the 1950s, as Spigel (1992) notes, was often associated with theater; this idea of a backstage space, contained within the box, supplying the screen with its material, further emphasizes its theatrical rather than cinematic antecedents: television as an electronic puppet theater.[5] It is this idea of a backstage location behind the screen whence the pictures come that supplies some of the uncanny effects of television as a separate, horrifying world that is more than merely virtual: the girl trapped inside the television in Spielberg's *Poltergeist* (1982) or Samara's terrifying emergence from the television set in *The Ring* (2002).[6] The horror of these images plays on the uncanny otherness, doubleness, and spatial proximity of the reality that the television set might contain, and that it might therefore unleash: its alternate world is more palpable when confined in a specific physical location.
[…]

The face of the future

Is this coarsely sketched physiognomy of the face of television in its mass-broadcasting era—based on the primacy of the head shot, the reflectivity of the screen, and the box-like design of the television set—likely to be sustained today? Perhaps one of the greatest impacts upon the head shot concerns the dimensions of the television screen, in particular its "aspect ratio"—the relationship between the width and height of a filmed image. Traditional television has consistently used an aspect ratio of 4:3 adopted from cinema (4 units of width to 3 of height). Known as Academy Standard, after its introduction as the standard format for sound film by the Academy of Motion Picture Arts and Sciences, 4:3 is a convenient and somewhat approximate shorthand for 1.37:1, where 1 expresses the height of the image: in other words, the image is 1.37 times wider than it is tall.[7] While television's adoption of 4:3 made it initially compatible with cinematic film, the development of wide-screen cinema (1.85:1 in the United States— Academy Flat)—one of the technical innovations introduced by the film industry to compete with television—meant that the dimensions of the image have also consistently been employed to distinguish between the two media. Technological changes in image display led to the introduction in the 1980s of a new standard aspect ratio of 16:9 (1.78:1)—favored by the large, flat LCD and plasma screens being sold today—a format that takes television firmly in the direction of wide-screen cinema.

How might all of this have affected the face on television, and particularly the use of the head shot? While neither 4:3 nor 16:9 exactly suits the orientation of the human face (they are both "landscape" rather than "portrait" formats: unlike the face, they are wider than they are tall), 4:3 encouraged and enabled an intimate focus on the face in close-up, with relatively little attention paid to the background within the same shot— even after the introduction of deep-focus cinematic techniques that allowed both face and background to be kept simultaneously sharp. In contrast, 16:9 necessarily includes more of the background and environmental surroundings of the human face, even in close-up. One of the implications is that the head shot—although by no means entirely eroded—has become less dominant in the televisual repertoire than previously, since it does not fully exploit the more contextual and epic dimensions of the wide-screen format. [...]

Screen reflectivity is another feature that has been altered and is considered a technical advance. Flat LCD or plasma screens do not have the same reflective surface as CRT consoles: my reflection never threatens to overlap or obscure the images they show, nor does it emerge from the depths of a three-dimensional virtual space that is permanently visible on the other side of the screen. There is no serendipitous sense of continuity between the worlds of viewer and viewed, no material correlate to the idea that television is the mirror of society. What we get instead is an opaque and inscrutable void that seems to absorb the surrounding light: television as a black hole.

Finally, these flat, depthless screens are obviously not boxes. They do not seem to contain society. Instead, they resemble framed pictures hung on walls or windows that look out onto the world, affinities that appear to embody the duality of spectacle and surveillance more acutely than the box that preceded them. Indeed, it no longer makes very much sense to talk about a "television set" at all—certainly not to a salesperson in an electronics shop. The "set" has disappeared. We speak instead of screens, monitors, or platforms, indications that the self-sufficient design rhetoric of the television box has given way to rhetoric of specific functionality (to screen, to view) and technical interdependence (platform). In contrast to the coherently integrated sociocultural unity between the three faces of traditional television that I have described—broadcast image, screen reflectivity, and physical dimensions—the future face of television becomes dispersed, like the medium itself, in a multitude of emerging contours and possible transformations, all of them, at the present moment, blurred and ill defined.

Notes

1 *Face*, incorporated here into "surface" and "interface," clearly refers to more than the human countenance, a reanimation of its earlier Latin associations with figure and form in general (*faciēs*).

2 Getrud Koch (n.d.) has written perceptively on the connection between cinema and the shifts in modern urban public life that foreground the "importance of face-to-face reading as a mutual but silent act."

3 The affinity is limited for two obvious reasons. First, if you are in a public place—a train or a bus—and a stranger looks directly at you for a prolonged period (as many faces do on television), this is a violation of civil inattention and can be interpreted as a potentially hostile act. Moreover, if that person speaks to you, ignoring him or her would violate conversational norms. The lack of copresence between viewer and viewed in the case of television—for all its ideology of immediacy—means that I can ignore or scream abuse at the face of the stranger with not the slightest effect (except perhaps on those watching with me).

4 See Frosh (2006) for a discussion of civil inattention and mismeeting that criticizes Bauman's pessimistic reading of Goffman.

5 Roald Dahl conveys the impression of television as a habitation for miniature people through the story of Mike Teavee in *Charlie and the Chocolate Factory*. Mike, desperate to be the first boy ever transmitted by television (or "Wonkavision"), finds that he has been drastically shrunk. It is, of course, the only way he can fit into the television set.

6 It is worth noting that the television sets shown in the US version of *The Ring* are cathode-ray-tube boxes, despite the fact that the film was made after the advent of flat LCD and plasma screens.

7 The reason for its approximate nature is that 4:3 is often quoted as a shorthand for 1.33:1, the aspect ratio used by virtually all films from the beginning of silent cinema until it was altered to 1.37:1 with the introduction of optical sound film around 1930. It is also a common aspect ratio used in photography.

References

Bauman, Z. 1990. Effacing the face: On the social management of moral proximity. *Theory, Culture and Society* 7: 5–38.

Frosh, P. 2006. Telling presences: Witnessing, mass media, and the imagined lives of strangers. *Critical Studies in Media Communication* 23 (4): 265–84.

Goffman, E. 1963. *Behavior in public places: Notes on the social organization of gatherings*. New York: Free Press.

Koch. G. n.d. Facing modernity: Facial expression and new reading. Manuscript.

Simmel, G. 1997. The metropolis and mental life. In *Simmel on Culture: Selected Writings*, ed. D. Frisby and M. Featherstone, 174–76. London: Sage. Originally published in 1910.

Spigel, L. 1992. *Make room for TV: Television and the family ideal in postwar America*. Chicago, IL: University of Chicago Press.

Uricchio, W. 2004. Television's next generation: Technology/interface culture/flow. In *Television after TV: Essays on a medium in transition*, ed. L.Spigel and J. Olsson, 163–82. Durham, NC: Duke University Press.

CHAPTER TWENTY-FIVE

From *Augmenting Human Intellect: A Conceptual Framework*

Douglas Engelbart

Introduction

By "augmenting human intellect" we mean increasing the capability of a man to approach a complex problem situation, to gain comprehension to suit his particular needs, and to derive solutions to problems. Increased capability in this respect is taken to mean a mixture of the following: more-rapid comprehension, better comprehension, the possibility of gaining a useful degree of comprehension in a situation that previously was too complex, speedier solutions, better solutions, and the possibility of finding solutions to problems that before seemed insoluble.

[...]

We see the quickest gains emerging from (1) giving the human the minute-by-minute services of a digital computer equipped with computer-driven cathode-ray-tube display, and (2) developing the new methods of thinking and working that allow the human to capitalize upon the computer's help. By this same strategy, we recommend that an initial research effort develop a prototype system of this sort aimed at increasing human effectiveness in the task of computer programming.

To give the reader an initial orientation about what sort of thing this computer-aided working system might be, we include below a short description of a possible system of this sort. This illustrative example is not to be considered a description of the actual system that will emerge from the program. It is given only to show the general direction of the work, and is clothed in fiction only to make it easier to visualize.

Let us consider an augmented architect at work. He sits at a working station that has a visual display screen some three feet on a side; this is his working surface, and is controlled by a computer (his "clerk") with which he can communicate by means of a small keyboard and various other devices.

He is designing a building. He has already dreamed up several basic layouts and structural forms, and is trying them out on the screen. The surveying data for the layout he is working on now have already been entered, and he has just coaxed the clerk to show him a perspective view of the steep hillside building site with the roadway above, symbolic representations of the various trees that are to remain on the lot, and the service tie points for the different utilities. The view occupies the left two-thirds of the screen. With a "pointer," he indicates two points of interest, moves his left hand rapidly over the keyboard, and the distance and elevation between the points indicated appear on the right-hand third of the screen.

Now he enters a reference line with his pointer, and the keyboard. Gradually the screen begins to show the work he is doing—a neat excavation appears in the hillside, revises itself slightly, and revises itself again. After a moment, the architect changes the scene on the screen to an overhead plan view of the site, still showing the excavation. A few minutes of study, and he enters on the keyboard a list of items, checking each one as it appears on the screen, to be studied later.

Ignoring the representation on the display, the architect next begins to enter a series of specifications and data—a six-inch slab floor, twelve-inch concrete walls eight feet high within the excavation, and so on. When he has finished, the revised scene appears on the screen. A structure is taking shape. He examines it, adjusts it, pauses long enough to ask for handbook or catalog information from the clerk at various points, and readjusts accordingly. He often recalls from the "clerk" his working lists of specifications and considerations to refer to them, modify them, or add to them. These lists grow into an ever more-detailed, interlinked structure, which represents the maturing thought behind the actual design.

Prescribing different planes here and there, curved surfaces occasionally, and moving the whole structure about five feet, he finally has the rough external form of the building balanced nicely with the setting and he is assured that this form is basically compatible with the materials to be used as well as with the function of the building.

Now he begins to enter detailed information about the interior. Here the capability of the clerk to show him any view he wants to examine (a slice of the interior, or how the structure would look from the roadway above) is important. He enters particular fixture designs, and examines them in a particular room. He checks to make sure that sun glare from the windows will not blind a driver on the roadway, and the "clerk" computes the information that one window will reflect strongly onto the roadway between 6 and 6:30 on midsummer mornings.

Next he begins a functional analysis. He has a list of the people who will occupy this building, and the daily sequences of their activities. The "clerk" allows him to follow each in turn, examining how doors swing, where special lighting might be needed. Finally he has the "clerk" combine all of these sequences of activity to indicate spots where traffic is heavy in the building, or where congestion might occur, and to determine what the severest drain on the utilities is likely to be.

All of this information (the building design and its associated "thought structure") can be stored on a tape to represent the design manual for the building. Loading this tape into his own clerk, another architect, a builder, or the client can maneuver within this design manual to pursue whatever details or insights are of interest to him—and can append special notes that are integrated into the design manual for his own or someone else's later benefit. [...]

Symbol structuring

[...] With a computer manipulating our symbols and generating their portrayals to us on a display, we no longer need think of our looking at *the* symbol structure which is stored—as we think of looking at *the* symbol structures stored in notebooks, memos, and books. What the computer actually stores need be none of our concern, assuming that it can portray symbol structures to us that are consistent with the form in which we think our information is structured.

A given concept structure can be represented with a symbol structure that is completely compatible with the computer's internal way of handling symbols, with all sorts of characteristics and relationships given explicit identifications that the user may never directly see. In fact, this structuring has immensely greater potential for accurately mapping a complex concept structure than does a structure an individual would find it practical to construct or use on paper.

The computer can transform back and forth between the two-dimensional portrayal on the screen, of some limited view of the total structure, and the aspect of the n-dimensional internal image that represents this "view". If the human adds to or modifies such a "view," the computer integrates the change into the internal-image symbol structure (in terms of the computer's favored symbols and structuring) and thereby automatically detects a certain proportion of his possible conceptual inconsistencies.

Thus, inside this instrument (the computer) there is an internal-image, computer-symbol structure whose convolutions and multi-dimensionality we can learn to shape to represent to hitherto unattainable accuracy the concept structure we might be building or working with. This internal structure may have a form that is nearly incomprehensible to the direct inspection of a human (except in minute chunks).
[...]

A quick summary of relevant computer technology

[...] For presenting computer-stored information to the human, techniques have been developed by which a cathode-ray tube (of which the television picture tube is a familiar example) can be made to present symbols on their screens of quite good brightness, clarity, and with considerable freedom as to the form of the symbol. Under computer control an arbitrary collection of symbols may be arranged on the screen, with considerable freedom as to relative location, size, and brightness. Similarly, line drawings, curves, and graphs may be presented, with any of the other symbols intermixed. It is possible to describe to the computer, and thereafter use, new symbols of arbitrary shape and size. On displays of this sort, a light pen (a pen-shaped tool with a flexible wire to the electronic console) can be pointed by the human at any symbol or line on the display, and the computer can automatically determine what the pen is pointing at.

A cathode-ray-tube display of this sort is currently limited in resolution to about 800 lines across the face of the tube (in either direction). The detail with which a symbol may be formed, and the preciseness with which the recurrent images of it may be located, are both affected by this figure so that no matter how large the screen of such a tube, the maximum number of symbols that can be put on with usable clearness remains the same.

The amount of usable information on such a screen, in the form of letters, numbers, and diagrams, would be limited to about what a normal human eye could make out at the normal reading distance of fourteen inches on a surface 3-1/2 inches square, or to what one could discern on an ordinary 8-1/2-by-11-inch sheet of paper at about three feet. This means that one could not have a single-tube display giving him an 8-1/2-by-11-inch frame to view that would have as much on it as he might be used to seeing, say, on the page of a journal article.

The costs of such displays are now quite high—ranging from $20,000 to $60,000, depending upon the symbol repertoire, symbol-structure display capacity, and the quality of the symbol forms. One should expect these prices to be lowered quite drastically as our technology improves and the market for these displays increases.

[...]

Hypothetical description of computer-based augmentation system

[... W]e shall present the following picture of computer-based augmentation possibilities by describing what might happen if you were being given a personal discussion-demonstration by a friendly fellow (named Joe) who is a trained and experienced user of such an augmentation system within an experimental research program which is several years beyond our present stage. We assume that you approach this demonstration-interview with a background similar to what the previous portion of this report provides— that is, you will have heard or read a set of generalizations and a few rather primitive examples, but you will not yet have been given much of a feel for how a computer-based augmentation system can really help a person.

Joe understands this and explains that he will do his best to give you the valid conceptual feel that you want—trying to tread the narrow line between being too detailed and losing your overall view and being too general and not providing you with a solid feel for what goes on. He suggests that you sit and watch him for a while as he pursues some typical work, after which he will do some explaining. You are not particularly flattered by this, since you know that he is just going to be exercising new language and methodology developments on his new artifacts—and after all, the artifacts don't look a bit different from what you expected—so why should he keep you sitting there as if you were a complete stranger to this stuff? It will just be a matter of "having the computer do some of his symbol-manipulating processes for him so that he can use more powerful concepts and concept-manipulation techniques," as you have so often been told.

Joe has two display screens side by side, but one of them he doesn't seem to use as much as the other. And the screens are almost horizontal, more like the surface of a drafting table than the near-vertical picture displays you had somehow imagined. But you see the reason easily, for he is working *on* the display surface as intently as a draftsman works on his drawings, and it would be awkward to reach out to a vertical surface for this kind of work. Some of the time Joe is using both hands on the keys, obviously feeding information into the computer at a great rate.

Another slight surprise, though—you see that each hand operates on a set of keys on its own side of the display frames, so that the hands are almost two feet apart. But it is plain that this arrangement allows him to remain positioned over the frames in a rather natural position, so that when he picks the light pen out of the air (which is its rest position, thanks to a system of jointed supporting arms and a controlled tension and rewind system for the attached cord) his hand is still on the way from the keyset to the display frame. When he is through with the pen at the display frame, he lets go of it, the cord rewinds, and the pen is again in position. There is thus a minimum of effort, movement, and time involved in turning to work *on* the frame. That is, he could easily shift back and forth from using keyset to using light pen, with either hand (one pen is positioned for each hand), without moving his head, turning, or leaning.

A good deal of Joe's time, though, seems to be spent with one hand on a keyset and the other using a light pen on the display surface. It is in this type of working mode that the images on the display frames changed most dynamically. You receive another real surprise as you realize how much activity there is on the face of these display tubes. You ask yourself why you weren't prepared for this, and you are forced to admit that the generalizations you had heard hadn't really sunk in—"new methods for manipulating symbols" had been an oft-repeated term, but it just hadn't included for you the images of the free and rapid way in which Joe could make changes in the display, and of meaningful and flexible "shaping" of ideas and work status which could take place so rapidly.

Then you realized that you couldn't make any sense at all out of the specific things he was doing, nor of the major part of what you saw on the displays. You could recognize many words, but there were a good number that were obviously special abbreviations of some sort. During the times when a given image or portion of an image remained unchanged long enough for you to study it a bit, you rarely saw anything that looked like a sentence as you were used to seeing one. You were beginning to gather that there were other symbols mixed with the words that might be part of a sentence, and that the different parts of what made a full-thought statement (your feeling about what a sentence is) were not just laid out end to end as you expected. But Joe suddenly cleared the displays and turned to you with a grin that signalled the end of the passive observation period, and also that somehow told you that he knew very well that you now knew that you had needed such a period to shake out some of your limited images and to really *realize* that a "capability hierarchy" was a rich and vital thing.

[…]

CHAPTER TWENTY-SIX

It's All about the Fit: The Hand, the Mobile Screenic Device and Tactile Vision

Heidi Rae Cooley

[...]

I identify the term *fit* to account for the particular relationship between a hand and a MSD [mobile screenic device], which opens onto a relation of interface through which vision becomes and remains tactile. I propose that the interaction of *fit* enables a more direct and vital mode of experiencing one's surroundings, which, while not directly about televisual space, is in conversation with it. Of course, it might seem easy to posit a connection between *fit* and televisual space; after all, the MSD is a screen-bearing device, which means it is possible to associate it with the television screen (as well as computer monitor), but it would be a mistake to do so. Televisual space is not simply a matter of the television screen and should not be confused with or reduced to what is presented on a television screen or where such a screen is located. Rather, it is possible to understand televisual space in terms of the relation that is produced between a screen and its surroundings (including the viewer) and/or the space that appears on the screen. Other screens participate in and qualify the *relation between* that constitutes televisual space. The MSD screen likewise participates but does so differently since it is handheld and mobile and, therefore, gains access to places beyond the reach of other screens. With MSD in hand, the most mundane and inconsequential of everyday places becomes the potential site for screenic engagement. Insofar as *fit* provides an opportunity for such engagement, it speaks to televisual space. However, because *fit* involves the physical and active relation between a hand and a MSD, it is something quite distinct from televisual space.

Fit

Fit, as I use it here, draws upon the discourses of biomechanics and industrial design.[1] It proposes to define the particular relationship between the hand and the MSD as a happening, which occurs at the instant of contour when the hand forms to the MSD and the MSD *gives* to the hand. In which case, *fit* is not a condition or quality but a moment of acting in, and through, a moment that reveals the potential for dynamic and reciprocal engagement. When hand and MSD articulate, the surfaces of the palm and the MSD mold each to the other, they interpenetrate. Thenar (thumb) and hypothenar (pinky) muscles cup the rounded edges of the MSD, which in turn sidles into the cradle of semi-flexed digits. The experience is tactilely pleasing, as hand and MSD fold into each other. Technically speaking, a 'blending of hand and wrist movements' allows 'the hand to mold itself to the shape of an object being palpated or grasped' (Bejjani and Landsmeer, 1989: 277). But, effectively, the hand and the device undergo a 'becoming one'
[…]

Screenic seeing

The soft and malleable meeting of hand and MSD in *fit* refuses the constricting tension that a grasp or clutch forces upon its object. Because *fit* is about the release and expansion of acquaintance, it intervenes in the flat and flattening vision that has become standard; it installs users within what they are seeing and thereby allows them to experience the transition, the interval that is seeing in its presencing (as opposed to being faced with an aggregate of discrete images). In other words, *fit* opens onto a different manner of seeing. The experience of *fit* coincides with the moment of contour; it emerges out of the articulation between the hand and the MSD, wherein the hand and device meet. Since *fit* presupposes a continuous merging, or becoming-one of hand and MSD, the experience is one that is dynamic and always happening. With regard to MSDs with imaging capabilities, this correspondence between *fit* and seeing often transpires in direct and explicit relation to the screen (whether it be an LCD screen of a digital camera or camcorder, or that of a PDA or mobile phone), a screen that is a distant relative to other imagebearing screens (including television and cinema screens). In this instance, vision is not a practice of seeing through, i.e. a window, but looking at, i.e. the screen.[2] And this shift from window-ed seeing to screenic seeing reconfigures one's relationship to that which is seen.[3] Whereas a window distances viewers from what they are looking at, the screen draws them toward the images that are displayed on the screen (not beyond it). In which case, window-ed seeing institutes a detached engagement, while screenic seeing encourages an experience of encounter. Vision, no longer a property of the window and its frame, becomes an extension of the screen. Likewise, that which is being viewed (and perhaps recorded) no longer exists separate from that which is framing it. The object, formerly located on the other side of the frame, converges or fuses with the screen, its physicality becoming the physicality of the screen. In this way, vision involves opacity, not transparency.[4] Screenic seeing acquires a sort of tangibility, a physicality of its own. In looking at the screen, the MSD user engages the screen and, subsequently, enters into a relationship with the screen. This relationship is material and unfolding; it does not involve containment but contingency. And yet, not all engagements with MSDs involve this opacity of screenic engagement, particularly since not all MSDs have imaging capabilities (and even if they did, not all people would make use of the feature). What I am describing as tactile vision does not necessarily require a seeing that is directly associated with the MSD screen. Rather, tactile vision involves seeing that coincides with a hand engaging a MSD: the seeing that accompanies *fit* is seeing in which the hand (or maybe hands) always participates.

In their mutual contouring, the hand and MSD expand; in their acquaintance, they open onto something else, which subsequently influences vision. *Fit*, then, cannot be understood as a self-contained, although ongoing, experience, meaning that *fit* is never an end in itself. Instead, it dilates into something larger or more encompassing than itself; it opens onto what can be understood in terms of interface, the threshold at which users and their surroundings meet and interact. Thresholds, as liminal spaces, are permeable; they are without definitive borders, even though they function as the boundaries between spaces. Because *fit* instantiates a very permeating and material relationship between MSD users and their surroundings, it is a mechanism of interface. In those instances wherein the MSD user engages the screen, the surroundings onto which interface opens are integrally related to, if not an extension of, the MSD screen. However, *fit* is never separate or distinguishable from the interface onto which it opens, even though it marks the beginning of the experience. And *fit* must be maintained in order for interface to continue; consequently, it becomes one with the happening of interface.

Vision that transpires in relation to *fit* and as filtered through interface is seeing that is simultaneously distracted and sensual. Finger, hand and wrist muscles synergistically flex and extend, abduct and adduct accordingly in order to maintain the integrity of contour between the hand and MSD and, thereby, sustain *fit*. But to the extent that *fit* happens without intention, and without assistance from the eyes because the hand is familiar with the MSD, the eyes are freed from the task at hand and can look on surrounding scenes (as well as screens) and events. The acquaintance materializing *fit*, the spreading of hand and MSD into one another, expands into interface and permeates the eyes' engagement with the surroundings. In this way, vision is never really free of the hand, insofar as it is always infused by *fit*, but also because of the analogous geometry of movement between the eye and the shoulder. According to Wilson (1999), the shoulder and eye move synchronously in acts of pointing (p. 328, n.4), with which it is plausible to compare the wrist's positioning in screenic mode – slightly extended and ulnarly deviated (in supination).[5] Because of this correspondence between hand and eye, it is possible to read vision as tactile in a double sense. First, the automatic yet intimate[6] contouring between hand and MSD that coincides and is integral with a seeing that is, as a result, never fully concentrated, but rather tangential and diffuse, comprises a tactility of vision. But also, the work executed by the hands in relation to the MSD screen, i.e. engagements with the screenic content by way of jog knob, stylus or even finger, constitutes a literal manifestation of tactile vision; the hand is directly and actively involved in the seeing that the eyes practice, in relation to screen and surroundings. A material experience of vision results as hands, eyes, screen and surroundings interact and blend in syncopated fashion. […]

Notes

1   Although *Gray's Anatomy* and Frank H. Netter's *Atlas of Human Anatomy* inform my understanding of biomechanics in general, for the purposes of this article, I refer to work by Bejjani and Landsmeer (1989), Chapman et al. (1996), Norkin and Levangie (1992), and Wilson (1999). In attending to matters concerning industrial design, I cite Kunkel (1999), Lupton (2002), Martegani and Montenegro (2001), Norman (1990), and Papanek (2000). (In many ways, design, in general, and the more specific categories of digital design and industrial design are usefully considered in relation to each other; I have chosen to do so here.)

2   Here it is important to distinguish between the MSD screen and its distant cousins just mentioned. Both television and cinema present screens that offer views onto other worlds; in which case, television and cinema screens function as windows. MSD screens, as I interpret them, do not open onto other worlds but merge with the world as it happens. In the case of camcorders with LCD screens, the screenic unfolding of the world supplants the actual world; the experience, while material and dynamic, is that of simulacra.

3   In thinking about the distinction to be made between window-ed and screenic seeing, it is important to recall Anne Friedberg's (2003) discussions of windows and screens, as well as Paul Virilio's (1988) 'third window'. By extension, one might also consider Jean Baudrillard (1988[1987]), Beatriz Colomina (1992), Anna McCarthy (2001), Marshall McLuhan (2001[1964]) and Lynn Spigel (2001).

4   I am borrowing heavily from Brown's (2001) distinction between transparency and opacity, which he discusses briefly in 'Thing Theory'. As Brown explains, window-ed seeing proceeds according to conceptions of objectivity, wherein the observer looks through the object in order to arrive at details, facts, etc. However, seeing that involves looking *at*, or what I am calling screenic seeing, engages the viewer in the thingness of objects, which is the 'contingency' that 'discloses the physicality of things' (p. 4).

5   Even though Wilson (1999) speaks about the shoulder, it is important to recall that positioning of the hand requires the entire upper extremity, including the shoulder. Perhaps also important to note here is the comparative treatment by the brain of the sensitive portions of both the digits and the retina (Wilson, 1999: 97–8), such that when an object is actively and simultaneously explored tactilely and visually, the brain is doubly engaged in like processes.

6   Wilson (1999) cites Jeanne Bamberger who discusses a process called 'felt path', in which the internalizing of familiar activities is interpreted as 'our most intimate way of knowing' (see p. 347, n.2). I contend that this intimate knowing is a way of understanding the acquaintance between hand and MSD operating in *fit*.

References

Baudrillard, Jean (1988[1987]) *The Ecstasy of Communication*, trans. Bernard and Caroline Schutze. New York: Semiotext(e).

Bejjani, Fad J. and Landsmeer, Johan M.F. (1989) 'Biomechanics of the Hand', in Brown, Bill (2001) 'Thing Theory', *Critical Inquiry* 28(1), Autumn: 1–21.

Brown, Bill (2001) 'Thing Theory', *Critical Inquiry* 28(1), Autumn: 1–21.

Chapman, C. Elaine, Tremblay, François and Ageranioti-Bélanger, Stacey A. (1996) 'Role of Primary Somatosensory Cortex in Active and Passive Touch', in Alan M. Wing, Patrick Haggard and J. Randall Flanagan (eds) *Hand and Brain: The Neurophysiology and Psychology of Hand Movements*, pp. 329–47. San Diego, CA: Academic Press.

Colomina, Beatriz (1992) 'The Split Wall: Domestic Voyeurism', in Beatriz Colomina (ed.) *Sexuality and Space*, pp. 73–130. Princeton, NJ: Princeton Architectural Press.

Friedberg, Anne (2003) 'The Virtual Window', in David Thornburn and Henry Jenkins (eds) *Rethinking Media Change: The Aesthetics of Transition*, pp. 337–53. Cambridge, MA: MIT Press.

Kunkel, Paul (1999) *Digital Dreams: The Work of the Sony Design Center*. New York: Universe Publishing.

Lupton, Ellen (2002) 'Skin: New Design Organics', in *Skin: Surface, Substance + Design*, pp. 28–41. New York: Princeton Architectural Press.

Martegani, Paolo and Montenegro, Riccardo (2001) *Digital Design: New Frontiers for the Objects*. Bäsel: Birkhauser.

McCarthy, Anna (2001) *Ambient Television: Visual Culture and Public Space*. Durham, NC: Duke University Press.

McLuhan, Marshall (2001[1964]) *Understanding Media: Extensions of Man*, intro. Lewis H. Lapham. Cambridge, MA: MIT Press.

Norkin, Cynthia C. and Levangie, Pamela K. (1992) 'The Wrist and Hand Complex', in *Joint Structure and Function: A Comprehensive Analysis*, pp. 262–99, 2nd edn. Philadelphia, PA: F.A. Davis Company.

Norman, Donald A. (1990) *The Design of Everyday Things*. New York: Doubleday.

Papanek, Victor (2000) *Design for the Real World: Human Ecology and Social Change*, 2nd edn. Chicago: Academy Chicago Publishers.

Spigel, Lynn (2001) *Welcome to the Dreamhouse: Popular Media and Postwar Suburbia*. Durham, NC: Duke University Press.

Virilio, Paul (1988) 'The Third Window: An Interview with Paul Virilio', in *Global Television*, pp. 185–97. Cambridge, MA: MIT Press.

Wilson, Frank R. (1999) *The Hand: How Its Use Shapes the Brain, Language, and Human Culture*. New York: Vintage Books.

CHAPTER TWENTY-SEVEN

The iPhone as an Object of Knowledge

Alexandra Schneider

In the 1990s the mobile phone, rather than the digital image, emerged as "the economic-technological basis for a vast industrial and infrastructural expansion."[1] Now, the (moving) digital image has become an integral part of mobile telephony. With an object like the iPhone, film history, the history of telecommunication, and the emergence of the digital intersect in complex ways that traditional film historiography never anticipated. Over the last ten years, concepts such as "media convergence" or "remediation" have proven to be useful starting points to account for the multilayered dynamics of the digital image in the age of mobile telephony. In exploring the iPhone as technological object and media platform, I follow Nanna Verhoeff's approach to what might be called "gadget analysis," an approach that permits one to "articulate the intertwinement of historical and theoretical thought, allowing us to turn from the one to the other."[2] Speaking of the Nintendo DS console, Verhoeff underlines the hybridity of the object, its materiality and "interface utility." My interest follows hers in discussing the iPhone as a theoretical object within a cinema studies framework. Much like the Nintendo console, the iPhone "hovers between three things": it is "a device we hold in our hands," "a screen we look at as well as through, and it is a screen we touch," and, finally, the iPhone is "at once an invisible and visible platform—a machine for haptic output of the applications one can play on it."[3] Like Verhoeff I take my cue from Hubert Damisch and propose to study the iPhone as a "theoretical object." In particular, I am interested in what the iPhone as a theoretical object tells us about an emerging new order of visual and sensory perception, not the least in relation to established modes of verbal and visual communication. […]

To pinch or not to pinch

When Apple launched the iPhone in April 2007, it was first and foremost a telecommunication device, providing mobile phone connections and Internet access. Two years after the iPhone's first appearance on the market, with the 3GS version released in 2009, Apple added video-recording features. The initial lack of a video camera did not impede the new device's impact. The iPhone was successfully marketed as "the revolutionary mobile phone," which proved to be true on two accounts. While consumers reacted enthusiastically, competing manufacturers of mobile communication devices apparently reacted with fear. At the point of the iPhone's initial release, executives at RIM, the manufacturer of the Blackberry device, were in a state of denial and refused to believe Steve Jobs's claim that Apple was able to provide sufficient battery power to light a screen the size of the iPhone's on a mobile device.[4]

Perhaps the most revolutionary aspect of the iPhone, however, was the substitution of traditional phone dials and the Blackberry miniature keyboard with a touch screen. Touch screens had been developed and used in various devices such as subway and railway ticket-vending machines for years, and it seems clear in retrospect that before the iPhone the potential of the touch-screen technology for mobile telephony had not been realized. What makes the iPhone touch screen distinctive and marks a significant advance over ticket-machine varieties of the touch screen is that the surface is completely touch sensitive, i.e., the touch-sensitive areas are not limited to certain proscribed icons. Depending on the application, the iPhone surface can be touched, rubbed, and even caressed. It is a surface that asks for an entire repertoire of tactile gestures rather than merely a functional handling.

When he first introduced the iPhone and its touch screen at one of Apple's now legendary product-launch ceremonies, Jobs strategically, and cleverly, introduced a specific verb to describe the kind of touch that the screen of the iPhone required: "to pinch." "To pinch" means to squeeze between the finger and thumb or between the jaws of an instrument. "Pinching" may be associated with a modest form of pain. The idea of being "pinched" does not necessarily evoke the sense of a tender touch, and the etymology of the corresponding French verb *pincer* (from which the English word derives) confirms this intuition. In the seventeenth century, when the verb first appeared, a "*pincer*" was also a *saisir d'amour*, a state of being touched (or moved) by a feeling of love. Rather than a piece of glass that supplants a series of buttons, icons, or a keyboard, the introduction of the verb "to pinch" suggests the touch screen surface of the iPhone is rather like a skin, a touch-sensitive surface that registers my every touch in its specific degree, direction, and expressiveness.

Whether Steve Jobs's proposition will become established as a figure of everyday speech remains to be seen. At the moment it appears that most

FIGURE 27.1 *Commuters using their smartphones while waiting on a metro platform, Washington, D.C., 2011. Photo: Jeffrey.*

people refer to the pinching mode (enlarging and scaling down of images) more in terms of zoom in and zoom out rather than in terms of "pinching" the visual object. It seems clear, however, that Jobs's choice of words intended to mark a shift from a merely visual approach to a haptic approach to visual objects. The semantics of "zooming in" and "zooming out" and the camera metaphor are no longer entirely adequate to this type of object and process. Again, the digital calls for the digit, the finger.

Yet at the same time the iPhone is now, in its third and fourth generations, also a camera and a portable cinema, complete with a "Cinemascope" application for film viewing. In this context, it is interesting to note that if the iPhone marks a shift from the knob to the switch to the screen as a semantically loaded technical skin, the etymology of the word "screen" reaches back to its earliest uses as a shield for warriors made of animal skin. Not only was the screen originally a protective skin, but in a media-historical genealogy, the current becoming-skin of the screen may be traced back to the nineteenth century and to early optical toys such as the flip book, where the physical contact and manipulation was a prerequisite of the visual experience. What the "pinchable" iPhone screen points us to, then, is a realignment of sight and touch around the sensitive surface of the screen. As I would argue, this realignment amounts to a specific kind of the return of the culturally repressed. The "pinchable" touch screen marks the reintroduction to the field of visual media of a tactile dimension of vision that was part and parcel of what we have come to call "pre-cinema" but had no place in the cinema when it became the culturally formative medium of the early twentieth century. Film theorists have been thinking about the tactile dimensions of the film experience for more than a decade now (i.e., for as long as telecommunications corporations have associated the digital with the digit and touch). In many ways the emergence of the iPhone and its touch screen valorizes the intuitions of such theorists as Vivian Sobchack and Laura U. Marks.[5] At the same time, the iPhone as a theoretical object forces us to rethink the configuration of moving image and embodied experience along the lines of how, through new technologies, touch and the tactile have once again become a key aspect of the visual experience.

Touch and visual perception

A visit to an art exhibition in a traditional museum space in the company of small kids will teach you not only about art but also about culture more generally. The most striking, and probably also most obvious lesson, concerns the issue of looking as opposed to touching. As a parent in an exhibition with small kids who are not yet quite able to read, you find yourself repeating one basic rule: "Look, don't touch" (or, as the Swiss German version goes, "Nur mit dae Augae luagae, noed mit de Fingaer"—"Look with your eyes, not with your fingers"). Communicating this rule becomes necessary for two reasons: first, art exhibitions usually feature objects that we are not supposed to touch, as even grownups find out when they get too close to a painting and are reprimanded for it by a museum guard, and, second, small children explore the world through the tactile and olfactory senses as much as through the sense of vision, by putting objects in their mouth and touching them rather than by merely looking at them.

Conventional exhibitions of paintings usually do not feature signs instructing the visitors that they are not supposed to touch the exhibited material. This rule is implicit in the practice of exhibiting artworks. But in some contemporary art exhibitions you are either explicitly invited to touch the exhibited artwork or reminded not to touch it. The basic ethos is still the same: hands off! The invitation to touch the artwork has to be made explicit because it is commonly understood that we are not supposed to do that. Interestingly enough, this has not always been the case. As Constance Classen has shown, the traditional hands-off ethos of the museum came into practice only in the mid-nineteenth century. Early museums, she writes, "were not exclusively hands-off affairs."[6]

"Touch had an advantage over sight in that it was understood to be the sense of certainty, an association symbolically grounded in the biblical tale of Thomas, who needed to touch the risen Christ to believe in his reality."[7] Until the eighteenth century, at least, touch remained one of the master senses. It verified perception and gave solidity to other, less reliable impressions.

According to Classen, the end of the nineteenth century marked the end "of the use of the proximity senses of smell, taste and touch," and they were relegated to the realm of the nursery and the "savage." Civilized adults were deemed to comprehend the world primarily through sight, and secondarily through hearing.[8]

The shift from the tactile to the visual coincided with the emergence of a new regime of scientific knowledge and, in particular, an ideal of "objectivity" evolving around the figure of the scientist as a detached observer. In short, during modernity close contact between visitors and exhibits was no longer allowed, as looking had become a central human feature—a fact that naturally can be linked to the emergence of moving images. In a broader cultural perspective on cinema history it can, thus, be argued that cinema was both complicit in, and a driving force of, the shift away from the tactile dimension of knowledge acquisition. In a related argument, film scholar Wanda Strauven has claimed that "the institutionalization of the cinema gradually got rid of all the features that determined the (potentially) interactive *dispositif* of early cinema, such as hand-cranked projectors." Strauven describes early rube films, for example, *Uncle Josh at the Moving Picture Show* (1902), as "a turning point in this institutionalization process that inevitably suppressed the more active conditions of the nineteenth-century observer and turned the viewer mode into the dominant mode of moviegoing. Porter's rube film confronts the 1902 audience, in this sense, with a form of spectatorship in extinction."[9]

In line with Strauven's point, one can argue that from the moment of its emergence cinema helped to enforce a regime of visual and nontactile knowledge, which today is undergoing a process of reconfiguration. In fact, if the argument that cinema played a role in the establishment of a new discipline of the body and the senses at the dawn of the twentieth century has any merit, then the emergence of a popular gadget that reintroduces and relegitimizes the once-common link of vision and touch must be seen as a shift in terms not only of media technology but also of epistemology. In order to illustrate and explain this shift, another Spielberg example[10] can be referred to: *Minority Report* (2002), based on a story by Philip K. Dick written in 1956. Produced five years before the release of the iPhone, the film features Tom Cruise as Chief John Anderton, a criminal investigator with prophetic capabilities working for a "pre-crime" prevention unit in Washington, D.C. Anderton's primary work tool is a command post with a set of fluid, immaterial touch screens. In a dynamic and almost feverish choreography of body and hand movements relating to these screens Anderton can draw up images of past, current, and even future events, alongside other information, texts, statistics, mathematical formulae, and so on. Like an iPhone user Anderton "pinches" images and information displays. He basically dances with the images that appear at the touch of his hands and disappear according to his movements. Anderton's office, or work station, is, if you will, a nonportable version of the iPhone.

How does Anderton's office tool relate to the current epistemological shift in media culture? The immateriality of the images and the information, as well as the screen itself, can be read, I would argue, as presaging and explaining the epistemological shift epitomized by the iPhone. As a handler, a "pincher," of immaterial images and immaterial surfaces and interfaces, Anderton turns out to be two steps remote from Uncle Josh. Uncle Josh wants to touch the object but finds out that there is no object, only a screen. Anderton never actually touches the screen—because the screen he uses is not a material surface—yet he reliably obtains the object (or information) he wants. It is therefore perhaps somewhere in between the fictional characters of Anderton and Uncle Josh that one comes close to the figure of the iPhone user: she is part Uncle Josh, part John Anderton. Like Uncle Josh, she actually touches the screen, since the touch screen is a material object, but like Anderton, she can make any object of knowledge appear on the screen at the touch of her finger.

Three regimes of touch, vision, and knowledge

In view of a historical epistemology of media, the settings and figures presented above [...] can be seen as emblematic for specific regimes or alignments of vision, touch, and knowledge that have emerged and succeeded one another over the last two hundred years. One can, in fact, distinguish between three major regimes: At first, there is an alignment of material object, touch, vision, and knowledge. It is culturally permissible and technically viable to gain knowledge of an object by both looking at and touching the material object. The emblematic figure of this regime is Uncle Josh, the rube, before he ever gets to the cinema. Second, one might see the emergence of a regime with which both the art museum and the cinema are thoroughly complicit, where vision and touch become separated and knowledge becomes scientific, objective knowledge of both material and immaterial objects based on distant observation and measurement. The emblematic figure of this regime is the educated, well-behaved spectator who has learned that she is supposed to look and not touch. She represents the norm that Uncle Josh, once he enters the cinema, fails to obey, or the ideal toward which Uncle Josh should educate himself. Third, today we witness the emergence of an alignment of touch, vision, and immaterial objects of knowledge, which becomes accessible by way of a screen, a nonspecific material object. *Minority Report*'s Anderton is the emblematic figure of this new regime, in which we mere mortals participate thanks to touch-screen devices like the iPhone.

The difference between Anderton and the iPhone user is that the latter still touches and operates a material device. However, the touch screen is a hybrid object. The screen itself may be a material object, but the objects to which it provides access are immaterial and devoid of physical consistency.

The iPhone invites an analysis similar to that proposed by Nanna Verhoeff in her discussion of the Nintendo playstation: "The console is best understood as a thing, instrument and interface at the same time. It is in this multiplicity that it is perhaps less a medium than a carrier of mediality." Moreover, Verhoeff continues, unlike other mobile "media players, a console is, in part, an empty interface. The software application determines part of the interface, in dialogue with the hardware elements. The complex of characteristics of the portable console as a versatile object, a thing/medium, demands a theoretical grasp on the phenomenon."[11]

Similarly, the iPhone as an object and the objects that the iPhone produces call into question our very definitions of medium and mediality. For a long time, and quite successfully, media studies have operated based on technological definitions of the medium. German media studies, *Medienwissenschaft*, for example, evolved from a focus on hardware, on the history of technology as media technology, and proceeded to analyze power relations and aesthetic phenomena as mere aftereffects of the technological base. Less stringently, but quite as cogently, film and television studies have based their epistemologies on quasi-technological definitions of their object of study: the cinematic *dispositif*, the television set, and so forth. Yet the scholarly challenge of the iPhone is not its effect on media convergence nor its multifunctionality and multiple formatting. Rather, the iPhone calls into question a number of basic distinctions, particularly the distinction between materiality and immateriality and that between (material) object and (social) action. Thinking about the iPhone thus forces us to acknowledge the hybrid nature of the devices and the practices that the device enables along the lines of the theoretical framework of actor network theory. It also forces us to acknowledge a fundamental instability and fluidity of the (im)material object—or medium—itself. In the new regime of vision, touch, and knowledge we have indeed become parts of a Deleuzian machine, elements in an assemblage, a set of couplings and connections that can, and do, redefine the sense and purpose of the individual element.

Let me illustrate this point by relating a final anecdote. In Switzerland, Apple has failed in their attempt to register iPhone as a trademark. The court argued that unlike the brand name iPod, which is a new verbal coinage without precedent in any natural language, iPhone is a homophone of an English language sentence that, in a colloquial abbreviation, describes the activity of using a telephone in the first-person singular. This sentence, the court argued, belongs in the public domain and cannot become the property of a person or other legal entity. As far as I know, the court's decision has so far not been detrimental to Apple's business interests. No competitor has dumped low-priced smartphones named iPhone on the relatively small market of Switzerland as yet. One could, of course, argue that it was never Apple's intention to own a part of a natural language or the practice thereof. But I would claim that the court's intuition was basically correct. In a way, an ownership stake in what the buyer does with the device is precisely what the iPhone (and other smartphones) are all about. Smartphones in general, and the iPhone in particular, are operated through apps that allow for specific activities and come in many varieties—but also at a price. As a customer, you pay for the license to do what you want with the device you already own. In a way, this is not much different from the introduction of pay TV at the end of the 1970s. But then again, the app is something fundamentally new. It expands the market for media beyond devices and programs and extends into the realm of social behavior. Apple sells gadgets and software, but, perhaps more importantly, it also sells patterns of activity and behavior. The iPhone calls into question the distinctions among medium, format/program, and user. We are now free to look and touch, but we pay a price for access to that new regime of knowledge.

Notes

1   Thomas Elsaesser, "Early Film History and Multi-Media: An Archaeology of Possible Futures?" in *New Media, Old Media: A History and Theory Reader*, ed. Wendy Hui Kyong Chun and Thomas Keenan (New York: Routledge, 2005), 15.

2   Nanna Verhoeff, "Theoretical Consoles: Concepts for Gadget Analysis," *Journal of Visual Culture* 3(2009): 290.

3   Ibid., 280, 296.

4   http://www,tagesanzeiger.ch/digital/intemet/iPhone-Stunde-Null/story/10695895 (February 10, 2011).

5   Vivian Sobchack, *The Address of the Eye: A Phenomenology of Film Experience* (Princeton, NJ: Princeton University Press, 1992); Sobchack, *Carnal Thoughts: Embodiment and Moving Image Culture* (Berkeley: University of California Press, 2004); Laura Marks, *The Skin of Film: Intercultural Cinema, Embodiment, and the Senses* (Durham, NC: Duke University Press, 2000);Marks, *Touch: Sensuous Theory and Multisensory Media* (Minneapolis: University of Minnesota Press, 2002).

6   Constance Classen, "Museum Manners: The Sensory Life of the Early Museums," *Journal of Social History* 4(2007): 896.

7   Ibid., 900.

8   Ibid., 896, 907.

9   Wanda Strauven, "The Observer's Dilemma: To Touch or Not to Touch," in *Media Archaeology: Approaches, Applications, Implications*, ed. Erkki Huhtamo and Jussi Parikka (Berkeley: University of California Press, 2011), 177.

10   [In a portion of the original essay not included here, Schneider invokes Spielberg's *E.T.: the Extra-Terrestrial* (1982). —Ed.]

11   Verhoeff, "Theoretical Consoles," 295–96.

CHAPTER TWENTY-EIGHT

The Smartphone Screen in All Its States

Virginie Sonet

Since the launch of the first 3G cellular services in 2004, and to a greater extent since the release of the iPhone[1] in 2007, we have access to a great variety of applications (communications, access and creation of contents, games) on a single device: the smartphone.[2] The possibility of using it to consume audiovisual contents—the object of this study—earns it the title of "third screen." The smartphone concentrates multiple preexisting technologies (telephony, web, music player, television). This hybrid genealogy encourages personalized forms of mobilizing and appropriating this screen. In addition, the device's mobility allows the user to diversify the contexts of use (places, moments) that in themselves can become deciding factors of use (opportunities and limitations related to the network or the presence of others).

We hypothesize that this is the result of these variable and ad hoc factors of use of the smartphone and that these contribute to the access of audiovisual contents on this screen by smartphone users [*smartphonaute*].[3] This multidimensional screen confronts the idea of flexible frames of use theorized by Flichy (1995, 2008). We therefore seek to study in what ways the accessing of audiovisual content on the smartphone form of mobile device consists of different dimensions, detectable through the individualized practices of users.

In light of the very recent nature of the phenomenon we have chosen to study, our path is necessarily mostly exploratory. For this, we have undertaken a qualitative study[4] of twenty-seven smartphone users (from 17 to 37 years old, of varied professions, living situations, and income levels).

We have conducted semi-directed interviews backed up by self-executed journals in which participants recorded all of their audiovisual consumption, regardless of the viewing device, for a week.[5]

We will start by briefly considering the properties of the smartphone that we considered key to accessing mobile audiovisual content. We will then analyze the different uses of this screen in relation to the consumption of such content.

Accessing audiovisual contents on a mobile, interactive, and networked device

The smartphone crystalizes the convergence of technologies and uses of previous devices: cellphone, computer, television, personal music player, video game console (Gonord, Menrath, 2005). Accordingly the smartphone, as a communication device, offers both services and spectacle.

Unlike the portable televisions studied by Spigel (2009), this telephone is truly a mobile audiovisual screen, kept in the pocket. Its mobility contributes to the adoption of the smartphone as an audiovisual screen by allowing an unprecedented variety of contexts of use and the consumption of available content (watching a TV show on the bus, sharing a viral video from a social media site while walking). It also allows the reinforcement of the individualization and privatization of these practices.

Its interactive, tactile surface[6] eliminates the components previously needed for screen interaction (remote control, keyboard, mouse). As Coutaz has emphasized, "[in the case of] a digital interface, the instrument is eliminated. The hand alone controls the system-entity represented on the surface" (Coutaz 2002: 115). Thus the smartphone contains at least the illusion of directly manipulating contents and information. According to Grossman (2007), this is typically what the iPhone permits: "Apple's engineers used the touchscreen to innovate past the graphical user interface … to create a whole new kind of interface, a tactile one … Touching is the new seeing."

These initial aspects show us the extent to which the smartphone user is able to access the communication, service, and entertainment functions of this apparatus, as well as its associated contents, in both a variety of spatial and temporal frames and a more direct and engaging manner.

As a connected device, the smartphone acts as the archetype of technical, digital objects characterized by their polyvalence, their openness, their systemization, the loss of their dominant function and the flexibility of their uses (Paquienseguy 2009). Paquienseguy identifies another fundamental trait of the smartphone: its hybrid genealogy. Indeed, the author demonstrates that very often these objects bring together previous information and communication technologies that reflect existing uses and are variable, important references in their appropriation by users.

As an "enhanced" cellphone, the smartphone, through its hybrid genealogy (personal music player, web navigation, audiovisual screen), is also one of those objects that everyone carries with him and that Boullier states "extend the individual and signify their belonging to diverse worlds" (Boullier 2002: 52). As such, the smartphone—unlike the cellphone that it remains at first degree, but also unlike the web and its communication applications—mobilizes the entire personal network of the user. Boullier suggests the neologism "habitèle" to stress "this phenomenon that belongs in fact to a human ability to instrumentalize our sense of belonging and through this create a new skin ... In the case of the habitèle, numerous systems allow us to build a skin from our multiple networks of belonging" (52). Lastly, in the lineage of the television and computer, the smartphone integrates in turn what can hereafter be called the culture of the screen (Messin 2005). Its inscription in the genealogy of the evolution of uses of the television monitor seems pertinent, in line with the work of Chambat and Ehrenberg on television and screen culture (1988). For them, "the social imagination of the all-electronic affects the traditional experience of television in its two modalities [interactivity and fascination with the screen] and explodes it in two distinct directions...: Ambience Television and Communication Television" (Chambat, Ehrenberg 1988: 120).

Thanks to the list of types of consumption of mobile audiovisual contents, our study has allowed us to demonstrate two major types of smartphone use—the Ambience-Screen and the Communication-Screen—for which we have detected five aspects, according to the contexts and uses in which they are found.

Ambiance-Screen

The two forms of access that emerge with mobile audiovisual content demonstrate, to our mind, the sedimentation of practices of ambiance as much audio as audiovisual, already found with the Walkman or the drifting sound of the television. We believe they point to an Ambiance-Screen, inheriting this use of the television already identified by Chambat and Ehrenberg, where "the image is heard as much as seen and [where] attention is as often fading and disengaged as it is active and focused" (121).

The Show Screen

Within this frame, the smartphone user deliberately employs this third screen to view audiovisual or televisual contents. The user makes little use of the interactivity and connectivity of the screen, which here functions principally as a viewing surface. The contents are generally rather long, involving series, TV shows, and the news, but also films and podcasts. These derive from two types of sources: those that require a network connection (such as

3G television and TV network apps) and those that are prerecorded and therefore require no such connection.[7] Although this practice of sideloading is time-consuming, and the learning curve is steep, it was done by most of those surveyed who use the smartphone in this way.

The Show Screen is employed in specialized viewing situations (public transportation, waiting, limits on time and space for the user). This use is therefore similar to that of the personal music player for creating personal ambiance (Thibaud 1994), but also resembles that of the flow of home television, across uses of the "canal lock" variety between two spheres of activity as observed by Le Goaziou (1999) and illustrated in the example of Anaïs:

> TV series run 40 minutes, about the same time it takes me to go to work. It's a good fit. (museum assistant, 24 years old)

These users share an anticipation or nuanced understanding of the viewing situation, especially the terms of the trip they are making (duration, network, comfort, schedule). With the contents selected, often having been converted and transferred ahead of time, this commonly corresponds to the true tastes of the user. Viewing is generally planned or even a routine.

> *The Shining* is two hours, ten minutes long and I saw it in five installments. The iPhone also has the advantage of picking up where it has left off, which is good. I select my film from the internet during the week, I convert it and the next day it's ready. In fact, on Sunday I usually put together my films for the week. (Julien, waiter, 26 years old)

The uses of the Show Screen are related to the mastery and delinearization of the consumption of audiovisual contents that began with the VCR, digital recording, DVDs and, more recently, with video on-demand and binge-viewing. This is particularly so when these uses correspond to a form of anticipated self-programming, as with Julien, which consists of preparing a personalized weekly viewing schedule.

The Phonic Screen

This use of the smartphone involves accessing music-video content for listening. It is found particularly in contexts where viewing is awkward (while walking, on cramped public transportation, or where there is a risk of theft) and the desired song is not available in the smartphone's playlists.

The smartphone user searches for a song in a video-sharing app such as YouTube. Once the video is found, the screen can be covered for the sole benefit of listening, in a selective aural environment that has already been identified with personal music player use (Thibaud 1994).

You have plenty of noise around you and … you put on your headphones, you listen to your music and you do what you have to do without hearing anyone else. (Sandra, micro-electronics technician, 31 years old)

The use of this screen in social environments recalls those of the personal bubble, of managing co-presence and the distracted listening identified with personal music player use (Bull 2000; Pecqueux 2009), in addition to those of portable television notably observed by Figeac (2009).

In these first two methods of application, the use of mobile audiovisual contents is shaped by a double genealogy: the personal music player and the detached listening of television. In a way the smartphone produces the "ambient television of tomorrow" envisioned by Chambat and Ehrenberg: "If the television of yesterday was broadcast into the family home in the dual tradition of wireless radio and cinema, the television of tomorrow—pushed by a taste for technical feat, actually extends both models simultaneously. Giant and high-definition, it mimics the cinema screen. In miniature, it copies the transistor in crossing individualized use and distracted listening" (124).

The Communication-Screen

Multifunctional media devices symbolize the television of communication, a product of the convergence of the audiovisual, telecommunications, and computing sectors. Ideas of networks and interactivity are at the heart of this communicational consumption. The interactivity of objects that supports these networks engages the user in a conative relationship. As such, what is consumed is no longer just the show, but also service and dialogue. In television use with the first cellphones linked to 3G networks, Hübel (2007) and Lejealle (2010) observed little user interest in the interactive properties of these services. Today, the development of more sophisticated devices like the smartphone encourages more interactivity. In the case of the smartphone, we observe the use of the Communication-Screen where, more than its mobility, it is the connected and interactive aspect of the smartphone that contributes strongly to the accessing of audiovisual contents. We have identified three forms.

The Collective Screen

We have observed that the smartphone is used to view audiovisual contents collectively, primarily in bars, restaurants, at school, or when visiting friends. The length of the contents ranges from two to twenty minutes. The smartphone allows for instantaneous video searches (excerpts from TV shows, sporting events, humorous clips) while with the group (of friends, family members, colleagues …). This use reinforces the social links of the collective:

> I have more use for videos to share with my friends at parties. (Myriam, communications manager, 32 years old)
>
> Sometimes I visit Koreus[8] with friends. But when I'm alone I don't feel like watching funny videos. (Rémy, design student, 17 years old)

As O'Hara (2007) already observed in his work on the consumption of mobile videos, this use functions on a relational basis of sharing, but also on the construction of individual and collective identity, of peer recognition, *in praesentia* through specific contents.

The Relational Screen

This use is observed during multimedia connections and interpersonal communications. Video is received through interpersonal communication features of the smartphone (SMS, MMS, emails, social networks) or encountered while browsing (apps or sites). These are short informational, commercial, or personal videos.

In this way, the smartphone extends the digital social practices of the web and the cellphone. One of the widest uses, very common during the day[9] and strongly associated with the cellphone, this practice takes place as much while commuting as when at home, at school, or between activities. Accessing audiovisual material is done through communication functions and the applications that support them, such as mobile social networks, as well as through the condition of permanent connectivity (Jauréguiberry 2003).

> For example, I'm on Facebook, I click on a link, and it opens immediately. So, let's just say that makes me watch more videos, like news reports, short things three minutes long that are causing a stir. (Jeanne, twenty-two year old student)

If viewing is individual, then the taste-level of the contents is not an issue. The decision to watch the video is the conclusion of a personalized action of evaluation of the contents by the smartphone user, who takes into account the length, the relevance, or, in the case of social networks, the relational potential based on who posted it or the number of comments generated.

The Advisory Screen

The advisory screen emerges in the use of multimedia services and reacting to notifications[10] that lead to accessing another screen, either immediately or at a later time. These situations of prescription and recommendation are not only interpersonal, but also come from "electronic" third parties (news sites or online communities, for example).

Upon receiving a notification, the user chooses to deflect the viewing of the video to another screen (PC, TV) or to postpone it.

> If there's something interesting, for example at work, I resort to the PC. (Nicolas, developer, 24 years old)

> In fact I mark the video as "unread" to run it later on my Mac. (Damien, actor, 32 years old)

Mobility constraints strongly shape the choices of the smartphone user. Even more than with the Relational Screen, this use really follows a logic of practicality that engages the user in a situated program of action where he establishes a personalized viewing schedule according to his surroundings. As such, he takes into consideration network availability, the autonomy of the device, the given span of time, the setting, who is present, and the format of the video and the nature of its contents (too long or poorly suited to the context).

The smartphone user can also create a kind of self-advising. He resorts to his screen to access a live broadcast that will lead, if he remains interested, to viewing on a more comfortable screen.

> I like the show *90 mn Enquêtes* [90-minute investigations] on TMC, so I'll check to see if it's on tonight. Before I even open an app such as Télé Loisors or Télérama I quickly connect to the network. If it's on and seems interesting I switch to the PC. (Thomas, student, 21 years old)

Conclusion

Communication Screen uses were clearly the most common in our study. We also found at the heart of such use that Relational Screen practices generally involved the consumption of mobile audiovisual contents. In fact, all those interviewed watched at least some audiovisual contents by means of received contents through interpersonal communication practices: an email, an MMS, private messaging, or a post on a social media platform.

This primacy of Communication Screen use clarifies the concept of the habitèle, which Boullier associates with communicative objects. The author explains that these communicative objects constituting the habitèle become a part of us. They perform the multiplicity of networks to which they give us access as terminal devices. As such, "there is also something of the other that approaches us, that we take with us, that becomes part of our body" (Boullier 2002: 53). In this regard the smartphone is an access device not only to our personal network, or "list of contacts" embedded in the telephone's SIM card but, additionally, through its ability to connect to the web it offers access to all our other networks, whether they be our personal networks—private as well as professional—or our network of interests. Through the ensemble of communication tools crystallized in this terminal (mail, SMS, MMS, notifications, alerts, social media apps, content aggregators, rss feeds) the smartphone user is able to receive outward signs of these different networks more or less continually. As such, the study of the consumption of mobile audiovisual contents tells us that the smartphone will be a device constituting the "habitèle," particularly through the Communication Screen, a situation within which what is consumed, to cite Chambat and Ehrenberg, involves relationships.

In conclusion, the uses of the smartphone are flexible enough that each user consumes audiovisual contents in a personalized way. Some study participants engaged in the five types of use we have identified here. Most participated only in two or three, while all made use of the Relational Screen. We therefore have not addressed the issue of types of mobile viewers: the smartphone user is only a mobile viewer at specific moments when he privileges the audiovisual or televisual function of his screen. According to a combination of his prior practices, his habits, and his context of use, he can in fact be, from one moment to the next, a participant in a telephone conversation, a mobile reader, mobile listener, mobile browser, but also, beyond our observations, mobile player, mobile buyer, or mobile creator of contents.

Notes

1   In France 31 percent of cellphone users have a smartphone. This number has tripled in two years.
2   [A smartphone is] a cellphone that can connect to the Internet through different networks (3G and Wi-Fi) and provides access to a wide range of applications.
3   We have employed *smartphonaute* as a neologism to describe smartphone users.
4   From September 2010 to February 2011, in collaboration with Orange Labs.
5   Our sample is not intended to represent an otherwise little-known population of users. In light of their relative weakness, CREDOC (2010) is not yet in a position to pass these mobile television practices through socio-demographic filters.
6   This is defined as any physical surface linked to computation capacities, such as a computer screen or PDA.
7   The contents are described as "sideloaded": transferred to the smartphone from a computer or downloaded in anticipation of viewing.
8   Koreus is a platform for unusual videos and user-generated content (UGC).
9   The average French person sends around 186 texts a month (ARCEP, June 2011). Facebook is first in the Top 20 of cellphone audiences in France, with nearly ten million unique visitors (Médiamétrie, last quarter, 2010).
10 These are short alert texts (notably news items) received directly on the smartphone screen from sites or apps. By "clicking" on them the smartphone user is redirected to the site or the contents in question.

References

Boullier D. (2002). "Objets communicants, avez-vous donc une âme? Enjeux Anthropologiques." *LCN*, volume 3, no. 4: 45–60.

Bull M. (2000, 2006). *Sounding out the City*. New York: Berg.

Chambat P., Ehrenberg A. (1988). "De la télévision à la culture de l'écran." *Le débat*, no. 52: 107–132.

Coutaz J. et al. (2002). "Quand les surfaces deviennent interactives … " *LCN*, volume 3, no. 4: 101–126.

Figeac J. (2009). "L'appropriation de la télévision mobile personnelle autour des réseaux de communication." *Réseaux*, no. 156: 81–111.

Flichy P. (2008). "Technique, usage et représentation." *Réseaux*, no. 148–149: 147–174.

Gonord A., Menrath J. (2005). *Mobile Attitude, Ce que les portables ont changé dans nos vies*. Paris: AFOM/ Hachette.

Grossman L. (2007). *The Invention of the Year: the iPhone*, Time, 30/10/07.

Hübel AK. et al. (2007). " 'I Just Want to See the News'—Interactivity in Mobile Environments." In P. Cesar et al. (Eds.), EuroITV 2007, *LNCS* 4471: 205–214, Berlin: Springer-Verlag.

Jaureguiberry F. (2003). *Les branchés du portable*, Collection Sociologie d'aujourd'hui, Paris: Presses Universitaires de France.

Le Goaziou V. (1999). "Le corps des téléspectateurs." *Réseaux*, no. 92: 293–314.

Lejealle C. (2010). "La télévision sur mobile est-elle interactive?" in *tic&société*, volume 4, no. 1.

Messin A. (2005). *De l'usage d'Internet à la culture de l'écran*, 3èmes doctoriales du GDR TIC et Société.

O'Hara K. et al. (2007). "Consuming Video on Mobile Devices," CHI '07, 28 avril-3 mai: San Jose, California.

Paquienseguy F. (2009). "Questionner les pratiques communicationnelles. Offre, pratiques, contenus." In *Nouveaux médias, nouveaux contenus*, sous la direction de Delavaud G., 153–164. Paris: Éditions Apogée.

Pecqueux A. (2009). "Embarqués dans la ville. Les déplacements préoccupés des auditeurs-baladeurs." *Réseaux* no. 156: 49–80.

Spiegel L. (2001). "La télévision portable: enquête sur les voyages dans l'espace domestique." In *La télévision du téléphonoscope à Youtube*, pp. 249–271, Lausanne: Éditions Antipodes.

Thibaud J.-P. (1994). "Les mobilisations de l'auditeur-baladeur: une sociabilité publicative." *Réseaux*, no. 65: 71–83.

CHAPTER TWENTY-NINE

In the Flesh: Space and Embodiment in the Pornographic Peep Show Arcade

Amy Herzog

Within cluttered media landscapes, littered with an infinite variety of screens, the pornographic peep show arcade is a singular and ubiquitous format. Clustered in tenderloin districts in virtually every metropolitan area, peep show "movie machines" can also be found in suburban porn shops and the truck-stop adult markets that skirt highways throughout rural North America. Peep show arcades provide a motion-picture viewing experience unlike any other contemporary medium, one in which the distinction between public and private is inverted on a number of different registers. The filmed body on-screen lays bare its most private attributes, yet it does so in a self-conscious, formulaic, and exhibitionist manner. The apparatus of the peep show subjects the body of the patron to a highly individualized and intimate mode of address, compelling in return an active and equally intimate corporeal response. At the same time, this exchange takes place in public, with the patron's own body rendered visible as it circulates through the arcade (to greater or lesser degrees, depending on the architecture of the venue and the booths). The peep show's voyeuristic, personalized viewing mechanism presents a further historical anomaly, its coin-operated interface and selection of exotic novelties harking back to the earliest Kinetoscope parlors. Despite this unusual and somewhat anachronistic exhibition format, peep arcades have provided a consistent revenue stream for the adult film industry. Peeps are historically one of the most profitable outlets for adult retail businesses, and they have survived the seismic shift from film to video with relatively few changes in their basic design.

Given the prevalence of peep arcades in both urban and rural areas, their historical longevity, and their unique mode of exhibition, it seems strange that the format has not received more critical attention. In the 1970s several studies were conducted on the sociology of adult bookstores and peep shows, providing thick, if at times suspect, descriptions of these spaces (see Karp; Kornblum; McNamara; Nawy; Sundholm). More recently, a number of scholars have pointed to the political and social significance of porn theaters and arcades, particularly in relation to queer culture and the policing of public sex (see Berlant and Warner; Cante and Restivo; Capino; Champagne; Chauncey; Warner). Yet the peep show arcade has remained relatively marginalized within the larger field of porn studies, and the content of peep show films is almost never discussed.[1]

This lack of attention may be a result of the inherent difficulties involved in the study of peep show films. As is the case with the pornography industry in general, peep show producers and distributors were unlikely to maintain archival records, particularly when their businesses existed on the margins of legal acceptability. Because peep machines brought in large quantities of small, hard change, it was easy for owners to mask the precise amount of revenue earned. Peep parlors would rarely advertise themselves, and the films shown in the machines were short and often regionally produced. It is thus nearly impossible to estimate the size and structure of the peep industry, and there are few printed advertisements or reviews to provide a sense of the content of films in different regions or at different historical moments. The ephemeral status of the format makes it equally challenging to determine which films might or might not have been run in the arcades. While a number of producers created films expressly for use in peep machines, these loops might later be sold over (or under) the counter after they were removed from circulation, often being edited or reprinted in the process. Loops produced for home use would also be loaded into peep machines in bookstores as a means of marketing those films to patrons. For a contemporary researcher searching through private collections or uncataloged caches within film archives there are few clues as to where a loop might have originated or whether it was ever shown in a peep machine.

The difficulties associated with studying the peep show might also result from the highly situated status of the format. Peep arcades are social spaces defined by their apparatus and architecture, their physical placement within a community, and the various regulations, enforcement policies, and mores at play in their geographical locale. While these are factors that must be considered with any pornographic material (or any media format, for that matter), issues of architecture and space literally define the peep show as a medium. Despite the pervasiveness of the peep show format, there are significant regional and historical distinctions in terms of design, display, film gauge, placement, degrees of privacy, and film content. These factors make it incredibly difficult to discuss the nature of peep shows with any degree of empirical accuracy.

Yet peep shows remain an important phenomenon to discuss, particularly in terms of theorizing the intersections of cinema and space. Peep show arcades have generated fierce debates about public decency and zoning and have been subject to much legislation. Peep shows also have a strong hold on the cultural imagination. Images of neon peep show signage remain one of the most efficient means of signifying urban decadence, especially that associated with the late 1960s and 1970s. As literature on the diverse social dynamics of "sex districts" has indicated, commercial venues such as adult bookstores, theaters, and arcades are traversed by a broad cross-section of users and are of tremendous social and political importance to various marginalized communities for whom such districts provide public visibility and relative freedom of movement.

This paper will explore questions of spatiality in the pornographic peep show, focusing on the widespread establishment of the adult arcades in the mid-1960s through the early 1970s. Space will be considered from a number of perspectives: in terms of the evolution of the spatial dynamics of the apparatus, in terms of the regulation of the social and cultural space of the arcade, and in terms of the performative spaces engendered by a series of 16 mm loops from this era. Within the arcade numerous cinematic and physical bodies are rendered open to display, enacting a vexed and often self-conscious web of exhibitionism, surveillance, and social exchange. These exchanges are rarely complete, however, and on every register are marked by inconsistency, disruption, distraction, and disavowal. An examination of the range of contradictory accounts of the peep show arcade provided by sociologists, entrepreneurs, journalists, and the courts in this era reveals a great deal about the complexity of the peep arcade as a public space. Even the most reticent of these accounts acknowledge that the 1960s peep arcade was a site inclusive of a range of sexual practices (albeit not inclusive of many practices geared toward female customers or of media created by female producers). The fluidity of this atmosphere, however, stands in contrast to the highly politicized manner in which arcades were monitored and regulated. And the film loops, too, especially those created exclusively for peep machines, bear marks of tension and contradiction, particularly as registered in their performances and in their unique mode of address. If we are to make sense, as Vivian Sobchack insists, of "the carnal foundations of cinematic intelligibility," the peep show arcade seems an ideal venue for doing so (*Carnal Thoughts* 59).

Given the dearth of information available on the pornographic peep show industry, it might be helpful to outline my methodology at the outset. Descriptions of peep show machines and the layout of arcades have been compiled from direct interviews with arcade owners and employees, interviews published in trade books on the pornography industry, sociological studies from the era (including those compiled in the U.S. Attorney General's

Commission on Pornography reports), accounts published in newspaper articles, and data included in local and federal court decisions. Access to 16 mm films, stills, and distribution cards from the Starlight Film Series was provided by Albert Steg, an archivist and ephemeral film collector. Additional Starlight loops are available on home video; Something Weird Video includes a large number of Starlights in their vintage erotica compilations. I viewed collections of uncataloged loops at the Kinsey Institute for Sex, Gender, and Reproduction in Bloomington, Indiana, and at the Museum of Sex in New York, and I consulted the extensive vertical files at the Kinsey covering the porn industry during this period.

My findings are nascent and reveal, more than any conclusive answers, the tremendous lack of reliable information regarding peep shows. Nevertheless, several central questions emerged during the course of this research that I wish to explore here. The peep arcade is an anomalous space within the realm of porn studies precisely because of the manner in which public and private become enfolded. Peep shows are social environments, sites of exchange between on-screen performers and cameras, between spectators and texts, and, in certain instances, between spectators in the arcade. Moreover, the systems of surveillance and regulation that attempt to police these exchanges indicate the degree to which peep arcades pose a threat to privatized, normative notions of sexuality. In the sections that follow I outline the ways in which public and private are subverted within these diverse registers. My hope is that these preliminary gestures might generate further research into spatiality and peep show culture.

A brief history of the arcade, 1966–1970

The rise of the modern-day peep arcade in the 1960s is subject to much mythologization. Coin-operated motion-picture "peep" machines were hardly a new invention at that time, with Kinetoscope and Mutoscope parlors dating back to the late nineteenth century. Early peep machines frequently flirted with salacious material (or at least with salacious-sounding titles); this trend increased exponentially as technologies lost their novelty and migrated to down-market amusement arcades catering to "sporting" crowds (see Nasaw 130–34). Periodic references to peep-related obscenity cases and the appearance of vintage loops in private collections suggest that pornographic motion-picture peep machines have enjoyed a fairly continuous presence on the North American entertainment landscape.[2] What changed in the 1960s, however, was the scale and ambition of the peep industry and its visible intrusion into the public sphere.

There are several regional accounts of the "invention" of the 1960s peep show booths that share a similar narrative, one centered on entrepreneurial recycling. In 1967 Martin Hodas, the "King of the Peeps," installed his first set of coin-operated film machines in Carpel Books at 259 West 42nd

St. (Bianco 162–63). Hodas had been working in the jukebox and coin-op amusement industry, installing and servicing machines. In an arcade in New Jersey in 1966 he encountered a large Panoram film jukebox machine that had been outfitted to show "girlie" striptease loops.[3] Panorams were launched in the early 1940s by the Mills Novelty Company to show three-minute "Soundies" musical performances. The Panoram consisted of a large wooden cabinet and a ground-glass screen on which the film was rear projected, maximizing visibility of the musical shorts in the restaurants and bars in which the machines were installed. This presented an obvious problem for peep purveyors, who needed to convert the machines for individual customers. The glass screens were replaced with a binocular viewer that looked onto the reflected image, and the remainder of the opening was either partially or fully boarded over. Despite the musical origins of the format, the peep loops were silent, and the machines contained no curtains or doors, such that the body of the user remained fully visible to the outside (paradoxically, unlike the body of the performer on film).

Hodas clearly did not invent this technology, as Panorams had been converted in this manner since the demise of the Soundies enterprise in the late 1940s. Other forms of peep machines existed in numerous amusement arcades throughout the country, and references to police raids on arcades with "obscene" peep shows date to at least the early 1950s.[4] A description of a 1950s arcade refers to a front room, with pool tables and "machines of skill"; a central counter for magazines, cigarettes, and change; and a back room with a large number of Panoram-style peep machines (*State v. Silverman*). While this model of the divided storefront with segregated peep area and a highly visible change counter remained the norm, Hodas's primary innovation was the relocation of peep machines from amusement arcades into adult-themed bookstores in large quantities and in a number of locations in a concentrated area. According to Anthony Bianco, adult bookstore owners had been pressured by the police department to obtain licenses to show films, which they had avoided rather than opening their businesses to additional scrutiny. Hodas hired a lawyer, who discovered that licenses for coin-operated movie machines were not required, and Hodas began to install Panorams in the backs of adult bookstores around Times Square. By 1968 he was reportedly depositing $15,000 in quarters in the bank per day (Bianco 162–64). His business soon expanded to film production, and he switched from the bulky 16 mm machines to 8 mm and to privatized booths with hard-core films by the 1970s. He was constantly dogged with charges of involvement with organized crime (charges he vehemently denies), and his involvement in the industry declined after he was convicted of tax evasion in 1975.

Other entrepreneurs began large-scale peep show operations across the country. In Atlanta, Michael Thevis built a massive multimedia porn empire largely funded by the distribution of peep show machines, reportedly developing his machines based on children's cartoon booths designed by

Nat Bailen.[5] Reuben Sturman is credited with mass marketing the privatized peep booth through his Cleveland-based company, Automated Vending. According to one of his former employees, the booths were constructed out of plywood and paneling, with a closing door. Each booth contained a screen and two to four 8 mm or Super8 projectors triggered by a circuit board when a user selected a button for a particular film. The projectors operated via electrical circuitry, and, rather than working via a continuous loop, they would stop, advance, and rewind the films automatically (McNeil and Osbourne 104–10). Such innovations in privacy and selectability held an obvious appeal for most users. Sturman's operations spread throughout the United States and Canada, later including partnerships in Europe, and separate corporations under his supervision controlled the production of films and the collecting of change. The 1986 report of the U.S. Attorney General's Commission on Pornography stated that Sturman was "widely believed to be the largest distributor of pornography in the world" (pt. 4, chap. 4, sec. 5; see also McNeil and Osbourne 104–10; Schlosser 128–32).

According to the 1970 report of the U.S. Commission on Obscenity and Pornography, peep show booths were primarily 8 mm and offered viewers three to four minutes of a reel for each quarter deposited, although 16 mm machines were equally common in the 1960s, and the amount of time allotted per quarter was often closer to two minutes. The films, the report notes, "usually depict fully nude females exposing their genitals, and many depict sexual foreplay between couples," both male–female and female–female (1:101–2). A 1970 study of porn outlets in San Francisco similarly found that the arcades "tend to limit their assortment of film to the less graphic, single girl, 'beaver' variety. In cases where two persons are shown, their sex play is more suggestive than actual" (Nawy 149).[6] Both studies noted that women were not permitted to enter the arcades at any of the venues observed. The report's conclusion, that the peeps "exceed the return from sales of books and magazines," providing the primary profits for these establishments, echoes numerous statements by law enforcement officials and bookshop owners. Peeps were to a large degree funding the operations of the adult retail industry.

Descriptions of arcades from this period seem to indicate that the industry was highly decentralized. Arcades seem to have been designed in an ad hoc manner, some utilizing rear-projection machines of varying gauges and others booths with projectors and screens. Despite these inconsistencies, several patterns emerge from the existent accounts of peep arcades, and it may be possible to point toward general trends in the evolution of arcade architecture.

Peep show arcades are frequently located in darkened sections in the backs of bookstores, coin-operated amusement centers, and, in later years, adult movie theaters. Warrens of booths are laid out in a manner that allows users to circulate with a degree of privacy and autonomy while at the same time providing mechanisms for surveillance by arcade employees. In 1973

Charles A. Sundholm described a San Francisco arcade consisting of a brightly lit front section containing pinball machines and other nonpornographic amusements and a darker section containing a "labyrinth" of 8 mm machines. A hexagon-shaped cashier desk separated the two sections, with mirrors that allowed employees to monitor the passageways between sections and machines. The bodies of the viewers in these arcades were fully visible as they peeped at films through slots (suggesting a Panoram-like viewing mechanism), although wooden panels on the sides of the booths could be adjusted to shield the viewer's face from those standing next to him. Machines closest to the front of the arcade were more visible and cost ten cents per view, while the more private booths near the rear of the store charged a quarter. A red light on the top of each machine indicated that it was in use, providing cashiers with "an index of legitimate occupancy and appropriate involvement on the part of patrons" (Sundholm 86–88). Although different machines made use of curtains or other privatizing measures, this general layout seems consistent in descriptions from this era.

Throughout the 1970s, while antiquated machines persisted in some locations, the general trend was toward privatization as Panoram-style machines were replaced with fully enclosed booths with closing doors. 16 mm projectors were gradually replaced by 8 mm and Super8 models, which were upgraded to video as that technology became available. The film loops, too, evolved into hardcore territory, some with mininarratives and others catering to various fetish audiences. The line between peep loop and home-use films grew increasingly blurred as producers attempted to maximize their distribution and profits. The decentralized nature of the industry, however, meant that many different types of peep machines existed concurrently and that local regulations would restrict content inconsistently. The evolution of the peeps was not entirely linear, then, and the few user reviews of peep arcades in print oscillate between praise for novel material that had slipped past censors and frustration with the endless repetition of the same ("what isn't bland is very ancient…arcades are showing the same old junk from 1964").[7]

A cinema of distraction

The roots of the motion-picture peeping machine, of course, extend far beyond the 1960s. This larger history is particularly significant to an understanding of the peep show's modus operandi. The arcade booths of the mid-twentieth century share much in common with Tom Gunning's descriptions of the nineteenth-century cinema of attractions are as follows: the spectator here "does not get lost in a fictional world and its drama, but remains aware of the act of looking, the excitement of curiosity, and its fulfillment" (121). In the peep loops the filmed body is highly aware that it is being watched. It addresses the camera directly, enacting an intimate corporeal performance for an individual viewer. The association I draw between pornography and the cinema of attractions is not a new one, yet the interface of the coin-op film machine manifests this legacy in a highly specific manner. The body of the viewer, too, is explicitly acknowledged by the apparatus of the booth, machines in public foyers that seduce passersby with the promise of the curious and the new. The public display of the viewer's own body would almost surely generate sensations of self-consciousness that would discourage complete spectatorial absorption. And, much like early cinematic shorts, the pornographic peep show loops provide a "succession of thrills … potentially limited only by viewer exhaustion" (Gunning 122).

As is the case with most visual technologies, motion-picture peep machines such as Mutoscopes and Kinetoscopes drew upon scandalous subject matter almost from their inception. Earlier technologies such as the stereoscope had successfully married the shape of the device to the presentation of prurient content. Like these devices, peep machines moved beyond the mere content of photographic representation to incorporate into the design of the apparatus an active and physical engagement with the viewer. The act of peeping necessitates a degree of visual disengagement with one's immediate surroundings, assuming a pose that allows for an ocular encounter with a space (either real or representational) accessible through some threshold. This disengagement is hardly passive or involuntary, as the peeper actively peeps in the hopes of experiencing sensation and pleasure, whether or not the material viewed is prurient or not. The space viewed and the actions of bodies potentially performing within that space may ostensibly trigger a corporeal response in the viewer. Yet the eye must work, navigating and exploring the viewed scene to extract perceptions that the brain and nervous system answer to and amplify. Peeping apparatuses are designed to heighten such exchanges, utilizing perspective, depth of field, and framing in addition to content to provide the viewer with a sensational, sensuous encounter.

The link between the evolutions of visual technology and the eroticized gaze is well documented (see, e.g., Crary; Williams, *Hard Core*). I would like to stress this point, however, in relation to the specificity of peep show technology. Devices such as the stereoscope and the Mutoscope create a pleasurable illusion that is enacted within the body of the viewer (the synthesis of two photographic images into a perceived three-dimensional space, the animation of a series of still photographs into the perception of continuous motion). Such processes, of course, are at the heart of the cinematic apparatus in general, yet the early peep machines tended to draw attention to the machinations of the illusion rather than masking the means of production in an immersive cinematic space (Crary 127–36). In the peep show the act of peeping takes place simultaneously inside and outside the body, inviting a corporeal collision between spectator and text.

The diegetic spaces of peep show loops do vary considerably, particularly as quasi-narrative hard-core loops began to appear in the 1970s. The earlier striptease films, however, make use of an extreme economy of means to construct a space of sexual encounter. Certain more sophisticated loops utilized first-person perspective to encourage the viewer to identify with the cameraperson (it is perhaps fair to presume a male camera operator in most instances). Here the performer engages with the camera/cameraperson directly through eye contact, gesture, and posture. The settings are domestic, frequently limited to a single room, with a limited number of props. On-screen performers are typically positioned on couches or beds, flirtatiously removing their clothing in a performative display that resists readings of sadistic voyeurism. The camerawork is intimate and close, roaming up and down the performer's body, paying copious attention to textures and fabrics, lingerie, skin, eyelashes, lips, breasts, and, in the more explicit loops, genitalia. Ideally, these tactile images coincide with the viewer's own affective bodily experiences. This modality verges on what Laura Marks refers to as a haptic vision, where the distance between viewer and object is collapsed and the eye is "more inclined to move than to focus, more inclined to graze than to gaze" (162). Porn loops, unlike the intercultural experimental videos that Marks links with haptic vision, resist falling into pure abstraction and are clearly marked by commodification and objectification; this is indeed their fundamental modus operandi. Yet I would argue that the intense focus on surface and texture in certain loops, while by no means removed from a sexual economy that fetishizes the female body, shifts the dynamic from one of optical mastery toward an intersubjective, visceral exchange. Peep show loops are deeply compromised, but the bodily response that the films evoke might, for some viewers, be described as a "concomitant loss of self, in the presence of the other" (Marks 192–93).

Yet this encounter is not experienced unproblematically, and while the peep machine invites a certain interpenetration of space, it is not fully successful in delivering it. Vivian Sobchack has argued that every cinematic encounter is marked by a limit, an "echo focus" whereby viewers recognize the technological mediation of their experience (e.g., the limits of the frame or of perspective), thus preventing complete spectatorial absorption (*Address* 177–86). Awareness of such limits tends to remain relatively unobtrusive during most film events, as the "unnatural" effects of the camera and the projector are experienced by viewers as "a primarily transparent extension of an embodied perceptive act" (186). The limits of the peep machine are so great, however, that they at times overshadow or intrude upon the world of the screen. The peep show patron may try, perhaps desperately, to achieve an immersive, embodied experience through the apparatus. Yet absorption is thwarted at every turn by the quality of the image, by the distractions of the lights, sounds, and smells of the arcade, and by the constant movements of other bodies outside the booth. Inevitably, the experience will be cut short by the machine itself, violently severing the visual flow to demand the insertion of another quarter.

These intrusions are multifold and somewhat distinct from disruptive effects in other cinematic formats. Some of these disruptions are intentional and are built into the structure of the machine. Primary among these, of course, is the coin-operated interface that is the raison d'être of the peep machine. Even in avant-garde or structuralist films that aim to demystify the transparency of the apparatus, the actual flow of the projector is rarely interfered with unless there is accidental equipment failure. The coin-op interface does precisely this, yet the goal is hardly one of Brechtian detachment. The objective, rather, is a temporary jolt that will elicit the desire to pay more to reenter the space of the film.

And within the films themselves one encounters further disruptions. Low budgets and shoddy cinematography result in numerous unintentional intrusions whereby the means of production are made painfully obvious. In the case of striptease films with a solo performer, the viewer experiences a self-reflexive cinematic mode that aspires to relative transparency (such that one might experience, through the mediation of the camera, the film body as viscerally present). Yet the limits of the frame and of the medium remain absolute. As Jean-Pierre Oudart might argue, the cameraperson in the peep show loop functions as a disconcerting, unidentifiable controlling presence, an "absent one" who, in this instance, is not repressed via the introduction of a character to whom we can attribute the gaze. Just as the coin-op mechanism of the booth simultaneously promises and thwarts spectatorial control, the structure of space within the film is ambiguous and unresolved. The viewer is confronted by the insurmountable gulf between his (again I presume most peep users are male) body and the world of the film, particularly within the charged social atmosphere of the peep arcade.

In considering the phenomenology of the arcade, we should not assume that all viewers wished to fully disengage from the space of the present, particularly those who were cruising for more fully embodied sexual encounters. Nor should we assume that the tension between filmed and real worlds within the booth was experienced as pure frustration; given the continued popularity of the arcades, it seems more likely that this tension may evoke certain pleasures of its own. The body of the viewer hovers in a suspended existence between the body of the film and the space of the arcade, hyperfocused (at least in the case of certain viewers) on the tactility of the flesh on the screen as well as on the sensations of his own flesh. He is also conscious of the synaesthetic realm around him and the constant possibility of intrusion (either welcome or unwelcome) of this space of the booth by other patrons, by management or vice cops, or by the machine itself. The peeps, indeed, seem to revel in a contradictory, in-between space that on every register is governed more by disruption, surveillance, chance, and displacement (what we might call a masochistic mode) than by visual erotic mastery. If peep shows aim to be voyeuristic, they typically fail in achieving that state, offering the aspiration of ocular embodiment with only the partial fulfillment of that promise.

Peep spectatorship and the legislation of privacy

Peep show arcades are thus porous sites where the delineation between viewer and text is subverted and the site of performance is extended into the space of consumption. The peep show is in fact one of the few areas within cinema culture where the activities of spectators receive greater attention than the content of the films. A number of sociological studies on adult bookstores were conducted in the early 1970s that provide detailed descriptions of spectator practices within the arcade. These reports, however, tend to stress the lack of social contact between patrons and attempts by patrons to manage self-presentation by "privatizing" the body. The anxiety about contact appears to stem, according to these studies, from a fear of being identified as well as a fear of being implicated in unsanctioned sexual activity. Visible public masturbation would be one such activity, the studies suggest, as well as anxiety about being identified as gay or of being propositioned for a sexual encounter. The studies are less explicit about other potential anxieties: of being *caught* participating in sexual encounters with other men or even of experiencing arousal when viewing male bodies.

That these anxieties exist says something about the range of activities and media that were readily available in adult stores.[8] Every study, without exception, noted that both male–female and all-male pornography was offered for consumption along with a range of more specialized fetish subgenres. The adult bookshop offered a virtual supermarket of preferences and perversities. The gradual privatization of peep booths increased opportunities for the consumption of loops to coincide with live sexual experiences. Peep arcades were obvious locales for cruising, and enclosed booths contained "glory holes" for exchanges between patrons. What booth one stood in front of was an indication of what one was into, and the process of selection appears to have been made with the explicit understanding that one's performance was being observed and that, in effect, one's body was on display as one of the many options another might desire.

Several sociologists from the era register this zone of indeterminacy as a threat that many patrons warded off with defensive measures, closing off the self so as to discourage contact. When observing open peep machines, they described viewers' bodies as striving to appear as motionless and disengaged from the present surroundings as possible. One report by Sundholm describes a setting of near paranoiac avoidance, where customers strive for anonymity at all costs. Such readings, as José Capino has pointed out, problematically paint the adult bookstore as a zone of anonymity with no recognition that anonymity might be a guise by which patrons seeking encounters evade detection by those who might prosecute or judge them. Other studies approached the homosociality of the arcades with more subtlety (see Karp; Kornblum), and more recent work on peep arcades has analyzed the "dramaturgy" of exchanges that take place in the arcade with recognition of the complex motivations various types of patrons might have in "privatizing" their behavior (particularly those turning, or soliciting, tricks) (McNamara 57–66).

Peep arcades, with their wide selection of sexual offerings, are polymorphic sites that viewers can, potentially, appropriate for their own unsanctioned performances, including masturbation as well as activities performed with other arcadegoers. In both cases the patron subverts the role of passive spectator to partake in sexual acts that are deemed doubly perverse in their nonprocreative nature and in their public staging. I would argue that peep show regulations aim not to legislate content but to restrict or even eradicate spaces for public sex. This is an objective that can be mapped throughout wider legislation regarding pornography. While the motivation for this push toward privacy is not explicitly stated, I would suggest that it is rooted in homophobia in particular and in a more general anxiety regarding nonnormative sexual practices. If the peep show can be seen as a potential locus of intersubjective exchange, arcade regulations seem keen on inhibiting that potential.

And it is the social space provided by the peep show arcade that has generated the most animosity toward the format, far more than the content of any particular film that was shown there. Even though law enforcement officials would seize select film reels during raids, it seems clear that the motivation for such raids had little to do with objections to individual titles and more to do with impeding the operations of the arcades in general. As adult theaters, bookstores, and arcades proliferated in the 1960s and 1970s, outlets were subject to numerous criminal investigations, most often hinging on the possession and sale of obscene materials. One can read within the voluminous obscenity cases from this time period a complex dynamic. Sexually explicit material was increasingly granted protection under the First Amendment, while thresholds of social permissiveness were simultaneously expanding. Perhaps in response to this shift, anxiety regarding the consumption of pornography in public spaces led to a legislative push toward the privatization of sexuality. Shifts in allowable content, then, seem to be closely related to the movement of pornography out of the public sphere.

Of particular import here is the 1969 case of *Stanley v. Georgia*. The case stemmed from an investigation on illegal gambling during which the police obtained a warrant to search Robert Stanley's home for records of bookmaking activities. Officers discovered a film collection during the search; they deemed the works to be pornographic and arrested Stanley for the possession of obscene materials. The Supreme Court ruled in favor of Stanley, yet in doing so it did not appeal to the most obvious avenue— protections against illegal search and seizure (Tuchman 2273–74). Instead, the majority decision focused on the issue of freedom of *thought* and the rights of the individual against the interference of the state in the circulation of knowledge, ideas, or beliefs "regardless of their social worth." This right was inseparable, the court found, from "the right to be free, except in very limited circumstances, from unwanted governmental intrusions into one's privacy" (*Stanley v. Georgia*).

Despite the rather progressive implications this decision might have had for future obscenity cases, later decisions interpreted *Stanley* in an extremely narrow manner. The privacy protections offered by this precedent were consistently limited to the physical space of the home. In other words, one was free to utilize obscene materials within the home, but interactions with the identical products elsewhere were subject to prosecution.[9]

Pornography's greatest threat to the social order, these interpretations would imply, rests not in its representations but in its public presence. Shifting definitions of privacy resulted in a number of contradictory rulings on the status of peep shows, in each instance, however, with the goal of restricting any sexual activity that might occur there (see, e.g., *Department of Housing v. Ellwest*; *Sanza v. Maryland*). For example, at least one peep show operator argued, unsuccessfully, that the *Stanley* decision should protect the viewing of explicit materials in arcades, as the booths provided for private consumption. The court ruled that arcades were by definition public, commercial spaces fundamentally distinct from the "castle" of one's home (*Star v. Preller*). Despite the contradictory definitions of public and private cited in similar cases, the focus in each instance is a prohibition against the peep arcade as a communal sexual space. Peep show regulations, which typically concern lighting, the width of aisles, occupancy per square foot, and mechanisms of supervision, confirm that the policing of public sex is a primary concern (see *Antonello v. San Diego*; National Obscenity Law Center).

Popular histories of pornography or of adult districts such as 42nd Street tend to describe the decline of the peep booth as the inevitable result of technological advancement, and it is true that videotapes and DVDs have made it easy to build an immense home library of high-budget pornography. At the same time, the state-sanctioned move toward privatization was clearly guided by other factors as well; at the very least, obscenity cases in the wake of *Stanley* provided a significant incentive for the adult industry to shift to a home-based model of porn consumption. The performance of the body in the peep arcade takes place in a highly politicized context. It is thus critical to read the legal marginalization of "vice centers" with deep suspicion. If we are to speak of the peep arcade as a space of disruption and distraction, the intrusions of the state into the culture of public sex are potent forces to take into account.

Skin deep: Solo girls and split beavers

In the case *Kaplan v. United States* (1971) the District of Columbia Court of Appeals included, for consideration, an appendix detailing the content of a peep show reel that had been deemed "sexually morbid, grossly perverse, and bizarre, without any artistic or scientific purpose or justification":

This film depicts a young female stripping absolutely naked, then brazenly and shamelessly displaying her breasts as well as her genitalia ... The sceneric [*sic*] background is meager and is designed in such a fashion as not to distract nor to interfere with the viewer's concentrated attention focused upon the camera's long shots, close-up shots and very-close-up shots of the female participant's genitalia and astronomically large breasts. The female filmed simulates passion; and by her body movements, gyrations and undulations coupled with a banana, used as a phallic symbol and being larger than normally displayed for sale in the neighborhood food markets, suggests to the viewer that she is ... most willing to engage in sex play culminating with sexual intercourse. The apparent highlight of this film footage is a close-in view of the female performer's vaginal area and with the aid of a banana used as a replica of the male sex organ in an erect state, she suggests to the viewer rather graphically the act of sexual intercourse. The film concludes with the woman peeling and devouring the banana—the gist of which is intended to be illustrative of the performer's desire to participate in osculatory relations with the private parts of a male (*Kaplan v. United States*).

I find several aspects of this description striking (beyond the rousing descriptions of breasts and banana). As this account suggests, readings of peep loops often refer to the camera's "close-in" attention to the anatomy and gyrating movements of performers; sensationalism and novelty, then, manifested in edits and camerawork, are markers of obscenity. Other respondents, however, are just as likely to stress generic monotony and single-mindedness as evidence of indisputable prurience. The *People v. Culbertson* decision, for example, found that "the sheer volume and duration of the exhibits ... has dulled our ability to relate the identity of any particular performer. The atmosphere and the flavor of the performances in each case however are unmistakably the same." While I do not share in the aesthetic or political conclusions of these courts, I do find a certain tension between variation and monotony to be core to the peep show aesthetic. The apparatus, adorned in many cases with marquee cards and provocative titles, promises stimulation and the shock of the new, while the products themselves may fail to deliver. It is also true that repetitive viewing of large numbers of peeps can result in a desensitized ennui. And the structure of the peeps emphasizes repetition and postponement over a teleological climax; much like a phone sex operator, the most financially successful loops are those that tease their patrons into lingering just a little longer.

Even more so than the feature-length porn flick or the stag, peep loops are nonlinear by design, in particular, the soft-core loops from the 1960s. Richard Dyer has argued that arcade loops contain a strong narrative component and that even when one encounters a loop midway through, it is easy to discern where one is within the narrative (a product of the simplicity and codification of the genre); moreover, viewers are anxious to temporally reposition the film's (and, ostensibly, their own) climax as an endpoint (27–29). I would agree that most peep show films do have a clear structure and that in the case of later hard-core peeps both heterosexual and gay loops have a narrative trajectory that typically concludes with a visible ejaculation. Yet many of the earliest hard-core loops were extremely low budget affairs, shot with a palpable lack of directorial control. As a result, in numerous loops the roll of film runs out before male performers climax, or they climax midway through, such that the rest of the reel is comprised of oral sex, female masturbation, digital manipulation, or other activities less geared toward a visual telos. In loops with solo performers, both male and female, there are even fewer shreds of narrative structure. Even in the case of male performers who do masturbate to a visual cum shot, these climaxes often occur several times throughout the reel, displacing the centrality of the orgasm as a finale and coupling it with the tactile display of the male body as an object of desire.

And tactility, I would argue, is one of the most essential aesthetic qualities of peep show films. Exemplary in this regard is a series of 16 mm silent loops, Starlight Films, that were exclusively produced and distributed for peep machines.[10] The earliest film I have encountered in the series was from 1956 and the latest from 1972, although I am uncertain if the company produced films beyond these dates. Most are printed on Anscochrome film and have retained a stunningly saturated color. The films are flipped from left to right, indicating that they were shown in Panoram-style rear-projection booths.[11] Each loop is silent and approximately ten to twelve minutes in total length, interspersed with notched slug frames that would stop the projector, displaying the image of a nude Venuslike statue. These reels typically feature either individual women stripping and posing for the camera or two women engaging in soft-core lesbian groping sessions.[12] The loops all seem to take place in intimate, colorfully decorated interiors. The examples that I've seen seem to feature predominantly white actresses, with a smaller number of black, Asian, and Latina performers, although their ages, sizes, and appearances do vary significantly.

I would argue, following Thomas Waugh's analysis of classic American stag films, that peep show films are remarkable in their relentless failure to make visible "the unknowable 'truth' of sex" (128). Waugh points to the homosociality of the stag film experience, demonstrated both in the exhibition space and as represented on-screen. The peep arcade can be read as a homosocial space, and certain peep show films, particularly later hard-core loops, exhibit on-screen homosocial interactions identical to those that Waugh describes. Yet the female striptease films that dominated the peep machines prior to the 1970s operate via an entirely different modality, one that includes more than a few flashes of the female subjectivity that, according to Waugh, rarely surfaces within the stags (129). Given the very limited presence of women within the space of the film arcade, this subjectivity manifests itself primarily within the on-screen performances,

performances that seem to resist anonymous objectification through a direct visual engagement with the camera—and, by extension, the camera operator and viewer.[13]

Some of the loops did contain a loose narrative. In Starlight 138 a young woman is enjoying a cigarette, a scotch, and *Photoplay* magazine when her roommate arrives home, visibly drunk. The roommate collapses on the couch while recounting her evening but dissolves into giggles when she discovers her panties are in her pocketbook. Her friend helps her get ready for bed, and, inevitably, one thing leads to another. There are several moments of dissonance that prevent this performance from slipping entirely into the realm of cliché. Most notably, the drunken roommate is either a phenomenal actress or is really quite drunk, for by the time the couple make it to the bedroom, she has passed out, and much of the interaction involves rolling her limp body around on the bedspread. Her friend's legs part at one point to reveal a dangling tampon string. The loop closes as well with a genuinely affectionate exchange that transcends typical pornographic pseudolesbianism.

Stormy is perhaps more typical in its nonnarrative structure, yet it is also interspersed with disruptive elements. We see a woman slip out of her dress in a living room upholstered in gray tweed. She begins to play with a red hula-hoop—rather badly—and after a few minutes takes off her panties, leaving on her Lucite heels. She lolls about, flirting with the camera, although after about eight minutes is running short of material. She throws several questioning looks at the camera before biting the hoop (which in fact looks much goofier in motion than it does in stills). She begins to jump through the hoop as if it were a jump rope until she hits herself in the head and starts laughing. As the camera follows her we see a kidney-shaped coffee table and a record player behind her along with a collection of record albums, indicating that the space is not an anonymous motel room.

In many of the Starlights I find myself drawn to similar minutiae (a tiny bruise on an actress's hip, a broken fingernail) and in particular to the décor—the textures of the drapery and upholstery and walls. For this viewer, the mise-en-scène is anything but "meager," as the *Kaplan* ruling suggested. Much has been said about the sleazy, bare settings for porn loops—I find this not to be the case here, as there are numerous artifacts (loaded bookshelves, toiletries, textiles, and knickknacks) that make these seem like lived-in spaces. But there is also a decided lack of "naturalness," in the sense that we are clearly watching someone perform (rather than watching a document of an unmediated act), and there is no corporeal, climactic "real" event (as there would be, ostensibly, in a hard-core or all-male reel) that might absorb our or the performers' full attention (see Hillyer 54–56). For me, as the movements of the performers begin to blur into banal repetition, it is in fact within the décor that I locate certain moments of intimacy or even of intrusion: Where are we? Whose room is this? The interior private space of the room has been laid bare and in many ways feels more legible than the exposed interiors of the bodies on display.

The question of agency and exploitation is an obvious one here, vexed by the lack of reliable information regarding the production of these films. There is no doubt the female body is offered up as an object for male consumption, a focus that is apparent in the staging, cinematography, and direction. Yet the inadequacy of that direction breaks down during the course of the loops, and the actress is left, it seems in many instances, to perform what she *imagines* to be an idealized display. Her own gaze directly engages with both the camera and the off-screen cameraperson, enacting a complex and seemingly self-conscious interchange of intimacy, control, and vulnerability.

The most direct point of reference I can make here is to Andy Warhol's *Screen Tests*, films in which subjects were asked to sit still in front of a camera for the duration of a three-minute roll of film, their gaze confronting the viewer, who slowly observes the performance as it disintegrates before the unblinking camera. Peeps, at least of the direct-address Starlight variety, seem to enact a similar encounter. They exist at arm's length and invoke a self-conscious exchange that registers in both the viewer's body and that of the performer as she actively struggles to sustain her performance in the absence of a guiding directorial force.

It is important to acknowledge that my perspective on peep loop aesthetics is limited by the fact that I am not the target audience for the format. It is quite likely that the typical peep show patron would not pay such detailed attention to décor or textile patterns. As John Champagne has argued, some peep show customers might not watch the films at all. Nor are these loops typical of the manner in which peep loops subsequently evolved, with later examples more closely echoing the stagings of hard-core production numbers. Yet I find these early loops to be haunting and indicative of the peep show's inclination to create fetish objects. References to Panoram-style peep machines repeatedly made two comparisons: they looked like either refrigerators or coffins. This analogy is illuminating, I believe, and speaks to the modality of the peep loop. Within it there is a marked attempt to capture and reanimate a corporeal experience, an uncapturable moment; the results are at once poignant and perverse.

Conclusion

The peep arcade presents a highly anomalous media terrain. On each of the registers I have touched on (the legal, the textual, the space of the exhibition) I have been struck by a series of reversals and inversions stemming from the indeterminacy of space as well as of time. The past (filmic and technological) is reanimated, while the body remains rooted in the present. Interior spaces, both corporeal and domestic, are opened to view, while the exterior realm of the public foyer is enveloped within the enclosed space of the booth. Just as the filmed bodies exist in a suspended yet politically charged space between exposure and intimacy, the bodies in the arcade enact a self-conscious performance that is at once personal and socially contingent. Moreover, the structural and accidental glitches within the machinery threaten to disrupt the illusory act of peeping at the same time that they add to the pleasure of the schizophrenic experience.

My readings of 1960s peep loops are perhaps colored by the nostalgia that invariably accompanies antiquated technologies—an experience that might not be applicable to contemporaneous audiences. At the same time I would argue that there is something profoundly strange about the spaces in which early coin-op film machines were positioned and utilized. The peep machine makes visceral the incommensurate contradictions between here and there, then and now, seeing and knowing, perceiving and acting, exposing, to return to Tom Gunning, "the hollow centre of the cinematic illusion" (129). The impact of the peep machine is often one of disruption and failure, yet that failure is actively registered within the body of the viewer. Moreover, the viewer's body, in turn, engages a multisensorial, multispatial cohabitation that extends beyond an involuntary response and that is irreducible to a mere voyeuristic fascination with the image. The peep show's illusion may be hollow, yet its experience is deeply embodied, with far-reaching social and political implications, presenting cinema scholars with a provocative, if elusive, field of inquiry.

Acknowledgment

I am greatly indebted to those who generously assisted with this research, in particular Albert Steg, B. J. Woodman at the Kinsey Institute for Research in Sex, Gender, and Reproduction, and Elizabeth Mariko Murray at the Museum of Sex.

Notes

1   Richard Dyer provides a welcome reading of several all-male loops in "Male Gay Porn."
2   Despite the lack of archival data, evidence of pre-1960s peep machines is ample. See note 4 for information on 1950s obscenity cases related to peep machines. Vintage loops and machines are frequently posted on eBay.com. It is difficult to verify whether the distribution of films for peep machines overlapped with that of stag loops during this era, although the early peep loops I have encountered tend to be less explicit than stags. This is clearly an area that demands further research.

3   This story is recounted in Anthony Bianco's *Ghosts of 42nd Street* (160–62), and Hodas confirmed the narrative in a telephone conversation (March 4, 2007). Bianco calls the machines "Panasonics," and Hodas referred to them as "Panoramics," yet their physical descriptions of the devices matches precisely that of the Soundies Panoram. The widespread conversion of Panoram jukeboxes into peep show machines is evidenced by the number of existent machines that have peep viewers installed (some with peep loops still loaded on the projector) and was confirmed by conversations with several Soundies Panoram experts. Many thanks to Hodas and Larry Fisher for their assistance with this research.

4   A 1952 *Washington Post* article reports on the conviction of a peep show arcade employee on charges of possessing indecent films with the intent to exhibit them. This was part of a raid on fourteen arcades in the Washington, DC, area ("'Peep Show' Change Man"). In 1954 a Seattle arcade operator was arrested for showing "obscene" films in fifteen "Pan-o-ram" machines (*State v. Silverman*).

5   Thevis is a fascinating figure who began in the newsstand business and was the producer behind *Pendulum* magazine. He was convicted of arson (the warehouse of Nat Bailen's movie machine company mysteriously burned down) and for both direct and indirect involvement in the murder of several business associates. See the U.S. Attorney General's Commission on Pornography (1986), pt. 4, chap. 4.

6   The Nawy study is, in fact, cited in the 1970 report of the U.S. Commission on Obscenity and Pornography and may provide, in part, the basis for the report's assessment of arcade films.

7   See the review from *Artisex*. Markers of this uneven evolution persist today. References to Panorams exist in contemporary peep regulations, and at least one peep show film arcade exists on Granville Street in Vancouver (see Otis). An overview of key court cases and current peep show regulations (both for video and live performance booths) can be found in the report "Construction of Open Booth Ordinances" issued by the National Obscenity Law Center, affiliated with the antipornography group Morality in the Media.

8   The studies I have encountered from this era focused exclusively on stores that offered both male–female and all-male materials. I have not located any published accounts of all-male arcades from the 1960s or 1970s, although it seems plausible that such arcades would have evolved concurrently with all-male bookstores and theaters. See Capino, who includes a discussion of 1970s all-male theaters with arcades of booths as well as a cogent reading of these same sociological studies. See Champagne on contemporary video arcades.

9   For example, the courts in *U.S. v. 12 200-foot Reels of Super8 Film* (1973) found that travelers transporting materials to be used privately were still guilty of trafficking in obscenity, as the materials were found outside the home.

10   I am much indebted to Albert Steg for sharing his impeccably documented collection of Starlight films with me and to Mike Vraney of Something Weird Video. According to Vraney, the company was based in Seattle (as is further evidenced by the distribution slips that accompanied many of the reels).

11   This was confirmed by Mike Vraney and Lisa Petrucci of Something Weird Video.

12 I have not encountered any hard-core activity in the Starlights, although later films in the series did include male participants, some with visible erections, and in certain cases appear to depict nonsimulated intercourse (although, in the works I have viewed, without any shots of actual penetration).

13 The presence of women within the arcades was greatly limited during this era (and, indeed, still is today); rare references to female patrons, who were explicitly barred from many peep venues in the 1960s, are limited to descriptions of curious interlopers accompanied by male companions or prostitutes utilizing booths for transactions (see, e.g., Kornblum; Nawy). I have yet to locate any references to female producers of peep films or of arcade loops produced for female audiences.

Works Cited

Antonello v. San Diego. 16 Cal. App. 3d 161. Civ. No. 10200. Court of Appeal of California, Fourth Appellate District, Division One. Mar. 19, 1971.

Artisex 2.9 (Sept. 1969). Mimeographed newsletter reviewing adult films. Vertical Files, Erotica Dealers, U.S., 20th Century, Kinsey Institute.

Berlant, Lauren, and Michael Warner. "Sex in Public." *Critical Inquiry* 24.2 (1998): 547–66.

Bianco, Anthony. *Ghosts of 42nd Street: A History of America's Most Infamous Block.* New York: William Morrow, 2004.

Cante, Rich, and Angelo Restivo. "The Cultural-Aesthetic Specificities of All-Male Moving-Image Pornography." Williams, *Porn Studies* 142–66.

Capino, José B. "Homologies of Space: Text and Spectatorship in All- Male Adult Theaters." *Cinema Journal* 45.1 (2005): 50–65.

Champagne, John. "'Stop Reading Films!': Film Studies, Close Analysis, and Gay Pornography." *Cinema Journal* 36.4 (1997): 76–97.

Chauncey, George, Jr. "The Policed: Gay Men's Strategies of Everyday Resistance." *Inventing Times Square: Commerce and Culture at the Crossroads of the World.* Ed. William R. Taylor. Baltimore, MD: Johns Hopkins UP, 1991. 315–28.

Crary, Jonathan. *Techniques of the Observer: On Vision and Modernity in the Nineteenth Century.* Cambridge, MA: MIT P, 1990.

Department of Housing and Community Development v. Ellwest Stereo Theaters. 263 Md. 678. No. 105. Court of Appeals of Maryland. Dec. 13, 1971.

Dyer, Richard. "Male Gay Porn: Coming to Terms." *Jump Cut* 30 (March 1985): 27–29.

Gunning, Tom. "An Aesthetic of Astonishment: Early Film and the (In)Credulous Spectator." *Viewing Positions: Ways of Seeing Film.* Ed. Linda Williams. New Brunswick, NJ: Rutgers UP, 1997. 114–33.

Hillyer, Minette. "Sex Is the Suburban: Porn, Home Movies, and the Live Action Performance of Love in *Pam and Tommy Lee: Hardcore and Uncensored.*" In Williams, *Porn Studies* 50–76.

Kaplan v. United States. 277 A.2d 477. No. 5452. District of Columbia Court of Appeals. May 10, 1971.

Karp, David A. "Hiding in Pornographic Bookstores: A Reconsideration of the Nature of Urban Anonymity." *Urban Life and Culture* 1 (Jan. 1973): 427–51.

Kornblum, William, project director. *West 42nd Street: "The Bright Light Zone."* New York: Graduate School and University Center of the City University of New York, 1978.

Marks, Laura U. *The Skin of the Film: Intercultural Cinema, Embodiment, and the Senses.* Durham, NC: Duke UP, 2000.

McNamara, Robert P. "Dramaturgy and the Social Organization of the Peep Shows." *Sex, Scams, and Street Life: The Sociology of New York City's Times Square.* Ed. Robert P. McNamara. Westport, CT: Praeger, 1995. 57–66.

McNeil, Legs, and Jennifer Osbourne, with Peter Pavia. *The Other Hollywood: The Uncensored History of the Porn Film Industry.* New York: Regan Books, 2005.

Nasaw, David. *Going Out: The Rise and Fall of Public Amusement.* Cambridge, MA: Harvard UP, 1999.

National Obscenity Law Center. "Construction of Open Booth Ordinances." Morality in the Media. Sept. 2007 http://www.moralityinmedia.org/nolc/caseStudies/openBooth.pdf.

Nawy, Harold. "In the Pursuit of Happiness?: Consumers of Erotica in San Francisco." In "Pornography: Attitudes, Use and Effects." Ed. W. Cody Wilson and Michael J. Goldstein. Special issue, *Journal of Social Issues* 29.3 (1973): 147–61.

Otis, Dmitrios. "The Last Peep Show." *Vancouver Courier* Aug. 31, 2005.

Oudart, Jean-Pierre. "Cinema and Suture." *Screen* 18.4 (1977–78): 35–47.

"'Peep Show' Change Man Found Guilty in Film Case." *Washington Post* Oct. 4, 1952: 15.

People v. Culbertson. 242 Cal. App. 2d Supp. 916. Crim. No. 9125. Appellate Department, Superior Court of California, San Diego. May 25, 1966.

Sanza v. Maryland State Board of Censors. 245 Md. 319. Nos. 35, 152. Court of Appeals of Maryland. Feb. 8, 1967.

Schlosser, Eric. *Reefer Madness: Sex, Drugs, and Cheap Labor in the American Black Market.* New York: Houghton Mifflin, 2004.

Sobchack, Vivian. *The Address of the Eye: A Phenomenology of Film Experience.* Princeton, NJ: Princeton UP, 1992.

Sobchack, Vivian. *Carnal Thoughts: Embodiment and Moving Image Culture.* Berkeley: U of California P, 2004.

Stanley v. Georgia. 394 U.S. 557. No. 293. Supreme Court of the United States. Apr. 7, 1969.

Star v. Preller. 352 F. Supp. 530. Civ. No. 72-27-Y. United States District Court for the District of Maryland. Oct. 3, 1972.

State v. Silverman. 48 Wn.2d 198. No. 33267. Supreme Court of Washington, Department One. Jan. 19, 1956.

Sundholm, Charles A. "The Pornographic Arcade: Ethnographic Notes on Moral Men in Immoral Places." *Urban Life and Culture* 2.1 (1973): 85–104.

Tuchman, Claudia. "Does Privacy Have Four Walls? Salvaging *Stanley v. Georgia.*" *Columbia Law Review* 94.7 (1994): 2267–2306.

U.S. v. 12 200-foot Reels of Super8 Film. 413 U.S. 123. No. 70–2. Supreme Court of the United States. June 21, 1973.

U.S. Attorney General's Commission on Pornography. *Attorney General's Commission on Pornography: Final Report.* Washington, DC: U.S. Government Printing Office, 1986. Full text available online (with commentary) at http://www.porn-report.com/contents.htm.

U.S. Commission on Obscenity and Pornography. *The Report of the Commission on Obscenity and Pornography*. Washington, DC: U.S. Government Printing Office, 1970.

Warner, Michael. *The Trouble with Normal: Sex, Politics, and the Ethics of Queer Life*. Cambridge, MA: Harvard UP, 1999.

Waugh, Thomas. "Homosociality in the Classical American Stag Film: Off-Screen, On-Screen." In Williams, *Porn Studies* 127–41.

Williams, Linda. *Hard Core: Power, Pleasure, and the Frenzy of the Visible*. Berkeley: U of California P, 1989.

Williams, Linda, ed. *Porn Studies*. Durham, NC: Duke UP, 2004.

Systems and Networks

CHAPTER THIRTY

The Other Small Screen: Moving Images at New York's World Fair, 1939

Haidee Wasson

Cinema is a technology of compression and amplification, a cultural and expressive form that is always to some degree a play on scale. Filmmakers and writers have long understood the power of the apparatus to speed up, slow down, and make big or small all manner of motion, events, and things: Bela Balazs on the poetry of the close up; Dziga Vertov's kinetic tapestries of urban life; Jean Epstein on microcinematography; Erwin Panofsky on cinema's capacity to transform the spaces of the stage and canvas. Well before mid-century a rich vocabulary existed for thinking about the density of the moving image and its cognate capacity to expand our ideas about the relative proportion of things in motion and the pictures we have of them. Using the trope of scale, we can see the ways in which cinema was not just a mode of artful expression but also a method of condensing, reorganizing and then expanding images and information, sound and text, experience and idea in repeatable, mechanical and standardized form. The screen is the rectangular site that hosts this drama, shaping the moving image irretrievably with its own dynamic of seemingly infinite possibility and geometrical containment. These particularities and provocations of the screen have their cognate forms in the theater's proscenium arch, the canvas's frame, and the photograph's paper edges.

While a vocabulary exists for discussing scale and image, there is comparatively less work that helps us think through the ways in which the screen itself—a highly standardized, primary and formative component of the moving picture—serves as both a generative site and a physical force for cinema's long play with the dynamics of scale. To be sure, in recent years there has been a groundswell of compelling work on what we might generally call screen studies, mostly focused on digital work that emphasizes a new kind of fluidity in image creation, dissemination, and display.[1] Work on IMAX and on new architectural screens directly or indirectly addresses the question of screen giganticism; a very slight body of work addresses the dynamics of the very small, handheld screen or the site-specific gallery-based screen.[2] Logically, the great bulk of this work focuses on the contemporary moment, partly in response to what often seems like a sudden multiplication of screens in jewelry, telephones, cameras, cars, bathrooms, museums, and so on. But, of course, the present has no special claim on spaces and surfaces designed to be animated whether by live performance, artisanal inscription, technological reproduction, or some mix of the three. In film studies, Anne Friedberg's book *The Virtual Window* and essays by Charles Acland, among others, elegantly yet forcefully remind us of this.[3] Yet, we still know far too little about what Erkki Huhtamo terms the "archaeology of the screen," the manifold and mundane, sometimes magical and frequently corporate path to the screen's current state of multi-function and ubiquity.[4] This is particularly true for the film screen, a crucial and highly visible iteration of screened phenomenon that is crucial for understanding the past and present dynamics of screens more generally.

Building on the pressing need to understand historical screens and thus cinema in an expanded way, this essay will focus on a small part of what we might call, adapting Huhtamo, "film screen archeology." Here I will explore a few of the basic conditions, consequences, and contexts of the small, portable film screen during the interwar period, focusing primarily on the 1939 World's Fair in New York City. By way of surveying screens at the fair, large and small, this essay provides a snapshot of a uniquely rich and underconsidered event in the history of cinema. The essay proceeds to focus on the *small* film screen as a productive way to think more specifically about the history of film technology, film exhibition, moving image display, and mobility. Looking at small film screens demonstrates the deep links of cinema's technological apparatus to cognate media technologies, helping to index expanded iterations of, as well as functions for, film. Such an examination also helps to map cinema's enduring place in sites and venues well beyond the movie theater.

The film screen at New York's "World of Tomorrow" was one element of a technological tapestry exulting the virtues of corporate innovation, efficiency and benevolence. While connecting the film screen to the structures of capitalism may seem familiar to critics of Hollywood's vertical integration during this period, it is important to note that the pairing of film and industry at the fair entails a fuller idea about American business, including not just film and entertainment but all manner of enterprise: cars, chemicals, cosmetics and beyond. At the fair, a sizable number of corporate (and state) bodies made ample use of cinema. Not only did this include making and showing films, but it included a surprisingly nimble and dynamic technological apparatus: screens of varied sizes and degrees of portability, projectors that were automatic and continuous, as well as numerous hybrid displays that used film technologies along with photography, recorded and live sounds, lights, cardboard cut-outs—even live animals—to create appealing displays and attractions. Alongside spectacular multi-screen installations and 3-D films, as well as conventional theatrical exhibition, a whole range of other ideas about film display and practices of exhibition are evident. These portable screens, untethered to the conventional, structurally enduring movie theater, present new dynamics of scale and motion, distinct visual textures, and diversified functions for celluloid, projector and screen, alerting us to a range of ascendant film practices that both preceded the fair and continued on well after it.

This essay will focus on what I assert are fundamental developments in film technologies, which are both symptom and cause for a paradigmatic expansion of film display, exhibition, and culture as we conventionally understand them. This consumer-driven and wondrous fair, the "World of Tomorrow," was a textured and diversified event with no shortage of creative applications for portable film projection technology. Such projectors and screens animated a range of things and spaces, from bottles of antacid to panoramic colorscapes. They served multiple functions, from supplying rolling didactic text to directing pedestrian traffic. This other film culture was predicated on ease-of-use, automation, and adaptability, on electrical display and push-button playback systems. It was, in part, a culture of gadgetry and consumerism, which fed a demand for small moving image machines both on the part of those who made and sold things and those seeking to buy them. In other words, we can see at the fair symptomatic evidence that film technologies fully participated in an everyday consumer ecology, one that shows the easy integration of film projectors and films into a culture of buying and selling, of individual ownership, self-operated display and mobile, electrical entertainment. At the level of merchandising, retailing, and managing public relations, film became a common-sense element of a business culture predicated on the need to master the new art of telling compelling stories—about itself and to itself—with moving images and sounds and to harness the emerging methods of placing products in motion-bound, malleable dream worlds of mechanically reproduced sound and light. At the level of the consumer, the rise of the small film screen, along with its portable projector, speaks to the increasing common sense of visual expectations: what does and should this new world look like? What is my role in shaping it, or at least, helping to project and perform it?

The use of film technologies in the ascendant consumer culture was but one element of a more general shift. Small projectors and screens formed part of a new infrastructure, laying the groundwork for a post-war proliferation of everyday screens and venues for film presentation. This includes but goes well beyond the advertising industry's embrace of moving images vis-à-vis television. The fair, I contend, can be understood as a predictive and telling inventory for a paradigmatic shift in film culture, inserting cinema into an important history of mobility and small-scale moving image display that served an increasingly integral everyday role throughout the interwar period and beyond.

Film at 20th-century World's Fairs

We know that early cinema has long and deep relationships to expositions and fairgrounds with a shared history in exploiting techniques of visibility in order to attract crowds and induce wonder.[5] There is a recent surge of interest in the experimental use of cinema at venues such as the 1958 and 1967 World Expositions in Brussels and Montreal respectively, where the artistic and utopian merged in complicated ways with the projects of state and industry.[6] The specific context for the use of film technologies at New York's fair is worth rehearsing, partly because the conditions undergirding this use are absent from most film historical paradigms. Well known is that theatrical film exhibition had stabilized since the shift to synchronized and amplified sound that began transforming theaters roughly a decade earlier. Yet, the use of small screens at the 1939 fair punctuates, in fact, a period wherein the use of portable and small-scale projection technologies had been slowly and steadily increasing alongside permanent, purpose-built theaters. The introduction of 16mm in 1923 and of 8mm in 1932 paved the way for a very different film economy, one based on self-operated, portable, and highly adaptable projectors that were designed to be used in a range of spaces beyond what we think of as theaters proper. Often linked to amateur filmmaking, these small machines also entailed the rise of a newly organized field of non-professional film presentation in homes and well beyond. Already during the 1930s, the rise of small-gauge projectors supported a range of practices. For instance, department stores, drug stores, camera shops, commercial film libraries and schools rented or lent small-gauge films to a growing network of do-it-yourself showmen and women. There was also a slow-growing but certain sea-change in public and private institutions that formed or grew during this decade incorporating cinema into a diversifying array of sites and functions. Museums, galleries, universities, schools, public libraries, film clubs, and film societies all began or accelerated efforts to incorporate and hence transform what was widely known as a mainstreet amusement.[7] Businesses large and small joined this shift leading to changes in organizational communication, marketing, and merchandising.[8] During the 1930s, New York advertising firms began forming film departments, securing the gradual influx of moving images, first on celluloid and eventually on television, into empires of persuasion.[9] Considering these circumstances, the use of film and its portable technologies at the fair was a predictable outgrowth of extant practices.

There were three World's Fairs held in the United States during the 1930s: the 1933 Chicago World's Fair "World of Progress," the 1939 San Francisco "Pageant of the Pacific," and the better known and much larger fair held in Queen's, New York City, "The World of Tomorrow," also in 1939. Films and film screens played a role at each of these fairs. A few words about the Chicago fair helps to set an instructive stage for screen use in New York, demonstrating both continuity and change. The Chicago fair boasted a wide range of moving picture applications, including the use of film to record and monitor the movement of crowds around particular exhibits, an example of early consumer observation research.[10] The largest single use of film at the fair was nonetheless advertising. The bulk of films shown at the fair promoted products including automobiles, pocket flashlights, alloy metals, radios, radio batteries, dentistry, travel, safety glass for cars, refrigerators, stoves, tires, newspapers, pianos, shoes, paint, tractors, canned food, bread, yeast, and steel. Motion pictures were even used to implore fairgoers to see motion pictures.[11] That is, Hollywood advertised at the fair in the best way it knew how. 8mm, 16mm and 35mm films ran through both sound and silent projectors. Yet, small or non-standard gauges, that is gauges not adopted by the dominant industry for movie theaters (which used 35mm film), featured prominently at the fair. Indeed, 16mm projectors outnumbered 35mm projectors eleven to one, with the 35mm industry standard gauge being used primarily in the five or so larger theaters operating at the fair.[12]

The advantages of the smaller gauge which made use of non-flammable acetate were numerous and included the comparable portability of the smaller machines (i.e. no need for fireproof booths or large auditoria), the lower cost of prints and machinery, decreased fire hazard, less expensive projection apparatus, and ease of operation. Some of these projectors required an ever-present operator, but many others did not, and indeed ran continuously without intervention. Ten projectors operated by direct audience intervention: push-button cinema. Of the one hundred or so portable projectors at the fair, only six serviced conventional theatrical set-ups.[13] On the whole, projector and screen placement varied considerably. Roughly a third were hidden behind a wall, a sixth concealed by purpose-built cabinets, and a sixth placed in the open for all to see. Just over half of the small projectors utilized rear-projection technology—what were often called daylight film screens—in order to save space and to allow projection in full light, natural or artificial. Some other projection environments used mirrors or featured projectors mounted above the ceiling or beneath floors in order to accommodate projection in very small spaces.[14] Screen size also varied dramatically. Twenty per cent of film screens at the fair were no more than twenty inches across, roughly half were smaller than forty inches. There were only two screens as big as five to eight feet across.[15] In other words, the small screen dominated the film scene at the fair.

The many non-fiction films that were screened at the Chicago fair served several different functions. Many told stories about particular manufacturers and how their goods were made; others instructed salesmen or showed products-in-use. Still others worked to attract passers-by to a particular exhibit, working like automated circus barkers. One survey indicated that roughly a third of the projectors at the fair played to seated audiences while two-thirds played to standing or moving ones. The few purpose-built theaters there were ranged in size with seating capacities as low as twenty-four and as high as 224.[16] Clearly the Chicago fair offers a quick portrait of a diversified film viewing environment. Viewers walked by a screen far more often than sat in front of one. The mystical beam of light that spans the screening space back to front was frequently resituated, to come from below, above or behind the screen. And, the idea of a big, main attraction here is clearly incidental to a cinema that was small, provisional, and sometimes supplemental to other attractions.

Cinema in the world of tomorrow

While the Chicago fair demonstrates the integration of film technologies into fairground exhibition techniques, with a full range of screen sizes and types in use, the New York fair that followed six years later indicates a clear increase in numbers, creativity, and overall significance of the small—as well as large—film screen throughout the fairground. This technological dynamic is best understood when considered as integral to the whole of the fair and the predictable complexities of its vast undertakings.

Warren Sussman shows that the 1939 World's Fair in New York boldly continued the convention of all modern fairs: to display the triumphs of state, science, and industry. But during this tumultuous period of American history, the 1939 fair also worked to reassure visitors that after almost a decade of economic hardship, government and industry were successfully building a new world based on the principles of abundance, efficiency, self-fulfillment, consumerism, and technological innovation. The fair's future was a place of unlimited possibility, heralding more prosperous times.[17] Its considerable size entailed that exhibits and concessions pursued this broad imperative in many different ways, each differently shaping common cultural refrains of the period in the optimistic language of good times in the good future. For instance, Robert Rydell reminds us that the fair also inflected its utopianism with normative ideals of the body and the family, many of which were undergirded specifically by eugenics and more generally by the racism that permeated the culture at large. The future woman was differently modern, at times appearing as a kind of commodified spectacle, enshrouded virtuously in a sanitized world of home appliances, convenience foods, and beauty products and at others offered up as a kind of sexually liberated (and sexually available) figure in the numerous nudie and peep shows that populated fair concessions.[18] The fair's cultural politic was predictably complex.

General trends can, however, be identified. One of the more prominent was the strategy of address employed by American corporations. Cultural historian Roland Marchand argues that while fairs had up until New York long served as sites for businesses to sell their wares, and announce new innovations, the 1939 fair marked a clear shift away from an emphasis on the selling of things toward forwarding a particular and carefully crafted corporate image.[19] This change is marked most monumentally by the signature buildings erected by specific corporations throughout the fairgrounds. General Motors, Ford Motor Company, Westinghouse, RCA, and AT&T each erected structures that incorporated the latest practices of industrial architecture—structures that resemble the corporate mandate. For instance, RCA's building employed glass walls which were structured to form the shape of a radio tube. The company forwarded an image of itself that was modern, streamlined, and that embodied the wonder of the gadgets and systems it sold. The rising emphasis on corporate image ran parallel to changes in the tactics of the advertising industry: an increased emphasis on entertainment and spectacle rather than straightforward functional didacticism. Exhibitors at the fair were less focused on manufacturing processes (how things are made) and more often illustrated the marvels of research (look at this cool thing we discovered). According to Marchand, this shift away from education and toward entertainment is a gradual one evident in the early parts of the twentieth century; it culminated in the two great fairs of 1939, San Francisco and New York. Here, according to Marchand, corporate sponsors fully embraced a very particular assumption about fairgoers: they preferred "attractions in tabloid doses."[20]

Corporations continued the drive toward presentational simplification and showmanship, treating fairgoers in a manner similar to the ways in which they addressed the mass audience for magazines, newspapers, and radio advertising—based on highly gendered ideas about a mass of consumers, whose desires (rather than minds) could be appealed to with cheeky robots, talking cars, automatic appliances, and food that was oddly fast. In short, magic and wonder rose to the fore of presentational and exhibition strategies. The use of films at the fair can be understood loosely to parallel this trend. Relatively new color film as well as synch-sound animation figured prominently in fair films, as did the then-novel use of 3-D. To illustrate this larger shift, take the case of film use by car manufacturers. At the 1915 San Francisco fair, Ford Motor Company reproduced a fully operational assembly line on-site, demonstrating to fairgoers how a car was built by his revolutionary process. In contrast to this, in 1939 Chrysler projected a ten-minute, 3-D stop-motion film which featured a car magically assembling itself, an exhibit that was by far the most popular film exhibit at the fair.[21] While the exhibitors at the fair did not need film to associate products and corporate mandates with desirable ideals (progress, efficiency, prosperity), many chose film and its technologies as a tactic in this evolving communications strategy. As a result, many of the buildings at the fair had multi-use or dedicated film theaters for film programs; many other exhibitors orchestrated elaborate multi-media displays in gallery spaces, hallways, and other interstitial spaces. An array of new and old moving image and sound technologies helped to constitute this complicated dreamscape, extolling the virtues of a technologically enhanced, wholly electrified, automated world of abundance where not just things but people—or at least reproductions of their appearance or their voices—could move quickly and efficiently and in some instances instantaneously across a hopeful nation. Corporate benevolence paved a kind of virtual highway of hope.

To be sure, film was part of a whole exhibition environment, one that didn't just feature moving images but all manner of moving things. One study of the fair's exhibition techniques indicates that 77 per cent of fair exhibits employed moving parts in their exhibits.[22] This compliments the basic fact that many aspects of the fair's design incorporated the ideals of movement. The grounds were filled with fountains, waterfalls, and reflective ponds, many of which were not only lit at night but often animated by highly choreographed light shows and amplified sounds. Buildings constructed of glass, exterior and interior moving platforms, ramps, and electrical staircases accentuated the perpetual, machine-movement of people, spaces, and things at the fair. A kind of expanded cinema helped to augment this man-made world of movement; particular exhibits demonstrate this well.

General Motors' popular Futurama Building featured a moving 1586-foot "chair train" that mobilized thousands of seated spectators daily, carrying them through the whole of the pavilion's elaborately designed dioramas, illustrating the highway saturated future of 1960. A GM press release declared: "In moving sound-chairs, visitors will tour vast miniature cross-sections of America as it may conceivably appear twenty years or so from now. The 600 chairs—each equipped with a sound device, serving as a private guide on an Aladdin-like tour—will be mounted on a continuous, moving 'carry-go-round', extending for a third of a mile in and about the building."[23] The ride lasted about fifteen minutes but was in a sense endless, as it was enclosed in a kind of criss-crossing, quasi-circular, and continuous loop. GM reported carrying 28,000 people per day into the near future. Sound for this ride emanated from speakers placed underneath the seats. A recorded lecture secured optically on a filmstrip played from a nearby control room. GM's "chair train" and "carry-go-round" combined the latest sound reproduction and amplification technologies, the very ones being used in many of the new portable film projectors that littered the fairgrounds.[24] While Futurama was not cinema proper, technologies of cinema shaped the ride experience at its core. It employed coordinated, panoramic images and spatialized sounds that transported viewers on a thrilling kind of travel ride. Futurama's iconography echoes that of travel films and the much older Hale's tours. It also presages that which would become commonplace in the 1950s with the roll-out of Cinerama and other widescreen technologies and techniques that stretched the horizontal plane of theater and spectator alike, forwarding immersion as one of cinema's primary attractions.

Equally important as a complement to the cinematic elements of ride exhibits such as Futurama was a well-known exhibit orchestrated by Eastman Kodak. Dubbed "a quasi motion picture technique,"[25] this cognate experiment in motion and color gained frequent mention in fair literature. Kodak's Cavalcade of Color, also called Kodak's "World of Color," used eleven screens, mounted side by side on a curved wall. Constantly changing Kodachrome slides emanated from an armada of synchronized, dissolving slide projectors, yielding an automated, moving panorama measuring 180-feet wide and 20-feet high.[26] A notched sound film ran the show automatically, dimming the lights, bringing them up, and coordinating everything in between, including the varied timing for each slide. The still images appeared on screen, changing at intervals of up to 20 seconds each. The elaborate slide show was synchronized with music and a voiceover and could make use of more than two thousand individual slides. At times the screens displayed individual objects and at others combined to display elaborate single panoramas. The presentation resembled that of a travel film: a script was delivered in an earnest, friendly baritone, supplemented with music at appropriate pauses. No seats were provided. Despite that, people came and stayed for the whole of the show, a fact which commentators considered a further tribute to the exhibit's healthy appeal.[27] Color film, a moving automated display, and a large screen format combined to create an unusual and extremely popular attraction at the fair.[28] Fred Waller, a key designer for Cinerama, worked on the Kodak exhibit, citing the experiment as crucial for his later work.[29]

The nature of exhibits at the fair bespeaks an exhibition environment that paralleled and echoed some of the most basic qualities of cinema, as it was known and as it was developing. Importantly, these exhibits also demonstrate continuity with a history of cinema's hybrid and expanded manifestations, what Gene Youngblood would many years later call "expanded cinema."[30] But, one need not consider these expanded forms of screen experiment in order to recognize a more conventional if miniaturized understanding of film—celluloid, projectors, and screens—firmly in place at the fair. But, first a word on television.

The 1939 World's Fair is best known among media scholars as the theater for television's unveiling. RCA and NBC inaugurated the country's first regular television service with live coverage of the fair's opening ceremonies, watched by viewers in the New York area on an estimated 200 television screens.[31] RCA, a subsidiary of General Electric, and

Westinghouse each demonstrated the technology at the fair in part by giving people the chance to appear and speak in front of a camera, a performance that simultaneously appeared on nearby, very small television screens that measured nine by eleven inches.[32] The technological augmentation and transformation of the human body echoed other exhibits nearby. AT&T invited visitors to make free long-distance calls, instantly connecting by voice to loved ones or strangers across the country. The communications behemoth also offered visitors the chance to make vinyl audio recordings of their own voices, which they could then take home.[33] Westinghouse implored visitors to talk, sing, or whistle into a microphone, which then translated the sounds into electro-magnetic waves, which appeared on a nearby screen. Television was but one among many modern media working to transform how the world looks and sounds, and how our bodies (eyes, ears, voices) operate within it.

Nevertheless, in retrospect, it is easy to see the prescience of television in particular—the phantom teleceiver, as it was called—signaling the post-war dominance of the electronic frontier that was soon to follow. Yet, television was still an unpredictable technology in 1939. There was limited content; the screens were very small and the image quality uneven but uniformly poor compared to the more familiar film images of the time. Indeed, in a telling and prescient technological sleight of hand, RCA set up a 16mm film projector and a small local transmitter on the fair-site that could feed television receivers throughout the grounds by cable with reliable, constant content for fear that its live theaters and transmitters based at Radio City Music Hall would fail to supply steady and clear signals.[34] The ten-minute film played on a loop and featured current events to increase the illusion of liveness; the film constituted roughly one-third of the images that appeared on television screens at the RCA exhibit. While television can be seen as a small but wondrous indicator of the near future, emergent small technologies of cinema prove—upon more careful inspection—to have played a more prominent role in a whole range of fair exhibits, including that of television itself, a technology conventionally understood as signaling cinema's demise. Indeed, New York's 1939 fair was dominated not by the electronic screen—which was a very small, blurry immobile screen—but by the portable film projector and screen which demonstrated remarkable resilience, adaptability and utility for the display of information and the transformation of built space. More conventional theaters were but a small element of this broader exhibitionary landscape.

While the San Francisco Fair of the same year did have several dedicated theaters and over one hundred 16mm projectors in use, the New York fair was simply bigger and more fully integrated with a range of moving image technologies and related practices.[35] The basic fact of film's prominence at the fair featured in fair publicity. A press release just over a month before the fair's opening day averred:

The wide-eyed movie fan might spend his entire time wandering from theater to theater at the New York World's Fair 1939 and see everything from a full-length Hollywood feature to a foreign travelogue short without once opening his purse. The Fair corporation itself, the United States government, a number of states, a score of foreign nations and uncounted commercial exhibitors will utilize the moving image and the silver screen to an unprecedented extent to tell the story of their significance and amuse their admirers.[36]

Grover Whalen, the fair's president and public figure-head, extolled publicly that at the fair "[a] new high mark in the use of motion pictures for educational purposes, for the betterment of living conditions, for the advancement of science, for the improvement of health, and for the distribution of the products of industry, will be reached."[37] Film, according to Whalen, worked in perfect harmony with the new mediated frontier that the fair itself sought to realize.[38] These overlapping goals manifested at multiple levels, from specific on-site event planning to generic, nationally circulated publicity. For instance, events at the fair were choreographed to facilitate filming by newsreel teams; film crews were accommodated with special parking passes, advance notice of events and parade routes, suggested staging areas and shooting angles, and on-site lighting.[39] Collins reports that "several thousand feet" of floor space was given over to newsreel crews in the Press building.[40] In addition to regular appearances in nationally distributed newsreels, fair administrators used film to promote the fair. According to Claude Collins head of the fair's film activities, the NY Fair was the first fair to do this.[41] The fair's official publicity film "Let's Go to the Fair" (World Fair Corporation, 1939, 16mm sound, color) circulated nationally. Early in 1940, there were sixty-two prints of the film in active circulation, facilitated by so-called "non-theatrical" powerhouses such as the YMCA (fifteen prints) and by regional distribution and projection services that supplied the film to clubs, schools, and civic groups. The tourism industry had an active interest in the fair and the National Trailways bus company showed the official fair film daily in its Chicago hub.[42] Two railroad companies showed the film regularly at rail station theaters. It was also a regular feature at Grand Central Station (New York City).[43]

In addition to making and distributing this widely seen film, the fair also maintained its own official movie theater, which played select titles continuously throughout the fair's operation hours. The schedule for the so-called "Little Theatre" appeared in the special fair supplement published by the *New York Times* daily. It was primarily at this theater that the fair established its reputation as an unprecedented, sustained, and concentrated display of the educational, industrial, and documentary film. News of the fair's non-fiction film offerings was available in publications like *Film News*, which celebrated the "largest assemblage of non-theatrical films ever shown in one place at one time."[44] Local papers published screening schedules and offered further comment.[45] The Little Theatre was located in the Science and Education Building and sat 253 audience members, running a slate of some forty-three films, among them the well-known film made for the fair, Ralph Steiner and Willard Van Dyke's 1939 *The City* (35mm sound; shown twice daily, four days a week), *The Plow that Broke the Plains* (Pare Lorentz, 35mm, 1936), and *The River* (Pare Lorentz, 35mm, 1938).

At one glance, it seems that all manner of small and large, local or international exhibitors showed at least one film in theaters of varied sizes. This included local colleges and various elements of the New York municipal system, including the Fire Department and the Department of Sanitation. It also involved at least nineteen foreign governments. Among those using a conventional theatrical apparatus were Britain, Brazil, France, Russia, and also the United States. Each had large theaters with regular film screenings scheduled throughout the day. The number of films shown varied from pavilion to pavilion. The British Pavillion featured 141 different films, Brazil 82, and France 72. Of the thirty-six commercial exhibitors using conventional theatrical settings, the largest theater by far was that constructed by General Motors, with a seating capacity of 612. The Coca-Cola screen sat 350 in front of a ten-foot screen. Coty Inc. featured 16mm Kodachrome sound film with seating for seventy-seven. The fair authorities estimated that attendance for film screenings at all theatrical venues during the first year of the fair's operation ran well in excess of twenty million.[46]

The fair established a department specifically to handle all matters related to moving images: the Newsreel and Film Department. It officially reviewed and censored all film exhibited theatrically on the fair grounds. A survey crafted by the department indicates that there were 612 motion pictures shown in the fair's first year. Four-hundred-and-four of them showed on 35mm and 191 on 16mm. The majority were projected with sound.[47] In the second year of the fair, the use of films in conventional theaters continued. U.S Steel, Ford, Greyhound, and Westinghouse built new theaters. Other exhibits continued their programs, including Chrysler, General Motors, Coca Cola, National Biscuit, Eastman Kodak, Coty, Inc., and the Petroleum Industry.[48]

Small screens: The future in rearview

Thirty-four different large and dedicated auditoria showed films throughout the fair's typical day. But many more venues featured films as part of their programming and display techniques, including many small theaters, restaurants, outdoor gardens, open-air theaters, and individual projection rooms, as well as "various other unique locations."[49] According to *Business Screen*, 130-odd portable projectors operated on a near-continuous basis ten to twelve hours per day, seven days a week.[50] Some of these smaller screens measured no more than twelve inches in contrast to the largest theatrical screen in the Chrysler building which measured sixty-feet wide. Some worked with rear-projection technologies. Such units appeared throughout the fairgrounds, including some that promoted current fair events on film, showing fairgoers at one location what was happening at another. One exhibitor advertised twenty rear-projection devices, yielding eight-foot images, that were placed throughout the fairgrounds.[51] Some spectators sat but many stood or simply walked by projections. A whole range of projection technologies illuminated mannequins, multi-screened installations, and large improvisational screens such as ceilings. One exhibit placed a small screen underneath a thin sheet of water in order to create the illusion of viewing magnified cells *in situ*.[52] Portable film projectors showed old American silents in the concession area, and also provided rolling text panels to accompany exhibits and replace conventional didactic labels.[53] As mentioned earlier, many projectors worked automatically and continuously; some were user-operated by push-button.

Labor union documents offer another important perspective on the status of these small projectors and screens at the fair. For instance, the differentiation of an ever-increasing range of projector types and exhibition scenarios is in part reflected in the agreement fair administrators struck with the local 306 of the Motion Picture and Machine Operators' Union. This agreement governed six different basic film projection scenarios, stipulating wages according to the degree of skill and attention required. These categories included one for 35mm projectors, used most often in conventional movie theater settings, one for 16mm arc illumination and a category exempted from the agreement: any exhibit using fewer than eight automatic small-gauge projectors.[54] Portable projectors were forcing a change in standard labor agreements for projectionists, unsettling the hold particular unions had on public and private film shows. These new automatic projectors were exempt from union claims and protections as the idea of self-operation was a part of their basic design and function.

Such agreements and the other numbers cited above indicate that the fair was a kind of watershed moment for portable, small gauge projectors with which a majority of moving images appeared. The presence of these small cinema machines at an event like the fair signaled their arrival as an official element of film's public and institutional presence. Some of the contemporaneous screen discourse even fashioned the film screen as a basic element of the built environment, measured the way one would assess the expanse of concrete or glass.

Raven Screen Corporation, for instance, advertised: "Over 4000 square feet" of their screens were at the fair.[55] A report on film projector use, which does not include projection of still images—likely even more widely evident—indicates that of the projectors in use at the fair, about 10 per cent were conventional 35mm projectors, and the remaining were 16mm, "with some 90% being the automatic type."[56] Further adding to my argument about expanding and varied screen presence is the basic fact that the screens that worked in tandem with these projectors ranged dramatically in size. For instance, the screen used at Chrysler's extremely popular 3-D film show measured forty by sixty feet, making it likely the biggest theatrical screen in the country. This screen would easily have seemed gargantuan in relative terms, given that the theater in which it was erected only seated 339 people, an extremely small number compared to the thousands at Radio City Music Hall just over the river.[57] Yet, the fact remains that small portable screens from twelve inches to eight feet outnumbered conventional, 35mm, theatrical screens by a ratio of ten-to-one. Screen variability and multiple textures (indicated by 8mm and 16mm, as well as different screen surfaces) were common-sense elements of 1939's World of Tomorrow.

One of the more interesting and less understood aspects of what I am calling the portable film screen is the wide use of the rear-projection screen. Anne Friedberg reminds us that while we tend to think of cinema as a technology of light, it has also long been predicated on the need for darkness, and thus technologies of darkness and light are irretrievably linked.[58] The rear-projection screen rose to prominent use at the fair and elsewhere during this period precisely to overcome the challenges of daylight projection, or, in other words, to overcome the need for spaces that were dark. Because conventional projector and screen relations dictated a projector on one side of the room and a screen on the other, film projection required very particular spaces which needed to be both free of visual impediments such as columns or other obstructions and also relatively dark in order that the image achieve legibility. Rear-projection units promised to overcome this problem. They also provided a more adaptable screen, one that could not only be used in daylight or a conventionally lit room, but that could be used in more kinds of spaces not requiring a long clear line for the projector to throw images.

The rear-projection system most widely used at the fair was a system developed by Trans-Lux, a company best known as owner of a small theater chain that specialized in dedicated newsreel theaters. These theaters used 35mm films and special lenses that allowed the projector to operate at close range—behind rather than in front of the screen—and yet project an image up to twenty-feet wide. This further allowed the company to repurpose inexpensive and small spaces that didn't need to be fully darkened and didn't require elaborate balcony projection booths.[59]

One of three newsreel chains in the 1930s and 1940s, Trans-Lux Corporation began in 1923 as the Trans-Lux Daylight Picture Screen Corporation. Its initial business idea was simple: projecting all manner of information (words, numbers, images) in full light. The company's first innovation was a "Movie Ticker" at the New York Stock Exchange, which projected the small, constant flow of stock information on ticker tape. Douglas Gomery indicates that in the context of the roaring 1920s, this particular application proved very successful.[60] When Trans-Lux diversified and opened its first dedicated newsreel theatre in 1931, repurposing its business screen for pictorial rather than numerical content, the business model was quite different from the palaces that so dominate our imagination of the theatrical landscape during the 1920s. Trans-Lux Theaters often rented spaces rather than building them or buying them. Its theaters had significantly smaller seating capacity than their picture palace peers, generally seating fewer than 200 customers. Rear-screen projection allowed them to keep house lights high, minimizing the need for ushers. Shows ran continuously; theater traffic was utterly flexible and was staggered according to the foot traffic that characterized the theater's urban locations.[61] There were several such newsreel theaters in major cities throughout the east coast and at least one operating in Times Square until the early 1960s.[62]

It was precisely the same rear-screen projection technology that was employed so extensively at the fair. Fair exhibitors built upon the Trans-Lux system and idea, which was merchandized by a range of interests during the 1930s to businessmen, small and large companies, department stores, travelling salesmen, and all manner of exhibitors as the ultimate business machine. The General Cigar Company used the Trans-Lux system at the fair with a teletype machine that flashed world and sport news every minute.[63] And, to return to the contextual transformations in moving image culture provided at the beginning of this essay, it was this rear-screen technology that made inroads as a sales and merchandizing device, described by trade press at the time as common in public spaces for advertising, stock quotes, and product demonstration throughout the US.[64] One such device was the Kodak Business Kodascope, first marketed in 1928, which Kodak claimed could be carried in a "case as small as the average sample case."[65] The screen reflected light in the normal way but because it was translucent the projected image could be seen from either side, front or back.[66] The Kodascope further promised quick set-up (less than half a minute), adaptability to all modern offices (including those fully lit and with glass partitions). The device featured a screen that was five-and-a-half inches by seven inches which Kodak suggested was large enough considering the "close range at which it is viewed" and its comparability to "a full page illustration in the average-size book."[67] Kodak claimed that the projector and bulb were sufficient to illuminate a thirty-inch by forty-inch screen, thus rendering the device adaptable, good for "a one-man [sic] audience or a group."[68] The machine frequently appeared in Kodak's advertising atop a desk. Other rear-projection business machines include "the Merchandiser," a small, table-top or mounted, rear-projection screen that used 16mm film. The unit's design resembled a photographic camera: the screen appeared where a lens jutting out from a camera body might otherwise be placed. The portable machine worked automatically on a loop, repeating a short message over and over again. Its small size and self-contained set-up meant that it could be placed anywhere in a store: in a window, on a counter, in a showroom, day or night. This flexibility was a key feature in its sales literature. The company,

Akeley-Leventhal, also claimed superior reliability, smooth operation and easy film changes.[69] Montgomery-Ward implemented the unit nationally in its department stores.

At the fair, the smallest of these devices were used in what were at the time highly sophisticated product displays. For instance, the makers of Bromo Seltzer placed a small, rear-projection unit inside an over-sized bottle of its ant-acid.[70] In another example, a ride-film featured ponies walking on treadmills carrying brave children who watched rear-projection screens playing travel scenes "so that youngsters get the effect of riding along the paths and through the streets of foreign countrysides and cities."[71]

Many other such machines appeared during this period, some of them featuring motion pictures, some with accompanying sound, and others that featured slides with sound. The pages of *Business Screen* contain many examples of products such as the "Explainette," the "Illustravox," and the "Automotion" machine, sold to retailers and merchandisers as automatic image machines to enhance selling techniques. Some of these required the constant control of an operator, others needed relatively little intervention. The Flolite, for instance, was a stand-alone unit that claimed to be a "miniature theater" allowing "brilliant pictures even in broad daylight." The unit allowed that the film could be played as many times as desired on a loop. The screen was quite small at twelve inches by fifteen inches, though the whole of the unit itself was quite large, weighing eighty-five pounds. The Flolite was sold as suitable for "retail, food, drug and cigar stores, department stories, car depots, window and store displays, hotel, theater and club lobbies, conventions, public buildings, and numerous other similar places."[72]

What did the small projector say about the "World of Tomorrow" in 1939? In the context of film viewing its role at the fair said something very particular. For instance, we know that the number of movie theaters in the US gradually increased throughout the 1920s, decreased during the depression of the 1930s, and then increased to a peak in 1945. After this the number of theaters rapidly decreased by almost 50 per cent in the twenty years that followed (from 19,096 in 1945 to a low of 9150 in 1963). As a result, we have this received wisdom that at mid-century cinema declines and television ascends. And, ascend television did. Yet, so too did this other kind of cinema—the fair's cinema. Sales of small-gauge portable equipment roughly tripled in annual sales during the 1950s.[73] To take just one year, 1959, the SMPE estimated 4,195,000 portable projectors in use. This equates to one projector for every forty-two people. Compare this to the statistic for movie theaters: one theater to 15,627 people, 4.2 million projectors, 11,335 movie theaters. In raw crude figures, portable projectors outnumbered movie theaters by a factor of 370. In short, the small film projector and screen formed an inextricable and lasting element of the future—imagined and near—of 1939. At the fair, the portable projector and mobile screen, along with the non-flammable gauge of 8mm and 16mm film, declared the impending end to the dominance of the movie theater as the primary site for projected moving images and sounds. Encountering films depended far less on purpose built spaces, darkened and highly controlled theaters, a professionalized apparatus of presentation and showmanship, or Hollywood-dominated production and distribution practices. Rather we have a quick view to an economy of self-operated, adaptable, consumer-grade machines, perfectly at home in a knob-turning, electrified, gadget-driven world of technological expression.

The specifically corporate appropriation of small film projectors at the fair shows us that film and its family of technologies were being eagerly adapted by a range of corporate interests seeking to master a changing audio-visual landscape, harnessing the powers of light and dark, sound and silence to their respective agendas. It also shows us the powerful adaptability of celluloid, projector, and screen as a kind of exhibition triumvirate, used creatively to envision a particular kind of automated, efficient future in which film screens purveyed not just corporatism but also a sense of connectivity and technological savvy, and a persistent link to a panoply of other technologies furthering imperatives of persuasion, convenience, and performance.

This corporatism was the toll to pay for a form of moving image culture that expanded the articulation of projectors and screens from mainstreet amusement to a complex, self-operated light and sound machine, capable of addressing mobile and seated, big, small and smaller audiences, in a range of spaces. This was a whole other kind of cinema, one that provides not just a different view to particular kinds of films but one that constitutes a technological infrastructure which plainly challenges and expands how we understand cinema's apparatus. For this was a hybrid of media machines, as much linked to the history of information machines and consumer gadgets as to Hollywood spectacle, modernist art or grand narrative. Cinema here was a family of wandering machines, one we might do well to wander after.

Notes

1   See, for instance, Janine Marchessault and Susan Lord, eds., *Fluid Screens, Expanded Cinema* (Toronto: University of Toronto Press, 2007), or the recent issue of *Public: Art/Culture/Ideas* 40 (2009), entitled "Screens."

2   On IMAX, see Charles Acland, "IMAX Technology and the Tourist Gaze," *Cultural Studies* 12.3 (1998): 429–445, Alison Griffiths, *Shivers Down Your Spine: Cinema, Museums, and the Immersive View* (New York: Columbia University Press, 2008), and Greg Siegel, "Double Vision: Large-Screen Video Display and Live Sports Spectacle," *Television & New Media* 3.1 (February

2002): 49–73; for small screens, see Heidi Rae Cooley, "It's All about the Fit: The Hand, The Mobile Screenic Device and Tactile Vision," *Journal of Visual Culture* 3.2 (August 2004): 133–155.

3   Anne Freidberg, *The Virtual Window* (Cambridge, MA: MIT Press, 2006) and Charles Acland, "Curtains, Carts and the Mobile Screen," *Screen* 50.1 (Spring 2009): 148–166.

4   Erkki Huhtamo, "The Sky Is (Not) the Limit: Envisioning the Ultimate Public Media Display," *Journal of Visual Culture* 8.3 (December 2009): 329–348; see also, Erkki Huhtamo, "Elements of Screenology: Toward an Archaeology of the Screen," *ICONICS: International Studies of the Modern Image* 7 (2004): 31–82.

5   See Lauren Rabinovitz, *For the Love of Pleasure: Women, Movies, and Culture in Turn-of-the-Century Chicago* (New Brunswick, NJ: Rutgers University Press, 1998), Kristen Whissel, *Picturing American Modernity: Traffic, Technology, and the Silent Cinema* (Durham: Duke University Press, 2008), and Tom Gunning, "The World as Object Lesson: Cinema Audiences, Visual Culture and the St. Louis World's Fair 1904," *Film History: An International Journal* 6.4 (1994): 422–444.

6   Janine Marchessault, "Multi-Screens and Future Cinema: The Labyrinth Project at Expo 67," in *Fluid Screens, Expanded Cinema*, ed. Susan Lord and Janine Marchessault (Toronto: University of Toronto Press, 2007), 29–51, and James Kreul, "New York, new cinema: the independent film community and the underground crossover, 1950–1970," (PhD diss., University of Wisconsin Madison, 2004), 89–99, http://0-proquest.umi.com.concordia.ca/pqdweb?in dex=0&did=828412181&SrchMode=2&sid=1&Fmt=2&VInst=PROD&V Type=PQD&RQT=309&VName=PQD&TS=1282660058&clientId=10306 (accessed 18 August 2010).

7   A department store in New York had its own 300-seat auditorium and used it to show old movies, flashing shopping suggestions in between films. Zenn Kaufman, "Films in the Department Store," *Business Screen* 1.4 (1938): 17–18.

8   For an overview of sponsored films, see Daniel J. Perkins, "Sponsored Business Films: An Overview 1895–1955," *Film Reader* 6 (1985): 125–132. For a spectacular overview of industrial and corporate uses of film during the interwar period, see Petr Szczepanik, "A Network of Media in the Bat'a Corporation and the Town of Zlín in the 1930s," in *Films that Work*, ed. Vinzenz Hediger and Patrick Vonderau (Amsterdam: University of Amsterdam Press, 2010), 349–77.

9   "The ABC's of Agency Film Activities," *Business Screen* 1.6 (1939): 18.

10   Robert W. Rydell, *World of Fairs: The Century-of-Progress Expositions* (Chicago, IL: University of Chicago Press, 1993), 127.

11   "Report of the Committee on Non-Theatrical Equipment," *Journal of the Society of Motion Picture Engineers* 24.1 (January 1935): 23–26. For more on the history of sponsored films, see Daniel J. Perkins, "The Sponsored Film: A New Dimension in American Film Research?" *Historical Journal of Film, Radio and Television* 2.2 (1982): 133–140, and "Sponsored Business Films."

12   "How to Use Films in Business: How to Use Films in Exhibits," *Business Screen* 1.2 (1938): 21–28; "A Survey on the Use of Films at Recent Expositions," *Business Screen* 1.2 (1938): 23.

13   Ibid., 28.

14 Ibid., 23–24.
15 Of the roughly 100, 16mm projectors in use on the grounds, 61 of them were silent, 19 used the recent sound-on-film technology, and 11 used the soon to be obsolete sound-on-disk models. Seventeen were manually operated and seventy-four were in automatic and continuous use. "Report of the Committee on Non-Theatrical Equipment," *Journal of the Society of Motion Picture Engineers* 24.1 (January 1935): 23–26. See also "A Survey on the Use of Films at Recent Expositions," *Business Screen* 1.2 (1938): 23. Bell & Howell conducted this survey sharing its information with *Business Screen*.
16 "A Survey on the Use of Films," 24.
17 See Warren Susman, *Culture as History: The Transformation of American Society in the Twentieth Century* (Washington, DC: Smithsonian Institution Press, 2003), and particularly chapters 9, 10, and 11.
18 For more on this, see Rydell.
19 Roland Marchand, "Corporate Imagery and Popular Education: World's Fairs and Expositions in the United States, 1893–1940," in *Consumption and American Culture*, ed. David Nye and Carl Pederson (Amsterdam: VU University Press, 1991), 18–33.
20 Quoted in Marchand, 26.
21 Showmanship was considered key to the success of this film which included 3-D glasses cut in the shape of a Chrysler car's front grill which could be taken home as a souvenir. The film bore the title *In Tune With Tomorrow* (John Norling, 1939) and was followed the year later with another 3-D film titled *New Dimensions* (John Norling, 1940), shown in Technicolor. The Chrysler theater sat 339.
22 The display of moving parts reflects the trend toward active demonstration and dynamic illustration of products or principles as opposed to static display. See *Exhibition Techniques: A Summary of Exhibition Practice, Based on Surveys Conducted at the New York and San Francisco World's Fairs of 1939* (New York: New York Museum of Science and Industry, 1940), 21.
23 "A Comprehensive Description of the General Motors Highways and Horizons Exhibit at the New York World's Fair," Press Release (ND circa 1939) [Box 1851, File 10: New York World's Fair Collection] Manuscripts and Archives Division, NYPL.
24 *Exhibition Techniques*, 41.
25 The use of films at the fair drew the attention of Carlos E. Cummings who in addition to being Director of the Buffalo Museum of Science in 1939 was also commissioned by David Stevens, Director of the Humanities Division of the Rockefeller Foundation, to conduct a study from the viewpoint of museum exhibition of the two World's Fairs of 1939, San Francisco and New York. This study yielded two volumes, one entitled *Exhibition Techniques* and the other *East is East, West is West* (Buffalo, NY: Buffalo Museum of Science, 1940). The latter of these was authored by Cummings and discusses in a rambling fashion all manner of exhibition techniques used at the fairs and considers them in relation to how the museum might adapt them to its purposes. Among the many techniques addressed by Cummings, use of film at the fairs receives special notice.
26 Fordyce Tuttle, "Automatic Slide Projectors for the New York World's Fair," *Journal of the Society of Motion Picture Engineers* 34 (January 1935):

265–71. The Kodak screen was matched by an exhibit in the Production and Distribution Exhibition, located in the Consumer's Building, where seven synchronized motion picture projectors displayed an 8-minute film on a 10-foot high and 100-foot wide screen, billed as the "widest movie screen ever built." See *Business Screen* 7 (1939): 37.

27 *Exhibition Techniques*, 56; The Kodak Pavilion was not the only one with multiple projectors used to create the effect of motion. The report based on the fair, *Exhibition Techniques,* indicates that other such exhibits used grouped projectors in order to show dynamic change within and across illustrated subjects. One involved a curved wall which displayed images projected from at least five projectors, each showing images that projected onto a designated area of the wall with a label that grouped all images into a single category. Also, a model of a transparent woman was used in conjunction with rear-projection techniques, in order to conceal the apparatus and to seamlessly show biological change of internal organs (59).

28 Fordyce Tuttle, "Automatic Slide Projectors for the New York World's Fair," *Journal of the Society of Motion Picture Engineers* 34 (March 1940): 265–271. Notably bright colors featured prominently in many exhibits at the fair, with 40 per cent of them employing it in some way. Technicolor also featured prominently among the many films shown, particularly those that were animated, echoing but also furthering the color revolution underway in mainstream commercial cinema.

29 At the fair, Waller also arranged a synchronized display of ten marching figures on the inside walls of the fair's signature perisphere. For more on this, see Fred Waller, "The Archaeology of Cinerama," *Film History* 5.3 (1993): 239–297.

30 See Gene Youngblood, *Expanded Cinema* (New York: Dutton, 1970).

31 For more on the debut of television, see Ron Becker, "'Hear-and-See Radio' in the World of Tomorrow: RCA and the Presentation of Television at the World's Fair, 1939–1940," *Historical Journal of Film, Radio & Television* 21.4 (2001): 361–78.

32 For more on the Westinghouse exhibit, see *The Westinghouse Exhibit at the World's Fair of 1940 in New York* (Westinghouse, 1940) [Box 1858, File 5: New York World's Fair 1939–40 Collection] Manuscripts and Archives Division, NYPL.

33 The wonders of electricity and the thrill of electrically facilitated ideas of expanded embodiment thrilled fairgoers. For more such examples, see *Exhibition Techniques*, 41.

34 Becker, 369.

35 For more on the San Francisco Fair, see "The Films at the Golden Gate Fair," *Business Screen* 2.1 (1939): 22.

36 Press release "Movies-1" (March 13, 1939) [Box 398, File 7: New York World's Fair 1939–40 Collection] Manuscripts and Archives Division, NYPL. Note that I have found no evidence of a contemporary Hollywood film showing at the fair aside from an anthology film made for the fair by Cecil B. Demille titled *Land of Liberty* (Cecil B. Demille, 1939). See note #43.

37 Grover Whalen, "New Fields for Films at New York's Fair," *Business Screen* 1.2 (1938): 15.

38 While a few Hollywood films were shot on-site, using the fair as backdrop, Hollywood otherwise opted to stay away from the fair's exhibition venues

in what seems like a concession to New York area exhibitors. Its main contribution to the fair, aside from ample newsreels coverage, was to supply an anthology film, whose assembly was overseen by Cecil B. DeMille. For more on this, see Sara Beth Levy, "Land of Liberty in the World of Tomorrow," *Film History* 18.4 (2006): 440–58.

39 See for example a three-page memo by Claude Collins to Fox Movietone, Hearst Metrotone, Paramount, Pathe and Universal detailing a preview celebration at the fair. "To All Newsreel Editors" (April 29, 1938) [Box 1983, File 2: New York World's Fair 1939–40 Collection] Manuscripts and Archives Division, NYPL.

40 Claude Collins, "Fair Movies," *Business Screen* 1.2 (1938): 18.

41 Ibid.

42 "Letter" to George Hammond from Claude Collins (May 27, 1940) [Box 1983, File 1: New York World Fair 1939–40 Collection] Manuscripts and Archives Division, NYPL.

43 Ibid.

44 See "World's Fair Films," *Film News* 1.7 (July 1940): 8.

45 See, for instance, Howard Barnes, "The Screen: The Moving Picture's Part in the World's Fair," *New York Herald Tribune* (May 28, 1938). In this article, Barnes alerts readers to the fair's elaborate offerings despite Hollywood's absence, indicating that "the cinema is extensively represented" in the World of Tomorrow. For Barnes, this included televised "movies" in the GE exhibition, the puppet film *Pete-Roleum and His Cousins,* and the "remarkable repertory of old and new Soviet films showing in the handsome motion picture theatre of the U.S.S.R. pavilion."

46 Claude Collins, "Introduction," *Films Exhibited at the World's Fair 1939: A Survey* (1940) [Box 398, File 10: New York World's Fair 1939–1940 Collection] Manuscripts and Archives Division, NYPL, II.

47 Ibid., 7.

48 For Business Screen's second year fair report, see "Films at the 1940 New York World's Fair," *Business Screen* 2.7 (1940): 14–15.

49 Collins, "Introduction."

50 "The World's Fair Survey of Motion Pictures and Slidefilms at the Fairs," *Business Screen* 2.1 (1939): 21–25.

51 "Movies-1" Press release (March 13, 1939) [Box 398, File 10: New York World's Fair 1939–1940 Collection] Manuscripts and Archives Division, NYPL.

52 Projection on ceilings at the fair is discussed in Cummings, *East is East,* 255; on screens under water, see Cummings, *East is East,* 258. For more examples of unrealized proposals for screen experimentation, consult the New York World's Fair 1939–40 Collection, Manuscripts and Archives Division, NYPL.

53 Cummings, *East is East,* 258. Old American films starring Charles Chaplin, Mary Pickford, Fatty Arbuckle and Lon Chaney played daily in the Amusement Area of the fair in a one-hour show, in a small theater for 48. Admission was charged. See Collins, "Introduction" *Films Exhibited,* 12.

54 "To All Exhibitors" letter from Luther Reed (August 29, 1939) [New York World's Fair 1939–40 Collection] Manuscripts and Archives Division, NYPL. Reed was at the time of this memo listed as Chairman of the Exhibitor's Projection Committee. Claude Collins was head of the film department.

55 *Business Screen: Equipment Review* 1.9 (1939): 18.

56 This information is gleaned from a summary of negotiations with projectionists' unions regarding the use of film projectors by exhibitors at the fair. The overall number of projectors was much higher, given that the fair itself operated many of them. But, these fell under a different agreement. Automatic projectors did not require a projectionist per se, but the need for regular maintenance was assumed. "Exhibitors' Projection Committee, New York World's Fair 1939" (March 17, 1939) [Box 309, File 11; New York World's Fair 1939–40 Collection] Manuscripts and Archives Division, NYPL.

57 For Business Screen's second year fair report, see "Films at the 1940 New York World's Fair," *Business Screen* 2.7 (1940): 14–15.

58 Friedberg, 152.

59 W. Mayer, "SMPE Trans-Lux Rear Stage Projection," *Theater Management and Theater Engineering* 26.22 (October 1931): 3; on the development of special lenses, see also Wilbur B. Rayton, "Short Focus Lenses for Projection with Translucent Screens," *Journal of the Society of Motion Picture Engineers* 19.6 (December 1932): 512–521.

60 Douglas Gomery, *Shared Pleasures: A History of Movie Presentation in the United States* (Madison: University of Wisconsin Press, 1992), 145–149.

61 Ibid., 147.

62 Ibid., 149.

63 "Business Screen Reviews the New York World Fair," *Business Screen* 1.6 (1939): 19.

64 During the 1930s, the SMPE established a "Projection Screens Committee" and began publishing its report regularly in the association's journal in September 1931. See for instance, "Report of the Projection Screens Committee," *Journal of the Society of Motion Picture Engineers* 18.2 (February 1932): 248–249.

65 "The Eastman Business Kodascope," *Journal of the Society of Motion Picture Engineers* 12.36 (September 1928): 1175.

66 Such translucent screens were widely used by the Navy on ships that needed to maximize viewing space on the deck and so arranged sailors on both sides of the screen.

67 "The Eastman Business Kodascope," 1176–1177.

68 Ibid., 1177.

69 Developed by Akeley-Leventhal, a company founded by Carl Akeley, the well-known explorer and developer of cameras suitable for capturing images of nature. [Advertising Pamphlet] Akeley-Leventhal Corporation (1939) [New York World's Fair 1939–40 Collection] Manuscript and Archives Division, NYPL.

70 This display featured an animated short with a six-foot by eight-foot screen made to appear as the label of an oversized bottle of the anti-acid medication: "The World Fairs' Best Salesman!," *Business Screen* 1.8 (1939): 17–19.

71 Whalen.

72 "Flolite [advertisment]," *Business Screen* 1.1 (1938): 8.

73 All numbers from Department of Commerce, compiled by Augustus Wolfman, published as *1960 Annual Statistical Report—The Photographic Industry in the United States: Photo Dealer and Modern Photography* (report no. 4, June 1960).

CHAPTER THIRTY-ONE

From Screen to Site: Television's Material Culture, and Its Place

Anna McCarthy

[...]

As I will propose, site as well as sight is a crucial conceptual framework for any attempt to think through the televisual as a material scene of representation. Three aspects of TV's technological form in particular can be foregrounded in the intellectual history of the medium, as moments in which television opens up new ways of thinking about place. The first I have already mentioned: it is the indexical force of formal ideologies of television like "liveness" that, through a range of representational and electronic techniques, translates perceived temporal simultaneity into the sense of spatial collapse that Heidegger noted in "The Thing."[1] However, as Jane Feuer has proposed, the ontology of televisual liveness in actual occasions of the transmission and reception of signals from one place to another instantaneously is not a determining aspect of the medium's cultural effects. Rather, it is through the *ideology* of liveness—sustained in ways less spectacular than the "media event," and filtered through micro-level visual techniques of the broadcast text, whether literally live or not—that television sustains both the intimacy of its direct address to the subject and its claims to documentary truth and historicity.[2] Liveness might thus be seen as a temporal ideology that works to construct two fictive spaces for the viewer simultaneously. On a small scale, it is the space of imagined co-enunciation signified in the direct address of the talking head on-screen; on a larger scale, and in collective terms, this space is the familiar imagined space of the nation looking in on its key sites—a space always constituted, as Benedict Anderson famously noted, via perceived temporal simultaneity.[3] This is the spatial operation of television most often scrutinized in theory: space-binding, the "abolition of every possibility of remoteness."

FIGURE 31.1 *A bank of TV broadcast monitors at Democratic Headquarters on election night, Washington, D.C., 1964. Photo: Marion S. Trikosko.*

But another aspect of television that makes it a key heuristic instrument in the philosophical exploration of place, materiality, and technics is far less recognized. This is the fact that its material form is profoundly *site-specific*. As Weber points out, although it is commonplace to note TV's pervasiveness, "for all its ubiquitousness it is not very well understood".[4] I think this is because we have not yet addressed some of the implications of TV's ubiquity—not only that it is constantly available in the home but also that it is present in other places too, the everyday locations where we shop, eat and drink, wait, and travel in our daily itineraries. What is interesting about this ubiquity is the way it illustrates something specific about TV as a medium: its peculiarly malleable and heterogeneous physical *form*. It can encompass giant video walls and video banks, flat screens that look like illuminated signs, small and large consoles, and all sorts of signal forms, from live transmissions to prerecorded program cycles, to simultaneous mixtures of both. And such divergent forms of television coexist unproblematically; one need only take a cab ride through Times Square, populated with more forms of the televisual apparatus than one could possibly count, to grasp the inadequacy of theoretical models that attempt to address the medium's materiality via an abstracted or idealized sense of its technological manifestation on the level of the everyday. More often than not, such models turn away from the fact of television's multiple phenomenological forms, its ubiquity and difference across a range of spaces, installing instead a more idealist notion of TV and its place: the screen in the home. However, although the home may be economically central to the broadcast television apparatus, this does not mean that critics should accept the pervasive ideological association of television with the domicile as an adequate representation of the actual geography of the medium. When we take the diverse proliferation of material forms and places of television into account, the medium starts to look very different. It becomes impossible to argue that the TV set always organizes relations between, say, public and private, subjects and collectivities, participation and isolation, in identical ways across locations. Rather, television's heterogeneous materiality requires that we accept that its operations upon the subject and its use as a form of communication between individuals must change from site to site, institution to institution. If the flexibility of the technology allows the medium to disappear into the everyday places where it appears, then surely it must simultaneously disappear into the particular relations of public and private, subjects and others, that characterize these places.

The third crucial feature of TV's material relation to space is another form of disappearance, one anticipated in the second: it is the screen's peculiar ability to *dematerialize* at the point of its encounter with philosophy. Despite its integration into everyday life, something we ignore, in Toby Miller's words, "like a pet or a vaguely dotty relative," television embodies technics for philosophers in a total(izing) and a physical frame. As Weber notes, "the television transmission does not...as is generally supposed, simply *overcome* distance and separation. (This is the illusion of a 'global village.') It renders them invisible, paradoxically, by transposing them into the vision it transmits...the space defined by the television set is already fractured by the undecideability of that which appears on the screen. Is it taking place here, there, or anywhere?" (122). In this account of television's spatiality, the insistent localism and materiality implied in TV's site-specificity, and all the questions raised by this localism, recedes and is replaced by a theoretical model of TV as global epiphenomenon of modernity. The screen here is not a local object we put things on and move around in a space, nor is it even a network, really, in a Latourian sense, that is to say, something that is both global and local, an agent or actor in cultural and scientific definitions of particularity and universality, fetish and fact. It becomes a thing that, in Weber's words, "takes place" and not a thing that makes a place, or a thing that is made by a place.

I dwell on Weber's account because his concern with processes of site and place is unusual in philosophical accounts of television. Others read the disappearing acts that TV performs in the place it inhabits as a predictable series of remote operations performed on the subject—operations that have no material form at all, despite the overproduction of material, embodied metaphors to describe such operations, such as "brainwashing," or the expression "glued to" the TV set. A recent, highly nuanced critical account of modern ideas about human perception and mass influence suddenly takes on a paranoid voice when it addresses the topic of television and its immense powers, powers that are systematically denied, even by television's critics:

> Television...has become so fully integrated into social and subjective life that certain kinds of statements about television (for example, about addiction, habit, persuasion, and control) are in a sense unspeakable, effectively excluded from public discourse. To speak of contemporary collective subjects in terms of effects of passivity and influence is still generally anathema...There is usually a tacit a priori conviction that television viewers constitute a hypothetical community of rational and volitional human subjects. The contrary position, that human subjects have determinate psychological capacities and functions that might be susceptible to technological management...must be disavowed by so-called critics of those same institutions.[5]

The author, Jonathan Crary, breaks here from a careful account of the history of attitudes toward theories of behavior modification via perception into an act of witnessing, of speaking the truth (apparently axiomatic) about television's influence. The problem, of course, is that the statements he describes—statements about viewers as a suggestive mass—are far from excluded from cultural circulation. Rather, such statements fairly constitute the contemporary public discourse on television, especially in the media.[6] They form the basis of the media critiques that emerge in popular and academic journalism around violent events like school shootings, for example, critiques that often offer "the influence of the media" as a master hermeneutic. And such fears of manipulation are the basis of a long-standing Hollywood formula, in which media paranoia takes on occult and insidious forms-from the '50s "cult classic" film *The Twonky* [1953] to more "serious" middlebrow critiques, like *A Face in the Crowd* [1957], or more recently *The Truman Show* [1998].

Such free-floating and ever-present ideas about media influence are abetted, on some level, by the conflation of TV's pervasiveness with a sense of dematerialization and derealization. TV's ubiquity makes it possible to speak of its cultural effects and operations of television without having to address its material form, because these operations are so obvious, so clearly already "known," that they are curiously independent of the material place of the screen and the viewing encounter. This tension between materiality and immateriality, what Weber nicely calls TV's "ambivalence," is no doubt what makes the medium attractive as a figure for modernity's spatial ruptures. The ambivalence, as Weber notes, is in part a result of its liveness—ambivalent because liveness is an attribute that applies also to recording, as in the terms "live mic" or "live recording." But it is more centrally, I think, a sign of the conceptual challenge of reconciling the universalizing rhetoric of television (as brainwashing apparatus, as the disappearance of physical space and time) with its myriad site-specific uses and appropriations. It is the challenge of scale, in other words. When TV comes to defining modern technics, the sense of extreme material heterogeneity that I have sketched above must somehow conform to an epistemological condition characterized by broad homogeneity. Given this situation, it seems absolutely crucial to move in an alternative direction and *diversify* some of the paradigms through which the materiality of TV maybe understood, and its relation to historical subjects best grasped.

[…]

Notes

1 Martin Heidegger, "The Thing," in *Poetry, Language, Thought*, trans. and introduction by Albert Hofsadter (New York: Harper and Row, 1971).
2 Jane Feuer, "The Concept of Live Television: Ontology as Ideology," in *Regarding Television: Critical Approaches—An Anthology*, ed. E. Ann Kaplan (Frederick, MD: University Publications of America, 1983). On the banality of liveness, see Mimi White, "Site Unseen: CNN's War in the Gulf," in *Seeing Through the Media: The Persian Gulf War*, ed. Susan Jeffords and Lauren Rabinovitz (New Brunswick, NJ: Rutgers University Press, 1994).
3 On direct address and the construction of a fictive national space through the live, or live-coded broadcast, see John Ellis, *Visible Fictions: Cinema, Television, Video*, revised ed. (New York: Routledge, 1992); see also Mimi White, "Site Unseen," and Sasha Torres, "King TV," in *Living Color: Race and Television in the United States*, ed. Sasha Torres (Durham, NC: Duke University Press, 1998); and Mary Ann Doane, "Information, Crisis, Catastrophe," in *Logics of Television: Essays in Cultural Criticism*, ed. Patricia Mellencamp (Bloomington: Indiana University Press, 1990).
4 Samuel Weber, *Mass Mediauras: Form, Technics, Media* (Stanford, CA: Stanford University Press, 1996), p. 112.
5 Jonathan Crary, *Suspensions of Perception: Attention, Spectacle, and Modern Culture* (Cambridge: MIT Press, 1999), pp. 71–72. To be fair, Crary's position on the perfidious influence of television is somewhat ambiguous here; in a footnote to this passage he alludes to the uncertainty of "whether or not attention can be controlled or managed" even though the passage itself clearly comes down on the affirmative side of this question.
6 For a full discussion of these cultural fears about communications technology, see Jeffrey Sconce, *Haunted Media: Electronic Presence from Telegraphy to Television* (Durham, NC: Duke University Press, 2000).

CHAPTER THIRTY-TWO

Nollywood: Spectatorship, Audience and the Sites of Consumption

Onookome Okome

Nollywood on the rise

Nollywood, the cinematic phenomenon that was inaugurated in Lagos, has known an unprecedented measure of success in its homeland, Nigeria. It is beginning to make its mark outside this home turf. Since the year 2000, it has gone from one international Film Festival to the other, and the gain it has made in these years has been consistent. In 2002, this author was invited to the second edition of the Festival of African and Caribbean Film, which was held in Barbados. Tunde Kelani, the veteran camera man and producer, who is also one of the icons of Nollywood, was also invited to present one of his video films, *Thunderbolt*. Jane Bryce, one of the organizers of this Festival, was clearly excited to formally introduce Nollywood to the audience of the island nation of Barbados for the first time. Bryce's introduction of Nollywood to this audience rephrased what is now "common talk" in the scholarship of the video film to date. It did so from a critical and serious manner, pointing not only to the uniqueness of this medium in the visual culture of Africa but also in the world cinematic expression as a whole. Bryce's take on Nollywood as an art and industry shows how and why Nollywood compels attention from those outside its field of operation and cultural vision, not that the industry cares for any attention from the outside. In fact, one of the characteristics that marks Nollywood as an autonomous local cinematic expression is that it looks inward and not outward, and one can accurately argue that it does so in all aspects of the production and organization of its operation. Bryce also made the point about the difference between Nollywood and the Francophone cinema of French West Africa that was the touch-bearer of what was known as *the* African cinema before the emergence of Nollywood. Indeed, as Bryce notes,[1] Nollywood does not "have the opportunities for training and production financing" of Francophone cinema and does not "go to the biennial Pan-African Film Festival (FESPACO) in Burkina Faso." Yet, it is remarkable in very radical ways. As a result of this success, Nollywood has been able to circumvent the problems that African Francophone filmmakers whine about and has done so successfully in the last twenty years or so. It has moved the discourse of cinematic representation away from the blame game that is obvious and somewhat compellingly represented in the scholarship of cinema production and culture in postcolonial Africa.

Nollywood is commercially savvy. It values the entertainment of its clientele. The entertainment bit is primary to the mode of representation in the industry, yet in that pursuit, one cannot forget its sense of mission, which is to produce culture from the bottom of the street, so to speak. Nollywood provides the imaginary for certain marginal sections of the society where it operates. It is the poorer part of its postcolonial base, which is no longer restricted to Nigeria. This marginal clientele is now found among people on the continent and in the black diaspora where such postcolonial conditions prevail. However, this is not to argue that Nollywood clearly demarcates its potential audience along social and economic lines. Even if it tries, this will not be successful in a society where the gulf between the rich and the poor is often a fluid spectrum of negotiations for access to power and money. If the organizer of the Nollywood event at the second edition of the African and Caribbean Film Festival recognized the continental significance of Nollywood and its economic and social importance to the audience that it caters for, this cannot be said for other Film Festivals, especially in Europe and North Africa. The organizers of Barbados Film Festival showed a remarkable, and rare, sensitivity to Nollywood. Outside of Nigeria, and indeed Africa, Nollywood is still largely a curiosity. One typical example was the 2004 edition of the Berlinale Film Festival, which was held in Berlin, Germany. Another was the 34th edition of the Montreal Film Festival. Each of them privileged Nollywood as a "curio." In moments of doubt for these organizers, Nollywood became a piece of artefact-a piece of *something* from *somewhere* far away but something that is interesting all the same. In this regard, it is noteworthy to point out the 34th Berlinale Film Festival had a curious title for the Nollywood video films: "Hollywood in Nigeria or: How to Get Rich Quick." For the organizers, the visual practice of Nollywood cannot exist outside of the cultural and institutional framework of Hollywood even when this Festival program announces at the same time the undisputed difference that Nollywood has made to African cinematic life and discourse. That announcement also comes with a tinge of the "exotic." In the introduction to the screening of Nollywood video films, the Festival highlights the cobbling together of video films "on a shoestring budget." Of course, the second part of the title links Nollywood to the famous Nigerian scam, the advance fee fraud that is now commonly known as "419." This ambivalent attitude to Nollywood has obvious draw-backs. Even if it does nothing to dampen the enthusiasm of the local audience or shake the faith of video filmmakers in themselves, it does take the local audience for granted. This essay is about this local audience, and about the ways it consumes Nollywood. It foregrounds the collective gaze of this local audience, and contextualizes the sites of consumption and the regime of meaning which these sites give to the practice of Nollywood as well as the meaning of spectatorship in the industry. Furthermore, this essay seeks to demarcate and read these sites of consumption as popular rendezvous where social meanings meet with the fictional world of the video film, and are then recast into an unending spiral of other social texts. This essay will also highlight how members of this audience recoup and perform a peculiar postcolonial condition in its encounter with video texts in these popular spaces of consumption.

Nollywood is the latest strand of the Anglophone African cinema. The other prominent category is the Francophone cinema. Its "headquarter" is in the city of Ouagadougou, Burkina Faso. The most eloquent expression of Francophone African cinema finds outlet in the Biennial Film Festival, which is held in Ouagadougou, the capital of Burkina Faso. It is the Festival Panafricain Du Cinema et De La Television de Ouagadougou (FESPACO). Before the emergence of Nollywood, it was the African cinema. West African popular video film is different from this Francophone cinema industry. Popular video film, which is the cultural product of Nollywood, is unique in many ways. While there is no doubt that Nollywood exhibits the hybrid character that is obvious in many forms of African popular arts,[2] it is its acute notation of locality that gives it an unprecedented acceptability as *the* local cinematic expression in Nigeria and indeed in Africa. With the emergence of video film, the discourse of African cinema will need to be rephrased in very radical ways. While the wholesale adoption of video technology by practitioners in Nollywood has been an unqualified local success, it is the spirit to defy the economic malaise of the cinema industry in Nigeria that led to the adoption of this "new" technology. What this success signifies is the will to overcome the problems occasioned by economic and political hiccups in the 1980s with the slump in the local currency. Perhaps even more important is the desire expressed by video filmmakers to keep local stories in the narrative program of this local visual culture. By appropriating the terms of video technology the way that Nollywood has done in the last twenty or so years, this local cinema has demonstrated to its audience and to the cinema world at large that it "has not despaired of making some kind of sense out of its own hieroglyphics" (Gottesman 5). In the same vein, it has invested in its playful narratives of the social and cultural life of the Nigerian postcolony a nuanced essence of parody, which, according to Robert Frost, "opposes the dominant discourse" (quoted in Gottesman 1). Nollywood does this in the most subtle manner.[3]

Yet, the form and content of Nollywood narratives reminds the casual observer of the obvious ties it has to the complicated trade in global media images even when the point has been made of its unique place in world media culture. The social and cultural stimuli that enervated the industry in the late 1970s[4] also demonstrate why the text of popular video film stays close to the sociality of its less than elite majority clientele. My insistence on the importance of the peculiar sociality is a way of demarcating the uniqueness of this cinematic practice as well as expressing the will of those who patronize its cultural product.

The prevailing myth of the origin of Nollywood circulating among scholars is that a certain Igbo trader in the Idumota area of Lagos suddenly chanced upon an ingenious way of disposing a large cache of VHS cassettes, which he imported from Taiwan. Taking advantage of prevailing social, economic and political circumstances in the post-war Lagos of the 1970s, this trader diverted the use of these VHS cassettes into recording and retailing of local theatre performances and productions.[5] Not long after, other traders saw the financial benefits to be derived from the voracious appetite for popular video film shown by an army of subscribers, some of whom came from the emasculated audiences of popular Yoruba travelling theatres tropes in the western parts of Nigeria. Reacting to this need, popular video producers quickly redoubled their efforts, and before long, a string of popular video films were put into the market. Lagos quickly became the mecca of video production, making the sites of the consumption of the cultural product of Nollywood essentially parts of that cultural landscape. But if the origin of popular video film is linked to the Yoruba travelling theatre tropes of the 1970s, this was to change quickly in the coming years as popular video film become more and more cosmopolitan in outlook. The years following the crude representation of theatre productions on vhs soon vanished. Yoruba, the language of the itinerant performers of the Yoruba travelling theatre tropes, was replaced with the English and the Pidgin English, and the main themes that engaged early Yoruba video producers changed from the mythological world of the Yoruba pantheon into the "ghettoized"[6] world of the new urban world that Lagos represented. In this dynamic, a new audience was inaugurated and with it new sites of consumption. It was the cosmopolitan audience of popular video film.

Right from its inception, the debate around the cultural relevance of Nollywood was part of the larger question of this filmmaking tradition. This debate has a direct bearing on the place of the audience, and it is intricately connected to the social sites where video films are consumed. In this regard, I have elected to privilege the contribution of Pierre Barrot because the opinions he expresses represent some of the most salient arguments put forward on the matter. In his own words, Nollywood is "conquering new territories because the domestic market is becoming too small" (2). But he argues that the Nigeria film (meaning popular video film) is still deficient because it is still far from creating any "impact on national unity" the way other cinema industries have done elsewhere. He notes that the reason for this is that Nigerian films "are shown neither in the movie theatres nor on TV," and that most "Nigerians films cannot enjoy a large audience because of the Censors Board that is seen by many as perhaps too restrictive" (6). His prognosis is that "a new development could make the Board change its mind: the re-emergence of the cinema theatres" (6). He gives the example of the newly established Silverbird Cinema Complex located in Ikoyi, an affluent neighbourhood in upscale Lagos. Based on this example, and on the possibility of replicating the Silverbird example, Barrot concludes that "a new market is emerging that is less popular but more prestigious and in this market, [the] Nigerian films no longer enjoy the monopoly they were used to in the home video sector" (6). This comment touches the heart of the operation of Nollywood as an alternative narrative code of a popular art form. I will return to this point shortly. For Barrot, the catch then is that "the re-emergence of cinema theatres in Nigeria though it is starting with foreign films will surely help to revive people's interest in film and automatically compel directors to shoot better, bigger and, especially, in a more beautiful manner"(6). His position assumes that there is a lack of interest among the audience of popular video film in "foreign films." This is hardly the case. Field evidence points to the fact that there is a lot of interest in "foreign films" among members of video film audiences. For this audience, it is neither one nor the other. Interest in "foreign films" does not amount to a depreciation of the avid attachment to video film. Members patronize "foreign films" as much as they do local ones. Essentially, what marks the postcoloniality of this audience is the deep intention of being immersed in both visual cultures without being strictly compartmentalized into any one. Its interest in Nollywood is different from the interest it has for Hollywood or any other cinema culture for that matter. Barrot's suggestion that only the re-invigoration of the moribund "movie theatres" and the screening of Nigerian films in these venues and on television will assure the growth of this art form misses the point. This position surely smacks of a lack of understanding of the history of the audience of popular video film. It shows a lack of understanding of the economics of the venues of spectatorship in popular arts in Africa. More importantly, it writes over the important feature of the alternativeness of spectatorship which has come out of the art of seeing in Nollywood. This essay reads spectatorship from this position by confronting and exploring the alternativeness of this mode of visual consumption. It focuses on two sites where the consumption of video images takes place. It locates the sociality of these spaces and shows how they constitute another form of the production of knowledge in the postcolony.

"Public Spaces" and the audience of Nollywood

The audience of popular video film has a special role in Nollywood. But like most audiences of popular expressions in Africa, few studies have been done to deal with issues around the importance of this audience; there is no denying the fact that this audience is central and important to the production and consumption of art and literature, especially popular arts on the continent. Indeed, understanding the multiple dimensions of this audience is indispensable to the goal of problematizing ways in which knowledge is constructed, used, or circulated, dispensed and re-invented in Africa.

Karin Barber recognizes this lack in the field and points to the need to bridge critically the lacunae in scholarship if our desire is to "uncover histories of consumers in African popular genres" ("Preliminary" 347). One way to study popular audiences in Africa, she argues, is to understand the concept of the "'public" as a new form of "coming together" ("Preliminary" 353). Barber cautions that this act of "coming together" must be carefully qualified and can only be properly understood "if the specific forms of address, use of space, mode of staging, and expectations and interactions of performers and spectators are empirically established in their surprising and subtle details" ("Preliminary" 353). While it is true that this is not a peculiar characteristic of the Africa visual audience, what truly distinguishes the African popular audience from popular audiences elsewhere is the peculiar history associated with its formations. Barber points to the sources in the history of art criticism as academic discipline and to that overarching historical trauma—colonialism. If the audience of Nollywood is a peculiar category in Africa's cinematic history, so too are the sites where this audience consumes the visual dreams and despair that Nollywood produces. While it may be argued that these sites display the condition of postcolonial abnegation of desire and want, two of them present a more eloquent writing of this condition that the others. They are the sites located on the "street" and what I refer to as the "video parlour." "Street sites" of consumption are *ad hoc* spaces of seeing. On the other hand, the site of the video parlour displays another sense of "coming together." Each site presents the presence of an absence. For instance, it is the absence of capital that makes it possible impossible to engage in the consumption of these images in the more orthodox space of consumption such as the cinema halls. This is one of many absences. Although Nollywood is also consumed in the context of the domestic sphere, which renders the appropriation of the videoed world as a familial engagement of the fiction of Nollywood, it is the uncontrolled sites of consumption in the streets and the video parlours that account for the democratization of the narratives and purpose of Nollywood. It is not only that these sites of consumption render spectatorship in Nollywood as a fluid field of reading culture, it also privileges the presence of an absence as we know it in the production of culture that had been tightly controlled by the ruling and intellectual elite in Nigeria until the emergence of Nollywood.

There are two main kinds of "street audiences": the "street corner" and the "video parlour" audiences. "Street audience" is the umbrella designation for a special kind of audience that congregates on the streets. These audiences are commonly found in the cities and are essentially defined by the desire to enjoy the re-telling of the social and cultural existence of members in the temporality of these *ad hoc* meeting places. The first category of "street audiences" is the "street corner" audience. This category of the street audience converts street corners into veritable spaces for the consumption of the visual images from video performances. In this site of spectatorship, members do not have the comfort of a cinema house. Standing all the way through a screening, they literally "suffer" through the experience of viewing the same way the poor characters of video tales suffer in the rough and tumble of their unpredictable lives in the city. Since the advent of popular video films, "street corner theatres" have become part of the visual topography of the city, through which motorists must navigate to access roadways back home or to other destinations at the close of the working day. The act of this peculiar "coming together" is often effected during the evening, just when workers of the city are heading home for the day. The constitution of this audience is fluid, and this fluidity is in turn constitutive. Members of "street corner" audience are linked together primarily by the goal to see what is making headline news in the city, and elsewhere in the country. By paying attention to what is making the headline news in the city, members assert their collective place in the turbulence of Africa's tragic economy. This act of involvement implicates popular "street corner" audiences in the social turbulence that is the result of this economy of want and desperation. The symbolic and temporary conversion of "street corners" into social spaces of engagement with the visual world of the video film is only one of the markers of the economic poverty of this group of consumers.

"Street corner" audiences come together in front of video and music stalls. These are the main outlets for the rental of video and music cassettes, VCDs and DVDs in Nigerian cities. The proliferation of video and music stalls is a prominent character of Nigerian cities and towns since the emergence of Nollywood. These stalls have since become part of the visual topography of these cities and towns. In profound ways, these stalls have remapped social spaces in these cities and towns. Although this re-mapping may indeed be temporary, while it lasts the spaces that these "street corner" audiences inhabit are invested with cultural and political value, the kind which only the postcolonial condition can provoke. In these street corners, the flotsam and jetsam of the city and towns act out the performative essence and the social relevance of popular expressions in Nigeria. It is part of the performance of the postcolonial condition of want and desire.

The video parlour is a simple location where members of a community congregate for the sole purpose of consuming video narratives. The material technology of the video parlour is sparse. It can be anything from a small, stuffy room in the neighbourhood to a disused school hall. The essential quality that it must possess is that it has room enough to take in people who are willing to pay a small fee to see video films with other members of the community.[7] This screening room is fitted with a television set and a video recorder. Depending on the spending power of patrons and of the neighbourhood, the television set could be anything from a 14-inch screen to 27-inch one. The screening room is often "crampy" and uncomfortable. It is not a cinema hall and does not have the apparatus of a modern cinema hall either. Sidney Little Kasfir once described this space as the video theatre partly because of its link to the social roots of the practice of popular Yoruba theatre in Nigeria and partly due to the contention that "contemporary African art has built through a process of *bricolage* upon existing structures and scenarios on which the older, pre-colonial and colonial genres of African arts were made" (13). There is some truth in this. The suggestion is that this site of screening has obvious links to the performance structure of popular Yoruba theatre practice of the 1970s. "Video theatres," like the improvisational theatre stages, are patterned along the mode of improvisation employed by this theatre practice. This is also only partly true. Although the transition into video theatre from the informality and the improvisational structure of the itinerant Yoruba travelling troupes was particularly compelling in the late 1970s, the *bricolage* that Kasfir suggests has a broader implication for the audiences of video parlours. Like the local cinema halls, video parlours are still generally gender specific. Women may be admitted but are hardly seen as regular patrons. The social space of the Nigerian video parlour is masculinized. Women who venture to cross this social barrier are often tagged as "free women." In the years following the emergence of the video film as a distinct popular genre in its own right, this social space of spectatorship has remained completely male-dominated.

Reading Nollywood and its ironic sociality

Reading the African poplar audience is a complex task. The complexities are explainable. Francoise Bayart offers us a way of reading this audience in what he refers to as Africa's "ironic chorus." This description collectivizes the ironic location of this army of the abject that live dangerously in the tragic economy begotten by Africa's kleptomaniac leaders. In *The State in Africa: the Politics of the Belly*, Bayart describes the "public" as an "ironic chorus" (12). The performance of the ironic by this public is a critical one. It is also inevitable because it is a mode of survival as it is act of performing. It is a form of social and economic negotiation, a way of being for the vulnerable and weak. There are a number of reasons for this performance of the ironic but by far the main strategy is subversive in its interpretation of this political terrain and of governance. Its maps of engagement with social and political issues capture innovative ways of providing for the belly in difficult political situations and these "publics" do become the "popular audience" at very short notice as they do this. Deeply marginalized, the narrative options available to members of this public describes the phenomenal life that each member lives in this ironic sphere. As part of the world of the "ironic chorus," this category of the African audience is always on the lookout for creative ways out of the complex and tedious life that members live and the economic and cultural negotiations they perform traverse definable boundaries. In the realm of performative exchange between the narratives of debilitating lives and the strategies of circumventing the debilities perpetuated by the uncaring State, members often seek magical ways[8] out of mundane problems and mundane ways out of spiritual things. If political and economic powers are lost to this category of the popular audience, narrative power is not. Powerlessness in the roughly organized political and cultural spheres is converted into a peculiar narrative power in the realm of this existential disorder. What comes out of the various narrative acts of this ironic chorus is what we may refer to as "popular narratives." Often hiding under the subterfuge of abjectness, members of the popular audience negotiate and restate their desires, aspirations and dreams without the fear of institutional intrusion. This pragmatic method of telling the social and economic concerns of the abject gradually builds up into neighbourhood feelings, which then offers alternative means of survival for members in these popular neighbourhoods whose social and economic interests are often left unattended in the larger political dispensation of the State. These neighbourhood cells then inaugurate different kinds of economic and social belonging. As members re-think their places in the life they are forced to live, affiliation to specific neighbourhood communities become one of the crucial ways they define social belonging. In many African cities, this sense of belonging redraws the meaning of community, nation, nationalism and individuality in ways that inevitably signals the depletion of State as the platform for social and institutional order. Davis Hecht and Maliqalim Simone refer to these cultural and social formations as the "invisible governance, a frame of elliptical efforts that maintain competing agendas and aspirations" (13). It is in this zone of social activities that the public is transformed into the active *audience*. The audience that I refer to is not constituted as an *a priori* category but by the semantics of the peculiar needs of the moment, which are always but loosely inspired by social and economic contingencies. In other words, the newly constituted audience exists, as it were, in a flexible geography of desire. Proximity to scarce national resources is resoundingly absent to members of this audience, yet members always seek to attain that status of duplicitous politics even when they criticize the duplicity of the politics of the State. In many instances, this audience may give up specific class affiliations, education, age or gender differences for the purpose of a temporary "coming together" but it does not give up the aspiration of a social mobility that seek to replace or even come to the same economic status as the political ruling class, which is perceived as the stumbling block to its common welfare. This is one of the ways that members of this audience perform the helplessness of living in the world of "lottery existence." Popular video audience is clearly an example of this category of the African popular audience, which performs the "discontent" of Africa's postcoloniality. Part of the intention of this paper is to understand how and why Nollywood creates this sense of a community of suffering in the different sites of meeting.[9]

Street corner audiences in Lagos

Nollywood is the medium of the Nigerian city. It is indeed a cultural child of circumstances. Its sense of purpose is determined by the temperament of the city. It is a medium of the city. It is only a city like Lagos that could have engineered and nurtured its birth. Lagos, the birthplace of this phenomenon, is the quintessential postcolonial city. This city is heavy with its burden of the past but light-headed in its dizzy, if not boisterous, drive to look ahead. Its history is no less dramatic. Nesting rowdily on the Lagos Lagoon, and fed by the tidal uncertainties of the Atlantic Ocean, this "ocean-city" was once described as 'the malarial coast" by Eileen Thorpe.[10] But it has gone through a lot of changes since it was first made a crown colony of the British Empire in the 1860s. The trauma of colonial occupation and its aftermath; the repatriation of ex-slaves coming from as far away as Brazil and Cuba in the seventeenth and eighteenth century and the culturally diverse local population of the Lagos area, have all added colour to the social history of this community. Even today, Lagos exhibits the socio-psychological pathology of an ocean community that is always in search of itself. As an ocean community, its body, like it its history, remains fractured.

Lagos displays this fractured psychology in the cultural forms that it promotes and consumes. As a city, Lagos is loosely defined and like all postcolonial locations, both the built and dreamed environment display this fractured psychology. Framed on various notions of cultural *bricolage*, Lagos often welcomes the idea of change and mutation with a sense of a *déjà vu*. Always at war with itself, the cultural history of this city has been one of constant negotiations with itself and its parts. However, what marks Lagos as the quintessential postcolonial city is not so much the external history of colonial subjugation, and the resurgence of the cultural worth of the local population; rather, it is precisely its eccentricity, which is defined in its cultural and political renewals. Considered the "centre of excellence" in independent Nigeria, Lagos quickly established its status as the main city. In the realm of culture and the arts, it has always led the way and it has continued to do so because of the freedom it offers to everyone in it, especially to newcomers. Long before many of the communities in Nigeria truly got on the bandwagon of the so-called global village, Lagos had already established itself in the very nexus of that "village" as early as the late seventeenth century. As soon as its status was recognized as the crown colony, this city quickly attracted the good, the bad and the ugly; pastors and other men of God, sinners and madmen who, in search of the new freedom, were also searching for the will to overcome the malarial temperament of this city. By the late 1950s, Lagos was culturally positioned to lead the newly created nation in matters of culture, especially urban culture. It was here, in this ocean-community, that the experience of the first "magic lantern"[11] became a novelty that would stay on in the minds of Lagosians for a very long time. It was also here, more than half a century later that the energetic burst of cultural activities that led to the creation of Nollywood, one of Africa's most exuberant cinema cultures, was hatched.

The geography of Lagos is divided in two by the Lagoon; one affluent and the other not. The affluent neighbourhood is called Lagos Island. This is where all the embassies and foreign missions are located. The other part is called Lagos Mainland. It is the high density, low-income area of the city. On the Island, there is a noticeable lack of the proliferation of video parlours. There are hardly any sightings of "street audiences." Nonetheless, there is an impressive array of video stalls all over the Island. But activities in these video stalls are subdued. A lot more caution is observed in the blaring of music from loudspeakers in these stalls. A number of them have television screens facing the streets but there are hardly people in front of them. Once every while, street hawkers of sundry good and services come into view and then disappear. Men and women in business suits move briskly about. Most of them attached to business concerns with multi-national companies. In this part of town, the rich can afford to acquire the technology of video projection and so do not need the video parlours. Many of the video stalls located in this part of town mainly do the business of selling and renting video films and their poorly built structures add to the special colour of the city. In this part of town, the re-mapping of the visual and aural landscape of the city is as visible as it is in the other part of town. This visual alteration has also helped to create a sense of a local cultural form of expression that cannot be ignored. The exuberant presence of Nollywood in this part of town points to the fact that it reaches beyond its primary constituency of avid patrons—those from the bottom of the social and economic ladder in Nigeria. Yet, one could also argue that the re-mapping of the landscape in this part of Lagos, which the proliferation of video stalls instigates, shows how this local form disrupts the carefully planned world of this postcolonial city by the departed colonial government. Even if this re-mapping is not a conscious desire, the very act of mapping itself points to the ways that abjectness exercises power in the most opaque manner in this situations. Perhaps even more telling is the fact that the proliferation of these *ad hoc* viewing venues in Lagos is a clear indication of how, to quote Okwui et al., "the changes in the modern paradigm…challenge old colonial spatial design" as they "slowly began to lose their decisive functionalist parameters and became subordinated to the mutations wrought by new civic and urban culture" (15).

The experience of watching the character of "street corner" audiences was different in the Lagos Mainland area of Lagos. The common ground upon which these screening venues are recognized as viewing sites of the abject still remains the same in the case of Lagos Mainland. But on the Mainland, the proliferation of "street corner" audiences was much more apparent and obviously more widespread. One area of the Mainland where the proliferation of video stalls and "street corner" audiences was prominent is the notorious junction between Lawanson Road and Ojuelegba Road in the Surulere. Fela Anikulapo Kuti, the Afrobeat maestro, once described this junction as symptomatic of the chaos of Lagos in one of his popular songs. All day along and in all four sides of this junction, video stalls screen different kinds of video films. These screenings are done mostly in the evening when the sun has set and the atmosphere more tolerable for bystanders who casually stop for a while to enjoy the dramatic presentations coming out from television screens in the different stalls. During my visits to Lagos, there were always groups of people standing before these screens. They watched and talked animatedly about the visual world that unfolded before them. Like all "street corner" audiences, these meetings were very temporary. In all the times that I visited this area, there was no let up in the enthusiasm shown for popular video film.

In the Mainland part of the city of Lagos, video stalls do not need to be quiet. The video stalls were overly loud and nobody seemed to care. It was mostly in this part of the city that I observed clearly the character of the "street corner" audiences of Lagos, and the ways that members consume the cultural product of Nollywood. Unlike the report of the video film audience at the Warri video parlour, my report on the "street corner" audience in Lagos is rather indeterminate, a character which follows from the fluid nature of this audience. However, it is important to point out that in both sites of viewing, Nollywood and all that it stands for, clearly proclaims its importance in the life of the people—rich and poor. Perhaps, this is more so with those who live the abject debilities of Lagos and Warri.

Quite understandably, the audience of the video parlour is by far a more stable category of the street audience in Nollywood. While it shares a lot with "street corner" audiences, it is marked by the presence of a *place*. The physical space of the video parlour has a lot in common with the domestic sphere of video film spectatorship. If the extremely fluid nature of the "coming together" of "street corner" audiences makes it rather difficult to truly follow members of this audience through one or more screenings, this is not always the case with the audiences of specific video parlours. Video parlours are generally run for profit. Proprietors aim to keep the business going by providing some of the basic necessities such as electricity and the convenience of a permanent location. Nollywood's "street-corner" audiences do not have these luxuries. I will now discuss my experience of seeing one video film, specifically, *Domitilla*, in a video parlour located in a village at the outskirt of Warri.

In the Warri video parlour

Domitilla was released in 1997. By the standards of Nollywood, it was a huge box-office success. It was produced by DAAR Communication Ltd., Lagos and the story was written by Zeb Ejiro, a veteran in the video industry. The screenplay was by the late Ken Oghenejabor. The blurb on the jacket of *Domitilla* is as telling as the story of this prostitute girl is dramatic. The real drama of reading this video film should begin here. This dramatic blurb, which has a literary parallel in the blurbs of the Onitsha market pamphlets of the 1950s and 1960s, directs the attention of the reader to the main characters in the story that "had to make a living. And the business turned sour, [*sic*] just when they beat a retreat, she [*sic*] wasn't to know the worse is yet to come." *Domitilla* describes the story of Domitilla as "[c] ruel, gruesome, revealing the life of a prostitute." Domitilla's story is indeed a cruel one by all accounts, yet it is not so different from the many stories of the city in Nigeria, especially the city of Lagos, in which women are victimized and sometimes callously murdered in the streets. The story opens in the red-light district of Lagos. It is night. Domitilla is plucked out of the pack of girls waiting to "catch their moogu." She is beautiful. She is one with the street and the city and as she goes into conversation with the "potential client," we hear her speak the poetic Warri-pidgin. She leaves with the client once she determines that the price is right. Not long after, a pimp comes along, asking for Domie. He is told by one of the "good time girls" that Domie has just gone away with her "moogo," which is the pidgin word for a "fool." The pimp laments Domie's absence, saying she has missed out on the prize catch of the night, which the pimp describes as a "whitey," meaning a white client. The picture of Domitilla as a prostitute comes out quite clearly in these opening scenes.

As the narrative progresses, we notice that Domie is not only a "good time girl." She is also a working-class office girl. She does her day-job in a depressing office under a boss who is cruel. After work, Domitilla goes back to her lodging in a decrepit and squalid neighbourhood. She lives desperately. Saddened and carrying the burden of the family back in Warri, Domie constantly negotiates the needs of her family and her own in Lagos by selling her body for money to "men who want to play boys all over again." Domie sees a chance to hit it big. She meets a local politician in one of the parties she is invited to attend as "a good time girl." He is Chief Lawson, the rich and influential politician. At first, this is merely a meeting with one of her "moogu" but she soon falls in love and as she becomes emotionally involved for the first time in her life, she begins to nurse the possibility of "settling down" with the Chief. She is briskly serenaded as "the Greek Goddess" by Chief Lawson who is, according to one of the "girls," the "dream of every ashewo"[12] in Lagos. Her hope of settling down is short-lived. Domitilla's dream turns out to be one of the mirages of the city. In time, Chief Lawson's wife gets her revenge. Colluding with the steward employed by Chief Lawson to wait on the desires of his mistress, Mrs. Lawson poisons the glass of wine, which Chief Lawson drinks while visiting with Domitilla in her apartment. Chief Lawson dies from poisoning and all hell breaks loose. Domie is utterly confused. She runs into the waiting hands of priest who looks more like a *marabou* than a Christian priest. She is prayed for before she is taken away by the police and charged with murder. She appears in court a little later.

The lawyer who initially takes up the case is a complete imbecile, making way for brief moments of clowning in the court room. A second lawyer is hired by Domitilla's friends. She is a woman who has more than a professional stake in the case. She goes through every bit of the evidence of the case and when she discovers that Domie is pregnant for the late Chief Lawson, she makes capital of this point in the proceedings. However, the case turns around only when, under intense cross examination, the daughter of Chief Lawson owns up to knowing of the plot by her mother to kill Chief Lawson with the intention of framing Domitilla for the crime. Domitilla is freed of the charge and there is a huge uproar in the court-room from the friends and family of Domitilla. A second video film, *Domitilla 2* was made soon after, a gesture that is common in the industry.

The audience of the Warri video parlour has a lot in common with the "street corner" audiences that I observed at the Ojuelegba outpost in Lagos. One remarkable fact that came out during my experiences with the Warri audience is the empathic connection, which members established with the content of *Domitilla*. Like the members of the "street corner" audiences in Lagos, responses to the world of this video film came with a sense of familiarity with the story. The audience of the Warri video parlour responded to it as a story it already knows. From the discussions that went on in the "parlour," I noticed that the city was contracted as a place that has an overwhelming presence in the lives of members. There were persistent discussions relating to women and religion in the city. The overwhelming contention on the floor of the screenings was that religion was "a market"[13] and that, as a commercial enterprise, only those who can weather the storm of this highly competitive business are able and likely to profit from it. Weathering the storm also means the ability to engage in inordinate social and economic vices to get desired results, including ritual sacrifices involving human lives. This comment on religion must be seen in the context of the upsurge of dubious religious activities in the country at the time this film was made. Domitilla's dubious connection to the church and the comments that it elicited from members of this video parlour audience reveals the essence of the "lottery economy" economy in which Domitilla operates as a sex worker. This criticism of the church as an institution that lacks social and moral credibility was also linked to ideas of wealth accumulation in the society. Comments on the activities of churches (not just the church that is depicted in *Domitilla*) by members focused on the return of profit rather than on the glorious "return of Jesus Christ." The point of this discussion, which members hammered upon at some length, also stressed the morality of Domitilla and her flippant return to a church. Her dubious return to the church is further highlighted in the background of what members thought of as the "business" of the so-called prosperity gospel churches in Nigeria. However, at the other extreme, this audience was touched by the predicament of Domitilla. The attack on the duplicity of the church is constructed as a narrative of pity for those that these religious institutions prey on due to the inscrutability of the city. Domitilla is a fine example.

The ambivalent location of Domitilla as a "free woman" in the city was another flashpoint in the discussions. Needless to say, this aspect of the discussions went on during the screenings of the two films. It was energetic and boisterous. As the audience engaged the primary visual representation of Domitilla, the prostitute, a number of constructed texts jumped out of the primary visual text during this act of reading. There was no agreement on the moral status of Domitilla in society. She was constructed as a marginal figure and a plaything in the hands of the rich and powerful in the city. Some energy was spent talking about her marginal ethnicity in the larger configuration of the ethnic politics of the Nigerian city. Members drew attention to the very fact the Domie is from the Niger Delta, the rich oil region that constantly suffers social and economic neglect. Others questioned the sociology of the poverty of the Niger Delta that drove Domitilla to Lagos in the first place, and lamented the fate of ethnic minority groups in the power politics of resource control in the Nigerian Federation. What came out quite clearly in the ensuing discussions about the life of Domitilla was an obvious reaction to the marginalization of this section of the country. The feeling of intense anger and despair was obvious. It came from the very fact that members saw themselves as being cheated out of the wealth that is taken from their territory.

This reaction from the audience at the Warri viewing centre privileged an aspect of video spectatorship which I consider unique. The content of *Domitilla* was transformed into a platform of critical inquiry. Comments from this audience went outside the social and ethical references that this video film privileged. *Domitilla* inspired the criticism of the state and its system of governance, and the primary text was then construed as a "real story" in the same way that television soap opera operates as social barometers of the things that matter to its consumers. The reaction to the world of Domitilla became the basis of a social critique of governance and the "big men in Abuja." By engaging in this kind of interpretation of the video-ed world, members assigned to the filmed world real social equality to the text of the video film. I would argue that while the primary visual text was important in this critical engagement and indeed indispensable to the audience's performance of its own social reality, the critical note we ought to make of this is that members read from a marginal social and economic status as representatives of the ironic chorus. What was positive about this engagement though was that it forced members into a critical introspection of those things that matter to them but were not expressed in the so-called enlightened vehicles of public debates that are controlled by the state. The downside of this critical engagement would be that while it offered a sense of freedom for members to say what they want, this freedom was only a pyrrhic victory of some sort. There is little doubt that the phenomenon of the video parlour has opened up the spectrum of social debate to include some members of the abject section of the Nigerian society but the agency which the "freedom" of this venue offers is achieved only in the temporal constitution of that space of spectatorship. Even in the energetic but high digressional discussions that ensued at the Warri venue, popular agency can only be but temporary.

Ideas of the postcolonial city and the place of women in it were also largely articulated during the screening of *Domitilla*. Domitilla was the scapegoat, the victim of the nebulous city of Lagos. There was talk about the evil of the city, the evil of rich men who derive wealth and influence from using people's private body parts. As the energetic discussions around the issues of women and the city went on, a number of constructed texts erupted from the primary video text. Discussions around the evil of rich men in the city often veered far away from the ideas presented in the primary video text itself. Reference to the sales of body parts and how these body parts are transformed—or, if you will, alchemized—into money through magic found its way into the contending narratives emanating from the video primary text. Domitilla is connected to this ritual practice because she escapes being a victim of "ritual murder." Her unfortunate friend and colleague in the prostitution trade does not. She is killed in the attack by what the Nigerian print media has dubbed the "ritualist." Although there is hardly any aspect of the Domitilla story that is connected directly to this ritual practice, it serves as a flashpoint for the discussion of the inscrutable city of Lagos, which is constructed as a frightful place for women and the less privileged. The source of fascination with the urban text of missing body parts comes from the culture of video film itself. Since *Living in Bondage 1&2*, which was released in 1992 and 1993, this urban myth in Nigeria has become the stable of popular video culture itself, so that it is hardly conceivable to see any video film without some remote reference to it. *Living in Bondage* was the first big hit in the industry and not the first video film produced in Nigeria as Bond Emerua contends in the newly released documentary on Nollywood, *This is Nollywood*.[14] It was followed by *Glamour Girls 1&2*, and then *Ritual*. All three films were made by Chief Kenneth Nnebue. *Blood Money 1&2* reified this urban myth and concretized its place as part of the tentative sub-genre of the city video film. As part of this cultural backdrop, the Warri audience can only explain the sudden accumulation of wealth in the city from the perspective of "ritual murder" and the magical alchemy of body parts into paper money—local and foreign. In this conversation, members refer to the wealth that is generated from these ritual exercises as "blood money." For this audience then, the city is a place to be feared. But there was also the obvious and palpable acknowledgment of the paradoxical and enigmatic pull which the city exacts.

Reading the audience of popular video film

Focusing on the two spatial arenas where the audiences of Nollywood consume popular video film, I wish to draw a number of conclusions as a way of pointing to the importance of these sites of seeing and what it means to the study of African cinema and to African visual spectatorship in general. The conclusions that draw from my observations of the "street corner" audiences in Lagos and of the more stable video parlour audience in Warri can only be tentative. In the very act of engaging with these audiences as members divine their individual and collective places in the social and cultural debate in contemporary Nigeria, the most noticeable undercurrent is the pronouncement of their abject status. Members acutely play out the status of their ironic chorus in these viewing venues as well as their ironic ambition of becoming part of the corrupt ruling class, which Nollywood often critiques. As part of this ironic chorus, members are inevitably implicated in both the discourses of postcolonial cities and in the performance of the malcontent of their postcolonial modernity. From the sites of spectatorship to the performance of the reading of video films, the scholar of popular art is confronted with the difficulties of assigning absolute knowledge to both forms of performances in these sites of seeing. Yet, the bold presence of the abject debating abjectness is never lost to the scholar, nor is the valuable presence of the video medium in the lives of the abject. In this dialectics of performance and reading, it is the content of the video films that mattered and not the medium. This is the point that Bond Emerua, one of the directors of Nollywood, made obvious in *This is Nollywood.*

There are bold and obvious similarities between the audiences of the video parlour in Warri and that of the "street corner." Perhaps, the most obvious is that they are both defined by a strong desire by those left out of public narrative of life in Nigeria to be part of the story of the city and of the nation. A large chunk of the membership of the two audiences is also denied access as part of the hegemonic narrative put forward by the State. Lacking access to State controlled media, they turn to the video film. They give freely of their collective consent to use this medium as the alternative platform to achieve an alternative narrative goal. Clearly then, the history of the emergence of popular video film is connected to the deep-seated desire by this group of Nollywood consumers to have a voice in the social and cultural debates of the time, which is why they give their unprecedented support to the pioneers and pathfinders of Nollywood. It is this support that has sustained the industry thus far. It is no surprise therefore that the predominant theme of popular video film revolves around the stories of the city, especially stories about the inexplicable *magic* of the city. Membership of the "street corner" audiences in Lagos as well as those of the video parlour in Warri was fluid, very temporary, and indeterminate. Members appeared and disappeared as if by magic. While this special kind of meeting is important to the industry, my reading is that it is the possibilities that popular video films provide as a way of escape and a as a platform for critical judgment on social conditions that recommend the massive patronage, which Nollywood enjoys in these site of seeing. The geography of these meeting places also has a telling presence in the world of the city. The ubiquity of "street audiences" in cities and in rural Nigeria attests to the popularity of the medium. More importantly, it reshapes the aural and visual topography of the city as well as that of the rural areas. In the city, "street corner" sites of spectatorship admit of the flotsam and jetsam of society, and in the rural areas, video parlours admit the poor and young. By bringing this group of socially and economically marginal viewership into this social discursive formation, these sites of screening help the enhancement of the democratization of video stories in contemporary Nigeria. In a country where media ownership was, until recently, tightly under the hold of the State, this shift in the dispensation of and the engagement with public debates is significant, if not crucial. As social centres, "street corners" and video parlours provide alternatives to the orthodox space of cinematic spectatorship. While they announce the material poverty of its audiences, these venues are open and the debates that go on in them are unfettered, unrestrained, and sometime very vociferous. In the very short time that members come together to look at themselves through the mediatory lens of video films, these sites offered a world which is outside what the State configures for public consumption. Outside the influence of the State, they are able to see themselves differently and to rethink their places in the scheme of things. Mobile in space and in time, "street corner" and the video parlour audiences bring their abjectness to these sites where members play out their temporary will to speak about things that matter to them.

The one clear difference between the two posts of spectatorship is in the payment of entry fees. In the case of the "street corner," members are not charged any fees to see a video film and they do not have any influence over what is screened either. What is projected at any time is entirely left to the proprietor of the video stall. As venues for screening the latest video releases, proprietors know all too well the advantages of positioning television screens to face the streets. This positioning is also an advertisement strategy. It is a way of announcing the availability of new video releases. Conditioned by the exigencies of the street, members may respond to this videoed world in way that can spring cultural and political surprises.

Perhaps the most enduring conclusion that I draw from my observation of these "street audiences" is the way they force us to rethink the whole idea of spectatorship in Africa and the special uses of popular expressions such as the video film in Africa. Besides the remapping of the aural and physical landscape of the city, audiences of popular video films repeat for us the ways that the economics of spectatorship is defined as a strategic means of coming to terms with an abject status. My experience with audiences in Lagos and Warri point to the unique ways members of these marginal audiences see themselves and the world created about and for them by Nollywood. It also points to ways of understanding why and how members look beyond the images of the video films as they try to make meaning of the miseries in which they live. For the audiences of video films in Nigeria, the medium is more or less a mirror into two distinct but interrelated worlds: the real world in which they live out their ironic reality, and the wish-world that they seek to achieve within the magic of despair inscribed in the stories. The first of the two worlds is a painful one. The second world exists only as a dream but it is a dream world that reinforces the desire of this abject-audience to keep the narrative of social transformation and renewal on the narrative agenda. In the final analysis, both worlds are defined by the eccentricities of the city. It plays a very crucial role in determining how these audiences redraw the map of spectatorship. My experience with these audiences opened my eyes to the uniqueness of the social place that members inhabit as spectators in this cinema tradition and, as I reflect on these experiences, I could not help feeling that I do not agree with Anthony Kwame Appiah who argues that African popular arts "are not concerned with transcending, going beyond, coloniality" (348–352). My reading of these audiences *reading* video images clearly shows *why* and *how* these images function as active agents of the political economy of desire. In the end, it is not the medium or how it manipulates the stories that Nollywood tells that matter to the people who consume Nollywood. The focus is on the stories. The medium may be important but the stories are even more so. There is the need to study many more sites of viewing popular Africa.

Notes

1   Please see the program website <http://humanities.uwichill.edu.bb/
    filmfestival/2003/films/kelani&okomi.htm>.
2   This point is well made in two very influential essays dealing with popular
    arts in Africa. They include Anthony Kwame Appiah's "Is the Post-in
    Postmodernism the Post-in Postcolonialism" and Karin Barber's essay on the
    subject, "Popular Arts in Africa." The polyglot "man on the bicycle" example
    is the typical expression of popular arts in Africa.
3   This impression is very deeply etched in the careful reading of the text. It is
    most obvious in what Bond Emerua, a producer in Nollywood, has to say
    about this in the newly released-documentary film, *This is Nollywood*.
4   See the essay "Preliminary Note on An African Popular Art: The Video Film
    in Nigeria" *Voices: Wisconsin Review of African Literature*. 2 1999:51–69.
    See also "The Popular art of African Video-Film." *New York: New York*

Foundation for the Arts, 2001. (See the web site www.nyfa.org/fyi/fyi_summer2001.)

5   See Ebun Clark's study of the father of this theatre tradition, Hubert Ogunde, in her book, *Hubert Ogunde: The Making of Nigerian Theatre*. Biodun Jeyifo's *The Truthful Lie: Essays in Sociology of African Drama* is also a useful reference in this regard.

6   For a fuller and well-informed discussion of the transformation of Lagos in the 1970s into a huge "ghetto" of an army of squatters and the jobless, see Jeyifo.

7   Fees are usually very inexpensive by international standards but not by local standards. At the Warri video parlour, I paid N20 for one of the screenings, which translates to about US$0.16.

8   Achille Mbembe and Jean Comaroff and John L. Comaroff have provided telling manifestations of how African localities in the new millennium express the depressing psychosis of the magic of despair. In many African localities of the new millennium, "magic" is the buzz word, and anything and everything is linked to this word on the symbolic and realistic realms, with a result of what Jean Comaroff and John L. Comaroff describe as "lottery economy." In these localities, life itself becomes a lottery of some sort and magic, the catalyst of the lottery existence. See Mbembe's "African Modes of Self-Writing" and Jean Comaroff and John L. Comaroff's "Millennial Capitalism: First Thoughts on A Second Coming."

9   See Jean Comaroff and John L. Comaroff, "Millennial Capitalism: First Thoughts on a Second Coming." I draw the reader's attention to page 271. Their definition of this social and political existence fits well into the character of the audience of the video film. For instance, "lottery economy" is defined as the social and cultural zone of existence where, "life is assimilated to a game of chance, a lottery, in which the existential and temporal horizon is colonized by the immediate present and prosaic shot term calculation." This is also part of what defines the "ironicity" of the actions of members of the video audience that I mentioned earlier on in the body of this essay.

10 See Eileen Thorpe, *A Ladder of Bone: The Birth of Modem Nigeria from 1853 to Independence*, Ibadan: Spectrum Books, 2002.

11 See the account of the first screening of documentary shorts in Alfred Opubor et al., *The Growth and Development of the Film Industry in Nigeria* (2–4). It is reported that the first screening was done in 1904 at the Glover Memorial Hall, which was located in the Lagos Island area of the city. The Alake of Abeokuta was said to have been in attendance.

12 This is the pidgin word for a prostitute. Its origin may have come from the Yoruba language but it has now gained currency as an urban usage.

13 This is another pidgin expression that refers to the commercialism of the church or that sees the church as business.

14 Released in 2007, this documentary film is one in the plethora of documentary films that have recently focused on the Nollywood phenomenon. Bond Emerua, who is a very significant director in Nollywood, gives the impression that *Living in Bondage*, one of the classics to come out of Nollywood, is the first video film produced in the industry. This is not quite the case. There is ample evidence to suggest that Chief Kenneth Nnebue, who is obviously the "father" of Nollywood, had sponsored some Yoruba video filmmakers before he ventured into making *Living in Bondage*. See Emerua, *This is Nollywood*.

Works Cited

Appiah, Kwame Anthony. "Is the Post-in Postmodernism the Post-in Postcolonial." *Critical Inquiry*. 17.2 (Winter 1991): 336–357

Barber, Karin. "Preliminary Notes on the Audience in Africa." *Africa*. 16.3 (1997): 347–362.

Barber, Karin. "Views from the Field: An Introduction." *Readings in African Popular Culture*. Ed. Karin Barber. Indiana and Oxford: Indiana University Press, 1997: 1–10.

Barrot, Pierre. "Censor, Lies and Video: 'Making Sure We Do Not See the Blood.'" *ITPANNEWS*. 12/6 (2004): 6.

Bayart, Jean-Françoise. *The State in Africa: The Politics of the Belly*. Legman: London, 1993.

Clark, Ebun. *Hubert Ogunde: The Making of Nigerian Theatre*. Oxford: Oxford University Press, 1970.

Comaroff, Jean and John L. Comaroff. "Millennial Capitalism: First Thought on a Second Coming." *Public Culture*. 12.2 (2002): 291–343.

Enwezor, Okwiu et al. "Introduction." *Under Siege: Four African Cities-Freetown, Johannesburg, Kinshasa, Lagos*. Kasel, Germany: Hatje Cantz, 2002: 13–20.

Forster, Till. "Seeing Visual Images: Video Technology and Ancestor Worship in West Africa. Unpublished presentation delivered at the Video Workshop, University of Bayreuth. June 7–9, 2001.

Gikandi, Simon. "Reason, Modernity and the African Crisis." *African Modernities*. Ed. Jan-Georg Deutsch, Peter Probst and Heike Schmidt. New Hampshire and Oxford: Heinemann and James Curry, 2002: 135–157.

Gottesman, Ronald. "Film Parody: An Immodest Proposal." *Quarterly Review of Film and Video*. 12 (1990): 1–2.

Hetch, David and Maliqalim Simone. *Invisible Governance: The Art of African Micropolitics*. New York: Automedia, 1994.

Jeyifo, 'Biodun. *The Truthful Lie: Essays in the Sociology of African Literature*. London: Bacon Books, 1985.

Leys, Colin. "Confronting the African Tragedy." *New Left Review*. 204 (March/April, 1991): 33–47.

Mbembe, Achille. "African Modes of Self-Writing." Trans. Steven Randall. *Public Culture*. 14.1 (2002): 239–273.

Okome, Onookome. "Preliminary Notes on an African Popular Art: The Video Film in Nigeria." *Voices: Wisconsin Review of African Literature* 2 (1999): 51–69.

Opubor, Alfred E., Onuora E. Nweneli and O. Oreh (Ed). *The Development and Growth of the Film Industry in Nigeria*. Lagos: Third Press International, 1979.

Powdermaker, Hortense. *The Dream Factory: An Anthropologist Looks at the Movie-Makers*. Boston, MA: Little, Brown and Co., 1950.

Thorpe, Eileen. *A Ladder of Bones: The Birth of Modern Nigeria from 1853 to Independence*. Ibadan: Spectrum Books, 2002.

Videography

Domitilla 1. 120min; color, English; Story by Zeb Ejiro. Screenplay Ken Oghenejabor. Prod. DAAR Communication, Ltd, Lagos, VHS. DAAR Communication, 1997.

Domitilla 2. 130min.; color, English. Story by Zeb Ejiro. Screenplay Ken Oghenejabor. Prod. DAAR Communication, Ltd, Lagos. VHS. DAAR Communication 1997.

Glamour Girls 1. 125 min.; color, English; Screenplay Kenneth Nnebue. Prod. NEK Video Link. VHS. Infinity Merchants, Onitsha/NEK Video Links, 1994.

Glamour Girls 2. 160min.; color, English. Screenplay Kenneth Nnebue. Prod. NEK Video Link. VHS. Infinity Merchants, Onitsha/NEK Video Links, 1994.

Living in Bondage 1. 140 min.; color; Igbo (subtitle English); Script Kenneth Nnebue; Prod. NEK Video Links. VHS. NEK Video Link, 1992.

Living in Bondage 2. 120min.; color; Igbo (subtitle English). Script Kenneth Nnebue. Prod. NEK Video Links. VHS. NEK Video Links, 1992.

This is Nollywood. 56min, color. Dir. Franco Sacchi and Robert Caputo. Prod. CDIA and Eureka Films. Ltd. DVD. California Newsreel, 2007.

CHAPTER THIRTY-THREE

"Culture: Intercom" and Expanded Cinema: A Proposal and Manifesto

Stan VanDerBeek

It is imperative that we quickly find some way for the level of world understanding to rise to a new human scale. This scale is the world. The risks are the life or death of this world. Man is running the machines of his own invention, while the machine that is man runs the risk of running wild. Technological research, development, and involvement have almost completely outdistanced our emotional and socio-"logical" comprehension. It is imperative that every member of the world community join the twentieth century as quickly as possible. Technical power and cultural "over-reach" are placing the fulcrum of man's intelligence so far outside himself, so quickly, that he cannot judge the results of his acts before he commits them. The process of life as an experiment on earth has never been made clearer. Man does not have time to talk to himself, man does not have means to talk to other men—the world hangs by a thread of verbs and nouns. It is imperative that the world's artists invent a non-verbal international language.

I propose the following:

That immediate research begin[s] on the possibility of a picture-language based on motion pictures.

That we combine audio-visual devices into an educational tool: an experience machine or "culture-intercom."

That audio-visual research centers be established on an international scale to explore the existing audio-visual devices and procedures, develop new image-making devices, and store and transfer image materials, motion pictures, television, computers, video-tape, etc.

That artists be trained on an international basis in the use of these image tools.

That prototype theatres, called "Movie-Dromes," be developed immediately, incorporating the use of such projection hardware.

I shall call these prototype presentations: "Movie-Murals," "Ethos-Cinema," "Newsreel of Dreams," "Feedback," "Image Libraries."

The "movie-drome" would operate as follows: In a spherical dome, simultaneous images of all sorts would be projected on the entire dome-screen. The audience lies down at the outer edge of the dome, feet toward the center; thus almost the complete field of view is taken up by the dome-screen. Thousands of images would be projected on this screen.

This image-flow could be compared to the "collage" form of the newspaper, or the three ring circus (both of which suffuse the audience with an abundance of facts and data). The audience takes what it can or wants from the presentation and makes its own conclusions. Each member of the audience will build his own references and realizations from the image-flow.

A particular example: an hour-long presentation using all sorts of multiplex images, depicting western civilization since the time of the Egyptians to the present through a rapid panoply of graphics and light calling upon thousands of images, both still and in motion, with appropriate "sound-images." The last three thousand years of western life would be compressed into such an aspect ratio that the audience could grasp the flow of man, time, and forms of life that has led us up to this very moment, using the past and immediate present to help realize the likely future.

Endless filmic and imagistic variations of this idea are possible in science, math, geography, art, poetry, dance, biology, etc. This idea could be endlessly varied by each culture group and nationality that took it on as a project, and presented in turn to other groups.

The purpose and effect of such image-flow and image density (also to be called "visual velocity") are both to deal with logical understanding and to penetrate to unconscious levels, to reach for the emotional denominator of all men, the non-verbal basis of human life, thought, and understanding, and to inspire all men to goodwill and "inter-and intro-realization." When I talk of the movie-dromes as image libraries, it is understood that techniques such as video tape and computer inter-play would be used and thus they would be real communication and storage centers. Each dome could receive its images by satellite from a worldwide library source, store them, and program a feedback presentation to the local community. "Intra-communitronics," or dialogues with other centers, would be likely, and instant reference material via transmission television and telephone could be called for and received at 186,000 mps from anywhere in the world. Thus I call this presentation a "newsreel of ideas, of dreams, a movie-mural, a kinetic-library, a culture de-compression chamber, a culture-intercom." My concept is in effect the maximum use of the information devices that we now have at our disposal.

If an individual is exposed to an overwhelming information experience, it might be possible to re-order the structure of motion pictures as we know them. Cinema would become a "performing" art and image library. Such centers would have artists in residence who will orchestrate the image material at their disposal, integrating it with live actors and performers, leading to a totally new international art cinema form. In probing for the "emotional denominator," it would be possible by the visual "power" of such a presentation to "reach" any age or culture group regardless of background. There are an estimated 700 million people who are unlettered in the world: we have no time to lose or miscalculate.

CHAPTER THIRTY-FOUR

The Aesthetics of the Arena: Live and Recorded

Robert Edgar

Introduction

The physical space of the arena confers a sense of legitimacy on the performer/s which is both at one with and at odds with the nature of economic success. The intimate venue is the preserve of the few or rather the deceit of the many, as evidenced by the number of people who claim to have been present at the infamous Sex Pistols gig at the Manchester Free Trade Hall in 1976.[1]

The arena thus provides a space for the majority to have access to the performer/s who can command this kind of space. This chapter explores the nature of aesthetic authenticity as the defining factor in the relationship between audience and performer/s which, while evident in the smaller venue, is legitimized by an appearance in the arena as a site of 'success' and mass appeal. Furthermore, this analysis identifies the recorded arena concert as an aesthetic entity in its own right, rather than being simply a recording of a 'legitimate' performance. In this sense, this chapter argues, the arena concert film cannot be understood in straightforward postmodern terms; it is not a copy without an original, it is the original.

The topography of the arena

The arena is a simple space to map out, and while there are differences between different arenas in terms of size and seating, such arenas remain fundamentally the same. The audience is largely distant from the performer/s, but sit or stand looking at one central staging area as often flanked by screens. And, while occasionally there may be a thrust or curtain stage, this is by no means the norm. This arrangement is no different to the smaller and more intimate venue; an equivalent staging area often exists with an audience facing forward in ranks. Often the real difference is in the repurposing of the arena venue, and its potential for rearrangements: transforming it from one thing to the next. This quantitative difference in physical space between the arena and the smaller venue of course allows for a different kind of access to the performer, and a different kind of access to the show. The smaller venue suggests intimacy, although access to the performer is still limited. In fact proximity, rather than access, is provided by the space—but there is a conceptual conflation of the two. While the pleasure inherent in proximity should not be underestimated, there is, however, an inherent paradox in this. The smaller venue allows for proximity to the performer, but by virtue of seeing this performer in such a setting, the performer is effectively of a different standing to the act that can command an arena.

An analysis of topography is not limited to discussion of physical space; this would be to negate a large part of the experience of the concert event. More difficult to identify is the semiotic space that the arena occupies and confers. By this I mean the process of signification that occurs from the recognition and unification of multiple signifiers. To borrow from Christian Metz, in developing an understanding of the channels of communication of the arena, it would prove useful to provide a list of signifiers that are allowed, in part by the architecture of the arena itself. Metz identifies: 1, The Visual Image; 2, Print and other Graphics; 3, Speech; 4, Music; 5, Noise (SFX) (see Metz 1974). Without question there are expectations held by an audience before they arrive at the venue, and these are the expectations that have to factor in shaping the experience. But that experience itself can be broken down into several strands, or 'channels of communication', that make up the arena event:

The Arena Concert Channels of Communication:

- The performer/s
- The ticket (real or virtual)/Wristband
- The entrance lobby/stairwells
- Video screens plus what then appears on the screens
- Specifics of staging
- Support bands
- Other visual FX
- Walk-in music

- Support and guest performer/s (playing with the main performer/s)
- Merchandise
- 'Unofficial channels' including audience costume, social media, etc.

The physical environment then provides the parameters of meaning and the individual channels of communication become unified within its walls. What is significant is that even at the base level of signification the band/performer is only one element of the communication in operation. But, in similar fashion to Metz's prioritization of the visual image in cinema, the band/performer, it must be argued, find themselves assuming just such a priority in these channels. (And they also have an extra-'textual' function in that they are known about prior to the concert.) Many of these facets of the performance could apply to live events in other venues but only acts of a certain stature will play an arena, and in these terms the space itself functions like a genre in framing certain expectations which are met, or not. The physical space of the arena thus acts like a cinemascope screen; we are free to look wherever we want but everything within our gaze is part of the performance. Part of the communicative dimension of the space is in its physical shape and size—a 'channel' not afforded to the recorded medium. However, in terms of a process of signification, the smaller venue may have many of these elements as well.

On the part of the audience there is inevitably knowledge of a band prior to seeing them on stage, and there will be an aesthetic on entering which frames the experience, and there will be walk-in music, and so on. The difference between the general run of live popular music events as they have occurred and the relatively new phenomenon of the multimedia-heavy arena concert is the scale of that which happens on the stage. And yet, nominally, the performance is more about the music and the band than the show. This suggests that the simple process of signification in itself is not enough in terms of theorizing arena concerts. That process provides a framework to consider the elements of the concert but is not sufficiently wide-ranging, and so its results fall short of a definitive status and engender further questions of an aesthetic response to arena and the performer/s who work in them.

The mediated arena

Mediation as a concept is not as simple as the idea of the recording of an event. The mediation of an arena concert is undertaken by the business machine that surrounds performer/s. This evidences important questions about the economic pressure of the arena concert tour; a concert is inevitably part of a tour and has to be seen by many people. The recent tour of Jeff Wayne's 1978 *The War of the Worlds*, that landed at the Leeds First Direct Arena, was witnessed on one night (6 December 2014) by some

13,500 people, with the venue sold out. However, this mass was only a fraction of those who would see the show on tour, which took in another seventeen venues in the UK alone. And this is, of course, only the most recent incarnation of a show which has previously been seen by countless thousands, with only minor variations in performance; your age dictates whether you see/didn't see Richard Burton or Liam Neeson, Justin Hayward or Jason Donovan. The subsequent recording of the live event is intended to meet the needs of those who went to the concert, those who couldn't get to the concert and those who would wish to revisit the performance. The event is at once a kinetic act which, while rehearsed and polished to the nth degree, is transient. The performance is also an advert for a DVD/download, as well as the t-shirt and the album, and all the previous albums.[2]

The nature of contemporary mediated performance has been theoretically undercut by the democratization of media—by the ability we have to record the event ourselves. The act of recording on a mobile phone is of a different order to the concert film; the pushing and shoving of a small venue allows for the aesthetic of the venue to be captured on the device, as countless YouTube bootlegs attest. This focus is something that cannot occur in the arena. If the vantage point or zoom setting is up close, then all that might be captured is an extreme high angle shot of Sting's knee or The Edge's digital delay pedal; to be at the back of a raked seating bank captures the reality of the arena venue but also the feeling that you are watching ants on the stage. What tends to be captured in this instance is the video screen: a video of a video of something that might be happening on stage. Watching through screens is part of the act of viewing, and the sight of the mobile phone is now quite normal in all venues. It is the universal presence of this mode of recording that further legitimizes the arena concert film as being of a different order.

The crucial facets of the arena concert film arise partly from the geography that defines the film, and partly the perceived experience that the film captures, but also from the fact that someone else has recorded this event—a professional, and not a fan lost in the audience. This dynamic is immediately apparent in the arena concert film *Who Put The 'M' in Manchester?* (Bucky Fukumoto, 2005), documenting Morrissey's 'homecoming' Manchester Arena concert of 2004, on the occasion of his birthday. The film opens with a close-up of a Morrissey tattoo, followed by a pan up the arm to the interview subject, an emotional fan, standing outside the entrance to the arena itself ('He's always meant the world to me...We came from California, we flew all the way here from San Diego, me and my girlfriend, and we're so happy to be here. We know that we just couldn't miss this day...Nothing can beat this day.'), and then to shots of the city and locale, and news report-like footage of fans queuing and finally to Establish Shots from the back of the arena as Morrissey enters. This smooth reportage, melding witnesses and event, the intimate with the enormous, provides legitimacy to the recording, as sanctioned and conferred by the band, by the venue and by the fact that someone deemed that event and that moment in time to be captured, and so employed a crew of professional film-makers to do so. This furthers the sense of a sociocultural value to what is in essence a product for sale, 'just' a commodity. This is the difficult irony inherent, then, in Peter Gabriel's talk of Steve Biko's fate as intrinsic to his concert and artistic formation and the wider agency of popular music, or Bono bemoaning the plight of the Global South, a trait now inseparable from his public persona. At the end of this process is sales and dissemination: both are simply paid for such proclamations. Thus worthy proclamation and tawdry promotion shade into one another.

There are then differing levels of mediation, from the 'unofficial' footage of the moment in which the audience member captures a performance 'as it happens' to the professional and 'official' reconstruction of the event for commercial release. But in whatever form it may take, mediation of the live concert occurs at a communicative level (the meaning imbued by the band being in that space) and through the nature of the recording (the spatio-temporal facet of the recording). The archived recording of the arena concert then functions as a separate artefact, to be enjoyed/utilized/cherished later—and, perhaps once uploaded onto the Internet, forever. The professional recording and the fan-filmed video both function as ways of shaping memory rather than capturing a moment in time. The fan video is the personal memory, even when posted to a public forum like Vimeo or YouTube. This is 'as it was seen by me'. The official arena concert recording is effectively the public face of the band: 'as it is meant to be seen'. The authorized view of the band thus functions as (or, more accurately, aspires to) collective memory. It is the single source which is then hyped and advertised, is associated with an album, which appears on broadcast television, and which is timeless and repetitive—becoming, eventually, the only available document of that performer's moment in history. And even the performer begins to find that the official narrative is, somehow, incredible:

> Meanwhile, somehow alive, I am New York's 'hottest ticket', as a stinky and steamy July brings me to the [Madison Square] Garden's vast and lavish dressing rooms. I sit by a grand piano awaiting the evening's call-time…I am afforded all of the luxuries and attention and private bathrooms where Elvis Presley had soaked before me, and as I lower myself onto the very toilet that where Elvis had no doubt whistled away the call of nature, I wonder how all of this could possibly be, yet at the same time I am confused by its naturalness and its *right* to be. (Morrissey 2013, 192)

The arena stands as different to other forms of concert: the venue is, as it were, as big as the band (in size, if not always in name). And there is a particular cultural cache associated with venues such as Madison Square Garden. But these venues are few in number. For other sites of performance, particularly the open-air festival, the performance is limited by the available geography of the layout, and the available technology in the field (reference pretty much any headline act on the Glastonbury main stage, with its vast hinterland of massed audiences, for whom the video screens are the only access to the event). Other events such as Live Aid venues, in 1985, presented similar problems for bands. Such sites allow the artists to perform but they don't allow them the control over their performance that the arena affords. In these terms the festival field, the open air stadium or the small dub venue function in the same way, where the performance is central. In creating a visual recording of the arena concert—now pretty much de rigueur for all arena world tours—this level of control is vital, and the opportunity to evidence the full nature of the show via showing such control is crucial. This suggests a conceptual relationship between the arena, as a venue, and the recording that happens therein. However, this relationship is a problematic idea in respect of the concert film, and to suggest that the concert film is simply a recording of an event is to negate its existence as an aesthetic object distinct to the performance to which it is perceived to relate.

The arena concert instinct

In *The Art Instinct*, Denis Dutton outlined his view of evolutionary aesthetics. In part, this approach takes a view on art (and in this case the concept he develops is being applied to the arena concert as such a form of 'art') which stands as separate from the ideological or cultural analysis of music. Dutton identifies twelve potential functions of the object in respect of artistic status, which Torres (2010) lists as:

Direct pleasure

Skill and virtuosity

Style

Novelty and creativity

Criticism

Representation

Special Focus

Expressive Individuality

Emotional Saturation

Intellectual Challenge

Art traditions and Institutions

Imaginative Experience

The tradition of assessing, for instance, subcultures and music, is well established, and there have to be enough reminiscences, academic texts, and documentaries on the importance of, say, punk rock and its contexts (i.e. its times and places). In terms of the present discussion, it can be said that what popular music allows for is an established analysis of music/ image/ performance as in unity—that is, with all the elements of style and performance and musicality as integrated. It is in this unity, and in the creation of the arena concert film, that it is possible to see direct connections with Dutton's perspective on the development of the aesthetic object.

There is something fundamentally specific about the arena and the function that environment serves. This specificity is in relation to the sense of a form of grandeur—in a comparable way in which there is 'gritty' legitimacy conferred on an artist exhibiting in a pop-up gallery, for a performer playing music in CBGBs in New York, King Tut's Wah-Wah Hut in Glasgow or even the Adelphi on DeGrey Street in Hull. The arena functions as a national gallery might; a sense of heightened status conferred by the exalted environment. And with this comes the placing of a set of artistic values on the performer/s. This is different from the cultural capital a band may or may not have and, paradoxically, may be inversely proportionate to their critical appeal (as with Justin Bieber's 2012 Believe tour for instance, in which the massed fans seemed to wrong-foot the dismissive critics). The very status, as 'artist' or 'artists' (indeed the very term: as opposed to 'band' or 'group' or 'singer'), is enhanced by the arena venue. This seems to be a fact not lost on Morrissey: the poster of his 2014 tour of North America pronounced him playing venues such as the Barclays Center with Sir Cliff Richard and the Los Angeles Sports Arena with Sir Tom Jones while Moz, sporting a pinstriped suit, leans casually on an alabaster statue. Morrissey is no longer toying with distinctions between different levels of aesthetic value (one thinks of his idiosyncratic engagements with 'low culture' across the 1990s): he is playing arenas, and this is, self-consciously, an 'event', and he is performing as a work of art.[3]

This is a performance that is understood to have no intrinsic value other than as artistic object, and in fact it may hold back the evolution of the form.[4] Dutton's consideration of the nature of the aesthetic object is one that looks to 'skill, style and a sense of accomplishment—[as those] values we admire in art. It is human intelligence and creativity that transforms appealing landscape scenes and plot outlines into works of painterly or literary art' (Dutton 2010, 136). And this is what Morrissey achieves in composite fashion. He himself precedes the event with a body of work (songs, performance and legend) and this becomes part of the arena performance. This is no different from Jack White at the Leeds First Direct Arena in November 2014: blues heritage and indie superhero here unify in a performance that is predicated on knowledge and understanding of both of these aspects from the audience. And the fact that this tour only took in four UK venues forces the audience to travel to stare in awe at this particular work of art (possibly in the same way that people travel to the Louvre and stare at the Mona Lisa, just to say they have); enjoying the performer's work may be secondary. However, this is to focus on the live performance and it is noteworthy that these performers often try to ban the recording of their performances, even on mobile devices (as with Prince's UK tour in 2014)—thus the (enforced) mystique of the transitory performance remains. Until, of course, the official recording is released for sale.

The arena concert film: Even better than the real thing

To view an arena concert film is not, of course, to view a concert. It is not even to view the recording of a concert. To risk a tautology: to view an arena concert film is to view an arena concert film. And to view one as 'original' and the other as a 'fake' is, in Jean Baudrillard's terms (1994), a fallacy; to read the recording of the arena concert as a simulation is to fail to recognize the separate and distinct function it serves. The arena concert film is not a facet of the hyperreal, in being an ontologically questionable copy of something authentic—a process of reproduction which positions the concert itself as the 'original'. Indeed, the notion of the original is not as straightforward as the existence of the one Mona Lisa: the arena concert film captures one concert of many in a tour, or assembles bits of each as blended into one. The sense of one point of origin begins to slip away, and so this line of argument is therefore of negligible use. The arena concert film is an object in its own right and the recording of the event highlights it as an artefact of a different order. The concert film functions in addition to and separate to the physical performance, and is a wholly different aesthetic object. In *The Critique of Pure Reason* (1781/1787), Kant observes:

> When we say that the intuition of external objects, and also the self-intuition of the subject, represent both, objects and subjects, in space and time, as they affect our senses, that is, as they appear—this is by no means equivalent to asserting that these objects are mere illusory appearances. For when we speak of things as phenomena, the objects, nay, even the properties which we ascribe to them, are looked upon as really given: only that, in so far as this or that property depends upon the mode of intuition of the subject, in the relation of the given object to the subject, the object as phenomenon is to be distinguished from the object as a thing in itself. (Kant 1993, 66)

In reductionist terms, a useful distinction here arises: the object as phenomenon (the live concert), and the object-in-itself (the live concert film). And the relationship between the two is muddied by a series of perceptions and values imparted by the concert-goer/film-watcher.[5] And these values, as I've argued here, predate the live event. Thus, in aesthetic terms, the arena concert film is predicated on sociocultural knowledge of the performer/s and the ritual of the arena performance, despite the subtle differences that might exist. The dependence of the arena concert film on a sense of a veracity of reportage is predicated on the perception of the performance.

There is a clear facet to the recognition of the concert film being of a wholly different order to the experience of the live concert itself. The camera allows access that an audience would have otherwise missed. In an age of digital recordings of concerts presented in 3D on IMAX screens, this access can best be described as forensic. The sensory overload associated with the live experience in the arena space is replaced by the clarity of the recording, and unimpeded vision. However, this wholly different order is about more than this; it is about a sense of authenticity as endowed by the recording itself. The film of the event is not a record of something which is understood to be authentic or legitimate. The arena is already a space where the performer is distant, and thus both removed and objectified. It is a space where the event is already lacking when compared to the concert film, and yet the space is the space of this event (it allows it, and it houses it), so both of these matters occur at the same time. The recording of the event is more than a record of something that happened and was witnessed by others. It is an aesthetic object in its own right, and one which serves a social function in which a unity of audience and performer are the essence. To refer to the arena concert film as an artefact would be to imply it is in existence as a result of a preceding concert or tour. This is true in a literal sense, that one object could not exist without the other, but this is a necessity of production rather than an influence on viewing. In a fiction film it is essential that actors are sought, scripts finished, locations dressed and so on. All of this work is hidden and it is better that an audience doesn't know about this so that the object stands in its own right. The same is true of the concert video; confusion between forms may exist where there is a use/ creation of a sense of preparation for a performance, or direct interaction with the audience. These are constructions or selections and are established to give the illusion of a connection to a 'real' event when this is forever absent—it has to be as the arena concert film is of a different aesthetic order.

Dutton identifies the difference between nominal and expressive authenticity in respect of an audience's aesthetic appreciation of an event. The sense of nominal authenticity is conferred on a performance by the presence of the performer/group; this suggests an intention and that there is provenance to the work. In these terms the intention is to perform for an audience and the provenance is the visual evidence that an event took place, even though the film doesn't provide connection to that event. A sense of expressive authenticity is conferred by an individual witnessing that performance. Audiences, even on a large-scale arena world tour, are limited and access to the concert and thus the experience of the performance is also limited. The recording of the event therefore serves a second-level aesthetic function, in that the image of the performance and the audience witnessing that performance become one unified object, sutured together, and this in turn represents an expressive authenticity. This is to suggest that the earlier identification of the cinema screen in a semiotic sense (i.e. the use of semiotics in terms of the analysis of cinema) collapses in the wake of the aesthetic function of the recorded artefact. Or, put another way: a semiotic consideration provides a viable method of analysing how meaning is communicated, but it does not capture the experience of viewing a concert film. It is in the viewing of the concert film that expressive authenticity is conferred but the perception of it existing within the film means it remains as nominally authentic.

In Dutton's terms, evolutionary aesthetics allows for the consideration of different acts and the qualities they embody for an audience and it is these qualities that further confer a sense of authenticity for and of a recording. This is the case after the passage of time or after a group has disbanded or a performer has died. Bands such as Dire Straits (for *Alchemy: Dire Straits Live*, directed by Peter Sinclair and first released in 1984) or Queen (for the film of the 1986 performance *Queen at Wembley*, directed by Gavin Taylor and first released in 1990) have slipped in and out of public favour. The music may not necessarily be enjoyed, or even liked. But the close-ups of Mark Knopfler's virtuoso guitar playing, or Freddie Mercury's showmanship, are respected. In these terms, the aesthetic authenticity of the whole remains intact.

The question of reception and aesthetic appreciation can be interrupted, or even overwhelmed, by a difference in temporal location. That is, years later we may find things funny when they were supposed to be deadly serious. Thus there is a fracturing of the authentic: we can see the mechanics of the performance, as if suddenly revealed in isolation, and this shatters the unity of the whole. Nowhere is this more evident than in *Peter Gabriel: Live in Athens* (Michael Chapman, 1987). There is pomposity in the performance which is accentuated by the production values, and an 'excessive' over-choreography; these risible qualities in the film transcend the performance of the songs. A live album version would stand as another aesthetic object and, blind to the 1987 performance, would probably work. As it is, the negotiation of the status of the arena has an effect which subsumes the music and negates its positive qualities. The film is, in theory, underscored by the aesthetic quality provided by Michael Chapman and the fact that the executive producer is Martin Scorsese. It is undeniable that there are high production values, and many people may enjoy the music, but together they lack the authenticity required of the artistic artefact. In this example there is a loss of authenticity in respect of a perceived live event, and more particularly a sense of fakery as a concert film: 'Forgery and other forms of fakery in the arts misrepresent the nature of the performance and so misrepresent achievement' (Dutton 2010, 187). The status of the authentic is never fully conferred on *Peter Gabriel: Live in Athens* where the performance loses its reference to the environment and to the audience. In fact the 'performance' seems wholly out of context for an arena venue—an irony when compared to the theatrics of Gabriel's earlier stage endeavours, particularly with Genesis. The result is that concert film creates its own signifiers which do not relate to the arena concert or the concert film; Tony Levin's coat has a lot to answer for. The presence of the audience in an arena concert film remains as a vital aspect for the film's viewing audience. The presence of the audience signifies a liveness and kineticism (in a perceived original) and ensures the perceived connection to the live event; *Live in Athens* focuses attention on the performers and while an audience are clearly there (we glimpse them and can hear some cheers) they fail to be referenced by the performers, or the performance, in the way we might expect from a live performance— and certainly not integrated in the way that we see in other arena concert films. This further fractures a sense of authenticity and makes the live performance look fake, and this perception of forgery then extends to the film. While one would be tempted to look to Brecht's 'Alienation' technique, in terms of an aesthetic discourse that reveals its own workings (consciously or otherwise), and contrast this favourably with the sutured 'Spectacle' that Debord diagnoses [...], a more useful comparison can be made with film critic and painter Manny Farber's 1962 dichotomy of 'white elephant art' and 'termite art' (1998, 134–144). The former is self-consciously important, hubristic and bloated, and essentially redundant (and so, for Farber, fairly natural for Hollywood film-making of certain periods). The latter holds no direct claims to importance or artistic integrity but, having adopted a given vernacular at the outset, begins to subvert meaning, usurp expectations, derail narrative and so burrows into the substance of (and from there destabilizes) the expected discourse. For Farber, such 'termite' artistic strategies were often and intriguingly present in film noir and Hollywood B-movies. A termite art in the arena concert film would seem to need the film to be achieved on its own grounds: acknowledging, at the outset, a need to construct a language that is self-contained and exploratory of this new form of film, and not aggrandizing and 'cashing in on' the legitimacy that the arena space confers on the performer. The standing of Jonathan Demme's *Stop Making Sense* (1984) is as a film, along with it being a film of a concert, as well being a film of the group Talking Heads, and it has equal levels of nominal and expressive authenticity. Here the status of the film as an object in its own right is more fully realized. The performer and the audience fuse into one and this renders the film as nominally authentic in its aesthetic function. The person witnessing the performance is the person at the cinema/at home who thus confers the expressive authentic aesthetic function. This is different from the simple semiotic reception of a series of signifiers. The function is the conferment of a sense of beauty which, in terms of pop/rock music, is essentially about witnessing something that stands in its own right.

Notes

1 Indeed, the contested nature of this specific has become the subject of a book in itself—*I Swear I Was There*; see Nolan (2006).
2 The original album, which has been reissued in various restored and high-performance formats, has also had foreign language, remixed and re-performed releases. In these respects, Wayne's continual live explorations of the album are comparable to Roger Waters's returns to *The Wall*, as discussed elsewhere in this volume. The original concept album was loosely based on H. G. Wells's 1898 science fiction novel *The War of the Worlds*.
3 See, for example, 'The National Front Disco' (from 1992's *Your Arsenal*), 'The Boy Racer' (from 1995's *Southpaw Grammar*), or 'Roy's Keen' (from 1997's *Maladjusted*). This notion of importance finds a place, rather crassly, in the concert film *Morrissey 25Live* (recorded at Hollywood High School, Los Angeles in 2013, and directed by James Russell). A microphone is passed around emotional audience members, mid-concert, who address Morrissey directly, in terms of the importance of his music for them. This is qualitatively different, in formal terms at least, from the opening interview of *Who Put the 'M' in Manchester?* since Morrissey is now present, as if a feudal lord receiving the expected praise from his subjects. The idea seems lifted from a spontaneous trope of gigs by The Fall in the 1990s, in which the microphone, wrested from or abandoned by singer Mark E. Smith, would be used by rowdy audience members sympathetic to the marginalization (rather than elevation) of the singer, announced with their now amplified cries of 'He is not appreciated!' For Goddard and Halligan (2010), Morrissey and Mark E. Smith effectively represent polar opposites in terms of cultural baggage, sentimentality, nostalgia for the 1970s North of England and so on, and how this relates to their audiences. The difference seems to be between wanting to be told of one's worth and finding oneself told of one's worth, respectively.
4 This is akin then to the issue of peacock's tail, as discussed by Dutton (2010, 136–137).
5 Dutton also draws on Kant's perspective on dependent beauty; see Dutton (2010, 189).

Bibliography

Baudrillard, Jean. 1994. *Simulacra and Simulation*. Translated by Shelia Faria Glaser. Chicago: University of Chicago Press.
Dutton, Denis. 2010. *The Art Instinct: Beauty, Pleasure and Human Evolution*. Oxford: Oxford University Press.
Farber, Manny. 1998. *Negative Space: Manny Farber on the Movies*. New York: Da Capo Press.
Goddard, Michael and Benjamin Hallgan. 2010. *Mark E. Smith and the Fall: Art, Music and Politics*. Surrey: Ashgate.
Kant, Immanuel. 1993. *Critique of Pure Reason*. London: Everyman.
Metz, Christian. 1974. *Film Language*. Translated by Michael Taylor. New York: Oxford University Press.

Morrissey. 2013. *Autobiography*. London: Penquin.

Nolan, David. 2006. *I Swear I Was There: The Gig That Changed the World*. London: Independent Music Press.

Torres, Louis. 2010. 'What Makes Art Art? Does Denis Dutton Know?' *Aristos*, http://www.aristos.org/aris-1-/dutton.htm accessed April 2015.

CHAPTER THIRTY-FIVE

Performative Cartography

Nanna Verhoeff

[...]

Cartographic interface

With touchscreen, camera, compass, GPS, network connectivity and the divergent mapping applications that are being developed for it, the smartphones such as Android devices and the iPhone can be considered a fundamentally cartographic interface. The hybrid interface of the gadget not only allows for navigation within the machine, and on the screen, but also within the physical space surrounding the device. It provides an interface for navigating bits, pixels, and spatial coordinates.

A wide range of innovative navigation software is being developed for the handheld devices such as the iPhone, enabling new ways of navigating urban space. Interactive tours, augmented reality, social locative media, and mobile navigation contribute to an expanding and transforming field of cartographic screen practices that not only represent space, but also truly make space—operating as performative cartography by generating a hybrid screenspace.

The hybridity of the interface compels us to investigate the complexity of navigation as it is taking shape as a prominent cartographic and epistemological model, or a visual regime of navigation in today's culture of mobility. This navigational model, as I argue, entails a shift in cartography. Originating in the art of making maps, but as such putting forward a regime of understanding and representing space, a new mobile cartography infuses spatial representation with a temporal and procedural dimension: a performative cartography, a dynamic map which emerges and changes during the journey. Moreover, divergent spatial categories of information or data space and physical space are connected in the map as a hybrid screenspace. The physical engagement of the user-navigator with the iPhone in this temporally dynamic and spatially layered process of making maps while reading them entails a collapse of making images and viewing them. This brings forward the co-operation of the device's (hardware) specifications, the applications' (software) affordances and the user's activity (the interfacing) in processes of connectivity, participation, and mobility.

The iPhone—a handheld, mobile, and hybrid device, and a console for multiple uses—invites us to interrogate the characteristic of the screen gadget as interface for mobile use. However, simply asserting that smartphones such as the iPhone are hybrid devices glosses over the complex and layered structure of characteristics and affordances of the interface of the device, as well as the different interactive practices involved in this hybridity. The iPhone raises questions about the specificity of this type of screen gadget as a *hybrid object*. In this sense, it is just as much a theoretical object as the Nintendo DS I alleged as such in chapter 3 [of *Mobile Screens*]. To be specific, because it is a mobile device, questions about the iPhone's hybridity are intrinsically related to movement, touch, and the process of spatial transformation. This is situated in an entanglement of technologies, applications, and interactive practices that iPhone *interfacing* entails.

Handling the iPhone takes place within what we have called a mobile screening arrangement or dispositif. As a hybrid object, the device is embedded within a mobile dispositif that encompasses both the perceptual positioning of the (mobile) user, and the physical (interactive) interfacing with the screen. The screening arrangement in motion, taking place within public space and making connections with this space, establishes a *mobile sphere*: a space that is marked by mobility and connectivity, and constructed within the (mobile) arrangement of the user, location, and device.

This mobility in space is intricately bound to the mobility, or flexibility, of the on-screen space itself: the interactive touchscreen that in fact requires physical manipulation for its operation. Considering the use of the iPhone as machine for navigation, the mobility of the device makes it a visceral interface: the entire body of the user is incorporated in mobility and making space.

The iPhone has a cartographic interface for the simultaneous navigation of both on- and off-screen space. As a machine, it enables navigation within the machine itself, as well as the navigation within physical space with the machine in hand. This makes the screen use of the iPhone distinct from historical screen uses such as televisual or cinematic viewing. The multi-touchscreen and the divergent practices of mobile touchscreening problematize the distinction of making, transmitting, and receiving images. Moreover, characteristic of the mobile screen is positioning within a mobile sphere—or dispositif—implying an ambulant locatedness and, hence, flexible site-specificity.

This mobility and physicality, I argue, point toward a performative and embodied notion of interactivity as characteristic of navigation, not only as a spatial decoding of map information, orientation and mobility, but as a cultural trope structuring our sense of (spatial) presence—as well as (temporal) present—as hybrid and flexible categories. This establishes a new spatial category, screenspace, which is activated by the simultaneous construction of on- and off-screen spaces when traversing in fluid motions with navigation devices in our hands (Verhoeff 2008).

As a device for navigation, the iPhone comprises a layered interface. While phenomenally intricately connected and hard to separate or isolate, conceptually we can discern three (non-hierarchical) levels that are all essential for navigation. First, it encompasses the level of the *internal interfacing* of applications: the backend operating system and software. This includes so-called application programming interfaces (API), making communication between applications possible, as well as the communication of the software with the graphical user interface (GUI) that enables the human user of the applications to "read," or understand, and use them.

The Google Maps API is a good example here. The fact that it is open source makes Google Maps a highly adaptable framework for all kinds of implementations. This is very suitable for mapping applications, because it provides the tools for mash-ups, or web-application hybrids: the integration of data from different sources within, in this case, the mapping environment of Google Maps. This level is the *processing* of data.

The second layer of the interface is the spatial positioning and connectivity of the apparatus in relation to physical as well as data space: the interface of internal instruments of the iPhone that connect with the external space. This entails the digital camera, GPS, Wi-Fi/3G connectivity, compass, and motion sensor or accelerometer, calculating the position, orientation and velocity, and the screen. This level of the interface communicates between the hardware of the device and "the world."

It includes what is called an *inertial* navigation system, defined by Oliver J. Woodman as follows:

> Inertial navigation is a self-contained navigation technique in which measurements provided by accelerometers and gyroscopes are used to track the position and orientation of an object relative to a known starting point, orientation and velocity. (2007: 4)

This inertial positioning system is combined with the absolute positioning system of GPS which is based on triangulation of geographical coordinates (which currently only works outdoors). This ability to calculate position and orientation is necessary for e.g. gravimetric (rather than marker-based) augmented reality applications as interface for location-based data, or *ambient intelligence*. Moreover, Internet connectivity also positions the device via wireless connection. The second layer of the interface, then, concerns *connecting* and *positioning* the interface, whether based on inertial, absolute, camera-based or wireless technologies.[1]

This positioning, then, is communicated to the user who might, for example, see the on-screen image tilt, or find a representation of position and movement signified by an arrow-shaped icon in the on-screen maps, and can then read this orientation and subsequently act or move. This is taking place on a third level of the interface of *user interaction*, enabling the communication between the user and the internal operation of the device (first level) as it is connected to the space surrounding it (second level). The first level of the applications interface also includes software operation of the graphical user interface (GUI). However, the way in which this data is visualized and made understandable, its output, operates at this third level of user interaction. This level contains the user feedback input options such as the touchscreen, buttons, the "shake control" (making use of the inertial system), but also representational conventions of the GUI. In the case of navigation, this means the way that spatial information is represented on the screen and interacted with by the user.

Significant for the touchscreen of the iPhone is that at the level of user interaction it is both an instrument for input and for output. This is the level of "access" (to data) and of the "experience" of it. Where the action takes place is, literally, on the screen. Moreover, it is a multi-touchscreen in a technological and practical sense: multi-touch technology allows for multifarious ways of touching such as swiping, virtual scrolling or swirling, and two-fingered pinch movements for enlarging or shrinking. Moreover, the dynamic horizontal or vertical scrolling of screen content establishes a connection between the image on the screen and its off-screen spaces: the frame is always a detail of a larger whole. The map is always larger than the part that is displayed on screen. Objects can be moved outside and brought into the frame by the swipe of a fingertip. Moreover, tapping the screen to give commands make more buttons, keys, sticks, or a mouse controller redundant. For example, pressure can make the screen image zoom in, simulating a virtual camera lens.

Seen within a layered constellation of the interface, the iPhone requires a triple perspective: it is a machine that processes and combines data, it is a sensor that connects and positions data, and it is a medium that produces perception. Within this constellation, its products, results, or yields received as visuals on screen by the user cannot be approached as fixed entities, or "texts," both in a temporal sense and in terms of authorship, or better, of agency. While walking and using the iPhone for an interactive tour, for example, the different layers of the interface operate together: location-based information is processed and communicated to the user via the screen. This complex layering of the interfacing process is not experienced as such because it is filtered by the user interaction interface. However, the integration of these processes (data processing, spatial positioning and connectivity, and the communication with the user) is the condition of possibility for creative navigation: an integration of the mechanisms and affordances that underlie our actions, but that are not experienced as discrete layers. As such, the hybridity of the iPhone interface provides the conditions for creative navigation of screenspace as a performative cartography.

These creative practices that make use of the affordance of the (layered) interface of the iPhone as navigation device involve different interactive engagements with an array of cartographic applications. We can discern three different ways in which the broad concept of interactivity becomes specific for navigation, as the point where interface and agency meet and where performativity is actualized: navigation understood as a constructive form of interactivity, as a participatory form of interactivity, and as yielding a haptic engagement with screenspace.

Let me explore briefly how this performative cartography constructs an urban space in which pervasive presence, embedded pasts, and evolving futures intersect, according to my triple interpretation of the index. I take locative media, or geomedia practices, and augmented reality navigation as popular and (at the moment of writing) innovative uses of mobile screens and sketch the way they revamp some cartographic principles. I first address the three aspects of tagging, plotting, and stitching in the following section before elaborating on augmented reality navigation.

Tagging, plotting, stitching

Interactive tours using online connectivity, GPS navigation, and interactive maps show us how both space and time unfold in the practice of navigation. The basic principle of screen-based navigation is that we see how we move, while how we move enables vision. This mutually constitutive, discursive relationship between seeing and moving is a new principle in real-time, digital cartography. It is the movement that establishes the map; reading space requires navigation, rather than the other way around. Digital maps make use of the logic of tagging, plotting, stitching as forms of interaction.

Tagging is essentially labeling objects or locations with metadata. Tags are clusters of digital data and primarily operate on the interface level of internal applications. Usually we refer to "tags" in relation to the way they appear: as textual or visual information or visual on our screen. It is, however, important to distinguish the tag as data and tag as symbol (visual or in words). The different levels on which tagging works correspond to levels of interfacing incorporated in the map: as metadata linked to objects, as inserts on screen providing information in relation to specific objects or locations, or as a visual layering of hybrid screenspace.

This warrants a precise terminology when analyzing how tagging is a central principle of digital cartography. Although tags primarily operate on the level of data processing, when visualized as clickables, they activate the level of user interaction. On maps they often function as geotags: location-specific hyperlinks that make a connection between data/objects and location.

The specific practice of tagging objects in space, and inserting tagged objects in the map, we can call the plotting of space. This entails marking locations and giving them a layered presence and hence, an added meaning. When these are "read" and used for navigation, we can call this tracing. When integrated into a navigable whole, this process I call stitching. While originally a term used for the montage of separate images into a seamless panoramic image, a more horizontal (two-dimensional) stitching, it also applies to a broader practice of "sewing together" visual layers in digital cartography. In similar terms, the developers of the AR browser Junaio speak of "glue" for this practice:

> Junaio has extended its capabilities beyond the usual location based internet services. Not only may the user obtain information on nearby POIs such as shops, restaurants or train stations, but the camera's eye is now able to identify objects and "glue" object specific real-time, dynamic, social and 3D information onto the object itself. Enrich your packaging, books, posters, flyers, magazines or whatever you can think of with junaio glue.[2]

Tagging, plotting, and stitching operate on the multiple levels of the interface: tagging on the level of software communication (data connecting to data), the spatial positioning (spatially connecting the objects) of plotting, and stitching, become effective on the screen, where the user actually perceives the connections as a navigable space.

Locative media activate different temporal layers within a set of spatial coordinates, which can be activated by tags. Dots on the map unfold, like spatio-temporal hyperlinks. The city becomes a clickable screenspace, a terrain of pop-ups that are triggered by real-life avatars in the physical world whose movements are tracked on-screen by GPS. In contrast to two-dimensional maps, which are a flat and still representation of space within a fixed frame, based on a fixed scale, and a fixed, abstract perspective, the digital tour-map is dynamic, layered, expandable, mutable, and flexible. It is now possible to attach geographical coordinates (geotags) as digital information, placing data back on a map of physical space, as well as tracking one's current location. Geotags bring together all levels of the hybrid interface: they combine data, they are locative and activated by positioning and/or connection, and they are perceived and activated on the screen.[3]

Geotagging photographs—attaching GPS coordinates of the time and place of photographing—underscores the geographical as well as a temporal aspect of tagging. It allows for a mnemonic mobility by placing (plotting) and tracing of digital footprints. We can understand this implication of memory as reinstating indexicality that digital photography is said to have lost when we can attach geographical coordinates as digital information:

adding data about the exact location from where the picture was taken. This location is not necessarily close to what is photographed, to the object of the image—the GPS tag marks the location of the camera, locating the object as well as the photographer in reality. These coordinates constitute the digital footprint of the image-making: its trace.

But it is also its deictic positioning in the present. The main use of this is in applications that integrate geotagged objects or images in mash-ups or in navigation software. Navigation systems like TomTom or Garmin, or smartphone applications using GPS maps, enable downloading POIs (points of interest) uploaded by other users, marked by geotagged images. Online one can find a lot of so-called POI collections or applications that make use of them. Geotags make it possible to retrace these digital footprints and turn the past into a destination: a deixis to the future.

The constructive quality of tagging, plotting, and stitching as several aspects of the making of locative, semiotic connections entails possibilities for participatory engagement. People can make their own personal archives or use them for exchange or for the building of a collective archive. Tagged "mobile mementos" (de Vries 2009) make a subsequent (online) exchange of data, or a collective image gathering or stitching possible. This is essentially collecting information from large social databases.

Photosynth is an example of an online collaborative image collection, also providing the software to stitch together multiple photographs of the same object, space, or event taken from slightly different points of view into a navigable, panoramic whole. In the company's words, it is a "viewer for downloading and navigating complex visual spaces and a 'synther' for creating them in the first place. Together they make something that seems impossible quite possible: reconstructing the 3D world from flat photographs."[4] The company's slogan is, in fact, "use your photos to stitch the world." Images can be stitched together and users can navigate by scrolling through the interactive panoramic rendering of the image. The website offers pre-fab collections, showing buildings, animals, natural reserves, or interiors—basically anything that works in an interactive panoramic image, and gives space to upload one's own synths to the database. The application *iSynth* takes this navigational model and database logic of stitching to the iPhone. The iPhone screen interface, then, allows for a touch-controlled visual navigation in a composite stitched image field. In the company's words:

> Capture, upload, share, and view Photosynth panoramas wherever you go with our new Photosynth app for iOS. These panoramas, which are the same as the ones created using our desktop panorama tools, can be created anywhere, from your favorite restaurant, a space station, or wherever inspiration strikes. From just a few stitched photos up to full spherical panoramas, the Photosynth app allows you to take Photosynth on the go and use it anytime.[5]

Stitching is a useful term for the activity of connecting individual elements to create a larger whole, a cooperative collage. Large databases such as Photosynth, much like the online photo-sharing site Flickr, serve the double purpose of creating and sharing one's own, individual archive, and using the network as a larger repository. This makes longer-running events or games possible. Geocaching, for example, is a treasure-hunt game that uses GPS coordinates tagged to "real" containers that hold objects. This is a clear case of tagging and plotting, and the user's reading of the map as a form of tracing. Moreover, when found, these may be taken if they are replaced by new objects. The user thus becomes a participant. Waymarking is based on a similar concept, to "share and discover unique and interesting locations on the planet," but does not use "real" containers for treasures. It only offers POIs, marked by other users.[6]

Yellow Arrow is a famous and long-running project that is a cross between a game, a database, a map, and a locative art project:

> Yellow Arrow is a global public art project of local experiences. Combining stickers, mobile phones and an international community, Yellow Arrow transforms the urban landscape into a "deep map" that expresses the personal histories and hidden secrets that live within our everyday spaces.[7]

Geocaching is an example of a similar, yet slightly different and also very popular formula: it is a treasure-hunt game that uses GPS for treasure hunts or other tours that involve the search of real-world objects using GPS software.[8]

These examples of locating the (physical) object of the image and the possibility of retrieving it (as image), and subsequently repositioning, collecting, or sharing it—or better: tagging, plotting, and stitching—have consequences for our conceptions of time and space. The integration of photography in applications on hybrid devices contributes to a cut-and-paste worldview: a being in the world that consists of endless possibilities. It makes it possible not only to practice limited ways of framing pictures, to crop and thus make cut-outs, but also to transpose, translate, transform, and paste these cuts into new contexts. As such, the world becomes a digital, clickable scrapbook that consists of different forms of data, overlapping information, connected dimensions, and multidirectional navigation. This transforms our sense of how we can engage in and with the world.

In an analysis of contemporary digital image-making practices, Uricchio (2011) proposes to distinguish an "algorithimic turn" exemplified by software applications like Photosynth and augmented reality, which, as I will discuss below, point towards a performative cartography. This turn in visual culture entails a radically new relationship between the image of the world and the viewing subject. He clarifies how we should on the one hand recognize the algorithimic operation in the constructing of images, but on the other hand also recognize the activity of the beholder of that image, as co-constructor. He states:

> Although of a different order than the clearly defined subject-object binary that characterized the modern era for the last few hundred years, the algorithmic turn remains rooted in human experiential and semiotic practices. (34)

Here, I am particularly interested in the creative activity as the co-operation of the different levels of the interface and the user as navigating agent in this semiotic practice. Tagging, plotting, and stitching constitute a networked and temporally expanding cartography, based on a "cooperative connected performativity" (de Vries 2009), or as I call it in the context of spatial practices, performative cartography. As such, the constructive aspects of this creativity, as I will argue below, are also inherently participatory. While practices in their own right, tagging, plotting, and stitching also converge in layering in augmented reality applications, which I will discuss next.

Layering in augmented reality

In the hybrid interface of mobile screens, tagging, plotting, and stitching converge in augmented reality browsing. Augmented reality is a container term for the use of data overlays on real-time camera view of a location, a term coined by Claudell and Mizell (1992). Originating from developments in virtual reality, using bulky head-mounted displays and later backpacks with equipment, the use of augmented reality is currently taking off in applications for mobile phones. This is a fast-developing field at the moment of writing: from marker-based augmented reality and QR codes, to image recognition technologies and experiments with haptic feedback to create a sensation of material depth of objects. AR browsers Layar and Wikitude and, more recently, Junaio are rapidly expanding the possibilities of (consumer) AR browsing for smartphones such as the iPhone. They offer browser applications on devices that have a video camera, GPS, a compass, and an orientation sensor, entailing a new way of engaging with screenspace and navigation of digital space, by effacing the map representation and using direct camera feed with a layer of data superimposed. AR browsing entails a new way of engaging with screenspace that converges the practices of touring, tagging, and navigation of digital maps.

Augmented reality browsers make it possible to browse data directly within "reality" as it is represented on the screen, showing objects within their spatial context. The camera eye on the device registers physical objects on location, and transmits these images in real time on the screen. On-screen this image is combined with different layers of data in different media: still image, text, moving image. These layers have various scales and dimensions within one master frame. We see information superimposed on a real-time image on screen. The screen is not actually transparent, but in effect, through real-time, simultaneous display of the camera feed, it seems to be. It looks like and functions as a transparent window, framed only by the edges of the screen. This framing is temporary and directly changeable by the user wielding the screen. As such, in terms of screen-based representation, augmented reality browsing provides a complex sort of framing of this "reality." We could say that the screen itself frames the video image on screen, yet the information is layered on the image, and in a sense frameless. The frame is the camera image that brackets off the contours of the world-as-image. With this new mode of "reality browsing" by means of camera feed, the map on the screen has been rescaled to the same proportion as our vision through the camera lens. Like that vision, it depends on the relative distance between ourselves and the objects seen, and the perspective changes according to our movements.

AR browsers such as *Layar*, *Wikitude* and *Junaio* offer platforms with different uses for this layering, ranging from commercial applications of location-based services showing where restaurants, banks, or shops are located, or what real estate is for sale, to more artistic interventions such as virtual expositions, galleries on location, or museum tours. Augmented reality offers a new platform for exhibition in public space, as is being discovered by museums, archives, and other cultural institutions. *ARtours*, for example, is an initiative by the Stedelijk Museum in Amsterdam to develop an AR infrastructure for art tours. In the summer of 2010, the Stedelijk Museum collaborated with the MediaLAB to hold a virtual exhibition of AR art on the Museumplein. The first augmented reality flashmob was organized in April 2010, also in Amsterdam. There and then, people could "encounter" all kinds of virtual statues or other characters on the street by wielding their mobile phones. These initiatives explore ways to bring AR applications to the public space for (scheduled) public events that can be shared. There is, however, a tension between the size of the individual screen, and the space available for multiple participants.[9]

The location specificity of augmented reality based on the tagging and plotting of space is, paradoxically perhaps, highly transportable to other locations. Tags can be moved easily. Time- and space-specific events—like festivals—can be used as settings for temporary virtual exhibitions, as *ARtours* experimented with such concepts at a music festival. In augmented reality, exhibitions can travel, infinitely multiplying and coexisting in space. A less time-based programming of augmented reality tours, but dealing with time nonetheless, is the Urban Augmented Reality (UAR) application launched by the Netherlands Architecture Institute (NAi). The tour shows large 3D buildings that were either once there in the past, will be there in the future, or were designed but were never actually built at all. In the hybrid screenspace this tour establishes, the present, past, future, and even the "past future" do in fact coincide. Using the reality browsing property of real-time camera vision, the navigation software Wikitude Drive shows new directions in consumer navigation. The map has disappeared in favor of direct on-screen visual and acoustic feedback. While this application uses the mobile screen of phones for live camera vision layered with data, this combination of real-time video feed and on-screen layering on transparent screens has been developed in the military and aviation, much like the integration of data-layering into special glasses or contact lenses, and *heads-up display* (HUD) layering of information on the windshield of our cars. The possibilities for commercial applications of this type of on-screen navigation are readily apparent. In boasting rhetoric, CEO of Mobilizy (developers of *Wikitude Drive*) Philipp Breuss-Schneeweis suggests:

> [Wikitude Drive] is a light-weight navigation system which takes a different approach than all other navigation systems: You see the real street on your mobile phone, instead of 2D or 3D maps. […] There is a lot of room to grow in this area when you imagine the possibilities by having access to the huge number of mobile services and points of interest that are already available on mobile devices. Imagine driving by virtual billboards of your favorite fast food chain, or simply having an alert when one of them is nearby. This is going to happen within Wikitude Drive. The Wikitude platform offers […] a fantastic base to sell premium content or to display location based ads.[10]

According to this rhetoric, the device will be a true competitor, rivaling for first place with spatial reality itself. This disregards the question of whether anyone really needs "millions of POIs."

Despite the commercial nature of the latter application, these examples generally demonstrate that augmentation is a form of creative contribution, which not only adds to space but inherently also modifies it. It creates hybrid space. I wrote above that this use of the word *creative* does not always imply artistic creation, but simply the act of making. Nevertheless, the word also suggests that the categories are porous. The possibility of activating the more traditional sense of creativity has the advantage of debunking an exalted, romantic vision of art that traditionally accompanies the qualifier "creative" and bringing out the participatory potential of creation. Margriet Schavemaker (2010), Head of Research and Collections at the Stedelijk Museum in Amsterdam and initiator of the earlier mentioned *ARtours*, the museum's project for AR tours for modern art, has pointed this out. She intimates that augmentation itself is at the core of art in general.

The mash-up logic we can recognize in the navigation of a layered reality entails mnemonic, temporal, and experiential aspects of mobility. First of all, it engages with objects in their specific place, while adding temporal layers: a form of mnemonic spacing. This logic requires some sort of spatial stability: objects need to be in their place for some time in order to function as markers for their tags. As such, the logic relies on archival information attached to a spatial presence. AR applications are built on databases (archives) of metadata attached to geospatial information. Secondly, the mash-up logic provides means to experience a "different" city. It adds, changes, enhances, and constructs a city of difference. The augmented reality navigator is an interactive performer, erecting a city of difference.[11]

These AR browsers and applications construct a particular kind of cartography. Like any kind of cartography they are information-based, but this information can be modified and personalized. Moreover, it is an interactive cartography in that it is responsive to input. The navigator operates it individually on a small, handheld touchscreen and the cartography activates a subjective perspective on the directly surrounding space, unlinking the abstracted bird's-eye view of space in traditional paper maps. The layeredness of the augmented-reality image is a superimposing of different spatial representations: one based on photographic/filmic framing, and the other a dataspace.

Discussing new-generation AR navigation systems for cars, Tristan Thielman makes the comparison with Edward Soja's (1996) conception of first, second, and thirdspace:

In accordance to [Soja] the new generation of navigation systems that project the travel route onto the windscreen can also be described as the rise of the perspective of a third space. The driver is himself in the first space and through the windscreen sees a first space that can be experienced physically. Via the head-up display, a second space is simultaneously projected before his eyes as a mental concept of space. These spaces, when overlaid and integrated into each other, represent something like a "both/and" instead of an "either/or" through this hybridity, mobility and simultaneity. Such a complex understanding of space opens up new spaces. (2007: 70)

The analogy with Soja's thirdspace is that of a conceptual and experiential category. As Thielmann seems to suggest here, this spacing is a quality of the experience of hybridity. Augmented reality thus brings about not the sum of layers, but a whole new dimension to the experience of space.[12]

Like cartography in de Certeau's sense, augmented reality provides a practiced narrative in that it tells spatial stories in the making: it makes experiences unfold in space at the moment of their occurrence. Hence, it is procedural, in the sense that movement through space and interaction with on-screen layers of digital information to off-screen geographical and material presence unfolds in time. But not only does it take time, it becomes over time. A conception of time that includes the productive, or literally creative aspect of time, is relevant here; it includes change in time.

This puts us with our historical feet back on the ground. This new technology has much in common with the age-old habit of walking, and in this links back to, say, Baudelaire's flâneur as leisurely stroller. The cartographic principle of (AR) browsing is a synthesis of the two other models, that of touring and tagging. Incorporating geotagging as a principle, the spatial logic is that of cut-outs and layers of information. Being structured as tours, the engagement is not visual, fixated, and distanced, but haptic, fluid, and procedural.

[…]

Notes

1 About ambient intelligence see Aarts, Harwig and Schuurmans (2001) and also Crang and Graham (2007).
2 http://dev.junaio.com/publisher/junaioglue (accessed October 2011)
3 Tuters and Varnellis speak of two kinds of cartography in the broader "genre" of locative media: annotative (based on tagging) and phenomenological (tracing movement) (2006: 359). This is close to my terminology here, although I wish to analyze the merging of these two forms in performative cartography, as it is made possible by the hybrid of interface.
4 http://photosynth.net/about.aspx (accessed October 2011).
5 http://photosynth.net/capture.aspx (accessed October 2011).
6 From the perspective of an outsider making use of the assembled database, this is also called, like a business model and with a different and more top-down connotation, crowdmining or crowdsourcing. The use of multiple amateur image feeds can also create a new, cooperative "YouTube aesthetic." In 2010 rock band Radiohead supported a fan initiative to make and distribute online a movie made by about 50 cellphone cameras of their 2009 concert in Prague. It shows a do-it-yourself concert movie compiled from a multitude of low-resolution camera views. See http://stereogum.com/495031/download-radioheads-prague-concert-film/video/ (accessed October 2011). Jeremy Crampton discusses crowdsourcing as part of the digital transformation of cartography in his essay "Cartography: Maps 2.0" (2008).
7 http://yellowarrow.net/v3/ (accessed October 2011).
8 See, for example www.geocaching.com (accessed October 2011). Geocaching is a treasure-hunt game that uses GPS coordinates tagged to "real" containers that hold objects. When found, these may be taken if replaced by new objects. Waymarking is a similar concept, to "share and discover unique and interesting locations on the planet," but does not use actual physical containers to hold treasures, instead offering points of interest that have been marked by other users. www.waymarking.com (accessed October 2011).
9 About the exhibition, see http://ikophetmuseumplein.nl/ (accessed October 2011). For the flashmob, see http://sndrv.nl/ARflashmob/ (accessed October 2011).
10 Philipp Breuss-Schneeweis, CEO of Mobilizy. Quoted in "Winning the Navteq Challenge 2010 Grand Prize with Wikitude Drive" on http://www.wikitude.org/en/demobilizy-gewinnt-den-hauptpreis-der-navteq-challenge-

2010enwinning-navteq-challenge-2010-grand-prize-wikitude-drive (accessed October, 2011).

11   An analogy can be made between locative media practices and pervasive games, and the project of the Situationists International, led by Guy Debord between ca. 1957–1972. From a more radical and political perspective, the Situationists' ambition was to provoke a new urbanism with their psychogeography of drift, or *dérive*, and cartography of experience. For this comparison, see e.g. Nieuwdorp (2005), McGarrigle (2010), and Tuters and Varnelis (2006). About the Situationists, see Sadler (1998).

12   In her study on what she terms nomadic theater, Liesbeth Groot Nibbelink also uses Soja's ideas about thirdspace as a lived space—in addition to a first (perceived) and second (conceived) spatiality. For her analysis of the "cartography" of nomadic performances, she uses Soja for a rethinking of presence, performance, and representation as layers rather than categories in the theater (in preparation).

Bibliography

Aarts, Emile, Rick Harwig and Martin Schuurmans 2001 "Ambient Intelligence." 235–250 in Peter Denning (ed.), *The Invisible Future: The Seamless Integration of Technology in Everyday Life*. New York: McGraw-Hill.

Claudell, Thomas and David Mizell 1992 "Augmented Reality: An Application of Heads-Up Display Technology to Manual Manufacturing Processes." *Proceedings of 1992 IEEE Hawaii International Conference on Systems Sciences*: 659–669. http://ieeexplore.ieee.org/search/srchabstract.jsp?arnumb er=183317&isnumber=4717&punumber=378&k2dockey=183317@ieeecnfs [retrieved August 2010].

Crampton, Jeremy 2008 "Cartography: Maps 2.0," *Progress in Human Geography* 33, 1: 91–100.

Crang, Mike and Stephen Graham 2007 "Sentient Cities: Ambient Intelligence and the Politics of Urban Space," *Information, Communication & Society* 10, 6: 789–817.

Groot, Nibbelink, Liesbeth (in preparation) *Nomadic Theatre. Movements in Contemporary Performance* (working title). PhD Dissertation Utrecht University.

McGarrigle, Conor 2010 "The Construction of Locative Situations: Locative Media and the Situationist International, Recuperation or Redux?" *Digital Creativity* 21, 1 (March): 55–62.

Nieuwdorp, Eva 2005 "The Pervasive Interface: Tracing the Magic Circle." Proceedings from the International DiGRA Conference Changing Views: Worlds in Play. Vancouver, Canada. www.digra.org/dl/db/06278.53356.pdf [retrieved August 2010].

Sadler, Simon 1998 *The Situationist City*. Cambridge, MA: MIT Press.

Schavemaker, Margriet 2010 "AR(t): Learning from the Paradox." Lecture given at AR: *Artistic Explorations*. Rotterdam, The Netherlands: V2: Institute for the Unstable Media, June 4.

Soja, Edward 1996 *Thirdspace: Journeys to Los Angeles and Other Real-and-Imagined Places*. Oxford: Basil Blackwell.

Thielmann, Tristan 2007 "'You Have Reached Your Destination!' Position, Positioning and Superpositioning of Space Through Car Navigation Systems," *Social Geography* 2: 63–75 www.socgeogr.net/2/63/2007/ [retrieved August 2010].

Tuters, Marc and Kazys Varnelis 2006 "Beyond Locative Media," Networked Publics Blog http://networkedpublics.org/locative_media/beyond_locative_media [retrieved August 2010].

Uricchio, William 2011 "The Algorithmic Turn: Photosynth, Augmented Reality and the Changing Implications of the Image," *Visual Studies* 26, 1 (March): 25–35.

Verhoeff, Nanna 2008 "Screens of Navigation: From Taking a Ride to Making a Ride," *Refractory* 12 http://blogs.arts.unimelb.edu.au/refractory/2008/03/06/screens-of-navigation-from-taking-a-ride-to-making-the-ride/ [Published March 2008].

Vries, Imar de 2009 "Mobile Mementos: Expanded Archives, Fragmented Access." Paper delivered at MiT6 at MIT, Cambridge, MA. http://web.mit.edu/commforum/mit6/subs/abstracts.html.

Woodman, Oliver J. 2007 "An Introduction to Inertial Navigation," *Technical Report* 696. University of Cambridge.

FURTHER READING

Section One

Chapters 1–5

Cavell, Stanley. *The World Viewed*. 2nd ed. Cambridge, MA: Harvard University Press, 1979.

Cubitt, Sean. *The Practice of Light: A Genealogy of Visual Techniques from Prints to Pixels*. Cambridge, MA: The MIT Press, 2014.

Eckmann, Sabine and Lutz Koepnick, eds. *Window/Interface*. St. Louis: Mildred Lane Kemper Art Museum, 2007.

Friedberg, Anne. *The Virtual Window: From Alberti to Microsoft*. Cambridge, MA: The MIT Press, 2006.

Paul, Christiane. "Mediations of Light: Screens as Information." In *Digital Light*, edited by Sean Cubitt, Daniel Palmer, and Nathaniel Tkacz, 179–92. London: Open Humanities Press, 2015.

Virilio, Paul. "Dromoscopy, or the Ecstasy of Enormities." Translated by Edward R. O'Neill. *Wide Angle* 20, no. 3 (1998): 11–22.

Youngblood, Gene. *Expanded Cinema*. New York: Dutton, 1970.

Chapters 6–10

Cubitt, Sean. "LED Technology and the Shaping of Culture." In *Urban Screens Reader*, edited by Scott McQuire, Meredith Martin, and Sabine Niederer, 97–107. Amsterdam: Institute of Network Cultures, 2009.

Gere, Charlie. "Genealogy of the Computer Screen." *Visual Communication* 5, no. 2 (2006): 141–53.

Higgins, Hannah B. *The Grid Book*. Cambridge, MA: The MIT Press, 2009.

Huhtamo, Erkki. "Behind the Messages on the Wall: An Archaeology of Public Media Displays." In *Urban Screens Reader*, edited by Scott McQuire, Meredith Martin, and Sabine Niederer, 14–28. Amsterdam: Institute of Network Cultures, 2009.

Huhtamo, Erkki. "Screen Tests: Why Do We Need an Archaeology of the Screen?" *Cinema Journal* 51, no. 2 (2012): 144–8.

Huhtamo, Erkki. *Illusions in Motion: Media Archaeology of the Moving Panorama and Related Spectacles*. Cambridge, MA: The MIT Press, 2013.

Kress, Gunther. "'Screen': Metaphors of Display, Partition, Concealment and Defence." *Visual Communication* 5, no. 2 (2006): 199–204.

Manovich, Lev. *The Language of New Media*. Cambridge, MA: The MIT Press, 2001.

Musser, Charles. "Toward a History of Screen Practice." *Quarterly Review of Film Studies* 9, no. 1 (1984): 59–69.

Shaw, Jeffrey and Peter Weibel, eds. *Future Cinema: The Cinematic Imaginary after Film*. Cambridge, MA: The MIT Press, 2003

Section Two

Chapters 11–16

Friedberg, Anne. "Urban Mobility and Cinematic Visuality: The Screens of Los Angeles—Endless Cinema or Private Telematics." *Journal of Visual Culture* 1, no. 2 (2002): 183–204.

Gorky, Maxim. "The Lumière Cinematograph." In *The Film Factory: Russian and Soviet Cinema in Documents, 1896–1939*, edited and translated by, Richard Taylor and Ian Christie, 25–6. New York: Routledge, 1988.

McLuhan, Marshall. "Television." In *Understanding Media*, 336–68. New York: Routledge, 2001.

Metz, Christian. "Secondary Screens, or Squaring the Rectangle." In *Impersonal Enunciation, or the Place of Film*, edited and translated by Cormac Deane, 52–9. New York: Columbia University Press, 2016.

Mulvey, Laura. "Rear Projection and the Paradoxes of Hollywood Realism." In *Theorizing World Cinema*, edited by Lúcia Nagib, Christopher Perriam, and Rajinder Kumar Dudrah, 207–19. London: I.B. Tauris, 2012.

Shipley, Jesse Weaver. "Selfie Love: Public Lives in an Era of Celebrity Pleasure, Violence, and Social Media," *American Anthropologist* 117, no. 2 (2015): 403–13.

Turnock, Julie. "The Screen on the Set: The Problem of Classical-Studio Rear Projection," *Cinema Journal* 51, no.2 (2012): 157–67.

Chapters 17–22

Barthes, Roland. "Leaving the Movie Theatre." In *The Rustle of Language*, translated by Richard Howard, 345–349. Oxford: Basil Blackwell, 1986.

Bazin, André. "Three Essays on Widescreen Film." *The Velvet Light Trap*, no. 21 (1985): 8–17.

Belton, John. "The Curved Screen." *Film History* 16, no. 3 (2004): 280–2.

Bordwell, David. "CinemaScope: The Modern Miracle You See Without Glasses." In *Poetics of Cinema*, 281–325. New York: Routledge, 2008.

Eisenstein, Sergei. "The Dynamic Square." In *Film Essays and a Lecture*, edited by Jay Leyda, 48–65. New York: Praeger, 1970.

Fowler, Catherine, and Paola Voci. "Brief Encounters: Theorizing Screen Attachments Outside the Movie Theatre." *Screening the Past* 32 (2011). http://www.screeningthepast.com/2011/11/brief-encounters-theorizing-screen-attachments-outside-the-movie-theatre/ accessed 1 February 2016.

Heath, Stephen. "On Screen, in Frame: Film and Ideology." *Quarterly Review of Film Studies* 1, no. 3 (1976): 251–65.

Kracauer, Siegfried. "The Cult of Distraction: On Berlin's Pleasure Palaces." In *The Mass Ornament: Weimar Essays*, edited by Thomas Y. Levin, 323–8. Cambridge, Mass.: Harvard University Press, 1995.

McLuhan, Eric. "The Fordham Experiment." *Proceedings of the Media Ecology Association* 1 (2000): 23–7.

Moholy-Nagy, László. "Simultaneous or Poly-Cinema." In *Painting, Photography, Film*, translated by Janet Seligman, 41–3. London: Lund Humphries, 1967.

Smithson, Robert. "Cinematic Atopia." In *The Collected Writings*, edited by Jack Flam, 138–42. Berkeley: University of California Press, 1996.

Wasson, Haidee. "The Networked Screen: Moving Images, Materiality, and the Aesthetics of Size." In *Fluid Screens, Expanded Cinema*, edited by Janine Marchessault and Susan Lord, 74–95. Toronto: University of Toronto Press, 2007.

Section Three

Chapters 23–29

Bruno, Giuliana. *Surface: Matters of Aesthetics, Materiality, and Media*. Chicago, IL: University of Chicago Press, 2014.

Bush, Vannevar. "As We May Think." *Atlantic Monthly* 176 (1945): 101–8.

Farman, Jason. *Mobile Interface Theory: Embodied Space and Locative Media*. New York: Routledge, 2011.

Galloway, Alexander R.. *The Interface Effect*. Cambridge: Polity, 2012.

Johnson, Eric Arthur. "Touch Displays: A Programmed Man-Machine Interface." *Ergonomics* 10, no. 2 (1967): 271–7.

Moggridge, Bill, ed. *Designing Interactions*. Cambridge, MA: The MIT Press, 2007.

Mondloch, Kate. *Screens: Viewing Media Installation Art*. Minneapolis: University of Minnesota Press, 2010.

Morse, Margaret. "Body and Screen." *Wide Angle* 21, no. 1 (1999): 63–75.

Norman, Donald A. "Natural User Interfaces Are Not Natural." *Interactions* 17, no. 3 (2010): 6–10.

Perlow, Seth. "On Production for Digital Culture: iPhone Girl, Electronics Assembly, and the Material Forms of Aspiration." *Convergence* 17, no. 3 (2011): 245–69.

Richardson, Ingrid. "Pocket Technospaces: the Bodily Incorporation of Mobile Media." *Continuum: Journal of Media & Cultural Studies* 21, no. 2 (2007): 205–15.

Richardson, Ingrid. "Faces, Interfaces, Screens: Relational Ontologies of Framing, Attention and Distraction." *Transformations* 18 (2010). http://www.transformationsjournal.org/journal/issue_18/article_05.shtml accessed 1 February 2016.

Rogers, Ariel. "'Smothered in Baked Alaska': The Anxious Appeal of Widescreen Cinema." *Cinema Journal* 51, no. 3 (2012): 74–96.

Sobchack, Vivian. "The Scene of the Screen: Envisioning Cinematic and Electronic 'Presence'." In *Materialities of Communication*, edited by Hans Ulrich Gumbrecht and K. Ludwig Pfeiffer, 83–106. Stanford, CA: Stanford University Press, 1994.

White, Michele. *The Body and the Screen: Theories of Internet Spectatorship*. Cambridge, MA: The MIT Press, 2006.

Chapters 30–35

Acland, Charles. "IMAX Technology and the Tourist Gaze," *Cultural Studies* 12, no. 3 (1998): 429–45.

Belton, John. *Widescreen Cinema*. Cambridge, MA: Harvard University Press, 1992.

Griffiths, Alison. *Shivers Down Your Spine: Cinema, Museums, and the Immersive View*. New York: Columbia University Press, 2008.

Kelley, Andrea. "From Attraction to Distraction: The Panoram Machine and Emerging Modes of Multi-sited Screen Consumption." *Continuum: Journal of Media & Cultural Studies* 28, no. 3 (2014): 330–41.

Klinger, Barbara. *Beyond the Multiplex: Cinema, New Technologies, and the Home*. Berkeley, CA: University of California Press, 2006.

McCarthy, Anna. *Ambient Television: Visual Culture and Public Space*. Durham, NC: Duke University Press, 2001.

Siegel, Greg. "Double Vision: Large-Screen Video Display and Live Sports Spectacle," *Television & New Media* 3, no. 1 (2002): 49–73.

Spigel, Lynn. "Installing the Television Set: Popular Discourses en Television and Domestic Space, 1948–1955," *Camera Obscura* 6, no. 1 (1998): 9–46.

Spigel, Lynn. *Welcome to the Dreamhouse: Popular Media and Postwar Suburbs*. Durham, NC: Duke University Press, 2001.

Sutton, Gloria. *The Experience Machine: Stan VanDerBeek's* Movie-Drome *and Expanded Cinema*. Cambridge, MA: The MIT Press, 2015.

Takahashi, Tess. "Experimental Screens in the 1960s and 1970s: The Site of Community," *Cinema Journal* 51, no. 2 (2012): 162–67.

Verhoeff, Nanna. *Mobile Screens: The Visual Regime of Navigation*. Amsterdam: Amsterdam University Press, 2012.

Wasson, Haidee. "Suitcase Cinema," *Cinema Journal* 51, no. 2 (2012): 148–52.

CONTRIBUTORS

Charles R. Acland is Professor and Research Chair in Communications Studies at Concordia University, Montreal.

Sarah Atkinson is Senior Lecturer in Digital Cultures at King's College, London.

Lara Baladi is an Egyptian-Lebanese multidisciplinary artist, the Ida Ely Rubin Artist in Residence at MIT's Center for Art, Science & Technology (CAST) and a lecturer in MIT's Art, Culture & Technology program (ACT).

Jean-Louis Baudry (1930–2015) was a French novelist and theorist. He was a principal proponent of apparatus theory.

Ron Burnett is President and Vice-Chancellor of Emily Carr University of Art and Design, Vancouver.

Francesco Casetti is Thomas E. Donnelley Professor of Humanities and Film and Media Studies at Yale University, New Haven, Connecticut.

Uta Caspary is Assistant Curator at Neue Nationalgalerie—Staatliche Museen zu Berlin (National Museums in Berlin).

Brad Chisholm is Professor of Film Studies at St. Cloud State University, St. Cloud, Minnesota.

Heidi Rae Cooley is Associate Professor in Media Arts in the School of Visual Art and Design at the University of South Carolina.

Harper Cossar is Visiting Lecturer at Emory and Georgia State Universities.

Edmond Couchot is an artist and former Director of the Department of Arts and Technologies of the Image at the Université Paris VIII.

Sean Cubitt is Professor of Film and Television and Joint Head of the Media and Communications Department, Goldsmiths, University of London.

Louis-Jacques-Mandé Daguerre (1787–1851) was a French artist, inventor of the daguerreotype photographic process, and co-creator of the Diorama, which flourished in Paris and London in the 1820s.

Giambattista della Porta (1535–1615) was an Italian scientist and scholar. His *Magia Naturalis* was first published in 1558 and translated into many languages during his lifetime.

Robert Edgar is a senior lecturer in the Faculty of Arts at York St John University.

Douglas Engelbart (1925–2013) was an engineer and pioneer in interactive computing. He is perhaps best-known as the inventor of the computer mouse.

Anne Friedberg (1952–2009) was Chair of the Critical Studies Division in the School of Cinematic Arts at the University of Southern California.

Paul Frosh is a senior lecturer in the Department of Communication and Journalism at the Hebrew University of Jerusalem.

Amy Herzog is Associate Professor of Media Studies at Queens College, City University of New York.

Erkki Huhtamo is a shared professor between the Departments of Design Media Arts, and Film, Television, and Digital Media at the University of California, Los Angeles.

Frederick J. Kiesler (1890–1965) was an Austrian-American architect and theater designer.

Lev Manovich is a professor of computer science at The Graduate Center, City University of New York.

Anna McCarthy is Professor in Cinema Studies in the Tisch School of the Arts, New York University.

Stephen Monteiro is Assistant Professor of Sociology and Anthropology at Concordia University, Montreal, Canada.

Onookome Okome is Professor in English and Film Studies at the University of Alberta, Edmonton.

Plato (428/427 BCE–348/347 BCE) was a Greek philosopher and founder of the Academy of Athens.

Marcel Proust (1871–1922) was a French writer. *Swann's Way* is the first volume of his seven-volume narrative *In Search of Lost Time*, published in France from 1913 to 1927.

Alexandra Schneider is Professor of Mediendramaturgie im Fachgebiet Filmwissenschaft at Johannes Gutenberg-Universität, Mainz.

Virginie Sonet is Lecturer at the Institut Français de Presse, Université Paris II, Panthéon-Assas.

William Henry Fox Talbot (1800–1877) was a British scientist and inventor. His negative-positive photographic process was the basis for most analog photography.

Stan VanDerBeek (1927–1984) was an American filmmaker, animator, and intermedia pioneer. He built his Movie-Drome in Stony Point, New York, between 1963 and 1965.

Nanna Verhoeff is Associate Professor of Comparative Media Studies at the Department for Media and Culture Studies at Utrecht University.

Haidee Wasson is Associate Professor of Cinema at Concordia University, Montreal.

Mitchell Whitelaw is Associate Professor in the Faculty of Arts and Design at the University of Canberra.

INDEX

absorption 23, 110, 178–9, 350–2, 375. *See also* attention
Academy ratio 246–8, 250, 252–3, 259–61, 272, 274. *See also* aspect ratio
accessibility 7
Acland, Charles 15–16, 368
advertising. *See also* marketing
 audiences and 51, 256
 of media products 100, 106–7, 271–2, 297, 344, 379, 381–2, 424
 on-line 159, 205–6, 208, 245, 249–51
 on-screen 32, 145, 148, 262
 production of 97, 370–1, 373, 412
 television 253
African and Caribbean Film Festival 395–6
African cinema 395–7, 399
airports 289
Al Arabiya 174
Al Jazeera 174
Alberti, Leon Battista 17, 56, 58, 134
allegory 18
Alloway, Lawrence 270
Althusser, Louis 234
ambient intelligence 437
anamorphosis 274
Anderson, Benedict 389
Android 435
animation 147–9, 256–62, 292, 373
Anscochrome 357
APP 208–11, 214
apparatus 25, 79, 201, 211, 233–41, 344, 350, 367–71
apparatus theory 79–80, 158–9
Apple 269, 287, 326, 331, 334
apps 156, 199–202, 204–5, 207–9, 332, 336, 338, 437–46
AR. *See* augmented reality

Arab Image Foundation 169
Arab revolutions 172
architecture 19, 59, 143–50, 158, 229–30, 292, 344, 349, 373
archives 205, 344, 425, 441–2, 446
Arnheim, Rudolf 187
arrays 160, 288–93
ART+COM 289
aspect ratio 125, 159, 246–55, 257–62, 267, 272, 274, 310–11
AT&T 376
Atkinson, Sarah 158
attention 35. *See also* absorption
audience. *See also* audience experience; spectator; user; viewer
 commodification 51
 formation 145, 302, 396–8, 402–3, 430
 interaction 8, 86–7, 207–8, 297, 305–6, 422–3, 425, 429
 intervention 371
 needs 178, 202, 399, 403–4, 422
 performativity 402–3, 411–12
 placement 84–5, 90, 189, 204, 229–30, 251, 299, 301, 372, 399–402
 size 383, 399, 426
 tracking 211
 Western 173
audience experience 93, 192, 198–9, 200–1, 206–14, 230, 276–7, 290, 405–12, 418–19, 427–9
augmented reality 443–7
authenticity 198, 201, 428–30
avant-garde 103, 270, 276, 282, 352, 359
avatars 25

Bakhtin, Mikhail 34
Baladi, Lara 157
Barber, Karin 400

Barr, Charles 251, 275–6
Barrot, Pierre 398–9
Barthes, Roland 26–7
Baudelaire, Charles 447
Bauder, Christopher 289
    ATOM 289
Baudrillard, Jean 167, 428
Baudry, Jean-Louis 79, 159
Bayart, Francoise 402
    The State in Africa 402
Bazin, André 251, 255, 270, 276, 279,
    283
    "Painting and Cinema" 270
    "Will CinemaScope Save the Film
        Industry?" 276
Being There 188, 193
Bellour, Raymond 206
Belton, John 257
Benjamin, Walter 59
    "The Work of Art in the Age of
        Mechanical Reproduction" 59
Berg 292
    Making Future Magic 292
Berger, John 170
    Ways of Seeing 170
Berlin 148–9
Berlin International Film Festival 396
Bianco, Anthony 347
Big Trail, The 246–8, 259
Bishara, Nina 205
BIX 149
Blackberry 326
Blackle 41
Blinkenlights 148
blogs 33–4
Blu-ray 49–50, 205, 207–8
Bolter, Jay David 249, 250, 253
books 203
Bordwell, David 207
Boullier, Dominique 335, 339
Bourdieu, Pierre 252–3
BRAVIA 272
Brecht, Bertolt 431
Breuss-Schneeweis, Philipp 445
Broadcast News 189
browsers 440, 443–5
Bruno, Giuliana 104
Bryce, Jane 395
Bug's Life, A 257–61

Buijs, Jan Willem 148
Burkina Faso 396–7
Burnett, Ron 157
Burns, R.W. 95
    Television: An International History
        of the Formative Years 95
bus stations 377

Cable News Network 167–8, 174
Cage, John 135
Cairo 157, 167, 169–71
camera 26, 186–9, 192, 194, 198, 200,
    233–5, 240, 351–2, 359, 429,
    443–5
    Simulcam 25–6
camera obscura 85, 96, 104, 225, 234
Cameron, James 25
Cape Cod network 130
Capino, José 353
cartesian space 51–2
cartography 435–6. See also maps
Casetti, Francesco 16–17
Caspary, Uta 19
cathode ray tubes 40–1, 44–5, 49, 106,
    109, 297, 308, 311, 313, 316
Cavell, Stanley 8, 279–82
CCTV. See closed-circuit television
Chambat, Pierre 335, 337, 340
Champagne, John 359
Chanel 147
Chaos Computer Club 148
Chassaing, Xavier 292
    Scintillation 292
China 42, 99, 171
China Syndrome, The 189
Chisholm, Brad 157
Chrysler 373–4, 380
cinema of attractions 350, 360
CinemaScope 246, 250–1, 261, 274–6,
    327, 423
Cinematograph 305–6
Cinerama 275, 375
closed-circuit television 200
clouds 297
CNN. See Cable News Network
code 57
codecs 49–50, 52
colonialism 404–5
color 43, 46, 48–50, 291

composition. *See* images; shots; mise-en-scène
computers 55–62, 108–9, 313–18
concert films 424, 428–31
concerts 301–2, 421–31
convergence 27
Cooley, Heidi Rae 299
Cooper, H.J. 84
copyright 47–8
Cossar, Harper 159
Couchot, Edmond 18–19
Coutaz, Joëlle 334
Cranach, Lucas 279
    Lucretia 279
Crary, Jonathan 391–2
CRTs. *See* cathode ray tubes
cruising 352
Cubitt, Sean 17

Daguerre, Louis-Jacques-Mandé 156
Damisch, Hubert 347
de Certeau, Michel 446
De Stijl 148
De Volharding 148
Dead Man's Tracks 214
Debord, Guy 167, 431
    The Society of the Spectacle 167
Deleuze, Gilles 48
della Porta, Giambattista 158
Derrida, Jacques 269, 278–9
design 43, 229–30
diaspora 396
digital micromirror device 46–7
diorama 90, 92–3, 156, 163–6
dispositif 79–80, 104, 110, 329, 331, 436
distraction 214, 351–2, 359
dividing screens 82–4, 87
DMD. *See* digital micromirror device
Doane, Mary Ann 202
Domitilla 406–10
Doom 262
downloading 30, 35, 50, 198, 200, 207–9, 246, 441
drawing 15, 108, 227, 314, 316–17
Drupsteen, Jaap 145
Du Maurier, George 96–7
Dutton, Denis 426–7, 429–30
    The Art Instinct 426

DVDs 29, 50, 205, 208, 249, 252, 336, 355, 401, 424, 429
Dyer, Richard 356–7

ebooks 203, 214
Eco, Umberto 56
Edelstein, Neal 200–1
Edeson, Arthur 246, 261
Edgar, Robert 301
Edison, Thomas 96
editing 233, 238
Edwards, Paul 130
Egyptian revolution 156, 167, 169–75
Ehrenberg, Alain 335, 337, 340
electron gun 40–1, 46
electroscope 98
el-Hamalawy, Hossam 170
Elsaesser, Thomas 206
Encyclopedia of Cottage, Farm, and Villa Architecture, An 83–4
Engelbart, Douglas 299
environment 43, 300–2, 305–6, 319–22, 336–7, 347, 353, 368, 371, 374–80, 389–92, 418–19, 421–8
    cinema 25, 158–9, 229–30

Facebook 34, 174, 338
Farber, Manny 431
Feuer, Jane 186, 389
Figuier, Louis 98
filesharing. *See* uploading
film 59, 206, 370–1, 377
    8 mm 347–9, 370–1, 380, 383
    70 mm 246–7
    16 mm 247, 345–9, 357, 370–1, 376, 378–9, 380–1, 383
    Super8 348–9
    35 mm 197, 246–7, 274–5, 371, 378–80
Film Arts Guild theater 103
film festivals 395
Film News 377–8
film studies 24–5
film theory 25, 79
filmmaking 425–31
    mobile phone 197–214
fire screens 82, 84, 155
Firefox 7
flâneur 447

Flickr 201
Flolite 382
flow 35–6, 107, 277, 301, 418–19
Fludernik, Monika 200
Flusser, Vilém
  *Towards a Philosophy of
  Photography* 172
formalism 249, 280–1
Foucault, Michel 31, 48, 51–2
frame 125, 158–9, 178, 188, 230,
  234–7, 249, 258–62, 267–84,
  316–17, 351–2, 438–44
Fried, Michael 280
  "Shape as Form" 280
Friedberg, Anne 6, 17, 270, 278, 368,
  380
  The Virtual Window 270, 368
Frosh, Paul 299
Funke, Cornelia 202–4

Gadney, Guy 248–50
Galloway, Alexander 48
  The Interface Effect 269
gamers 33, 177–83, 250, 255–6
games 33, 36, 157, 168, 177–83, 250,
  253–5, 262. *See also* MUDs
Gates, Bill 55
  The Road Ahead 55
Gateway 273
gaze 9, 31–2, 92, 203, 249, 277, 350–2.
  See also vision
  gender and 357–9
Gelernter, David 55–6, 59
General Motors 374
genre 197
geocaching 442
George Washington University 61
Gernsback, Hugo 101
Gilje, HC 291
  blink 291
  shift 291
global positioning systems 31–2, 435,
  437, 439–43
Good Morning America 186
Google Earth 36
Google Maps 437
Gottlieb, Carla 283
GPS. *See* global positioning systems
Grandeur (format) 246–7, 259

Grant, Catherine 207
graphical user interface 55–7, 58–9,
  131, 437. *See also* interface
green screen 198
Grey's Anatomy Sync 205
Grossman, Lawrence 334
Grusin, Richard 249, 250, 253
GUI. *See* graphical user interface
Gulf War 167–8
Gumbrecht, Hans Ulrich 293–4
Gunning, Tom 349–50, 360

habitèle 335, 339
half-tone printing 44
handheld screens 299–300
hapticity 203, 351, 443, 447. *See also*
  tactility
hardware 43, 49, 88, 157, 201, 331,
  436–7
  hacking 294
Haunting Melissa 199–202, 210
HD. *See* high-definition
Heidegger, Martin 389
Henke, Robert 289
Herzog, Amy 300
High Treason 104
high-definition 25
Hodas, Martin 346–7
Hollywood 51, 159, 187–8, 192, 214,
  246, 368, 371, 383, 392, 399,
  431
homosexuality 357
How to Marry a Millionaire 274
Huhtamo, Erkki 6, 18, 23, 275, 368
  "Elements of Screenology" 18
  Illusions in Motion 86
Husserl, Edmund 237–8
  Cartesian Meditations 238

icons 59, 326, 438
ideology 234, 239–41, 389, 391
IM. *See* instant messaging
iMac 297. *See also* Macintosh
image
  adaptability of 159, 267–71,
  440–4
  definition of 129
  function of 240, 277–8, 418–19,
  440–4, 446

mobile device 198–209
  qualities 155–6, 188, 235–7, 305–6
  stitching 442
  types 134–5, 138–40, 274
IMAX 429
immersion 35, 92, 94, 99, 110, 157,
    178–80, 350–1, 375, 399. *See*
    also absorption
indexicality 201
India 7
instant messaging 200, 210. *See also*
    texting
interactivity
  computer 313–22
  and format 248–50, 299, 334
  game 178, 183
  image 273, 284, 326
  and narrative 206–8
  of objects 267–8, 337, 437–8
  televisual 307–11
interface 7, 140, 267–8, 299. *See also*
    graphical user interface
  culture of 56–9
  and environment 302, 435–43
  experience of 133, 203, 206, 273–4,
    283–4, 313–22
  with facades 148–50
  game 178–83
  human-computer 126–30
  mobile 9, 326
  pre-digital 55, 92, 94, 99–100
internet 171–4. *See also* downloading;
    networks; uploading
iOS 199, 201, 205, 208, 273
iPad 199–201, 269, 292
iPhone 197, 269, 273, 325–32, 334,
    435–43
Israel 169
iSynth 441

Jenkins, Charles Francis 102
Jobs, Steve 267, 273, 326–7
Johnson, Samuel 82, 84
  Dictionary of the English Language
    82, 84
Judd, Donald 280, 282–3

Kandinsky, Wassily 136
Kant, Immanuel 278–9, 428

Critique of Judgment, The 278
Critique of Pure Reason, The 428
Kaplan v. United States 355–6
Kendrick, James 249–50
keyboard 314–17
Kiesler, Frederick 103, 158
Kinder, Bill 258
Kinetoscope 346, 350
Kittler, Friedrich 80
Klinger, Barbara 26, 207
Kodachrome 378
Kodak 168, 375, 381
Kodascope 381
KPN Telecom headquarters 146

Lacan, Jacques 239
Lagos 398, 404–13
language 233, 236–7, 315, 331, 422
  visual 417
Late Fragment 208
Latour, Bruno 43
Laurel, Brenda 57
LCD. *See* liquid-crystal display
Lebanon 169
LED. *See* light-emitting diode
lens 225–7, 234, 275
Lessig, Lawrence 47
letterboxing 159, 245–6, 249–56, 262,
    273. *See also* image
light 73–7, 145–9, 155–6, 165–6, 227,
    234, 288–93, 305–6, 372, 381
light-emitting diode 147, 272, 289–90,
    294
Lincoln Laboratory 130–1
Linux 57
liquid-crystal display 41–2, 44–5, 49,
    272–3, 311
lithopane 90
liveness 198, 422–8, 431
Living in Bondage 410
locative media 6, 302, 435, 439–42
London 84, 168
Looper 207

MacCullough, Campbell 247–8
Macintosh 55–7. *See also* iMac
Mackenzie, Adrian 50–1
Macworld 273
Madison Square Garden 425

magic lanterns 85, 87, 91, 94, 99, 158, 219–20
Manchurian Candidate, The 189
Manovich, Lev 6, 18, 30, 81, 253, 257, 281
maps 435–41, 443, 445–6. *See also* cartography
Marchand, Roland 373
marketing 25, 206, 348, 368–9, 371–3, 377, 382. *See also* advertising
Marks, Laura 203–4, 328, 351
materiality 39, 159, 330–1, 390–3
Matrix, The 262
Max Headroom 157, 189–93
McCarthy, Anna 301
McLuhan, Marshall 23, 136, 171
media archaeology 78–80, 300, 368
media studies 3
Medienwissenschaft 331
megalethoscope 93
mercury 41
metaphors 16–17, 30–4, 58–9, 80, 179
Metz, Christian 198, 207, 422
Micromax 269
Microsoft 55–6, 269, 271
Miller, Toby 391
Mills, C. Wright 23
minimalism 270, 280, 283–4
Minitel 29
Minority Report 329–30
Mirada 202
mirrors 100–2, 203–4, 288–9
MirrorWorld 202–4
mise-en-scène 239–40, 246–8, 252–6, 259–61, 358. *See also* images; shots
mobile phones 7, 109–10, 297, 299, 302, 319–22, 325–32, 333–40, 424, 445. *See also* iPhone; smartphones
mobility 5, 9, 197–9, 298–300, 319–22, 333–40, 368–71, 372–9, 381, 435–43
Modern Screen 3–4
monitors 30–1, 129, 131, 185–6, 189–93, 245–6, 248–9, 297
montage. *See* editing
Morrissey 424, 427
Morsi, Mohamed 173–4

Motion Picture and Machine Operators' Union 379
movie theaters 59–60, 103–4, 158, 207, 229–30, 276, 297, 378, 380–1, 399, 418–19
Movie-Drome 276–7, 301, 418–19
MP3 42, 207
MPEG 49–50
MS-DOS 55–6
Mubarak, Hosni 167, 170, 173, 175
MUDs 62. *See also* games
multiframes 56
multi-screens 185, 194, 317, 369, 375
multitasking 56, 59–61
Mulvey, Laura 202
Munsterberg, Hugo 187
museums 328, 330, 445
Musser, Charles 86–7, 91
Mutoscope 346, 350
Muybridge, Eadweard 305

Nadar, Félix Tournachon 127
navigation 435–43
Nelson, Ted 109
Netherlands Institute for Sound and Vision 145
networks 7, 30, 214, 278, 292, 297–8, 300–1, 337, 339, 435–43. *See also* flow; internet
Wi-Fi 437
newsreels 377–8, 380–1, 418
Nigeria 395–413
9/11 168
Nintendo 181, 325, 331, 436
Nokia 197
Noland, Kenneth 280
Nollywood 301, 395–413
Nostradamus 100
Nöth, Winifried 205

Obama, Barack 173
ODM. *See* original design manufacturer
OEM. *See* original equipment manufacturer
Okome, Onookome 301
Olympics 288
ombres chinoises 91
Onion, The 287

operating systems. *See* iOS; Linux;
     MS-DOS; Windows
original design manufacturer 42–3
original equipment manufacturer 42–3
Oscilloscope 40, 52
Oudart, Jean-Pierre 352
Oxford English Dictionary, The 82,
     84, 91

painting 19, 59, 125, 134–6, 139,
     163–5, 234, 269–70, 278–81,
     283–4, 292, 311
Panofsky, Erwin 62
panopticon 31
Panoram 300, 347, 349, 357, 359
panoramas 86–7, 92–3, 96
Paquienséguy, Françoise 334
parergon 269, 278–9, 281–2
peep devices 91–4
peepshows 300, 343–60, 373
perspective 134
Peter Gabriel: Live in Athens 430–1
Peter Marino Associates 147
phantasmagoria 84–7, 91
Philips, Tom 147
phosphors 40–1, 45–6
photography 19, 127, 155, 157,
     167–74, 234–5, 292
Photoshop 36
Photosynth 441–2
Piano, Renzo 146
Pixar 246, 256–62
pixels 46–7, 50, 136–7, 147, 281, 288
plasma 46–7, 311
Plato 18, 159, 239
pointer 314, 317
porn studies 344, 346
pornography 300, 343–64
   U.S. Attorney General's Commission
     on 348
   U.S. Commission on Obscenity and
     348
postcolonialism 167–75, 301, 396–401,
     404–13
post-screen 288, 290–4
presence 293–4, 437, 439–40
Presley, Elvis 425
Prince, Stephen 256
privacy 353–5

production 205–6, 233–4, 246, 250,
     256–7, 344, 377, 398
productivity 62
projection 85–7, 156, 225–8, 233–9,
     269–70, 305–6, 372, 375, 379,
     381–2
   digital light processing (DLP) 47, 49
   rear 46, 348, 371, 379–82
projectors 47, 101–2, 269, 291, 305–6,
     329, 352, 357, 369–72, 374–83
Prometheus 205–7
protocol 48
Proust, Marcel 158
   In Search of Lost Time 158
Pudovkin, V. I. 187, 238
punctum 206

Quetelet, Alphonse 51

radar 40, 127–30
Radiation Laboratory 129–30
radio 101–2, 135
Radio City Music Hall 376, 380
Radio Corporation of America 373,
     375–6
Radio News 101
Radiovisor 102
Rage 198–9
railroads 377
rare earths 9, 42
raster grid 44, 46–7, 51, 288–90, 293,
     316
Rauschenberg, Robert 135
RCA. *See* Radio Corporation of
     America
realities:united 149
reality 73–7, 137, 239–40, 444
recording 423–6, 428–30
recycling 10–11, 41, 44
reflectivity 308–11
Renaissance 234
Research in Motion 326
Retina (display) 269, 287
RIDES 211–13
Robida, Arthur 96–7, 101–2
Rodowick, D.N. 25
Rosenblum, Robert 280
Rozin, Daniel 288–9
   Mirrors Mirror 289

Trash Mirror 289
Wooden Mirror 288–9
Ryan, Marie-Laure 213

SAGE. *See* Semi-Automatic Ground
    Environment
Samsung 272
scanning 136
Schavemaker, Margriet 445
Schneider, Alexandra 300
Schupli, Susan 201
Scott, Ridley 207
Scott Brown, Denise 143
screen. *See also* dividing screens; fire
    screens; multi-screens
    archaeology (*see* media archaeology)
    as bulletin board 32–3
    classification systems 18, 300
    definition of 15, 24–6, 77, 125
    as display 35, 56
    and government regulation 43–4, 52
    material composition of 40–3, 88,
        101, 163–6, 220, 225, 228, 267,
        281, 299, 305–6, 379
    as mirror 239–40
    on-screen 185–94
    origins of term 80–2, 327
    outdoor 19, 301
    as scrapbook 33–5
    shape 102–7, 245, 248, 280, 283,
        367
    size 199, 366–8, 371–2, 378–82,
        402, 423
    space 156–7, 159, 307–11, 435–43
    split 186
    technical specifications of 23
    as window 17, 55–6, 58–62, 134,
        269, 278
    windshield as 446
screen studies 3–4, 24–6
screen theory 4
screenology 78, 80
screen-o-scope 103, 158
second screens 158, 204–11, 213, 298
self 62
Semi-Automatic Ground Environment
    130–1
semiotics 430
Semper, Gottfried 146–7

*Style in Technical and Tectonic Arts,
    or Practical Aesthetics* 146–7
senses 182–3. *See also* hapticity;
    tactility; vision
shadow theater 87
Shining, The 336
shots 136, 186, 189–93, 199, 233–5,
    248, 274, 299, 310–11, 351–2,
    356–7, 389
    close-up 202
    first-person 198–200
    handheld 197–8
    pan-and-scan 257, 261, 274
Silver Goat, The 199
simulation 131, 137–40, 179, 181–2
Sketchpad 131
slide shows 375
smartphones 15, 157–8, 197–215, 297,
    300, 331–2, 333–40, 435–6, 441,
    443. *See also* iPhone; mobile
    phones
smartwatches 111
Sobchack, Vivian 271, 281–3, 328, 345,
    351
Social Commentary 207
social media 34–5, 168–9, 174, 201–2,
    207, 211, 334, 339–40, 423, 435.
    See also Facebook; Twitter
Socrates 73–7
software 43, 48, 55, 58–9, 255, 257,
    290–1, 294, 302, 331–2, 435–42.
    See also apps
    hacking 197
Soja, Edward 446
Sonet, Virginie 300
Sontag, Susan 173
    On Photography 173
Sony 272
SOTCHI 255 198
sound 26, 96, 135, 191, 200, 290, 335,
    347, 418, 422
spectator 59–60, 73–7, 158, 301–2,
    397–413. *See also* audience;
    viewer
Spigel, Lynn 310
Stanley v. Georgia 354–5
Star Trek 194
Starlight Films 346, 357–9
Stella, Frank 280